WHITE TERROR

In the last days of 1917, a fugitive Mongol-Cossack captain brashly led seven cohorts into a mutinous garrison at Manchuli, a roughneck bordertown on Russia's frontier with Manchuria. The garrison had gone Red, revolted against its officers, and become a dangerous, ill-disciplined mob. Nevertheless, Captain Grigorii Semenov cleverly convinced the garrison to lay down its arms and board a train back into Bolshevik territory. Through such brash action, Semenov and a handful of Cossack brethren established themselves as the warlords of the Russian Far East.

Like inland pirates, they menaced the Trans-Siberian Railway with fleets of armored trains, Cossack cavalry, mercenaries and pressgang cannon fodder. They undermined Admiral Kolchak's White government, ruthlessly liquidated all Reds, terrorized the population, prostituted themselves to the Japanese Army, antagonized the American Expeditionary Force and Czechoslovak Legion and orchestrated the frenzied last spasms of the Russian Empire's Götterdämmerung. Historians have long recognized that Ataman Semenov and company were a nasty lot. This book details precisely how nasty they were.

White Terror describes the major events and trends during this dark era when Siberia became hell on earth. It offers a taste of daily life in the *atamanshchina* – the realms of Atamans Semenov and Kalmykov, and depicts the byzantine web of relationships and conflicts in a desolate land that suddenly teemed with warlords, revolutionaries, counterrevolutionaries, refugees, prisoners, foreign troops and relief workers, while describing the ever-changing orders of battle, key officers and armored trains. It is the story of a forgotten Russia in turmoil, when the line between government and organized crime blurred into a chaotic continuum of kleptocracy, vengeance and sadism.

Jamie Bisher is a graduate of the United States Air Force Academy with a masters degree from the University of Maryland and more than 25 years experience in international security programmes. His fascination with Russia's revolution dates back to his first childhood visit to the Soviet Embassy in Washington in 1968.

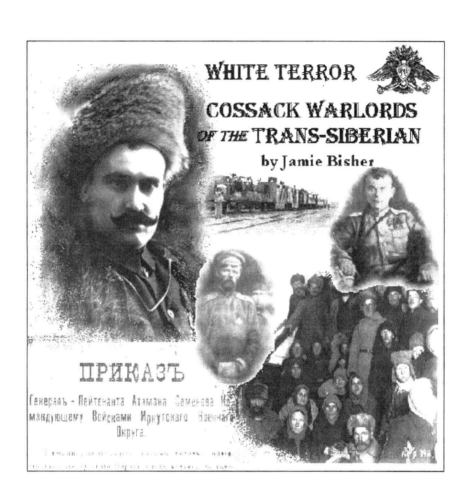

WHITE TERROR

Cossack warlords of the Trans-Siberian

Jamie Bisher

LONDON AND NEW YORK

First published 2005
by Routledge, an imprint of Taylor & Francis
2 Park Square, Milton Park, Abingdon, Oxon, OX14 4RN

Simultaneously published in the USA and Canada
by Routledge
270 Madison Ave, New York NY 10016

Routledge is an imprint of the Taylor & Francis Group

Transferred to Digital Printing 2009

© 2005 Jamie Bisher

Typeset in Times New Roman by
Newgen Imaging Systems (P) Ltd, Chennai, India

All rights reserved. No part of this book may be reprinted or
reproduced or utilised in any form or by any electronic,
mechanical, or other means, now known or hereafter
invented, including photocopying and recording, or in any
information storage or retrieval system, without permission in
writing from the publishers.

The publisher makes no representation, express or implied,
with regard to the accuracy of the information contained in this book and
cannot accept any legal responsibility or liability for any errors or
omissions that may be made.

British Library Cataloguing in Publication Data
A catalogue record for this book is available from the British Library

Library of Congress Cataloging in Publication Data
Bisher, Jamie, 1956–
White Terror: Cossack warlords of the
Trans-Siberian / Jamie Bisher – 1st ed.
p. cm.
Includes bibliographical references and index.
1. Siberia (Russia) – History – Revolution,
1917–1921 – Protest movements. 2. Russian Far East
(Russia) – History – Revolution, 1917–1921. I. Title.

DK265.8.S5B57 2005
957.08′41–dc22   2004012577

ISBN10: 0–714–65690–9 (hbk)
ISBN10: 0–415–57134–0 (pbk)

ISBN13: 978–0–714–65690–8 (hbk)
ISBN13: 978–0–415–57134–0 (pbk)

Publisher's Note
The publisher has gone to great lengths to ensure the quality of this reprint
but points out that some imperfections in the original may be apparent.

TO PALOMA, BULLY, BUTTERCUP AND DADDY

CONTENTS

List of illustrations   xi
List of abbreviations and acronyms   xiii
Preface   xvi
Acknowledgments   xix

1 Prelude to terror: Creation – November 1917   1

Battleground of the Gods 1
Frontier Siberia 8
Russia's Asian neighbors and the Iron Road 13
Mongolia and the Tournament of Shadows 19
Ensign Grigorii Mikhailovich Semenov 23
Semenov in the Great War 26
Commissar Semenov 32
Bolshevik coups across Siberia 37

2 Revolution and Red Terror: November 1917–May 1918   40

Revolutionary days in Dauria and Harbin 40
Semenov's eight-man Counterrevolution 42
First offensive 46
Recruiting Mongols 48
Red Takeover and Terror 49
Harbin – the Paris and Gomorrah of the Orient 53
Strategic ambitions and the Austro-German threat 56
Bullets, guns and money 59
Japanese advisors, internationalists and the April offensive 60
Kolchak and Semenov 66
Lazo's May Counteroffensive and the Kolchak–Semenov meeting 70

3 Counterrevolution: May–October 1918   75

Czechoslovakian saviors 75
July defeat and new foreign assistance 77

CONTENTS

Battles for Lake Baikal 81
Anarchist locusts descend upon Chita 84
Semenov's third offensive: the conquest of Transbaikalia 85
Czech liberation – or occupation? – of Vladivostok and Nikolsk-Ussuriisk 90
Internationalists and interventionists 91
Russian Railway Service Corps 94
Ataman Kalmykov 96
Allied liberation of Khabarovsk 98
Blagoveshchensk – the last Red Bastion 101

4 The White Terror begins: October 1918–December 1918 104

Semenov's realm 104
Chita 106
Semenov's army 109
Provisional Siberian Government and the 5th Corps 113
Semenov, Incorporated 115
Reactionary backlash 116
Kalmykov's Khabarovsk 118
White nightmare in Blagoveshchensk 120
Japanese Siberia 122
Death trains 125
The Ataman versus the Supreme Ruler 127
Gloomy Omsk at its peak 131
Attempt on the Ataman's life 132

5 Rodomontade and girls with diamonds: January–April 1919 134

Likin, diamond-studded mistresses and Jewish Cossacks 134
Rodomontade, martinets and sadists 138
Crime, punishment and the Shumov–Natsvalov affair 140
White hell in Kalmykov's wild, wild east 143
Allies and the atamans 146
Serbian mercenaries and Slavic legions 151
Foreign voluntary organizations 152
Spring and White victory in the air 153
Inter-Allied Railway Agreement 155

6 White Terror on the *Magistral*: May–September 1919 157

War on the rails 157
Semenov's armored train division 159

CONTENTS

Strategic railway resources 162
Reign of terror on the rails 163
Red partisans of Transbaikalia 166
Face-off at Verkhne-Udinsk 170
Semenov's golden days in Chita 174
OMO interference on the rails 177
Trouble on the Chinese Eastern 180
Refugees 182
Killing fields 183
Dreams of a Pan-Mongolian empire 188

7 The White collapse begins: Summer 1919–January 1920   192

A black summer for Siberian Whites 192
Partisan growth in the Russian Far East 194
Atamans' plot against the Americans 196
Battle of Khada-Bulak 199
The Ataman versus Lieutenant Ryan 201
The fall of Omsk 202
Gajda's plot against the Whites 203
Panic on the Trans-Siberian 205
Battle of Irkutsk 208
A treasonous White commander and murders on Baikal 213

8 Red onslaught: January–April 1920   216

New Year in White Siberia 216
Selenga River valley and Verkhne-Udinsk 219
Counter-counterrevolution in Vladivostok and Nikolsk 223
Semenov and the Americans 225
Kalmykov's Waterloo 230
White breakdown in Transbaikalia, Red liberation in Irkutsk 232
Firesales, strikes, mutinies, collaboration and a coup 238

9 White–Japanese resurgence, panic and disaster:
   April–December 1920   243

Massacre at Nikolaevsk and the Japanese offensive 243
Frontline Transbaikalia 249
The Hailar incident 251
Forging a Japanese–Mongol buffer state 255
Red panic, Lazo's fiery martyrdom and White panic 258
The fall of White Transbaikalia 261

CONTENTS

10 Götterdämmerung: October 1920–November 1922 266

*Ungern-Shternberg's liberation of Mongolia
(October 1920–January 1921) 266
White Götterdämmerung in Mongolia
(January–September 1921) 274
Ataman's exile and White Russia's last spasms
(October 1920–November 1922) 282*

11 Diaspora, Manchurian revival and legacy: June 1921 to the present day 286

*White diaspora and ambush by New York lawyers
(January 1921–June 1922) 286
Red dawn (1922–1930s) 292
Semenov in Dairen (1922–39) 295
Semenov, godfather of Manchukuo's Reactionary
Whites (1939–45) 306
Epilogue 311*

Appendix 1: The *Magistral* 314

Appendix 2: Cadre and Staff 317

Appendix 3: Proclamations of the Atamans 319

*Proclamation of the Temporary Government of Transbaikal
Territory, May 1918 319
Proclamation of Ataman Kalmykov in Grodekovo District,
July 1918 319*

Glossary	322
Notes	330
Select bibliography	402
Index	441

ILLUSTRATIONS

Plates

1. Dom Nikitin
2. Czechoslovak armored train
3. Bridge over the Angara river at Irkutsk
4. Mongol caravan
5. Onon river bridge
6. Vladivostok city center
7. OMO armored train 'Ataman'
8. Manchuli Station – the center of intrigue
9. Ataman Ivan P. Kalmykov
10. OMO Buryat cavalryman
11. OMO Cavalry
12. Semenov's train with gaudy 'Summer Car'
13. Ataman Grigorii M. Semenov
14. Soldiers and refugees in Vladivostok Station
15. The Cossack and the Cowboy
16. 'Death Train' and defiant peasants
17. Leaders of US technical assistance
18. Japanese soldiers
19. Japanese Imperial Army staff in Siberia
20. Lieutenant Colonel Charles B. Morrow, at 27th Infantry Headquarters in Khabarovsk
21. Nikolsk-Ussuriisk Station
22. Russian Naval Train, Vladivostok
23. OKO armored railcar

Figures

1. Order of Battle – OMO, April 1918
2. Order of Battle – Transbaikal Front, April 1918
3. Order of Battle – Chinese Eastern Railway, July 1918
4. Order of Battle – OMO, July 1918
5. Order of Battle – OMO, May 1918

ILLUSTRATIONS

Maps

1 Russian Far East
2 Southern portion of Russia's Maritime Province
3 Transbaikalia

ABBREVIATIONS AND ACRONYMS

1LT	First lieutenant
2LT	Second lieutenant
ADM	Admiral
AEFS	American Expeditionary Forces Siberia
Agitprop	Agitation and propaganda
AP	Associated Press
ARC	American Red Cross
ASMPR	Academy of Sciences – Mongolian People's Republic
ASTP	Army Specialized Training Program
BREM	*Byuro po Delam Rossiiskikh Emigrantov*, Bureau for the Affairs of Russian Emigrants
Britmis	British Military Mission in Siberia
CAPT	Captain
CBMO	Central Bureau of Military Organizations
CER	Chinese Eastern Railway
COL	Colonel
CSEF	Canadian Siberian Expeditionary Force
Dal'buro	*Dal'nevostochnoe Buro*, Far Eastern Bureau (Russian Communist Party)
DMI	Director of Military Intelligence
DVSV	*Dal'nevostochnyi Soyuz Voennykh*, Far Eastern Union of Servicemen
ESC	Eastern Siberian Commissariat, anti-Bolshevik resistance organization based in Harbin
FER	Far Eastern Republic
FO	Foreign Office
FRUS	*Papers Relating to the Foreign Relations of the United States*
FSB	*Federal'naya Sluzhba Bezopasnosti*, Federal Security Service, the successor to the KGB
GEN	General
Gospolokhrana	*Gosudarstvenaya Politicheskaya Okhrana*, State Political Police of the FER
gulag	Slang for Soviet labor camp network, from *G(lavnoe) u(pravlenie ispravitel'no-trudovykh) lag(ere)*, Chief Administration (of Correctional Labor) Camps

ABBREVIATIONS AND ACRONYMS

GVO	*Gosudarstvennaya Vnutrennaya Okhrana*, Mongolian State Internal Security
HQ	Headquarters
IARC	Inter-Allied Railway Committee
IATB	Inter-Allied Technical Board
LT	Lieutenant
LTC	Lieutenant Colonel
MAJ	Major
MGB	*Ministerstvo Gosudarst'vennoi Bezopasnosti*, Ministry of State Security
MID	Military Intelligence Division
MILREVKOM	Military-Revolutionary Committee
MPP	Mongolian People's Party
MVD	*Ministerstva Vnutrennich Del*, Ministry of Internal Affairs
n.d.	No date
n.p.	No place of publication given
NARA	National Archives and Records Administration
NCO	Noncommissioned officer
NKVD	*Narodnyi Kommisariat Vnutrennikh Del*, People's Commissariat for Internal Affairs
ObRevKom	*Oblast Revolyutsionnyi Komitet*, Regional Revolutionary Committee
OGPU	*Obedinennoe Gosudarstvennoe Politicheskoe Upravleniye*, All-Union State Political Board
OKO	*Osobii Kazach'ii Otryad*, Special Cossack Detachment
OMO	*Osobii Manchzhurskii Otryad*, Special Manchurian Detachment
ONI	Office of Naval Intelligence (USA)
OSS	Office of Strategic Services (USA)
PGAS	Provisional Government of Autonomous Siberia ('[Petr] Derber Government', January–September 1918)
POW	Prisoner of war
PREDREVOYENSOVIET	*Predsedatel' Revolyutsionogo Voenogo Soviet*, President of Revolutionary Military Soviet
Pri-Amur	*Primorskaya* (Maritime) and Amur Provinces
PSG	Provisional Siberian Government ('Omsk Government', June–November 1918)
QM	Quartermaster
RG	Record Group
RGIADV	*Rossiiskii gosudarstvennyi istoricheskii arkhiv Dal'nego Vostoka*, Russian State Historical Archives of the Far East
ROA	*Russkaya Osvoditel'naya Armiya*, Russian Liberation Army
ROVS	*Russkii Obshche-voinskii Soyuz*, Russian All-Military Union
RRSC	Russian Railway Service Corps
RSFSR	Russian Soviet Federated Socialist Republic

ABBREVIATIONS AND ACRONYMS

RTA	Russian Telegraphic Agency
SGT	sergeant
SKDV	*Soyuz Kazakov na Dal'nem Vostoke*, Union of Cossacks in the Far East
SMERSH	*'Smert'Shpioni!'* Soviet counterintelligence units during the Second World War
SOVDEP	Soviet of Cossacks', Workers', Peasants' and Soldiers' Deputies
SR	Socialist-Revolutionary
UKGB	*Upravlenie Komitet Gosudarstvennoi Bezopasnosti*, Administration of the Committee of State Security
UMVD	*Upravlenie Ministerstva Vnutrennich Del*, Administration of the Ministry of Internal Affairs
UNKVD	*Upravlenie Narodnyi Kommisariat Vnutrennikh Del*, Administration of the People's Commissariat for Internal Affairs
USAT	US Army Transport
USSR	Union of Soviet Socialist Republics
WIA	wounded in action
WSC	Western Siberian Commissariat, anti-Bolshevik resistance organization based in Novonikolaevsk
YMCA	Young Mens' Christian Association

PREFACE

Historians have long known that the Cossack warlords of Russia's civil war era were a nasty lot, but no one seems to have assembled a coherent and accurate picture of them. They are often relegated to the footnotes of Russian revolutionary history, even though they set the stage for many crucial turning points when they themselves were not at the forefront of history-making events, as they were in 1918 and from 1920 until 1922. This book aims to describe the Cossack warlords by their actions, words and the impressions on those around them, to flesh out their role in the Russian Civil War, to dispel common rumors and disinformation, and to place the conflict in the Russian Far East in strategic perspective.

This book focuses on the infamous warlords that operated along the Trans-Siberian Railway in the vast expanse between Irkutsk at the southwest corner of Lake Baikal and Vladivostok on the Pacific coast: Transbaikal Cossack Ataman Grigorii Mikhailovich Semenov, Ussuri Cossack Ataman Ivan Pavlovich Kalmykov and Baron Roman Ungern-Shternberg. They stepped into Russia's revolutionary arena as young war heroes, appalled by the Reds' destruction of traditional institutions, incitement of class hatred, brutality and anarchy. They boldly raised the White banner of counterrevolution when most generals and politicians had retreated in confusion into exile. There ended their positive contributions to modern Russia.

The Cossack warlords actively undermined Admiral Aleksandr Kolchak's government and military until its collapse in autumn 1919, although the admiral's fiery temper and tactlessness salted the Whites' self-inflicted wounds almost as much as Japanese treachery and manipulation of Tokyo's pliable protégés, Semenov, Kalmykov and Ungern-Shternberg. The Cossack warlords' sadism and avarice caused Western powers to accept the vicious Bolsheviks as the inevitable lesser of two evils, and the warlords' legacy branded White refugees as reactionary suspects or even *persona non grata* during the post-war Diaspora. Ungern-Shternberg and Semenov managed to discredit not only Russia's White movement but the Pan-Mongol unification movement as well.

Blinded by his hatred of revolutionaries, the sparkle of loot and the intoxicating taste of absolute power, Semenov survived the Red onslaught to undermine Russia's eleventh-hour White governments and to entrust Russia's riches to her conniving enemies. As if this miserable legacy was not black enough, Semenov ungratefully undermined law and order in his Manchurian refuge, becoming a kingpin in one of the century's most diabolical criminal enterprises, the extortion, prostitution and narcotics syndicate run by Japanese intelligence and the Kwantung Army. This racketeering paved the way for the 1931 invasion and enslavement of Manchuria, which eventually contributed to the emasculation of the League of Nations and set the stage for the Second World War. In contrast to his vile accomplishments, Semenov was, according to those who knew him, intelligent, brave, personable, a sadist who was a warm, loving father, a womanizer who was kind to all his wives and mistresses, a pirate who was generous with his purloined treasure.

Sources

The primary source material for this book – indeed, its impetus – includes memoranda, reports and a variety of other documents written on the spot by people who had to work alongside the armies of the Cossack warlords. Most of these documents now reside in the National Archives record groups for the US Army American Expeditionary Force – Siberia, the US War Department's Military Intelligence Division, the US Office of Naval Intelligence, and the US Department of State's Russian Railway Service Corps. Many documents had never before been declassified or examined by an outsider. Most were not written by desk-bound bureaucrats in Washington, but by engineers, soldiers and humanitarian aid-givers from many nations. These records also included telegram and cable traffic from the lines running alongside the Trans-Siberian and Chinese Eastern Railways, communications which conveyed the drama, excitement, fear and confusion of the moment. The old files also contained a wealth of valuable newspaper summaries from *Dalekaya Okraina, Primorskaya Zhizn, Novosti Zhizn, Sibirskii Put', Osaka Mainichi* and other newspapers, with translations and analysis of the articles by in-country intelligence analysts. Some recently released Russian archival material was also obtained, but the author relied more upon recent books and papers published by many industrious Russian researchers who have enjoyed the access and time to pore through the old files of the intelligence services and regional archives, in particular V.I. Vasilevskii's extensive compilation of documents pertaining to Ataman Semenov.

Other sources poured into this book include the synthesized research of Russian and Western writers: Smele, Morley, Fleming, Snow, Dotsenko, Dvornichenko, Borisov, Shereshevskii, Gutman, Ablova, Manusevich, Shishkin and scores of others; and memoirs of eye-witnesses: Ataman Semenov, US Major General Graves, doughboy Jesse Anderson, Czechoslovak legionnaire Henry Baerlein, Canadian Captain James M. Bell, General Baron Aleksei Budberg, socialist revolutionary Paul Dotsenko, Polish prisoner of war Roman Dyboski, Polish refugee Ferdinand Ossendowski, Dutch journalist Lokewijk-Hermen Grondijs, YMCA secretaries Edward Heald and the Reitzels, British Colonel John Ward, Manchurian intelligence officer Amleto Vespa, *et al.*

Geography, language, political labels, ranks and dates

Note that geographic references to western Siberia refer to everything west of the River Ob, references to eastern Siberia refer to territory between the River Ob and Lake Baikal, the Russian Far East includes everything east of Baikal. Anglicized, pre-revolutionary provincial names are used, for example, Transbaikal, Amur and Maritime Provinces.

A standard scheme of transliteration and romanization of Russian terms and names is adhered to, which, to the author's annoyance, results in mispronunciation by readers who have not studied the Russian language, making no distinction between the Russian *e* and *ë*, for instance. Thus 'Semenov' is normally used, even if original documents cited him as 'Semionov', 'Semenoff', or any of the other many variations. However, there are some necessary exceptions dictated by common usage or quotes from other citations, for instance: Bolshevik versus *Bol'shevik*, soviet versus *sovet*, Alioshin (as cited by Peter Hopkirk) versus Aleshin, Harbin instead of Kharbin, and Horvath instead of Khorvat. Also, foreign language terms are italicized except for those which have come into common usage in English, like Bolshevik and soviet.

Note that the term 'Red' evolves with the ambiguous White and Allied usage of the term, which sometimes (but not always) included most rank-and-file Socialist-Revolutionaries (SRs) in the Russian Far East until about January 1920, although many SRs – notably Colonel A.A. Krakovetskii – served with the Whites for the duration of the civil war. Similarly, the 'Bolshevik' label was often generously applied to include not only all members of the Russian Social-Democrat Labor Party (including Mensheviks), as Lenin's party was formally known in its early years, but everyone who supported party endeavors, and the term continued in use after the March 1918 introduction of the 'Communist' brand.

The author made an effort to state participants' military ranks in Russian because of differences between Russian Army and Cossack rank titles and additional officer ranks that are not present in Western militaries, and also because of the unusual and confusing new rank titles of the revolutionary forces.

Japanese names are presented unadulterated (i.e. last name first).

Vladimir Ilyich Lenin changed Russia from the Julian Calendar to the Gregorian on 1 February 1918, adding 13 days to Julian dates. This is especially confusing during the threshold period of autumn 1917–spring 1918, although an effort has been made to cite new calendar dates during these months.

ACKNOWLEDGMENTS

Many people deserve my most gracious thanks for their unselfish assistance in the research and writing of this book, which has relied heavily upon the kindness of strangers...

Dr Jonathan Smele, for his infectious enthusiasm, priceless encouragement, frank opinions, expert knowledge and encyclopedic reference book, *Civil War in Siberia*; Andrei Bukin, modern Transbaikal Cossack, for his generous support and invaluable contributions; Linda Kaufman, genealogical researcher extraordinaire, for her sleuthing into the background of US Army Captain Harold V.V. Fay and her generous mentoring in the mechanics of genealogical research; Major Craig Martelle for finding answers to my prickly questions about Russian Civil War military details; Pavel Yelkin, Eugene Levin, Molly Golubcow, Dr Alicia Campi, Dr Denys Voaden and fellow members of the Washington area Mongolia Society, for their continuing encouragement over the years and indulgence in hearing out my over-heated reports of snail-like progress; Furman Bisher, for the click-clacking of his Royal typewriter into the night, like a train into dreamland, teaching me by example how a writer works; Veronica, Jamie and Natalie, for quietly accepting all of the missed hours we could have shared together, and for giving me a reason to write this book.

1

PRELUDE TO TERROR

Creation – November 1917

> 'The history of little Chita was the history of all Russia.'
> (Prince Petr A. Kropotkin)

Battleground of the Gods

Long before Siberia's forests echoed with the ringing swords of Mongols, Tatars, Cossacks, Reds and Whites and the cries of their victims, the land was terrorized by vicious flying serpents, gigantic snarling canines, invisible evil spirits called *shalmos*, and multi-headed beasts called *mangathais* – according to the myths of the Buryat Mongols. These creatures fought constantly for territory and for power over the Marat, the people who inhabited the world that preceded our world. Boundaries between the natural and supernatural blurred in the old world where even mortal Marat transformed into supernatural wolves, ravens and swans. Buryat myths spin a relentless and confusing web of sacrifice, politicking, deceit and betrayal, punctuated by vicious atrocities traded by forces of both good and evil. Siblings turned against siblings and, motivated by self-preservation, thirst for power or revenge, men even cut deals with *mangathais*, who were usually busy boiling, impaling or disemboweling people.

It was not an idyllic world. In one case, a deformed, frog-faced infant with supernatural powers lured enemies close enough to rip out their tongues and bludgeon them to death. In another, the World White God, Esege Malan, found it necessary to spy on his own earthly emissary's activities and attitudes. Esege Malan created the world, but could not even control his own human sons, much less the plethora of other hideous creatures running amok over the land. Evil and disorder reigned. At one point so much carnage smothered the earth that Esege Malan created flies and maggots to clean up the blanket of putrefying bodies. Epic battles raged for days and nights on end. Gargantuan combatants gouged out hills and gorges with their slashing claws and hooves, hammered out valleys where they tumbled, and pitched immense projectiles that became rocky outcrops and landmarks for the ensuing centuries of warriors, rebels and pirates.[1]

Epic struggle cast its shadow across the Transbaikal plateau again between 1917 and 1921, when Reds and Whites fought ferociously for the souls of humanity. Infernal flying machines hurled fire from the sky, and giant belching locomotives roared like *mangathais* and pitched projectiles that tore shelters asunder and shredded people into fodder for wolves and crows. Assassins and spies lurked in the shade, modern *shalmos* wreaking doom upon mortal enemies. The stench of mass graves and burning flesh, rivers swollen with corpses, screams of the tortured and raucous hilarity of sadists raping, mutilating and tormenting, reveling in quarterings, hangings, whippings, brandings, beheadings and multitudinous methods of slaughter – the horrors of Buryat mythology had come to pass in Verkhne-Udinsk, Chita and hundreds of satellite villages and settlements hugging the Transbaikal plateau, nestled in river valleys, buried in the green taiga, or perched above Lake Baikal.

This modern pestilence was ordained by Russia's conquest of Siberia and the shifting fault lines of Russo-Japanese tensions. The background of the civil war in Russia's Far East was shaped by its history as the cradle of Mongol culture, a land of freedom and opportunity for Cossacks, runaways, fugitives and the oppressed, and a land of exile for troublemakers and criminals. An irregular flow of people, commerce and ideas, moving in and out along Siberia's interlaced rivers, the Great Post Road and the Tea Road, kept the region in ferment and conversely swayed events in distant parts of Asia, Europe and even America.

The White Terror that extinguished so many lives was shaped by a frontier society, where the cultural chemistry of Buryats, Evenks, Russians, Old Believers, Poles, Koreans, Chinese and other societies fused to spawn a culture of endemic violence. Cossack society and tradition, as altered and practiced by the isolated and relatively young institutions in the Russian Far East, overlaid this complex embroidery and set the stage for warlords and banditry.

Siberia is immense enough to be the gods' battleground. The swamps and plains of western and central Siberia engulf an area as wide as Australia and the Russian Far East lies as far from the Urals as Newfoundland is from Britain. Russia's Far East rears up like a *mangathai* from the eastern tendrils of the Altai mountains and the basin of the Lena river to nestle Lake Baikal between jagged alpine peaks of the Sayan mountains. From this confluence of alps around Baikal, interlocking spines of mountain ranges – the Yablonovii, Borshchovochnii, Udokan and Stanovoi, among others – fan out east from the lake to collect water for the Lena river's long journey to the Laptev Sea in the frozen north.

No less than a quarter of a million years ago, our world supplanted the mythological world of the Marat. Some early human clans were hardy and advanced enough to settle and thrive in the Altai mountains and even in the Arctic tundra during the Upper Paleolithic period more than 35,000 years ago. By the modern era, Siberia was the home of more than 30 indigenous ethnic groups of diverse origins, but classified linguistically as mostly Turkic, Manchu-Tungus, Finno-Ugric and Mongolic. Newcomers tended to enter Siberia from central Asia, forsaking the steppes for the richer, yet colder forests of the north. The memories of some groups' ancient migration treks from central Asia still survive in folklore.

The rich forests and waters of the Baikal region fostered cultural development. Formal burial sites around the lake evince rituals that date back 8,000 years. Paleolithic tribes such as the Mal'ta scattered carvings of birds, deer and women in mammoth ivory, bone and antler across an area from west of Lake Baikal to the Amur basin. Prehistoric clans of the Evenki clustered in Transbaikal, the region east of Lake Baikal, before scattering across the taiga to the Pacific coast and as far west as the Yenisei river.[2]

Nomadic tribes that would eventually become known as the Mongols had settled along Baikal's shore and in valleys south of the lake by 500 AD. They flourished along the Selenga, Kherlen and Onon rivers. Mongols came to be defined more by geography, language and way of life than by racial characteristics. By the eleventh century, they comprised a number of fractious clans of nomadic herdsmen vying with each other for the sparse grasslands bounded by the Altai and Tian Shan mountains in the west, the Great Khingan mountains in the east and the Gobi desert in the south. They were loosely bound by a common spiritual tradition of animist beliefs, where shamans interpreted dreams, visions, omens and natural signs of the many good and bad spirits lurking in the water, ground, air, fire and other dimensions. In the life-or-death competition for livestock, water and pastures, individuals perfected the arts of horsemanship and hunting, tent-living and frequent moves. These skills were also valuable in coping with the ceaseless drama of feuds between tribes, clans and families. In contrast to settled communities where men wielded agricultural and construction implements, Mongol men mastered the lasso, dagger, saber, battle-axe, mace, javelin, hooked lance, bow and arrow. Likewise, constant competition and conflict honed clan leaders' expertise in shrewd negotiation, spying and tactical thinking.

The heartland of Mongolian peoples is the Lake Baikal basin, *Barguzin Tukum* to the ancient Buryats. In Buryat mythology these kinsmen were known as *Burte Chino* – the Blue Wolf People. 'The Buryats have characteristic Mongol features', wrote one European adventurer, 'but they are taller and more strongly built than the tribes met further east and have much more energy of character.' This energy shone in all aspects of their rich and ancient culture. Even long after firearms came into popular use, mounted Buryats hunted wolves with bow and arrow, running down and shooting their formidable prey at full gallop. Temujin, the most famous of Mongols, was said to have been descended from the Blue Wolf clan.[3]

At a site on the Onon river in 1206, a *khuriltai*, an assembly of Mongol tribal leaders, pronounced the great warrior Temujin as Ghengis Khan, the Lord of the Earth.[4] As a boy Temujin learned life's harshest lessons on a desolate stretch of the Onon after Yesugei, his respected father, was poisoned and his family cast out of their clan to subsist on berries and occasional bits of marmot and dormice. The 1206 *khuriltai* culminated Temujin's struggle for his family's survival and revenge against the Mongols who betrayed them. The event also forged Mongolian national identity and Temujin's subsequent brutal and brilliant campaigns fortified it. Ghengis Khan's first campaign was to unite – by the sword – all Mongol tribes by attacking the last hold-outs not under his control, the Urianhai and Merkit. His second major campaign set out to pillage, plunder and subjugate China's Jin empire. In May 1215, the Mongol army razed the opulent Jin capital at Zhongdu (Beijing), and then, during the next 12 years, swarmed over central Asia and the Caucasus like locusts, ravaging its rich erudite cities, driven by lust for battle, power, flesh and immediate pilferageable loot, although some modern writers insist that Genghis Khan also possessed some spiritual motivation for the apocalypse he wrought.

The entire Mongol nation, estimated at between 700,000 and 3 million people, mobilized for predatory warfare and the bacchanalia that followed. Women followed the armies onto the battlefields to slit the throats of enemy wounded while children darted about the corpses retrieving arrowheads to launch against the next unfortunate foe. Military units were structured on the decimal system so that no commander had to give orders to more than ten men. The building block of the huge Mongol armies was the *arban* and *bagatur* – a ten-man squad and its leader, which could be rapidly deployed in a ten-*arban* squadron – the *jagun*, then as a ten-*jagun* regiment – the *minghan*, and on so forth up to 10,000-man divisions. Captured technologies – catapults, giant crossbows, gunpowder, incendiaries, combat engineering and psychological warfare techniques, to name but a few – were expertly exploited and applied in battle.

After Ghengis Khan died in August 1227, the Mongol whirlwind raged for two more generations. The bloody tide of the Mongol invasion ebbed at the gates of Vienna in December 1241, halted not by defeat, but by the death of the current khan, Temujin's grandson Ogedei. The army of another grandson, Mongke, penetrated as far west as Ain Jalut, Palestine in September 1260, before his death and a powerful Mameluke army deflated its vigor. Within two centuries of Temujin's triumphant 1206 *khuriltai* on the Onon river, successors to Mongol rule who had not assimilated into local societies lapsed into squabbles, debauchery and irrelevance. In the Mongols' 'glorious slaughter' and sacking of Samarkand, Bukhara, Herat and other central Asian cities, they abruptly halted development and reshaped the landscape with the massive heaps of their victims' bones. In western and central Siberia, their empire dissolved into a number of Turkified khanates and by the fourteenth century the region was labeled Tataria on Italian maps, Sibir in Arabic chronicles, the origins of both names being obscured by time. Mongol territory quickly receded back to the heartland between Lake Baikal and a rising Manchuria, and the yak-tail banner became a symbol of barbarity and sadism. Yet, in Mongol folklore, Genghis Khan became a national icon.

By 1580, when the bellwether Cossack expedition under Yermak Timofeyevich marched into Siberia, the land was still predominately inhabited by numerous clans of pastoral nomads and hunter-gatherers. Tatar khans, Turkic heirs to Mongol power, still ruled large patches of western and central Siberia, although the growth of the Muscovy principality into a Russian power center was eroding Tatar territory. After the Russian conquest of the khanates of Kazan and Astrakhan in 1552 and 1554, the borders of the White Tsar (then Ivan IV, 'the Terrible') were pressing against the Ural mountains and Caspian Sea to the east and a strong Polish kingdom and Crimean khanate to the west and south. Along the periphery of Tsar Ivan's kingdom lived communities of iniquitous pirates, renegades, fugitives from cruel and arbitrary laws and runaways from vassalage, the flotsam of scores of different tribes and cultures, predominately Orthodox Christians, known as the Cossacks.

Yermak was a Cossack warrior originally hired and outfitted with modern firearms by the Stroganov family, rich salt-merchants on the Kama river, to defend its property. With the Tsar's blessing, Yermak led a band of Volga Cossacks as far as the Irtysh river, defeating numerically superior detachments of the Tatar khanate of Sibir in several battles along the way. His small force captured Tyumen and Khan Kuchum's capital, Kashlyk, before Yermak drowned in battle in about 1585, pulled under the Irtysh by a suit of heavy chainmail bestowed upon him by the Tsar. Yermak's legend spread quickly, advertising the vulnerability of the vast lands to the east, rich with furs. The seeds of Cossack conquest for God and Tsar had been planted.

Expansion into Siberia handed the Tsar an opportunity to simultaneously employ Russia's restless Cossacks against the troublesome Tatars on his eastern frontier and to tap into the treasures of Siberia's forests. The push to the east would offer the added benefits of siphoning off Cossacks away from the burgeoning frontier of Russian commerce and population where they engaged in banditry and inspired disobedience and disperse the explosive concentrations of troublemakers in the Volga and Don river basin *voiskos* (hosts), the unruly communities that were swelling with runaway serfs and tax-dodgers. Siberia provided the pressure-relief that made it possible for Russia's property-owning elite to tighten the screws upon the peasantry, institutionalizing feudal relationships by indenturing serfs to land and landowner, and constantly increasing the tax burden.

Thus, Cossacks, trappers and traders bore into Siberia's forests in search of freedom as much wealth from furs. Allured by the scent of new revenue, the Tsar began dispatching settlers and exiles to reinforce the territorial gains of the Cossack vanguard within ten years of Yermak's first expedition. Throughout the seventeenth century, the oppression of Russian and Polish governors, nobles, priests and bureaucrats enkindled violent upheaval among the Cossacks. Cossack aversion to authority and the grind of feudal life drove them east into the forests, despite Siberia's threats of scurvy, starvation, frostbite, snow-blindness and hostile natives. Some Cossacks exchanged the uncertain life of trader or robber for service as garrison soldiers or government agents (*prikazchiki*) – service Cossacks, the backbone of Russian imperial expansion. Service Cossacks were paid in cash, grain, salt or sometimes land and titles, however Siberia often extracted payment of its own in misery, blood, sanity and life.

As Cossack camps evolved into settlements and then towns, attracting colonists and meddling Russian administrators, Cossacks drove deeper into Siberia to escape the stifling influence of the latter. Within 60 years of Yermak's expedition, Cossacks had swarmed over the 4,000 miles of Siberian wilderness between the Urals and the Pacific. The steady march across Siberia left a string of fortified settlements at strategic, defensible sites along major rivers: Tyumen in 1585, Tomsk in 1604, Krasnoyarsk in 1628, with dozens of *zimov'e*, small cabin outposts, to collect the *yasak*, in between. In 1689 the Russian–Chinese Treaty of Nerchinsk halted the Cossack advance at the Amur river, the natural boundary between Siberia's forests and the Manchurian badlands. By the middle of the eighteenth century, armies of China's Qing dynasty coincidentally removed the biggest threats to Russia's vulnerable chain of outposts by defeating the Kalmyk and Kyrgyz princes of the Turkestan steppes. Offshoots from the Mongol family tree, they had refused to pay the *yasak* – an age-old tribute paid in furs and commanded formidable nomad cavalry that proved lethal to the small Cossack detachments.

Of course, Siberia was not unoccupied, virgin territory, and the inhabitants were not eager to share the forests and waters with the newcomers. Cossacks became adept at pitting tribes against each other, a task made easier by generations of squabbling over hunting and fishing rights. They made alliances with many tribes, took hostages when expedient, instituted loyalty oaths, and, to the tsar's delight, collected the *yasak*. There were fierce battles between combatants, enslavement of natives, forced labor, smallpox outbreaks among isolated clans in the far north, and incidences of mass murder of locals and cannibalism among stranded, starving Cossack detachments. Their tiny parasitic colonies were precarious footholds in a vast green sea brimming with hostile inhabitants. Cossack survival relied upon pacts with local chiefs and the loyalty of local mercenaries as much as it did on imported foods.

An expedition under Yakov Khripunov brought Russian encroachment to Buryat Mongol territory in 1622, but the Buryats would not willingly submit to Russian rule for another 80 years even though they were eager to trade. Khripunov dispatched a Cossack envoy named Kozlov to invite the natives to become Russian subjects. Apparently the Buryats refused the offer, because in 1627 an expedition under one Perfilyev set out to unsuccessfully extort tribute from the Buryats.[5] Yet another expedition, led by explorer Piotr Beketov, was attempted the next year, but, for the time being, the Russians sidestepped the Buryats and continued east up the Angara river, then the Ilim, then the Lena to establish Fort Yakutsk in 1632. Six years later, the Altyn Khan, who ruled from Lake Ubsa in northwestern Mongolia, warmly received a Russian envoy, yet opposition to the invaders from the West continued.[6] Resistance faltered in 1643, when Cossacks broke the Buryat siege of a Russian fort at Verkholensk near Lake Baikal's western shore, ransacked local villages and crossed the lake to squeeze tribute from Buryats on the Irkut river. The following year, a Russian expedition was allowed to visit the Setsen Khan's capital, Urga, on the Mongolian plateau and shortly thereafter the Setsen Khan sent an emissary to Moscow, formally launching a cautious courtship with Russia. Sometime during these years of tension, shamans noted that when a great forest fire destroyed an expanse of dusky pines, white-barked birch trees grew out of the ashes, an omen that Russians would supplant the Buryats. Thus, perhaps it was inevitable that in 1648 Barguzin was founded on Lake Baikal's eastern shore 'as a place to receive tribute from the Buryats'.[7] Uprisings against the Russians occurred in 1650, 1695 and 1696, but in a few short years the Buryats agreed to a Russian protectorate to avoid Manchu rule by an expanding Qing dynasty in China. The first 60 families of Russian colonists settled in Buryat country at Fort Balazansk in 1653. Nevertheless, Buryat *taishas* (chiefs) maintained some authority until the twentieth century, although this arrangement did not prevent Russian expropriation of lands for distribution to settlers and exiles.

Despite all of their freedom-loving discourse, the Cossacks were no less brutal than Spain's *conquistadores* in the Americas and they eagerly became the bloody instruments of 'ruthless colonial exploitation'.[8] Armed resistance against the Russian conquest begat slaughters by both invaders and the original inhabitants, but the worst cases led to genocide of indigenous groups such as the Dauri people on the Amur river, who were hunted down and butchered during campaigns by Vasilii Poyarkov about 1645 and Yerofei Khabarov in 1650. Cossack settlers in Kamchatka so exploited and ravaged the natives that wholesale murder, massacres and waves of suicides reduced the indigenous population from 20,000 to 8,000 in the first five decades of the Russian conquest.

The Cossacks were a remote threat to the Khalka Mongols who lived in the region that is now modern Mongolia. A Dzungar Mongol army under Galdan Khan was pressuring them from the west in an effort to conquer and reunify the entire Mongol nation. In desperation the Khalka appealed to the Manchus for assistance, who routed Galdan's army with modern artillery then, in May 1691, summoned major Khalka chiefs to a *khuriltai* at which the Qing monarch, Kangxi, received their pledges of loyalty in return for his protection. The Khalka lands furnished Kangxi with a buffer against Russian expansion and a base for offensive operations against the Cossacks.

North of the Khalka lands, the Buryats and Evenki were preyed upon by Khalka raiders who stole cattle and horses, and drew closer to the Russians for security. In 1727 China and Russia agreed upon a line between east and west that roughly shadowed the boundary between Evenki and Buryat territory to the north and Peking's Khalka vassals to the south. On the Russian side of the line Evenki and Buryat clans living near the delineating rivers and 63 stone border posts were employed to guard the border in exchange for some enticing privileges. Evenki, for example, received lances from the Cossacks, exemption from paying tribute and 6 rubles per year. In 1772, Cossacks were ordered to homestead along the border and soon lived alongside Evenki and Buryat families in budding villages.[9]

In the 1760s construction of the Great Siberian Post Road, the *trakt* linking Moscow to Yakutsk, facilitated migration, communications and supply to settlements, so that by the end of the century approximately 1.6 million Russians were scattered across Siberia. All who ventured into the depths of Siberia, from nobles to convicts, shared the *trakt*, the single artery that bore into the green frontier. They all experienced Siberia's physical sense of loneliness and desolation, the monotony of the endless taiga, the claustrophobia between the morose walls of pine and cedar that seemed ready to smother the *trakt* in verdant boughs. As travelers penetrated deeper into central and eastern Siberia, they felt the palpable vastness – a thousand miles between cities (for example, Tomsk–Irkutsk), hundreds of miles between towns, and 15–20 miles between post stations, the sturdy cabins where travelers exchanged horses, drank tea and passed on news.[10] Travelers with means rode in a *tarantass*, a notoriously uncomfortable carriage where the rhythmic plod of horses' hooves, muffled crunch of the vehicle's four wheels on roadbed and incessant vibration that jarred every bone and organ might mercifully lull the fortunate into a trance. On the *trakt* west of Lake Baikal, the tedium might be relieved by the passage of a clinking column of somber convicts or procession of big-wheeled barrels of vodka heading east, or a westbound procession of tea carts.

It is difficult to say whether the *trakt* spawned development along the Tea Road, or vice versa. Russians had savored their initial taste of Chinese tea during the first half of the seventeenth century and quickly adopted it as their national drink. Their voracious demand gave birth to the Tea Road, the trade route that funneled precious bales of tea to the thirsty masses in Europe. From its origin at Kalgan behind China's Great Wall, camel caravans lumbered across the Gobi desert to the Outer Mongolian city of Urga, thence to Kyakhta, a Russian border town made rich by the trade. Sledges, boats and other conveyances carried the tea to Irkutsk via Verkhne-Udinsk and Lake Baikal. Naturally the profitable tea trade generated subsidiary commerce in leather, sheepskins, furs, horns, woolen clothes, coarse linens, manufactured silks, nankeen cloth, porcelain, rhubarb, cattle and Chinese produce. Cossacks were thinly deployed along the Tea Road, the *trakt* and frontier not only to protect traders but to legitimize the tsar's claim on the new territory.

The *trakt* and Tea Road accelerated the growth of Irkutsk, which, since Spiridon Lingusov's caravan passed through with a load of Chinese wares in 1698, had already grown into a prosperous regional trading hub and showed signs of becoming a budding center of industry. Cossack and settler farms thrived on the fertile earth nearby, and the city prospered enough to replace its village church with Bogoyavleniya Cathedral in 1718. In 1719, Irkutsk earned the mantle of provincial capital over a domain that stretched east along a chain of towns and villages originally seeded by Cossack *ostrogi* (forts) in the seventeenth century, principally Verkhne-Udinsk, Chita, Sretensk and Nerchinsk. On the heels of Irkutsk's newfound prestige came a city hall, courts, magistrates, merchants, tradesmen, shopkeepers and all of the trappings of civilization that most Cossacks tried earnestly to avoid.[11]

Nevertheless, the Cossacks had now become an instrument of the government instead of its nemesis, and although this unusual marriage did not tame them, it did institutionalize their society and traditions, making them subject to a special body of law, setting forth conditions for military service, elections of *atamans* (chiefs), property ownership and other aspects of life. Yet, beneath the thin veneer of explorer, frontiersman or farmer lay the dormant beast of Cossack brigand, libertine or rapist. Stefan Petrovich Krasheninnkov, a scientist who accompanied Vitus Bering through Siberia about 1740, wrote:

> The Cossacks, a people rude enough themselves, seemed to be pretty well pleased with the manner of living here, using the natives as slaves, who furnished them with sables and other furs in abundance, and passing the greatest part of their time at playing cards. Their only want seemed to be that of brandy. In gambling for brandy...the gamesters wagered their furs and when they had no furs, even their slaves. What the poor slaves endured is almost incredible, being obliged sometimes to change their masters twenty times a day.[12]

Just as the Cossacks reshaped the societies they invaded, Siberian conditions gradually molded Cossack society to better accommodate the hardships and demands of frontier life. The loneliness of wilderness living led to Cossack intermarriage with local women, and the melding of Cossack traditions with local ones. Likewise Siberia's demands on Cossack services differed quite a bit from those expected of the older *voiskos* in the Don and Volga river basins, so a Siberian Cossack Host was established, tailored to Siberian measurements. While Cossacks continued to swear loyalty only to God and Tsar, the manner in which God was worshipped gradually became less important in Siberia as Shamanists, Lamaists and Buddhists seeped into the ranks which had traditionally been all Orthodox Christian. Also, in contrast to their western brethren, Siberian Cossacks were paid individually, were granted personal rather than communal freedoms and were overseen by Russian governors. The close living of the interconnected communities that intimately bonded Don, Volga and Caucasian Cossacks to their brethren was impossible in Siberia, where communities were often separated by hundreds of miles of wilderness and hostile natives. Siberian Cossacks were scattered across the map, acting as 'official tribute collectors, guides and militiamen', and sometimes serving as the sole representative of tsar and his vast imperial administration, a lone beacon of Christendom and Western culture in a dark green sea of shamans and pagans.[13] Anyway, the village, the core social unit of Cossack life in the west and font of communal property, was weakened by an 1869 law allowing all individual Cossacks to own property.

A century after the European invaders appeared east of Lake Baikal, independent units of Evenki and Buryats were formed to perform security and administrative functions that had traditionally been the domain of the Siberian Cossacks. These units formed the catalysts for an Evenki regiment that was organized in 1762 and for four Buryat regiments of 600 men each established two years later.[14] On 17 March 1851, the Governor-General of eastern Siberia, Nikolai N. Murav'ev, established the Transbaikal Cossack Host with its headquarters at Chita and regional centers at Verkhne-Udinsk in the west and Nerchinsk in the east. Its ranks were built around the existing Evenki and Buryat regiments, and buttressed by an infusion of 29,000 peasant emigrants.[15] A Western traveler described them as 'wild, untaught, and savage to the backbone', even 50 years after their formation.[16]

Similarly, in 1857, when General Murav'ev led an armed flotilla down the Amur to take the river basin territory for Russia, he took 12,000 supposed 'volunteers' from the Transbaikal Cossacks. They gave birth to the Amur Cossack Host, which, owing to its extreme isolation and danger, was recruited with special incentives – exemption from military service, cash, timber to make rafts and other enticements. Coming at a time when the creaking Qing dynasty was preoccupied with the Second Anglo-French Opium War and the Taiping Rebellion, Murav'ev's aggressive colonization forced the Chinese to recognize the Amur river as the Sino-Russian border in May 1858. To keep the diplomatic accounts of favors and counterfavors straight, China 'owed' Russia for the latter's role in mediating an end to British and French aggression.

In subsequent years, 6,500 Amur Cossacks were drafted or enticed to foster the Ussuri Cossack Host, which surged to the Sea of Japan and founded Vladivostok in 1860 for their ambitious master, Murav'ev.[17] The lines of the empire had been drawn, impelled by lust, hunger for freedom, greed and patriotism.

Frontier Siberia

As the dawn of the twentieth century loomed on the horizon, daily life for most people in Siberia stumbled along to a monotonous rhythm unchanged in centuries. A handful of large towns strewn through the taiga between Lake Baikal and the Pacific coast carried the torch of progress, reaping the riches of commerce, administering and taxing the outlands, and tinkering with new ideas that arrived from the West. The native peoples had been subjugated or assimilated, but Russia's growth along the Amur river and Pacific were causing new tensions with their Chinese and Japanese neighbors. Yet old, internal tensions stood poised to change or disrupt everything in the twentieth century.

By 1897, more than 4.5 million Russians lived in Siberia, though most had not ventured far beyond the *trakt* in western Siberia. Three major waves of immigration had swept new faces into eastern Siberia and the Russian Far East: Cossacks in the seventeenth century, Old Believers in the eighteenth century, and Peasants in the nineteenth century. The abolition of serfdom in 1861 swelled the numbers, although officially Russians needed permission inscribed in an internal passport to relocate. Peasant immigrants who resettled with official blessing after 1889 received 15 *dessiatins* (40.5 acres), a three-year tax holiday and nine years exemption from military service. However, it was easier for immigrants to be declared 'Siberians' by bureaucrats than by their new neighbors. Prince Kropotkin sneered dramatically, 'He is a "Russian" – a term of contempt with the *Sibiryak*.'[18] In the first two decades of the twentieth century, the term 'Siberians' referred to European immigrants who settled in Siberia before the railway arrived with tens of thousands more homesteaders.

Exiles had reluctantly followed closely on the heels of the first settlers in Siberia.[19] Beginning in 1754, the systematic exile of convicts, prisoners of war and political malcontents was used to populate villages and labor camps. Nobles who plotted the unsuccessful December 1825 uprising against the autocracy added an elite class to Siberia's social strata of exiles when they were banished to villages in the Irkutsk and Transbaikal regions. The Polish revolt of 1863 and peasant revolts in the Ukraine infused a number of villages with Siberia's largest Catholic congregations. Still, political exiles never comprised more than 2 percent of the exiles; most were peasants charged by landowners, clergy or other non-judicial authorities with imprecise misdeeds such as 'vagabondage' or 'vile behavior'.[20] Violent criminals and social deviants – heretics, homosexuals and the like – fleshed out the body of exiles.

Staroveri, Old Believers, comprised one of the largest exile groups in Transbaikalia. They were the byproducts of a traumatic 1653 schism (*raskol*) in the Russian Orthodox Church, which pitted traditionalists, the *staroveri* (or *raskolniki*), against reformers backed by Tsar Alexei Romanov and the Russian Orthodox patriarch, Archbishop Nikhon of Novgorod. Nikhon intended to modernize Russian rituals to conform with those of other – foreign – Eastern Orthodox churches, but a 1666 council of Eastern Orthodox patriarchs that assembled in Moscow to resolve the conflict aggravated the situation by excommunicating millions of Russian Orthodox Christians. Nikhon virulently purged the clergy and flock of Old Believers, zealously promoting his reforms with flogging, burning at the stake and exile. To the Old Believers, following Nikhon's errant flock and accepting the modernized church rituals entailed nothing less than damnation; the contentious 1666 council signaled an alien takeover of their church and heralded the coming of the Antichrist. During ensuing years, the *raskolnikis*' Western European farmland lay fallow while 'the faithful adorned themselves in burial clothes and awaited the end of the world in their cemeteries at night, singing hymns and sitting in wooden coffins'.[21] Some communities committed mass suicide. In 1682, Tsar Peter III ('the Great' to non-Believers) took the throne and in 1706 launched his personal crusade to Westernize Russia, forcing foreign customs, dress and the shaving-off of beards upon the obstinate peasantry, while targeting Old Believers in particular for violent persecution because of their obstruction. They sought refuge from the blasphemous modernization, often among the Cossackry in Russia's border areas and the autocracy obliged die-hard Old Believers by exiling them to the fringes of the empire. The first *staroveri* moved into Irkutsk in 1756 and by the early nineteenth century exiles from Ukrainian, Belorussian and Polish points of origin had established successful settlements along the Uda and lower Selenga Rivers in Transbaikalia. In Transbaikalia they became known as *semeiskie*, literally the family ones, because whole families were exiled.[22] Warm bonds developed between Old Believers and Cossacks and the Believers' 'defense of the old ritual became the defense of Russia's history, [and] as western influence continued to grow, it became a defense of native cultural tradition as well'.[23]

Other sizeable minorities at the turn of the century included about 40,000 Chinese and no less than 25,000 Koreans usually living in small communities on the outskirts of towns in the Russian Far East. Several thousand Japanese migrants were widely dispersed between Irkutsk and Vladivostok. Asian immigration exploded during the next two decades, easily swelling these numbers fourfold. The population of the indigenous Evenki had declined to 70,000, but the resilient Buryat Mongols had made the best of the Russian invasion.

In 1897, somewhere between 220,000 and 300,000 Buryats lived in Russia's Far East, most in the region around Lake Baikal and in Transbaikal Province. Though largely pastoral nomads on the Transbaikal steppe – packing up their eight-sided yurts twice a year to migrate between summer pastures and winter camps – the Buryats' patrilineal clans living closer to Lake Baikal included many skilled farmers, hunters, fishermen, lumberjacks and artisans. Some Buryats had joined the tsarist civil service, and many lived in towns alongside 'Siberian' neighbors and adopted European dress when it suited them. Buryats in traditional garb were a common sight in Transbaikal cities: pig-tailed men with fur-rimmed hats shaped like yurts, wrapped in fur robes secured by ornate belts; women in derby hats, ankle-length skirts, and goatskin coats, overladen with silver, coral, malachite and mother of pearl jewelry. Buryat culture owed its strength to its people's willingness and ability to fight total subjugation by the Russians, as demonstrated by their exemption from the *yasak* in earlier times.[24] By the turn of the century, Buryats enjoyed a symbiotic relationship with the government and escaped convicts and exiles made a point of avoiding their settlements to avoid being turned in.[25]

Perhaps the endemic violence in Russia's Far Eastern society comes as no surprise considering that the population was drawn from convicts, exiles, fugitives, peasant migrants torn away from their family roots in European Russia and descendents of Genghis Khan, not to mention that the authorities themselves, the Cossacks, were the offspring of a culture of piracy and rebellion. Indeed, during the infancy of Siberia's settlements, flogging, lip- and nose-slitting and burial alive were still officially sanctioned punishments among the Cossacks.

Exile and *katorga* – hard labor – stimulated Siberian demographics with a rich diversity of criminals and dissidents, who shaped the region's attitudes toward the state, law and order and life. By 1896 some 17,000 to 20,000 convicts – along with their hapless spouses and children – were herded east on the *trakt* each year to forsaken Siberian mines and villages.[26] The unfortunate, who could not adjust to the stresses of 10-hour workdays in winter or 14 hours in summer, faced death from overwork, exposure, brutal beatings, starvation, a variety of diseases, or suicide (drinking the toxins of matches soaked in water was a popular escape according to Trotsky). Their sufferings christened Siberia as the 'land of exile'.

As of 1901, no less than 17,000 men and women had been 'transported for life' to Transbaikalia and the increasing pace of revolutionary activity in European Russia during subsequent years swelled the numbers.[27] They included 'some of the vilest criminals of the human race', a fact attributed to Russia's infrequent application of capital punishment.[28] They also included many innocents, exiled to Siberia for some slight against a property-owner. Upper class reliance on the tsarist exile system to enforce the exploitation of peasants and workers stoked the caustic violence of class hatred. Runaways from the system took to the forests each spring – 'when the cuckoo cried'– and the hills around Chita sparkled with their campfires. Thousands of escaped convicts and exiles – 'the terror of the Transbaikal province' – skulked in the forests or marshes, desperate enough to kill to relieve a citizen of a legitimate passport.[29]

Governors-General of Siberian provinces had no trouble relieving citizens of their rights and property and, so conveniently far from St Petersburg, ruled their domains like 'personal fiefdoms'.[30] Given the vast distances between settlements, local authorities could transform into petty tyrants, and power and justice was often distorted in the myopic world of an isolated village. 'Private and especially romantic, conflicts frequently took on the proportions of drama', wrote an exiled Leon Trotsky of life in the dismal villages of Ust-Kut and Verkholensk, Irkutsk *Guberniya* (Province). Even Ust-Kut, a tiny 'village comprised [of] about a hundred peasant huts, had seen "days of wild debauches, robberies, and murders"'.[31]

Siberia's sexual mores were warped by isolation, the absence of family, authority or religious pressure and by an aching shortage of women that inspired Cossacks (and centuries of forlorn men before them) to kidnap and trade in indigenous women.[32] As settlements grew, Cossack women influenced the budding Siberian society with their 'high degree of sexual license'.[33] The large numbers of convicts and exiles reinforced this trend, particularly as they included many 'dissipated women, bloated with self-indulgence and apparently dead to every consideration except that of personal profit and enjoyment'.[34] Rumors were whispered of renegade Christian cults in Siberian villages that engaged in sexual orgies such as the *khlisti* (whippers), in which a wanderer, destined to notoriety, named Grigorii Efimovich Rasputin indulged.[35] Immigrants quickly adjusted to the milieu. Siberia's sexual appetites would eventually pose a strategic conundrum, as the daughters of Korean and Japanese farmers, sold by their fathers to prostitution rings, staffed a vast chain of brothels that began spreading west from Vladivostok in 1883.[36]

Further loosening of Siberia's inhibitions was fueled by 'the great propensity which the Russians generally had for strong liquors, the ladies as well as the gentlemen'.[37] Vodka inflamed passions from shared bottles in post stations on the *trakt* and from barrels in wild Cossack bacchanalias. No Buryat homestead was complete without a barrel or more of *tarasun*, a 'highly alcoholic colorless liquid' distilled from mare's milk, fermenting under a lean-to by the house (although such home production of *tarasun* was technically illegal).[38] Celebrations, notably Easter, brought out 'fantastic head-dresses and pink-flowered gowns of the women, and the red blouses of the men', and days of round-the-clock carousing fueled by liquor.[39] In colder months, the harsh climate and ennui of being snowbound for days at a time – on top of the daily peril of life in the wilderness, encouraged tippling.

The land itself could be cruel. Summer's warmth casts a deceiving glow upon the Transbaikal taiga and steppe. July is the only frost-free month. Winter freezes rivers to the bottom and snow softens the shade until the summer's peak. When Trotsky crossed the Lena during his springtime escape from Ust-Kut, the river was full of 'loose timber and dead animals' and whirlpools.[40] For anyone unfortunate enough to become stranded or lost, starvation usually beckoned long before rescuers knew of any problem. The lonely 'runaway paths' leading away from labor camps were dotted with the bones of those who 'vanished like a cloud in the sky on a hot summer day', as Prince Kropotkin referred to those who fell ill, broke a bone or starved to death on the run. Around Lake Baikal, the usual Siberia hazards were compounded by earthquakes, unusually powerful thunderstorms and other bizarre natural phenomena that could kill the unwary.

Tales of the empty *tarantass* rolling into a village, all aboard having been devoured by some predator, attest to the fear inspired by the taiga's denizens. Man did not stand at the top of Siberia's food chain. Brown bears (*Ursus arctos*) standing 10 feet tall and weighing over 1,500 pounds generally roamed unsettled areas, but, in years of poor pine nut crops, searched wherever they pleased for substitute menu items, such as livestock or man. In Transbaikalia's harsh, dry habitat, man-eating bears were more prevalent than in other parts of Siberia.[41] Massive tigers also prowled east of Lake Baikal, especially in the Ussuri district, but wolves were the 'most numerous and destructive beasts of prey in Siberia' and did not hesitate to attack men when desperate for food.[42] Yet, the predators that made life most miserable came in 'overpowering swarms' of mosquitoes and midges voracious enough to drain the life out of livestock.[43]

Village life could exacerbate Siberia's risks. The typical, unpainted wooden house, each looking as if it had endured a hundred winters, underlined the grim monotony. Some sagged into the mushy soil until the window sills, ablaze in geraniums during summer's brief blush, grazed tired paths daubed with garbage and manure of roaming livestock, pigs and cats. Some wretched, chained mongrel usually snarled at every passerby when not curled into a dusty cavity scratched into the dirt yard. Beyond the lucky iron horseshoe inevitably set into the principal threshold of each peasant *izba*, the houses were often dark, overcrowded, poor ventilated and filthy. A cornucopia of deadly diseases flourished in unsanitary dwellings: plague, typhus, 'relapsing fever', typhoid fever, scarlet fever, measles, mumps, whooping cough and 'malignant sore throat'. Infant mortality amidst such squalor was 'very great'.[44] Tedium and isolation could breed psychosis or dangerous behavior like alcoholism, chronic abuse or incest.

Typhoid and other diseases transmitted by drinking contaminated water were endemic. In any settlement of substantial size, water was distributed by Chinese vendors who served the public with 'filthy water carts'. Wells, streams and even sizeable sections of rivers were sometimes polluted with animal waste. 'Sometimes it was green, and sometimes brown, and always tainted with decayed organic matter', wrote Charles Wenyon of the drinking water he was offered during a late nineteenth-century journey on the *trakt*. 'But as the average Siberian peasant only uses water to dilute his vodka and infuse his tea', reasoned Wenyon, 'the danger may have been less serious than it seemed.'[45] Luckily the drinking of *chai* (tea) was a common social ritual at all hours; samovars gurgled day and night in every public establishment.

Until civil war cast its shadow across Siberia, food was 'abundant and cheap'. Luxuriant vegetables thrived, especially fertilized as they were by 'liquefied night soil' – human excrement, a detail that many uninitiated newcomers would belatedly discover when the wrenching cramps and chills of dysentery soon followed an undercooked meal. Alas, as the last years of the nineteenth century faded the menu of hazards to human health dished out by Siberia had remained unchanged for millennia.

In past millennia invading armies and great migrations traditionally brought change into Siberia, but the twentieth century rushed into Siberia on iron rails. Nikolai Murav'ev, the empire-builder who engineered Russia's final expansion to the Pacific, had begun clamoring for a Far Eastern Railway soon after his 1857 conquest of the Amur basin and appointment as Governor-General of the new territory. In 1886, Tsar Alexander III, looking to cement and bolster Russia's presence in Asia, committed funds of the Russian treasury to the engineering and construction of the Trans-Siberian Railway. Wasting no time, survey teams set out to plot the railway's course during the following year. On 19 May 1891, the tsarevich, Nikolai Alexandrovich, ceremoniously laid a symbolic first stone of Trans-Siberian construction on the future site of the Vladivostok train station. When his father, Alexander III, died of kidney disease in November 1894, the 26-year-old Tsarevich was crowned Nicholas II and inherited humanity's most grandiose engineering project, along with one-sixth of the world's landmass and 100 million illiterate, superstitious, impoverished and restless peasants. Like the young untested Tsar, the bold Trans-Siberian Railway project seemed to embody Russia's aspiration to emerge from its feudal gloom into a new century of promise.

The entire nation threw its savings and the minds of its best scientists and engineers into Trans-Siberian construction. Within two years of Alexander's death, nearly 90,000 men – laborers hired out of European Russia, convicts and soldiers – were crashing through the taiga and marshes, east from Chelyabinsk and west from Vladivostok, paralleling the *trakt* where possible, wielding the simplest of tools – axes, handsaws, picks, shovels and wheelbarrows. Despite their primitive implements, they would lay approximately 15,000 miles of track by the end of the decade, including, of course, branches, spurs, sidings and other peripheral lines and countless bridges, some of them engineering marvels in their own right that defied Asia's most powerful rivers.[46] Nevertheless, to keep costs down and meet their aggressive schedule, they took shortcuts that would eventually return to haunt the railway. For example, on stretches of the Ussuri and Western Siberian lines, specifications were relaxed to allow for narrower railbeds, thinner layers of ballast and lighter rails than were necessary.[47] Many bridges were constructed of wood, though engineers preferred metal. The engineering challenges were not only compounded by tight budgets, marshy terrain dissected by alternately frozen or raging rivers and work gangs of illiterates and convicts, but by pressure from the Tsar himself.

The monumental construction of the Circumbaikal Line, in the shadows of the frosty Khamar Daban mountains between the lakeside towns of Baikal, Slyudyanka and Mysovaya, faced the most obstacles. Though only 162 miles (244 *versts*) in length, it took five years and 220 rubles per *verst* to build, three times as much as any other stretch that length, because of the need to blast 41 tunnels through the precipices alongside Lake Baikal.[48] When it finally opened for regular traffic in October 1905, it would take a train four hours to skirt the lake's crystalline waters, clinging to cliffsides, tumbling over stony ridges, diving through tunnels, all the while twisting, coiling and uncoiling over tight turns like a wandering snake.[49] Still, it made for an easier journey than the alternative, taking the train ferry-icebreaker *Baikal*.[50]

By 1899, the Trans-Siberian Railway connected Irkutsk to European Russia, and by 1903, it linked Vladivostok to St Petersburg, although construction was far from finished in the Amur district, so that just east of Chita the railway took a shortcut through Manchuria to the Ussuri line. Regardless of its sociopolitical disappointments and economic shortcomings, the Trans-Siberian Railway was a marvelous engineering feat.

To Russia's government, the Trans-Siberian Railway promised prestige, a solid presence in the new Amur and Ussuri territories on the Pacific, security as a national defense asset, revenue from expanded commerce and pressure relief from the poor and explosive masses in Europe begging for a piece of land. To businessmen, the Iron Road (*zheleznaya doroga*) opened new markets, broadened sources of supply and offered a new source of profits. To the poor, it offered an escape route to land of their own, a chance to gamble the future on eastward migration. But the railway could not solve Russian society's ills. Indeed, electric lighting from the weekly *Train de Luxe* literally cast a stark light on the gulf between rich and poor, as railside hovels quivered and flashed in the golden glow from the luxurious *coupés*, 'where you can shut your door and sleep all day if you prefer it, or eat and drink, smoke and play cards if you like that better', wrote one well-off 1901 traveler who was amazed by individual electric reading lights and separate electric bells to summon a waiter or attendant.[51] Alas, the railway by itself could 'not substantially relieve the pressure for land in European Russia; it merely intensified the peasants' craving for land of their own and hastened the end of the communal system'.[52]

As for the railway's economic shortcomings, Russian planners realized before the system was completed 'that in the competition for through-freights, the Trans-Siberian Railway may not cope with the steamship lines to Europe, either in rates or time ... The time between Vladivostok and Hamburg, under present conditions, will be about the same either by rail or steamer, with the advantage of uninterrupted passage and fragmentary rates in favour of the latter.'[53]

Of course, the Tsar did not invest 1.5 billion rubles to lay a pair of iron rails across Asia merely to gamble on unpredictable returns from the freight-carrying business. Russia had its eye on real estate – Manchuria, Korea, Mongolia and Tibet, rich untapped natural resources and even more so on the geopolitical advantage such desolate real estate offered during an age of empires.[54] 'One of the most potent instruments of world-dominion to-day is the railway', wrote the sensationalist travel writer Burton Holmes at the turn of the century. 'Russia wields modern weapons. The Trans-Siberian Railway is the latest acquisition in her arsenal of conquest.'[55]

Russia's Asian neighbors and the Iron Road

Sixty-one miles east of Chita the double-tracks of the Trans-Siberian Railway split at the town of Karymskaya. One line headed southeast through the Transbaikal steppe toward China, 300 miles away, where, at the frontier, the line became the Chinese Eastern Railway as it cut across northern Manchuria.⁵⁶ The other line bore northeast in a wide loop around Manchuria, shadowing the Amur river on Russian territory and passing 1,248 miles (1,997 kilometers) through Russia's Amur and Ussuri districts to the city of Khabarovsk and on to the Pacific coast. The two lines met again at Nikolsk-Ussuriisk, then terminated 60 miles south at the docks of Vladivostok. The shorter and faster Chinese Eastern route was preferred by most travelers.

Manchuria, the native soil of the ruling Qing dynasty and its Manchu bureaucracy, was, of course, Chinese territory. However, at the turn of the century, Manchuria's absorption into the Russian Empire seemed to be a fait accompli to some observers. An 1899 article in *Scientific American*, a popular US magazine, declared, 'Port Arthur is destined to become the great city of Siberia' and referred to Russia's 'recently acquired territory of Manchuria'. British expatriates in Manchuria, mostly merchants and missionaries, considered the territory 'Russian in all but name'.⁵⁷ However, Manchuria was *not* Russian territory, though it was an 'extraterritorial zone' where Russian laws and control prevailed.

Manchuria's strange situation was the result of China's growing social disorder, internal division and weakness. In 1857, Nikolai Murav'ev and his Cossacks had plowed into the Amur river basin planting Russian flags and settlements with little fear of Chinese retribution, in spite of the 1689 Treaty of Nerchinsk and 1727 Treaty of Kyakhta, both of which defined the limits of Russia's expansion. China's Qing emperor was preoccupied with the sixth bloody year of the Taiping Rebellion, coming on the heels of catastrophic droughts, famines, floods, economic failures, boiling public disgust against the Manchu rulers, and the stinging disgrace of the 1842 Treaty of Nanjing. The Treaty was the final humiliating slap of the Opium War – the First Anglo-Chinese War, in which the defeated emperor ceded Hong Kong to Britain and opened the door for European colonialists to sow China's coast with extraterritorial treaty ports and carve peripheral states from its carcass. By 1885, France had swallowed most of southeast Asia – Cochin China, Cambodia and Annam and Britain controlled Burma.

In the 1890s a new player came to the fore in the east Asian fray – Japan. A harbinger of Japan's heightening competitiveness was the celebrated ride of Captain Fukushima Yasumasa. Supposedly on a challenge from some German officers, Fukushima, the Japanese Military Attaché to Germany, rode his horse from Berlin to Vladivostok, traversing European Russia, Siberia, Mongolia and Manchuria on the way. Fukushima was feted as a hero upon his arrival in Tokyo in 1893. Fukushima's 15-month excursion propelled his career as a leading military intelligence officer, and, most of all, spotlighted all of Japan's primary areas of strategic concern but one – Korea.⁵⁸

Unfortunately for Korea, both Russia and Japan coveted it. Following the lead of the European bullies in China, Japan gradually muscled its way onto Korean soil and into its internal affairs through a series of treaties: Kanghwa in 1876, Chemulpo in 1882 and the Li-Ito Convention in 1884. A populist anti-Japanese and anti-Western movement, Tonghak (Eastern Learning), which blended Confucian religious tenets with Korean nationalism, was penetrated by agents provocateurs controlled by the Genyosha, a Japanese terrorist organization advocating aggressive imperial expansion.⁵⁹ Genyosha, acting on behalf of the Japanese Army Intelligence Service, 'used the *Tonghaks* for agitation and disruption and generally weakening [Korean] government influence'. In 1892, the Tonghaks began orchestrating large-scale demonstrations against Korea's King Kojong that led to brutal suppression. At the request of King Kojong, Chinese forces were dispatched to Seoul's aid in 1894 and Tonghak leaders responded positively to conciliatory promises by the government. However, Japan seized the opportunity to feign helping its little neighbor defend its sovereignty and, on 25 July 1894, sank a Chinese troopship near Asan Bay. This began the first Sino-Japanese War, although Japan did not declare war on China for another six days.

PRELUDE TO TERROR

The Japanese soundly beat the Chinese on land and sea, while crushing the Tong movement and beheading its leader, Chon Pong-jun.[60] China sued for peace after a disastrous nine months of war and in the April 1895 Treaty of Shimonoseki, agreed to give Japan Formosa and choice morsels of Manchuria – Port Arthur and the Liaotung peninsula.

Russia had no intention of letting Japan take possession of any part of Manchuria. Within one week, Russia compelled France and Germany to join it in pressuring Japan diplomatically to renounce its claims to the Manchurian prizes. The Japanese public howled about the 'triple intervention' cheating them of their rightful prize of war, then watched with disgust during the next five years as Russia, France, Germany and Britain carved colonial chunks out of China. Japan's bitterness would simmer for decades.[61]

Meanwhile, Japan wasted no time consolidating its hold on Korea, part of which involved training 800 Korean military men assigned to the palace in Seoul. This literally opened the doors for Japan's next brazen move. At dawn on 8 October 1895, Genyosha assassins charged into Kyongbokgung Palace in Seoul, murdered Queen Min, then incinerated her body with kerosene. The Japanese Minister to Korea, Miura Goro, shamelessly repatriated the perpetrators before they could be apprehended by Korean authorities.[62] The queen's killing sounded the deathknell for the 'greedy, cruel and rapacious personal despotism' of the Korean throne, and for the next half century of Korean independence as well.[63] Year after year, Japan imposed more controls on the Korean population while introducing – and expropriating land for – its own emigrants in pursuit of a 'hopeless ideal – namely the integration of the Koreans with the Japanese'.[64]

Likewise, the Tsar relished the opportunity to 'help' his weak neighbor on the Qing throne, because China's repayment for each Russian 'favor' was so generously out of proportion to the original good deed. In part to assist China to pay Japan a 200 million tael indemnity stipulated by the Treaty of Shimonoseki, Russia arranged for a 400 million franc loan at 4 percent interest, payable in 36 years from issue in July 1895.[65] The loan gave birth to the Russo-Chinese Bank, which in 1910 became the Russo-Asiatic Bank and one of the world's most powerful financial institutions with 30 branches throughout east Asia. A year after issue of the loan, the Chinese were 'induced to contribute' 5 million taels towards the bank's capital. Any separation between the bank and the Russian government seemed a mere legal technicality. The statutes of the bank (approved by a Qing court softened up with generous bribes from Russian lobbyists in Peking) permitted it to receive taxes, manage local finances, mint coins and, last but certainly not least, to construct railways and telegraph systems in China.[66] It was hard to say whether the Russo-Asiatic Bank was a corporation with government powers, or a shadow government with corporate powers.

In March 1896, a Chinese newspaper leaked startling reports of a secret military agreement between Russia and China, not two weeks after the Russian Foreign Ministry had assured Japan that such a pact did not exist. More surprising news was in store for Japan as China's newfound intimacy with Russia came to light. A quiet 1896 Sino-Russian agreement, the Cassini Convention (named after the Tsar's minister in Peking), had, in addition to fleshing out details of the Manchurian Railway concession, promised Russia a treaty port in Kiaochow Harbor. However, in December 1897, the murder of two German Roman Catholic missionaries in Shantung province gave Kaiser Wilhelm II a pretext to invade and claim Kiaochow Harbor and nearby Tsingtao as compensation.[67] So, a jilted Russia informed China that it would 'take hostile measures' if, by 27 March 1898, China did not agree to the lease of Port Arthur and the Liaotung peninsula.[68] China agreed. For partners who had taken the vows of a secret military agreement, it was a strange way to behave. Russia's Pacific fleet, previously icebound in Vladivostok each winter, could henceforth dock in the ice-free Manchurian harbors of Port Arthur and Darien, the latter now known by its new Russian name, Dalny. The Japanese fumed.

15

The Chinese fumed as well. Although railways generated local jobs and commerce, they exemplified the evils of alien origin that were invading China. 'The enmity of people and officials alike seemed to be chiefly directed against two classes – Roman Catholics and mining and railroad engineers', declared a Western missionary.[69] Trains aroused the primitive superstitions of the uneducated millions who loathed the roaring mechanical 'fire-carts' and their endless iron tentacles that uprooted family burial places, upset the *feng shui*, and, according to popular rumor, rested upon foundations of entombed Chinese babies. The telegraph, the railway's constant companion, was no better. Telegraph wires moaned and hummed as if in pain, dripped rusty, blood-colored water after rains or heavy dew and were carried deferentially atop ranks of menacing poles that marched across the horizon, reinforcing the peasants' paranoia that the foreign devils were up to something diabolical. Apart from the supernatural peril, a modern transportation system threatened the rice bowls of merchants, sideroad innkeepers, tax collectors and hordes of teamsters and porters whose work relied on the old patterns of commerce. The Chinese Eastern's 1,464 bridges often choked or completely blocked traffic on canals and waterways, disturbing centuries-old patterns of movement.

It is no wonder that the first mayhem of the Boxer Rebellion occurred at Fengtai, a junction of the Peking – Tientsin Railway, where xenophobic fanatics swarmed over the Empress Dowager's railway coach and destroyed it on 28 May 1900.[70] About 800 miles of the Chinese Eastern Railway had been laid when the Boxers erupted in an anti-Western frenzy in summer 1900.[71] Two years of construction went up in smoke as new stations were torched, warehouses were plundered, tracks were uprooted and assets and personnel were attacked. Troops were rushed over the Trans-Siberian to relieve the beleaguered engineers, missionaries and diplomats in China.

One event in early September 1900 illustrated the unique hazards of the new railway's savage environment, when 'a band of desperados lifted the rails in front of a train that was on the way from Lake Baikal to Chita' (Transbaikalia's administrative and commercial center). Unfortunately for all concerned, it turned out to be a troop train. Eleven soldiers died in the derailment; the bandits got nothing.[72]

The bloody tide of the Boxer pandemonium swept right up to Russia's doorstep. 'On the other side of the [Amur] river, drums began to beat and banners waved and then bullets came dropping into the Blagoveshchensk streets', terrifying the citizens and the small 60-Cossack detachment that was the city's only defense. The government would later claim that an 18-day bombardment took 40 lives, while other accounts say that only windows were broken. In an effort to not appear impotent, the governor, one Chichegov, ordered the city's 8,000 or so peaceful Chinese residents to go back to China. Having no boats with which to cross the Amur, they hunkered down in their homes hoping to ride out the storm of xenophobic vengeance. Eager to strike back at anything Chinese, Chichegov had the Cossacks herd groups of 100 men, women and children down to the banks of the Amur where they were ordered to swim back to China. People who refused to enter the river's swift icy waters were murdered on the shore with bayonet and sword. Some 5,000 souls perished.[73]

Although the Boxer Rebellion added 70 million rubles to construction costs, Russia transformed this negative turn of events into an opportunity to sink its claws deeper into Manchuria. Protection of the railway was originally assigned to the Chinese army by the Cassini Convention, except in unspecified remote areas where Russia might be allowed 'to station special battalions of Russian infantry and cavalry'.[74] During the bedlam of summer 1900, however, Russian soldiers deployed across wide areas of Manchuria. After the Boxer Rebellion, the Chinese Eastern was allowed to expand the railway guard force into its own private army.

By 1902, Russian railways crisscrossed Manchuria. The Chinese Eastern Railway was 920 miles long, entering from Transbaikalia at Manchuli, crossing the Manchurian steppe to Harbin and reentering Russian territory at Pogrannichnaya, not too distant from Vladivostok. The southern Manchurian line stretched south from Harbin 650 miles to Port Arthur. A six-mile spur linked Port Arthur to Dalny. Both railways seeded new Russian settlements and helped to subtly graft the territory onto Siberia.

Similarly in Korea, a Japanese-built railway between the port of Pusan and Seoul accelerated the infusion of Japanese immigrants and influence, and the extraction of exports. Meanwhile a fault line of Russian and Japanese imperial pressures was building up at the Manchurian-Korean border. Russia sought to extend its power via an extension of the railway from Mukden on the southern Manchurian line to the Korean port of Masanpho. Diplomats negotiated for two years to avoid the imminent crisis to no avail. On 7 February 1904 the countries ominously severed diplomatic relations and went to war.

By mid-summer, Russians were disillusioned with their military's lackluster performance against the Asian upstarts: 'Gallant little Japan' had pinned Russia on two fronts, besieging Port Arthur and holding it along the length of the southern Manchurian line.[75] For ten years, liberals, disgruntled workers and idealistic students disappointed with Nicholas II's apathy towards poverty and land reform had been demonstrating occasionally in the streets for a loosening of Russia's autocratic shackles, sometimes bold enough to raise traditional red flags of revolt before gendarmes and Cossacks charged into them with sabers. Now moved by the government's lumbering uncertainty in its campaign in Manchuria, new voices joined the chorus of opposition. Even the *zemstvos* (local elected assemblies first introduced by Tsar Alexander II in 1864) began to call for a constitutional monarchy. From the shadows of illegal opposition, the Socialist Revolutionaries, the loose association of secret political groups formed four years earlier, increased agitation and propaganda against the government. On 28 July 1904 terrorists celebrated the killing of the Minister of Interior – 'the greatest statesman in Russia', in a bold assassination with a hand-held bomb on a St Petersburg thoroughfare cordoned by police. Minister von Plehve, his carriage, coachmen and horses were shredded by the blast.[76] Assassinations had become commonplace, but the brashness of this particular incident emboldened radical reformers. By 1906 and 1907 the tempo of assassinations would climb to 4,000 a year.[77]

That number of men would be slaughtered in a morning in places like Nanshan and Mukden, Manchuria. The Russo-Japanese War was a chain reaction of disasters for Russia. For 18 months, combatants on both sides struggled heroically with frequent displays of chivalry that obscured the horrors of modern warfare. Reinforcements from European Russia began trickling through the narrow pipeline of the Trans-Siberian Railway, but it took until autumn 1904 to accumulate enough men on the front for a counterattack. While Russia faced the daunting test of sustaining logistics for a war front situated a continent away from its supply base, corruption and ineptness better explain the empire's failures.

Problems at chokepoints in the Trans-Siberian supply chain illustrated the failures and foretold future tribulations. 'A hectic time' prevailed at Listvinichnaya and Mysovaya, where the transit of men, munitions and materiel transformed the quiet lakeside villages into boisterous frontier boomtowns.

> Champagne flowed like water. Bedizened vice flaunted itself at every turn. Graft was rampant. Each evening found everyone – generals, colonels, lieutenants, conscripts, Manchurian coolies, and even the numerous uniformed convicts who were drafted to put a shoulder to the wheel of the chariot of Juggernaut – totting up the day's non-official earnings. Everyone demanded, or expected, extra rubles for doing his duty...[78]

In one case a theft ring misdirected seven carloads of champagne, which was transported in 'sealed ammunition cars' to both ensure smooth handling by illiterate soldiery and discourage tampering. A ring of army officers shuffled the seven freight cars out of Irkutsk's jumbled railyard, unloaded them, changed their identification markings and attached them to a westbound train while the champagne was smuggled into southern Manchuria. The ring's larceny cleared about 100,000 rubles.[79]

The concentration of military and civilian resources made the rail corridor a vital target for hostile intelligence and an irresistible lure for counterintelligence. George Digby, an adventurous scholar in the Far East, wrote, 'The Japanese were kept perfectly informed about affairs by scores of intelligence officers, looking like Khalka Mongols, Buryats and Manchus, who had been studying the requisite languages for years, in order to get jobs as coolies and transport workers when the long foreseen struggle with Russia should at last materialize.' They were the forward elements of an elaborate system of Japanese espionage that extended to the frontlines in Manchuria, generating detailed orders of battle and reports of troop movements, attitudes and technical vulnerabilities.[80] But Listvinichnaya and Mysovaya also offered splendid perches for Russian counterspies, who detected and summarily executed 'quite a number' of undercover Japanese agents – 'and a number of [innocent] unfortunate Mongols, Buryats and Manchus, as well'.[81]

The siege of Port Arthur ended suddenly in January 1905 with a scandalous surrender. Huge armies fought the grand finale on land at Mukden between 23 February and 16 March 1905, ending in a Russian withdrawal. At sea, the Tsar's Baltic fleet sailed halfway around the world in a well-publicized six-month voyage to be promptly sunk on 27 May 1905 by Admiral Togo Heihachiro's British-trained and equipped navy in the Battle of Tsushima Straits.

Japan had possessed the foresight to arrange an endgame by arranging with the United States before the war to officiate a peace treaty. The Treaty of Portsmouth rewarded Japan with Russia's railways, bases and treaty rights in southern Manchuria: the Liaotung peninsula, Port Arthur, Dairen and the southern Manchurian line as far north as Changchun. Japan was also given the southern half of Sakhalin Island and free license to continue her domination of Korea.[82]

In 1907, Russia and Japan would secretly agree to boundaries of their respective spheres of influence in Manchuria.[83] An intensifying focus on brother Slavs in the Balkans promised to consume Russian attention during the subsequent seven years. Japan would soon find an excuse to buy out Korea's young King Yi and annex his kingdom in August 1910, after Ito Hirobumi, 'the greatest of Meiji leaders', was gunned down by a Korean nationalist inside the Chinese Eastern Railway station in Harbin.[84]

The Russian government's abysmal conduct of the war caused a tremendous loss of prestige at home and abroad. In the eyes of the public, the army that could not defeat little Japan seemed all too anxious to gun down its own unarmed countrymen in peaceful demonstrations. The 'Bloody Sunday' slaughter on 22 January 1905 sparked strikes and rebellion throughout the empire. Throughout the next week, while anti-government mobs torched factories in St Petersburg, fighting broke out in Warsaw, Lodz, Riga, Finland and the Caucasus. In a dramatic encore to von Plehve's slaying, a Socialist Revolutionary terrorist blew up Grand Duke Sergius, the Tsar's uncle and 'chief of the reactionaries', within the walls of the Kremlin on 18 February.[85]

Chita, of all places, emerged as a center of revolutionary activity in the Russian Far East. It seemed an unlikely locale for radical political thought, having taken 300 years since the Cossacks first settled it to even become officially classified as a town in 1870. The newspaper *Aziatskaya Rossiya* sneered at it as a place of 'dilapidated wooden houses, dirty unpaved streets with cattle and stray dogs wandering here and there. The only decent buildings are the Governor's house, Vostochno-Daurskoe Podvore Hotel and three churches.' However, for a short time in 1905, it became the capital of the Chita Republic. The general strike in October paralyzed the Trans-Siberian Railway. Three Bolsheviks, V.K. Kurnatovsky, I.V. Babushkin and A.A. Kostyushko-Volyuzhanich organized the railway workers to take over the town and throw open the gates of Chita's notorious prison.[86] Kurnatovsky was a chemical engineer who had forsaken his career to pursue revolutionary activities, had shared one of his three previous terms of exile with Vladimir I. Lenin and Nadezhda K. Krupskaya at Shushenskoe, and had become acquainted with young Iosif Stalin in 1900.[87] The strikers persuaded soldiers of the Chita garrison to join them, and in December 1905 published and distributed 10,000 copies of one of Russia's first 'red' newspapers, *Zabaikalsky Rabochi*.[88] At the same time an assembly of Buryats gathered in Chita, demanding self-government and linguistic freedom. Japanese agents were suspected of stirring up the assembly and Pan-Mongol sentiments to destabilize Russia.

In Verkhne-Udinsk a strike committee sprang up in October 1905 and a subversive newspaper, *Verkhneudinskii Listok*, was passed out in the streets. In early December 2,000 people joined the strike, but within a month the authorities had shut down *Verkhneudinskii Listok* and arrested radical leaders. The uprising inspired local garrison soldiers to form the Transbaikal branch of the All-Russia Military Union in March 1907.

Even Irkutsk saw her workers and soldiers join in the general strike. On 8 November the entire 4,000-man garrison turned out for a meeting that demanded the election of a Constituent Assembly. It was a common demand during the revolution of 1905, put forth not only by the Socialist Revolutionaries and Peasants' Union, but by 14 professional unions. However, one week prior to the meeting Tsar Nicholas II took the wind out of the revolution's sails with an imperial manifesto that called for convocation of a popularly elected state duma and promised 'freedom of conscience, speech, union and association'. Nevertheless, a march on 30 November in Irkutsk turned violent as armed demonstrators fought the gendarmes.

The authorities soon terminated the Chita Republic and Kurnatovsky, according to Krupskaya, was 'seized by [Baron Alexander] Meller-Zakomelsky and handed over to [Major General Paul von] Rennenkampf' for execution.[89] In a similar fashion the revolution of 1905 was quelled in cities and towns across the empire, but the lines had been drawn between the 'reds' and the 'whites'.

Mongolia and the Tournament of Shadows

At the turn of the century, Outer Mongolia was described as a place of squalor, slothfulness and degeneracy, in contrast to the industrious Buryat communities in Russia. It was a dusty, rocky wasteland, a natural reservoir of plague bacilli, that hardly seemed worthy of any interest whatsoever, much less like a target of high stakes international geopolitics.[90] Yet it became entangled in Russia and Britain's strategic maneuvering for central Asian spheres of influence that came to be known as 'the Great Game' (to the British) or the 'Tournament of Shadows' (to the Russians).

The unlikely catalyst of this commotion was Agvan Lobsan Dorzhiev, an energetic Buddhist lama born near Verkhne-Udinsk and educated at Drepung Monastery in Tibet. Since the late sixteenth century, the Gelug ('Yellow Hat') school of Buddhism had overlaid ancient Mongolian shamanism, binding Mongols in Siberia, Inner Mongolia and Outer Mongolia with Tibetans. Dorzhiev, an advisor to the thirteenth Dalai Lama in Lhasa, the xenophobic capital of the Tibetan theocracy, was dispatched to establish relations with Tsar Nicholas II. In contrast to the autocracy's wickedness towards Jews, Old Believers and other persecuted sects, Buryat Buddhists enjoyed a measure of sympathy, since their clergy had enjoyed legal status in Russia since 1741, when Empress Elizaveta authorized the establishment of 11 *datsans* (Buddhist spiritual centers). In fact, Buryat Buddhists venerated the tsar and his Romanov predecessors as incarnations of White Tara, a merciful Buddhist deity. A tract distributed by Dorzhiev glowingly describing Nicholas II as an 'emanation of the King of Shambhala'. Envoys of the Dalai Lama were warmly received by the Tsar and Tsarina, who were said to be intrigued by the mystique of Buddhism.

Unfortunately for the Tibetans, the British grew alarmed at the loud publicity of Dorzhiev's third mission to St Petersburg, which trumpeted the blossoming courtship between Lhasa and her Russian suitor.[91] Meanwhile, the Dalai Lama refused to even speak with British representatives. So, fearing that a Russian-sponsored Tibetan–Mongol nation might break free of China's suzerainty and become a threat to British interests in India, London dispatched Francis Younghusband and 3,000 troops into the Himalayas in the winter of 1903 to speak with the Dalai Lama. Around Zongshan Castle at Gyangze Younghusband's expedition defeated an outnumbered Tibetan militia equipped with pikes and other medieval weapons, then marched into Lhasa on 3 August 1904, where modern machine guns quickly subdued the populace.[92] The Dalai Lama fled to Mongolia. Tibet was forced to bow to British territorial demands on the India – Tibet frontier and, at Whitehall's insistence, to the continuing presence of China's *amban* (imperial advisor) Yu Tai in Lhasa.[93] Better a Tibet controlled by China, than an independent Tibet that might spin into the Russian orbit reasoned the Foreign Office. In August 1907, Russia and Britain formally reiterated their mutual recognition of China's domination over Tibet.

Mongolia seemed to face an even tougher fight in throwing off the Manchu yoke. In recent years, China had embarked upon a 'new course' of forced colonization through mass resettlement of Chinese, intensification of the military occupation and isolation of Mongolia from the rest of the world, especially the mischievous Russians. Plans of the Bureau for Resettlement in Beijing laid claim to 5.3 million hectares of Mongolian territory and a Chinese commercial invasion had already begun. The number of Chinese merchants and money-lenders swelled from a few dozen to nearly 500, running up Mongolia's debt to China to 11 million lan, and reducing the entire country to penury.[94] Such exploitation prolonged Mongolia's feudalism, backwardness and squalidness.

Resistance against Manchu rule had been stirring in Mongolia since the late eighteenth century when Prince Amarsanaa and Prince Chingunjav led unsuccessful uprisings against the Qing occupation. In 1837, discontent with Manchu rule combined with an uproar against the feudal oppression by Mongolia's theocratic nobility to fuel a three-year revolt in Setsen Khan *aimag* (province). More recently, in 1900 when Mongol reservists were called up by Manchu authorities to quell a revolt, they instead annihilated the Chinese garrison in the western town of Uliastai, then ransacked offices of merchants and usurers. Simultaneously a similar but separate anti-Manchu uprising erupted in eastern Mongolia. Seven years later a wiry *ard* (peasant herdsman) named Ayush led another foiled rebellion, this one against the onerous feudal system that smothered *ard* families in poverty. Perhaps encouraged by Ayush, *ard* uprisings arose but were crushed in Barga and Setsen Khan *aimags* in 1909.[95]

At this time Russia revealed the intensity of her enchantment with her Mongol and Buddhist neighbors when the Tsar blessed Agvan Dorzhiev's plans to construct a Buddhist temple, Khram Kalachakri, in St Petersburg. Among the prominent academics and artists on the construction committee sat Prince Esper Ukhtomsky, the same young associate of the Tsar who bribed the Qing court to accede to the formation of the Russo-Chinese Bank and who accompanied the Tsarevich to lay the first stone of the Trans-Siberian in 1891.[96] The temple became an unofficial embassy for the Buddhist flocks of Tibet, Mongolia and Siberia.[97]

Anticipating the revolutionary storm to break in China, an anti-Chinese assembly of *doyons* and ranking lamas convened in Urga in July and drew up a petition for Russian assistance. The following month Tsar Nicholas II received a Mongolian delegation and promised them arms and ammunition.⁹⁸ Finally, on 10 October 1911 the long-awaited republican revolution in China ignited among modernized army units in Hubei province, and within six weeks inflamed 15 of the 23 other provinces which declared their independence of Qing authority. China's internal turmoil in 1911 so paralyzed the nation that little could be done to thwart Mongolian independence. On 1 December, a committee of princes and high priests declared independence, called up militia from four Khalka *aimags* and demanded the departure of the Qing *amban*, Sando. Just over two weeks later, the eighth incarnation of Buddha, Jebtsundamba Khutuktu, was declared Bogdo Khan (Holy Ruler) of a Mongolian government that merged Church and state in the Tibetan model.⁹⁹

The Khutuktu and Mongolia's theocracy of lamas were unable to comprehend the vicious milieu in which independence had tossed them. Daily life in Mongolia was indiscernible from medieval existence except for the appearance of the occasional modern firearm or Tea Road trinket. Most people were chronically poor, subsisting by hunting or hiring out 'for a bit of grain'. Venereal disease afflicted most of the population. Healing was in the hands of 'itinerant magicians and quacks, working from grubby handbooks of divination' and, in similar fashion, the Khutuktu sought to cure society's ills by exorcisms and magic.

In contrast, the nobility and lamas lived lives of extravagance and debauchery. So pronounced were the excesses of the Bogdo Khan that he was even notorious in the Western world as 'a drunken profligate', with whom the Dalai Lama had refused to communicate during his four years in Mongolian exile (1904–08). The Bogdo Khan suffered from the advanced stages of syphilis and was blind, but still devoted more attention to his eccentric sexual appetites than to his newborn government. At the time of independence, when diplomatic efforts seemed to have been in great demand for pursuing security and assistance for Mongolia, Prince Khandadorji, Urga's ambassador to Russia, was busy fundraising 330,000 taels of silver to purchase a special Buddha statue that might restore the Bogdo Khan's vision.¹⁰⁰ A few months later, in preparation for services to pray for the Bogdo Khan's long life, Mongolia's new government wasted precious energy and money in purchasing thousands of statuettes of Ayushi (the Buddha of Long Life), even importing 9,000 of them from Poland at a cost of 23 rubles apiece. They blissfully chose to ignore the realities of modern politics and their people's stifling pauperism and hardship.

Despite the prevalent ignorance and superstition, Mongolia was not completely devoid of contacts with the outside world. New ideas and gadgets seeped in from the commercial traffic between Russia and China on the Tea Road as it snaked through eastern Mongolia. There were even Americans in Mongolia, engineers who worked for the gold mining company Mongolore in several provinces.¹⁰¹ It was not like Tibet, where mobs chanted 'Kill the foreigners!' outside guesthouses and desperately curious Western adventurers were forced into deep disguise to tour the barren country.

The Japanese demonstrated their strong interest in Mongolia in typical fashion – by setting up a secret society, Roninkai, a subsidiary of the Black Dragon Society, to gather intelligence and create a Mongolian cell of pro-Japanese activists.¹⁰² This led to the formation in 1911 of Kanzan So, the Mountain of Sweat Society, formed with the goal to forge a Manchurian–Mongolian nation 'under Japanese jurisdiction with [Manchurian police official and agent of Japanese intelligence] Prince Su Chin Wang as head of state'. Two powerful *noyons* (Mongol prince or chieftain) in Mongolia, identified as K'e-la and Pa-lin, signed agreements with Naniwa Kawashima, a samurai and exceptional covert operator, for Japanese arms, military advisers and agricultural specialists in exchange for control over their new state.¹⁰³ Japanese intelligence set up Su in a headquarters at Dairen and began smuggling arms to followers in Manchuria and Mongolia, though the former surely received the bulk of the weapons. Nevertheless, some 50 Japanese agents were said to have been killed while engaged in arms smuggling, confirming the aptness of Kanzan So's descriptive moniker.[104]

Any arms were welcomed by the Mongolians, because, despite China's domestic confusion, the Chinese garrisons occupying Mongolia had no intention of simply vacating the country. Not only that, it was a long road back to China through hostile territory. Outer Mongolia's insubordination to Beijing had set off a series of secessions that could not be ignored: 35 out of 49 Inner Mongolian *khoshuun* announced their voluntary allegiance to the new state.[105]

The fighting fell squarely upon the shoulders of the *ard* to attack and drive out the Chinese garrisons throughout western Mongolia, although no Mongolian drama is complete without magic and mysticism. Separatists captured Ulaangom in May 1912, but a 10,000-man Chinese army remained firmly entrenched in western Mongolia. The Khutuktu (reincarnate lama) charged Hun Baldon, a 'simple shepherd' who was nonetheless 'ferocious, absolutely without fear and possessing gigantic strength', with capturing Khovd (also known as Kobdo), regional headquarters of the Chinese army. The Chinese fortress-headquarters looked impregnable to the poorly armed Mongols, with six-foot thick walls 12 feet high, surrounded by a moat filled with water from the nearby Buyant river. After several futile attacks against Chinese machine guns, an illustrious Kalmyk sorcerer and nationalist named Tushegoun Lama inspired the Mongols with mass hypnotic visions of the rich afterlife that awaited them should they fall in battle. On 6 August four detachments under Dandisuren, Magarjav, Gun Khaisan and Dambijantsen 'fought furiously, perished by the hundreds but not before they had rushed into the heart of Kobdo'. It was the debut of Mongolia's fledgling modern army. Hun Baldon's force also liberated Uliastai in 1912, crashing through the gates of the Chinese fortress and torching the official quarters and barracks.[106]

In December 1911, the ruling nobility had decided to form a 20,000-man army with conscripts contributed from their domains. Their martial heritage notwithstanding, the *doyons* could not comprehend the urgency for a modern military, nor did they even make a serious effort to bring 20,000 men to arms. They contributed mostly 'misfits and sick men' to the new army, figuring that China was too distracted with her own affairs to attack and that anyway Russia would take care of Mongolia.[107] The questionable recruits were hastily trained, then half were rushed to the Chinese frontier and the other half to a reserve force around Urga. Only 2,000 men formed the ranks of the budding Mongolian army, organized into two cavalry regiments, a machine gun company and a four-gun artillery battery. The Mongolians' awkwardness in modern military matters stands in stark contrast to the ruthless efficiency and mastery of their thirteenth-century predecessors.

In early 1912, Russia dispatched a colonel with a small military training mission to Urga under a one-year agreement with the new government. It was a difficult marriage of cultures trying to cast a reborn Mongolian army in the mold of the Russian Imperial army. The harshness of the Russian instructors and their insensitivity to cultural differences clashed with the Mongolians' freedom-loving and relatively egalitarian steppe lifestyle and stunting backwardness. Ignoring the Mongolians' unsurpassed expertise in horsemanship, the narrow-minded imperial officers stubbornly hammered their recruits with ceaseless infantry drills. Naturally the Mongolian conscripts began bucking the harsh regimen of the Russian training and the bitter taste of barracks life. Several deserted and one unit even mutinied against its Russian trainers, requiring Cossacks from the Legation Guard in Urga to quell the disturbance. By the time the mission's one-year term was finished, the Russo-Mongolian courtship had soured so much that the training agreement was allowed to lapse. However, the suitors needed each other, and Russians continued to train Mongolian soldiers, but mission staffing was halved.[108]

In the meantime, diplomats concluded a secret agreement in early November 1912 that affirmed Mongolia's autonomy from China and supported her right to establish her own army and expel China's. A protocol to the agreement created a Russian protectorate over Outer Mongolia. Recognition of Mongolia's independence came only from Tibet via a pact signed two weeks later that had been negotiated by the tireless Agvan Dorzhiev. Nevertheless, the following February Russia demonstrated her devotion with a 2 million-ruble loan (about US$1,000,000) for training and maintaining the new army. Apparently this sum was squandered because the Russians soon lent another 3 million rubles in a loan that came with a financial officer to oversee its use. The staff of the Russian consulate in Urga, established in 1860 to facilitate trade, was also bolstered to pursue decidedly non-commercial activities.[109]

Ensign Grigorii Mikhailovich Semenov

A young imperial army *praporshik* (ensign) stood out from the Caucasian faces of the Russian officers in Urga in 1912. Grigorii Mikhailovich Semenov (СЕМЁНОВ – pronounced sem-YO-nov) stood five feet nine inches tall, had mild blue eyes with the slightest hint of an Asiatic contour that revealed his Cossack– Buryat roots.[110] While an imperial officer of Cossack stock was not so common, an officer of mixed race was a novelty. The ensign's epaulets and his cocksure manner bore testimony to the youth's insatiable and undaunted ambition.

Semenov was born on 13 September 1890 at Post Kuranshi in the settlement of Durulguevskaya stanitsa, a village on the Onon river between Chita and Nerchinsk in the second department of the Transbaikal Cossack Host.[111] Semenov's face reflected the features of his Buryat mother, Evdokia Markovna Nizhegorodtseva, the daughter of a prominent local family.[112] Rumors claimed that she was a tribal princess. His Cossack father, Mikhail Petrovich Semenov, was a wealthy cattleman, a model farmer and agricultural innovator who was popular in his village and among neighboring Buryat and Mongol tribesmen, although he enjoyed 'no particular standing or influence' far beyond his *stanitsa*.[113] He ran a self-sufficient operation without many hired hands, was known for fielding McCormick harvesting machinery and other modern farm equipment and annually returned 250 to 300 *poods* (9,780 to 11,735 pounds) of meat to the government.[114]

Military service was a family tradition, of course, but in, contrast to most Cossack families where enlisted service was the norm, Semenov's family boasted a number of distinguished officers. At least one paternal uncle was a field officer and a second cousin, Dimitrii Frolovich Semenov, was destined to rise to the rank of major general.[115] Grigorii was 14 years old when his community was mobilized for service in the Russo-Japanese War. It turned out to be a dramatically formative emotional event for the teenager, who took the surrender of Port Arthur as a personal humiliation and thereafter dreamed of redeeming Russia's military glory.[116]

As a child, Semenov was imbued with a hunger for learning but, after two years attending the local settlers' school and then a school of limited capability in Mogotu, he was denied entry to the *gimnazia* (secondary school) in Chita. This denial is certainly evidence of his family's lack of social standing beyond his home village, which makes his subsequent achievements all the more remarkable. Grigorii Mikhailovich was educated at home, thanks to a large library assembled by his father. With a single-mindedness that would become his trademark, father and son aggressively rounded up precious books in this Transbaikal backwater and the student Semenov just as aggressively devoured them, especially when they concerned his favorite subjects: war, philosophy and religion. Despite the cultural isolation of his home, he developed a broad range of interests, including, for example, paleontology and archaeology. As a teenager he worked on archaeological digs that recovered mammoth bones and fossil of prehistoric sea creatures for the Kuznetsov Museum in Chita. He also developed fluency in Buryat, Mongol and Kalmyk languages, learned a little English and of course became an expert horseman.[117]

The Transbaikal Cossack Host was one of the few Cossack hosts that did not have its own cadet corps. Thus, Semenov applied to the Orenburg Cossack Military School in 1908, passed a rigorous examination and was admitted in the autumn. Orenburg was a provincial capital of the Kazakh steppe, a crossroads between Europe and central Asia as a busy river-port on the Yaik and a major junction of a new railway that linked Tashkent and Turkestan to Russia. The growing city had been a center of the Kalmyk Cossacks since the eighteenth century. In addition, it was the hub of suppressed pan-Kyrgyz and Kazakh nationalist aspirations.[118] Perhaps this nourished dormant seeds of Buryat nationalism in Semenov's subconscious.

As a cadet he became known for 'remarkable physical toughness', and, though surrounded by children of the more privileged classes, he expressed pride in his peasant background. When chided by his fellow cadets about a newfound fascination with economics, Semenov declared, 'Do not forget that I am a peasant, and, for a peasant, economics is the one essential branch of learning.' During his three years in Orenburg, he came to consider himself an intellectual. In his academic life he demonstrated the ability to submerge himself completely in a subject to achieve mastery. He wrote poetry, broadened the scope of his voracious reading and was exposed to a structured academic regimen, new subjects, city life and different cultures.[119]

Upon graduation in August 1911, Semenov was commissioned an ensign and assigned to the 1st Verkhne-Udinsk Regiment of the Transbaikal Cossack Host at Troitskosavsk, on the frontier of Khalka Mongol territory.[120] His father had died earlier in the year but Grigorii Mikailovich's two elder brothers 'kept the household going' so that he could perform his military duties.[121] David Footman, a senior British intelligence official and Russian history scholar, surmised that Semenov 'left the Military School much as he had entered it', with 'great curiosity, a mass of ill-digested reading, an aversion to any form of discipline and only the sketchiest knowledge of educated society or of social usage'.[122] Historically, most officers in Cossack units were not Cossacks themselves and a 'good deal of prejudice' arose against those who were.[123] There had been strong opposition to commissioning Cossacks; they were considered ignorant and, given the rank and opportunity, likely to abandon themselves to 'all the vices of a parvenu'.[124] Most Cossacks who became officers were selected from the ranks based on heredity, intelligence and NCO tests. Semenov, as a graduate of the Orenburg military school, was a rare breed in the imperial officer corps.

After a mere three weeks in Troitskosavsk, Semenov, owing to his fluency in Mongol languages, was assigned to perform military topographical surveys that gave him a chance to travel from one end of Mongolia to the other during the turbulent period preceding the break from China. When he finished this task in early October 1911, he was posted to his regiment's 6th *sotnia* (a traditional Cossack unit of 100 men) which formed the consulate guard detachment in Urga.

Semenov could not help but notice that the city of Urga bore little resemblance to the European concept of a city, much less a capital, being mostly a sprawling, odiferous assemblage of smoky yurts and animal pens. Yet, in autumn 1911, this dusty encampment was the capital of a rudimentary Mongolian nation and the focus of tribal politics for hundreds of miles in all directions. The Bogdo Khutuktu, visiting *doyons* and other leaders were pleasantly surprised to meet a sympathetic Russian officer who was as comfortable speaking Mongolian as he was speaking Russian, and could swallow a ladle of *tarasun* (fermented mare's milk) as easily as a glass of champagne. They flattered the young ensign by asking for his advice and assistance. Namsarai-Gun, an aspirant for the position of war minister in Urga's embryonic theocratic government, persuaded Semenov to translate Cossack regulations into Mongolian for the future national army.[125]

He was immediately drawn into the political intrigue and scheming that prevailed during Mongolia's first year of independence. 'Urga boiled in a whirlpool of political passions and new aspirations', wrote Semenov and he eagerly jumped right in. In December 1911, disorder swept through Urga's streets after Outer Mongolia's declaration of independence on the 11 December. The Russian Consul ordered Semenov and a small detail of Cossacks to rescue the Chinese *amban*, whose palace was on the verge of being sacked by an excited Mongolian mob. He not only rescued the *amban*, but, on his own initiative, deployed his troops to disarm and disperse the Chinese garrison, which, he said later in his own defense, was agitating the crowds and making a volatile situation worse.[126] Soon after that, his platoon raced over to the Daitsin Bank in Mai-mai chên, Urga's Chinese quarter, where they prevented a violent robbery.[127] Semenov discovered the power and influence that even a young ensign could wield upon events and subsequently received cables and gifts of gratitude for restoring order in the city. The Daitsin Bank lavished gifts upon Semenov, giving him 5,000 lan in cash, a 4-*pood tsibik* of 'fragrant tea' (a bale sewn into a raw bull hide), swaths of silk and 'ten well-fed bulls', all of which he contributed to the 'collective property' of his *sotnia*. Unfortunately, Russia's Ministry of Foreign Affairs deemed that Semenov's actions constituted meddling in China's internal affairs and had compromised Russian neutrality. Therefore, for exceeding his orders, the Russian Consul demanded the young ensign's recall after just four months in Urga and gave him 48 hours to leave the city.[128]

Semenov turned his recall back to Russia into a triumph of sorts. He set a mid-winter speed record for the 232-mile journey from Urga to Kyakhta, riding relays of horses provided by his Mongolian friends to arrive in 26 hours. Such an accomplishment did not go unnoticed in a country where everyone above the age of 5 was a skilled equestrian. An investigation by the Irkutsk Military District into Semenov's actions in Urga was thwarted by his regimental commander (a 'brilliant officer' in the accused ensign's eyes), Colonel Baron Artur Arturovich Keller.[129]

The next two years passed like the quiet before the storm. Semenov yearned to return to Mongolia, and his Mongolian friends, now high officials, petitioned the Russian government to second Semenov to Urga to help organize their new national army. Semenov's superiors, wary of aggravating the thin-skinned foreign affairs bureaucrats, endeavored to keep him away from Mongolian intrigue. 'Bad luck followed him and he was obliged to be transferred often from one regiment to another', declared a sympathetic biography published years later, which suggested that he was scapegoated by unethical superiors. 'His morally tender soul could not agree with the many dark sides of modern military life and he protested against every injustice and always told the blunt truth.'[130] For a short spell he served in a little artillery battery in Troitskosavsk, then in a military school in Chita, and then on border duty with the 1st Nerchinsk Regiment (of the Transbaikal Cossack Army) along the Ussuri river. There at the far edge of the empire in the Maritime Province, Semenov got his first taste of guerrilla warfare hunting clever bands of *hunghutze* (Manchurian bandits), and he learned many a nook and cranny of the Chinese–Russian border area, tactical knowledge that would come in handy years later. He also married a girl named Zenaida and fathered a son, Vyacheslav, but any domestic life was soon to be doomed by the clouds of war gathering over Europe.[131]

Russia soon had second thoughts about her hastiness in plunging so deeply into Mongolian affairs. In the tit-for-tat of great power geopolitics, Russian pressure on Mongolia was bound to result in counterpressure from Britain elsewhere (probably Persia, where both Russian bear and British lion sniffed oil). With this in mind, just one year after Russia and Mongolia formalized their vows to one another, the relationship was dampened by the Sino-Russian Declaration of 5 November 1913. Russia recognized China's preeminence over Mongolia and, in return, China's new republican government promised Mongolia the right to self-rule and control over her own commerce and industry. Most importantly, China pledged not to send troops into Mongolia.

By the end of 1914, Russia's military mission to Mongolia had been recalled, but the Sino-Russian Declaration had little to do with it. Earlier issues compelled the withdrawal: continuing friction between Russian advisors and Mongolian students had bred irreconcilable resentment and, in spite of the Sino-Russian Declaration, Mongolia's naive leaders still had a lackadaisical attitude towards building the army. Regardless, in August 1914, Russia's interest shifted to the Great War and thousands of miles of war fronts arcing from the Baltic Sea to Azerbaijan.

Semenov in the Great War

On 4 August 1914, Cossacks, their families, railway employees and villagers of Grodekovo gathered to hear a colonel read aloud the mobilization telegram that meant war with the Central Powers – Germany, Austria–Hungary and the Ottoman Empire. The crowd roared a loud 'hurrah' for Tsar Nicholas and the border village packed up its fathers and sons and put them aboard trains to Europe in mid-month. Their cross-country train ride at harvest time, as the 'fields and woods of Siberia donned the gold brocade of autumn', filled them with pride. A three-day stopover in Moscow gave them their first taste of a metropolis and they took advantage of free tram rides for soldiers to sightsee. Semenov walked with three Buryat soldiers to the Kremlin, where they encountered a trio of European Russians who refused to believe that they were not Japanese. Their fellow citizens in Moscow had never heard of Buryats, and had no idea that they were part of the Tsar's domain.[132]

The regiment disembarked in Poland and Semenov received his baptism of fire in operations west of the massive citadel of Novo Georgievsk, defending Warsaw against Austro-Hungarian attacks in September and German assaults in October.[133] While leading a reconnaissance mission northwest of Novo Georgievsk, Semenov's *sotnia* crossed paths with a German patrol and he personally captured two Germans. The brigade commander, Major General Kiselev, congratulated Semenov for snagging the 'first trophies' of the war for both his regiment and brigade.[134]

Semenov built a reputation for courage under fire and quick thinking, proving himself a bold leader of small raiding and reconnaissance units. On 11 November 1914, Uhlans of a Prussian regiment captured the brigade baggage train – 150 transport vehicles including ammunition of the artillery battalion, the regimental flag of the 1st Nerchinsk Regiment and 400 Russian soldiers. *Khorunzhi* (Sublieutenant) Semenov was returning to base from an overnight reconnaissance with nine Cossacks and did not realize that his brigade had moved on ahead without him and the now-captured baggage column until a breathless, half-dressed rider galloped up with the news. Semenov followed the sound of desultory gunshots and brashly spurred his little party into a gathered squadron of dismounted Uhlans, scattering their horses and creating a panic. Remarkably, Semenov achieved such surprise that alarm spread through two adjacent German squadrons. Displaying his best Mongol horsemanship, Semenov led his Cossacks right through the German column. Not realizing the size of the Russian threat and startled by the sheer audacity of the Russian attack, a whole German cavalry brigade began a sloppy withdrawal that turned into a hasty retreat and the captured Russian baggage train was discarded in the rush to get away.

For this deed, Semenov was decorated with the Order of St George, 4th Class. Three weeks later, he led 11 men in an overrun of a Bavarian infantry outpost, taking 55 prisoners. That feat earned him another Cross of St George.[135] Semenov was a modern-day *bagatur* who excelled in practical combat skills and reveled in war.

After ten months on the Polish Front, the Ussuri Division was moved to the Northern Front near Dvinsk, then shifted to Riga. Here in 1915, Semenov participated in two daring raids in the extreme rear of the enemy which – according to Semenov's earliest biographer, Borisov – wreaked such havoc that 'afterwards the name of the "yellow [Buryat] Cossacks" induced horror' amongst the Germans. The Ussuri Division moved south into the Carpathian Mountains to support the Brusilov offensive, which was launched in summer 1916. Semenov distinguished himself in a breakthrough around Chernovitz, and in a raid into Hungary itself, in the heart of hostile territory. In another instance, when isolated in mountainous terrain, Semenov showed exceptional heroism in leading 40 Cossacks in the defense of a critical pass, repelling four attacks with hand grenades.[136] His exploits earned him a warrior's reputation among senior officers, and he eventually came to the attention of General A.M. Krymov, the corps commander, who promoted him to *pod'esaul* (junior captain). At one time Semenov was entrusted with command of a detachment befitting a colonel, consisting of two infantry companies, four Cossack *sotnias* and a section of artillery.

Semenov's leadership of the 5th Squadron of the 1st Nerchinsk Regiment during the winter of 1916 attracted the eye of General Baron Petr Nikolaevich Vrangl. Vrangl later wrote,

> Semenov was... dark and thickset, and of the rather alert Mongolian type. His intelligence was of a specifically Cossack calibre, and he was an exemplary soldier, especially courageous when under the eye of his superior. He knew how to make himself popular with Cossacks and officers alike, but he had his weaknesses – a love of intrigue and indifference to the means by which he achieved his ends. Though capable and ingenious, he had received no education, and his outlook was narrow. I have never been able to understand how he came to play a leading role [in the civil war].[137]

Of course, Vrangl was wrong about Semenov having received no education, but the statement hints at a coarseness in Semenov's character that his limited education in the Orenburg military academy could not smooth over.

It was on Vrangl's Galician Front that Semenov cemented his friendship with Baron Roman Fedorovich von Ungern-Shternberg, commander of the 1st Nerchinsk Regiment's 6th Squadron. Ungern-Shternberg was a pale wisp of a man with reddish blonde hair, darting blue eyes and small head dominated by an oversized forehead, who shared Semenov's reputation as a courageous combat leader and mutual interests in central Asian people, history and religion. He claimed the bloodline of a warrior caste that dated to Attila the Hun, and recited a litany of fighting Ungerns including one killed 'under the walls of Jerusalem' during an early Crusade, 11-year-old Ralph Ungern who perished during the Children's Crusade, Baron Halsa Ungern-Shternberg of the twelfth-century Order of Teutons, two more Teutonic Ungerns slain by Polish and Lithuanian troops in the Grünwald, a sixteenth-century gladiator named Heinrich 'the Axe' Ungern von Shternberg, Baltic pirates Ralph and Peter, and eighteenth-century alchemist Wilhelm Ungern. He was the descendant of a notorious 'sea robber', Count Otto Reinhold Ludwig von Ungern-Shternberg, who moved from a plantation near the village of Vana-Kuuste, Estonia, to the Baltic isle of Hiiumaa in 1772, where he set fires to lure ships onto the shoals so he could plunder them, even though he owned several estates. In 1804, the count was convicted of piracy and the murder of a Swedish skipper, and banished to Tomsk where he 'built a Lutheran church, perused books on economics and flying machines, [and] wrote touching letters to his wife, round which he painted garlands of forget-me-nots'. Roman Ungern-Shternberg claimed that his grandfather was an Indian Ocean privateer who extorted tribute from English traders until he was captured, handed over to the Russian Consul and deported to Transbaikalia.[138] He credited this ancestor for introducing him to Buddhism.

Ungern-Shternberg's background is clouded by different versions. It seems that he was born in the Austrian city of Graz on 29 December 1885, while his parents were traveling through Europe, and grew up in Revel (now Talinn).[139] In 1921, he told Ferdinand Ossendowski, 'I am also a naval officer but the Russo-Japanese War forced me to leave my regular profession to join and fight with the Transbaikal Cossacks.' Baron Vrangl related a slightly different version. As a teenager Ungern dropped out of school to fight as an infantryman during the Russo-Japanese War, being wounded and decorated for valor. After the war, his relatives pressured him into military school and, noted Vrangl, 'He passed his officers' examinations only with great difficulty.' He chose assignment to a Cossack regiment in Siberia where he was struck on the head with a saber during a drunken quarrel. The latter 'undoubtedly upset his mental balance... for the rest of his life'. He left his regiment and, with a small rifle, hunting dog and horse, set out from Vladivostok for a year-long hunting and camping expedition that ended in Harbin. When war broke out between China and Outer Mongolia in 1912, Ungern-Shternberg rushed to offer his services to the Mongols and, according to Vrangl, became 'commander of the whole cavalry force of Mongolia!'[140] An updated version states that Ungern became a naval cadet in St Petersburg in 1896, served as an infantryman on the Manchurian front during the Russo-Japanese War, then attended the elite Pavlovsk infantry school and was commissioned into the Transbaikal Cossacks in 1908. On a bet with his fellow officers, he made a 400-mile journey across the wild taiga from Dauria, near Russia's frontier with Mongolia, to Blagoveshchensk on the Amur river, equipped with only a horse, rifle and cartridges. Like Semenov, he served in some nebulous capacity in Mongolia, allegedly fighting the Chinese around Kobdo in 1913, and became enamored of the culture and spirituality.[141]

Ungern-Shternberg maintained that he had dedicated much time to 'the study and learning of Buddhism', and during the pre-war years, he founded an Order of Military Buddhists, into which Semenov and a number of other Transbaikal Cossack officers were drawn. 'I gathered round me and developed 300 men wholly bold and entirely ferocious', he told Ossendowski. Ungern's regimen for spiritual development entailed celibacy and 'the limitless use of alcohol, hashish and opium' to produce fighting men who became 'heroes in the war with Germany', or so he claimed.[142] In any event, the bond between Semenov and Ungern sprouted before the First World War, was shaped by Ungern's mysterious clan and forged in combat on the Eastern Front.

Ungern-Shternberg joined the Nerchinsk regiment at the beginning of the First World War, served in East Prussia and, like Semenov, distinguished himself early on as a daring leader of raiding parties behind the Austro-Hungarian lines in Galicia and the Carpathians. Wounded several times, he earned the St George Cross, Russia's highest decoration for bravery. To his fellow Russian officers, he was an eccentric who 'turned up his nose at discipline, and was ignorant of the rudiments of decency and decorum... He was dirty and dressed untidily, slept on the floor with his Cossacks, and messed with them'. Vrangl himself tried to convince Ungern-Shternberg to affect some semblance of military bearing – to adopt 'at least the external appearance of an officer' – to no avail.[143]

The coincidence of Ungern-Shternberg and Semenov's experiences in Mongolia, their passion for war, their unconventional paths into the officers' corps, and camaraderie on the frontlines bound them closer than brothers. The mere occurrence of their friendship is fertile ground for advanced psychological study: two brash and remarkably successful outsiders in the ultra-conservative and restricted fraternity of the Russian officer corps, tolerated only because the dire necessity of war made them indispensable. As Vrangl wrote, 'He [Ungern-Shternberg] was of the type that is invaluable in wartime and impossible in times of peace.' The same could be said of Semenov.

January 1917 found Semenov in command of the 3rd *sotnia* of the 3rd Verkhne-Udinsk Regiment in the mountains cradling Lake Urmia in northwestern Persia, holding the Turks while General N.N. Baratov advanced across the Mesopotamian plain to link up with Lieutenant General Sir Frederick Stanley Maude's British expeditionary force.[144] It was a forgotten theatre of war compared to the grand fronts across Flanders and Galicia, but no less vicious.

In the opening moves of the war, General Baratov had advanced into northern Persia and engaged a Turkish army under Hussein Raouf Bey, while the British landed at Basra and moved north to secure the Anglo-Persian Oil Company's pipeline.[145] In northwestern Persia, the Russians armed a number of Christian communities of Assyrians and Armenians and drafted men for military service. Then, tragically, on 1 January 1915, the Russians abruptly withdrew their 2,000 troops from Lake Urmia as Khalil Pasha's 1st Turkish Corps drew near. Thousands of frightened Assyrian and Armenian families tried desperately to keep up with the retreating troops.[146] All Christians were now branded as traitors, and any caught behind the Turkish lines were liable to be savaged by Turkish troops and their Kurdish auxiliaries in a cruel jihad sweeping Asia Minor. Many Kurdish families sheltered fleeing friends, but did so knowing that they could meet a terrible fate if discovered by Turkish authorities or informers.[147] Thousands of refugees sought protection in US missionary stations, but many more perished in a wave of genocide that hemorrhaged throughout the region for several months. The Russians recovered the area in the summer, but abandoned it again in early August 1915, when the genocide began anew.[148]

In November 1915, during General Sir John Nixon's ambitious effort to conquer Baghdad, link up with the Russians and sever Persia from the Ottoman torso, the British 6th Poona Division suffered a startling defeat at Ctesiphon. The division's epic retreat was cut off and it was besieged at Kut al-Amara, a grubby hamlet squatting in a bend of the Tigris river. During the next four months, 23,000 British Commonwealth soldiers perished trying to relieve the 13,000 men at Kut. Baratov advanced deep into Persia to help his allies, forcing the Turks to withdraw a corps of their 6th Army from the siege, but in vain. With starvation looming, the Poona Division finally capitulated to Khalil Pasha on 29 April 1916. Turkish captors sadistically butchered more than 2,000 of the soldiers who had surrendered.[149]

After Kut, Khalil Pasha turned his attention to the Russians and halted their southward advance in June 1916, but again relinquished the mountains around Lake Urmia to Baratov. By January 1917, when Semenov and the Transbaikal Cossacks arrived in the area, the Ottoman jihad had disfigured the landscape with scorched villages, wells stuffed with decaying corpses, meadows littered with human bones and tufts of drifting hair, gorges lined with mummified cadavers of the menfolk, and river banks coughing up the swollen remains of children. The countless crime scenes of brutal, individual murders contrasted sharply in scale and emotion with the endless fields of mass slaughter wrought by machine guns and artillery on the Eastern Front. Gaunt survivors, Assyrian and Armenian men and boys for the most part, weakened by typhoid and hunger, stumbled out of the hills to hail the Cossacks as saviors and beg for food. Girls and women were few and far between; most had been gang-raped and carted off to slavery in neighboring Muslim villages.

Semenov's impressions of Urmia's hellish surroundings are unknown, although the scene was certainly impossible to ignore. In Gulpashan, the ghostly town where the

3rd Verkhne-Udinsk Regiment eventually made camp, a single grave containing 51 bludgeoned elders served as a reminder of the recent blood-orgy.[150] Nevertheless, the Buryat Cossack warrior was pleased to be campaigning where Alexander the Great and Emperor Darius had marched centuries before. He also enjoyed the companionship of Baron Ungern-Shternberg. Ungern-Shternberg came up with the idea of raising an army from the Assyrians around Lake Urmia, a notion that evolved into Semenov's scheme for an all-Buryat regiment and further entwined their fates.[151]

In March 1917, General Baratov's vanguard linked up with the British northeast of Baghdad. At the time, Maurice Paléologue, the French Ambassador in Petrograd, lauded the Imperial Army's Mesopotamian Campaign, 'In the general schemes of the war, this brilliant operation is obviously but an episode; but quite possibly it is the last exploit which historians will have to record in the military annals of Russia.'[152] Apart from Mesopotamia, it seemed that Russia and the Imperial Army were coming apart at the seams.

Since 1916, a slow, irreversible rot had eroded morale in the Russian Army. The Great War had consumed nearly one-quarter of Russia's male workforce: an estimated 4,500,000 men had been killed or disabled, and more than 2 million others languished in prison camps in Germany, Austria–Hungary, Turkey and Bulgaria. 'Too often the Russian infantryman had been called on to retake with blood what the German had taken with high explosive, and by the beginning of 1917, there was little blood left.'[153]

On 8 March the soldiers' wives, mothers and sisters unwittingly ignited the February Revolution with the simple spark of an innocuous Petrograd procession to mark International Woman's Day. That innocent procession bred a spate of ill-planned strikes by 90,000 workers the next day. Although revolutionary committees and police planning teams had been preparing for this moment for years, with both sides intent on improving their 1905 performances, their blueprints and timetables for carefully calculated movements and actions did not take into account the emotions of the mounted Cossacks on Sampsonievskii Prospekt when ordered to stampede through 2,500 Erikson millworkers on the cold morning of 10 March 1917. First with a wink, then with the flash of a smile, the Cossacks signalled the crowd that they would neither attack the workers nor flagrantly disobey their officers. When their flustered officers formed a wall of Cossacks to block the street, the men stood 'stock-still in perfect discipline', not allowing their horses to stir while demonstrators squeezed between their legs. 'The revolution...made its first steps toward victory under the belly of a Cossack's horse', wrote Trotsky. Stories about sympathetic Cossacks inspired the dark masses in the streets: the Cossacks who chased away policemen that had flogged a woman marcher, Cossacks who whispered promises not to shoot, Cossacks who fired on police that shot into a crowd at the Alexander III monument... 'It seems that the break in the army first appeared among the Cossacks, those age-old subduers and punishers', smirked Trotsky, who had little love for them. Spontaneous strikes punctuated by demands for bread and peace jammed the city, unleashing pent-up hatreds and frustrations that had been suppressed by tsarist police for more than 20 years. Cossacks sent to subdue demonstrators joined them, and mutiny spread through Petrograd's 150,000-man garrison like an epidemic.[154]

Suddenly the hated police abandoned some areas of the city and the old order just seemed to collapse. The provisional government and Petrograd Soviet emerged from the shadows, each competing to fill the vacuum. On 14 March 1917, *Izvestia* published Military Order No. 1, a decree of the Petrograd soviet which undermined military discipline by transferring authority from officers to individual units' soldiers' committees of men elected from the ranks.[155] Upon hearing that he had been forsaken by his beloved army, a melancholy Tsar Nicholas II abdicated the throne aboard the imperial train at

Pskov station on the night of 15 March 1917. In subsequent weeks hundreds of thousands of men deserted the army, clogging the roads and hanging from packed trains.[156] Whole regiments mutinied en masse. The largely illiterate soldiery arrested and often murdered unsympathetic officers. Some officers went into hiding, and others reluctantly feigned solidarity with the soldiers' committees.

It took several days before the collapse of the military chain of command was felt by the 3rd Verkhne-Udinsk Regiment and the nearby 2nd Argun and 2nd Chita Regiments, but while Order No. 1 caused confusion, anarchist and Red agitators eventually stirred up dissension in the previously cohesive Cossack ranks.[157] Semenov was emotionally untouched by the tsar's abdication; 'his loyalties were to the Russian Empire, not to the Imperial House'.[158] They were at Gulpashan when a soldiers' committee took over the regiment in March and held elections for commander. Semenov won, although he did not seek election. Not only that, but he was elected Deputy of the 1st Nerchinsk Regiment, as well. He refused both positions, saying that there was no time for such activities on the field of battle.[159] Semenov could not fathom abandonment of the struggle that had consumed his energies and the lives of so many comrades for two and a half years.

Likewise, the provisional government refused to abandon the war. Despite the disastrous state of the armed forces – indeed, naively unaware of the extent of it, Alexander F. Kerensky, the inexperienced and vain socialist lawyer who became Minister of War in mid-May, refused to back down from a promise to the Allies to launch a massive offensive in summer 1917 to divert Central Powers pressure away from France. Kerensky believed that he could bolster the front with new regiments composed of indigenous people of Siberia, Transcaucasia and central Asia. Nearly 10 million men of military age in non-Christian minorities were not subject to the military draft.[160] However, such a desperate recruiting scheme presented some risks. A decree dated 25 June 1916 calling up Kazakhs for duty in the rear led to uprisings and a sudden Kazakh emigration to China's Sinkiang province.[161]

Semenov, drawing from Ungern-Shternberg's idea for an Assyrian Army in April 1917, drew up a proposal for an all-Buryat regiment and sent it to Petrograd in May 1917.[162] The proposal struck a responsive chord among the wishful thinkers in the provisional government and War Ministry officials who realized the army's dire need for men willing to fight and immediately summoned Semenov to the capital. About this time, the 2nd Cossack Corps was disbanded and Semenov was ordered back to the Ussuri Brigade, so, one way or another, Semenov was leaving his regiment.[163]

He arrived in Petrograd on 8 June, which, in the three months since Citizen Nicholas Romanov signed his abdication letter, had degenerated like a grande dame gone to seed. Its streets were strewn with stinking garbage, rife with crime since the dismissal of most police weeks before, and full of raucous soldiers – more than 100,000 of them, garrison troops and deserters who had come to 'defend the revolution' and carouse.[164] Luckily he befriended a naval officer, one Lieutenant Ul'rich, who invited Semenov to stay in his apartment on Vasil'evskii Island and filled him in on the revolutionary insanity that had brought Russia's capital to her knees.[165] The chaos irked Semenov.

With some difficulty he found the All-Russia Revolutionary Committee for the Formation of the Volunteer Army in a small office on the second floor of No. 20 Moika Street and reported to Colonel Murav'ev. For two weeks he reported each morning at 9 a.m., making his way through the uncouth hooligans in muddled uniforms loitering amidst the rubbish, rubbing shoulders with senior Bolsheviks on the sidewalks, and getting a taste of the complex societal changes the revolution promised for Russia. It was a taste that sickened and infuriated him. He proposed a coup to install General Brusilov and offered to arrest the members of the Petrograd Soviet – the proletarian sirens who had seduced his army – and shoot them all. Semenov was not joking. Murav'ev – perhaps even War

Minister Kerensky himself – refused the offers, but listened with interest to his proposal to raise a new regiment in Transbaikalia.[166] On 26 July Semenov boarded a train bound for the Far East, entrusted with 60,000 rubles, the title of Military Commissar and the authority to create a Mongol–Buryat regiment.[167] The exact sanction and responsibilities that came with this title were vague, though Semenov suggested that he carried the Petrograd soviet's 'full authority' for all military matters in the Irkutsk and Pri-Amur (*Primor-skaya* – Maritime and Amur provinces) military districts and the Chinese Eastern Railway zone.[168]

Commissar Semenov

Semenov's train pulled him away from the Great War just as his Russian Army gasped its last breath on Kerensky's ill-conceived summer offensive. On 29 June, 31 divisions charged into the German armies threatening Riga and Petrograd. Although backed up by 1,000 artillery pieces and months of staff planning, their advance stalled within 72 hours, three days before the southern offensive started against the Austro-Hungarian line in Galicia on 3 July. By 26, July when Semenov traveled east, the trains were bulging with deserters from the front.

The disastrous offensive produced more mutinies than victories.[169] Since the tsar's abdication, many army units had fallen under the control of soldiers' soviets, which insisted on voting whether or not to obey any particular order from above. A German-led counteroffensive tore into the Russian lines just as the equally devastating news of an unsuccessful Bolshevik coup d'état against the provisional government swept through the ranks in mid-July. Discipline and morale in the Russian ranks evaporated, but, to the soldiers' credit, not as fast as had their rifles and ammunition. Months of staff planning still could not provide something so basic as a rifle in the hands of each infantryman who was expected to run at the German machine guns. Meanwhile, 2 million tons of military supplies sat on the docks of Archangel and Murmansk, and even more at Vladivostok.

As the Central Powers gained the upper hand in battle, the Russians began melting away so fast that 300,000 new soldiers were needed every month to fill gaps in the porous 2,000-mile front that snaked from the Baltic Sea to the Black Sea. No recruitment was possible amid the bread riots and strikes in the cities of European Russia where streets teemed with deserters and revolutionary agitators. Semenov's mission took on added urgency if Kerensky, who became Prime Minister on 22 July, intended to keep up the war effort.

Russia was drunk with its first taste of weak democracy. Joyous anarchy reigned in every city and town along the railway. Fluttering banners of a plethora of political parties trumpeted intoxicating concepts of freedom and equality that few peasants comprehend, much less read, though many could parrot the words of *Rabochaya Marsel'eza* – the Russified 'Workers' *Marseillaise*'. No more tsarist insignia – the Romanov dynasty's double-headed eagles, nor haughty policemen, nor shuffling columns of chained convicts were to be seen. All symbols of the old authority had become objects of scorn or targets of violence. As Semenov's train wheezed over the Urals into Siberia, the revolutionary fever seemed to lessen. Yet even in Siberia's dreary towns and villages, red activists spread the revolutionary contagion among the colorful mix of hardy Russian frontiersmen, entrepreneurs, recently released convicts and exiles, native traders garbed in skins jingling with amulets, Mongols, Chinese, prospectors, adventurers and fugitives from all corners of Eurasia. All around Semenov, on the train and on the platforms of stations big and small, loitered deserters on their way home to claim or forcibly take a plot of land from the nearest estate. In better times, the decorations on Semenov's chest and the German bullets embedded in his shoulder would have marked him as a hero. But in the dizzy days of revolutionary fervor, such badges of valor meant little. His epaulets only marked him as a suspect in the eyes of many soldiers, who considered every officer a reactionary. Most soldiers refused to salute anymore, and addressed officers like everyone else, *'Továrishch!* Comrade!'[170]

On 1 August Semenov debarked in Irkutsk and called on Major General Samarin and his assistant, Colonel Krakovetskii, at the Irkutsk Military District headquarters. After four days of coordination with Samarin's staff, he took the overnight Siberian express to Chita, arriving on the morning of 6 August, and proceeded to the contentious Transbaikal Cossack Host *krug*, the decision-making assembly of the Cossack community. Semenov worked closely with the president of the congress, Sergei Afanas'evich Taskin, who had been Transbaikalia's representative to the national *duma*, and Taskin's assistant, Major General I.F. Shil'nikov, to preserve the traditional character of the Transbaikal Cossack Host, which was under attack by revolutionary representatives.[171]

The Transbaikal Cossack Host was not only a military organization, but the dominant social, political and economic force in Transbaikalia. In 1914 it encompassed 255,000 people living in 63 *stanitsa* areas with 516 satellite settlements, all divided into four regional administrative departments that competed for influence and resources within the host. They were one of the primary economic engines of Transbaikalia, generating income and taxes from agriculture, cattle and horse breeding, and cross-border trade with China, as well as smuggling and industrial enterprises. As with Russia's other Cossack hosts, in exchange for their military service to the state, they enjoyed their own public health and educational systems, a separate tax structure and a variety of opportunities that were unavailable to the grey masses of peasants and workers.[172]

Semenov proposed that a fifth all-Buryat and Mongol department be created, but the *krug* became distracted by more compelling revolutionary issues.[173] Since the February Revolution members of the Host's third and fourth departments had been crowing about disbanding the Transbaikal Cossack Host altogether as an unjust remnant of the old regime. The third and fourth departments occupied eastern Transbaikal regions populated by descendents of peasant miners who had been easily radicalized by revolutionary idealism. The first and second departments, which had larger Buryat and Mongol constituencies, were situated in western Transbaikalia and became labeled the *karaul'tsy* – the 'old guard'.[174] Their differences polarized the Transbaikal Cossacks and deepened during the heated debates of the August 1917 *krug* in Chita's Mariinskii Theatre. This estrangement would fester as the months passed and traditionalists struggled to preserve their way of life while revolutionaries pushed to usher in a new socialist era. Another estrangement also cast its shadow over Semenov's life at this time. He sent for his wife, Zenaida, to return to Siberia from south Russia, but she would not – or could not – come.[175]

Semenov soon departed for a Buryat congress in Verkhne-Udinsk, the city of 30,000 sprawling across rolling hills of pine above the confluence of the Selenga and Uda Rivers. The Selenga paralleled the main street, defined by the railway station at the north end and a modest cathedral at the south. In between, three more churches and several chapels stood as reminders of the waning power of Russian Orthodox priests. The Nicholas Memorial Arch was now the object of derision or sympathy, around which was clustered the London Hotel, post and telegraph office, and north end of the shopping district. Pungent aromas wafted out of a brewery and several tanneries, candle shops and soap factories. Weather-beaten wooden houses rose out of a gridiron of wide, sandy streets like stubby shadows of the surrounding Ulan-Burgasy and Yablonovy mountains. A bazaar in the center of town was lined with little shops run by Jews banished from European Russia. One wealthy merchant, Gdali Itzkovich and his six sons owned and operated silk, leather, soap and shoe factories as well as a well-stocked department store that employed 30 workers.[176] Yet the richest merchant was a Mr Zgelnitski, 'merchant, automobile owner, capitalist'. The local economy revolved around Tea Road trade and wool – some 75,000 tons were harvested annually between the city and Lake Baikal, but was retarded by troublesome currency problems. The only currency in circulation were 50-ruble banknotes that had been printed by the Bolsheviks and had to be individually registered, numbered and rubber-stamped by the banks to guarantee payment, with chits used for smaller denominations.[177] Camel caravans from Mongolia, exhausted by the 40-day cross-desert trek from Kalgan (now Changchia Kow, China), paused here in the summer to trade.[178] The streets' poplars and green-berried *cheromki* may have stirred a pre-war memory among returning soldiers, but the town was vastly different now.

Inflation was felt in the astronomical price of tobacco, and war shortages caused a scarcity of staples like sugar. In almost all occupations, even dirty, back-breaking work in the railway shops, women performed the jobs of men who had been called into army service. The place was swollen with troops returning from the front. A Soviet of Workers and Soldiers had evicted the top ranks of the imperial bureaucracy just after the tsar's abdication in March and now governed the town through an Executive Committee of Public Organizations. Similar committees of soldiers, peasants, workers and other citizens had already taken over the administrations of most Russian towns and cities.

Most of the railway men and troops who composed the Verkhne-Udinsk soviet were not Bolsheviks, though agents of the Bolshevik party sat among them. A cell of the formerly illegal Social Democratic Labor party, the parent organization of Bolsheviks and Mensheviks, had been formed in Verkhne-Udinsk in 1902. Most of the Soviet leaned toward either the Menshevik party or the Socialist-Revolutionary party, the latter being the most popular political organization in Siberia despite the fact that the *Eser* (SR) label had been appropriated by so many that it came 'to connote little more than general support of the Provisional Government'.[179] The Socialist-Revolutionaries were far from united in their beliefs and political endeavors, but they generally agreed that a Constituent Assembly should be democratically elected to rule the land. Many of them strongly supported an autonomous Siberia, and some bent towards extremist policies that mirrored Bolshevik demands, such as a radical redistribution of wealth.[180] On the other hand, Siberia's Socialist-Revolutionary constituency focused on a markedly different agenda from that of their European kin. 'The [Siberian] peasants were not cowed drudges, eking out a dull existence on cramped plots of land', wrote Peter Fleming, 'they resembled, rather, pioneer settlers, and their farms, averaging a hundred acres, were ten times the size of their counterparts in European Russia.'[181] Some moderate Socialist-Revolutionary factions even advocated staying in the war against Germany and Austria–Hungary.

Siberian Russians were less prone than their European brethren to prefer peace at any price when they believed that an honorable peace could still be sought on the battlefield. Many believed the widespread disinformation about the Bolsheviks' alleged collusion with the German Kaiser and considered Lenin and his associates to be traitors. Nevertheless, Semenov's recruiting mission in Verkhne-Udinsk and other locales in Transbaikalia would not be easy. People were sick of war and numbed by the endless political tirades in the gritty streets. Even patriotic Russians now dreaded military service and no one wanted to be at the front when the government might begin distributing land.

In Verkhne-Udinsk, Semenov convinced a five-day conference of southern Transbaikal Buryats to accept his proposal for a Mongol–Buryat regiment.[182] From there he traveled around the province meeting with local military and civil authorities and holding rallies to convince Cossacks and Buryats to join his hollow regiment. The provincial commissar appealed to district commissars to render assistance, specifically lodging and grain, to 'Commissar *Pod'esaul* V.V. Semenov, representative of the Central Committee of the

Organization of the Volunteer Revolutionary Army'.[183] Before the long, hot summer days of August 1917 passed, frost was already glazing the meadows of Transbaikalia but Semenov's ranks were still largely vacant. By the end of September he opened recruitment to anyone, not just Buryats and Mongols.[184]

Undaunted by the lethargy he encountered in Transbaikalia, Semenov called on old friends from his 1912 assignment in Urga and arranged secret meetings with chiefs across the frontier in Outer Mongolia.[185] This foreign intrigue clearly exceeded the scope of his orders from Petrograd but he recognized a rich source of recruits among the Mongols, many of whom realized that their fragile autonomy, promised by the 1915 tripartite Treaty of Kyakhta, was really guaranteed by the Russian Army.

Even so, Semenov's Mongol–Buryat regiment was slow to materialize. As the chill of approaching autumn sharpened, people's moods grew gloomier. Families feared for loved ones gone to the front, whence came no good news. Prices kept rising, and fewer goods appeared on store shelves. Mobilization of horses made the provisional government no new friends. The lower classes became enchanted by slogans of radical socialists. Wealthy and conservative citizens discreetly formed leagues to defend their threatened interests. New faces began to emerge on town and regional soviets in Transbaikalia – political organizers from European Russia with no bonds to local communities. Under these circumstances it seems remarkable that Semenov was able to enlist anyone, yet somehow he managed to entice more than a handful of Cossacks into the ranks.[186]

At the end of August 1917, distrust boiled over into violence between Kerensky and his supreme commander, the heroic Siberian Cossack General Lavr Kornilov. General Krymov and his 3rd Cavalry Corps marched on Petrograd to support Kornilov and defend the provisional government and ran up against revolutionary troops who were marching to *defeat* Kornilov and defend the provisional government. The ensuing confusion among the troops turned to fraternization, and, hours later, after a shouting match with Kerensky, Krymov, Semenov's former commander and mentor, penned a letter to his wife, turned his revolver to his chest and committed suicide. A total of 25,000 bolshevized soldiers sprang to Kerensky's defense while their radical brethren throughout the army declared a hunting season on officers. 'The Germans were at Riga, and the Russians were busying themselves killing their officers', wrote historian Brian Moynahan in summing up the disastrous situation. At this point, Semenov, a protégé of Krymov's and, like many Russian officers, a devotee of the brave Kornilov, was faced with the choice of supporting or betraying them. Kerensky ordered Semenov to stop recruiting in Transbaikalia. Semenov ignored him.[187]

While Semenov hurried to build his regiment, Bolshevik agitators were quietly forming Red Guard detachments among workers and soldiers in Transbaikalia.[188] Chita was a regional center of the Bolshevik underground. Mikhail Frunze, who would eventually command the Red Army's Siberian front, had edited a Bolshevik weekly in Chita, *Vostochnoye Obozreniye*, for a short period after his escape from exile in 1915. Many of the Red recruits in Chita, like 29-year-old locksmith Boris Pavlovich Clark, were veterans of the futile 1905 workers revolt (Clark was eventually made commander of a *sotnia* of the 1st Argun Red Guards Regiment).[189] Since the 'bourgeois-democratic revolution' in March, the Bolsheviks had been gradually infiltrating the police and other institutions with party members and sympathizers. Vasilii M. Sokol-Nomokonov, a 38-year-old Evenk veteran of the Chita Republic, was assigned by his Red leadership to infiltrate the railway *militsia* (police), which provided good training for his future role as leader of a special partisan detachment.[190]

While extremists in the shadows geared up for a violent showdown, in the foreground Russia staggered toward its date with democracy. 'The great day was approaching – November 28th, 1917 – when deputies of the whole of Russia were to have arrived in

Petrograd to meet in the Constituent Assembly', wrote a young army captain named Ivan Kalmykov a few months later. 'This assembly was to have determined and settled the life of all Russia, just as the local self-governing organs were to have settled local life in villages and towns. This assembly of the best elements of the Russian people was to have settled the question of war or no war [with the Central Powers].' However, before the Constituent Assembly could gather, the Bolsheviks secured the support of the army with the irresistible promise of 'immediate termination of the war', sweetening their sales pitch with the allure of bread and land.[191]

During the first days of November before the Bolshevik revolution, Red Guard and bolshevized army units in western and central Siberia began disarming troops who would not recognize Bolshevik authority.[192] Suddenly, news flashed from Petrograd that Vladimir Ilyich Lenin had launched a coup d'état on 7 November 1917 that overran the Winter Palace.

The announcement of the Red coup found Semenov and his 50-man shell of a new regiment in Nizhnyaya Berezovka, a small garrison town near Verkhne-Udinsk. Confusion reigned. V.M. Serov, a young Bolshevik who had maneuvered to become legal head of the local soviet, not only denounced the provisional government for failing to convene the Constituent Assembly, he also condemned his own party's seizure of power.[193] In other parts of Siberia, armed Bolshevik detachments concentrated in cities, disarmed the befuddled opposition and arrested vociferous leaders, then dictated terms to the surrounding countryside.[194]

On 16 November Semenov took the train to Irkutsk where Major General Samarin agreed with his plan to continue raising the Mongol–Buryat Regiment on behalf of the provisional government. Bolshevik sympathizers in Irkutsk government offices had already begun to reveal themselves however, among them a clerk in the military district headquarters. During a pointless squabble with this clerk, a naive and indiscreet Captain Kubnitsev blurted out something to the effect of 'Captain Semenov will soon show you Reds a thing or two'. This foolish bluster resulted in Kubnitsev's prompt arrest and Semenov's secret and hasty departure from the city, accompanied by five Irkutsk Cossacks.[195]

Semenov arrived in Verkhne-Udinsk expecting his arrest at any moment, and, sure enough, the station commandant had received a telegram from Irkutsk to detain him. About 750 soldiers had also recently shown up in Verkhne-Udinsk from the west, their ranks permeated with Bolshevik agitators and anti-war activists who were proselytizing with great success among the four regular battalions in town. A company of these Red troops were in the vicinity of the train station on the afternoon of 18 November when the station commandant and two guards accosted Semenov, demanding to see his papers. He punched the commandant in the chin and kicked him in the leg as the Irkutsk Cossacks rushed the guards, wounding them both with their sabers. The other Reds around the station backed off and scattered while Semenov and his group boarded an eastbound train and ordered the engineer to depart a bit early. Semenov and his fellow fugitives made it to Chita the evening of 18 November, and to their relief found that the 'liberal-pink elements of the local intelligentsia' had not yet succumbed to the Bolsheviks.[196] However, Semenov realized that the Bolsheviks would not tolerate the local socialist coalition government for much longer, and had begun making preparations for an 'active struggle' against them.

Likewise, the Reds did not expect to take over without a struggle. Workers from Chita's electric power station and sprawling railway shops and miners from nearby coal pits had formed a substantial Red Guard commanded by Konstantin Grigorevich Nedorezov, a senior railway worker. About 40 POWs joined Nedorezov in December.[197] The Red Guards remembered the heroic 1905 Chita Republic and General Rennenkampf's iron-fisted suppression of it, and were eager to vent the class hatred that Bolshevism endorsed. The only obstacle was Chita's People's Soviet, a coalition of Mensheviks, moderate and left SRs with a Bolshevik minority, a tenacious symbol of Russia's chaotic experiment with democracy. The Bolsheviks had no intention of allowing the experiment to continue.

Semenov, as a Cossack officer and commissar of the provisional government, risked arrest in Chita should the 'liberal-pinks' try to placate the Bolsheviks with his apprehension. Yet he feared not because he had an agent that kept him abreast of every step of the ruling revolutionaries. His source was a soldier named Zamkin, an actual member of the Chita *SovDep* (Soviet of Cossacks', Workers', Peasants' and Soldiers' Deputies). Semenov's helper, Junior NCO Burdukovskii, acted as the intermediary for communications between the two. For a short spell Semenov considered brashly storming and arresting the *SovDep* with Burdukovskii. However, a waiting telegram from the General Staff that had been received before his escape from Irkutsk and Verkhne-Udinsk convinced him otherwise.[198] It ordered Semenov to regroup his Mongol–Buryat formation at Dauria near the Manchurian border, where there was a well-appointed military base with ample barracks. Somehow he managed to wheedle funds out of the regional treasury that had been appropriated for his recruiting activities, and he found a secure means to send word to his cadre in Berezovka to rendezvous at Dauria. On 28 November Semenov fled 250 miles south to the town of Dauria. That same day in Verkhne-Udinsk, the Bolsheviks rigged an electoral victory that gave them a majority on the local soviet, and soon began redistributing property and liquidating 'class enemies', aided by an influenza epidemic in December. At this point, it looked as if the battle for Russian democracy rested on the shoulders of this brave young captain and a handful of Cossack friends and associates.

Bolshevik coups across Siberia

The Bolshevik coup d'état cast its shadow slowly but steadily across Siberia, like a Red tide sweeping east along the railway. In some places provincial and local officials were quickly deposed at gunpoint and replaced with pro-Bolshevik commissars, Military Revolutionary Committees or Committees for the Defense of the Revolution. In a few places, the Bolsheviks met resistance, such as at Orenburg where a recently elected Cossack *ataman*, Lieutenant Colonel Aleksandr Il'ich Dutov, immediately issued a call to arms that echoed through the empty *stanitsas* – all the fighting men were at the Fronts. In other places the Reds moved 'in a quiet way' to gradually take control of local soviets and various government departments, in the same way that weeds take over a garden.[199]

Bolshevik penetration varied widely from one city to another. In Khabarovsk there was

> a gradual letting go of the professional official intelligentsia, always unpopular figures among the workers of the lowest categories, until eventually the entire intelligentsia, with small exceptions, would boycott the transformed offices, which began to be filled with a hastily chosen element, half illiterate... The intelligentsia, of course, secretly smiled at the Soviet authorities, boycotting the whole outfit and expecting it all suddenly to end.

A young tailor named Tobelson (who went by the pseudonym Alexander Mikhailovich Krasnoshchekov) had returned from the United States for the revolution and became the chief of the Council of People's Commissars of the Far East – DALSOVNARKOM in the fashionable new workers' jargon. The council promptly created an extraordinary investigational committee led by 'a grim individual of typically bandit physiognomy and churlish manners', a primitive local secret police to fill in until the CHEKA professionals could arrive.²⁰⁰

In Vladivostok, Red agents spread like a subtle infection through the city administration throughout November, but, for six months after the coup, the Bolsheviks and their obedient soviet, wary of inciting a Japanese backlash, had to wrestle over power with a *zemstvo* council and a municipal duma (HMS Suffolk steamed into Vladivostok harbor on 14 January 1918 and the Bolsheviks also had to be wary of provoking a British reaction).²⁰¹ Similarly, Bolsheviks in Chita and Verkhne-Udinsk still shared seats on local soviets with Socialist-Revolutionaries and Mensheviks.

A variety of factions from across the political spectrum, including other revolutionary parties, opposed the Bolshevik takeover, but few managed more than a whimper before Red Guards suppressed them. Irkutsk was different. Five weeks after the red flag went up over the Winter Palace, and three weeks after Semenov's escape from town, Irkutsk blew up. Its fate would determine that of Verkhne-Udinsk and other towns and cities down the line in Transbaikalia.

'The great wave of anarchy came sweeping down from the west with great rapidity', an American engineer in Siberia wrote to his home office, 'Irkutsk was caught in the current, and for days severe fighting was in progress on its streets'.²⁰² Irkutsk Bolsheviks gained control of the city soviet on 28 November and set up a Military Revolutionary Committee under A. Rydzinski, which took over city offices on 17 December 1917, and set out to collect all weapons from possible opponents. In the process, the Bolsheviks excited the opposition when they turned over security of a sizeable prisoner of war camp to a group of 300 'revolutionary POWs'.²⁰³ Russian officers, military cadets from two local military schools, and various other soldiers and citizens loyal to the democratic soviets resisted Red attempts to disarm them.

On 21 December loyal cadets and officers attacked Irkutsk's White House, where the Military Revolutionary Committee had set up shop. The Whites set up machine guns on the Museum of Regional Studies across the street and rolled in a cannon to besiege 153 Red Guards and a handful of party chiefs holed up behind the six powerful columns of the old Governor-General's residence. It was a historically ironic setting for this revolutionary drama. Decembrist exiles had called on the austere mansion in the 1840s soon after the first tsarist governor moved in. Years later Governor-General Nikolai Murav'ev-Amurskii hosted his relative Mikhail Bakunin before the latter was exiled for his anarchist beliefs. Petr Kropotkin, the prince who turned anarchist, had visited also.²⁰⁴ A Cossack *sotnia* joined the spontaneous White uprising. Vicious street battles raged for a week, paralyzing the city's 100,000 inhabitants and freezing traffic on the Trans-Siberian Railway.

The Bolsheviks mustered the 'revolutionary soldiers of a few reserve regiments' and a number of newly formed Red Guard detachments. The Irkutsk Red Guards included not only local workers from the city's working class suburb, Znamenski, but Cheremkhovo miners, army deserters, Polish exiles and refugees, Koreans and Chinese. Two separate detachments were raised from socialist POWs, one of them commanded by a 'German revolutionary' named A. Shtiller.²⁰⁵

On 28 December the badly mauled Bolsheviks agreed to a truce which acknowledged the existing city government. It was just a ploy to gain time until reinforcements could arrive. Two days later, trains began arriving with carloads of Red Guards and internationalists from Krasnoyarsk under Ensign Sergei Georgievich Lazo. The Bolshevik leader, Boris Shumyatskii, tore up the truce agreement and announced that he would raise the red banner 'over the ruins of Irkutsk' if he had to. Shumyatskii then allowed the outwitted opposition forces to depart on eastbound trains.²⁰⁶ By 4 January, Shumyatskii could claim control over the city and province of Irkutsk.

The deployment of *internatsionalisty* – internationalists – in Irkutsk marked one of the first applications of a Soviet innovation in recruiting that would be employed for next seven decades: enlisting sympathetic (if not ideologically pure) warriors from war prisoners, foreign workers and refugees. Most internationalists were recruited from Russia's prisoner of war camps, where up to an estimated 1.6 million men languished.[207] Of this flatulent number, at least 51,000 soldiers of the German, Austro-Hungarian and Turkish armies were held in stockades east of Irkutsk.[208] Recruiting internationalist POWs ranked high on the Bolsheviks' agenda. Their military training and experience, discipline and diverse origins made them a natural vanguard for Lenin's world revolution. On the very day of the Bolshevik coup, 7 November 1917, the Petrograd Military–Revolutionary Committee took time to appoint a commissar for POW affairs and order the reorganization of the Central Committee of POWs of the Russian Society of the Red Cross.[209] Detachments of Germans, Hungarians, Latvians and Poles would become the shock troops of Red offensives in Siberia. With their military training, combat experience and knowledge of weapons, they became the 'most solid and reliable military support' that the Bolsheviks had in the east.[210] Their success in Irkutsk encouraged the formation of Red Guard detachments among POWs and Asian workers in Moscow, Petrograd, Voronezh, Simbirsk, Penza, Tversk, Tsaritsyn, Kazan and other cities.

The Bolsheviks took over Khabarovsk in a similar fashion. Left SRs gained control of the soviet in mid-December and began to organize Red Guard detachments among radical trade unionists, garrison soldiers and sailors of the Amur river flotilla. On 24 December they arrested the provisional government's commissar and within three days were gloating over their control over the entire Russian Far East, except for Vladivostok. There, although the Bolsheviks had wormed their way into control of the soviet, Allied warships bobbing in the harbor kept them from exerting their power.[211]

Far from Irkutsk, in northwestern Persia, news of the Bolshevik takeover demoralized Semenov's old command, the 3rd Verkhne-Udinsk Regiment, and contaminated the army of Russian saviors who had brought peace to the area. 'The hitherto brave and well-disciplined Russian soldiery were, at this stage, irrecognizable', wrote an Assyrian clergyman. 'They became transformed into bandits...[and] fled in disorder, burning and destroying bazaars in their wave of anarchy, everything indeed which presented an obstacle to their return [to Russia].' The Bolsheviks ordered the troops to abandon the Caucasus Front, but most of them would have gone home anyway. A hastily assembled army of 20,000 Assyrians inherited the front at Lake Urmia.[212] The Russians gave them eight guns, several machine guns and ammunition, wished them luck, and shamelessly left them to their fate with the Turkish regulars and Kurdish and Persian auxiliaries.[213] The Cossacks trudged back to Transbaikalia, eager to claim a plot of distributed land, not comprehending the storm that was brewing.

2

REVOLUTION AND RED TERROR

November 1917–May 1918

'All semenovtsy, as persons outside the law, will be subjected to merciless extermination.'
(*Tsentrosibir* pronouncement in Irkutsk newspaper, *Rabochii i Krest'yanin*, 14 May 1918)

Revolutionary days in Dauria and Harbin

Dauria was a dusty little Transbaikal town on the line to Manchuria, sitting 50 miles north of the border on a barren, knobby plateau. It served as a flashpoint for invasion from Russia's Asian neighbors and accordingly hosted an oversized complex of one- and two-storied red brick barracks that could accommodate a mobilization. In the world of Russian military architecture, Dauria's pseudo-Gothic structures were unique in that they were comfortable, fashionable and new – built in 1907 during the retrospective defense overhaul that followed the defeat to Japan.[1]

Grigorii Semenov took refuge at the military base here for about two weeks in late November 1917. He was pleased to find that a number of officers from his Mongol–Buryat Regiment cadre could make it to Dauria from Berezovka: *Khorunzhii* (Sub-lieutenant) Madievskii, *Podkhorunzhii* (Junior Ensign) Shvalov, *Mladshii Uryadnik* (Junior NCO) Batakov, *Starshii Uryadnik* (Senior NCO) Medvedev and *Kazak* (Cossack Private) Batuev. The situation looked gloomy. With each passing day the militia detachment that composed Dauria garrison became more and more 'bolshevized' and unruly, while the prisoners themselves had taken control of the sizeable POW camp at the base.[2] Semenov's old friend, *Voiskovoi Starshina* (Lieutenant Colonel) Baron Ungern-Shternberg, had also reached Dauria, after having been demoted (to captain) in August for assaulting a senior officer's aide de camp and partaking in General Kornilov's aborted coup shortly thereafter.[3]

Unable to rely upon any of the Dauria garrison's Russian soldiers, Semenov could only count on a few Turkish and German prisoners-of-war 'whom the German-speaking Ungern-Shternberg had dressed up as military policemen', in addition to his five-man Berezovka cadre and a handful of Russian followers. While the myth that Semenov started the counterrevolution with 'three junior officers, a warrant officer, a minor official and a clerk' is not exactly correct, it does not change the David-versus-Goliath dimensions of his struggle to add that a few other sympathizers offered their services at critical times, usually officers, Cossacks and minor officials who had tasted the Bolsheviks' cold, stern fanaticism.[4]

One dubious volunteer was a 'muddle-headed' Cossack named Berezovskii, who was serving time in the 'discipline battalion' the last time Semenov heard of him before the war. Now the misfit sat on the Chita soviet and, as a plum result, had become the Dauria commandant. Semenov was amazed – and amused – to find out that he could be bought with the offer of an officer's rank (which meant, in the miscreant's eyes, acceptance back into the Cossack fold), so he enlisted Berezovskii, promising him that if he performed his tasks wonderfully, Semenov, as commissar of the provisional government, would commission him as a *praporshchik* – an ensign. He began by eagerly telling Semenov all he knew about the Chita soviet and its activities. Though Semenov thought Berezovskii was 'inclined to get carried away', he put his heart into his new position and was soon rewarded with the commission that he coveted.[5]

The other officers of the garrison lacked Berezovskii's shifty background, but were competent and anxious to join any effort to brake the revolutionary descent into anarchy. They included the garrison commander, Staff Captain Oparin, his second-in-command, Staff Captain Usikov, and perhaps a few others.[6]

Semenov allowed one POW onto his cadre, a 'captain of the Turkish general staff', whom Semenov referred to as Prince Al-Kadir.[7] Al-Kadir would work with Semenov for about one year. After the armistice in November 1918, Semenov helped Al-Kadir communicate with his family in Baghdad via the British Consul in Harbin. Soon Al-Kadir was on his way home to 'a notable position' in the British–Mesopotamian government, courtesy of the British Embassy in Peking.[8]

It was only a matter of time before the Dauria garrison mutinied outright, so in early December 1917, Semenov sent a Lieutenant Zhevchenko to Vladivostok, Shanghai and Peking to seek assistance from Russian and Allied consuls and military representatives. Prince Nikolai Alekseevich Kudashev, Russia's Minister to China and his military attaché were pleased with Semenov's plan to recover Transbaikalia, but had nothing to offer. Zhevchenko also paused in Harbin to ask the Chinese Eastern Railway administration for help, then he returned to Semenov with bad news: Harbin's hands were full with its own problems.[9]

The railway line through Dauria fed the Chinese Eastern Railway, which was still free of Bolshevik control and without which the Bolsheviks would have difficulty governing Russia's provinces on the Pacific coast. The railway held immense strategic value and most of the stations offered tactical strongpoints, having been reconstructed as stockades complete with gun ports (usually around the station master's house) after they were torched during the Boxer Rebellion. Although the railway traversed Chinese territory, the Russian government had, during the course of the past two decades, gradually extended its authority into the parts of Manchuria covered by the Chinese Eastern Railway zone. The titular chairman of the railway's board was a token Chinese, but all directors and administrators were Russian, and most shares were owned by Russia's imperial treasury. A paramilitary Russian brigade guarded the railway and its facilities and diplomatic agreements even permitted the Russian military to enter certain areas. While the power of the Chinese Eastern Railway Company centered on the railway zone, a commercial empire of auxiliary enterprises stretched its tendrils throughout Manchuria and included a telegraph service, lumber camps, coal mines and steamship lines on the Amur and Sungari rivers.

A legal pretense for Russia's creeping expansion lurked in the ambiguous wording and liberal translations of the original 1896 Railway Agreement – the 'Cassini Convention' – between Count Sergei Witte's Ministry of Finance and the Chinese government.[10] However, after China's tumultuous Boxer Rebellion in 1900, Russians curtly took over civil administration along the line, and even began levying local taxes and operating their own judicial system.[11] Since Tsar Nicholas II's abdication, railway company executives had struggled to coexist with radicals of a newborn Union of Railway Employees and Soviet of Workers' and Soldiers' Deputies, while the Chinese warlord of Manchuria, the Machiavellian General Chang Tso-Lin, watched and waited expectantly as the railway company's power inside and outside the zone shriveled.[12]

To thwart a Bolshevik takeover of the railway, the railway administration in Harbin cut a deal on 5 December to share power with a multiparty Committee of Public Safety. The railway militia was rebellious, having been cannibalized by conscription of its best soldiers for the front, leaving only a lax, understrength force of middle-aged men and teenagers who were gullibly enchanted by revolutionary propaganda. They were clamoring to take over the railway as Lenin had ordered on 21 November. Allied consuls implored the Chinese government to prevent a Bolshevik takeover, and the ranking local official, Sze Sheo-Chang, called for troops to be sent from Kirin province. The situation presented a splendid opportunity for China to reassert her sovereignty in northern Manchuria.

The Bolsheviks could wait no longer. They took over the Harbin soviet on 12 December, coercing the remaining Mensheviks and Socialist-Revolutionaries to walk out, publicly declared, via the revolutionary newspaper *Golos Truda* (*Voice of Labor*), that the soviet was now the sole government of the Russian zone and dispatched Bolshevik militiamen to take over the railway by force. Chinese troops, who had already begun massing in town, engaged the militia, and disarmed and immediately deported many of them back to Russia. Ensign M.N. Riutin, the chairman of the soviet, had gone into hiding hours earlier.[13] Six days later Riutin announced the dismissal of railway administration officials and their replacement with Bolsheviks.[14]

About this time, Semenov received a telegram from General R.A. von Arnold, the chief of police in Harbin, asking him to detain a Bolshevik named Arkus, whom Riutin had appointed as commissar of the Chinese eastern militia brigade and who would soon be passing through Dauria on his way to Irkutsk for instructions. Duly authorized as a commissar of the provisional government, Semenov plucked Arkus from the train, intending to simply hold him a week or two until the unrest in Harbin died down, realizing that if the Manchurian railway zone fell to Arkus' comrades, his position in Dauria would soon be surrounded by Reds. However, Arkus cursed and threatened Semenov and shouted in vain to rile up mutinous troops milling around the station. Semenov's compatriots responded to his vulgar outbursts with a *voenno-polevoi sud* – a field court martial, during which they found documents in his baggage ordering Semenov's arrest. These papers sealed Arkus' death sentence and he was immediately executed.[15]

On 13 December 1917 Lenin moved to abolish special privileges and obligations of all Cossacks. It would have made little difference to Semenov.[16] The traitorous Bolshevik despoilers had already made clear their intention not only to destroy all that was precious to traditional life, but also to destroy Semenov's life as well.

Semenov's eight-man Counterrevolution

It was time for action. In the early morning hours of 18 December Semenov and two Cossacks (NCOs Burdukovskii and Baturin) caught a train south to Manchzhuriya, popularly referred to as Manchuli or Manchuria station, just inside Chinese territory.[17] Manchuli was destined to become one of the Far East's epicenters of international tension during the next three years. 'The hills around Manchuria Station are the bleakest-looking brown hills you can imagine, much like the dry lands of eastern Colorado', wrote an American traveler. '[It] is a dust-swept town of fifteen thousand inhabitants of whom two-thirds are Chinese and the other third Russians and various others. The Russian side of the city is on one side of the railroad, the Chinese on the other. The main streets are lined with peddlers and little bazaar shops. Gin, whiskey, *sake* and vodka bottles beckon to passing travelers from half the windows …'[18] Commerce – and intrigue – in Manchuli centered around an ornate train station with snarling gold dragons writhing atop its long tile roof. 'A few of the more pretentious buildings ... [like] the Nikitin Hotel and some of the railway yard buildings' were of modern brick construction, but apart from these and a small number of wooden edifices, weary sun-baked, mud-plastered architecture dominated. For centuries Manchuli had prospered as a crossroads between China and the wilds of Mongolia and Siberia, an oasis on the parched, treeless steppe. Long caravans of pack-horses and camels hauling two-wheeled carts still plodded through the streets of the walled town like wanderers from a medieval dream.

Manchuli's railway facility was a strategic asset, being the junction and a turning point for the Chinese Eastern and Trans-Siberian railways, from whence trains of the former returned to their divisional headquarters at Hailar, and trains of the latter to Olovyannaya. The railyards had a 12-stall roundhouse and several large repair shops which had long been infected with Bolshevism and other revolutionary ideas. Similarly troops in six barracks of the town's military complex and coal miners at the Djalanur colliery 15 miles east had gone Red.

Upon their arrival from Dauria, Semenov, Burdukovskii and Baturin first visited passport control for processing where they found two officials, I.I. Kulikov and his assistant Kyunst, 'veritable patriots who did not hesitate to make sacrifices for the good of their Motherland'. They filled Semenov in on the local situation. Manchuli's garrison, consisting of the 720th Militia group and a company of Chinese Eastern Railway troops, was irretrievably 'bolshevized', demoralized and unmanageable. A Chinese Army brigade had just arrived to disarm them and assume security duties on that section of the railway, but its commander, Major General Gan, thinking his force insufficient for this sensitive task, was awaiting further orders and reinforcements from Harbin before proceeding.[19]

Kulikov also informed Semenov that the Reds had already begun to haul officers and officials before a revolutionary tribunal on the second floor of the train station. Minutes later, when the tribunal staff tried to march a prisoner through passport control, Burdukovskii jumped them with ursine ferocity, clubbed the two escorts with the butt of his rifle, freed the captive official and scattered the Red functionaries to meek protestations of 'Cossack brute!' In the afternoon Semenov scouted the barracks and noted how loosely they were guarded.[20]

Meanwhile Kulikov invited Manchuli's four senior Chinese officials – Major General Gan, the chief of the Tsitsihar Province diplomatic office, the mayor and local police chief – to visit the passport control office to hear a proposal from Commissar Semenov of the provisional government. When they gathered, Semenov suggested that the mutinous garrison be disarmed without bloodshed by Russians, rather than risk an international incident and civilian casualties in Manchuli should gunfire occur as Chinese troops tried to take the Reds' weapons. Gan immediately agreed and offered the assistance of his brigade if necessary.[21] Of course, the Chinese assumed that Semenov had a sizeable military force at his disposal.

Semenov and his seven counterrevolutionary cohorts set to work at once. First he had the station master assemble a train of 30 *taplushki* (standard Russian boxcars for freight, soldiers and peasants) equipped with bunks and stoves, telling him that it must be dispatched to Dauria immediately to retrieve his regiment and deliver them to Manchuli by dawn the next day. He sent Burdukovskii on this train to Dauria with a message for Ungern-Shternberg to round up anyone he could find, have them fire up the stoves and lanterns in each *taplushka* and take the return trip to Manchuli. In the meantime Semenov counted on gossipers, Reds and spies among railway workers and hangers-on at Manchuli station to spread the word to the Bolshevik and Chinese chains-of-command that the Mongol–Buryat Cavalry Regiment was arriving.[22]

At 4 a.m. on 19 December, the 30-car echelon carrying the imaginary cavalry regiment arrived at Manchuli, faintly aglow with lanterns, smoke rising from each stovepipe.

A handful of men exited the train, including Lieutenant Colonel Ungern-Shternberg and Sub-Lieutenant Madievskii. Ungern-Shternberg quickly tracked down the chief of the railway militia, Captain Stepanov. He told the captain to show him the barracks of the railway troops, explaining along the way that he and the single Cossack accompanying him intended to disarm them. Stepanov was utterly amazed that two fools would try to take the guns out of the hands of two companies of mutinous soldiers and informed Ungern-Shternberg that he was going home. Ungern-Shternberg whacked Stepanov convincingly in the gut with the scabbard of his *shashka* (Cossack saber) and informed the incredulous captain that he was going to help them. Thus began the infamous counterrevolutionary career of the soon-to-be notorious Stepanov.[23]

When the Manchuli garrison awoke shortly after 6 a.m., news of the regimental echelon's arrival spread quickly. In the barracks of the 720th Militia group, Semenov assembled the drowsy rabble. 'As I expected', he wrote, 'the disarmament proceeded quickly and easily, without any incident, if you don't count an attempt by one of the members of the unit's [Bolshevik] committee to call his confused comrades to arms.' Perhaps this Bolshevik was the only soldier who did not notice that a single small chain ran through the trigger guards of all the rifles. No one was passionate enough to answer his lonely appeal. Private Batuev held his rifle at the ready and Semenov drew his pistol, announcing that they would shoot anyone who did not cooperate. He added that they were being demobilized and sent home by the provisional government, and gave them 20 minutes to collect their belongings and reassemble. Anyone who was late would be arrested and court-martialed. Upon hearing of home, the soldiers joyfully began to gather their belongings and were ready to march to the station in half an hour. Ungern-Shternberg, his Cossack assistant and a nervous Captain Stepanov disarmed several hundred railway troops in a similar fashion. In a short time 1,500 happy mutineers were jostling each other on the station platform to board a waiting train home. Only the long faces of the zealous Bolsheviks tarnished the glow of this homecoming excursion.[24]

Sub-Licutenant Madievskii had not bothered to deliver the demobilization speech when he and two Cossacks burst into the apartments of the garrison's Bolshevik leaders and agitators. They arrested them – a few radical teachers, workers and, as Semenov described them, men 'of uncertain profession, specializing in political speculation'. They were pushed into a separate, sealed *taplushka* in which, they were told with a sneer, 'they could ride proudly into Russia ... just like their god Lenin'.[25]

By 10 a.m. the train was ready to pull out, but not before the passengers were told that if anyone stuck their head out a window or tried to disembark they would be shot by the guard detail in the last car. Unbeknownst to the 37 carloads of homesick Reds, that detail consisted solely of Junior Ensign Shvalov and a Mosin-Nagant rifle. He jumped off the train just before Dauria, where the troop train skipped the station and accelerated through town faster than normal, giving Dauria mutineers the impression that the Mongol–Buryat Cavalry Regiment was on the move to squash more Bolshevik uprisings.[26] Thus, armed only with a fertile imagination, convincing bluster, fearlessness and a handful of men, Semenov neutralized two hostile bases and captured his first two towns. On 19 December 1917 Semenov telegraphed the Chinese Eastern administration: 'Have disarmed and demobilized the bolshevized garrison of Manchuli and evacuated it to Russia. Garrison's duties have fallen on my regiment. Awaiting your orders. Captain of the Cossacks, Semenov.'[27]

By 20 December, somewhere between 3,500 and 4,500 Chinese troops were swarming through the streets of Harbin. Sze Sheo-Chang compelled Lieutenant General Dmitri Lionidovich Horvath, the administrator of the railway, to demand the departure of both Bolsheviks and *semenovtsy* from the railway zone. Of course, both parties refused and

Horvath had no control over the railway militia anymore. An 'alarming atmosphere' developed as Chinese soldiers added another unpredictable variable to the increasingly explosive mixture of soviets, monarchist refugees and other armed groups.

At 3 a.m. on 25 December, the Chinese staff presented the soviet with an ultimatum demanding that the 618th Tomsk Infantry be disbanded and all Bolsheviks leave China. The soviet executive committee decided to comply; the revolutionary troops were well-equipped with small arms but were outnumbered and outgunned by the Chinese. Nevertheless, violence broke out, as was almost inevitable with so much tension, animosity and weaponry crammed into a small place. A two-hour gunfight between Russians and Chinese wounded several innocent bystanders and killed a school teacher. The death of the 618th's acting commander, Lieutenant Colonel Davidov, seemed to turn the battle. A Chinese colonel, Tsao-Zhi-Gan, managed to step up to Davidov while the Russian officer was talking on the telephone with company staff and shoot him at point-blank with his revolver. It alarmed the men, who began to think that the 618th was jinxed. During the first flurry of revolutionary madness in March 1917, Davidov had joined with the mutineers in arresting the original commander, Colonel Fridrikhov, who hung himself with a towel in the guardroom several days later.[28]

The Chinese rounded up and disarmed the Bolshevik combatants, including Red Guards of the Union of Railway Employees, then shipped them out of the city, destination unknown.[29] An Asian historian noted that it was 'the first time in history that any group of Europeans, having reduced themselves to anarchy, had been brought under control by the Chinese'.[30] General Pao Kuei-ch'ing began replacing Russian railway guards with Chinese troops along the length of the railway.[31] However, to the Chinese' chagrin, Semenov still operated inside their borders.

His successes in Manchuli and Dauria attracted new men to his anti-Bolshevik vendetta. By 25 December, another army officer, 35 Cossacks and 40 Mongols had joined his party of seven. The next day a train full of homeward-bound troops of the Ussuri Cossack Division passed through Manchuli on its way east. These men had been among the 700 Cossacks under General Petr Nikolayevich Krasnov, who had been routed by Bolshevik troops at Pulkovo Hills on 13 November as they marched on Petrograd. General Boris Rostislavovich Khreshchatitskii accepted a subordinate position as Semenov's chief of staff, whereupon a number of other senior officers of the division followed the young general's example. Khreshchatitskii was a combat hero and military leader who inspired men, having been commander of a Don Cossack regiment before the war, and who rose through achievements on the battlefield to the rank of major general by the time he was 30 years old in 1915. Semenov enticed ten officers and 112 Cossacks to enlist with his band.[32]

A few days later a battalion of Italians came through Manchuli en route for a transport ship out of Vladivostok. Presumably they were *irredenti*, ethnic Italians (from Trentino, Trieste, Istria, Fiume and parts of Dalmatia) unwillingly conscripted into the Austro-Hungarian Army who had deserted or been captured in the Carpathians. It seems that they donated their arms and ammunition to Semenov.[33]

Rather than charge into Transbaikalia with his 205-man army, Semenov next focused his attention further down the Chinese Eastern Railway on the rebellious Russian garrison at Hailar, Manchuria, 115 miles east of Manchuli. He sent a small group to Hailar but initially they did not try to take any action against the soldiers' committees or governing soviet. They simply observed the chaos, taking notes of the leaders, schedules, discipline and locations of arms, while making contact with the few officers and men uninfected by the Bolshevik dementia.

On 28 December 1917 three congresses of regional soviets met in Chita to reorganize the local government and decide what to do about the Bolshevik seizure of power in

Petrograd. In the meantime they declared Semenov a counterrevolutionary and reiterated the order for his arrest.[34] Soviet histories later miscast this event as proof of the broad solidarity between leftist parties, obfuscating the distrust between Socialist-Revolutionaries and Mensheviks on one hand and Bolsheviks on the other and thus, subsequent discreet negotiations with Semenov by socialists on Chita's people's soviet are cited as examples of the latter's treachery. Similarly, it is not accurate to say that Semenov had a pronounced dislike of all socialists – he would deal with many brands of socialists for years to come, while he certainly developed an indelible hatred for Bolsheviks during the first months of the revolution.

Semenov gave fair warning of his intentions to all members of the Chita soviet in an undated telegram sent from Manchuli:

> Bolsheviks! Witting and unwitting traitors of the Motherland! You have sold out Russia, launched a military campaign and undertaken civil war. I demand the disarming of the Red Guards and that their leaders leave the boundaries of Transbaikalia. If these demands are not met, I will be compelled to use force of arms to enforce them.

Semenov addressed both the citizens of Chita and his brother Cossacks, calling on them to stand behind him. He closed with the rallying cry, 'Long live the Constituent Assembly!'[35]

First offensive

On or about New Year's Day, 1918, Semenov launched his first offensive into Russia.[36] Months later he would proclaim for the benefit of foreign correspondents and diplomats that he merely intended to restore law and order, not to crush the democratic revolution. Regardless of his motives, to Semenov goes the distinction of launching the counterrevolution against the Bolsheviks in Transbaikalia and the Russian Far East.

However, before he thrust very deep into Russia, he had to secure his rear at Manchuli, where he had tolerated a secretive town soviet full of Bolsheviks since the eviction of its supporting Red garrison. Accompanied by three new volunteers from the regular army, Lieutenant Colonel Skipetrov, Captain Tierbach and Lieutenant Tskhovrebashvili, Semenov entered the soviet's meeting hall shouting '*Ruki vverkh*!' – 'Hands up!' After a short diatribe by Skipetrov about the White revolt in Irkutsk, whence the newcomer had recently escaped, Semenov informed the soviet that there were three categories of Bolsheviks: first – brazen traitors like Lenin; second – hangers-on angling for personal gain; and third – 'fools and jackasses'. He intended to 'annihilate' the first two categories, while he could excuse the third. So the members of the Manchuli soviet earnestly confessed to being fools and jackasses and were thrown onto a train to Chita.[37]

Semenov's army now numbered about 600 men: 51 Russian officers, three former officials (including Sergei A. Taskin), 300 Buryats, 135 Cossacks, 80 Mongolians and 'a few military cadets, university students and schoolboys from passing trains'.[38] On 9 January 1918 he christened his little horde the *Osoboi Manchzhurskii Otryad* (OMO) – the Special Manchurian Detachment. The name had nothing to do with the large number of Buryats and Mongolians in the formation, nor with Semenov's latent Pan-Mongol aspirations. The 'Manchurian' part of the unit designation referred to OMO's place of origin, the town of Manchzhuriya.[39]

There was not much armed opposition in the dreary frontier towns Semenov attacked, where the little Red Guard units dispersed along the railway 'had no great military value and little stomach for a fight'.[40] Yet it was a time of almost daily skirmishes, when OMO fought without the luxury of artillery or machine guns, on an unconventional front that was but a 'ribbon of railway'. Semenov's anti-Red reputation preceded him, and some active Socialist-Revolutionaries and Mensheviks melted away from the towns with the Bolsheviks before OMO's arrival. From Manchuli Semenov issued separate appeals to Cossacks and other citizens to resist the 'Bolshevik usurpers'.[41] As word of Semenov's rebellion spread through Siberia and the Russian Far East, an unknown number of men eager to fight Bolshevism tried to make their way to OMO territory and, in response, *SovDeps* and *chekisty* (CHEKA agents) established control points on the railway lines to ferret them out. A youth named Dashkov became a semenovist martyr after his trek to OMO was interrupted at Slyudyanka by a Red execution squad.[42]

OMO pushed north out of Dauria 41 miles up the railway to take Borzya on 11 January. Borzya's small size belied the tactical importance that its mundane railway facilities and proximity to the border afforded it and would figure prominently in Semenov's activities during the next three years. It was neatly laid out with about 110 Russian houses and a small church on one side of the railway tracks and a Chinese–Mongol village on the other side. The train station had a small roundhouse and between eight and ten side tracks, essential facilities for assembling and disassembling trains, or for sorting out and routing traffic.[43]

By 12 January 1918 an OMO unit under Baron Ungern-Shternberg had advanced 60 miles further to take Olovyannaya, on the Onon river midway between the Chinese border and Chita, where it captured scores of rifles and four ammunition wagons before Red Guards pushed them out of town.[44] Three or four days after that, Captain Savel'ev and a 100-man OMO cavalry detachment recaptured Olovyannaya (and 78 rifles and 12 swords) and drove northwest all the way to Adrianovka, just one station short of the big railway fork at Karymskaya and only 75 miles from Chita.

For a fleeting moment, the thought of a 'dash for Chita' must have been seductive. The 1st Chita Cossack Regiment had returned home from the front during the first week in January, and, in support of the elected Soviets, had disarmed Bolsheviks who were organizing Red Guard units.[45] The returning Cossacks also plucked the 40 or so POW internationalists from the Red Guard detachments and threw them into prison.

Soviet histories accuse Chita's people's soviet of taking a conciliatory path at this point in January, even of conspiring to bring Grigorii Semenov to power. Semenov unsuccessfully invited the 1st Chita Cossack Regiment's commander to join him, and the people's soviet rushed a delegation to Adrianovka 'to plead with Savelev to withdraw'.[46] It was a critical time when a few dozen more men on either side may have swept their opponents from the field. Semenov was unable to swing the moderates to his side, and some moderates were already wary of associating with Semenov, perhaps out of fear of Bolshevik wrath or because Semenov's reputation already tilted too far to the right. Semenov wrote that 'in war generally, and especially in civil war, the human factor plays a decisive role', yet the only incentives he could offer were booty, a return to democracy's hectic status quo and threats.

Without support inside Chita, an OMO march on the city in mid-January threatened to stretch Semenov's resources too thinly. He had already spread his 600 soldiers over more than 200 miles of railway spanning 13 train stations and, he had no supply line. His hopes that OMO's invasion might ignite a spontaneous anti-Bolshevik uprising among the peasantry had been dashed. Most Transbaikal peasants still had no idea what inconveniences Bolshevism entailed and just wanted to be left alone – by all parties.

Meanwhile in distant Petrograd, Russia's Constituent Assembly actually convened in Taurida Palace on the afternoon of 18 January. Transbaikalia, Amur and Irkutsk had voted solidly moderate socialist – about 61 per cent of the returns (compared to about 40 per cent across the old empire).[47] Unfortunately, the Bolsheviks and their left SR comrades dominated the boisterous military and naval units and grey-uniformed rowdies made up most of the gallery at Taurida Palace. For a few hours they amused themselves watching the moderate socialists earnestly go through the legislative motions of political debate and passing laws, accompanied by the drab mob's whoops, catcalls, cursing and the dissonant metallic percussion of Mosin-Nagant bolts slamming shut, triggers clicking and butts banging the floor.[48] After that single session, however, the Bolsheviks tolerated no more democratic charades in European Russia. The Taurida Palace was padlocked and the Constituent Assembly scattered wider than the eddies of political leaflets blowing through the streets.

Recruiting Mongols

Semenov's anti-Bolshevik campaign had begun as a vengeful retort by Russian officers, most of whom, it was said, had escaped the initial wave of Red roundups and executions, and were enraged by the murders of their wives, children and other family members. Semenov restrained 'the revengeful zeal of his fellow warriors and ennobled them by imbuing their struggle with the ideal of a fight for the Constituent Assembly'.[49] He realized that the salvation of democratic Russia was at stake, not merely primitive retribution, and OMO needed many more men for the struggle.

Since August 1917, when he attended the assembly of the Transbaikal Cossack Host, Semenov had been pondering how he could make use of a large number of Karachen Mongol warriors stranded and unwelcome in Barga, the homeland of the Bargut Mongols in northwestern Manchuria. Barga had formally seceded from China in March 1912, but, like Outer Mongolia, accepted autonomy after the Russians stepped in to mediate and prevent a Chinese invasion to reassert Peking's authority. Many Barguts aspired to unite with autonomous Mongolia on their western border, but the flight of the Karachen Mongols into their territory complicated matters.

The Karachen émigrés in Barga had joined the short-lived 1916 rebellion of Chinese General Babu-Dzhan against the Peking government. Unfortunately for the Karachen, Babu-Dzhan was killed in one of the first clashes with Chinese regulars, so his deputy, Prince Fu Shin-Ga, led the tribe into the region around Barga to escape the pursuing Chinese Army. The sudden influx of Karachen fighters, amplified by their extended families and herds, caused friction with the native Barguts. By the summer of 1917, the Barguts and Karachens were at each others' throats in all-out war when Semenov, disappointed by poor recruiting in Transbaikal province, first contacted an old acquaintance in the Karachen camp about joining his Mongol–Buryat Regiment.[50] Semenov did not pursue the matter until he set up camp in Manchuli in December and contacted the Barga prince, Gui-Fu, to arrange peace talks. The three-day talks were welcomed by both sides and resulted in an agreement of friendship as well as amnesty from the Chinese government. For his part, Semenov received one brigade of Karachens, volunteers from the Barguts and a tremendous boost in prestige among the Mongols.[51] The Mongols' contributions of their men to Semenov reflect the insecurity they felt about the downfall of their traditional protectors in St Petersburg and the resurgence of their age-old nemesis in Peking. Compounding the threat of Chinese invasion was the menace of Bolshevik interference in Mongol affairs.

Regrettably, the Karachen Brigade was unavailable for OMO's first offensive, being more than 500 miles away, but in January 1918 some Bargut nationalist units were incorporated into a new Mongol–Buryat Regiment and assigned security for the western segment of the Chinese Eastern Railway from Manchuli to Hailar. The Chinese were upset and demanded that Semenov disband the units. Prince Kudashev and General Horvath, who preferred to turn over railway security to the Chinese, were annoyed by Semenov's independent action and sent him a verbose telegram protesting that the Bargut units infringed upon the sovereignty of China.[52]

In late December 1917 some of Semenov's people had established a presence in Hailar, the next major city to the east of Manchuli in the Chinese Eastern Railway zone. Law and order had broken down in the Russian quarter of the city since the October Revolution with the garrison leading the descent into chaos. Most of the garrison's officers had cast their lots with the Bolsheviks and, to Semenov's disgust, 'appeared to be the initiators and leaders' of Red mutinies. To their vociferous protests, Semenov appointed Lieutenant Colonel Baron Ungern-Shternberg as the new commandant of the city of Hailar, with complete confidence that he would bring order back to the city. Ungern-Shternberg had at his disposal a handful of officers, 250 green Bargut cavalrymen and the only loyal unit in Hailar, a cavalry *sotnia* commanded by Shtab-Rotmistr (Staff Captain) Mezhak. The garrison mustered 800 seditious troops of the Chinese Eastern Railway Brigade and border guard cavalry from Pogranichnaya. Near midnight one evening in mid-January, while the Red leadership was pontificating about revolution in yet another session of never-ending meetings, the Baron 'painlessly' disarmed the riotous garrison in about two hours and emptied the barracks into boxcars headed back to Red Russia.[53]

Since Bargut territory extended eastward beyond Hailar to Khingan, Ungern-Shternberg and 150 Barguts moved a few days later to occupy Bukhedu, the next major station to the east. Upon their arrival the commander of Bukhedu's Chinese garrison warmly invited Ungern-Shternberg to lunch, where he was arrested while his men were disarmed. Semenov was furious. In Hailar, he quickly rigged up a train with a platform car mounting a huge dummy howitzer half concealed by a tarpaulin and applied superficial 'armor' to two freight cars, then rushed to Ungern-Shternberg's defense. The Chinese commander was apologetic and released both the Baron and his men's weapons.[54] Like the Manchuli bluff, it was another victory achieved by sheer guile and audacity.

Red Takeover and Terror

Events in distant cities shaped the gathering storm in Transbaikalia. To Vladimir Lenin and the Bolshevik leadership in Petrograd, Siberia's sole reason for existence was to produce the bread which Red propaganda had promised to the urban masses in European Russia. On 13 January, a Bolshevik delegation from the city of Omsk pulled into hungry Petrograd with a trainload of grain. The delegation informed Lenin that 1,000 more carloads of grain were being held up in western Siberia by anti-Bolshevik railway workers. Lenin ordered about 50 CHEKA agents to ride back with the Omsk delegation and man key stations along the railway to expedite the stalled grain. The CHEKA agents performed their mission with ruthless efficiency; grain shipments from Siberia to European Russia skyrocketed in the month after their arrival.[55]

Bolshevik terror crept east out of European Russia like a biblical pestilence, months before Dzerzhinsky publicly declared 'We [Bolsheviks] stand for organized terror' and an official government terror campaign was formalized by the order 'On Red Terror' in September 1918. Arbitrary arrests, mass shootings, torture and imprisonment were an integral element of Bolshevik policy long before anti-Bolshevik armies gathered.[56] A typical display of this policy occurred in the western Siberian town of Kansk, where the mayor, a moderate Socialist-Revolutionary named Stepanov, was 'implicated' in an anti-Bolshevik protest that had erupted one day late in December 1917. The mayor had had nothing to do with the protest, which bore signs of a Bolshevik provocation. Nevertheless, he was jailed for several weeks, even after a Bolshevik military commission determined his innocence.

One day he was suddenly led through town to the train station with a large crowd, his wailing wife and children following. At the station, Bolshevik soldiers tightened a noose around his neck as he shouted, 'Long live the Constituent Assembly!' and heaved him into the air. Stepanov dangled from a corbel of the Kansk depot for 29 hours, his corpse twisting in the breeze of passing trains, whose eastbound passengers now carried the crystal-clear message: if the Bolsheviks could hang the mayor, they could hang anyone.[57]

The Bolsheviks immediately confiscated church and monastery real estate, terminated subsidies for clergy and churches, relaxed divorce laws, legalized civil marriage and assumed responsibility for registry of births and deaths. They preached 'a new sort of faith in the bright future of all mankind, along with an impassioned rejection of God'.[58] Churches were sacked and clergymen and pious believers were targets of violence and murder. Despite the Church's standing as the old empire's largest and, as judged by some, most oppressive, landlord, the faithful or superstitious among the peasantry were nevertheless horrified by the Bolshevik revolution's blasphemous acts. Patriarch Tikhon issued a pastoral letter on 1 February 1918, calling upon 'faithful children of the Orthodox Church...to have nothing in common with these outcasts of the human race' – the Bolsheviks.[59]

Anti-Bolshevik opposition was forced underground by the Red Terror as increasing numbers of Bolshevik thugs and assassins spread east along the Trans-Siberian. On 26 January 1918, the Bolsheviks shut down and arrested many members of the Siberian regional duma in Tomsk, the largest body of elected representatives in Siberia. Forty Socialist-Revolutionary members who avoided arrest gathered during the night of 27–28 January to form a secret Provisional Government of Autonomous Siberia (PGAS) under Premier Petr Yakovlevich Derber. Within 48 hours, Derber hastened to relative safety in the Far East, leaving the shells of an underground government behind: the western and eastern Siberian commissariats (WSC and ESC). Semenov claimed to have sent a telegram about this time to the 'President of the Government of Autonomous Siberia', presumably Derber, 'expressing [Semenov's] complete readiness to attain your [Derber's] Government's aims'.[60]

In early February 1918 the PGAS commissariats decided to 'overthrow Bolshevik authority', though it would be months before they mustered the organization and military strength to do so.[61] Despite its solid socialist orientation, the western Siberian commissariat (based in Novonikolaevsk) accepted former Imperial Army officers into its clandestine military cells. These officers included men from the far right of the political spectrum, such as the Group of Thirteen, a secret gathering of military officers from Cossack communities in the Omsk area, among them men whose names would soon be synonymous with counterrevolutionary terror – Lieutenant Colonel Boris Vladimirovich Annenkov, Major Pavel P. Ivanov-Rinov and Colonel Vyacheslav Ivanovich Volkov.[62] Other future White leaders who worked with the WSC included Lieutenant Colonel A.N. Pepelyaev in Tomsk, Lieutenant Colonel A.V. Ellerts-Usov in Irkutsk and Captain A.N. Grishin-Almazov in Novonikolaevsk.[63]

Semenov gave the PGAS opposition more than just sympathy and for the time being seemed to operate independently of right-wing groups in western Siberia. 'Intending to organize the struggle against the Bolsheviks on a broad scale', explained an OMO history, 'Ataman Semenov naturally was obliged to enter into contact with the [PGAS] military cells in Siberian towns.' He not only coordinated with the ESC's Socialist-Revolutionary 'Minister of War' in Harbin, Lieutenant Colonel Arkadii Anatolevich Krakovetskii, but provided generous 'material and moral support', including money to buy arms, to ESC cells. For example, in the weeks to come, Semenov would deliver 50,000 rubles to anti-Bolshevik cells in Irkutsk via a network of 'special agents' distributed through Transbaikal Cossack *stanitsas*.[64]

This network of agents and other sympathizers reveals that Semenov's little insurrection was not only growing, but exceeded the face value of his army. His force in Transbaikalia now numbered around 1,000 men: 180 Russian officers and cadets, 270 Cossacks, 300 Mongols and 300 Serbian prisoners of war, not including Inner Mongolian allies, such as Ungern-Shternberg's Bargut detachment.[65]

In early February 1918, soviets in Verkhne-Udinsk and Chita still included moderate Socialist-Revolutionaries and Mensheviks as well as Bolsheviks. However, three Cossack regiments returning from the front now had Bolshevik commissars with orders to end Transbaikalia's experiments with democracy. As they had traveled through soviet territory, the 1st Verkhne-Udinsk, 2nd Chita and 2nd Nerchinsk Cossack Regiments were bombarded by constant Bolshevik tirades, which incited them to arrest their officers and put them off the train in Irkutsk.[66] Suddenly, on 16 February 1918, Vyborni Komandir (elected commander) Yakov Zhugalin of the 2nd Chita Cossack Revolutionary Regiment and local Red Guards took over the Chita government at bayonet-point.[67] Well-disciplined internationalists helped.[68] They arrested so-called 'reactionary' officers of the garrison, dispersed the elected people's soviet and 'raised the red banner of the [Bolshevik] Soviets over Chita.[69] The Bolsheviks would later claim that the deposed Chita soviet was intending to negotiate with Semenov. A thoroughly bolshevized provincial Soviet of Workers', Peasants', Cossacks', Soldiers' and Buryats' Deputies took over administration. Its hard-nosed chairman was Ivan Afanasevich Butin, a former Sretensk schoolteacher of Cossack birth (from the Transbaikal village of Daya), who had just emerged from a decade in a St Petersburg prison and exile (in a village on the Angara River) for revolutionary activity.[70]

A similar coup raised the bloody red banner over Verkhne-Udinsk, where the 1st Verkhne-Udinsk Cossack Regiment, under elected commander Vasilii Kolesnikov, led the takeover. 'All money was taken away, and only small amounts of food allotted each family; no one [was] permitted in the streets after nine o'clock', wrote an American who visited the town a few months later.[71] During the next six months the Bolsheviks executed about 150 townspeople in Verkhne-Udinsk. The intelligentsia – 'anybody that had any book learning' – was marched away first. The Bolsheviks preached venomous class hatred and even menaced peasants with modest holdings. Homes were inspected nightly. Anyone found with arms was promptly shot. Concealing food without Bolshevik permission was likewise punishable by immediate execution. Reportedly the Bolsheviks dispatched many of their victims with axes 'in order to save bullets'.[72]

A senseless act of violence at a Chita jeweler's shop illustrates the venomous nature of the class warfare that followed the Red coups in Transbaikalia.

> The Soviet Commissar, with Red soldiers, visited the shop one day to loot the stock. The [owner's] mother, an old lady over sixty years of age who was then looking after the business, protested against the robbery of her property. The commissar ordered one of the Red Guards to bayonet her, which he did. They then proceeded to remove everything of value, locked up the premises with the dead woman lying on the shop floor and for several days refused permission to her neighbors to give her a decent burial on the plea that she was just a counter-revolutionist.[73]

In Blagoveshchensk 'the Bolshevik terrorism...massacred over one thousand' when it fell upon the Amur province in February 1918, setting an example for sullen extremists in more remote settlements.[74] Such outrages were inevitable when the head of state himself incited violence by referring to wealthy peasants as 'spiders' who grow fat at the expense of other peasants ruined by the war, 'leeches' who suck the blood of starving workers and 'vampires' who had snatched the landed estates of the rich before the party could grab them.[75]

The Red regiments holding off OMO were soon bolstered by the arrival of the 1st Revolutionary Transbaikal Cossack Division. Elected Commander Frol Balyabin and Commissar Georgi Bogomyag led their men in armed fights against Semenov's troops, the first well-organized military opposition that OMO encountered. Buryat scholars later noted that Soviet histories ignored the fact that the first determined resistance to Semenov came from Buryat Cossacks.[76]

The second session of the Pan-Siberian – and all-Bolshevik – Congress of Soviets gathered in Irkutsk during late February to proclaim a Red victory in central Siberia and pay homage to *Tsentrosibir'*, the Central Executive Committee of Siberian Soviets that had evolved from a convocation of revolutionary agitators in early November 1917 to become the regional center of state power. However even this all-Bolshevik gathering soon illuminated the gulf between Siberian and European Reds when, upon hearing rumors of Moscow's negotiations to conclude a separate peace with Germany, delegates unanimously objected to the upcoming Brest–Litovsk Treaty. Such thoughts threatened subservience to Moscow's dictates, particularly when a populist Cossack war hero like Grigorii Semenov was roaming the countryside calling on supporters of the Constituent Assembly to reject self-seeking Bolsheviks 'in service of Germany'.[77] Thus, Moscow engineered the appointment of N.N. Yakovlev, an obedient disciple of Lenin, as *Tsentrosibir'* chairman, to enforce revolutionary discipline among the obstinate Siberians.[78]

The Pan-Siberian Congress of Soviets empowered Ensign Sergei Lazo to cleanse the newly declared Transbaikal Front of Semenov and his followers.[79] It was Lazo and his Krasnoyarsk Red Guards who had rescued Irkutsk Bolsheviks' from rebellious Whites in December. At 24 years old, Lazo was even younger than Semenov and had been a student at the St Petersburg Technological Institute until he was commissioned for duty in the First World War. He projected the youth, vitality and intelligence that most of the slovenly, surly Red soldiery lacked – he was handsome, broad-shouldered and sported a neatly trimmed mustache, 'black leather *furazhka* [peaked military cap], worn-out *gimnasterka* [traditional high-collared military blouse], khaki riding breeches and soldier's boots', with a 'small Browning' pistol hanging from his officer's belt. In contrast to many dour, aloof commissars, he was personable and accessible and inspired revolutionary units full of older, cynical veterans as well as radical intellectuals.[80] The most reliable Bolshevik workers and soldiers in western and central Siberia were organized into Red Army units under Lazo for the campaign against Semenov.[81]

Lazo quickly assembled his legion in Chita: the 1st Argun Cossack Regiment (commanded by Z. Metelitsa), the Chita Red Guard, the Transbaikal Railway Red Guard (a detachment of Chita railwaymen), a 'combined detachment' of Red Guards from Irkutsk, and the stalwart internationalists, predominantly Hungarians.[82] The Reds were on the move by late February.

Neither side took prisoners, but Semenov claimed to have strictly forbidden 'the killing of prisoners on the spot, and ordered them to be delivered to the judicial department to investigate whether the prisoners were real Bolsheviks...[or were] persons enlisted by force'. OMO accused the Reds of introducing and regularly practicing torture upon captives. One of the first victims was a Serbian named Radoslavovich, who was captured at Dauria in February, stripped, and placed naked in the snow to die. When he lost his senses and collapsed, his guards lost interest and left him, whereupon he escaped back toward the White lines. Frostbite claimed his hands and feet. 'The Bolsheviks carve epaulets and stripes on the naked bodies of captured Cossacks', pointed out a White text, and castrated Chinese prisoners. An unfortunate Cadet Chernyaev, captured at Borzya, was found with his nose and ears sliced off and eyes gouged out. Some officers committed suicide upon seeing that their capture was inevitable, and no one thought the worse of them for it. 'Thus perished the brave Ensign Epov near the station of Kharanor.'[83]

The Reds easily took Dauria from Semenov on 1 March, and defeated him at Sharasun on 5 March. OMO was sandwiched between the Bolsheviks and the border, and the only obstacle that kept Lazo from annihilating Semenov's exhausted troops was the Chinese Army.

The Chinese commander at Manchuli, Major General Lin Fu-man, sent a representative to speak with Ensign Lazo on 5 March, then at Dauria. The Chinese wanted to avoid a clash at the border with Semenov's pursuers, and had moved 4,000 troops into Manchuli (combining detachments from Heilung Jiang and Kirin provinces) as a precaution. Lazo insisted that Semenov be disarmed and withdraw beyond Jalai Nur, the Chinese station 18 miles east of Manchuli. On 8 March, as Bolshevik soldiers marched into Matsievskaya, Major General Lin closed the border to all parties, moved his troops a short distance inside Russia, built a defensive position at Railway Siding No. 86 (situated on the 13-mile stretch between Manchuli and Matsievskaya), and declared that the Chinese Army would enforce a one-week armistice.[84] As tempers cooled during the next few days, Lazo agreed to withdraw to Dauria by 23 March, and although the Chinese Army declared Semenov interned (until 5 April), it did not disarm him or restrict his travel.[85]

Semenov had to get help if he were to stay in the fight for Transbaikalia. He needed men, guns, money and a supply line. Contrary to popular rumors that Semenov had flourished without any early outside support during his first weeks on the warpath, he had been 'generously supplied' by local industrial groups, particularly mining interests, according to General Petr N. Vrangel.[86] In addition, he 'received appreciable assistance in cash, provisions and stores from the Chinese Eastern Railway at the instructions of the Administrator General [Horvath]', probably in January after Ensign Riutin's Bolshevik mutiny was crushed.[87] Nevertheless, OMO needed a system of supply and support geared for wartime. Within days of his defeat at Sharasun, Semenov and a number of Mongol bodyguards headed for Harbin to seek more assistance.[88]

Likewise, Lazo returned to Chita to recruit more Red Guards. The Bolsheviks organized rallies of thousands in Chita's Atamanovski Square to drum up public support and round up recruits. Lazo exhorted a meeting a railway workers in March 1918 to enlist for the fight, saying, 'He is preparing for battle with us! He's buying horses and weapons with the money of imperialists, he goes running to hired fighters from the lowest strata of society. Semenov is the hunting dog that imperialist predators have loosed upon the land of the soviets.'[89] Transbaikalia mobilized for civil war.

Harbin – the Paris and Gomorrah of the Orient

Six hundred miles east from Manchuli along the Chinese Eastern Railway sprawled the city of Harbin, the heart of Manchuria, a thriving hub of commerce with 70,000 cosmopolitan residents during peacetime – '34,000 Russians, 23,500 Chinese, 5,000 Jews, 700 Japanese, 560 Germans', and a smattering of Poles, Greeks, Englishmen, Americans and other assorted nationalities. References to Harbin usually implied inclusion of its twin city, Fu Chia Tien, which lay outside the railway zone and was undergoing frenetic growth, from a pre-war Chinese population of 30,000 to 120,000 in 1918. The Chinese Eastern flew over the Sungari river on a towering eight-span bridge of iron, and provided connections to the terminus of the Japanese-controlled Southern Manchuria railway. 'Many substantial business houses with extensive commercial connections' relied upon these arteries to engage in lucrative international trade, smuggling and profiteering.[90] It was a city of contrasts, modern and medieval, the 'Paris of the Orient' overlaid with an Asian Gomorrah.

In the Harbin neighborhood of Novyi Gorod, wide boulevards punctuated with tree-lined cobblestone streets, plush lawns, mansions with spires, cupolas and scalloped turrets, and baroque and art nouveau structures looked as if they had been lifted out of a fine neighborhood in European Russia. From elegantly appointed edifices adorned with statuary, I.I. Churin's department store competed with the Japanese-owned Matsuura's on Ulitsa Kitaiskaya. On the streets, only the occasional rickshaw and deferential Chinese workers suggested that this garden city was not in Russia. However, Harbin's true character was best typified by the range of her culinary offerings, which extended from French haute-cuisine to grilled bear paws, deer nostrils and Siberian tiger testicles. Residents of Harbin (*Kharbintsy*) often spoke Chinese as well as Russian and French, and had acquired an entrepreneurial and egalitarian vitality absent in Mother Russia. Socialist ideology had more difficulty taking root in this environment where high stock was placed in commerce and an individual work ethic.

Nevertheless, socialist ideology *did* take root among the susceptible Russian railway workers and soldiers. Until December 1917, Harbin harbored a 'distributing center for pro-Bolshevik funds' and was an assembly point for Red fighters waiting to return to Russia and Russian immigrants from America anxious to join the Bolsheviks.[91] One such returnee was Aleksandr Mikhailovich Krasnoshchekov, a 38-year-old lawyer accused of 'a criminal past [and] who had been a small restaurant owner in Chicago' (and who would rise to rule Russia's Amur and Maritime provinces in 1920).[92] The Bolsheviks neutralized the Mensheviks and Socialist-Revolutionaries on 12 December, and the Chinese Army rounded up all armed Bolsheviks on 25 December. By March 1918 Harbin's remaining Reds operated deep underground.

In its seedier districts – Pristan and Fu Chia Tien, Harbin was proclaimed 'one of the world's moral cesspits' by Canadian Major James Mackintosh Bell, who seems to have thoroughly surveyed the city's salacious amusements, while scrupulously avoiding any decent part of town. From the shadows of 'dives of almost every description', sirens 'from almost every quarter of the globe' ('French *demi-mondaines*' and Japanese geishas being the most popular) cooed to passers-by. Harbin's low-end lodgings were noted only for their 'ubiquitous filth'. Dazed Russian refugees, rich, poor and the recently impoverished, mingled aimlessly among shysters, smugglers and fugitives in warrens of opium dens, brothels, cheap tea houses and saloons. During the long, harsh winter even nature seemed to conspire with the city's wicked humanity when 'the wind blew the finely powdered snow with the dust and microbes of Harbin into one's eyes and ears'.[93]

The *hunghutze*, infamous gangs of Manchurian bandits, skulked on the outskirts of town in wait for someone to rob or kidnap, often a target identified by their informants inside Harbin. They traced their origin to the seventeenth century, when disciples of the fallen Ming dynasty began raiding government outposts of the new Qing rulers, and occasionally a *hunghutze* chief earned a reputation as a local Robin Hood, robbing from the rich, giving to the poor and fighting for the oppressed, although noble deeds never supplanted piracy as a primary activity.[94] Chinese authorities sometimes lined a road into town with the heads of recently beheaded *hunghutze* as a warning to their compatriots. Manchuria's ambitious strongman Chang Tso-Lin was himself rumored to have been a *hunghutze* chieftain in the Kirin mountains, before fate steered him into a life of respectability. He was born in 1876 in a small village called Haichen in Fengtien, the southernmost of Manchuria's three provinces, and built a reputation as a fearless fighter and *hunghutze* leader. Japanese intelligence contracted his services during the Russo-Japanese War when his band performed sabotage, ambushes and spying against the Russian Army behind enemy lines. The Japanese were so impressed with his performance that, after the war, they pressured the Court of Peking to grant Chang a complete pardon, and even had him named governor of Fengtien province. On the other hand, they could not dominate Chang Tso-Lin, although he soon rose to dominate all of Manchuria's three provinces.[95] Nevertheless, he was powerless to override Peking's grants of extraterritoriality to the Japanese in the ports of Dairen and Port Arthur and along the Southern Manchurian Railway, and to the Russians in the Chinese Eastern Railway zone. Having watched Harbin grow from a river village to an international city, he surely longed to bring the metropolis under Chinese jurisdiction, but understood the political forces against him enough to bide his time.

Russia's troubled shadow loomed over the city like the massive byzantine tower of St Nicholas Cathedral, its onion domes sprouting on the skyline like invading mushrooms. The Russian quarter was home to 30,000 expatriates before revolution deluged the 'execrable' hotels and flophouses with countless thousands more. 'The place was filled with officer refugees', noted Major Bell, 'the dissipated excesses of whom were notorious.'[96] A half-dozen small private armies coalesced from the armed gangs of stranded Russian military men, answerable to no one, who operated their own 'counter-intelligence units' engrossed in 'vendettas, extortion and the traffic in opium', and which littered the dusty streets with corpses of their rivals.[97] Semenov was justifiably indignant at the noisy salons full of generals and senior officers jabbering endlessly about war against the Bolsheviks, when they only had to take a short train ride west to actually join the war. British author Peter Fleming, who spent a number of years in Manchuria a decade later, painted a disreputable picture of 1918 Harbin:

> In the overcrowded public rooms of the Hotel Moderne, spurs continued to clink, patriotic toasts to be drunk, eyes to fill with tears. Rumours were anatomised by pundits, intrigues were carried on by knaves, fortunes were made by speculators. Salute were exchanged, hands kissed, sword-hilts polished. But, save for a few shady and regrettable adventurers, nobody left the scene of this martial-patriotic *tableau vivant* and took a train for Manchuli.[98]

Above the growing chaos in Harbin's streets soared the bastion of the last vestige of Russian imperial institutions, the Chinese Eastern Railway Company. From his palatial office in the Chinese Eastern headquarters, Lieutenant General Dmitri L. Horvath, a retired tsarist army engineer, had presided over this commercial powerhouse since 1902. His flowing white beard (which made him look older than his 59 years of age), piercing black eyes and towering, sturdy frame called to mind an ancient prophet. Horvath was 'magnificent, suave, urbane and distinguished', and no less gracious to Bolshevik visitors than to monarchist ones. 'Accustomed to being the recipient of large political favors from the old regime, he was loathe to recognize the revolutionary government', said Major Bell, 'but with that skillful strategy which ordinarily characterized him he did so with alacrity once he realized that the new state of affairs was a fait accompli.'[99] At the same time, the shrewd old fellow covertly headed a toothless anti-Bolshevik organization called the Far Eastern Committee for the Defense of the Fatherland and the Constituent Assembly.[100] Until the roundup of the rebellious railway militia in Harbin in December 1917, everyone – including the Bolsheviks – tried to curry favor with General Horvath. After all, his immense corporate empire still controlled the largest labor force in Manchuria, its own private army (in the form of the now emasculated railway militia), a substantial intelligence network and a fat treasury.

In March 1918 Semenov 'put up in some style at the Orient Hotel' and officers of his entourage dismissed to the saloons. During the binge that ensued, one of these men was tossed into jail for some drunken infraction. Semenov and his Mongol bodyguards surrounded the police station and coerced the carouser's release. The event reaffirmed the breakdown of discipline in the Chinese Eastern militia brigade that allowed Harbin to degenerate into a 'gangsters' paradise'.[101]

Strategic ambitions and the Austro-German threat

Harbin, the Manchurian Babylon, had also become a seething nest of intrigue. Spies of every major power and every Russian faction prowled the dusty alleys, while intelligence officers schemed and fretted in the consulates, salons, hotels and commercial offices. 'The place was literally packed with enemy agents', wrote Major Bell, referring to scores of thinly veiled Bolshevik, German and Austro-Hungarian operatives.[102] Until recently the most widespread web of spies and informers worked for General Horvath's Chinese Eastern Railway Company. 'His emissaries were everywhere, in the big shops and warehouses, among the Chinese merchants and coolies, in the better hotels and in the lowest resorts...'.[103] They could not possibly keep tabs on the sudden deluge of competitors. Harbin was suddenly a magnet for agents of British and French Military Missions, the Japanese and American foreign and war ministries, Asian secret societies, Chinese warlords, Czech nationalists, central Asian separatists, and a cosmopolitan cornucopia of syndicalists, maximalists, lamaists and a dozen other philosophical stripes who believed that affairs in this overgrown Manchurian railway town were of world-shaking strategic importance.

Indeed, the world war had not bypassed Asia, and the breadth of German operations had ingrained a lingering paranoia early on. Japan boldly declared war against Germany on 23 August 1914, without waiting to see the outcomes of the Europeans' opening moves and dutifully fulfilled her obligations to Britain under their 1902 mutual defense agreement.

Japan launched a campaign against the fortified German colony at Tsing-Tao, China, a stronghold that was touted as 'a second Port Arthur'. It was also the homeport of Vice Admiral von Spee's East Asiatic Squadron, where the Germans intended to service commerce raiders and mount hostile operations against Allied colonies in the Far East. Lieutenant General Kamio Mitsuomi led an arduous campaign across flooding gullies and mountains of mud to attack a chain of modern fortifications and small fleet of German and Austro-Hungarian warships in Tsing-Tao harbor. As in the Russo-Japanese War, the combatants conducted themselves chivalrously. It ended with General Yamada Yoshimi, leading a dramatic charge into the crumbling central redoubt, caped in a Japanese flag, 'Banzai's!' resounding around him, and siege artillery thundering in the background.[104] The Germans surrendered on 7 November, and the Japanese gladly laid claim to the colony's 117 square-miles of prime real estate and lucrative infrastructure.

Elsewhere in the war, Japan's First Fleet occupied Germany's Marshall and Caroline Island groups in the western Pacific, and the Third Fleet escorted British Commonwealth troopships across the Indian Ocean, hunted for the German light cruiser *Emden* and commerce raider *Wolf* in the East Indies and Indian Ocean, pursued von Spee through the Pacific Ocean, helped British forces stamp out a mutiny in Singapore, and even sent 14 destroyers with cruiser flagships to the Mediterranean to serve as anti-submarine convoy escorts. Japanese merchant ships were targets of German raiders and submarines just like those of the European Allies. When Captain August Nerger's raider *Wolf* caught the 6,557-ton *Hitachi Maru* near the Maldives in September 1917, at least 14 Japanese seamen died defending her before she was overpowered, stripped and scuttled.[105]

German mischief even extended to Manchuria and Mongolia. Early in the war the German consulate in Mukden was suspected of inciting *hunghutze* to raid the Chinese Eastern Railway. Not satisfied with this, the German Military Attaché in Peking, Captain Werner H.K. von Pappenheim, undertook the sabotage effort himself, and set out in

January 1915 with seven other Germans, four Chinese, a Mongol, 20 camels and five horses on a supposed hunting trip into the Khingan mountains. The caravan packed explosives to blow up tracks, bridges and tunnels between Tsitsihar and Hailar. Pappenheim also carried a small treasury to bribe Mongol tribes into conducting raids – he offered one Mongol chief 50,000 rubles for the use of 300 men.

Two Russian merchants, Grigorii Shadrin and Abraham Berkovitz caught wind of the expedition and informed the Russian consul in Hailar. Spies tracked the Germans along the Tea Road between Kalgan and the railway, advising Russian intelligence officers in Irkutsk. A special detachment of the 5th Transamur Border Cavalry Regiment was sent to intercept von Pappenheim, and friendly Mongol princes were offered rewards for the Germans' capture. Unfortunately for the Germans, the Mongols found them first. Eighteen warriors (of a Mongolian prince identified as Babush-shab) caught and slaughtered the Germans on 20 February 1915, then incinerated the bodies and other evidence with benzol (an impure benzene incendiary) from the saboteurs' own stores. When the Chinese government inquired about von Pappenheim's tragic mission, the German embassy pleaded ignorance and stated that he had 'left China for the theater of war'.[106] China eventually declared war on Germany on 14 August 1917.[107]

In spring 1918 the perception of a new German and Austro-Hungarian threat arose in the Russian Far East – that of a huge internationalist army raised from the POW camps. Widespread reports about German and Austro-Hungarian internationalists circulated, exaggerating the numbers, reviving suspicions of a diabolical secret pact between Lenin and the Kaiser. Allied intelligence experts had difficulty comprehending that the Bolsheviks were not mere proxies of the Central Powers, and overestimated and eventually overreacted to the internationalists because they expected the entire POW population in the Russian Far East could conceivably take up arms by order of Berlin and Vienna.[108] Japanese War Minister Oshima Ken'ichi estimated that 11,000 POWs were armed, and that more soon would be, based upon intelligence gathered by Japan's diligent espionage network in Siberia.[109]

In reality, only a small percentage of prisoners joined – idealistic socialists, Bolshevik converts and adventurers. Trotsky insisted that foreign volunteers were accepted into the Red Army only if they accepted Russian citizenship.[110] Lenin envisioned the internationalists as the nucleus of a world revolutionary legion who would 'make the international brotherhood of nations a reality by fighting together with [their] front-line enemies of yesterday...'.[111] When the Japanese Ambassador to Italy declared that German prisoners of war were 'armed and ready to seize the Siberian railway', newspapers around the world published his words in March 1918. Red military authorities toured a pair of British and American army officers along the Trans-Siberian Railway to 'convince themselves of the falsity of the official Japanese statement'.[112] Regardless of the actual number of German and Austro-Hungarian internationalists, their discipline and experience magnified their performance in combat in Irkutsk and Transbaikalia, where Red commanders relied on them more than all but the best Red Guard detachments. The internationalist ranks included not only Germans, Austrians and Hungarians, but Czechoslovakians, Bulgarians, Rumanians, Poles, Yugoslavians, Chinese and other nationalities, as well.

Apart from the POW camps, the Korean émigré population also stocked a fertile pool for Red recruitment. By 1917, approximately 300,000 Koreans lived in northern Manchuria and the Russian Far East, their decades old settlements swollen with refugees escaping the iron fist of the Japanese occupation in their homeland. Their presence was noticeable in every city from Vladivostok to Irkutsk, and Korean homesteads dotted the countryside from Lake Baikal to the Pacific. Desperate to find any allies in their liberation struggle, Koreans were found on all sides of the Russian Civil War, but were especially enchanted by the Reds' anti-colonial and anti-Japanese propaganda. For example, Alexandra Petrovna Kim, a 32-year-old Korean–Russian woman born and educated in the Maritime province, rose to prominence in Red circles and in 1917 traveled from one POW camp to another preaching world revolution and recruiting internationalists.

The internationalists created a feeling of insecurity, but the Red contagion inspired hysteria in Japan, where rapid industrialization and capitalism's increasingly glaring inequities excited small circles of the intelligentsia with a fascination with socialism, Marxism and other forbidden political fruit. A 1908 Tokyo parade of anarcho-syndicalists 'carrying red banners and chanting revolutionary songs' shocked the nation, as did the sharp words of Katayama Sen's socialist propaganda, 'I will be the bleeding mouth from which the gag has been snatched.' Public outrage against an alleged socialist assassination plot against Meiji Reform Emperor Mutsuhito in 1910–11 inoculated Japan against radical ideology for a few years as homegrown Reds were rounded up by police, committed suicide or fled the country.[113]

The Japanese General Staff entertained the notion of carving a buffer state out of the Russian and Chinese hides that would shield Korea and Japan from the Bolshevik contagion and inject Japanese influence deeper into the weak Chinese republic. Wistful strategic thinking aimed to bring Manchuria and Inner Mongolia – Man-Mo in the parlance of the Japanese press and officialdom – into Tokyo's orbit and transform the Sea of Japan into *Shin-naikai*, a New Inland Sea framed by a Japanese empire sweeping over the Asian mainland.[114] Japanese diplomats had prepared the way in 1913 by arm-twisting China into acceding to extension of Japan's Southern Manchuria Railway into Inner Mongolia. In 1915, giddy from the victory at Tsing-Tao, Japan arrogantly issued the infamous 'Twenty-one Demands' in a brazen but unsuccessful attempt to force an unwilling Republic of China to succumb to Japanese control. Japan's ambitious goals could be attempted under the guise of helping her European friends relieve pressure on the Western Front, but both Japan and the Allies preferred that a Russian force engage the Bolsheviks and internationalists in Siberia, at least in the beginning.

By the end of 1917 Britain and France were single-mindedly doing everything in their powers to weather the German onslaught and reopen the Russian Front against the Central Powers, while Japan's strategic agenda aimed for territorial growth and commercial expansion at the expense of Russia and China. Japan's economic incentives to contain Red power and control the Whites were compelling. First of all, Japanese companies – small firms as well as the powerful *zaibatsu* (huge industrial and banking networks) – had invested a tremendous amount of money and commercial energy in the Russian Far East; their storefronts and branch offices dotted the map from Vladivostok to Irkutsk. On top of that, Tokyo had nearly 256 million yen tied up in Russian government bonds, and lucrative wartime trade through Vladivostok had provided a boon to Japan's industry and her treasury.[115] Japan was willing to fight to protect her investments.

Japanese intelligence networks strained to expand their depth in anticipation of an imminent imperial army expedition. Harbin was the hub for many of the 3,000 intelligence officers and agents operating in Manchuria for the Japanese General Staff or secret societies of Japanese militarists and expansionists like the Black Dragon Society and *Kanzen So* – the Mountain of Sweat Society.[116] Several Japanese commands were running independent intelligence operations that overlapped in Harbin: the Army General Staff in Tokyo, the Kwantung governor-generalcy, Japanese armies in Tsing-Tao, Korea and other places. Japan had carefully tended the region's intelligence networks for several years, nurturing their growth into Russia where 'a number of Japanese [intelligence] officers actually worked...as barbers, cooks and ordinary domestic servants'.[117] They even maintained 'safe houses' in obscure villages, although most operations emanated from Japanese trading posts and branch offices of Japanese firms scattered throughout the Russian Far East.

A legion of Japanese prostitutes working between Irkutsk and Vladivostok gathered intelligence and performed special tasks.[118] Information filtered up through local intelligence officers to regional commanders to ministers in Tokyo. The theatre was of sufficient importance for the intelligence chief of the Japanese General Staff, Major General Nakajima Masatake, to tour it personally. Nakajima was well qualified for the mission: he had been military attaché in Petrograd and spoke Russian (in addition to French). He landed in Vladivostok with his assistant, Lieutenant Colonel Sakabe Tosuho, on 22 January and visited Blagoveshchensk on 27 January before continuing on to Harbin.[119] They were among the first of 'a regular procession of intelligence officers' shuttling between Tokyo, the Russian Far East, North China, Mongolia and Manchuria.[120] The findings of Nakajima's tour convinced his superiors that the theatre was of sufficient importance to return him as chief of the Japanese military mission in Manchuria.

Bullets, guns and money

In December 1917 and January 1918, Japanese agents were busy checking out the bonafides of the many anti-Bolshevik Russians soliciting money and guns in Harbin. The Japanese preferred to cast their lot with General Horvath, but only if he would form a government. However, Horvath insisted that the Japanese send troops before he would declare a government in exile. Meanwhile, Chinese officials, who had watched the Russians' Manchurian railway evolve into a foreign colony over the past 20 years, let it be known in March 1918 that a Horvath government was not welcome on Chinese territory.[121] Other prime contenders for Japanese assistance were Lieutenant General Domanevski, who had recently fled from Khabarovsk, and Colonel Nikitin, former commandant of an officer's school at Irkutsk. Domanevski had no men, and Nikitin's army was mostly paper, based on a mid-February announcement of the formation of an army for Horvath's Far Eastern Committee for the Defense of the Fatherland.[122] A refugee from the Ussuri area, General Mikhail Mikhailovich Pleshkov, and a Captain Orlov, were also trying to raise detachments for the Far Eastern Committee, but Grigorii Semenov had the only tangible anti-Bolshevik force that was actively engaging the enemy.

Semenov's representative, Lieutenant Zhevchenko, first contacted the Japanese in December, and in late January traveled to Tokyo to begin negotiating a 'concrete agreement' with Japan's war ministry. During January 1918, Semenov himself had made at least two trips to Harbin to ask the Japanese – as well as Horvath and anyone else who would listen – for arms and money. Meanwhile, the Japanese government was being pressured to support anti-Bolshevik forces: the Russian embassy in Peking asked Japan's Charge d'Affaires Yoshizawa for a small arsenal on 1 February and the Japanese military attaché in London received a similar request three days later.[123] On 4 February Semenov returned to Harbin to meet with Lieutenant Colonel Kurozawa Jun, 'the chief Kwantung Army staff agent'. Kurozawa was sent by Lieutenant General Baron Tanaka Gi'ichi, vice chief of the Japanese Army General Staff, to size up Semenov and evaluate his plan to drive the Bolsheviks out of Transbaikalia. Semenov impressed both Kurozawa and the Japanese Consul General in Harbin, Sato Naotake, who praised Semenov as 'a man of sound ability'.[124] Kurozawa dispatched a Captain Sakabe to Manchuli to work with OMO and, on 17 February wired General Baron Uehara Yusaku, the Japanese Army chief of staff, advising that Semenov be funded immediately, reasoning correctly that 'if he is helped now when his funds are about exhausted, he will rely heavily on Japan'.[125] That same day, the Charge d'Affaires in Peking, Yoshizawa, recommended to Foreign Minister Motono that Japan support Semenov. Four days later Major General Nakajima returned to Harbin, and met with Domanevski and Nikitin, who assured him that Semenov would subordinate himself to Horvath's Far Eastern Committee. On 24 February, Nakajima wrote the crucial recommendation that opened the spigot of Japanese support to OMO, and the following day the Japanese finance ministry approved the necessary funding. Many of the expenses were allegedly picked up later by the Kuhara *zaibatsu*, which had business interests in the Russian Far East.[126] In February–March 1918, Semenov allegedly received 3,106,408 rubles from his new Japanese friends.[127]

The British and French, driven to desperation by the stalemated trench warfare with Germany, pursued a dual policy of negotiating with the Bolsheviks in Moscow with one hand, and helping the anti-Bolshevik opposition in Siberia with the other. In January 1918, Captain R.B. Denny, Assistant Military Attache at the British Legation in Peking, made his way to Manchuli to investigate Semenov while French officers in Harbin, Peking and elsewhere pondered bringing in colonial troops from southeast Asia for a punitive march on Irkutsk to avenge the rumored murder of the French consul there by the Reds. Fortunately for all concerned, the rumors were false, and French plans for a 2,000-mile march from Tientsin to Irkutsk, which promised to be more punitive on the avenging Allied troops than the Reds, were quietly scrapped.[128] In early February, Prince Kudashev presented Semenov's plans to the British and French military attachés in Peking, and a French Captain Pelliot then made the pilgrimage to Manchuli.[129] Within days, British diplomats informed Washington and Tokyo that London had decided to bankroll Semenov's 'scallywags' (as the Foreign Office referred to OMO) as an anti-Bolshevik movement 'of purely Russian origin' to the tune of £10,000 per month for clothing and ammunition, after an initial grant of £30,000.[130] Supposedly the French Military Mission donated a comparable sum of cash to OMO each month, though they had the good sense to funnel it through Prince Kudashev and the Russian legation in Peking, until Semenov eventually demanded direct payments to himself.

Britain's dalliance with Semenov 'was not a happy one'. From London, OMO looked like 'a posse of Chinese ex-bandits, Mongol cattle-rustlers, Japanese mercenaries, Serbian prisoners and Cossack adventurers' that threatened to derail Bruce Lockhart's efforts to mend fences with the Bolsheviks and bring Russia back into the war.[131]

It is not surprising that, as large sums of money begin changing hands between diplomats, military officers and a rebel chieftain like Semenov, hushed accusations and wild numbers begin flying like bottles and bullets in a Harbin saloon melée. In October 1918, a Russian newspaper would relate a tidbit that was originally leaked to 'the Japanese Press' stating that Major General Alfred Knox, head of the British Military Mission in Siberia, had 'lent' Semenov the huge sum of £6,000,000. Soviet histories declare that in February–March 1918, Semenov received 500,000 rubles (approximately £52,000) from the British, and 4,071,000 rubles (approximately £426,000) from the French. Regardless of the exact amounts involved, a stream of pounds and francs would flow into Semenov's war chest until about October 1918.[132]

Japanese advisors, internationalists and the April offensive

In March 1918, the *semenovtsy* underwent a rags-to-riches transformation. First came a gift of two ancient, 5-inch howitzers from the military guard of the British Legation in Peking, which were 'secretly dispatched by rail,... then held up for some days at Mukden until the Japanese railway authorities had received a suitable bribe'. Similarly, French forces at Tientsin donated to Semenov 100 hand grenades and four 9-centimeter guns with at least 50,000 shells.[133] A small number of British and French officers and men accompanied these donations to provide initial training.

On 18 March, four Japanese officers and seven soldiers arrived at OMO headquarters.[134] From this time on, Semenov hardly seemed to make any major decision without consulting his Japanese advisor, Captain Kuroki (soon promoted to major). Kuroki Chikayochi was a 35-year-old intelligence officer who had been operating in Siberia since at least 1917. He had supposedly fallen out with the Japanese General Staff over some detail of Man-Mo policy but still received the prestigious assignment to OMO's staff. Interestingly, one of Semenov's visitors remembered, 'Kuroki openly criticizes the Japanese government, which he says, is not democratic and does not deal with Russia in a democratic manner. It is probable that his criticisms, so inconsistent with the usual Japanese procedure, have no other motive than to gain the confidence of the Ataman more and more, to remain with him, to advise him and...to direct him.'[135]

Another Japanese advisor to OMO, Captain Kuroki Shinkei, was said to be Chikayochi's son, making it difficult to discern of which Kuroki records speak.[136] 'Kuroki [presumably the father] is one of the most energetic of the Japanese officers in Manchuria', wrote Major Barrows, 'and has always been in favor of support being given to Semenov direct, probably because he felt that this was the best method of leading up to an early intervention.'[137]

In addition to the Kurokis, two more officers and 36 enlisted men borrowed from the 7th Division in Korea arrived wearing Russian uniforms with the first shipment of Japanese arms on 20 March.[138] Most of these men had orders to train OMO on their new weapons, pack harnesses and other equipment and then depart, but a number of them would become involved in Semenov's next offensive up the Onon river.

Meanwhile, General Horvath was revamping the corporate board of the Chinese Eastern Railway to create an organizational catalyst for a new Russian government. It was a clever solution intended to avoid antagonizing the Chinese government, while satisfying Tokyo's prerequisite for committing Japanese troops in the Russian Far East. Consul General Sato made it clear that the Derber government was unpalatable to Japan: 'There is no difference between their principles and those of the Bolsheviks', he wrote to Foreign Minister Motono.[139]

On 23 March, Horvath put General Pleshkov in command of the Chinese Eastern Railway's military assets, who announced plans to unify all anti-Bolshevik detachments in the region, including Semenov's, and to raise his own army. US Army Major David P. Barrows, military attaché in Peking, understood Semenov's reluctance to submit to Pleshkov: 'His force is suited for operations in Transbaikalia, and he had no wish to be mixed up with Horvath's scheme...', for raising the force formerly quartered in the Railway zone. Thus Semenov submitted nominally to the authority of General Pleshkov, but resisted all of Pleshkov's attempts to draw away OMO troops from Manchuli to Harbin to seed a new railway militia officer corps.[140]

Major General Nakajima signaled Japan's tentative approval by giving Pleshkov 100,000 rubles and 20,000 rifles. Pleshkov's tenure lasted just over a month, in which time he gathered only 'a small motley corps...of Chinese soldiers, mounted bandits, Koreans and Mongolians', but managed to strengthen Captain Orlov's anti-Bolshevik detachment by upgrading their weaponry and arranging for eight Japanese machine gun instructors to train them.[141] Orlov had earned the St George's Cross for heroism in the First World War, and had become a company commander in a reorganized railway guard formed by General Mikhail Konstantinovich Samoilov in December 1917. Samoilov, a former General Staff officer, would soon leave in a huff at being subordinated to the Chinese Eastern Railway Board, and emigrate to France, leaving the detachment to Orlov.[142]

Horvath was wise enough not to become totally beholden to the Japanese. To the horror of General Muto Nobuyoshi, who came to sweet-talk Horvath with promises of railway 'assistance' aimed at coaxing the Chinese Eastern into Japanese hands, Americans emerged from Horvath's inner chambers just as Muto arrived to woo him. On 27 March, John F. Stevens, chief of the US Advisory Commission of Railway Experts, concluded an agreement with Horvath for American railwaymen of a recently formed Russian Railway Service Corps (RRSC) to instruct their counterparts on the Chinese Eastern.

The Japanese were horrified to find their friend Horvath in bed with the Americans. Generals Muto and Nakajima tried to change Horvath's mind, or at least to convince him to limit the territory in which the Americans would operate. In Tokyo, many strong statements were made, but a Japanese Railway Board councilor, Kanai Kiyoshi, expressed Japanese suspicions best when he brashly accused the United States of using the RRSC to claw a foothold in Manchuria.[143] About 100 RRSC men appeared in Harbin before the ink had dried on Stevens and Horvath's agreement.

Across the border, Lazo's army was growing as fast as Bolshevik recruiters could raise, organize and rush new units to the Transbaikal Front. In mid-March, the Omsk 1st and 2nd Proletarian detachments arrived, the former composed of 300 Russians and an equal number of Hungarian and Rumanian POWs, the latter of 100 Russians, 150 Lithuanians, 130 Czechs and 70 Germans.[144] Meanwhile the Bolsheviks consolidated their power throughout the bulk of Transbaikalia, and on 24 March declared 'the transfer of all power to the hands of the Soviet of Workers', Peasants', Cossacks' and Buryats' Deputies convening in Chita in the baroque Shumov Palace, the luxurious mansion of the owners of a gold-mining firm.[145] Twelve days later they replaced the Chita city duma with a Soviet of People's Economy. Ivan Butin, chairman of the Transbaikal executive committee, felt confident enough to begin taking over farms and nationalizing businesses.[146]

At dawn on 5 April, to everyone's surprise, two companies of Japanese marines and a handful of British marines went ashore at Vladivostok. The pretext for the landing was the killing of two Japanese clerks during a robbery on 4 April at the Ishido company store. Crime was on the upswing in the port since municipal administration vacillated between a moderate city duma and district *zemstvo* and a hostile Bolshevik soviet. The soviet was biding its time, taking control of the city piece by piece, and had raised tensions ten days before by seizing the post and telegraph office. However, the Japanese officials in Vladivostok who ordered the landing – Consul General Kikuchi Giro, Army General Staff representative Colonel Sakabe Tosuho, and Admiral Kato Kanji – seemed to be reading from the wrong sheet of music. Tokyo panicked. Japan's ministers and military planners simply were not ready to invade Russia, and the landing forced heated discussions about Russian policy in the villas of Japan's *genro* (elder statesmen) that resulted in the resignation of Foreign Minister Viscount Motono Ichiro.[147]

Lenin fired off a defiant, supportive message to the Vladivostok soviet, and even the moderate *zemstvo* council and city duma protested. The official Bolshevik condemnation of the landing went so far as to imply that Japan herself had the clerks murdered to fabricate an excuse for the landing. Moscow's statement declared, 'The murder of two Japanese, from this point of view, was most opportune... The course of events leaves no doubt whatever that all this was prearranged and that the provocative murder of the two Japanese was an essential part of the [landing] preparations.'[148] The incident ignited nationalist sentiments that played into the hands of Bolshevik recruiters and undermined the Allies' dual policy of negotiating with the Bolsheviks while hedging on the White opposition.

Newspapers in Moscow immediately linked the 5 April intrusion to Semenov.[149] The Red fears were not groundless. OMO personnel were reconnoitering eastern Manchuria near Vladivostok for the first time, specifically in the vicinity of Pogranichnaya where the Chinese Eastern Railway crossed from Manchuria onto Russian territory, and Japanese agents were very active in the area stirring up Ussuri Cossack resistance to the Bolsheviks.[150] General Pleshkov contributed to the Reds' paranoia by permitting the Japanese to take control of Harbin's wireless station on 7 April.[151]

April's first combat occurred in an unlikely locale, about 25 miles west of Manchuli at Kolusatai, a Cossack *stanitsa* located on a large lake near the Mongolian border. The Bolsheviks had learned that a Semenov officer named Zolotukhin was organizing a detachment at Kolusatai, and dispatched a Red Guard detachment to arrest or liquidate them. When the Red Guards approached the settlement on 20 April they were surprisingly greeted with shells from a four-gun battery that Semenov had hastily dispatched from Manchuli. Zolotukhin's new company enthusiastically routed the Red Guards and advanced north. At midnight on 20–21 April they attacked a Bolshevik outpost on the railway at Kharanor. The Red Guards tried to flee by train but were derailed – 25 were killed and 23 captured. All of the prisoners were soon executed.[152]

The actions at Kolusatai and Kharanor launched Semenov's second invasion of Soviet Transbaikalia, a campaign undertaken against the advice of his Japanese advisors but with the reluctant approval of General Horvath, even though a prime reason for Semenov's haste was to keep Horvath's nascent army from siphoning OMO officers off to Harbin.[153] In previous weeks, the British Army's Captain Denny had also warned Semenov 'forcibly' against undertaking this offensive while Allied diplomats in Moscow were making their final, and ultimately unsuccessful, pleas for a Soviet reopening of the Eastern Front against Germany.[154] On 23–24 April, Semenov's main force advanced cautiously out of Manchuli up the Railway into Red territory, meeting strong resistance, according to Semenov. From the comfort of his Harbin hotel, General Baron Alexei Pavlovich Budberg, a cynical tsarist exile, remarked, 'The *semenovtsy* advance where there are not any enemy'.[155] They easily recaptured Dauria on the morning of 23 April owing to a Red evacuation, and continued north through Kharanor that evening. Budberg sneered, and likewise Semenov mocked him as part of 'an element preferring Harbin to the dangers and inconveniences of the marching [and] fighting life'.[156]

General Pleshkov, chief of the Chinese Eastern Railway's military staff, came to Manchuli on 23 April to meet with Semenov. Even though relations had 'not been wholly harmonious between Semenov and Pleshkov', the latter sent – as proof of Horvath's support – Colonel Orlov's 400-man mounted detachment – described as the 'least disreputable of the local White private armies' – to reinforce OMO.[157] Although numerous White detachments had formed in Harbin by this time, OMO accounts of the offensive mention receiving assistance only from 'one company of Colonel Rakhil'ski and the mounted Jaeger *sotnia* of Rotmistr (Captain) [Viktor] Vrashtel', although during the next few days Pleshkov would also contribute a field battery and a detachment of engineers and signalmen.[158] It may have been between 23 April and 28 April that a 'scuffle' between OMO and the Orlov Detachment almost turned into a shootout inside Semenov's front lines.[159]

With minimal resources, Semenov and a handful of officers had successfully assembled a highly mobile cavalry expedition, albeit with underdeveloped infantry, artillery, ordnance, engineer and railway sections inadequate to support or consolidate the horsemen's gains. These officers formed a skeleton headquarters staff, with the young, handsome and bright Colonel Nikolai Georgievich Natsvalov as chief of staff, a Captain Verigo and Second Lieutenant Pontovich in charge of inspection, and lieutenants Sergei and Mungalov as operational quartermasters, while other 'independent departments' dealt with finance, railway, political and mobilization functions. Lieutenant General Nikonov became his military assistant, and Colonel Ogloblin took charge of the rear echelon in Hailar and Harbin.[160] Captain Shiroki, a very quiet, serious Cossack, headed the intelligence service, which generated constant reports from a network of 'scouts, secret agents and particularly Buryat leaders'. As exemplified by its staff, OMO began as a grassroots anti-Bolshevik movement of young officers, uninhibited by the secret political horse-trading that handicapped conservative cabals in Harbin. Major Barrows remarked, 'I wish to emphasize the essential simplicity and entire loyalty of his command'.[161]

While Barrows noticed that OMO enjoyed abundant food, especially 'bread baked in great loaves and fresh meat', sanitation and medical care was horrendous. There were a few box cars painted white and labeled 'sanitary cars', a handful of Red Cross 'sisters', a medic or two, one doctor and clouds of flies.[162]

Fighting seems to have been heavier than the Bolsheviks expected, and on 27 April, US Consul Jenkins at Chita reported the arrival of 14 dead Red guardsmen 'from the Manchurian Front'. He added, 'Evidently considerable fighting, and Semenov is gaining ground'. Even Moscow newspapers were strangely silent about Siberian military developments.[163] However, around the end of April, rumors that were almost certainly generated by the Bolsheviks declared that Semenov had been killed.[164]

On 27 April Major Barrows left Harbin to follow the OMO offensive. He had spent 11 days in mid-April observing anti-Bolshevik organizing in Harbin and noted that only Semenov's group had moved into Transbaikalia to 'escape from the disadvantages of occupying Chinese territory' and find an atmosphere more conducive to discipline and training. While Semenov retained a support office in Harbin and a skeleton crew in Manchuli, he had moved all of his operational forces out of Manchuli into Transbaikalia by 26 April, most of them aboard 14 echelons of 25–40 small box cars (*taplushki*).

Barrows quickly befriended Semenov and wrote an incisive profile of this energetic and hard-working commander:

> While always cool, he undoubtedly has a passionate disposition and is capable of intense anger and fixed resentment. He had three and one half years of fighting in Europe and many stories are told in his camp as to his prowess. So far as I can judge, he is completely independent of the influence of those around him and other Russian leaders with whom he has relations. His personality easily dominates. His feelings toward the *Bolsheviki* and the prisoners who have joined their ranks is very strong. He detests their undoing of Russia...He is devoting his life to their destruction and, after that, to the resumption of the warfare against the Central Powers. He is capable of great severity toward his enemies and toward the disobedient in his own ranks.[165]

Semenov's main force quickly caught up to Zolotukhin's company at Kharanor and moved northwest to attack Borzya on 28 April. Red Guards held a chain of hills running about a mile east of town, but scurried away at the first blasts from OMO artillery, which fired before they had even finished preparing positions for their four Japanese field guns and pair of howitzers on the north side of the tracks, and a pair of Russian 3-inch guns and trio of French mountain guns on the south side. Semenov's battalion of Chinese infantry spilled across the hills and hastened the Red Guards' flight to town. The Red commander tried to assemble and rally his men, but his garrison of revolutionary Russian troops and Hungarian internationalists excitedly elected to abandon Borzya when they noticed an OMO mounted detachment emerge from the hills and trot towards town. The American observer Major Barrows noted, 'They lost all courage and fled in their trains', leaving many railcars behind and failing to destroy a little bridge over a stream just northwest of town. The Borzya station master estimated their numbers at 3,000–5,000, 'over half Magyar' and enough to fill 11 trains.[166]

OMO's Chinese infantry soon entered town, a few of them looting dwellings along the way. Semenov heard about the pilferage and promptly shot eight thieves to death, then laid out the stolen property at the train station for its owners to retrieve it. He made a sincere effort to discipline his men, even executing 'one of his own officers commanding the Chinese battalion for dishonesty in the payment of his troops'. There was no mercy for suspected Reds and it seems that, as the campaign progressed, Semenov ordered a number of men from his own ranks shot as spies. Thus Semenov launched his 'law and order' agenda with his own men.[167]

Semenov declared the establishment of 'a provisional administration for Transbaikalia' at Boryza on 29 April, merely intending to fill the vacuum of retreating Red power and restore order in his home province, not to take over Russia. Major Barrows arrived with the first two trainloads of Orlov's Detachment that night and was informed of Semenov's proclamation the next morning by 'Mister Eltekov, the Russian political representative', although word of it would not reach Harbin for a few days.[168] Reports from Transbaikalia grew sketchy towards the end of April, as OMO raced in hot pursuit of Lazo and Semenov even outran his publicists.

During his brief stopover in Borzya, Major Barrows got Semenov's permission to accompany the *orlovtsy* (the Orlov Detachment) into battle. Their train reached Khada-Bulak by 2 p.m. on 30 April, finding the town occupied by Chinese foot soldiers under Colonel Likhuchev, 'a young man of about 35 with an exceptional fine face and bearing' whose glasses made him look more like a doctor than an infantry commander. 'The place was being carefully secured', noted Barrows, 'Outposts were located on the hills north and south and patrols were constantly moving'. Ten miles further north, the Kolusatai Cossacks had liberated Birka the day before. A locomotive pushing an improvised armored car preceded the *orlovtsy* train out of Birka and led them to a valley of the River Gurga about 10 miles south of Olovyannaya, 'where the Bolsheviki were expected to make a firm stand'.

An 80-man *sotnia* of *orlovtsy* detrained, mounted up, split into three columns – one along the tracks and the others on each side. Barrows joined the Russian commander, Captain Vrashtel, in the armored railcar and ran ahead of the cavalry into the broad valley of the Onon. The armored car was one of two that Barrows saw in OMO's inventory. He described it as:

> a steel platform car on which was erected a steel house with walls made of one-half inch steel plates riveted together. It was partly roofed over, leaving several inches of space between the top of the wall and the eave of the roof. There were casements for guns closed by swinging doors on each side and at both ends. The car was equipped with two Hotchkiss [guns] firing three-inch shells and two machine guns.

Normally the armored car advanced a couple of miles ahead of the forward cavalry patrols, providing reconnaisance while boosting the patrols' morale.[169]

A Cossack *sotnia* had already established outposts in a small house and hills overlooking Olovyannaya, about four miles distant. There was a 'considerable force of the Red Guard' on both sides of the Onon, some entrenched in 'easily defensible' strongpoints. Colonel Natsvalov joined Barrows on May Day. 'Considerable activity was to be observed in the town itself', reported Barrows, 'and once during the morning an armored car came across [the bridge] and under cover of the bluff advanced within the line of our outposts, exchanging a few shots.'[170]

The bridge over the Onon at Olovyannaya was a strategic asset and the waters themselves held an emotional significance for many Buryats. Semenov called the Onon 'my native river', and it had been Genghiz Khan's native river as well. In this area it was 'about 200 yards wide and not easily forded', meandering and sprawling across expansive valleys except at Olovyannaya, where the river-bed narrowed and bluffs rose 'steep and bold' over the waters. Four 350-foot steel trestles rested on five great stone piers strong enough to stand up against the spring floods.[171]

Semenov was determined to not only take the bridge, but to cut off and kill or scatter the entire Red outfit. During the night of 1–2 May, he sent Zolotukhin's company to ford the Onon several miles upriver. Zolotukhin's objective was to stealthily swing around the Reds' rear and take the town of Aga, about ten miles northwest of Olovyannaya. Some Buryat soldiers prepared 'a swinging pontoon' near the mouth of the Gurga river, and ferried men across the Onon. On 2 May, Barrows accompanied Semenov and his staff on a horseback reconnaisance of the hills in front of OMO's outposts. A Bolshevik battery fired on them, but they saw that Lazo had abandoned all positions on Semenov's side of the river. Apart from five shells landing in or near its forward outpost, OMO saw no Red resistance. That night Semenov sent most of his troops across his two Onon bridgeheads, keeping back only 'a few troops and the heavy cannon' to hold his position on the railway. To Major Barrows it was 'a dangerous dispersal of his force', but, thanks to Shiroki's intelligence network, 'he [Semenov] knew that the Red Guard had not the slightest idea of taking the offensive'. Lazo's soldiers sought refuge behind the swift and icy spring currents of the Onon after dynamiting the railway tracks on the east side of the river, then blowing the third span of the bridge into the river as they retreated on the morning of 3 May. Four trains of Red Guards sped away from Olovyannaya as an OMO company of Serbian volunteers clambered over the debris of the bridge and entered town. The Zolotukhin detachment reached Aga the next day, but not in time to seal off the Reds' escape.[172]

Ensign Lazo and his Red commanders learned that it was more difficult to lead troops in combat than to lead a revolutionary mutiny. 'The [Red Guard] leaders appeared unable to bring their units into cooperation and doubtless each element judged itself the final authority to determine when and whether to fight', concluded Major Barrows. The same unruliness and lack of discipline that had 'bolshevized' the Russian Army now undermined the Red Guards.[173]

Although critics would charge during the months and years to come that Semenov's April offensive was a rash venture launched prematurely, it appeared neither rash nor premature on 4 May. He had gained two strong lines of defense – the Aga and Onon rivers, could conceivably threaten Moscow's line of communication to the Pacific by attacking Karymskaya or just cutting the Tran-Siberian's nearby northern branch, had liberated large sections of Transbaikalia inhabited by his natural constituency, Buryats and Cossacks, had struck a powerful blow against Bolshevik rule and demoralized the Red Guards. Thwarted but undaunted by the destruction of the span over the Onon river, OMO cavalry units under Major General Matsievski and Lieutenant Strel'nikov assaulted Bolshevik positions 60 miles apart within 12 hours to convince the Reds that his White army was much larger than it actually was.[174] Major Barrows estimated Semenov's strength at 2,300 officers and men on 1 May. Yet, his army was growing: Semenov's call for Cossack mobilization within the liberated areas had already been answered by 850 men. According to Shiroki's intelligence, Semenov had cleared out no less than 2,500 Red Guards and '1,000 Magyars' in the drive from Dauria to the Onon.

Semenov told Major Barrows that he hoped to capture Chita in two weeks, notwithstanding 'the presence of 6,500 Red Guards and 2,100–2,200 armed prisoners [internationalists] with 30 field guns' barring his way.[175] Within weeks, they would be bolstered by Cossacks who were willing to fight to resist Semenov's mobilization order.[176]

Kolchak and Semenov

The arrival of a famous polar explorer in Harbin on 28 April changed the entire situation in the Russian Far East. Admiral Aleksandr Vasilevich Kolchak was a slight, aristocratic fellow 'with a permanently worried expression on his face', renowned for his bravery, leadership, chain-smoking and explosive emotions. Born in St Petersburg in 1873, he graduated from the Naval Academy in 1894, served as a line officer on the cruisers *Rurik*, *Kreiser, Knyaz Pozharskii* and battleship *Petropavlovsk*, then became interested in hydrology and plunged into scientific work. His subsequent exploits in arctic exploration and naval warfare earned him the Konstantinov Gold Medal of the Russian Geographic Society, the Orders of St Anne and St Stanislav and a golden sword from Tsar Nicholas II. During the Russo-Japanese War, he commanded the cruiser *Askol'd*, destroyer *Serdityi* and torpedo boats until a serious bout of rheumatism forced his reassignment to a 75-millimeter shore artillery at the fortress of Port Arthur. He personally experienced his nation's humiliation at Japan's victory by being taken prisoner and held captive by the Japanese for five months. When only 41 years old, he had been promoted to vice admiral and given command of the Russian Black Sea Fleet.[177]

Nineteen months later, in February 1918, he was a post-revolutionary exile anxious to begin a new life in service of the British crown on the 'staff of the Mesopotamian army' when his very roundabout journey deposited him in Shanghai for 'three or four weeks'. During his sojourn, he received and decline an urgent invitation from Prince Kudashev to come to Peking. He also received a visit at his hotel from Lieutenant Zhevchenko, Semenov's traveling arms buyer. Zhevchenko told Kolchak about Semenov's counterrevolution in the railway zone and that he was shopping for arms in China and Japan and insisted that the admiral 'go to see Semenov and talk this matter over', as Kolchak later remembered it. Kolchak replied, 'I fully sympathize, but I have undertaken an obligation and have received orders from the English government and am going to the Mesopotamian Front'. Before departing Shanghai, Kolchak advised a British representative to 'give Semenov funds for the purchase of arms', but his advice was ignored.[178] Years later it was written that Zhevchenko asked Kolchak to join a 'Cossack government to be based in Manchuria', and that the admiral declined because he already knew of and strongly objected to the latter's 'Japanese orientation', however this appears to be a Japanese version of events that is not supported by either Kolchak or Semenov's testimony.[179]

Upon reaching Singapore on 11 March Kolchak's tight-fisted employers ordered him to turn around and report (at his own expense) to Prince Kudashev in Peking.[180] Upon landing in Shanghai again, Kolchak learned that he had been appointed the 'military director' of the Chinese Eastern Railway Board (replacing General Pleshkov) effective 27 April, and was told to proceed to Harbin. He realized that he would be responsible for more than just rejuvenating the railway militia; Horvath hoped his new board would become the seedling – the organizational catalyst – of a new Russian government (excepting the figurehead president of the railway, Kirin province Governor Kuo Tsung-hsi, of course). Kolchak reluctantly accepted the new assignment, muttering something about the 'swindling merchants' among Horvath's backers, investors and profiteers tied to the Russo-Asiatic Bank.[181] Also while passing through Shanghai, an emissary of the derber government offered Kolchak a job as minister of marine, which the admiral declined – he loathed Derber and his socialist orientation.[182]

'Matters naturally grew worse [with Kolchak's appearance] in the fetid atmosphere of intrigue which had developed at Harbin with the arrival of so many senior officers', noted the Canadian Major Bell, 'most of whom wished to lead, not to be commanded.'[183] Kolchak found the situation appalling. 'As for our [Chinese Eastern] militia men, they were mostly licentious drunken men', wrote the Admiral, 'absolutely unacquainted with any police duty. The Chinese very often beat them up...'[184] Kolchak's prime concern, however, was OMO: 'I wanted, first of all,' he said, 'to clear up my relationship with Semenov.'[185]

'As for Semenov', testified Admiral Kolchak,

> it was known there [in Harbin] that he...received material support in arms and money from the Japanese; that his detachment so far had not been especially successful; that it was on the Manchurian frontier, near Transbaikalia, as far as the Manchurian boundary line; that it expected an influx of volunteers that would swell the ranks.

Kolchak asked Kudashev to define his relationship with OMO. Kudashev drew a geographical boundary between OMO in Transbaikalia and Kolchak's responsibilities in the Chinese Eastern Railway zone, but added that he wanted foreign financial aid and arms to be channeled through a single source, which would have the effect of forcing a fusion of the chaotic anti-Bolshevik movement. Reckless actions of the latter caused concern with the Chinese Eastern Railway Board that the Chinese government might be provoked into taking over the railway.[186]

Before they even met, a harsh disharmony undermined Kolchak and Semenov's relationship. A culture clash was inevitable between the intellectual, technocrat admiral from the salons of Petrograd and the unrefined, half-Mongol lieutenant from the saloons of the Manchurian frontier. 'For us', Semenov would say, 'an admiral is a kind of civilian'.[187] In addition, Kolchak suspected that his chivalrous Japanese captors of 1905 had evolved into devious, acquisitive fair-weather friends and he was wary of their shallow benevolence, while Semenov may have been anxious to mask his growing subservience to Tokyo with a personality clash.[188] 'The qualities which had recommended him [Kolchak] to the British – his integrity, his powers of leadership – automatically made him persona non grata to the Japanese', noted Peter Fleming.

Apparently between 28 April and 4 May relations between Grigorii Semenov and Admiral Kolchak deteriorated rapidly. According to Kolchak's vague and rambling description of this critical period, Semenov was 'requisitioning' property of the Chinese Eastern Railway at gunpoint, and supposedly wanted to 'militarize' the railway, both of which smacked of revolutionary behavior that was no different from that of the Reds.[189] The admiral allegedly ordered the Cossack to Manchuli for a conference to rein him in, but Semenov, having led his troops nearly 150 miles into hostile territory and being at a critical juncture in his campaign, insisted that Kolchak come to him in the field. Besides, OMO was not part of the Chinese Eastern Railway chain of command. Kolchak, in his efforts to bring Semenov under the control of the Chinese Eastern Railway Board, eventually cut off the supply line to OMO that his predecessor General Pleshkov had opened.[190] This harsh act put Semenov and his men in jeopardy. Kolchak's later recollection of events declared that he 'conversed several times' with Major General Nakajima, but, with a imprecision that seemed almost deliberate, slurred the timeframe across several weeks in April and May.[191]

On 4 May everyone in Harbin was stunned to learn that a Cossack captain named Semenov had proclaimed an autonomous government in Transbaikal province.[192] General Muto, Japan's senior officer in northern Manchuria, and Major General Nakajima, the former intelligence chief and now head of Japan's military mission in Harbin, seemed genuinely surprised by it and, regardless, were unlikely to have supported such an audacious declaration without at least some delicate diplomatic preparations.[193] If the Temporary Government of the Transbaikal territory was the brainchild of some Japanese faction – a deep-cover scheme of Japanese intelligence or a rogue operation by a Japanese secret society like *Kanzen So* or the Black Dragons – then they certainly miscalculated.

Nevertheless, Semenov's small circle of Japanese advisors may have independently encouraged his maverick tendencies. When Britain withdrew support for OMO during its negotiations in Moscow and trouble with Kolchak was brewing in April, Japan reconsidered her assistance to Semenov, drawing indignant protests from the Japanese officers who worked day-to-day with him. They took offense at the notion of abandoning their Buryat comrade along with their 'Asia First' principles.[194]

Semenov was undaunted by the fact that the territory he held – a roughly 10,000-square-mile triangle of Buryat and Cossack grazing lands and villages – was considered by Harbin as well as Moscow to be a wasteland of only symbolic political value. On their maps, it appeared that he was merely squatting on a shoestring tract along the railway from Manchuli to the Aga river, little wider than the maximum effective range of a rifle. However, for three months Semenov had heard the Japanese tell General Horvath that if he were to set up a new Russian government, Japan would support it. Semenov believed that his risky proclamation of a Transbaikal government would garner more Japanese support. Indeed, under the current circumstances on the Transbaikal Front, he must have thought that the proclamation would force Japan's hand to become more involved or risk losing OMO. In addition, as Semenov's propagandists later explained, 'All our Allies were on the eve of recognizing the Soviet authority [as the legitimate Russian government].' Semenov's rebellion undermined this acquiescence to 'Bolshevism [and]...the low, animal passions of the uncivilized masses'.[195]

Of course, the proclamation further distanced Semenov from Admiral Kolchak and the White establishment in Harbin, but that entailed little immediate loss to OMO. To what degree Kolchak restricted the flow of reinforcements and supplies to OMO before 4 May is unclear, but the handwriting was on the wall. The British, who were still negotiating with the Bolsheviks in Moscow, had withdrawn support from Semenov, and that added to Kolchak's resolve to squelch OMO's offensive. In addition, China passively opposed the Transbaikal government and any military action originating in Manchuria until the anti-Bolshevik forces mustered 'superior strength'. Kuo Tsung-hsi, the governor of Kirin province and the new president of the Chinese Eastern Railway, was leery of provoking Red attacks or counterattacks into Chinese territory.[196]

As evidenced by the content of Semenov's proclamation, planning for the Transbaikal government had been in the works for at least a week, probably longer. Some careful thought had gone into the agenda unveiled in the proclamation – it was not a spontaneous, haphazard pronouncement. The proclamation expressed gratitude to the Allies – not just Japan – for respecting Siberia's territorial integrity. It made clear its focus was on a government for an autonomous Siberia, not an all-Russian entity and called for a democratic regime with a legislative assembly that would 'restore by degrees laws established by the Russian provisional government'. The proclamation emphasized the importance of straightening out Siberia's economic disorder by promising 'to take particular care...to restore banking facilities...and to readjust agriculture'.[197]

Semenov's government was not just paper. The former commissar of Transbaikalia under the provisional government, Sergei Afanas'evich Taskin, agreed to serve as civil administrator and a Cossack, Major General I.F. Shil'nikov, became chief of military-administrative, Cossack and mobilization affairs.[198] In coming weeks, up to 2,000 Transbaikal Cossacks flocked to Semenov's standard on the Onon to volunteer and some 148 officers 'constituting the Blagoveshchensk organization' (presumably the Amur Cossacks) also joined. In addition, at Progranichnaya, the eastern terminus of the Chinese Eastern Railway, a new Ussuri Cossack leader, Ivan P. Kalmykov was said to be 'in close understanding with Semenov, [and] is building up a force to take Nikolsk and Vladivostok'. Major Barrows predicted, in the sole analytical error of a lengthy 9 May 1918 report, 'I believe the end of the Bolshevik regime in Siberia is near'.[199]

Lazo's May Counteroffensive and the Kolchak–Semenov meeting

Semenov could not afford to be cocky, despite having surprised the Reds and broken their Onon river defense line, routing the Bolsheviks and pursuing Lazo across the Aga river, all but opening the gates to the rail junction at Karymskaya. Despite Semenov's astonishing success, his push to Aga unsettled his Japanese advisors who had advised that he hold up at the Onon river and consolidate his position. By mid-May, OMO could progress no further without a supply line and additional troops to protect its flanks.

Ensign Lazo established the Red headquarters at Adrianovka and, advised by his chief of staff, Major General Baron Taube, assembled the reinforcements that he had called for weeks before.[200] A number of new units finally arrived at the front: the Tomsk 1st and 2nd Internationalist Battalions, the Chita Internationalist Battalion, the Transbaikal Internationalist Detachment, and new Red Guard units raised in eastern Transbaikalia. The Tomsk 1st Internationalist Battalion consisted of '250 volunteers with a number of POWs', and the Transbaikal Internationalist Detachment contained 500 internationalists of various nationalities from Nerchinsk, Sretensk and Verkhne-Udinsk. The composition of the other internationalist units is unknown, but they were presumably about the same size – 300–500 men each.[201] A Japanese military intelligence agent reported that about one-third of Lazo's army consisted of POWs.[202] More difficult to gauge is the number of new volunteers that arrived in eastern Transbaikal Cossacks' and peasants' Red Guard detachments. The Bolshevik party ordered institutions and organizations to create and contribute volunteers to constitute new Red Guard detachments. Notwithstanding the rural isolation of eastern Transbaikalia, its mines, factories and villages were saturated in a sweaty, bloody history as the purgatory of *katorga* (hard labor), and finding anti-elitist, anti-tradition recruits posed no great problem. When internationalist and Red Guard detachments arrived in Chita, they were screened for undesirable elements, such as anarchists and hurried to the front. From Irkutsk, *Tsentrosibir'* tried to fan the flames with a fresh pronouncement to reiterate that Semenov was an outlaw and *vrag naroda* (enemy of the people).[203]

On 14 May, Lazo's long-awaited counterattack commenced against Semenov's camp at Aga. It was imperative that the Bolsheviks deny Semenov the vital rail junction at Karymskaya, where the Trans-Siberian Railway split into the Chinese Eastern and Amur lines, or the umbilical between Moscow and the revolutionary committees in Blagoveshchensk, Khabarovsk, Vladivostok and the towns in-between might be severed.

The following day, Admiral Aleksandr Kolchak and Grigorii Semenov met for the first and only time. It was an awkward and defining moment in a relationship that would trouble the anti-Bolshevik household for years to come. Both men had anticipated and contemplated the encounter for quite some time beforehand, yet a third, unseen party stage-managed the unhappy event.

Sometime during the previous days, Admiral Kolchak tried to prepare the ground for the meeting by first speaking with Semenov's principal Japanese patron, General Nakajima, head of the Japanese military mission in Harbin. When Nakajima offered Kolchak machine guns and other equipment, he also intimated that he expected payment, not in cash, but in 'some form of political concession'. Kolchak ignored Nakajima's subtle extortion attempt. As to Semenov's detachment, the admiral suggested 'channeling all Japanese support for independent Russian detachments through a central organization', and naturally Kolchak's Chinese Eastern Railway military organization was the most capable for managing such transactions. Nakajima ignored Kolchak's request. Both men parted unfulfilled and annoyed.[204]

Thus prepared, Admiral Kolchak traveled to OMO headquarters at Manchuli on 15 May 1918 to reason with the young captain-cum-warlord.[205] 'Kolchak, or someone on his staff, had announced his coming in a telegram which is said to have been unfortunately worded', delicately noted Peter Fleming. Kolchak recalled – perhaps selectively – that he had telegraphed to announce his visit as if it were merely a courtesy, not a threat or condescending dressing-down of a subordinate as it seems to have been. No one was at the station to greet the arrival of the admiral's special train, which was a particularly insolent discourtesy since Semenov's personal coach was parked nearby.[206] Kolchak described the next several minutes:

> When I arrived, I was told that Semenov was not there. This surprised me, since I had telegraphed three days ahead and everything was quiet on the front; yet Semenov had not come. After a while I became convinced that there was some queer play in this. I was informed that Semenov was present at Manchuria station after all... The fact of Semenov's absence surprised me exceedingly. Nevertheless I stayed there and waited. Finally I was told very definitely that he was there but did not wish to come to me. I then decided that the question was so important that personal pride should be disregarded. I went to Semenov myself, in order to speak with him. I was quite positively informed that Semenov had received instructions [from Nakajima] not to submit to me in any case.[207]

Thus, before Kolchak even met Semenov face to face, the damage between them was done. An upstart army officer of low rank in the employ of a rival foreign power had kept a national hero waiting hat-in-hand at a grim Manchurian train station in hope of an audience. A short-tempered admiral – a relic of the old regime – had tried to cut off supplies to anti-Bolshevik fighters during the heat of battle in order to make them obey a private railway's board of directors. Nakajima had manipulated the meeting with Machiavellian mastery.

The admiral said that he had not come as a superior, but simply wished to know Semenov's objectives and what material assistance OMO needed and, by the way, offered him 300,000 rubles from the Chinese Eastern Railway. 'He replied to me rather evasively that he was not in need of anything at present, that he received funds and arms from Japan, that he was not asking me for anything or expressing any wishes', recalled Kolchak. 'I then saw that there was really no use talking to him...' Kolchak concluded by saying, 'Very well, I shall not discuss this question with you, but bear in mind that, since you are unable to come to terms with me and cannot make matters clear, I relinquish all responsibility for the help that the railway might give you, and I shall apply its means and resources to those units which are under my command.' The men parted. Their sole encounter lasted minutes and the bitter taste of their poisonous antipathy persisted for years, tainting their decisions and distorting historical accounts. It is difficult not to imagine Kolchak stridently accusing Semenov of treason, however, the unusual circumstances in which the admiral would eventually be forced to regurgitate the details of his fateful meeting with Semenov were not conducive to confessions that could aid the soviets.[208]

While Captain Semenov was humbling Admiral Kolchak and refusing Harbin's conditional offer of assistance, Lazo and his Red Guards were shoving OMO out of Aga. Misguided by his pride and immaturity (and, no doubt, by his Japanese advisors), Semenov could not bring himself to accept Kolchak's offer for assistance no matter how much his men needed it, presumably because Semenov would have had to subordinate himself to

Harbin in exchange for promises of more reinforcements and ammunition. The American observer Major Barrows believed that

> the support given by the local Japanese military officers direct to Semenov encouraged him to take up an independent attitude. Semenov and a number of the officers surrounding him, being young and somewhat irresponsible, are much averse to superior control, which they consider to be merely a hindrance to energetic action in Transbaikalia and, in addition, as Cossacks, they resent control by officers who are not themselves Cossacks. They are thus easily influenced by the Japanese.[209]

During the five days after Semenov's meeting with Kolchak, the Red assault pushed OMO back across the Onon. Luckily for Semenov, the river checked the Bolshevik advance for a while. Lazo's armored train was idling in Olovyannaya on 19 May when Japanese General Muto arrived at OMO's headquarters across the river during a three-day tour.

Muto advised Semenov not to sever all contact with Horvath 'lest Horvath cut him off from his supplies'.[210] The Japanese general reassured Semenov of his continuing support – Japan's cabinet had recently approved 1,000,000 rubles (about 300,000 yen) in funding – but it took time for men and material to trickle through the supply pipeline, and OMO was also short of time.[211] Indeed, Captain Kuroki and the other Japanese officers serving with Semenov were adamant that Japan should not abandon him despite the cutoff of British aid, Chinese hostility and the quarrel with Kolchak.[212]

Alas, while Semenov faced his greatest military challenge on the Onon, trouble with Kolchak arose again. About this time, a Kolchak representative in Tokyo assured Lieutenant General Tanaka that the admiral and Semenov had a 'complete understanding', when in reality their only mutual understanding was an acidic loathing for each other.[213] By some accounts, Semenov was repeatedly pleading for supplies and reinforcements, while Kolchak attests that Semenov told him he needed nothing from the Chinese Eastern Railway. Muto's tour report suggests that the former was closer to the truth.

In spite of the 1902 Anglo-Japanese mutual defense agreement, Horvath and Semenov's Japanese sponsors were concerned about Kolchak's pro-British bias. Instead of coordinating their separate agendas among themselves, Britain and Japan tried using their Russian proxies to settle policy differences, quite brusquely in the case of the admiral and the Cossack captain. Personal problems ballooned into international issues (and vice versa). After Kolchak returned to Harbin from his degrading mid-May meeting with Semenov, his rage spilled over during an encounter with Major General Nakajima, whom he allegedly berated and insulted. While fingers can be pointed at the hypersensitive personal prides and egos of the individuals involved, the dominant regional partner, the Japanese war ministry, energetically avoided a leadership role and allowed petty quarrels to fester into infectious lesions. While Lazo was eyeing OMO across the Onon River on 19 May, Nakajima took the time to write a scathing, fateful opinion of the admiral to Lieutenant General Tanaka at the General Staff:

> I must admire his [Kolchak's] gallant spirit, but how unfortunate! He does not understand the situation; he lacks knowledge about the army, consideration and tolerance and is quick-tempered…I am worried about his being able to handle such complicated affairs as the mustering of forces, organization, command, supply and civilian administration.

Consul General Sato endorsed Nakajima's opinion a week later, adding, 'I am afraid that in the end, Japan will get nothing' (for her efforts with the Russians), reflecting fears that when post-war prizes would be shared out sometime in the future, Britain might cheat Japan in a repeat of the 1895 Treaty of Shimonoseki swindle. Sato's blunt statement summed up Japan's reservations about dealing with Admiral Kolchak in particular and its distrust of Britain in general.

Around the end of May Kolchak sent Colonel Orlov's Detachment to arrest an OMO officer who had been 'requisitioning' Chinese Eastern property at small stations along the line. A furious Semenov promptly stormed into Harbin in an armored train to demand the officer's release. A tense standoff unfolded between the Russian commanders. The Chinese Army and Bolshevik underground were quite amused, no doubt. The situation was eventually defused and Semenov left Harbin empty-handed, but from now on Kolchak required a bodyguard (recruited from Colonel Orlov's Detachment) to protect him from Semenov.[214]

While Semenov was bickering with Kolchak, his two-week face-off with Lazo on the Onon River came to an abrupt halt. During the night of 27 May, men of the Far East Red Guard detachment swam across the Onon and crept up to surprise Semenov's rear, just as Semenov was preparing to launch his own attack against Lazo.[215] Once across the river, the 1st Argun Cossack Revolutionary Regiment and Red Guard detachments of Chita railwaymen and Chernovskii miners spearheaded the attack on the front, while small units of Reds harassed the White's flanks. The Associated Press (AP) reported that 'a large force of Austrians and Germans, former prisoners of war' – a cavalry brigade and four infantry companies – had flanked Semenov and begun to operate behind his lines. OMO retreated to Borzya.

The Bolsheviks were determined not to let Semenov escape across the border to shield himself with Chinese sovereignty again, raising concerns on all sides that cross-border pursuit by the Reds might precipitate an invasion of Transbaikalia by Japan and China.[216] Beginning in late May, the Soviet government began asking Peking for permission to chase Semenov across the border when the inevitable retreat occurred.

Some said that OMO suffered a breakdown of order and loss of nerve. By the end of the first week in June rumors circulated in Harbin that Semenov had 'left the Transbaikalia front' because of 'dissension among his forces'.[217] Tales of mutiny in OMO mingled with predictions that Semenov would disband his army and flee to Mongolia. Indeed, about this time Semenov issued an order 'On Officers Who Betray the Name of Semenov', threatening officers with court-martial for insubordination.[218] Semenov's short-lived image as a national liberator had already evaporated. The European allies had come to believe that he represented no one but himself and was becoming 'wholly subservient to the seamier side of Japanese policy'.[219]

OMO's travails may have gone unnoticed behind the White lines, because Harbin was distracted by an internal political battle for control of the Chinese Eastern Railway's military resources. A few days after Consul General Sato and Major General Nakajima gave Tokyo the 'thumbs down' on Kolchak, Horvath demoted the admiral to commander of the Orlov Detachment, reinstated Pleshkov, and, to add insult to injury, skipped town for a board meeting in Peking and left Pleshkov to break the news to Kolchak. On about 8 or 9 June, Kolchak exploded in a tantrum: he recalled the Orlov men from the front, took personal command of a portion of the detachment at Harbin, then embarked on 'a campaign of his own', moving eastward on the Chinese Eastern to set up an advance headquarters at Muling 'in preparation for a descent on Vladivostok'. The Kalmykov Detachment, an independent unit of Ussuri Cossacks that was loosely associated with Semenov, was able to halt the mad admiral and his loyal *orlovtsy* at Pogranichnaya, the last Manchurian town before the Chinese Eastern Railway passes from China into Russian territory, 400 miles east of Harbin.[220]

On 10 June, a Bolshevik official repeated the request for permission to pursue the *semenovtsy* into China and also asked Chinese Commander Chang at Manchuli if Red soldiers could buy provisions at Jalai Nur, 18 miles east of Manchuli. OMO was surrounded on three sides and had to relinquish Borzya on 11 June. Semenov's army was cornered, its back pressed against the Chinese border again.

On 17 June Chinese border guards received instructions from the provincial military governor to disarm any OMO soldiers who tried to retreat across the border.[221] Upon hearing of this order, Major General Saito Kijiro, the Japanese military attaché in Peking, scurried between the offices of Heilung Jiang Province Military Governor Pao in Tsitsihar and China's Premier Tuan Ch'i-jui to have the order rescinded. Within a day or two, Tuan and Pao agreed to look the other way if OMO crossed the border, and wired appropriate instructions to Commander Chang at Manchuli. If, on the other hand, Bolshevik troops entered China, Chang's troops were to engage and drive them out. Nevertheless, Semenov did not trust the Chinese Army and did not send any of his soldiers into Manchuria just yet.[222]

Once again, events in distant cities were transforming the military situation in Transbaikalia. Just as newspapers around the world heralded Semenov's defeat, fate intervened.[223] Some of Lazo's units were suddenly ordered back to Irkutsk and rushed to central Siberia to put down an uprising in Omsk. This gave Semenov a brief interlude to rally OMO for a counterattack around 21 June in which he carved out a small sanctuary on Transbaikal territory hugging the border.[224]

The Japanese were encouraged by his tenacity and on 25 June they contributed 500,000 rubles to him via General Horvath. Kolchak was in no position to block the aid this time. After the admiral's outburst in early June, Pleshkov and Horvath appealed to their Japanese friends – Consul General Sato and Major General Saito, respectively – to persuade the Japanese foreign ministry to pressure the Chinese Eastern Railway Board into accepting Kolchak's dismissal without too much fuss. Thus, just five weeks after he arrived, Admiral Kolchak was removed from his post of military director on the corporate board of the railway, and departed for Japan on 30 June. While Semenov was fighting for survival on the fringes of Transbaikal badlands, Kolchak was pacing the lawn of the Russian chancery in Tokyo, chain-smoking and grumbling about Japanese duplicity.[225] Kolchak's trust in the Japanese was destroyed, and he left behind in Harbin 'a core of embittered Russian leaders who later helped destroy the Admiral's own regime at Omsk'.[226]

3

COUNTERREVOLUTION

May–October 1918

'*Za zakon i poryadok*' – 'For law and order.'
(Ataman Semenov, 10 September 1918)

Czechoslovakian saviors

During the first three weeks of June 1918, Semenov's future looked grim. After striking 220 miles into Bolshevik Transbaikalia in April and May, his volunteers were once again squatting among the ruins of the ramparts of Genghis Khan that wound along the Mongolian, Russian and Chinese frontiers, undermined by their own White comrades in Harbin. OMO's respite during the third week of June 1918 had been inadvertently prompted by widespread attacks against the Reds by some 55,000 Czechoslovak soldiers strung out along the Trans-Siberian Railway from Samara on the Volga river to Vladivostok.

These attackers were men of the Czechoslovak Legion, originally a corps-size, Russian Army unit recruited by the provisional government and made up of Czech and Slovak soldiers who had deserted the Austro-Hungarian Army or been taken prisoner.[1] They hoped that their military efforts against Germany and Austria–Hungary would promote the creation of an independent Czechoslovak nation. Noted an American observer, 'They wear the same uniforms as the Russians, but are distinguished by the snappy way they salute and by the red and white ribbon in their hats, these being the Czech national colors'.[2] Russians and Westerners looked favorably upon them as 'a democratic army' with strict discipline and 'the absence of a sharp division between officers and men as in the old Russian Army'.[3]

In the weeks after the Bolsheviks catapulted to power, Czechoslovakian and Allied political leaders decided – after much waffling – to transfer the legion to the Western Front, and placed the stateless legion under nominal control of the French in the person of General Maurice Janin. Because the German Army barred passage through the Eastern Front, this transfer would involve a 6,000-mile movement on the Trans-Siberian Railway to Vladivostok, where Allied ships would embark the legion for the long voyage to France.

Nearly three months earlier, on 18 February 1918, an armistice between the Bolsheviks and the Germans on the Eastern Front expired. Trainloads of German troops promptly rolled across the Russian border to occupy the Ukraine, while others crossed the Dvina river and marched on Dvinsk and Lutsk. The Czechoslovak Legion fought alongside the Bolsheviks to repel the invasion until the Treaty of Brest–Litovsk was signed on 3 March and ended hostilities between Russia and Germany.[4] On 14 March the Soviet government ordered that the Czechs be allowed to head east, then immediately reversed itself, then again on 26 March decided to let them leave. The Bolsheviks were in no rush to get rid of the legion – the longer they stayed, the more of them could be convinced to join Czech internationalist detachments. Of course, the Bolsheviks were also wary of allowing a foreign armed force to traverse Russia, even though it was generally believed that most Czechoslovaks leaned towards socialism.

On 21 March 1918, the Germans launched a massive assault on the Western Front. Fifty-four German divisions, freed from the Eastern Front by the Brest–Litovsk Treaty, were thrown into a hellish offensive across a 50-mile front between the Sensee and Oise rivers. British defenses crumbled at Saint Quentin, German shells fired from huge railway guns terrorized Paris, Dunkirk was shelled by German ships, and destroyers clashed off the coast of Flanders. Within a week the Germans were crowing that they had captured 70,000 Allied prisoners and artillery pieces. They were the darkest days of the war for the French and British, who yearned for the arrival of the Czechoslovak Legion as much as the Czechoslovaks yearned to get into the fight, but the most expedient way out of Russia was via the Trans-Siberian Railway to Vladivostok.

On 17 May a Czech on the platform at Chelyabinsk station was struck and seriously injured by an iron bar tossed from a passing train by a Hungarian POW (some say the Hungarian was an internationalist). This single spiteful act sparked an international incident that changed countless lives. The Czechoslovaks halted the train, pulled off the assailant, and, in a fit of vengeance, killed him. Bolshevik militiamen arrested the killers, whose jail was soon liberated by Czech soldiers after they disarmed the local Red Guards. On 25 May, Red Army chief Leon Trotsky ordered the Czechoslovak Legion to disarm. The Czechoslovak Legion had tried hard to remain neutral in Russia's revolutionary affairs, but Trotsky's order exhausted the legion's patience. Within 24 hours of the order, the Czechs lashed out against the Soviet government along the length of the Trans-Siberian Railway, from the Urals to eastern Siberia, taking over train stations and large segments of the railway. In their shadow, anti-Bolshevik Russians from a wide range of organizations spanning the political spectrum emerged into the streets to depose the Red radicals. As a result, the Bolsheviks withdrew from Novonikolaevsk on 26 May, Penza on 29 May and Petropavlovsk and Tomsk on 31 May.[5]

The Czechoslovaks would have faced much tougher Bolshevik resistance had not thousands of the most reliable and battle-hardened Red organizers and soldiers been dispatched to the wilds of Transbaikalia to squash Semenov's rebellion. Western Siberia had been stripped of Red fighters for the Transbaikal campaign, and 'official information of the Chita revolutionary staff' indicated that as many as than 26,000 men had been brought to bear upon OMO, complimented by a corresponding arsenal of small arms, machine guns and shells. According to OMO's own history of the spring campaign, 'Sailors were called forth from Kronstadt; cannons were taken from warships; agitators arrived from Lenin and Trotsky; all of the Red Army east of Samara was concentrated against Semenov's detachment'. Accordingly, while Semenov necessarily focused his main thrust up the railway line on the Daurski Front, he had wisely extended his operations across a 200-mile front, west from Manchuli to Aksha, roughly paralleling the Onon river, with another *semenovtsy* band operating as far west as Kyakhta, and sympathizers along a chain of Cossack border settlements stretching into western Transbaikalia, trying to draw the Reds in many directions at once as ephemeral traces of White guerrillas appeared, then vanished.[6]

In Omsk, 2,000 miles west of Semenov's battlefields, a 290-man Red Guard detachment was waiting to meet a Czech echelon when it pulled into Kulomzino station. The Red commander, one Comrade Uspensky, demanded the Czech's weapons. They handed over 30 rifles. Uspensky then demanded to inspect the train. The Czechs tossed the engineer out of the locomotive and roared out of the station. Uspensky gave chase and caught up with them about 50 miles from Omsk, only to be severely routed, loosing 70 men killed and 30 wounded. This bloody event unleashed a storm of anti-Bolshevik sentiment in Omsk. During the next several days railway workers tore up the tracks to prevent the Bolsheviks from fleeing, took over the railway and prison, and thwarted a Red attempt to blow up local bridges.[7]

Red troops were withdrawn from Lazo's campaign against Semenov and dispatched to quell the Omsk uprising.[8] They would never make it there. Small Czech echelons had already taken several stations in their path. For instance, Nizhne-Udinsk station was captured by two Czech companies armed with just rifles and clubs.[9] Meanwhile in Omsk on 7 June, leading Bolsheviks emptied the bank of 279 million rubles, loaded up several steamships and evacuated in such a rush that they left behind 1,300 Red Guards. By the time a Czech detachment arrived in town two days later, Socialist-Revolutionaries and their allies had taken over the city in the name of the Provisional Government of Autonomous Siberia.[10]

Within days, small groups of well-organized Czechoslovaks crushed, disabled or scattered any nearby Bolshevik forces that might impede their eastbound trek to Vladivostok. Their success was made easier because so many Red Army and Red Guard units had been drawn from throughout Siberia and the Far East into the fray against Semenov in Transbaikalia. Within days, most of the Trans-Siberian Railway from the Urals to the Irkutsk area was in the hands of the Czechoslovak Legion.

Initially Derber's Provisional Government of Autonomous Siberia (covertly formed in Tomsk during February) was supported by secret military organizations that also sprang from their hiding places in early June 1918.[11] Besides their mutual hatred of the Bolsheviks, however, the revolutionary parties of the Derber government and the right-wing militarists had little in common. General Horvath joined the militarists in showing open disdain for the predominately socialist Derber government. Conservative officers scorned the Siberian government's egalitarian army, led by Colonel G.N. Grishin-Almazov, where positions were filled according to ability (and popularity, no doubt), not former rank, and white and green ribbons were worn instead of the hated epaulets.[12] Against this background, several members of the PGAS met in Omsk on 29 June and decided to form the Provisional Siberian Government (PSG), a more politically balanced administration under the premiership of Petr Vasil'evich Vologodskii, a democratically minded lawyer described as being gentle, very proper and a hypochondriac.[13]

July defeat and new foreign assistance

The lightning-like Czech uprising and anti-Bolshevik rebellions did little to alleviate Semenov's plight in Transbaikalia until late June. The withdrawal of some Red troops gave Semenov a chance to muster an attack on about 21 June, but it came to nothing. Sergei Lazo's army, driven by revolutionary zeal, class hatred and death threats, kept up the pressure.[14] On 28 June the Reds unleashed a powerful attack against Matsievskaya, supported by heavy guns that had recently arrived from the West. OMO suffered the 'great loss' of Captain Mallachikhan, commander of the 1st Manchurian Regiment, but did not crumble. This may have been the same action where the Bolsheviks sent rolling a railway carriage full of 'explosives and balloons of suffocative gas' toward the OMO lines. The carriage struck one of Semenov's armored trains, but the explosives failed to detonate.[15] Nevertheless, the battle's outcome was so predictable that Lazo was able to take a short vacation, leaving the front for three days' leave with his 'combat girlfriend' Olga in a deserted *zimove* (winter hut) in the forest at Kruchina, near Chita. A local

Red Guard detachment commander, Boris Clark, also took leave and met his family at Lazo's cabin.[16]

Soon after their return to the front they noticed a new unit in the White enemy's forces, the first Japanese volunteer battalion. It appeared on the front lines on 7 July, commanded by infantry Captain Okumura Naonari. Major General Muto conceived of the battalion in early June and drafted two organizers from the expatriate community: the leader of the Japanese residents' association in Manchuli, Ansho Jun'ichi, and a Japanese mine operator in Siberia, Seo Eitaro. On a whirlwind tour of south Manchuria, the recruiting duo offered Japanese reservists 60–130 yen per month (plus food and clothing) to join. Nearly 500 men signed up although British sources reported that '100 had to be sent home for taking part in drunken brawls and other acts of insubordination'.[17]

Despite months of setbacks, casualties and desertions, Semenov's army had grown since his first incursion into Siberia six months earlier. Despite Semenov's call for mobilization of all Transbaikal Cossacks, the majority of his force remained predominantly Asian – 'Mongols and Chinese', serving under Russian and Cossack leadership. Since the May defeats, a number of Japanese officers and NCOs had been seconded 'to stiffen the Chinese formations, especially the 2nd Daurski Mounted Regiment'.[18] In the first week of July, OMO consisted of:

5,000 officers, men and support personnel (including the Japanese battalion)
armored train battalion with at least 1 armored train with a crew of 32
1 double-company of 190 Serbian cavalryman
1 pioneer company of 140 Koreans
1 motor (automobile) company of 53 men.[19]

Some of the riff-raff that flocked into OMO's officer corps were not eager for combat. On 29 June, while the Reds were pummeling OMO on the front, General Budberg wryly noted a shameful event in Harbin: 'Last night in the Palermo Bar our [OMO] saviors got superlatively drunk and finished up with shooting. A Semenov officer concerned with freight car allotments was killed: he had 130,000 rubles in his pocket.'[20] A few of OMO's swashbuckling officers preferred to fight over *zakuski* (hors d'oeuvres) and vodka in Harbin's big railway club, gambling joints or cabarets than chase Reds in the Transbaikal wastelands.[21]

On 13 July, Semenov's men assaulted Sharasun and Dauria, intending to break through the Red line of defense and pin down Lazo's army to help the Czechoslovaks 'to break the Bolshevik opposition at Verkhne-Udinsk and move to Chita'. Soldiers on both sides understood the importance of this action and fought tenaciously, enjoying 'neither rest, nor breath' for 15 days. The *semenovtsy* 'sometimes passed several nights without sleep, several days without hot food, in permanent contact with the enemy...justifiably thinking that every hour of the battle would contribute to the success of the Czechoslovaks'.[22]

The brutal battle turned on 26 July when a Bolshevik assault force entered Manchuli, in spite of the secret agreements hammered out between the Japanese military attaché and Chinese officials weeks before. 'Rumors are current at Semenov's headquarters that General Chang Kuan-hsiang, Chief Staff Officer to the Military Governor of Heilung Jiang [Province], and in command of all Chinese troops at Manchuli, has received bribes from the Bolsheviks', reported Major Barrows, the American observer.[23] Still the Red Guards were not able to evict OMO from Russia altogether. Semenov was pinned against the border, the Red Army in front of him and the Chinese Army in back. He hunkered down in his headquarters train '*Atamanovskaya*' at Matsievskaya, a hilltop station that dominated the Reds' approaches, just seven miles from Manchuli, with armored trains providing artillery and machine gun cover on his left flank and fighters in a chain of hills overlooking the railway.

Suddenly, to Semenov's surprise, the commander of OMO's armored train battalion, one Captain Shelkov, bolted to Harbin with his men, where he was warmly greeted by General Pleshkov (under pressure from the foreign consuls in Harbin, according to Semenov, the trains were returned to him). With his flank thus exposed to the enemy, Semenov even appealed to a Chinese general to stop Shelkov, but the Chinese was forbidden by his superiors in Harbin to intervene.[24] Major Barrows noticed another bit of treachery from the same quarter – the withholding of the Officers' Corps, a unit 'raised originally by Colonel Orlov under the direction of the Russian Consul at Harbin, in connection with [Horvath's] Far Eastern Committee'. The corps was made up of several hundred Poles, Serbs, Chinese and other mercenaries fleshed out with a few Russian officers and cadets from Irkutsk and Khabarovsk military academies and armed with Japanese weapons, and had been intended 'to form a reserve for Semenov or to operate against Vladivostok'. Yet while OMO fought for its life, Horvath held back the Officer Corps to support his self-proclaimed dictatorship.[25]

With the artillery support of Shelkov's trains now absent, the Bolsheviks charged in to overrun OMO's positions. Only a determined counterattack by OMO's battalion of Japanese volunteers, led by Semenov's military advisor Major Takeda, prevented Semenov's outnumbered army from being annihilated by the Red Guards. Semenov decorated Takeda with an OMO version of the Cross of St George, 4th Class.[26]

It must surely have seemed to Semenov that, apart from his Japanese friends, he was surrounded by treachery, while the Chinese also had reason to be wary. 'The Chinese see that we [Allies] are not supporting Semenov openly', wrote Major Barrows, '[and] they have also a very shrewd suspicion that we had dealings with the Bolshevik Government at Moscow, and they are hardly likely therefore to take up the cudgels on behalf of Semenov until they see what the Allies do'.[27]

It looked as if OMO was doomed at the 'three-cornered negotiations' that followed – the Bolsheviks demanding, the Chinese agreeing, and Semenov differing, that the *semenovtsy* hand over their arms and be transported back to Harbin.[28] Luckily for Semenov, these talks were never consummated. Before the Chinese and Bolsheviks could agree to the terms of his surrender, he engineered a sudden withdrawal during the dead of night, marching most of his troops around Manchuli to board hijacked trains in Jalai Nur which carried OMO east into Manchuria.[29] It should be noted that OMO was not entirely lacking for Chinese allies, because months later *semenovtsy* publicly expressed thanks to Chinese General Chang Kui-Vu 'for rendering a valuable service' about this time.[30] Meanwhile, the counterrevolutionary and Czechoslovak Legion uprisings on the Trans-Siberian Railway distracted the Bolsheviks, just as they were about to finish off OMO.

OMO's unsuccessful performance in July 1918 may have had far-reaching implications. During that same month some Japanese intelligence officers contemplated a plot to rescue the tsar and the royal family from their Bolshevik captors in Ekaterinburg. Semenov's assistance would have been expected during the getaway.[31] However, whether the plan died with Tsar Nicholas and his family when they were gunned down 16 July, or with OMO's waning fortunes on the battlefield is unknown.

On 2 July 1918, the Allies' Supreme War Council had agreed to send troops into the Russian Far East.[32] Their declared mission was to rescue the Czechoslovak Legion, and to fight a rumored legion of German, Austro-Hungarian and Turkish internationalists whom the Bolsheviks had mustered from prisoner of war camps. All Allied participants in the Siberian adventure believed that the treacherous Bolsheviks were simply proxies of the German enemy, and would be dealt with as such. Other factors bolstered Allied hostility to the Bolsheviks: militant atheism and persecution of the Church, and, of particular concern to Allied businessmen and investors, the Reds' 8 February repudiation of all foreign debts.[33] In addition, Bolshevik propaganda calling for world revolution amounted to a blanket declaration of war on all governments and fanned the flames of allied paranoia. The possibility of world revolution did not appear to be a Red fantasy to allied intelligence and security officers. A huge international network of maximalists, syndicalists and varying shades of Marxists applauded the Bolshevik revolution and was encouraged by it.

Allied soldiers in British Hong Kong and the US Philippine colony began gearing up to embark for Vladivostok while Japan's 7th Division began moving into Manchuria from Korea in July. The Red Army's pursuit of OMO into Manchuria at the end of July 1918 gave the Japanese General Staff grounds to accelerate its army's deployment and overt activities, even though the Chinese government insisted that its borders had not been violated by Lazo's incursion.[34] On 5 August the Japanese cabinet approved the movement of regular army units into the Manchuli area.

In the meantime, Semenov gathered his men in Hailar and, with considerable Japanese assistance, put OMO back together again. The Japanese volunteer battalion was abruptly disbanded between 23 and 31 August.[35] Although White and Soviet histories credit it with saving Semenov, Japanese records indicate nothing more than a lackluster existence. Of the 500 men enlisted in June and July, some 200 supposedly 'dropped out' before 23 August, although it is unclear whether they dropped from Bolshevik bullets, disinterest, disciplinary problems or continued to serve in another capacity.[36]

The Japanese continued trying to help OMO assemble an improvised staff that could handle operations, administration, inspection and supply. Since Semenov had not been able to obtain a Russian general staff officer to take the lead in operations planning, he relied heavily on Captain Kuroki. 'There is not much doubt that the plans of operations are drawn up to a large extent by Captain Kuroki', wrote Major Barrows in late July.[37]

A 'trickle of Cossack recruits' took up arms for OMO, but the majority of Semenov's men were Asians: Buryats and other indigenous tribesmen – 'Tungus and Chunchus brigands and other unruly elements', many Chinese and a noticeable number of Koreans.[38] Semenov had been particularly successful recruiting Buryats, who, apart from being naturally drawn by Semenov's Buryat heritage, were incited by a rumor that their lands would be confiscated by the Bolsheviks and divided among European Russians.[39] Men from their own ethnic groups commanded the OMO soldiers in the barracks; Russian officers took over only in battle.

By mid-summer 1918, even OMO appeared more palatable than the increasingly ruthless Bolsheviks. The long-awaited Constituent Assembly had tried to convene in Petrograd on 18 January 1918 but the non-Bolshevik delegates, who composed the majority, were rounded up by the CHEKA and incarcerated.[40] During the spring, food battalions of urban Bolsheviks roamed the countryside seizing farm products for the restless cities and antagonizing the rural folk.[41] On 6 July CHEKA agents who, up to this point, had belonged to the pro-Bolshevik faction of Left Socialist-Revolutionaries (LSRs) revolted in Moscow, assassinated the German ambassador, Wilhelm von Mirbach, and even took over CHEKA headquarters for a short while.[42]

Consequently the Bolsheviks branded all non-Bolshevik organizations as subversive. Anyone who muttered against the Bolsheviks' requisitions of food, livestock or other property was liable to be shot on the spot as a 'counterrevolutionary agitator'.[43] Some 12,000 refugees abandoned their homes and made their way to Semenov's camps, where they received shelter, flour, sugar, tea and other necessities.[44] For a time, the Bolsheviks' coldblooded cruelty was Semenov's best recruiting tool.

Battles for Lake Baikal

On 12 July the Bolsheviks (reinforced by an internationalist unit of 3,000 Hungarian prisoners of war) were driven out of the city of Irkutsk by a detachment of the Czechoslovak Legion's 7th Regiment 'armed with only 30 carbines and a few grenades' and a small force of counterrevolutionary Russians.[45] The Red Army began withdrawing to the east of Lake Baikal in a colossal cavalcade of echelons and armored trains. The Bolsheviks took every serviceable locomotive and railway carriage they could find, and blasted spans of every major bridge. Close on their heels, a Czech detachment raced on foot to cut them off before they disappeared into the 41 tunnels that hugged the cliffs over the lake. Despite a dogged five-day march with hardly any rations, the Czechs missed intercepting the Reds' rear guard before they got to the tunnels.

A small force of anti-Bolshevik Russians joined in the pursuit. A number of hastily assembled, all-volunteer infantry regiments would become the nucleus of the Siberian Army. They included one regiment each from Omsk and Irkutsk composed of officers, cadets and students, and three regiments from Tomsk, at least one of them largely made up of Tomsk University students.[46] In contrast to the opportunists who later swarmed into the White ranks when victory seemed a fait accompli, the Russian officers who rushed to join the volunteer and Czech regiments during this uprising distinguished themselves with their self-sacrifice and bravery. After the campaign, one Allied officer would acclaim, 'To the Russian officers of superior military rank who recognized the Czechish [sic] superiority in both organization and training, and to the many Russian officers who fought as privates, we recommend the highest admiration'.[47]

One volunteer unit entered the lakeside town of Port Baikal and found a small number of Reds guarding two freightcars which they had planned to roll onto one of the lake's two large ice breakers – *Baikal* and *Angara*.[48] Apparently the Reds who commandeered the *Baikal* and *Angara* had steamed away with great haste, abandoning the freightcars and even their guards. 'The [White] Russian force fired on the cars with machine guns and succeeded in exploding them and practically destroying the whole town', reported an observer. The boxcars had been loaded with high explosives intended for destroying the railway tunnels. After several days repairing equipment that had been discarded by the Bolsheviks, the volunteers and their enterprising commander, a tsarist colonel, put some field pieces on rafts and set out across the lake in pursuit of the *Baikal* and *Angara*.[49]

The ice breakers were the mainstays of a makeshift flotilla assembled by the Red chief of staff of the Pribaikal Front, Meier Abramovits Trilisser ('Pribaikal' refers to the western part of Transbaikal province).[50] Other ships of the Red Baikal fleet included the *Krugobaikalets*, *Leitenant Malygin*, *Graf Murav'ev-Amurskii*, *Innokentii*, *Mikhail* and the steamboat *Volna*. The *Baikal* and *Angara* had been hastily loaded with coal, grease, spare parts and food, their wooden decks covered with sand bags, and mounted with machine guns and artillery – a few field pieces aboard the *Baikal* and two 6-inch guns on the *Angara*. The majority of gunners were Hungarian internationalists. The *Angara* also picked up the Listvenichnoye Red Guard detachment, and reconnoitered the lake, snooping around the White-occupied towns of Utulik and Mangutai and firing on a Czechoslovak echelon which darted for cover into a tunnel.[51] At Baikal, where the Angara river meets the lake, the *Angara* engaged in indecisive artillery duels with a Czechoslovak Legion howitzer ashore and the 'Czech Fleet', the steamship *Siberyak*. More Red Guards were taken aboard, including a detachment of Cheremkhov miners and Commissar Ivan Shevtsov, military commandant of Irkutsk and one of the heroes of the White House defense in December 1917. On 29 July the ice breaker *Angara* participated in an amphibious landing at Goloustnoe, putting ashore 150 Hungarians for a few hours. They tried to repeat this feat at Listvenichnoye, but were repulsed by withering fire from the Czechoslovak Legion's 7th Regiment.[52]

One unlikely witness to the battles for Lake Baikal was an American railway expert, Colonel George H. Emerson. Until the war broke out, Emerson had been general manager of the Great Northern Railway. Emerson was crossing Siberia to join John F. Stevens' advisory commission in European Russia when the Czechoslovak Legion revolted. His path west blocked by battles between the Czechs and Bolsheviks, Emerson began heading back to the Pacific Coast on Czechoslovak Legion echelons. By the time the legion reached Lake Baikal, Emerson's expertise in repairing the battered railway was constantly in demand.

Before the end of July the Czechoslovak Legion was fighting the Reds' rear guard for each tunnel along Lake Baikal.[53] When the Czechs took Tunnel No. 16, they discovered 1,450 *poods* (about 25 tons) of high explosives placed for detonation.[54] Using a similar amount of explosives, the Bolsheviks managed to blast a section of Tunnel No. 39, about one mile east of Sludyanka. Luckily for the Czechs, No. 39 was a small tunnel, but it still held up the Czechs for about two weeks while 300 German prisoners of war were brought in from Irkutsk to clear 4,000 cubic yards of fallen rock from the tunnel by hand (no machinery was available). Boulders loosened by the explosion frequently fell from the cliffs above. One day sporadic shells from the *Baikal* and *Angara* harassed the anti-Bolshevik forces and the unfortunate prisoners of war. A Czech detachment lugged a 3-inch field gun up the mountain overlooking Tunnel No. 39 to protect the laborers. When the *Angara* returned the next day, the Czech artillerists startled her with a number of close shots that convinced her wise captain, Vyacheslav G. Bazilevskii, to turn tail and run, vibrating furiously at full speed. Nonetheless, a Czech shell exploded right at the stern, splintering the deck and scaring the crew with a huge column of water.

On 2 August there was continual artillery action to the east of the tunnel until late into the night. All day, men of the Czech 7th Regiment and their Russian allies pushed over the mountain. Colonel Radola (Rudolph) Gajda, the Czechoslovak Legion's 27-year-old commander, joined them.[55] This was now the front. They forced the Reds to retreat, but a company of Russian volunteers from Tomsk lost half its men in battle.

Goloustnoe was the target of another Red amphibious assault on 4 August, when the *Krugobaikalets*, *Innokentii* and *Angara* put ashore several boatloads of Red Guards, silenced Czechoslovak machine guns with the ice breaker's 6-inchers, and routed the legion from the town. The battles for the lake were demanding increasing ingenuity and resourcefulness from both opponents.[56]

Colonel Gajda cleverly planted disinformation, eagerly believed by Bolshevik commanders, that his advance troops east of the tunnel were short on ammunition and provisions. Emboldened by this ruse, the Red rear guard backtracked and attacked the anti-Bolshevik Russian units that had been working their way up the railway line. The Reds chased the bait all the way back to the eastern mouth of Tunnel No. 39. Suddenly the steep hills overlooking the tunnel entrance rained bullets and shells down upon the Bolshevik pursuers. From their perches above the railway line, the Czech 7th Regiment decimated the Reds soldiers and their Hungarian mercenaries, and captured seven locomotives and a *bronevik* – an armored train.

Czech troops boarded the captured trains and resumed their pursuit of the retreating Red Army. During the night of 10 August Tunnel No. 39 was clear enough for eight echelons to make it through, although repairs were still unfinished. Rock slides and cave-ins would continue for another week, but 12 more echelons managed to pass through on 13 August.

Meanwhile the Czechs in the captured armored train caught up with the Bolsheviks again just east of the small lakeside town of Tankhoe and seized another armored train. In desperation, the Bolsheviks launched a locomotive and boxcar full of explosives at the approaching Czech *bronevik*. The Czechs pulled back, leaving a flatcar in their path. 'The explosion [was] terrific', reported an American observer, 'several buildings were razed to the ground, vegetation had been entirely obliterated in the immediate neighborhood.'[57] A ground battle ensued with Red infantrymen entrenched behind barbed wire entanglements. Czech troops flanked them from behind and routed them. By the time the fighting finished, much of the little town lay in ruins, including its docks.[58]

Early the next morning, 18 August, Colonel Emerson and other railway engineers were looking over a captured *bronevik* at Tankhoe when 15 or 20 exhausted Russians walked up to them. They were the crew of the *Baikal*, they explained. The innovative White unit at Port Baikal had crossed the lake in 'rafts mounted with field guns', they said, drawn up near the *Baikal*'s dock at Mysovaya (35 miles east of Tankhoe) during the night and shelled her. Her wooden superstructure and holds full of coal and grease roared into an inferno, even though quick-thinking Red sailors fought the fire with pumps aboard the *Krugobaikal'ets*. Afire and adrift, her crew abandoned her. A day or two later the *Angara* surrendered.[59]

In previous days another White colonel named Ushakov had crossed the lake with 80 men on the steamships *Siberyak*, *Feodosii* and *Buryat*. They landed behind Red lines at Posol'skaya, where Colonel Ushakov brazenly entered the Bolshevik commissar's headquarters, informed him that he and his 80 troops were Bolsheviks too, and requested ammunition, explosives and supplies from the stockpiles at Verkhne-Udinsk so he could return across the lake and blow the tunnels. The gullible commissar passed Ushakov's request on to Verkhne-Udinsk. After a while, Ushakov's detachment slipped out of Posol'skaya and marched about eight miles west in the direction of the advancing Czechs. They pulled up the tracks around *verst* 339 and caused several Red trains to derail, then marched a little further west.[60] Colonel Ushakov apparently tried to flag down an oncoming *bronevik* which he believed to be the Czech spearhead. Bolshevik and Hungarian soldiers jumped from the train and slaughtered Ushakov. His body was badly mutilated when found. Of his 80 men, only eight survived.

Ushakov's sacrifice was not in vain – 61 Red echelons stalled in the bottleneck behind the derailment at *verst* 339. The Bolshevik soldiers panicked and deserted their trains, but Whites and Czechs of the Barnaul Regiment cut off their retreat and annihilated them.[61] Subsequent reports estimated that about 6,000 Bolshevik soldiers perished and 2,000 were captured during the battles for the lake, most of these casualties falling between Mysovaya and Posol'skaya.[62] These losses devoured no less than 40 percent of the Red Army assigned to defend the heart of Siberia. The Reds' loss of 41 field guns dashed any hopes of entrenching against their pursuers again.[63]

Thereafter, the Czechs and Whites advanced through Transbaikalia almost unopposed. The Reds were on the run. The American engineers reported,

> All of their efforts from that time on [were] put forth in making a hasty retreat and in blocking and retarding the advance of the Czechs and [White] Russians; this they did by blowing up numerous bridges, derailing surplus equipment and protecting their rear by their armored train only to such an extent as to keep track of the progress being made against them while they made every effort to take with them high-class goods and provisions.[64]

Echelons loaded with Czechs and Whites raced 80 miles east of the lake to Verkhne-Udinsk, where the Bolsheviks were swept out of power on 20 August.[65] Pausing only to make slapdash repairs to the railway line, the echelons quickly rolled through a dozen more little towns where the train stations or pumping engines were ablaze. The Czechs had assembled a remarkable engineering echelon which seemed capable of fixing damaged tracks and bridges faster than the Reds could sabotage them. Occasionally the leading Czech *bronevik* got close enough to the last Red train to take a shot at it.

By 24 August, the Czechs drew near to the town of Mogzon, less than 100 miles west of Chita. They found the rural peasantry in dire circumstances, '... being entirely out of bread', according to one American observer. Shortly before the Reds evacuated Mogzon, the Bolshevik commander there informed a peasant leader that he had lost control of his troops in their frenzied flight to the east. No disciplined Red resistance remained at the tail end of their retreat, but a series of burnt out and disabled bridges frustrated the Czech advance late that night. Finally, during the early morning hours of 25 August, the restless Czech and Tomsk regiments marched the last nine miles into Mogzon. To their surprise, a train soon pulled into Mogzon from the east and offered to take them to Chita. It had been sent by anti-Bolshevik Cossacks inside Chita.[66]

Anarchist locusts descend upon Chita

After the abandonment of Irkutsk on 12 July, discipline eroded quickly in many fleeing Red Army units. Not surprisingly, the Anarchist detachment of Efrem Perezhogin led an infectious degeneration into banditry. As the Central Executive Committee of Siberian Soviets (*Tsentrosibir'*) resettled briefly in Verkhne-Udinsk, Perezhogin's band followed, bringing disorder to the city and plundering a nearby *datsan* (Buddhist temple), giving the local Buryat populace a taste of militant atheism while absconding with all relics and regalia made of precious metals. Indeed, Perezhogin and company seemed to worship gold, and the *Tsentrosibir'* commissars were toting 200 *poods* (about 7,220 pounds) of it, taken from the state bank in Irkutsk.[67]

As the Czechoslovaks and White volunteers cleared the lakeside tunnels, Perezhogin fell in with other slackers and deserters from the Pribaikal Front. They descended upon Chita like a plague of locusts, adorned with bandoleers, binoculars and trinkets 'like a gypsy horse', reported the newspaper *Zabaikalskii Rabochii* at the time. 'Everyone has orders in his pocket [stating] that his is a member or instructor of the Siberian military commissariat, not simply a private soldier...These gentlemen have taken over the Hotels Selekt and Dauria, where there is total revelry, [and] rivers of champagne flow.' Shadowed by an ever-present bodyguard, Perezhogin perambulated through town, an unforgettable giant with a untamed mane of grey curls, white canvas shirt, billowing khaki trousers and unusually high boots, a pistol and two grenades tucked in his belt, and a heavy club in his hand. Anarchist Red Guards were untouched by the much vaunted revolutionary discipline of the Bolshevik military. Perezhogin gathered around him a frighteningly colorful retinue of wayward internationalists, Red Army runaways and undisciplined Cossacks.

Most of the Chita garrison was away, fighting a losing battle against Czechs and Whites to the west, and Japanese and Whites to the south. Local security was under the jurisdiction of Red military authorities but the Chita police was still functioning until Perezhogin decided that the latter was an impediment to his next escapade. He had been haranguing the soviet to give his detachment 'the unlimited right of requisition and confiscation', and convinced them that the police ranks harbored 'counterrevolutionary elements' and that their revolvers would better serve the revolution on the Dauria and Pribaikal fronts. On 6 August to Perezhogin's delight, the soviet disarmed the Chita militia. However, he faltered on the next step of his scheme, when some of his Cossack followers bumbled their attempt to arrest Chita's military commandant for abuse of power. Perezhogin and his disciples were thrown into the regional prison, but not for long.

Verkhne-Udinsk fell to the Whites and Czechs on 20 August and the Pribaikal Front collapsed. Having not been paid their salaries for some time, the ignoble revolutionary mob was demanding that the soviet pay them their arrears before the Whites arrive and execute them. No one was foolish enough to accept paper currency, which would be worthless under a White occupation, so the authorities gradually began to dip into the state bank in Chita. Including the gold *Tsentrosibir'* had carted in from Irkutsk, the bank held about four tons of gold and six tons of silver.

Perezhogin was released from prison, apparently with the connivance of Bolshevik leaders including Ivan A. Butin, chairman of the Transbaikal Executive Committee. It was like unleashing a Siberian tiger to control a mouse problem, and the uncontrollable Perezhogin had no intention of taking orders from a Bolshevik ringmaster or anyone else. With Perezhogin on the loose, there was no way that evacuation of the gold reserves could perform according to soviet plans.

At dawn on 25 August Perezhogin led a large gang into the state bank, dispersed the security detail, and began hauling out scores of boxes and bags of gold. Chita Police Chief Borisov and his assistants, Boyarkin and Okolovich, were determined to prevent the plunder of national property and, no doubt, hoped to keep their jobs under the imminent White regime. They received word of the robbery by telephone at 6:30 a.m. and dispatched 50 policemen in three mobile groups, two to the bank and one to the Hotel Selekt. At the bank, Borisov and Boyarkin's groups arrested 60 Red Guards inside the building and quickly transported them to the police station. Okolovich faced a more chaotic situation at the Hotel Selekt, where his small force pacified an unruly Red Guard cavalry platoon in the courtyard, and then, moving on to the Hotel Dauria, succeeded in disarming an even larger force of Chinese mercenaries. A few minutes later a locomotive with a machine gun approached and several Hungarian internationalists hopped off to advance on the police position. Upon seeing the Magyar advance, the Chinese jumped the policemen and took their weapons. By mid-morning it was all over and the outnumbered and outgunned police had retreated to their headquarters.

Perezhogin and the first wave of bank robbers were already on an eastbound train to Blagoveshchensk. Later trains carried similar throngs of nouveau riche who celebrated their bank withdrawal in a marathon binge of alcohol. An atmosphere of drunken revelry prevailed at every train station between Chita and Blagoveshchensk, where passengers disembarked to shop, paying for their purchases by slicing slivers off their ingots. The Transbaikal Bolshevik boss, Ivan Butin, grumbled, 'The bastards have slapped Soviet authority'. The anarchist bacchanalia continued in Blagoveshchensk, seemingly mindless of the approach of the Japanese Army.[68]

Semenov's third offensive: the conquest of Transbaikalia

In mid-August, 2,700 Chinese troops left Peking to join Allied forces at Vladivostok and OMO suddenly reappeared on the Manchurian Front (as the Allies referred to the Red's Daurski Front). On about 21 August Semenov returned to Manchuli to face Lazo again on a narrow front stretching from the railway to Bagaita, a village about 16 miles east. OMO had established a position on a railway siding just seven miles inside Transbaikalia. A Lieutenant Shirek was marching towards Verkhne-Udinsk at the head of a 1,000-man column of Buryats he had organized in Urga since the July retreat. Semenov was well aware of the chaos reigning in Chita, and heard that the Red administration was trying to relocate to Sretensk.[69]

Bolshevik patrols were seen to the west and around Lake Kharanor, while two Red regiments and a battery were reported near Bagaita. Lazo's main body, some 4,000 men and a battery of 6-inch guns, planned a fighting withdrawal to natural defense lines behind the Borzya river, then the Onon river at Olovyannaya. A sketchy description of these forces still gave a good idea of Red order of battle:

> 2nd Verkhne-Udinsk Revolutionary Regiment
> 1st International Partisan Division or Detachment
> four *sotnia* of the 1st Argun Cavalry Regiment
> 2nd Argun Cavalry Regiment
> 2nd Zargol Detachment (Zargol is an Argun village near Byrka)
> 500-man internationalist cavalry (also referred to as the '1st Magyar Regiment')
> 450-man Anarchist Cavalry Regiment.

A 'unit of Siberian seamen' was expected to arrive, presumably from Commissar Trilisser's Baikal fleet, while a Red Chinese unit that had been raised recently was inexplicably 'dissolved'. A nervous Red field headquarters at Borzya waited for the White attack.[70]

In late August 1918, a courier from the Czechoslovak Legion made his way behind the lines to deliver a request to Semenov's headquarters 'for an OMO offensive to relieve pressure on the Czechs'.[71] The fleeing remnants of the Red Army could not arrest Gajda's aggressive eastward pursuit on the Trans-Siberian Railway, but the Bolsheviks had not lost the will to fight. On the other hand, the swift Czech advance from Verkhne-Udinsk relieved Red pressure on Semenov so that OMO could cautiously return to Transbaikalia, but resistance by the two remaining brigades of Red Guards was stiff.[72] Chita was still behind Red lines, but fighting in and around the city began no later than the third week in August. It was a confusing situation with separate groups of regular anti-Bolshevik forces advancing from the west and southeast, while irregulars operated behind the lines.

On 23 August 1918 Japan's 7th Division under General Fujii established its headquarters at Manchuli. Fujii's troops jumped at the chance to bully the Chinese. Major General Gao Fin Tchen, the local Chinese brigade commander, had

> telegraphed ahead for half of the [Manchuli] barracks to be vacated for them. On arriving, instead of quietly moving into the barracks already vacated, they went, under the command of NCOs and officers of low rank, to the barracks where the Chinese commanding general was located, and demanded that he come out and parley with them. He refused. The matter was finally settled by the Japanese taking the barracks assigned them.[73]

Such pointless intimidation seems inappropriate in light of the fact that Japan and China had signed a secret agreement for military cooperation just three months prior, however it became the Japanese behavioral norm when dealing with her allies in Russia.[74]

During the next few days, the main force of Semenov's small army spearheaded the 7th Division advance 'to dull the point of Japanese intervention'.[75] On 26 August the OMO cavalry screen was at Kharanor while Semenov was close behind at Dauria. Major General Matsievski's cavalry advanced so quickly that they took Lazo's staff by surprise near a place called Tin and dispersed them.[76] Japanese cavalry followed and close behind marched columns of Fujii's 7th Division infantrymen. A number of OMO troops tagged along with the bulk of the Japanese Division's infantry. The American summary of the campaign noted that the movement and location of these troops were obscure.[77]

The battle for Chita had begun heating up by 23 August, even though the anti-Bolshevik regulars were still days away. Cossacks led the uprising in Chita, and while they were probably composed of men from the 1st Chita Cossack Regiment (who clashed with their

Bolshevik brethren upon arrival in January), their numbers may have included OMO raiders and even renegades from the bolshevized regiments. Boris P. Clark, close friend of Sergei Lazo and a *sotnia* commander with the 1st Argun Cossack Regiment, was felled by a bullet on 23 August.[78] On 25 August, when the Cossacks sent a locomotive to Mogzon to welcome the Czechoslovak Legion, they 'claimed to be in control' of Chita, but the fight there was not over yet. During the night of 26 August, Czech legionnaires and White volunteers from Tomsk began entering Chita and found that local 'White Guards' had overthrown the soviets two days before. Most of Lazo's Red detachments – estimated to include 4,000 soldiers, 15 automobiles and three airplanes – pulled out just in front of the Czechs, however a number of Bolsheviks went into hiding in the sprawling city and forests beyond the suburbs.[79]

With Czechs and Whites beginning to swarm over the Chita area, the Red troops who were holding off the Japanese 7th Division and OMO's main body 200 miles to the southeast suddenly lost their avenue of retreat along the railway. They withdrew from Matsievskaya and Sharasun, poisoning all water tanks, wells and other stored water before they evacuated, a practice they would repeat during their retreat.[80] By 26 August, the Manchurian front had receded 70 miles into Russian territory to the village of Sokhtoi. OMO soldiers faced them at Sokhtoi, while the Japanese infantry was at Kharanor, the next village south from Sokhtoi. The Japanese cavalry, advancing across the dusty steppe west of and parallel to the railway line, ran into 'stubborn resistance' opposite Kharanor and took a few losses.

Semenov and General Fujii could afford to be cautious. The Red detachments in front of them weakened every day as Bolshevik soldiers deserted, demoralized by the news of Chita's capture and the onslaught of regular Japanese Army units. During the next two days, 27–28 August, General Fujii stationed troops in Matsievskaya and Sharasun, the towns between Manchuli and Dauria, and reinforced Dauria with an infantry battalion to guard against sabotage by Red stragglers. About this time, the Ussuri Front had become so calm that some Czechoslovak Legion troops were withdrawn from the march on Khabarovsk and put on trains to Transbaikalia.[81]

Meanwhile, the lead Czech *bronevik* and the engineering echelon pulled out of Chita to resume pursuit of the Reds early on the morning of 28 August. They covered about 50 miles in three hours. Mid-morning found them halted at a slightly damaged bridge just west of the vital railway junction at Karymskaya. A number of Cossacks approached the trains to inform the Czechs that the Reds had entrenched a short distance further and asked for arms to join in the fight. About 200 men set out on foot and horseback to encircle the Red defenses, but found their trenches empty. At 5 p.m. the *bronevik* crossed the bridge and charged into Karymskaya unimpeded. The engineering echelon followed an hour later. 'On our way in', recalled an American engineer, 'Cossacks and peasants climbed on [our] train, all anxious to see us occupy Karymskaya... We arrived at Karymskaya just at dark, people met us with cheers. A peace delegation informed us that the Czechs were welcome.'[82]

That night at the next major Trans-Siberian station to the east, Urul'ga, Bolshevik political and military leaders gathered and, after a brief session lamenting the looting of the Chita state bank by unruly anarchists and Red Guards, resolved to abandon open warfare and begin partisan operations against the Whites.[83] It was an event that would be immortalized in Soviet history books. Old comrades bid heartfelt farewells as they departed for their new underground lives, knowing that their circle would be quite smaller if they should ever meet again. Chita was to remain the center of Bolshevik activity, albeit underground, throughout the White occupation. Some local Bolsheviks, under the leadership of a commissar described as 'a railway workman of anarchist tendencies',...took to the forest, some engaging in running contraband over the Chinese frontier, others forming themselves into bands who not only robbed the isolated peasantry, but forced young men to join them, and afterwards levied toll upon large villages and small towns'.[84] From this time on, the fragile line between piracy and revolution was blurred as gangs emerged from the taiga to murder, steal and pursue other villainous activities in the name of the revolution, settling old scores along the way.

Meanwhile, OMO's advance guard pushed through the town of Borzya, where the Reds had ignited a 14,000-ton coal pile and destroyed railway equipment but left in such haste that they could not destroy the bridge over the Borzya river. The Bolsheviks were now in full flight, with the *semenovtsy* snapping at their heels, pursuing them more than 20 miles up the railway to take Khada-Bulak on 29 August, capturing 100 Reds, two machine guns and armored automobiles along the way. At 9 p.m. that night an OMO cavalry patrol caught a fleeting glance of the armored railway car at the enemy rear. One of Semenov's raiding parties was operating along the banks of the Onon river, at least 20 miles behind the fading Red lines.

A desperate evacuation was already underway at Olovyannaya. The surviving fragments of Lazo's Red Army in Transbaikalia abandoned the railway line and fled east into the desolate hills, making for the town of Aleksandrovskii Zavod. The only significant obstacle between Semenov and Chita was a flood at Olovyannaya, which seems to have washed out a temporary wooden railway bridge over the Onon. A small number of Red fighters and arms were captured there on 30 August, but most of the Bolsheviks had already retired eastward towards Sretensk. Semenov's units followed them along the banks of the Onon.[85]

Before sunrise on 31 August a Czech *bronevik* and soldiers of the 3rd Tomsk Regiment set out to link up with Semenov. About 30 miles south of the Karymskaya junction they found a deserted Bolshevik train with several guns and a large supply of 3-inch shells. The last 50 miles to OMO's advance position at Olovyannaya passed without incident. Semenov visited shortly thereafter, his forces augmented by 20 Czechoslovaks who had come from Vladivostok. The next day OMO soldiers began moving into Chita. General Fujii's cavalry details followed on 2 September 1918, yet it seems that Semenov remained near his temporary headquarters at Borzya for several days, receiving Czech staff officers and plotting with his Japanese advisors.[86]

In the ravines and gullies of the hills around him darted small groups of fugitives, scraps of western Siberian Red Army regiments, of revolutionary *sotnias* of eastern Transbaikal Cossacks' and of workers' and peasants' Red Guards. They carried their arms into the taiga, rendezvoused with other survivors and reorganized into partisan detachments. Each encampment became the seedling of a *lesnaya kommuna* – 'forest commune', – usually a well-concealed, defensible base near a sympathetic village. Veterans of the Daurski Front became the cadre for military, recruiting, agitation and supply teams.[87]

During the first week in September 1918, a large contingent of OMO Cossacks rushed to Verkhne-Udinsk and embarked upon a joint operation with the Czechs to sweep the Selenga River valley south to the Mongolian border of retreating Reds. Some 1,200 Hungarian internationalists surrendered to the Czech's Colonel Seinevich at the large town of Troitskosavsk on the Mongolian border. On the river itself, the Czechs reaped a rich bounty when they captured four steamers and three barges loaded with automobiles, machine guns, horses, food and other Red war supplies.[88]

Other OMO troops joined the Czechs and the Tomsk volunteer regiments in the eastward pursuit of the surviving Reds. They intended to sandwich the Reds against Allied forces moving west from the Pacific coast. Red commanders hoped to gather all of their remaining Siberian forces around the Amur river town of Blagoveshchensk for a last ditch stand.[89] However, the east–west vise was tightening faster than they could run. On 6 September the

Czechs occupied the eastern Transbaikal towns of Nerchinsk and Sretensk without resistance, declared martial law and continued their advance.[90]

In a strange turn of events, Nerchinsk had to be 're-liberated' four days later in a joint assault by OMO and Japanese units. The struggle for the ancient town must have been fierce, because an entire Cossack regiment, including its commanding officer, deserted Semenov on the battlefield and cast its lot with the Bolshevik side.[91] This fratricidal bloodletting was all the more bizarre considering Semenov's wartime service and post-revolution election as deputy in a Nerchinsk regiment. However, a clue to the cause of the intra-Cossack bloodshed may lie in a question posed by the Dutch journalist Lokewijk-Hermen Grondijs to Grigorii Semenov one year later: 'Why have the Nerchinsk Cossacks taken up arms against you, their elected leader? You, a Cossack, must know that to rape a worker's daughter is quite a different sort of crime from raping a Cossack's daughter.'[92]

OMO reoccupied Nerchinsk and rejoined the chase. Semenov appeared in Chita no later than 10 September, when he telegrammed the president of the government of autonomous Siberia, expressing his solidarity and stating that Amur and Ussuri Cossacks and other 'fellow countrymen' in eastern Transbaikalia had united under him and the slogan '*Za zakon i poryadok*' – 'For law and order'.[93] The telegram was published in Chita newspaper *Zabaikal'skaya Nov'* to pronounce Semenov's political stance. In the meantime the liberated areas grew when the Bolsheviks evacuated Magocha on 17 September, then Taptugary on 18 September. Transbaikalia was free of Red regulars.

During the first week in September, Mr Simpson, a correspondent for the Associated Press became concerned at the heavy-handed Japanese presence in Transbaikalia. First he noticed 'two very significant proclamations posted on the station and walls of the town' of Borzya and also in every Transbaikal railway village. In one of the Russian-language flyers, Japanese General Otani proclaimed:

> The operations of the Allied Armies on Russian territory have as their sole object the liberation of the friendly Czechoslovak troops from the power of forces organized from Austro-German prisoners and at the same time to give assistance to Russia, now suffering indescribable calamities under a misguided administration. The Allies have, therefore, for their only enemy, the forces of Austro-German prisoners and have no hostile intention whatever against the Russian people.[94]

The other proclamation stated that the populace must accept payments in gold yen banknotes which were being issued by Japanese military authorities in Manchuria, and promised that a branch of the Chosen Bank would soon open in Manchuli so that people could redeem them. Hoping to obtain a few copies of the flyers, Simpson went to the printshop that published them and left empty-handed, but found out that the Japanese had paid for 2,000 flyers with their new banknotes. Simpson pondered, 'Why is it that Japan wishes to pay for what she buys from the Russians in gold yen when she has got plenty of Russian paper?' The official exchange rate was five 'Romanov rubles' to the yen. Even more provocative were the prominent Japanese flags flying at every town from Manchuli to Borzya, and the Japanese soldiers who had taken over Chinese Eastern Railway stations, bridges and tunnels from Manchuli to Bukhedu. 'Former Chinese troops completely vanished', mused Simpson.[95]

Yet Semenov bristled at another foreign intrusion. At 2 p.m. on 5 September, a special train arrived at Olovyannaya from the east bearing Major General Mikhail Konstantinovich Diterikhs, the Czech Legion division commander in the Maritime province, Dr Girsa, the Czechoslovak political representative and military attachés from Britain, France and Japan.

The 'splendid 7th Regimental band' of the Czech Legion hammered out the national anthems of all present, including the chief of the American Red Cross, then all hushed for the speech of their host, the prodigious General Radola Gajda. The next day, Simpson, the AP correspondent, headed south and was startled to pass 'Horvath's train... hurrying in answer to Gajda's request to visit him [at Olovyannaya]'. Simpson expected his interview of Gajda to 'make a great scoop for the AP' owing to the young general's 'masterful feat... in dealing [a] death blow to the Bolsheviks'.[96]

A momentous, yet anticlimactic, day came on 22 September, 1918. One group of Reds dashed across the Amur river into Manchuria and Japanese and Chinese troops surrounded them near Mohe and forced their surrender. Meanwhile, pursuit of the main body of Reds along the Trans-Siberian Railway had extended into Amur province. That same day Japanese cavalry caught up with them near Ushumun station, inflicted heavy losses and captured '50 saddle horses, 20 pack horses and 100 rifles'.[97] Yet the most significant event occurred quietly at an Amur village called Lefrovo. There some of Fujii's 7th Division cavalrymen ran into a detachment from their own army's 12th Division. At Lefrovo, the Japanese pincers from Transbaikalia and the Pacific Coast closed.[98]

Czech liberation – or occupation? – of Vladivostok and Nikolsk-Ussuriisk

The anti-Bolshevik pincer from the Pacific coast had begun its westward movement on the Trans-Siberian Railway nearly three months before. On the morning of 29 June, the Czechoslovak Legion ousted the Bolsheviks in Vladivostok in a violent coup d'état. Although their relations with the city's Bolshevik administration had been relatively cordial, the Czechs felt pressured to take the port that guaranteed their exit from the Siberian morass. The Czechs had no territorial ambitions in Siberia – they just wanted to get out.[99] This meant holding Vladivostok until their transport ships came in, and clearing hundreds of miles of railway of stubborn Bolshevik resistance.

The night before the coup Major General Mikhail K. Diterikhs, the Russian officer in charge of the 15,000 or so Czechs in Vladivostok, informed the Allied consuls of his intentions. At 10 a.m. the next morning, a Czechoslovak Legion company formed up in front of the offices of the soviet, delivered a 30-minute ultimatum and, having received no reply by 10:30, broke into the building and confiscated all weapons.[100] They invaded the telegraph office an hour and a half later. The Czech takeover took the Bolsheviks by surprise. The Red headquarters, located in an old fortress opposite the Trans-Siberian Railway terminal, held out against the Czechs until 6 p.m. on 29 June. About 100 Red Guards resisted the Czechs while most of the Bolsheviks escaped, but there was some shooting and the day's casualties amounted to 83 dead and wounded on both sides.[101]

Three Japanese cruisers and single warships from Britain, France, China and the United States had been waiting in the harbor since late winter, watching over the enormous inventory of Allied supplies that had piled up beside Vladivostok's piers during the war. Small British and Japanese landing parties came ashore that day to show their support for the Czechs. In the afternoon the Chinese landed 80 men and the Americans dispatched 20 for the sole purpose of protecting resident nationals. On 30 June Admiral Kato Kanji, commander of the Japanese naval squadron, disarmed three Russian destroyers and one auxiliary. One week after the Czech coup, British, French and Japanese forces put the Vladivostok area 'under their protection'.[102]

The Canadian observer Major James Mackintosh Bell arrived in Vladivostok during these 'anxious days'. He recalled, 'The great majority of the population of the city was still strongly Bolshevik in sympathy and even many of those who were not resented what they considered the arrogant attitude of the Czechs. Enormous processions of Red mourners accompanied the funeral of the Bolshevik victims of the Czech attack on the Staff Headquarters'.[103]

As soon as they took Vladivostok the Czechs launched an offensive to clear the Reds from the railway. In the first 70 miles of their drive the Czechs encountered little resistance. Then they came to Nikolsk-Ussuriisk, junction of the Chinese Eastern and Amur lines. The Bolsheviks and their internationalist detachments put up a fierce defense of this strategic little city on the Suyfun river, peacetime population: 30,000. Heavy fighting raged for days. Finally, 'by dint of immense perseverance in the face of very considerable odds' the outnumbered Czech Second Division forced a Bolshevik withdrawal on 5 July.[104]

Back in Vladivostok, a provisional government sprang up, but it had no popular support and only a token military force christened 'the New Army', which consisted of a few hundred former tsarist officers under a Colonel Tolstov. General Horvath, his two Japanese advisors and a large entourage soon arrived from Harbin in a caravan of luxurious trains that planted itself on a siding about a mile south of Vladivostok's train station.[105] On 9 July he had proclaimed a new all-Russian government (which appropriately became known as the *Delovoi Kabinet* – the Business Cabinet) while his retinue sat in Grodekovo, the first town inside the Maritime Province on the Chinese Eastern. Accustomed to the duties of an exalted potentate, Horvath began making political appointments and receiving visitors.[106] Reactionary generals and colonels seemed to crawl out of the woodwork. The city was bloated with their oversized egos and glorious ambitions. Siberia's White movement had no shortage of governments: in Omsk, Petr Vologodskii's Provisional Siberian Government was struggling to set up shop and establish an administration, Petr Derber's Provisional Government of Autonomous Siberia 'lived on sufferance in some railway carriages at the [Harbin] station', and Semenov's temporary government of the Transbaikal Territory was poised in a handful of towns near the Russo-Manchurian border.[107] Meanwhile, the Czechoslovak Legion spearheaded the assaults against the Bolsheviks.

Despite serious losses and skimpy reserves, the Czechoslovaks pursued the Bolsheviks up the Amur line in the direction of the city of Khabarovsk, 400 miles north of Nikolsk-Ussuriisk. The Czechoslovaks bogged down four miles north of a little whistle-stop named Kraevski, about halfway to Khabarovsk. Both sides, exhausted by the chase, dug trenches, set up 'strong points in the hills with a light gun or two', positioned machine guns and lookout posts, and settled down to rest in late July.[108] The Czech lines were fragile; their artillery support consisted of three mountain guns which were 'old, worn-out, short in range and generally ineffective'.[109] Luckily the Bolsheviks were no better equipped. A semblance of chivalry still existed between combatants. When 2,000 Czechoslovaks captured the town of Ivanovka on about 11 August, 'There were no repressions from their side', wrote the young son of the local Bolshevik health officer. 'Life went on in its usual way, without any changes.'[110] Sheep and cattle grazed around a pastoral front line. 'Peasants were garnering the harvest, apparently quite uninterested as to whether Bolshevik or Tsar ruled in Petrograd.'[111]

Internationalists and interventionists

Calm settled across the Ussuri Front for several days in mid-August. Major Bell paid a visit to the front and observed a Czechoslovak armored train – just a locomotive hauling a freight car 'mounted with a light field gun and several machine guns'. The 'armored train occasionally sallied beyond this point [Kraevski] to exchange shots at a distance of five miles or so with its Bolshevik opponent, the maneuvers of which were extremely amusing to watch through a telescope, as their shooting, fortunately, was poor'.[112]

As in Transbaikalia and other Siberian cities, a number of 'internationalists', mostly German and Hungarian prisoners of war, were recruited by the Bolsheviks for the defense of the Russian Far East. The small internationalist detachments brought badly needed expertise to the inexperienced Bolshevik ranks. The Bolsheviks' Amur river flotilla was said to be directed by the German naval officer who had commanded the German light cruiser *Magdeburg*, which ran aground and was destroyed by two Russian cruisers off Odensholm Island in the Baltic in August 1914.[113] Amidst the pines and broad-leafed woods north of Nikolsk-Ussuriisk, Edward Heald, an American Young Men's Christian Association (YMCA) volunteer who had served recently on the Western Front, noticed evidence of German handiwork in the Bolsheviks' 'admirable' trenches. '[They were] not simple Russian trenches, but artistic, scientific trenches with trap doors and hidden passages.'[114]

Combat with the internationalists was loudly trumpeted in the Allied press, but the Allies still did not have a true picture of how many German and Austro-Hungarian POWs had actually volunteered, while their technical expertise, combat experience, discipline under fire and competent leadership magnified their presence far out of proportion to their actual number. For example, out of 2,500 prisoners of war at the Evgenevski camp near Vladivostok, only 120 Hungarians, 30 Germans and one Turk left with the Red recruiters.[115] It was surmised that the Hungarians joined out of animosity for the Czechs, and the Germans to continue the war against the Allies. The solitary Turk's motivations were a mystery. A German–Magyar–Bolshevik conspiracy theory held sway, not only among Russia's shrill reactionaries like Ussuri Cossack Ataman Ivan Kalmykov, but in respectable Allied diplomatic circles as well. Back in April 1918, the French ambassador to Russia had spoken of Germans organizing 'colonial centers in Siberia', and on 3 July a British assistant military attaché to China insisted that 'there is no doubt but that German influence is rapidly increasing in Transbaikalia'.[116] The myth that Lenin and company were financed by Kaiser Wilhelm II was still pervasive, and fostered paranoia and confusion among the Allies and anti-Bolshevik forces.

The reality was not so sensational. Most POWs had been in Siberia for between three and three and a half years, in which time several hundred of them had married Russian women and fathered children. Accordingly, few POWs were gullible enough to swallow the Red propagandists' sales pitches for world revolution. The American YMCA secretary Edward Heald concluded, 'They all seemed to want to go to America.'[117] Nevertheless, in the absence of accurate intelligence, heads of state in Tokyo, London, Paris and Washington based their July 1918 decisions in favor of Allied intervention partly upon this exaggerated German–Magyar threat to Asia.[118]

Before the interventionists even set foot in Siberia, the Allies had laid claim to large detachments of Rumanian, Serbian and Polish soldiers, separated from their homelands by hostile territory and anxious to demonstrate their solidarity with the anti-Bolshevik cause. Most had been in units of the Austro-Hungarian Army that deserted to the Russians during the First World War rather than fight for their oppressors against fellow Slavs.

In contrast, many men of the Polish Legion had served in the Russian Army, and had formed nationalist units as the empire and the army began to disintegrate. Bound by their Roman Catholic faith and the powerful call of their homeland, they occupied Samara with the Czechoslovak Legion and People's Komuch Army, fought a number of battles against the Bolsheviks near Ufa, and would stalwartly persevere on the frontlines until the very end. At its peak strength, nearly 12,000 Poles were fighting the Reds in Siberia.[119]

On 3 August Colonel John Ward and the British Army's 25th Middlesex Battalion arrived at Vladivostok from Hong Kong. At the wharf they received a lukewarm greeting from a small honor guard of Colonel Tolstov's 'New Army', a 1,000-strong army funded by the municipality and local *zemstvo*. Then the British marched through town, a Czechoslovak Legion band blaring in front of them, as sullen crowds of locals eyed them maliciously.[120] Only the prostitutes on Kopek Hill and the saloon-keepers welcomed the interventionists.[121]

Similar morose welcomes hailed the arrival of subsequent newcomers to Vladivostok's piers. Six days after the Middlesex Battalion landed, the first 300 of 760 French colonial troops arrived from their Saigon garrison.[122] On 12 August Japanese soldiers began swarming ashore. They would eventually number more than 70,000 throughout the Russian Far East, Siberia and Manchuria.[123] One week later, Vladivostok streets were clogged with yet another parade, this time of the first contingent of the US Army's American Expeditionary Force, Siberia (AEFS). The marchers belonged to the 27th Infantry Regiment who had been eager to leave their Philippine garrison to fight the Germans and contribute to the war effort. They were a bit surprised to discern 'passive hostility' from the onlookers which was attributed to 'a predominance of the Bolsheviki element', but were warmly hailed with cheers and applause as they neared the Czechoslovak Legion headquarters.[124]

By late August the first contingent of the AEFS was joined by the 31st Infantry Regiment, also coming from garrison duty in the Philippines and augmented by 5,000 men of the 8th Division from Camp Fremont, California.[125] To Polish prisoner of war Roman Dyboski, a product of Warsaw's intelligentsia, 'The soldiers were mostly of the Apache-hooligan type that, prior to the World War, made up the American Army'.[126] Dyboski attributed the coarseness of men of the 27th and 31st to 'service among the slothful inhabitants of the Philippines'. Dyboski recalled a conversation with an 'American medical Colonel' about the varieties of venereal disease among the US troops: '[the Colonel] took me by the hand and cried, "If only they had not brought so many here with them!" ' Of the American officers, the Pole said, 'With none of [them] was it possible to carry on a conversation that to any European would seem intelligent'.[127] Many of the hard-drinking, unrefined American soldiers sympathized with the Russian peasants and would enjoy consistently better relations with them than did their swaggering west European and Japanese allies.

The Allied contingents clung to divergent visions of their purpose in Siberia. The British and French hoped to reopen the Eastern Front against the Germans. Japan saw an opportunity to expand her area of political and commercial influence. President Wilson sent the US Army to Siberia to facilitate the Czechoslovak Legion's evacuation and, while they were at it, to keep an eye on the Japanese. No wonder that the chief purpose of the Allied intervention was unclear to the US commander, Major General William Sidney Graves.[128] Weeks earlier, during a brief rendezvous in the Kansas City railway station, US Secretary of War Newton Baker had handed Graves a copy of Washington's vague orders as the General boarded a train, saying, 'This contains the policy of the United States in Russia which you are to follow. Watch your step; you will be walking on eggs loaded with dynamite'. Major General Graves later wrote, 'I was in command of the United States troops sent to Siberia and I must admit, I do not know what the United States was trying to accomplish by military intervention'.[129] His troops were mystified as well. To confuse matters further, a US Navy landing party had gone ashore from the USS *Olympia* on 3 August at Archangel, a port on the Arctic Ocean several thousand miles away, and begun aggressively pursuing Bolsheviks down the railway line. No one was sure of what they were expected to do.

Russian Railway Service Corps

Among the throngs of US troops disembarking in Vladivostok in August 1918 were about 100 American railwaymen of the Russian Railway Service Corps (RRSC). Their Siberian landfall finally gave the Japanese and Bolshevik governments common cause, because both shared consternation at the appearance of these decidedly apolitical technical experts, albeit for very different reasons. The Japanese sensed only the commercial competition that these men symbolized, because Tokyo had hopes of extending its own railway networks in Korea and southern Manchuria into northern Manchuria, Transbaikalia and Russia's Far East, but the Russians – all except Semenov, it seems – recognized that the Japanese offering of technical assistance was merely a Trojan horse to absorb their railways. The Bolsheviks simply considered the RRSC the transportation arm for a White and Allied campaign to oust them. Originally intended to help a democratic Russia in the fight against the Central Powers, the RRSC became a strategic pawn in the Russian civil war and the international political games swirling through it.

The RRSC was the brainchild of the American Advisory Commission of Railway Experts, both of which operated under the aegis of the US State Department and under the personal supervision of John F. Stevens, the builder of the Panama Canal and the Great Northern Railway.[130]

The relationship with Russia began in April 1917 when the United States, having just enthusiastically recognized the fledgling provisional government, bestowed upon it $325 million in credit for the purchase of 1,500 locomotives and 30,000 rail cars. Stevens oversaw the transaction. Two months later, Stevens and a few other American railway experts arrived in Petrograd to help plan the modernization of Russian railways, with the specific goal of improving Trans-Siberian efficiency and repairing the military supply line from Vladivostok to the front lines in Europe. For seven weeks the Americans languished through interminable negotiations, first with minor bureaucrats of the Ministry of Ways and Communication (the railway and telegraph authority), then with the ministry's Council of Engineers and then with Comrade Minister L.A. Ustrugov. Finally, on 10 August, Stevens gained an audience with Premier Kerensky, who ordered that the Americans' recommendations be implemented at once.[131]

Back in the United States, the War Department quickly circulated appeals for RRSC volunteers 'over railway wires and roundhouse bulletin boards' to enlist experienced American railway men – superintendents, trainmasters, dispatchers, auditors and other specialists, who would be paid out of the credits to the Russian government.[132] George H. Emerson, general manager of the Great Northern Railway, recruited most RRSC candidates from northwestern states like the Dakotas and Montana, 'where long hauls and the rigors of the climate most closely approximated the conditions' the men would face in Siberia.[133] The RRSC was originally composed of 74 men from the Baldwin Locomotive Company and eastern lines in Philadelphia, 215 men from the Great Northern and Western at St Paul, Minnesota and about 30 Russian – American mechanics and interpreters from San Francisco.[134] Men selected for the RRSC were granted commissions by the War Department although they remained a State Department organization. They were also exempted from the draft and paid more than military officers, but the driving forces for the recruits, most of whom were family men and were older than the typical military recruit, were simple patriotism and the chance to employ their technical expertise in the fight against Germany.

The RRSC's transport ship USS *Thomas* steamed into Vladivostok harbor in December 1917, but owing to the Bolshevik takeover in European Russia and the resulting lawlessness in the port, not to mention a lack of housing, the *Thomas* sailed away to Nagasaki, Japan and deposited the befuddled engineers to await orders from the US State Department. John Reed ranted about the significance of this turnaround – in Red eyes:

> Mr Stevens, could have begun work in Siberia...long before March 1918, if they had really wanted to help the Russians and oppose the Germans. When the Bolshevik uprising took place, Mr Stevens and his Railway Corps fled to Japan, and sat there, in the best hotels, hobnobbing with the Allied and Japanese Imperialists. While the Brest-Litovsk negotiations were going on, the Soviet Government asked the American Government to send the Railway Mission into Russia. It promised to appoint Mr Stevens, or anyone else designated, to be Assistant Commissar of Ways and Communications, with complete authority over half the transportation lines of all Russia. But the American Government was not interested, evidently, in saving munitions from the Germans; it was more interested in upsetting the Soviet Government.[135]

Stevens' 27 March 1918 agreement with Horvath picked up where the American Advisory Commission and the provisional government had left off in November 1917. To howls of protest from the Japanese and the Bolsheviks, 110 men of the RRSC deployed on the Chinese Eastern Railway in March. Whites would soon join the plaintive chorus.

In early May 1918, Semenov asked for assistance from the RRSC unit on the Chinese Eastern. Secretary of State Lansing was firm in his response (via Ambassador Francis, then at Vologda), 'The work of these engineers should not be diverted to support any movement partaking of civil war nor to facilitate the military operations of Semenov'.[136]

Meanwhile, the remainder of the RRSC was forced to relax in Nagasaki, where, initially, their Japanese hosts rolled out the red carpet and feted them. In the acrid words of John Reed, they 'sat there, in the best hotels, hobnobbing with the Allied and Japanese Imperialists'. While the men fought boredom and filled their days with tennis, volleyball and soccer matches, baseball games, cultural lectures, tours, church services, teas, concerts, benefits and dances, the State Department hoped for a palatable pseudo-democratic government to appear. By the time the Provisional Siberian Government materialized in August, about 80 men had already returned to the United States, and US relations with Japan had become awkward and chilly, as was the RRSC's send-off, coming on the heels of a suspicious burglary of the Nagasaki Hotel.[137]

From Vladivostok the RRSC dispersed across the Trans-Siberian Railway in August, appearing in stations large and small, roundhouses, shops, railyards and, most of all, aboard the trains and locomotives – everything from 'small saddle-back tank switch engines to the large Baldwin decapods' – rumbling slowly through the taiga. Although they wore US Army uniforms and bore military ranks, they were, technically speaking, employees of the US State Department, but they viewed themselves as missionaries of American technology, there to make the Russian railwayman's life easier and more efficient. Once the men were deposited at lonely train stations on the frozen Siberian steppes and taiga, their only link to the world was via the fragile wires of a very vulnerable and unreliable telegraph system. Very soon they became witnesses to revolutions and the horrors of civil war, in which they also became tactical pawns.

Ataman Kalmykov

Major Bell met Ivan Pavlovich Kalmykov near the battle front of the Maritime Province in summer 1918, and described him as

> a little man, about five feet two inches in height, with a trim lady-like waist, small and delicate hands, and a face even more boyish than his twenty-five or twenty-six years would suggest. Clad in Cossack shirt, bright-colored trousers, and high fur cap, with sword attached to his gaily ornamented belt, he looked a striking and interesting figure, contrasting strangely with his huge, burly comrades. His manners were so courtly as to be almost elegant, so much so that in recalling him to memory at a somewhat later date, it seemed impossible to associate so apparently gentle a creature with the bloodthirsty excesses he committed.[138]

Kalmykov was not a Cossack himself, but his fate and that of the Ussuri Cossack Host became irretrievably entangled. The February Revolution struck an idealistic cord among many Ussuri Cossacks who, in the revolutionary excitement of mid-March 1917, convened a special meeting at Nikolsk that impulsively chose to not only get rid of the elected ataman, but to renounce the Cossacks' special status and merge with the peasant population, pending approval of the Constituent Assembly. Captain N.L. Popov was elected chairman of a temporary executive committee and assumed the responsibilities of ataman. With these events appeared a fractious schism between revolutionary and traditional Cossacks, the latter of whom were loath to relinquish their privileges, which, after all, had been paid for in lives, blood and heartache at the front. In a second *voiskovii krug* (traditional assembly of the Cossack Host) in Nikolsk in April 1917, a convocation of Ussuri Cossacks elected Popov ataman and maintained the momentum to abolish the Host's special status, while an October *krug* reversed the motion. In January 1918, the fourth *krug* convened, this time swollen with recently returned troops from the front, and, even though many of them were pro-Bolshevik, the delegates refused to recognize Soviet authority, condemned the dispersal of the Constituent Assembly, and elected a young traditionalist, *Pod'esaul* (Junior Captain) I.P. Kalmykov, as ataman.[139] Presumably Kalmykov was not an altogether unknown candidate to the Cossacks. His detractors would later claim that Kalmykov (or his Japanese cohorts) murdered the legitimate candidate for ataman and, abetted by covert Japanese pressure and bribes, muscled his way into the elected post.[140]

Major General Nakajima had assigned Captain Yokoo Noriyoshi, a young military intelligence officer from the army of occupation in Korea, to advise Kalmykov (as well, of course, as to report on him). Kalmykov later claimed that the Reds offered him 'supplies and money' if he would join them, but he refused.[141] In late February, Nakajima endorsed Kalmykov and formally requested money from Tokyo to bankroll him. In the meantime, the new ataman began making quiet preparations to take over the Iman train station, which was situated about 250 miles north of Vladivostok, roughly halfway to Khabarovsk.[142]

The schism yawned dangerously wide when the quarrelsome Ussuri Cossacks gathered for the fifth *krug* in Iman, on 3–5 March 1918, to decide on a collective approach to the Bolshevik takeover.[143] Britain and Japan sent agents to lobby for an anti-Bolshevik stance – a Major Dunlop from the British Army and three Japanese officers detailed by Major General Nakajima. Kalmykov also attended, where a Japanese agent named Alekshin (apparently a Russian national) persuaded the assembly to confirm him as ataman, based upon the young captain's ability to secure aid from the British and Japanese.[144] Regardless, a large body of veterans just back from the front refused to recognize Kalmykov and many pro-Soviet villages and settlements stood behind them.[145]

Red agents found out about Kalmykov's plot to take over Iman station and kindle an anti-Bolshevik uprising so they set out to arrest him. On 6 March he took refuge in the British Consulate in Vladivostok, where he continued conspiring with British and Japanese diplomats, military and naval officers and was the grateful recipient of a 1 million ruble grant from Major General Nakajima. Kalmykov announced a mobilization of the Ussuri Cossacks and escorted Nakajima to Iman on 9 March to see Japan's beneficiaries in action against the Reds. Unfortunately, the Cossacks did not respond to Kalmykov's call and the mobilization was a failure. A handful of followers fled with Kalmykov to Pogranichnaya where he announced the formation of the *Osobii Kazach'ii Otryad* (OKO) – the Special Cossack Detachment.[146] Pogranichnaya was a sleepy way-station on the Manchuria–Russia border consisting of a depot, customs house and a few small buildings, but it was strategically located 400 miles east of Harbin and just a short train ride from Nikolsk and Vladivostok.

General Gao, the local Chinese Army commander, objected to Kalmykov recruiting in the border area but could not prevent the Japanese from delivering 500 Arisaka Model 1905 infantry rifles with bayonets and ample ammunition on 13 March. Five days later, six additional Japanese officers were assigned to Lieutenant Colonel Sakabe's detail in Vladivostok to monitor local political developments and support Kalmykov.[147]

'France also supported me', stated Kalmykov, 'by opening a credit for the needs of the Ussuri troops amounting to 100,000 rubles monthly'.[148] During the spring of 1918, Kalmykov also established contact with Semenov and kept in close touch ever after. The British consul in Vladivostok purchased a vast amount of seedcorn to distribute to the Cossacks to cultivate goodwill, but it was not dispensed because it seemed that most of it would fall into Bolshevik hands. Kalmykov's critics later charged that he was authorized by the Ussuri Cossack assembly to seek a loan to finance their spring planting, and used the opportunity to cut his first lucrative deal with the Japanese.[149] Meanwhile, the pro-Soviet faction reconvened the fifth *krug* again at Iman on 8–14 May and reiterated the decision to disband the Host.[150]

OKO had about 150 men and attracted few newcomers as it lurked in the northeastern corner of Manchuria, stalked by a military train full of Red Ussuri Cossacks under G.M. Shevchenko. In early June Kalmykov got the opportunity to prove his worth when he blocked the path of Admiral Kolchak's temperamental dash towards Vladivostok with the Orlov Detachment, thus preventing the embarrassing domestic strife between General Horvath and Kolchak from exposing its ugly sores to the Bolsheviks and the world press, but marking OKO as a Japanese tool. Major Bell observed that, until the Czech coup in Vladivostok in June 1918, 'Kalmykov had taken refuge, with his small force, in the woods which surrounded the Cossack villages'.[151]

Ataman Kalmykov 'invaded' Russia on 4 July, taking the border town of Grodekovo then trying to make his way to Nikolsk-Ussuriisk to launch a mobilization campaign of the Ussuri Cossacks. General Khreshchatitskii, formerly of the Ussuri Cossack Division and presently in Horvath's employ, was said to have sent Kalmykov's train to Nikolsk to commence this mobilization without first consulting his new boss, General Pleshkov. Local Japanese commanders were suspected of encouraging Kalmykov and Khreshchatitskii to charge into Russia, fearing that the Czechoslovakians' penchant for democracy revealed military weakness and a softness for Bolshevism. Kalmykov issued a lengthy proclamation that elucidated his beliefs and intentions. It recalled the events and promises of the February and October Revolutions, and blamed the Germans for fomenting the Bolshevik pox and civil war. 'Citizens! It is impossible to live like this any longer!' screamed Kalmykov's manifesto, calling all to arms. Then he closed his proclamation with the slogans: 'Long live general, direct, equal and secret voting! Long live the Siberian

Constituent Assembly! Long live the All-Russian Constituent Assembly!' Apart from a single rambling reference to 'Jews and criminals of various degrees', he sounded like a reasonable fellow.[152]

On 7 or 8 July, Czechoslovaks of Major General Diterikhs' 2nd Division encountered OKO on the Chinese Eastern Railway between Golenki and Nikolsk-Ussuriisk, leading about 200 Cossacks aboard an armored train east into the Maritime province, to all appearances coming to claim territory for General Horvath, who was not far behind. The fiery lieutenant probably had no intention of claiming territory for General Horvath – he allegedly declared on 7 July that he would not serve General Pleshkov, Horvath's military commander. Kalmykov was dismayed that the Czechs did not allow him to pass, but the Allied consular corps had forbidden them to cooperate with any Russian political factions, a restriction that would very soon be impossible to observe. Paradoxically, the Allied consuls' action came at the request of 'the local Nikolsk civil authorities, the [Nikolsk] Municipality and the Zemstvo', which accused Kalmykov of shooting Cossacks who refused mobilization. Similarly, Nikolsk authorities opposed a proposal for Kalmykov to conduct joint military operations with the Czechoslovak Legion because 'it would alienate the population against the Czechs'. It was ironic that when Kalmykov finally got the chance to charge into Russia, he suffered the humiliation of being threatened with disarmament in his own country (or deportation) by a foreign army. Khreshchatitskii was relieved from Horvath's service and renewed his relationship with Semenov.[153]

Horvath and his unabashedly bourgeois Business Cabinet were already viewed with suspicion by socialists and liberals but stirred up fear and resentment by 'invading' the Maritime province with his officer corps. Indeed, Horvath seemed to have trouble making friends. Japanese officers accompanied the officer corps, but 'he does not speak in too friendly a tone' of them noted Major Barrows, adding that Horvath was also 'very bitter against the Americans, apparently mistrusting their motives'. He was allowing American railway experts to be employed on the Chinese Eastern Railway, but refusing to give them executive powers. On the other hand, the few Ussuri Cossacks who responded to Kalmykov and Khreshchatitskii's call for mobilization flocked to Horvath's officer corps rather than OKO.[154]

When the Czechs eventually began their drive on Khabarovsk, Kalmykov and his men eagerly joined them. He had been cleared of the charges of executing recalcitrant Cossacks by a commission (which included Kalmykov's sponsor, Major Dunlop) that convened on 17 July, and declared the rumors to be false.[155] Kalmykov's bravery and recklessness in battle endeared him to his Cossack disciples, and his viciousness and cruelty engendered fear in the populace.

Allied liberation of Khabarovsk

The relative calm on the Ussuri front began to dissolve at Kraevski on 24 August, when an attack by 5,000 Reds west of the railway failed, although they had managed to encircle Ataman Kalmykov's Detachment and force its fighting withdrawal.[156] The Bolsheviks started a gradual northward withdrawal towards Khabarovsk, destroying the railway and pillaging along the way.[157] Railway workers who watched the Reds retreat up the banks of the Ussuri river counted 4,000 infantrymen (about 1,000 Red Guards from Nikolsk-Ussuriisk, 3,500 from Grodekovo, and 500 of obscure origin), two squadrons of cavalry, and 19 artillery pieces (three howitzers, 12 field pieces and four mountain guns).[158] A few armored trains and ammunition cars accompanied them. This ragtag revolutionary army had managed to hold the Czechs since mid-August, but now the Japanese 12th Division (the Oi Division) was spearheading the drive on Khabarovsk.

The city had grown weary of its revolutionary experiment. The cost of living had grown unbearable and food was rationed through a 'meal-ticket system'. 'A workman who arrived from Khabarovsk says that the inhabitants are leaving... and going to the villages. The ranks of the Red Guards are full of undisciplined youths, and the spirit is a gloomy one', read an American intelligence report. The hysterical flight of Reds from Transbaikalia to the east had even prompted Amur province authorities to demand of Chita, 'Stop sending troops as there are plenty of them in Khabarovsk'. Loose Allied estimates put the number at 5,000 'Austro-Germans' and 3,000 Bolsheviks with two aircraft at their disposal.[159]

Allied officers in Vladivostok gave the AEFS staff the impression that a powerful Red horde built around a vengeful corps of released German and Austro-Hungarian prisoners had assembled to the north. The Americans rushed to join the other Allied forces massing along the Nikolsk-Khabarovsk railway: several battalions of Japanese under Brigadier General Mihara, the British Middlesex Battalion, a company of French *poilus*, Czechoslovaks of the Legion's 5th Regiment, and the 'friendly Russian forces' of Ataman Kalmykov.[160] Men of HMS *Suffolk* threw together an armored train equipped with two 12-pound naval guns and two machine guns, and raced into action.[161] Japanese field and heavy artillery harmonized with Czech mountain guns to rake the assault area from Dukhovoe. At dawn the Allies launched an attack across a river just north of Dukhovoe, and the Bolsheviks engaged them in a gory hand-to-hand fight where even a Japanese commander 'Captain Konsumi met a glorious death, being hit by an enemy grenade'. For most other combatants, bitterness far outweighed the glory as the Reds made the Allies bleed for every step forward until the vicinity of Kraevski. A Red armored train emerged to pin down a Japanese infantry company as it advanced across a marshy field, wounding 40 men before its commander, Captain Nishida, rallied them. They subsequently captured two armored trains, and the enemy broke, retiring with the Allies in pursuit, leaving some 300 dead on the battlefield. The Japanese lost about half that number. Documents taken from the dead Bolsheviks allowed Allied intelligence to piece together a Red order of battle:

1st through 5th Battalions of the Red Army
Shevchenko's Detachment
1st Khabarovsk International Partisan Detachment.

On 27 August, Japanese and OKO troops beat the Bolsheviks at Shmakovka, then pressed on about 35 miles further to reach the Tanga river in an effort to prevent the Reds from destroying any but small bridges.[162]

On 29 and 30 August, Major David P. Barrows, now the AEFS intelligence officer, led three enlisted men mounted on motorcycles to thoroughly survey the field of action around Kraevski. Corpses littered the abandoned trenches and bivouacs. Barrows and his men scrutinized the fields of fire, battle damage and locations of the rotting bodies. 'My judgment is that the strength of the enemy previous to the "Combat of Kraevski", as given to us by the Japanese General Staff and by Allied Intelligence Officers, was greatly exaggerated, as were also the current estimates of the enemy's casualties.'[163] The desperate picture of the Allied situation had been conjured up solely to draw the Americans into the Siberian quagmire more quickly.

On their way to the front the green doughboys' trains carried them past the old lines at Kraevski, where they could take note of the trenches and bomb craters marring the landscape, the hulks of locomotives and armored cars which the Bolsheviks ran off the tracks during their retreat, the repaired battle damage on the bridges over the Ussuri river, and the lingering aroma of gunpowder.[164] This just whetted their appetites for real combat. On

30 August they joined their Allied comrades on the front lines and, to their surprise, the Americans came under attack immediately – by swarms of fierce mosquitoes.[165] Kalmykov's OKO occupied Iman this day, while, on the Ussuri river in sight of the town of Muravev'-Amurskii, a Japanese naval squadron drove away a flotilla of five Red transports carrying 500 men, two artillery pieces and eight machine guns.[166]

During the first days of September, men of the US 27th Infantry Regiment helped OKO and the Japanese 12th Division to capture Khabarovsk. There was not much of a battle, as the Reds tried to abandon the city with their forces intact.[167] 'The Bolsheviks, in great part, melted into the farms and villages', said Major Bell, 'leaving their German, Austrian and Turkish mercenaries behind to be taken prisoners'.[168] Shortly after sunrise on 5 September, 1918 Ataman Kalmykov's cavalry galloped into Khabarovsk, followed closely by Japanese units.[169]

Bands of Reds took to the forests. 'The Red detachments of Mukhin, Krasnoshchekov, Shilov and others, under the "leadership" of the [recently freed] penal element of Sakhalin and eastern Siberia, were scattered throughout the [Amur and Maritime] region', wrote Anatoli Gutman. On 8 September, a Japanese destroyer landed a 300-man detachment under a Major Ishikawa to occupy Fort Chnyrrakh and protect Nikolaevsk-on-Amur, the administrative center of Sakhalin.[170] Life in most of Sakhalin and Kamchatka continued largely oblivious to the revolution and civil war, while the Reds hacked out camps in the taiga and gathered up survivors and stragglers from Khabarovsk.[171]

Most of Khabarovsk's liberators were Japanese, but the US Philippine garrison got to share in the brief glory of a victory for the war effort. In these first exuberant days in Siberia, the US soldiers thought their participation was simply an extension of the grand battle against Germany and its Bolshevik agents. Reality quickly soured their noble sentiments. Men of the US 27th Infantry and their commander, Colonel Charles H. Morrow, were horrified at atrocities perpetrated by OKO in Khabarovsk. Upon their entry into the city, Morrow's doughboys came across 11 naked bodies sprawled in front of the cathedral. They later found the corpses of 16 Austrian musicians. They were the handiwork of the *kalmykovtsy*, the reactionary followers of Ataman Ivan Kalmykov.

The story of the murdered Austrian musicians in Khabarovsk circulated in many forms. Major Bell heard that Kalmykov disliked their music, and flatly ordered, 'That music is awful. I order these players to be shot'.[172] But the Polish prisoner of war scribe, Roman Dyboski, related that the Austrians 'were all accomplished musicians', who had given 'twelve symphony concerts such as Khabarovsk had never dreamed of hearing before, and probably has never heard since'. They had requested – and received – permission from Kalmykov to play summer promenade concerts in the city park. Meanwhile, some information was forwarded to Kalmykov

> from some jealous rival musician to the effect that some of the [Austrian] musicians in the orchestra had given a night's lodging to a Bolshevik attempting to escape from the city... The next day, in the morning, the orchestra was going down the main street of the city, preparing to assemble for rehearsal. Kalmykov's Cossacks fell upon them, and, beating them unmercifully, drove them along the street to the park where they were to play.

There, on a precipice high over the Amur River – 'in full view of the public promenading in the park' – Kalmykov's brutes executed the musicians.[173]

'His killings continued', stated Colonel Morrow, the 27th Infantry commander, 'dead bodies being found all over the town and wherever the American troops were marching'.[174] The newspapers wisely reported nothing. Dozens of people were arrested each day, thrown into a railway car at the train station, then hauled out and 'shot during the night without a trial near the signal station, often after having to dig their graves with their own hands', according to Dyboski.[175] Among those gunned down in mid-September fell Aleksandra Petrovna Kim, a Korean–Russian woman who had been an internationalist recruiter in POW camps and had lately been an organizer of Korean Reds in Khabarovsk.[176]

Six days after the Allies captured Khabarovsk, a representative of the Swedish Red Cross walked into the US headquarters to seek protection for his small staff from Kalmykov.[177] As protocol dictated, a US colonel told the Swede to take his request to the Japanese general who was the supreme Allied commander in the area. So the Swede took his plea to General Otani.[178] Two days later, Kalmykov's men burst into the Swedish Red Cross mission, shot dead the three men and one woman working there, looted the place, and absconded with 3 million rubles.[179] So much for Japanese protection. Obviously the naive American staff had not yet realized how close the Japanese and Kalmykov were; as the Osaka Mainichi newspaper explained, 'General Otani especially sympathized with Colonel Kalmykov and assisted him to become garrison commander of Khabarovsk'.[180]

'One week after this...', testified Colonel Morrow,

> about 60 women appeared at our headquarters, stating that their fathers and sons and brothers were going to be executed by Kalmykov without any form of trial. Colonel Styer [of the American Expeditionary Force headquarters] protested against these executions, and asked a delay. Despite his protests, sixteen men were taken out of the jail and executed that night. They were cut all to pieces by saber blows and bayonet wounds. Their bodies, half naked, were left on the ground for several days, and were viewed by a large crowd of Russians and Americans. After this incident an Allied guard...was placed over the prison of Kalmykov to prevent his executions. Despite this, Kalmykov merely used other prisons, and continued his executions by the hundreds.[181]

About this time the British vice-consul from Vladivostok appeared in the Khabarovsk office of General Oi, 12th Division commander. The vice-consul protested Kalmykov's barbarous acts and pointed out that the 12th Division's backing of Kalmykov was stirring up anti-Japanese sentiment among Khabarovsk's populace. The Japanese countered that the vice-consul had not properly obtained permission to proceed past Nikolsk-Ussuriisk and simply ignored the diplomat. Japanese newspapers portrayed the incident as an affront to the dignity of the Imperial Army.[182]

Kalmykov's reign of terror was just beginning. He would eventually raise a fearsome horde of about 1,600 men, of whom only 250 or so were 'genuine Cossacks'. The remainder were 'former Red Guards, drifters, farmers, etc.', whom Kalmykov forcibly conscripted or who joined with him 'merely to be fed and clothed'.[183] Kalmykov established himself as an independent warlord, and, as of October 1918, after yet another reconvening of the fifth *krug*, answered only to the *pokhodnii ataman* of a newly created Union of Far Eastern Cossack Armies, Grigorii Semenov.[184]

Blagoveshchensk – the last Red Bastion

The Bolsheviks' days in Siberia were numbered – so it seemed in September 1918, anyway. The last stronghold of the Bolsheviks in eastern Siberia centered on Blagoveshchensk, capital of Amur province, the center of a gold-mining district, and an inland port on the Amur river border with China near the confluence of the Zeya river, about 460 miles west of

Khabarovsk. It was bustling town of squat, weathered shops and houses out of which rose an occasional stone office building. Telegraph, telephone and electric wires festooned wooden sidewalks that framed parallel streets of mud. More than 40,000 people lived in Blagoveshchensk, which was also home to several large factories, a large hospital, library and military base. No one expected a violent revolution to roll into town like a storm.

As in Irkutsk, Chita, Khabarovsk and Vladivostok, the Bolsheviks in Blagoveshchensk were not strong enough to snatch local power immediately after the November revolution, but their left Socialist-Revolutionary allies whittled away at the opposition until they acquired a majority on the Amur territorial soviet on 18 January. Moderate socialists still managed to keep their hold on the municipal duma, but were snubbed by General Nakajima when he visited Blagoveshchensk on 27 January, scouting for counterrevolutionaries to sponsor. He enlisted the Russian employee of a Japanese firm (Kuhara Mining Company) to scrabble together conservative support, but focused most of his hopes and energy on a 30 January assembly of the Amur Cossacks, where they were deciding their stance toward the Bolsheviks. Nakajima persuaded Ataman Gamov, the Amur leader, to oppose the Bolsheviks, and assigned Major Ishimitsu Makiyo, an intelligence officer from the Kwantung government, to help him.[185] They plotted to arrest the Amur soviet, but Red workers and peasants rallied to thwart Gamov on 18 February.[186] Blagoveshchensk became Russia's last territorial capital to go Red on 5 March, when the municipal duma gave in to the territorial soviet. Fighting erupted in the streets, and for one week a scrappy force of Russians, Cossacks, Chinese and Japanese irregulars battled the Red Guards in average temperatures of $-10°F$. By 13 March, remnants of the Amur Cossacks and Blagoveshchensk's other anti-Bolsheviks were slogging towards Harbin, as red flags fluttered mockingly over their town.[187] Red power would last six months, but only during the first two hectic months was there regular contact with Petrograd and Moscow.

The Red Army made a frantic attempt to regroup here. Only 3,000 Bolshevik troops were here at the beginning of September. This number increased as survivors of the Allied campaign against Khabarovsk (200 miles southeast of Blagoveshchensk) made their way here. Most of the tattered remnants of Lazo's Transbaikal Army never made it. However, Efrem Perezhogin and many plunderers of the Chita state bank entered the city like an apocalyptic circus in the final days of August, running amok and undermining the authorities in a frantic last effort to line their pockets before the Japanese invasion.

Blagoveshchensk frantically prepared for battle. The Bolsheviks armed loyal factory workers in the town, but ammunition was in short supply. Japanese communiqués warned that the 'poisonous menace' of 15,000 Austro-Hungarian and German prisoners-turned-mercenaries had joined the Reds at the barricades, but these alarms had no basis in fact. A more realistic report from the Asahi news service stated that some 4,000 Bolshevik fighters had retreated into Blagoveshchensk during the first days of September, and that the town was in anarchy. Reports from the city in mid-month stated, 'The anarchists are slaughtering the peaceful inhabitants and giving themselves up to continuous pillage in full daylight. However, their chief [presumably Perezhogin] has been murdered. The entire city is in the greatest disorder, the inhabitants terrified, the stores and shops closed'.[188]

General Oi's cavalry advanced on Blagoveshchensk in two prongs, one regiment moving up the railway and a smaller force following the banks of the Amur river. Opposition was minimal. On the afternoon of 17 September, the Bolsheviks made a futile stand near Alekseevsk, the junction of the Trans-Siberian and the branch line to Blagoveshchensk. En route to Alekseevsk, a Japanese cavalry squadron captured an armored train containing two machine guns and 'a few former Austro-German prisoners'. In the town proper, the Japanese captured 214 Russians, 1 Chinese, 42 'Austro-German prisoners', 6,000 rifles, dozens of machine guns and light artillery pieces, and a railyard full of rolling stock. Few of the 'Austro-German' captives participated in the skirmish, in which only seven Japanese were killed. Two days later seven Red gunboats approached the city and, according to the intelligence reports, a pair of them were somehow captured by a Japanese infantry company and cavalry regiment – in spite of Major Barrows' observation that these were 'poor cavalrymen, mounted upon very poor animals'. The others escaped.[189]

Ataman Gamov and a group of Amur Cossacks accompanied the smaller Japanese column as they entered Blagoveshchensk at midnight and took possession of two armored trains, seven automobiles and a modest cache of weapons and ammunition. The demoralized Reds were unable to muster a half-hearted defense of Blagoveshchensk, much less a defiant last stand.[190] Many of Perezhogin's anarchist cohorts died in Blagoveshchensk, though whether they were killed by Reds or Whites is vague.

Some Bolshevik soldiers slipped across the Amur river into China, others fled north along the Zeya river, but most evaporated into the interminable forests, joining Commissar Aleksandr Krasnoshchekov and about 3,000 survivors of the Ussuri Front.[191] A number of *Tsentrosibir'* commissars, a detachment of Hungarians and the last of Perezhogin's anarchists were hunted down on the road to Yakutsk, their dying screams swallowed by the 'deaf taiga'.[192] Thus ended the last Bolshevik administration east of the Urals. From western Siberia to the Pacific Ocean, the Red fanatics had been driven into the wilderness.

4

THE WHITE TERROR BEGINS

October 1918–December 1918

'The truth of any statement made by these [OMO] people is to be doubted.'

(Captain F.F. Moore, 1919)

Semenov's realm

By early September 1918, less than a month and a half after Sergei Lazo's Daurski Front cornered OMO near Manchuli and almost drove it completely out of Russia, Grigorii Semenov was back in Chita. While detractors would later try to pass off Semenov's conquest of Transbaikalia as an unremarkable occupation on the coattails of the Czechoslovak Legion, the opposite view was equally true, that the Czechoslovaks may never have been successful if OMO had not pinned down so many Reds on the Daurski Front. 'One without the other would not have been successful', admonished OMO propaganda. 'Both together brought victory'. This victory had not come without a cost: Semenov had lost about 1,500 men killed and wounded, with the biggest losses occurring among 'Chinese and Mongolian infantry detachments'. OMO officers attributed their losses not to any lack of bravery, but to poor comprehension of the Russian language of their officers, which led to fatal misunderstandings on the battlefield. About 100 officers had also sacrificed their lives during the eight-month campaign.[1]

Semenov's miraculous resurrection made him lord of Chita and the de facto ruler of Transbaikalia, a territory the size of France, roles which suited his Napoleonic ego and purported posturing. One British officer even described Semenov as 'a very small man with a very keen eye and rather like what I have always imagined Napoleon to be like'. Indeed, wrote Peter Fleming, some said that the ataman later 'tried to resemble Napoleon, with his hand thrust into the front of his coat and his pendant lock of hair arranged every morning by his mistress'.[2] One writer insists, 'He always carried Napoleon's *Maxims* in his pocket'.[3] However, in Semenov's defense, the original sources of these assertions are elusive while most Americans who met him complimented his bearing, warmth and manners.

Semenov's power soon extended beyond Transbaikalia, stretching over 1,000 miles from the east shore of Lake Baikal to the Pacific coast. His rail units roamed as far west as the villages on Baikal's eastern shore, and Major General Skipetrov, a staunch Semenov officer, was operating in Nikolsk-Ussuriisk, just 50 miles north of Vladivostok.[4] Semenov's area of influence cast an even wider net into the scattered territories of anti-Bolshevik Cossacks throughout Siberia who identified with Semenov the doggedly determined warrior. Under Semenov's scepter, Chita would become the *sanctum sanctorum* of Russia's most extreme reactionary and militarist cliques, the Mecca of *atamanshchina* – Cossack warlordism.

A new civil administration was instituted under Semenov's auspices, and former duma representative and provisional government Commissar Sergei A. Taskin returned to run it after an empty stint with Horvath's wilting Business Cabinet.[5] Local administrative bodies that had functioned under the provisional government, such as the Chita municipal duma, were resurrected to take care of the details. In Verkhne-Udinsk and other cities, officials who survived the Red Terror were returned to municipalities.[6] Outside the cities and towns, 'the countryside lived its own life and was governed by committees formed in Kerensky's time', wrote Paul Dotsenko.[7] Beyond the railway zones, government authority – tsarist, provisional, soviet or White – penetrated Siberia's feral green sea of forests and tundra porously at best.

Semenov's freebooting image made it difficult to attract new talent to associate themselves with his rule. In the early months of the *atamanshchina*, months before regular feats of grand larceny, corruption, shakedowns of individuals, or torture tainted OMO's reputation, the only grounds for distaste could have been Semenov's intimacy with Asian ethnic minorities, fraternization with the Japanese Army or his rabid anti-Bolshevism. The former commissar of Amur province, an honest and well-educated lawyer named Alexeievski, refused Semenov's offer of an appointment as 'civil head of the Amur', though he did not explain why.[8]

To its credit, Semenov's administration immediately reopened Chita's courts of law in the Starnovski House, although military courts under Semenov's control continued to preside over a wide range of offenses such as insurrection, treason, arson and destruction of military property, all liberally applied and punishable by shooting.[9] One of the first judicial matters before the new civil authorities concerned the soviet looting of the state bank, and whether Chita police did enough to try to prevent it. A special commission of the Chita municipal duma convened on 12 September 1918 and investigated the robbery for three months, concluding early on that, in the face of several well-armed detachments of anarchist, internationalist and regular Red Guards and Chinese mercenaries, Chita's 50 on-call policemen had done everything they could. For a while, the Reds' shameless piracy became the 'crime of the century' in Chita newspapers and made great propaganda against the Bolsheviks.[10] In the aftermath, everyone in Chita who had somehow acquired a piece of the loot buried it a little deeper, knowing that its discovery by White authorities could be used to implicate anyone as a Bolshevik. No one would ever know how much of the 10 tons of gold and silver was captured by Japanese soldiers when they overran Amur province, or how much was squirreled away by individuals.

Semenov's administration soon earned a reputation for twisting or ignoring the law, particularly when it came to questions of confiscated property and commerce. Yet, initially at least, Semenov cultivated a merciful image, for instance, loudly declaring in the midst of the 1918 trial of some captured Red Army men, that if the accused would just give their word of honor to break with the Bolsheviks, he would release them. Even if his gesture was solely for the benefit of attending journalists, it was a grand performance.[11] Semenov's word was law in Transbaikal and Amur provinces, but he was a soldier who cared little for the tedious administrative responsibilities of government. He seemed to be dazzled by the wealth and hedonistic lifestyle his sudden power bequeathed upon him, although he enjoyed holding court at the Hotel Selekt (at least until March 1919), receiving petitioners and complainants like a benevolent potentate.[12] Grigorii Semenov, a 28-year-old war hero and junior officer who, just ten months before, could not show his face on a Chita street without fear of arrest, now ruled Transbaikalia like a king.

In early summer Lieutenant General Nikonov, Semenov's military advisor, and the OMO staff decided that their youthful leader 'should assume the style and status of ataman'. As far back as January 1918, *Esaul* (Captain) Semenov had signed public proclamations with the modest title of 'Detachment Ataman', as local Cossack custom dictated. By June his orders and communications were being endorsed by 'Ataman Semenov, Ataman of OMO'. Around the same time, he was declared a *pokhódni ataman* (expedition chief) of the Transbaikal Cossack Host, but it was early September before foreign newspaper articles and allied intelligence reports first began to refer to 'Ataman' Semenov. Semenov and his patrons would deal with the technicality of his formal election by Cossack assembly later. Yet he was genuinely popular among traditional Cossack communities and, in fact, would eventually be elected *pokhódni ataman* of the Ussuri, Amur and Transbaikal Cossacks, and an ataman of the Ural and Siberian Cossacks.[13]

Likewise, even though the international press had already been writing about 'General' Semenov since at least April 1918, Semenov was technically still a captain, and something had to be done about his lowly title now that scores of officers senior in rank were serving under him. Nearly nine months had passed since General Khreshchatitski and a number of other superior officers from the Ussuri Division set an example by subordinating themselves to Semenov's command.

Semenov's dogged persistence and leadership in the conquest of Transbaikalia elevated him above the generals who were making bombastic proclamations from the comfort of hotels and office suites in Harbin in autumn 1918. General Otani, commander of all Japanese forces in Siberia, named Semenov commander-in-chief of Transbaikalia. Radola Gajda, the brilliant 26-year-old commander of the Czech Legion's 7th Regiment, 'appointed' Semenov 'commander of Russian troops in the territory east of the Onon river including the Pri-Amur'.[14] Neither Otani nor Gajda had legal authority to appoint or promote Russian military officers, but they did have the most powerful armies in the Russian Far East, where legality was meaningless and authority emanated from the barrel of a gun.

Nonetheless, Semenov was furious when he first read Gajda's proclamation in leaflets being handed out by 'a little Czech soldier' (as Semenov described him) on an eastbound passenger train. He railed about the young Czech general, whose ego was no smaller than Semenov's, subordinating OMO to his command. It took days of reciprocal visits between Semenov and Czech Legion staff officers, with guards of honor, lots of saluting and a dinner with Gajda before the misunderstanding was all sorted out and Semenov's Russian honor was restored.[15]

On 7 September 1918, Semenov issued an Order of the Day announcing that OMO troops had made contact with soldiers of the Provisional Siberian Government, and that 'all must now unite in the interests of Russia'.[16] Semenov had just spent several days meeting with Czechoslovak Legion officers at Olovyannaya and Borzya, and it was later written that the Czechs 'threatened to use force against him' if he did not recognize Petr V. Vologodskii's government. In addition, members of the Cossack League at Omsk also probably exerted some pressure on Semenov.[17] For his cooperation, Major General Pavel Pavlovich Ivanov-Rinov rewarded Semenov with appointment as commander of the provisional Siberian government's 5th Pri-Amur Independent Army Corps, which oversaw forces throughout the Russian Far East. He was also promoted to colonel, a rank ill-fitting for a corps commander, but that was irrelevant to a young hero with Semenov's budding Napoleonic ambitions.[18]

Chita

In mid-September Ataman Semenov settled into *Dom* Nikitin, a beautiful stone mansion capped by an extravagant cupola near the center of Chita. His troops were quartered in the huge redbrick headquarters of the Transbaikal Cossack Host on Atamanovski Square and throughout the city. OMO and Japanese staffs moved into Chita's finest offices and hotels.

THE WHITE TERROR BEGINS

Suddenly Grigorii Semenov was being dealt with like a great statesman and he made Chita the capital of his empire, although he was frequently on the road, receiving celebrity treatment wherever he went. In late September 1918, he and Major General Skipetrov embarked on an aid-seeking pilgrimage to Vladivostok, where Semenov met his American friend Major Barrows and was called upon by the US Ambassador to Japan, Roland S. Morris. They discussed Semenov's coordination with General Gajda to improve the quality of 5th Corps' men and material assets, and, when asked whether he contemplated levying taxes to sustain his troops, the ataman replied that he counted on the financial support of Omsk. He revealed no separatist ambitions, nor any quarrels with the Provisional Siberian Government or the United States. He expressed his desire for up-to-date, long-range artillery to replace the antiques OMO relied on, and for some aircraft. Morris mentioned something about humanitarian aid for destitute Buryat refugees, the two men parted amicably, and Semenov returned to Chita.[19]

For centuries Chita had prospered as a frontier trading post, Cossack garrison and end of the line for exiles from European Russia. The railway profoundly changed the sleepy town of 8,000 when it arrived in 1899, giving birth to industry and a working class that toiled in the large railway workshops and nearby coal mines, and who surged into the militant revolutionary vanguard that formed the defiant Chita Republic in 1905. A flour mill, saw mill and brick factory sprang up to service the fast growing population, wealthy merchants constructed ornate villas, and a few decent hotels opened to cater to affluent rail travelers. In 1906, a 650-kilowatt power station brought the modern wonder of electric lights to the city's most prominent offices and residences.[20] Several hundred telephones linked Chita's political bosses, bureaucracies, businesses and wealthy homes. Of course, these ultra-modern utilities were little more than curiosities to the lower classes, who still relied upon unsanitary Chinese water carts, lamp oil and candles.[21] Many neighborhoods of sturdy double-log cabins huddled behind stockades and appeared no different than a typical eighteenth-century village.

When Ataman Semenov arrived in autumn 1918, Chita had between 70,000 and 75,000 permanent residents, 2,800 Austro-Hungarian, German and Turkish prisoners of war, about 650 horses and a wildly fluctuating number of refugees. The city stretched across a bowl-shaped valley where the Chita and Ingoda rivers met, sheltered from raging steppe winds by rolling mountain ridges thick with pines where families spent leisure hours picnicking beside meadows of starry lilium aflutter with red-spotted parnassius butterflies. American engineers found it well laid out with broad parallel streets, all of them unpaved and very sandy, even in the winter since there was practically no snow fall. There were seven hospitals of various sizes and specialties, 60 free elementary schools, three male and four female high schools, a polytechnic institute, a seminary, a museum, three theatres, two tanneries, three flour mills, a brewery, a vodka distillery and several imposing buildings of bureaucrats. Chita rated two railway stations: station No. 2 in the heart of town had very few sidings, so most railway switching operations occurred a little over a mile west at No. 1, where huge military yards sprawled alongside shops and a roundhouse, the breeding ground of Red activists. Tracks between the stations crossed the Chita river on a 175-yard long bridge of brawny planks. The shallow, unnavigable river froze solid every winter, forming an excellent highway.[22]

People flocked back to the two cathedrals, synagogue and chapels. Bishop Safron led his Old Believer congregations in special public services to commemorate Chita's liberation from the atheists, and much of the citizenry hailed Semenov's arrival with heartfelt fanfare, although many liberals were reticent and left SRs and Bolsheviks utterly fearful if they were foolish enough to not already be in hiding.[23] Religious institutions welcomed the relief from Bolshevik insults and torment, and Kadets (members and supporters of the conservative Constitutional Democratic Party) breathed a sigh of relief, having been declared 'enemies of the people' after the October Revolution. Chita's leading Socialist-Revolutionaries, who had been hiding from the Red Terror for seven months, now fled west to Irkutsk to escape Semenov's inevitable White Terror.[24] Semenov later wrote, 'I did not refuse cooperation with socialists', and pointed out that he even 'employed' a prominent Socialist-Revolutionary party leader, Colonel A.A. Krakovetskii, as a liaison with anti-Bolshevik organizations in Irkutsk.[25] Colonel Krakovetskii was a dedicated Socialist-Revolutionary 'military organizer' who had pulled together Siberian anti-Bolshevik resistance in 1918, and even though he answered to Semenov's command, he stood miles apart ideologically.[26]

Nevertheless, 'Political life in the city is almost at a standstill', reported newspaper *Moya Gazeta* eight weeks after OMO marched in (although a temporary municipal Duma was in operation). Military authorities 'suppressed' the newspaper *Trudovaya Sibir*, shut down all socialist publications, and restricted but did not entirely prohibit public meetings. However, if anyone uttered the word *tovarishch* (comrade) during a meeting, it would be shut down by a military monitor. At a meeting of the cooperative association Ekonomist, a speaker drew a reprimand for declaring that Siberia would soon be a Japanese colony, but proved that people sometimes had more freedom of speech in Semenov's jurisdiction than in Bolshevik territory where such subversive statements might draw a bullet. In fact, such a semblance of normalcy settled over Chita by mid-October that Ataman Semenov lifted the state of siege.[27]

Transbaikalia's political future was nebulous, but elections for a new city council in Chita proceeded 'very orderly'.[28] Public opposition to Semenov surfaced occasionally, but only at great risk. In late October, one cautious newspaper cryptically alluded to an incident of opposition, saying, 'The conduct of the Semenov detachments and their misunderstandings with Commissar Flegontov in Chita called out energetic measures on the part of the ruling classes of Irkutsk'.[29]

In late October 1918 Semenov told a Vladivostok journalist from newspaper *Primorskaya Zhizn* that he intended 'to maintain the democratic victories of the revolution', but that his constituency of officers, having been insulted and humiliated during the revolution, tended to be monarchists.[30] Semenov's ideology was never clear, though in the beginning of his movement, his 'first allegiance was to the Great Russian state principle', and he simply intended to cleanse his Transbaikal homeland of the destructive Bolshevik contagion and install a caretaker administration that would restore the promise of the Constituent Assembly.[31] Beneath this he believed in the universal brotherhood of Cossacks, but did not entertain the notion of a Pan-Mongol nation at the time of his October interview. In his talk with *Primorskaya Zhizn*, he said that he and his officers would abide by the decisions of the Constituent Assembly whenever it would convene next, and that the army should stay out of politics. Whatever Semenov's beliefs were during these weeks of his meteoric rise to power, cabals of ultra-conservative militarists and self-serving opportunists flocked into his realm and steered it into a bloody era of reactionary repression, while Japanese advisors imbued with 'Asia first' ideology began implanting the vision of a Greater Mongolia in the Ataman's head.

Every night OMO and Japanese punitive detachments (*karatyélniye otryádi*) swept through Chita's streets carrying out round-ups of Reds and searches for those in hiding or incriminating material (such as purloined gold or silver from the state bank). By the end of September 1918, the Chita prison was filled to double its capacity, with 1,422 men and 122 women jammed into its dark cells.[32] Captured Reds and suspected sympathizers often disappeared into *zasténki* – torture chambers – scattered about Chita and her suburbs. At least ten *zasténki* sprang up in surrounding areas to handle the large volume of victims.

At nearby Lake Kenon, the corpses of 200 Bolshevik troops were later unearthed with bound arms and wire around their necks. Inside Chita, the Hotel Selekt and the mansion of the Badmaev family became notorious torture centers. One of the first to die was Vasilii M. Serov, the 'professional revolutionary' who had organized the Bolshevik movement in Chita and the surrounding region, and who, ironically, had condemned Lenin's 7 November seizure of power as being harmful to the revolution.[33]

A number of White intelligence units – *razvedki* – operated out of Chita and throughout Semenov's territory. Semenov gave these death squads free reign to do almost anything they pleased. Names of sinister *razvedka* chiefs became synonymous with sadism and terror: Colonel Tierbach, the Chita garrison commander (soon transferred to Makkaveevo); the Grants, a father – son pair of English mercenaries; Vasil'ev, Semenov's chief of staff; and Budakov the *kontr-razvyédka* (counterintelligence) head – the 'only general in Chita to look like a general'.[34]

Chita streets were dangerous. 'There were frequent occasions of sniping and individual executions', recalled one American observer. 'I was cautioned about going out after dark'.[35] No one was safe. Scarcely a morning passed when the rising sun would not illuminate a fresh corpse sprawled in the sandy streets, the victim of White soldiers, Red partisans or robbers. Some satellite towns, particularly Antipikha and Peschanka, were saturated with Russian and Japanese soldiers, all armed, and many indulging in never-ending binges and debauchery that capriciously sent fists and bullets flying. More than 70 taverns, gambling houses and other dispensaries of vice contributed to the lawlessness in Chita.

In contrast, there were five police stations. In November 1918, Semenov appointed former gendarme Lieutenant Colonel Aleksandr Mironovich Kamennov as Chita's chief of police (*nachal'nik militsii*), who promptly authorized police to shoot robbers and burglars on site. The order had little effect on soldiers who invaded homes and masked robberies as searches for subversive materials, and anyway about one-third of the policeman on duty were themselves involved in 'political searches' to eradicate Bolshevism.[36]

For the next two years, Semenov himself rarely strayed far from his well-guarded Chita headquarters except in an armored train convoy. In case everything fell apart, the ataman quietly made arrangements to flee. As early as November 1918, a US intelligence report noted, 'Semenov is always prepared to fly [presumably by Japanese Army aircraft] to Mongolia'.[37]

Semenov's army

The ataman planted his headquarters staff in Chita's finest hostelry, the Hotel Selekt, where it grew in size and sophistication, employing a number of respected senior officers including Generals Shil'nikov, Khreshchatitskii and Afanas'ev, the latter, for instance, a retired Imperial Army colonel who had been 'chief of the civil section of the Chinese Eastern Railway'. In December 1918 US Army Captain Frederick F. Moore, an AEFS intelligence officer, was detailed to Semenov's headquarters at Chita where he got acquainted with OMO's leadership. In his opinion, Major General Verigo, Semenov's popular chief of staff at the time, was an example of 'a very good type of Russian officer... He was wounded five times in the Russo-Japanese War, and four times in this war against the Germans', spoke English 'fairly well' and was married to a woman whose grandfather was American.[38] Nevertheless, 'Verigo makes no bones about displaying his hostile attitude toward the Allies', reported another American officer, because 'the Allies gave nothing but promises'.[39]

Ataman Semenov's conservative political platform even attracted civilian specialists from the region's talented pool of refugees. For example, a well-known writer, Nikolai Fridrikhovich Oliger, headed an 'information department' (*osvedomitel'nii otdel*), the innocuous title of which belied its broader functions, which corresponded more to a Red agitation-propaganda (agitprop) cell. Oliger had been involved in 'revolutionary activity' in his youth, but became so disillusioned by it that he became a Kadet after the February Revolution and a fugitive after the October Revolution, when Kadets were tarred as parasitic enemies of the toiling classes. He fled from the literary salons of Petrograd to Harbin and ended up in room No. 58 of the Hotel Selekt in 1918, poring over OMO combat reports and intelligence data gathered from clergy and loyal parishioners describing the mood of the population, and determining how to best package and market Ataman Semenov and his brand of Cossack law and order.[40]

Semenov's presence throughout most of his vast Transbaikal empire was patchy: a strong presence along the railway and isolated garrisons scattered in towns and villages augmented by an occasional punitive expedition. In autumn 1918, the largest concentration of OMO – 'over 100 officers and about 1,000 men, mostly Chinese' – was posted under Colonel Tierbach (recently promoted from *pod'esaul*, junior captain) in the vicinity of Semenov's Chita headquarters. Tierbach's detachment had relatively good discipline, but, like most Russian military units – Red and White, their reliability in combat could not be taken for granted. The other 4,000 men attributed to OMO five months earlier were either dispersed in garrisons along the railway to Manchuli, distributed as cadre to form new regiments or had deserted. As time went on, the OMO label was inconsistently applied not only to Semenov's core unit but to his entire politico-military organization.

In addition to the original OMO, an October 1918 inventory of Semenov's army listed the following units among its assets operating out of Transbaikalia:

1st Semenov Infantry Regiment
2nd Manchurian Infantry Regiment
Mongol–Buryat Cossack Regiment
Onon Cossack Regiment
2nd Daurski Regiment
Chita Cossack Regiment
Argun Cossack Regiment

Allied intelligence reports described the soldiers of the 1st Semenov and 2nd Manchurian Infantry Regiments as 'Chinese and Russians'.[41] However, most Allied officers could not tell the difference between Chinese, Buryats or other indigenous Siberian peoples, and tended to classify anyone with Asian features as 'Chinese' unless they happened to be distinguishable by costume or language. Most of the troops were probably Mongol nationalists or mercenaries recruited in northwest Manchuria. These two regiments totaled about 2,000 men, with 100 mounted scouts and a machine gun detachment.[42]

On paper, Semenov possessed a formidable Cossack legion called the 8th Transbaikal Cossack Division. However, regiments that supposedly constituted this division would appear in the order of battle for a few months and then disappear without explanation. Some of these phantom units – including, at various times, the Transbaikal, Nerchinsk, Onon, Chita and Argun Cossack Regiments and 2nd Daurski Regiment – had 'very many officers but few men'.[43] The units may have represented genuine mobilizations of Cossacks and conscripts who quickly deserted, or perhaps were efforts to pad the payroll (which was paid by Omsk). Two thousand Cossack cavalrymen of the 8th Division owed their allegiance to a pro-Kolchak ataman, Colonel Zimin, who was 'not in accord with

Semenov'. Zimin's name disappeared from reports after December 1918. Presumably, Zimin himself disappeared as well.

Semenov assigned Major General Verigo to form regiments of Ukrainian peasants, who made up a significant proportion of the Maritime province's new migrant communities. The hope was that the regiments would be a new base of support to counteract opposition in the Ussuri Cossack Host to *semenovist* influence in the Pri-Amur region. Initially many Ukrainians responded with enthusiasm to Verigo's overtures, but 'cooled off considerably' when they discovered that Semenov was behind the venture, which was postponed indefinitely.[44]

OMO also attracted its share of soldiers of fortune and adventurers. There were the two English torturers, the Grants, Serbian mercenaries in Semenov's bodyguard, five Belgian deserters, a Rumanian pilot and, no doubt, many others of nebulous background and dubious motivation.[45] 'A certain Dr Yugolewski, an American Jew' eventually became Semenov's private secretary and 'chief of his counterespionage department'.[46]

Newcomers to the Russian Far East were unfamiliar with regional demographics and expressed surprise at the overwhelmingly Asian character of OMO's rank and File. OMO recruited 'fringe elements of society – petty criminals, bandits, deserters and ethnic minorities' – precisely because Transbaikalia had been the empire's dumping ground for undesirables, a traditional frontier refuge for fugitives, and the ancestral home of many aboriginal peoples.[47] Like the Buryats, Tungus tribesmen, who were noted fur trappers and woodsmen, were attracted to OMO ranks by promises of self-determination in an autonomsus Transbaikalia. In addition, the aboriginal nationalities had a long association with the Russian military, as Semenov recalled in an appeal to Transbaikal Tungus to serve in the White Army:

> Tungus citizens! Two hundred years ago your forefathers composed the nucleus of the defenders of Transbaikalia from invasion by hostile powers of the Russian nation. Later from that nucleus, together with other nationalities devoted to Russia such as the Buryats, were assembled the Tungus and Buryat 5-*sotnia* regiments, which served as the foundation for the formation of the present-day, glorious Transbaikal Cossack Host.[48]

The command structure of Buryat, Mongol, Tungus and other indigenous and Asian units resembled the 'double command' system employed in colonial units of other imperial armies. Indigenous officers and non-commissioned officers were shadowed by Russians who supervised drill and training sessions, then commanded during battle, akin to the British Indian Army or French Senegalese infantry.[49]

Despite the occasional formation of all-officer units, experienced military officers were in short supply. Nearly four years of European combat had depleted the ranks, forcing the army and navy to promote capable enlisted men and to commission latent Reds (like Sergei Lazo) from the universities. Some were 'young boys who have had just enough education to be able to do the necessary paperwork', adjudged an American liaison officer, Captain Montgomery Schuyler. Shortly after the February Revolution the soldiers' soviets made officers superfluous, and the October Revolution declared them enemies of the people to be liquidated or harnessed. 'In the Black Sea massacre, it is stated that not less than 8,000 officers were murdered', noted Captain Schuyler, 'and at Kronstadt...between six and seven thousand were drowned at one time'.[50] The pool of officer material in a far-flung corner like Transbaikalia was shallow.

In November 1918 the Chita Ataman Semenov Military School was founded to mold new and replacement officers. The course of instruction for the first class lasted 13 months, whether by design or forced by events is not known because by graduation time Semenov's realm and the world around it would be vastly different. Cadets were counted among the ataman's most loyal servants, thus their zeal was not bottled up in lecture halls and classrooms. Some were siphoned from the school for duty on Semenov's bodyguard or to man the machine guns during executions of mutinous OMO troops.[51] Perhaps because of his youth, Semenov exerted a strong attraction to certain traditional, patriotic young men. An RRSC officer saw a group of 20 naval cadets traveling from Vladivostok to Chita in early December to volunteer for the ataman's crusade to save Russia.[52]

Early on Ataman Semenov experienced disciplinary problems with his officers, particularly the mob that congregated in staff and garrison positions in Chita, similar to the shameful situation in Omsk that would so frustrate the Provisional Siberian Government War Ministry. 'We find nothing military in their organization', chided Captain Conrad Skladal, a new US Intelligence officer who arrived just as Chita plunged into winter 1918. 'We find a majority of officers employed during the day in speculation, while during the nights in frolicking and drinking...I was informed that the gaiety at Chita is a repetition of the conditions of 1905 during the Japanese War.'[53]

It was only natural that similar merriment took priority over the war in other cities, too, considering that the officer corps was composed of green youths and war-weary veterans. While the rest of the economy sagged, the region's leisure industry boomed, as hotels, restaurants, bars, cabarets and brothels filled with soldiers. In Manchuli, the Japanese Army occupied four of the six hotels, and 'railway and commercial clubs with gardens and music and restaurants' swarmed with military personnel and flies during the day. At night it seems that a bomb tossed into the town's single cabaret would have devastated the Japanese and OMO officer ranks.[54]

Among the list of Semenov's assets in autumn 1918 appeared eight aircraft based near Chita, which he used to patrol the railway. However accounts of Transbaikal partisans do not express fear of being discovered by OMO air patrols, probably because snow and long periods of engine-freezing weather during the winter, or sudden squalls and treacherous gusts during the summer frequently grounded the delicate machines.[55] Semenov asked the Americans to donate aircraft and modern artillery to him but Major General Graves refused on the grounds that such aid would violate US neutrality.[56] A small but growing fleet of locomotives, each lugging one or more of OMO's fierce-looking armored railway cars, roved the rails to spearhead combat operations, provide artillery and machine gun support, pursue partisans and saboteurs and frighten or prod the peasantry and workers into submission. By late November 1918 OMO was operating no less than three armored railway cars out of the Chita yards alone.[57]

Thanks to Ataman Semenov's cosy relationship with the Japanese General Staff, OMO was the best outfitted Russian army in Siberia. By December 1918 the Japanese had reportedly shipped to OMO 'full equipment, rifles, ammunition and clothing for 10,000 men', and 17 field guns of different calibers to guard the junction at Karymskaya.[58] Interestingly, many artillery units were served by camels instead of horses. Despite Japanese generosity, when the first snows fell, Semenov had only enough winter boots to equip 1,000 men.

While Semenov himself was attired in a finely tailored Transbaikal Cossack uniform, his men turned out in a motley assortment of imperial and provisional government army, Cossack, British and Japanese uniforms. A common feature was 'a small shield of yellow cloth (the color of the Transbaikal Cossacks) with the initials "OMO" and with an indicator of military unit' worn on the left sleeve. Another form of insignia was a small badge (about 6-centimeters wide and 5-centimeters tall) of a silver double-headed eagle with a shield inscribed 'OMO', '19' and '17' impressed upon the wings, a writhing serpent in its claws and gold sunbeams above on which the cyrillic letters 'A' and 'C' (for Ataman Semenov) were raised.[59] OMO did not discard epaulets, the simple uniform accessory that aroused violent reactions from revolutionary soldiers who seemed to be possessed by a primeval hatred of the objects and the ranks that they stood for, and probably used similar monograms on them.

Semenov retained police investigators and militiamen who had not associated too cosily with the Reds, and established an extensive intelligence network to keep tabs on the citizenry. His intelligence service relied on pools of natural allies to provide voluntary informants – businessmen, former officers and bureaucrats, political conservatives, Cossacks, Mongols and Old Believers. Religion triggered strong emotions in revolutionary Russia, and, in the crusade against the militant Red atheists, the clergy and devoted parishioners of the Russian Orthodox Church collected information about the political winds at the grass-roots level, and fed assembled data through the church hierarchy to Semenov's military, intelligence and propaganda staff.[60] In Russia it seemed that the civil war often spilt over into heaven and hell.

Provisional Siberian Government and the 5th Corps

Three centers of power emerged in eastern Siberia and the Russian Far East: the Provisional Siberian Government (PSG) in Omsk, which inspired the most hope among the Allies and the war-weary Russian populace; Semenov's free-wheeling Transbaikalian entity; and a semi-autonomous city-state in Vladivostok, generally under Dmitri Horvath's influence. An uneasy mix of moderate Socialist-Revolutionaries and White militarists had run the Provisional Siberian Government since the Czechoslovak Legion and anti-Bolshevik forces ousted the Reds from Omsk on 7 June. As the pace of military operations quickened against large Bolshevik armies in the western foothills of the Urals, the scales of power in the Provisional Siberian Government tipped more and more towards conservative military elements. On 5 September 1918 these elements, promoted by persistent lobbying from Major General Alfred W.F. Knox, head of the British military mission, forced the replacement of the New Siberian Army's moderate, Socialist-Revolutionary commander, Colonel G.N. Grishin-Almazov, with Major General Pavel P. Ivanov-Rinov.[61]

Ivanov-Rinov was a mysterious figure, not widely known in the tsarist army.[62] He was a Cossack line officer – not a product of the General Staff, recently elected as ataman of the Siberian Cossack Host, and known for his iron-fisted suppression of the 1916 Kyrgyz revolt.[63] Apart from commanding a brigade on the Southwestern Front during the great war, he had 'little real military experience'. In September 1917 he had founded a League of Cossacks in Petrograd to save Russia and 'protect the Cossacks against the spread of Bolshevism'.[64] An American intelligence report dated 23 October noted ominously that, 'The efforts of Semenov and the other Cossack leaders [Dutov, Kaledin, Kalmykov, Annenkov, et al.] have been in line with the program of the Cossack League'. The word around Omsk was that, 'General Ivanov-Rinov is not a very clever man, but he is very ambitious and vain'.[65]

Ivanov-Rinov immediately instituted reactionary measures that shocked many moderate revolutionaries. The day after he took over the New Siberian Army, he authorized punitive detachments to shoot on sight.[66] Two days later he reversed two of the army's most emotional reforms by reinstating officers at their former rank and ordering that epaulets replace the simple green and white ribbons then worn by all ranks.[67] Soldiers were again required to salute officers, although saluting was deemed 'not obligatory' when off duty.[68] Military ritual was restored in the Siberian Army and the average soldier's spirit was dampened, but the Reds no longer offered them a refuge from the discomforts of military discipline.

In preparation for the bloody trials of the civil war, the Red Army had already begun reversing military reforms in the summer of 1918. The election of officers, which had been formally introduced in December 1917, but in practice since March 1917, was abolished, and strict discipline, such as execution for desertion was reinstated. In addition, professional military officers from the tsarist army were forced back into service, designated as military specialists, *voenspets*.[69]

After Ivanov-Rinov appointed Semenov as 5th Corps commander, the latter's order of battle now encompassed the 9th Infantry Division, 'composed of the 32nd, 33rd and 36th Regiments and a new Ussuri regiment', made up of European Russians conscripted in the Pacific coast provinces. The division chief was a Semenov devotee, Major General Skipetrov, but the commander of naval and military forces of the Maritime province (where Vladivostok was located) was a conscientious, regular army officer, Colonel Butenko, who was loyal to the Provisional Siberian Government and did not hide his loathing of Semenov. The feeling was mutual. Semenov loyalists treated men of the 9th Infantry Division with hostility. Other regiments in the coastal provinces nominally fell under the umbrella of Semenov's authority, although their commander, General Pleshkov, was loyal to General Horvath. These included one well-trained regiment of *plastuni* (Cossack infantry), a newly formed infantry regiment, one regiment of Chinese (recruited in the Manchurian railway zone) under Russian officers and the 2nd Cavalry Regiment of Mounted Jaegers.

Semenov's reactionary reputation preceded him and earned him no trust among soldiers of Butenko's 9th Infantry Division or the egalitarian men of Omsk's New Siberian Army. A New Siberian Army brigade at Troitskosavsk refused to serve under the ataman's command and had to be transferred farther west.[70] One 5th Corps command that *was* loyal to Semenov was the 'United Division of Amur and Ussuri Cossacks'. This designation seems to have been some Vladivostok staff officers' catch-all title for the Far Eastern units under the spell of renegade Captain Ivan Kalmykov.

Semenov's relations with the Provisional Siberian Government soon chilled when – at Major General Knox's insistence – Admiral Kolchak was named Minister of War in late October. Shortly before this, the admiral passed through Chita on a train bound for Omsk. Semenov refused to call on him, though he did have a tepid conversation with Kolchak's traveling companion, Major General Knox, who visited Semenov's headquarters before the train pulled out. Knox explained that Kolchak would have paid his respects also but for the fact that he was traveling 'incognito'.[71] For months, Major General Knox, who had been Britain's military attaché in Petrograd from 1911 until the Red coup, had been trying to orchestrate a single, disciplined anti-Bolshevik front out of the fractious White Russian cliques, yet, despite his Herculean efforts, he could not even prevail upon the minister of war and a corps commander to act civil to one another. Alfred Knox was a diehard autocrat, 'not averse ... to classifying the entire Russian peasantry as "swine", and an energetic, exceptional military officer who had served extensively in India and was fluent in Russian'.[72] To Knox, the fight against Bolshevism was not only to keep Russia in the war against Germany, but a crusade against rule by the unwashed and ignorant mob.

About this same time, the British halted their regular monthly payments to Semenov.[73] After all, Omsk's New Siberian Army was shedding blood in combat with formidable Bolshevik armies in western Siberia while OMO refused to dispatch troops to the frontlines in the west, and did not even hunt local partisans energetically, preferring to rob and terrorize peasants along the railway hundreds of miles from the war zone. Semenov vented his displeasure over the unexpected breakup with the British in a peculiar way. It was a minor incident, but one which revealed the vindictiveness of Semenov's character. Edwin Earle, a 25-year-old railway specialist in the British Royal Engineers, was aboard Kolchak and Knox's special train when it pulled into Chita that October. Earle reported to the OMO officer of the guard, who led him to Semenov's headquarters train where Earle extended courtesies on behalf of the British command. Earle asked Semenov if he would call on Major General Knox. The ataman replied, 'If he wishes me, I am here'. Earle made the innocent mistake of mentioning that the British train included two American Red Cross cars loaded with clothing for Kolchak's army at the front. Semenov turned to an aide and muttered a command in Buryat. While Earle continued chatting with Semenov, the ataman's aide had the OMO station commandant back a locomotive up to Earle's train and removed one of the Red Cross cars. 'A British sentry was killed in the cutting of it [the Red Cross car] off', testified Earle later. 'He stayed with his car and was never found, so I assume he was killed.'[74] Semenov could not pass up an opportunity for larceny and revenge, even if the victim happened to be his former benefactor, Alfred Knox.

Semenov, Incorporated

During his summer campaigns Semenov had come to realize the fabulous wealth that control of the railway could provide. Weeks before OMO advanced out of dusty Transbaikalian whistlestops near the border, Semenov was raking in huge amounts of money from 'confiscations, requisitions, levies and combinations with Harbin speculators'.[75] Some said that a bribe of 20,000–25,000 rubles could get an extra freight car attached to a military supply train.[76] However, Captain Moore heard the figure of 75,000 rubles mentioned 'for a single car from Harbin to Chita'.[77] General Budberg's diary entry for 29, November 1918 revealed

> Semenov is now earning up to 3 million rubles a day, plus the reputation of a public benefactor. He sells allotments of railway freight cars to Harbin merchants. These guarantee to pay over to the Ataman 20 percent of the resultant turnover, and undertake not to make any larger percentage of profit themselves. So everyone is happy – the businessmen, Semenov and the public.[78]

General Budberg understandably erred in this last observation – everyone in Semenov's fiefdom had to feign happiness to avoid ending up in the *zastenki*. Of course, Semenov and the OMO quartermaster corps were genuinely elated at the bounteous results of the extortionate 20 percent 'tax'. However, someone eventually had to pay. 'There is graft at every turn', observed Captain Moore. 'A speculator may lease a truck [railcar] at a high price to bring goods from Harbin to Chita, then he has to pay the station agent for the order to have it hooked to a train; [then] he has to pay the engineer before the train moves and he has to pay more graft to get the car [shunted] on a siding at Chita.'[79]

In an army where robbery and extortion were widely accepted practices, Semenov's lucrative quartermaster corps was clearly the elite. The powerful OMO supply officer was Colonel Burikov, a 'very cunning and avaricious man' (according to Semenov's disgruntled procurement agent in Harbin), who had been assistant to the chief of the Chinese Eastern Railway's counterespionage detachment. Burikov spoke a little Chinese, which surely helped him in negotiating deals with Harbin gangsters.[80] Burikov later earned a promotion to major general, perhaps for instituting the extortionate 'tax' on all merchandise brought through Transbaikalia. Burikov expanded the basis for this tax until merchants were eventually forced to cough up '20 percent of the original cost of goods' brought into Chita. 'When a merchant arrived with his car of goods', wrote Lieutenant Davidson, a US Army observer, 'he was immediately set upon by one of Burikov's officers, or the general [Burikov] himself and ordered to pay the money, which they said was going into the Fund for the Protection of the Trans-Baikal District by Ataman Semenov's Army. If the merchant refused to pay the required sum, his goods were locked up until he did pay'.[81]

Burikov reportedly '[did] not like the Japanese', but that did not stop him from doing a great deal of business with them.[82] Publicly Semenov denied making any concessions to Japan in exchange for aid, although as early as May 1918 he agreed with General Muto to try to prevent American technical assistance from extending onto the Transbaikal Railway.[83] Behind the scenes, however, Semenov granted the Japanese a monopoly in Transbaikalia in exchange for a cut of the profits.[84] The OMO quartermaster corps and the Japanese Army became business partners, bringing goods into Transbaikalia without paying duties to the Omsk government and selling them for substantial profits.[85] Often Japanese imports were even disguised as Red Cross supplies.[86]

Japanese goods were landed at Dairen, Manchuria, shipped through Changchun and Harbin on to Chita. Every day a Japanese train heaved 40 railcars laden with supplies into Transbaikalia from Manchuli.[87] Some of these supplies were bound for Japanese military units, but surely not all. The director of the Chinese customs office at Manchuli estimated that one-third of the Japanese traffic contained 'goods on which duty should rightfully be paid'.[88] At a time when everything was scarce in Russia, Chita's markets looked opulent to refugees and travelers from other towns. Burikov masterminded this racket.

Common items like leather, rope, string, sugar, lard and butter were precious commodities in other Siberian cities and, because of constant depreciation of the ruble, everything was usually priced exorbitantly. Laborers who earned 35 rubles per month could not afford to pay two rubles per Russian pound for bread or meat, three and a half rubles for butter and cheese or 25 rubles for sugar. One Russian railway employee remarked that, 'Trains are fearfully crowded because of people going from larger cities to villages to obtain food because of [the railway's] inability to handle flour'.[89] The purchases of relatively well-paid Japanese troops drove up food prices in Transbaikalia; local cattlemen preferred to sell wholesale to the Japanese Army rather than peddle individual cattle to Russian buyers.

'The Japanese headquarters is selling food products to the poorest inhabitants [to] thus gain their good will', reported a newspaper in October 1918, but this support was but 'a drop in the ocean'.[90] Nevertheless, despite increasing numbers of refugees from the west, life in Chita grew more bearable as provisions supplied by the Allies and booty from OMO's pillaging campaigns appeared in the markets. 'Semenov...had all the instincts of a *grand seigneur*', explained David Footman and 'set up an elaborate relief organization. Supplies were allotted from military stores and special shops [the Semenov "boutiques"] opened for the benefit of the needy.'[91] The ataman sincerely took pity upon the refugees.

Reactionary backlash

Just as a glimmer of peace and a new, post-war democratic order came into sight in central Europe, the disintegrating Russian Empire seemed consumed by wild eddies of chaos and veered further away from the path to representative government. On 19 October the Austro-Hungarian Prime Minister Count Tisza stood up in the parliament in Budapest to declare, 'We must admit openly that we have lost the war', while thousands of Austrian and Hungarian internationalists were widening a new war in Siberia. Turkish troops had invaded Azerbaijan and parts of Dagestan, a Rudobel Partisan Republic had flared up in German-occupied Belarus, a German protectorate was raising its head in Crimea, an Austro-Hungarian occupation in Khotyn was about to give way to a Rumanian occupation and the flags of separatist governments flapped over Bukhara, Georgia, Alash Orda (Kazakhstan), Ruthenia and Ukraine.

THE WHITE TERROR BEGINS

Meanwhile, rebellious German soldiers in occupied Ukraine and Russia killed their officers and paraded through the streets of Kharkov, Odessa and Belgorod waving red flags and for a fleeting moment Lenin's vision of world revolution seemed to be unfolding.[92] Along the railway just west of the Urals, the CHEKA was hunting down 50,000 rebels of a worker–peasant army that failed in a proletarian revolt against Bolshevik excesses in August.[93] In other areas under Bolshevik control, a zealous, now formalized campaign of Red Terror (announced on 5 September) was in full swing, unleashing the CHEKA upon the starving, sickly population with the ferocity of a medieval inquisition.

A smorgasbord of White polities was separated not only by hostile armies but by sharply different visions of post-revolutionary Russia. A befuddled government in Archangel under Nikolai Vasil'evich Chaikovskii presided over frozen strips of land extending a few hundred miles down the Dvina river and railway. A northwestern Russian Regional Defense Council in Pskov was preparing to appoint its own government and General Denikin's Volunteer Army had carved a White tract out of the Kuban region along the Black Sea. In territories of the Don, Kuban, Astrakhan and Terek Cossack Hosts, a union of United Highlanders of the Northern Caucasus and Dagestan was merging with a Don–Kavkaz union. In western Siberia, Transbaikalia and the Amur and Maritime provinces, White execution squads roamed the countryside and villages torturing and killing all 'Reds', a damning label applied inconsistently depending upon recent partisan activity, a soldier's opinions of Mensheviks, Socialist-Revolutionaries, democrats and the provisional government, etc. and a potential victim's desirable belongings. The reactionary backlash had begun.

The White military command had gradually taken over the reins of the Provisional Siberian Government, running roughshod over the last vestiges of democracy and rule of law. A five-member directory representing an 'All-Russian Provisional Government' formed in Ufa 8 September now resided in Omsk, but right-wing military cliques quickly bullied them into submission.[94] In Omsk on 18 October the White General Staff ordered 'the military execution of agitators on the spot' to break a strike declared four days before by railway workers. On 24 October a group of the supposedly democratic-minded Czechs forced their way into Krasnoyarsk prison in western Siberia, hauled out five communist captives and shot them.[95] Peasants in the western Siberian district of Mariinsk, who had earlier revolted against the Tsar and then the Reds, now revolted against the Whites.[96] In Omsk, the capital of free Russia, a lackadaisically concealed monarchist gang calling itself the Mikhaikovski Hunting and Fishing Society ferreted out Socialist-Revolutionary members of the Constituent Assembly and sent them to the 'Kingdom of the Irtysh', in other words, murdered them and fed them to the fish. A prominent hunter was Ataman I.N. Krasilnikov, renowned for leading a reluctant Omsk orchestra in 'God Save the Tsar' with his pistol, who orchestrated the kidnapping of Constituent Assemblyman V.N. Moiseyenko and presumably presided over the latter's torture and ritual tossing into the Irtysh. The names and militarist organizations of the perpetrators of crimes like this were an open secret in Omsk.[97] It did not bode well for a government that claimed to be striving to restore law and order.

The White militarists' brutish behavior knew no bounds, and extended to their fellow soldiers as well. In December 1918 a story circulated about 10,000 Russian soldiers who were released from German prisoner of war camps and returned en masse to Siberia. When they passed through Samara, Red Army authorities gave each of them 25 rubles, felt boots, a coat and a recruiting pitch. Three thousand veterans enlisted and the rest continued on their way east in four trains. When they crossed into White territory, soldiers of the Omsk government relieved all of the homebound veterans of their money, boots and coats.[98] Whether true or not, the story reflected the general public perception of Kolchak's army. Meanwhile, tales of systematic brutality and plundering by Semenov's soldiers were circulating far and wide. Japan's *Osaka Mainichi* newspaper whined that the Japanese Army's reputation was being tainted by rumors of 'barbarous doings' by 'a band of unknown Cossacks' posing as Semenov troops.

Kalmykov's Khabarovsk

Khabarovsk fell ever deeper into the surreal nightmare that had begun in August when the Japanese Army installed Captain Ivan Pavlovich Kalmykov as garrison commander and 'town commandant'. He worked with his Russian chief of staff, Nepenov and General Oi, the Japanese division commander, to run the city. In early October 1918 Kalmykov's OKO was, according to a sympathetic British officer, 'recruiting, collecting supplies and doing secret service work with his forces in the region around Khabarovsk'. What the British officer did not explain in his report was that 'recruiting' sometimes meant taking men off the streets at gunpoint and forcing them into the ranks; 'collecting supplies' often meant robbery and 'secret service work' entailed arresting and executing anyone who could remotely be considered subversive.

OKO's 'very busy secret service' arrested 18 army officers for 'being *Bolsheviki*' soon after the White liberation. Major Malcolm Wheeler, a local US Army commander, asked Kalmykov's adjutant about their disposal in October. '*C'est tres triste, quel dommage*', he replied, with a melodramatic lifting of eyebrows and a gesture indicating that they had been shot. Five more officers surely feared a similar fate when they were discharged from the army intelligence staff on 2 October for 'having aided the *Bolsheviki* by translating for them'. While Wheeler noticed that most officers were 'bitterly anti-Bolshevik' monarchists, he also gathered that they were 'lukewarm supporters of Kalmykov' and 'lukewarmly patriotic', too – being mostly 'fond of wine, women and song'.[99]

When the local military academy opened on 15 October the immodest junior officer renamed it the Ataman Kalmykov Khabarovsk Military School and found a general, M.P. Nikonov, to serve as commandant. Kalmykov was not so disreputable that he could not round up 22 young men to join the first class. Events would force their course to be accelerated and condensed into ten months of training.[100]

At this time Kalmykov's OKO contained about 1,000 men and 40 'picked officers'. 'Not more than 30 percent would remain loyal in case of a showdown', predicted one American officer a short time later.[101] Kalmykov hoped to add 700 more Cossacks to his gang in mid-October after he orchestrated the fifth Ussuri Cossack Conference.

At 11 a.m. on 22 October Colonel Kalmykov (he had recently exchanged his captain's epaulets for a colonel's) strode into Khabarovsk's Garrison Club, his delicate frame dwarfed by the fawning crowd of brawny, garishly uniformed Cossacks. Kalmykov took his place at the head table in the cavernous hall and everyone arose, hushed as the boyish, 25-year-old raised an ornate mace, the emblem of the ataman of the Ussuri Cossacks. He spoke, 'I greet you, delegates of the fifth Conference of Ussuri Cossacks, which I call the fifth because I, as ataman, elected by the fourth authoritative conference, cannot call authoritative the series of conferences which were convened after it as these, in fact, were not authoritative...'. Everyone knew that Kalmykov was not a Cossack and had allegedly acquired his position through murder and willingness to make himself a Japanese pawn.

Nevertheless, the hall of Khabarovsk's Garrison Club resounded with robust applause as the little ataman opened the conference, giving unwanted thanks to the Czechs 'who raised the battle standard against the Bolshevik traitors' and calling for a moment of silence for fallen warriors. Kalmykov directed his warmest praise to his benefactors in the Japanese Army. He led the delegates in 'long "hurrahs" and applauses' for Captain Okabe, attending on behalf of the Japanese command. A few minutes later, the president of the

Ussuri Cossack Conference 'rewarded' Kalmykov with the rank of major general. Amidst 'continuous and stormy applause', the young man graciously accepted the honorarium which he himself and his Japanese sponsors had discreetly arranged.[102] Then a representative from Semenov's staff (named as Captain Savel'ev in a US Army report) read a message of solidarity, noting that '[Semenov] was always in full contact with Ataman Kalmykov's Detachment'.[103] Savel'ev also reminded Kalmykov and his Ussuri horde in a most tactful manner that they answered to Semenov in the Cossack pecking order. In conjunction with the White factions of the Transbaikal and Amur Cossacks, Kalmykov's Ussuri group accepted the formation of a Union of Far Eastern Cossack Armies with Semenov named *pokhodnii ataman*.[104]

Kalmykov was labeled a Japanese pawn and a Russian officer in Vladivostok informed the American headquarters, '[Kalmykov] executes all their orders without demur'.[105] In stark contrast to the groveling obedience that Kalmykov showed the Japanese in exchange for their generous subsidies, he refused to deal with his fellow anti-Bolshevik Russians in the Provisional Siberian Government. Things came to a head on the same day that the fifth Ussuri Cossack Conference opened. Admiral Kolchak had just become the Provisional Siberian Government's Minister of War and he was determined to cleanse the officer corps of miscreants like Kalmykov. A General Sulevich, residing in Harbin, was ordered by Omsk's loyal commander in Vladivostok to proceed to Khabarovsk to take over the new ataman's command. Kalmykov was indelicately notified via a telegram copy of the order:

To: General Sulevich, Harbin   22 October 1918
By order of the Commander of the Army, Ataman Kalmykov is: (1) subordinated to me; (2) must turn over the garrison command to you; (3) the non-compliance with this order will lead Kalmykov into trouble. The arrival of the commander will solve all questions which may arise.
(Colonel Butenko, Commander of the troops of
Primorsky province)

Kalmykov immediately fired off a defiant response to Colonel Butenko, piously intoning the 'honor and dignity of the officers of the Russian Army' and the 'iron discipline' of the brigands under his command. Kalmykov declared: 'I, the Ataman of the detachment formed by myself, categorically refuse, not only to obey, but even to work together with you.'[106]

White Cossackry came out in support of Kalmykov. From Nikolsk, 405 miles south of Khabarovsk, Kalmykov received an encouraging telegram signed by Major General Skipetrov, a notorious brute who was aide-de-camp to Semenov and 'Chief of the Ninth Siberian Fusilier Division'.[107] It was a bizarre dilemma for the generals in Omsk: two young upstarts – until recently just junior captains – not only flaunting open defiance of their orders, but also hinting strongly that they would take up arms at any attempt to subordinate Kalmykov. The day after the bitter telegraphic exchange between Kalmykov and Butenko, the Union of all Far Eastern Cossack contingents – Ussuri, Amur and Transbaikal – was announced.[108] Unfortunately for Colonel Butenko, Skipetrov and other Semenov loyalists were positioned along the line between Vladivostok and Khabarovsk and he knew that they would just as soon kill him as discuss their differences.

A more formidable obstacle to Butenko's desire to rein in Kalmykov was the Japanese 12th Division, which was distributed up the railway from Vladivostok through Khabarovsk. Just four days before Butenko's telegram, the *Osaka Mainichi* newspaper ran an anti-British diatribe that pointed out that Colonel Butenko 'is living in the same house as General Knox' and mentioned how Japan's supreme commander in Siberia, General Otani, 'especially sympathized' with Kalmykov.[109] It was a strange attack of words in light of the long

British–Japanese alliance that predated the Russo-Japanese war. Polish prisoner Roman Dyboski noted, 'From its position on top of Cadet Hill, with its main quarters in the handsome building of the Cadet Corps, the Japanese division gazed down with inhuman quiet on the terror spread by Kalmykov throughout the city of Khabarovsk'.[110]

Kalmykov grew ever stronger with discreet Japanese support, notwithstanding the presence of a Chinese Army contingent.[111] He commandeered at least one armored train for his sinister crusade and amassed a substantial arsenal: two 6-inch Schneider howitzers, four 3-inch Russian Model 1902 field guns, six 75-millimeter Argentine mountain guns, a pair of 75-millimeter Japanese mountain guns and five Lewis machine guns. The Japanese doled out ammunition to Kalmykov as it pleased them. Regardless, Kalmykov's artillery officers were 'not well trained technically...hazy as to theory and the capabilities of their own guns'; they occupied their spare time with saber practice.

Kalmykov had little immediate need for artillery; the Bolshevik partisans that had survived were laying low. Nevertheless, the killings of 'suspects' on trumped up charges continued. An American intelligence report explained:

> Most of the citizens he put to death had nothing to do with Bolshevism, but were rich. Men were put to death and their money was taken from them by the Juridical Department of Kalmykov's Detachment, at the head of which was Commander Kandaurov. When Kandaurov had, with Kalmykov's knowledge, accumulated almost a million rubles–stolen money, Kalmykov arrested his whole Juridical Department, confiscated the money for his own use and had Kandaurov and all the other members shot.[112]

Kalmykov's territory extended south to Nikolsk-Ussuriisk, where the White counterrevolution had yet to bring law and order, much less stabilize the economy. In early December Austro-Hungarian prisoners were still 'running wild over the town'. The city's largest coal mine had been returned to its owners, but output remained closer to the paltry 36 tons a day that was the norm under Red mismanagement than to the pre-revolutionary level of 180 tons daily. Another mine had flooded during the period of revolutionary neglect. Few workers intended to exert themselves for pay in currency of dubious value, yet limited quantities of lumber, hay, oats, flax, soy bean oil and soap were being sold by wholesalers. Like many other commercial and industrial centers in the Maritime and Amur provinces, Nikolsk's 50,000 or so citizens were suspended in a discomforting political and economic limbo.[113]

Though elegant and articulate, Kalmykov lacked Semenov's charisma, and his unbridled cruelty and avarice made him many enemies. The most dangerous were not the Bolsheviks, but the Chinese, whom Kalmykov hated. The feeling was mutual. Major General Gao Sin Shan, commander of the Chinese Army regiment at Pogranichnaya, was 'engaged in [very profitable] opium traffic' but underneath was a staunch patriot. He openly called Kalmykov 'a stupid boy' and, in June, even conspired with the Bolsheviks to rid Manchuria of Kalmykov and his whole detachment until the Czech uprising spoiled his plans. He would pass up no opportunity to do the arrogant Kalmykov harm. He and his brother, Gao Fin Tonen, who was soon to be promoted to lieutenant general and division commander in Harbin, were focused on one overriding objective: to rid China of the Russian and Japanese parasites.[114]

White nightmare in Blagoveshchensk

Blagoveshchensk, a prosperous river port facing China across the Amur, had also fallen into Semenov's dark orbit. Although the city had unwillingly become the last redoubt of the Bolsheviks and Anarchists back in September, Blagoveshchensk had a notable record of resistance to Red extremism. Military cadets had once overthrown a Red-dominated soviet before being crushed by Bolshevik troops. In mid-November 1918 US Army Captain Roger W. Straus visited to gauge the situation there: 'The peasants were and are sick of Bolshevik ideas and desire a conservative democratic and stable government; they were particularly disgusted with the actions of the Red Guard. Into this favorable condition has entered an extremely dangerous factor.' That factor was Semenov's emissary, Colonel Shemelin.

'General Shemelin looks more like a Mongol than a Cossack', observed US Army Captain F.F. Moore, who attended a banquet with him a few weeks later. 'He is very dark, has a very wicked face and altogether appears to be a man of very poor caliber. At the banquet he got very drunk and made speeches when he was scarcely able to stand on his feet.'[115]

At the request of the provincial governor to raise some troops for local defense, Semenov had dispatched Shemelin to Blagoveshchensk in late October or early November 1918. Instead of reporting to Ataman Gamov as a subordinate, 'for unknown reasons [he] declared himself commandant of troops of the Amur region'.[116] Colonel Shemelin gathered up a throng of Cossacks and a few ex-officers and, refusing to answer to anyone but Semenov, went on the rampage. Captain Straus observed, 'He has now about 250 men, recruited from the worst possible elements, many have been recognized as ex-Red Guardsmen, others as members of the old Imperial "Black Hundreds". In short, Shemelin has gathered together a very good imitation of the *Bolsheviki* Red Guard made up of men who want to pillage and rob and keep gloriously drunk'. His punitive detachments struck nearby towns, first killing anyone in jail accused of being a Bolshevik, then going house to house to rob the inhabitants. Blagoveshchensk's chief of police 'resigned because he did not have authority to check this lawlessness', and murmurs of rebellion rippled through the populace.[117]

Shemelin's outrages upon farmers in the surrounding agricultural district typified his senseless brutality. The trouble began when Aleksandrovskoe's police chief ordered the confiscation of all firearms in the district. Farmers in the town of Aleksandrovskoe complied, but in the outlying village of Bochkarevo, five farmers convinced their neighbors that if they gave up their weapons, their crops and horses might be next. Then farmers in the nearby village of Tomskoe also decided not to surrender their firearms. Backed by Japanese troops stationed at Bochkarevo train station, the Aleksandrovskoe police chief arrested five agitators. On November 11 Shemelin sent a 50–80-man detachment of Cossacks to Aleksandrovskoe under Lieutenant Lepushanski. They immediately executed four of the agitators, and flogged the fifth one before releasing him. For some unknown reason, Lieutenant Lepushanski then arrested and killed 14 more persons before moving on to Bochkarevo. Since learning of the agitators' killings, the Bochkarevo farmers had a change of heart and turned in their weapons without the slightest show of obstinacy. Unmoved by the peasants' submission, Shemelin's men started searching the houses. '[The] Cossacks behaved themselves in a very bad brutal manner', reported Captain Straus' well-informed source, Nicholas Romanov, 'while searching the houses they robbed many of farmers, taking money, golden ring[s], crosses and other valuable small articles'.[118]

'The same expedition went to town Tomskoe', continued Nicholas Romanov. 'They met no resistance and all farmers brought all their arms to Cossacks. But Cossacks arrested two farmers, Mr Malzev and Mr Litofka, and executed them, then they started same as at Bochkarevo to search houses, but only rich farmers.' A Cossack would enter a home, point his pistol at the head of the household and demand all valuables. Romanov's report gave a glimpse at these victims' pitiful 'wealth:' 'money...watches, rings, good and new overcoats, gloves, caps, etc.'. One Tomskoe farmer robbed by this punitive detachment had gained prominence in the district as an anti-Bolshevik fighter. Until this day the people had expected the Cossacks to restore order. Now they realized that no one was on their side.[119] Lieutenant Colonel Barrows predicted, 'Smarting under the violent treatment of the Cossacks, [the peasantry of Amur Province] should form a fertile field for the *Bolsheviki* to work on now'.[120]

Ataman Gamov of the Amur Cossacks appeared in Blagoveshchensk to encourage Shemelin's removal. Japanese General Nakajima took a train to Chita to scold Semenov for Shemelin's poor behavior. Semenov relieved Colonel Shemelin of his command on 9 December and Ataman Gamov took over.[121] The Japanese whisked Shemelin off to Harbin, where their General Yamato staged a press conference on 12 December, promising that Japan had no territorial designs on Russia and branding Semenov's errant colonel as insubordinate.[122] Nevertheless, Shemelin not only went unpunished, but within two months was promoted in rank and position.[123]

Shemelin's short, violent tenure in Amur province erased much popular support for the Whites, and emboldened the underground pockets of Bolsheviks. 'A small force of *Bolsheviki*' was reported along the Amur river just three miles from Blagoveshchensk in early December.[124] The day of Shemelin's departure from Blagoveshchensk, 500 Red Guards with two field guns and 25 machine guns emerged from the taiga to threaten a town in the northern part of the province.[125] Fortunately for the Reds, Semenov's thugs preferred thievery and looting to engaging the partisans.

Japanese Siberia

By early October, the Rising Sun was flapping over cities, towns and villages from the Vladivostok to Chita. They seemed to be everywhere in the Maritime province and, apparently in league with Kalmykov, 'took possession of Pogranichnaya' in an awkward, heavy-handed manner that raised eyebrows amongst the Allies in late September. RRSC Colonel Lantry saw Japanese 'railway guards' at every station on the Chinese Eastern and between Manchuli and Olovyannaya, with a large cavalry detachment at Dauria alongside a 600-man OMO base. On 7 October he estimated that no less than 10,000 Japanese soldiers of the 3rd 'Nagoya' Division had been pumped into Transbaikalia via Chang Chun during the previous ten days, at a feverish rate of three 500-man echelons per day. Their abrasive conduct amplified their presence into an 'occupation'. 'Complaints have come in from every side of petty abuse on the part of the Japanese troops', wrote Major Barrows, 'largely insolent behavior towards inhabitants and small acts of plunder. These reports may be partly ascribed to Russian prejudice against the Japanese, but in some cases are obviously due to bad discipline...'[126]

While Semenov made few strenuous efforts to win over the Russian population outside of Chita, he exerted himself to cosy up to his benefactors in the Japanese Army. A Japanese divisional headquarters (initially the 7th Division, then, successively, the 3rd and 5th Divisions) eventually planted itself comfortably close to Semenov in Chita. 'General Oba, commanding the Third Japanese Division, was a great friend of the Ataman's and I am certain they were working in perfect harmony', reported First Lieutenant Justis Davidson, the US intelligence officer in Chita.[127] Semenov's friendship did not come cheap, however. Rumor had it that the Japanese Government paid him a monthly allowance of ¥300,000 – on top of all the other support heaped upon the Ataman.[128] Perhaps it was money well spent, because Semenov and Kalmykov were fast becoming Japan's only friends in Siberia. Common Russians cynically referred to the Japanese Army as the 'Army of Salvation'.[129]

In late October 1918 a Japanese military mission under Baron Muto was dispatched to discuss 'strategic questions' with the Provisional Siberian Government.[130] The Baron and his infantry company escort went no further than Irkutsk while a Major Miko continued on to Omsk. Miko proposed to the Russian General Staff that Japan furnish guards for the bridges and railway lines west of Chita. Suspicious of Japanese intentions, the Provisional Siberian Government refused Major Miko's proposal.[131] Despite Omsk's objections, Japanese Army operations would eventually extend as far west as Irkutsk.

Semenov obligingly tried to hush Russian suspicions of Japanese intentions. For instance, in late October 1918, Semenov's military censor in Chita 'proposed to the editor of *Zabaikalskaya Zhizen* [newspaper] to abstain from criticizing measures and operations of our Allied country Japan'.[132] Another disrespectful Chita newspaper had already been shut down that week, so the editor understood the thinly veiled meaning of the censor's 'proposal': any newspaper that criticized the Japanese risked being closed. Nevertheless, no censor could shut the Russians' eyes to the Japanese' frantic commercial activities in areas under their occupation.

'Close on the heels of the Japanese military occupation', observed stranded Polish POW Roman Dyboski, 'came a whole train of Japanese merchants, industrialists and businessmen... These civilian forerunners of Japanese power eagerly bought up, on terms highly favorable to themselves, houses, shops and factories in all the larger cities of the Far East'.[133] Their buying spree extended at least as far west as Verkhne-Udinsk, where the Japanese tried to cajole Gdali Itzkovich and other local businessmen to part with their factories and businesses.[134] Japanese military men and civilians were tactful, discreet, paid up front for all products, and rarely if ever created any conflict with Russian merchants. Nevertheless, their purchases raised eyebrows.

The Japanese were buying 'real estate containing iron mines' in Transbaikalia in October 1918.[135] 'Not long ago they negotiated with the local industrialist Rozenfarb for the purchase of his gold and iron mines', reported one bold newspaper. Yet, much to the chagrin of Japanese buyers, the export of Russian iron was blocked in Vladivostok by none other than Colonel Butenko, who was accordingly chided by the *Osaka Mainichi* for being pro-British at Japanese expense.[136]

The Japanese Army overshadowed railway operations in Semenov's territory and Japanese companies controlled the Southern Manchuria Railway that linked Transbaikalia with China's nearest ports, Dairen and Port Arthur. This situation favored Japanese traders operating in the Russian Far East and eastern Siberia in many ways: customs payments were overlooked by Semenov's friendly or easily bribed agents, Japanese Army supply trains transported Japanese goods gratis, and, with these and other advantages, Japanese products became readily available, undersold their competitors and took over the marketplace in about six months. 'Japanese influence, wares and currency are evident on every hand', wrote a frequent traveler to Chita. 'Russian counterfeit rubles, made in Japan, flood the markets. In the station newsstand the only picture postal cards are Japanese-made...'.[137] By December 1918 the director of Chinese customs at Manchuli estimated that '75 percent of the dutiable goods which enter... with proper payment of tax' was of Japanese origin, and, furthermore, that when duties or tax were paid at all, it was usually by a foreign consignor.[138] Some Russian merchants reluctantly agreed to pay Japanese middlemen a percentage of their profits for shepherding their merchandise from port to sales points. By summer 1919 this shady arrangement would be prevalent throughout Transbaikalia. Tokyo's commercial invasion thundered west in boxcars. Japanese products relentlessly conquered the store shelves and stockrooms of eastern Siberia. An American military intelligence officer surveyed economic conditions on a March 1919 journey from Harbin to Omsk and where stores had any goods at all, he found, 'The whole market today is practically Japanese, although I found at Krasnoyarsk two [trading] houses which had British woolens to the amount of 1,300,000 rubles lately imported'. Wholesale speculators could not have functioned without the Japanese, who shepherded goods through Semenov's customs and provided discount transport, thus saving duty and freight costs. 'This is done by giving "squeeze" to the train guards, Japanese trains mostly, but in some cases this has been done with Russians and Czechs.' The effects of Semenov's embargoes, extortion and theft were recognizable west of Novonikolaevsk, where the commercial supply picture worsened. By the time the officer reached Omsk, 'there [was] little or no supply of any goods, resulting in...prohibitive prices'.[139]

An American YMCA secretary in Verkhne-Udinsk, W.H. Blaine, befriended a local businessman, Gdali Itzkovich, whose son gave Blaine a tour of the family's large department store and an earful of Yiddish–Russian complaints about the unpleasantries of doing business with the Japanese. 'During the conversation I found that every bit of the merchandise was from Japan and had been shipped in during the past few months coming through as military supplies. Several of the boxes they were emptying while I was there had the Red Cross on their sides....They paid the Japs a certain percent of their profits in order to get the goods through.' Young Itzkovich chided Blaine for the astounding naivete of the Americans in Siberia. Blaine remarked, 'They [the Russian merchants] dislike the Japanese and the Japanese goods and do not want to do business with them, but are forced to on account of the difficulties of transportation'.[140]

Many Japanese Army officers had no qualms about making money on the side during their military campaign. An AEFS investigator discovered, 'Captain Kuroki does not content himself with being...an evil councilor; he is, as occasions require, a very practical Japanese and even a businessman'. He was angling to obtain 'a forestry concession of several thousand hectares in the vicinity of Argun' from Ataman Semenov, to whom he offered a 10 million ruble payment. The investigator did not seem surprised that a Japanese army captain of Kuroki's ilk could accumulate such wealth.[141]

Even other Allied forces in Siberia experienced Japan's heavy-handedness and arrogant bullying. On 16 October a petty misunderstanding between Japanese and Italian troops almost resulted in a pitched battle at a train station in Changchun, Manchuria.[142] An Italian Army echelon changing trains from the Southern Manchuria Railway to the Chinese Eastern placed sentries to guard its luggage as it was heaved from one train to another. A Japanese laborer who wanted to pass through the Italian guard line was not allowed to do so, and complained to a nearby Japanese captain. The latter attempted 'to take away' one of the Italian guards. The Italians took up their rifles and the Japanese called up a company of their soldiers. Luckily, quick talking between officers from both Allied armies averted a shootout for control of this Manchurian train platform.[143] No doubt Changchun's largely Chinese population was amused by this affront to the Japanese Army. The town had become the reluctant host to a huge Japanese military base of 'hospitals, large warehouses and barracks...crammed with Japanese soldiers'.[144]

About the same time, the British 25th Middlesex Battalion paused in Manchuli on its way to the frontlines beyond Omsk hundreds of miles further west. Colonel John Ward, the 25th's commander, was irritated because most of his officers had been riding in cattle cars. Intent that his officers should have some modicum of comfort before they went into battle, Colonel Ward secured the station commandant's permission to allocate two idle passenger cars to his men. Two hours passed, and the passenger cars were still not shunted onto the British echelons. Colonel Ward exploded when he discovered that the Japanese 'had given instructions that no "class" carriages were to be provided for British officers', and had 'spirited away' the station commandant to make sure. 'I informed the authorities that nothing should be shunted in that station until those two carriages were joined to my trains', wrote Colonel Ward, 'and proceeded to occupy the whole station'. For 23 minutes, the 25th Middlesex Battalion held Manchuli station. Then the Japanese agreed to relinquish the passenger carriages. Ward removed his guards, and sat down to dinner. When he emerged, eager to depart Manchuli, he found the idle carriages surrounded by Japanese soldiers. He promptly ordered more than 30 Tommies with fixed bayonets onto the disputed cars while they were shunted onto his trains. Meanwhile a contingent of Chinese soldiers had joined the act, surrounding Colonel Ward's car to defend it against any Japanese intrusion. The Japanese guards faded away one by one. However, before leaving Manchuli, a pair of Japanese officers harangued Ward's liaison officer for displaying the Union Jack on one of the trains without authority. 'I answered it was an English train carrying an English battalion to Omsk, and no authority was necessary', growled Colonel Ward. 'The Japanese officers replied that they considered the flying of any other flag than theirs in Manchuria or Siberia an insult to Japan. I told them they were fools.'[145]

The incidents at Changchun and Manchuli stations showed how volatile the Siberian situation could become, even among the Allied detachments, which now included Japanese, British, American, Canadian, Italian, French and Chinese units. Serbs, Poles, men from a variety of central Asian nations that had been swallowed and regurgitated by the tsarist empire, and released prisoners of war from the Central Powers were all serving under various Russian commands. Friction was inevitable between so many tired, armed men from so many different cultures pursuing diverse political and military agendas that sometimes varied from unit to unit. Soon it would be evident that tension between the all-Russian, anti-Bolshevik factions was growing even more explosive.

Another incident should have served to remind the Japanese and all of the anti-Bolshevik factions exactly who the enemy was, however. On 2 November 1918 an assassin crept into Chita's Red Cross Hospital, killed a *semenovets* torturer named Valyaev and escaped. It was the first slaying by a recently formed 'fighting group' controlled by the underground coordinating committee of left-wing parties. Russia's diehard revolutionaries had little fear of reactionaries like Semenov.[146]

Death trains

Capture during Russia's civil war often meant summary execution – or worse. Neither Whites nor Reds considered captured opponents as prisoners of war; prisoners were often considered subversives who were liquidated without fuss, although the Red Army and partisans would eventually make efforts to win over certain captured Whites through agitation, indoctrination and threats.[147] Reds captured in Siberia were not usually offered a chance to reconsider their affiliation, and only a fraction of them ever saw the inside of Siberia's substantial prisoner-of-war camp system that still housed thousands of German and Austro-Hungarian soldiers.

Ever since the White uprising succeeded in the autumn of 1918, 'death trains' trolled the Trans-Siberian Railway between Irkutsk and the Maritime province looking for some place to dispose of their miserable human cargo. Most of the unwilling passengers were believed to have been taken prisoner by White armies on the Volga and Ural battlefronts hundreds of miles to the west. Apparently, the trains were crammed full of captives near the front and sent east without coordination with their intended destinations (if any thought had actually been given to a destination). No one among the train crews or guards possessed authority or rank to requisition food or fuel, if any could be found. It became proof that the White generals made no effort to set themselves above the Bolsheviks when it came to the treatment of prisoners.

American railway experts first took notice of them in November 1918. A rancid-smelling train of boxcars sitting in the Vladivostok railyard on 13 November caught engineer Fred

Roberts' attention. It was full of 'Red Guard Russians' who had been loaded into the cars 37 days before and had 'not much to eat' since then. That train disappeared and others rumbled slowly through the yards, becoming so commonplace as to not warrant mention much concern.[148]

A typical 'death train' pulled into Nikolsk around 20 November 1918. More than 1,300 Austrian and Bolshevik prisoners were crammed into 40 *taplushkas*, where they had been loaded six weeks earlier in faraway Samara with 800 less fortunate prisoners who perished during the trip. The dead had been 'shot while trying to escape...lost their lives by throwing themselves from the car windows', or succumbed to 'disease, starvation and exposure'. The train carried no provisions or 'sanitary equipment' of any kind. When the train pulled into the railyard at Nikolsk, the *taplushkas* were oozing human waste and blood. The Japanese Army, the principal power in Nikolsk, refused to do anything. However, the American Red Cross rushed doctors in from Vladivostok to tend to the survivors. Many prisoners succumbed to death as they were unloaded. YMCA secretary Edward Heald said, 'I saw these wretched fluttering pale shadows of humanity, some of them too weak to lift a hand to carry bread to their mouths. The strongest staggered out to beg bread, which they brought back to their starving comrades.' Newspaper correspondents witnessed the horrible episode and filed the first stories about the 'death trains'.[149] The men on this train were lucky to have received any aid and attention, however.

About the same time, an eastbound train pulled into Chita carrying 1,000 people. Among them were not only common criminals and war prisoners, but also an unspecified number of 'innocent women and children'. For days the train sat in the railyard. General Ivanov-Rinov forbade concerned citizens of Chita to render assistance to the wretched passengers, even though they 'were starving and without heat in the cars'. After five days in Chita, the train was sent back to the west. US Army Captain Skladal tried to keep track of the train but to no avail.[150]

Edward Heald, the YMCA man who witnessed the 'death train' in Nikolsk days earlier, saw another on the Chinese Eastern line between Bukhedu and Hailar on 26 November. Russian and Czech Legion guards loitered around the carload of prisoners on a siding.

> Russian railway workers at the station asked me why the Americans allowed such a crime, for these prisoners were starving to death and no one was feeding them bread. 'Why don't the Russians feed them?' I asked... 'Semenov', he answered. 'Why do the Russians allow Semenov to do this?' I asked again. The reply was a shrug of the shoulders while they pointed in the direction of the Japanese soldiers standing on guard at the station. 'The Army of Salvation prevents it', they said.[151]

Two days later Heald saw another 'death train' full of tattered *Bolsheviki* at Olovyannaya.

> They looked more like animals than any group of human beings I ever saw. They fought with each other for the pieces of bread which some of them were able to buy... When I asked where they were going, the reply was, 'Back and forth.' The attitude of their captors, both Russians and Czechs, seemed to be that they were suffering just punishment for the cruelties they had perpetrated, and that to keep running them around the country would have a salutary effect of fear on the population.[152]

Since Captain Skladal arrived in Chita on 1 November 1918, he endeavored to monitor all shipments of prisoners through the local railyard. In the month of November, 5,689

Bolshevik prisoners passed through Chita to the east, however '2,478 were returned for lack of room near Vladivostok'. These captives were subsequently unloaded at Chita and various little Transbaikal stations west of Chita. Whatever happened to them after that was a mystery. On 2 December Captain Skladal reported, 'No more prisoners will be sent east from here.'[153]

Train No. 53 slipped through Transbaikalia before this last order took effect. This train pulled 38 cars packed with 800 Red prisoners, about one-third of whom were ill with typhoid, dysentery and influenza. Eight men onboard had gone insane. No. 53 pulled into Nikolsk and was turned back to the west. Chinese Eastern Railway officials refused to let the train unload in Manchuria, so it reluctantly chugged back into Transbaikalia.[154] Like the famished, ghost-like souls on most 'death trains', these 800 men vanished. Apparently the December 1918 stoppage was temporary and the 'death trains' continued their macabre service until the fall of Omsk in November 1919.[155]

The Ataman versus the Supreme Ruler

On 18 November just one week after the guns went silent on the Western Front and streets in London, Paris and Washington reverberated with jubilant mobs celebrating peace and victory over the Central Powers, a small group of White officers in Omsk engineered a coup against the Directory, the executive body of the Provisional Siberian Government. Semenov's nemesis, Admiral Aleksandr Kolchak, was thrust into the role of Supreme Ruler. The dark days of Siberia's 'rule by court-martial' had begun.[156]

Semenov had never accepted Kolchak's authority as Minister of War, and publicly labeled him a 'mediocre invalid' who 'had done nothing for the anti-Bolshevik cause beyond tossing his sword into Sevastopol harbor', referring to the Admiral's emotional June 1917 resignation of his Black Sea fleet command when sailors' soviets demanded that officers be disarmed.[157] Now the bitter rivalry between the old patriotic admiral and the young maverick ataman came to a head. The day after Kolchak took power, Semenov assumed 'total military authority' in areas under his control, cutting off Omsk from the Russian Far East.[158] In the days after the coup, Admiral Kolchak tried to get through via telegraph to Major General Alfred Knox who was visiting Vladivostok, but found that Semenov was interrupting all wire communications in Chita. Chita and Omsk began swapping hostile messages. Semenov renamed the 5th Pri-Amur Independent Corps as the Separate Eastern Siberian Army, and for the next several months issued orders under that breakaway mantle.[159]

On 26 November US Army observers reported that 'the Japanese are behind Semenov in his opposition to Kolchak...Japanese Staff Captain Kuroki has been urging Semenov to declare himself dictator of the Transbaikalia and to seize the [Lake Baikal] tunnels and the railway; and that Semenov has recently received 5,000,000 rubles, and he plans to issue his own currency'.[160] At least one Japanese newspaper (*Osaka Mainichi*) casually referred to Transbaikalia as lying within 'a sphere of Japanese influence'.[161] In addition to Major General Nakajima's belittling report on the admiral in May and the general Japanese view that he was too pro-British for their tastes, Kolchak had recently refused to allow the Japanese Army to garrison towns in eastern Siberia and obstructed the juicy commercial concessions that they savored in Russia's Far East.[162]

OMO and Japanese troops began holding up supply trains bound for Omsk. Kolchak was enraged. Workers on the Chinese Eastern Railway, no fond admirers of Supreme Ruler Kolchak themselves, then refused to handle any more war supplies for Semenov. Semenov was enraged. He wired his agents at each station between Manchuli and Harbin to rectify the situation with drawn revolvers and threats of 'court-martials' (i.e. execution) for all disobedient Chinese Eastern employees. The dissension rippled through all the Russian and Allied forces in Siberia, creating suspicion and a splintering into distrusting cliques: the Japanese and Semenov with their Cossack, Mongol and Manchurian allies; Kolchak with his Kadets, industrialists and big merchants, clergy, monarchists, democrats and traditional patriots supported by British advisors and Polish and Rumanian Legions; the Czechoslovak Legion and its French advisors; and the Americans, Canadians and Chinese toeing independent paths. Only days before, on 15 November, they had all marched together in Vladivostok's Armistice Day parade. It took less than two weeks for the world war's unity of purpose to evaporate.

On 1 December Admiral Kolchak issued Order No. 60, a directive relieving Semenov of command and ordering his court martial for 'banditry and insubordination'.[163] Captain Conrad Skladal, an US military intelligence officer who had arrived in Chita one month earlier and complained of 'constant trouble with Ataman Semenov since his arrival', reported high tension around the OMO headquarters and 'that his own Cossacks have sent a messenger to Kolchak reporting their adherence to him; that the Serb regiment at Chita had openly refused to obey, and that the infantry regiment here was pro-Bolsheviks. Nobody, in fact, remained loyal to Semenov except his Mongolian Buryats with whom he was ready to fly to Mongolia in case of need'. Even many among the civilian population were already rooting for Semenov's ouster 'on account of his brutalities'.[164] That night rumors circulated in Chita streets that Semenov had been 'arrested by his own officers'. Whether the tales were based upon an actual attempt by pro-Kolchak officers or merely upon the grumbling of the disenchanted is a mystery.[165]

'As early as 2 December 1918, after detailed information of the aims and substance of the [November 18] Omsk revolution were received, I decided to recognize Admiral Kolchak and I sent him a telegram to this effect', claimed Semenov a short time later. 'But on receiving at the same time telegraphic Order No. 60, I was compelled to change this decision.'[166] He received enthusiastic encouragement from his Japanese advisors.

A few days later, General Inagaki, a Japanese commander in Chita, stated that 'he did not believe that Kolchak could arrest Semenov because the Japanese would not allow Kolchak to use force'.[167] In other words, if the Serb mercenaries, half-hearted Cossack units and OMO's 1,000 Mongol warriors in Chita failed to protect the Ataman, Japanese troops would. General Janin, head of the French Military Mission, informed Kolchak from Chita that the Japanese would resist any attempt by the Omsk government to move troops east of Lake Baikal.[168] Exasperated, the Omsk government finally demanded on 5 December that Japanese diplomats publicly acknowledge their back-alley dealings with Semenov.

That same day Admiral Kolchak published a foreboding order to Major General Vyacheslav I. Volkov, military governor of Irkutsk, to seize Semenov:

> *To*: Major General Volkov   5 December 1918
> Commander of the Fifth Siberian Corps, Colonel Semenov for disobedience and infringement of the telegraphic service in the rear of the Army, which is an act of high treason, is hereby dismissed as Commander of the Fifth Corps, and relieved entirely from all duties imposed upon him of the Siberian Cossack Troops and subject the Fourth and Fifth Corps Districts in all regards and on the rights of a Commander of a separate Army, and with appropriation of the authority of General Tieverhor subordinate immediately to me. I order General Volkov to bring to obedience all renegades to the Supreme Authority according to the laws of wartime.
>
>   SIGNED (Admiral Kolchak)[169]

The following day, refugees on eastbound Trans-Siberian trains out of Irkutsk, who thought they had left the war hundreds of miles behind them to the west, were startled to see a battle raging between two White units. The combatants were Volkov's and Semenov's men.[170]

Major General Volkov was no liberal reformer or whiner about epaulets. He had been active in the Western Siberian Commissariat (WSC) and Cossack League, and was a member of the Siberian Cossack Host. While cynics expected Cossacks to put tribe before nation, Semenov's defiance suggested that he had a higher calling than even his Cossack tribe – power, gold and the almighty yen.

Volkov had quickly assembled a punitive expedition at Irkutsk where anti-Semenov sentiments ran strong, and headed east by train towards Chita, certain that he could dispose of the *semenovtsy* in three or four days.[171] He deposited a detachment alongside Lake Baikal with orders to blow up the railway tunnel at Sludyanka if any of the many Semenov units to his rear made a move for Irkutsk.[172] Volkov's echelons continued east and progressed as far as Mogzon, 87 miles west of Chita, where Semenov's garrison prevented them from going further. Volkov issued an ultimatum to Semenov to withdraw his men within 24 hours. Semenov responded by sending reinforcements to Mogzon with orders to attack Volkov. In case Volkov broke through, OMO troops ripped up the rails east of Mogzon to prevent him from advancing towards Chita.

Meanwhile, at Manchuli that night, OMO soldiers arrested Colonel Vsevolozhskii, a pro-Kolchak officer who was chief of the traffic bureau (and thus in charge of troop movements) for the Chinese Eastern Railway. All rail traffic was thrown into confusion.[173] General Horvath fired off a telegram to the 'neutral' Japanese commander, Semenov's friend General Fujii, pleading for Vsevolozhskii's release for the sake of the railway. General Fujii 'arranged bail' for Vsevolozhskii, but not before the railway convulsed with disorder.

The standoff continued for days in temperatures that hovered around $-20°F$. A trainload of pro-Omsk troops on the Chinese Eastern Railway, apparently intending to approach Chita from the south, was halted by the Japanese Army at Bukhedu, Manchuria (between Hailar and Tsitsihar) at 4 a.m. on 9 December. The Japanese even disassembled their train 'to prevent its surreptitious departure'.[174] Later that day it became obvious that Volkov's punitive expedition was fizzling out as his men began fraternizing with Semenov's. East of Chita, an anti-Semenov uprising in Nerchinsk was crushed. The young warlord was weathering the storm.

Nevertheless, the Omsk–Chita riff spawned strange disturbances and rare opportunities for dissent inside Semenov's realm. Provisional Siberian Government troops assigned to Semenov's 5th Corps command at Verkhne-Udinsk and other places gladly refused to obey the ataman after Kolchak's 5 December order.[175] A few weeks later an OMO colonel was arrested after he was overheard saying that Semenov would submit to Kolchak.[176] Semenov's purchasing agent in Harbin, an opportunist named Piper, defected from the ataman's service and cut off his supplies, figuring that his downfall was imminent. Piper passed on the strangest tale of recent events: 'At Chita [the] Japanese got frisky with some members of the Serbian machine gun company stationed there, finally trying to rush them. The latter turned a machine gun on them, incapacitating about a hundred. The rest fled. The Serbians lost six men killed. There is now talk of removing the Serbian M.G. Company to Harbin.' The American intelligence officer who interviewed Piper noted, 'This is certainly a good story'.[177]

Events along the Chinese Eastern Railway forced the Chinese Army to reluctantly get involved. The menacing antics of OMO thugs and heavy-handed Japanese soldiers had demoralized the railway workers. Regular traffic had been interrupted for weeks. It seemed to be a good time to reassert Chinese sovereignty while so many OMO and Japanese garrison troops had been called away to the standoff with Volkov at Mogzon. Thus on 9 December General Myn, Chinese commander of the Tsitsihar District, dispatched additional troops to stations between Manchuli and Hailar. They were not able to prevent Japanese and OMO bullying though. Just five days later, 50 OMO soldiers drove a locomotive into the railway yards at Tsitsihar itself and rode off with 25 embargoed carloads of military supplies right under General Myn's nose. Yet Semenov's most brazen trampling of Chinese sovereignty occurred at Manchuli, where the local OMO commandant, Colonel Isaev, and his 200 men relieved the Chinese Customs office of 650,000 rubles 'under threat of armed force', although they *did* write out a receipt for the money they took. General Myn could do nothing but protest without provoking the Japanese Army.[178]

The standoff at Mogzon ended in mid-December when Major General Volkov disarmed his Omsk troops upon receiving an ultimatum from General Fujii. The terms of Fujii's ultimatum were not made public, but the presence of thousands of combat-ready Japanese troops in the vicinity surely weakened Major General Volkov's resolve. English and French military observers demanded that Semenov also disarm – to no avail, of course.[179]

The tension persisted. 'Semenov sees personal danger. Is not supported by Cossacks. Wants Kolchak's Order No. 60 revoked', wired Captain Skladal on 17 December, just as new rumors of the ataman's arrest flew across the pages of Harbin newspapers.[180] The next day Semenov took the offensive, setting up OMO checkpoints and machine guns in the streets of Verkhne-Udinsk and arresting all public officials there. Japanese guards had obligingly withdrawn.[181]

Meanwhile Major General Graves sent his senior intelligence officer, Lieutenant Colonel David P. Barrows, to Chita to see what was going on. Lieutenant Colonel Barrows met with Ataman Semenov on 18 December and with General Oba the following day. Both meetings were cordial. General Oba convinced Barrows that White leaders in Vladivostok and Harbin 'exaggerated the seriousness of the situation'. Barrows, somewhat naively it seems, accepted General Oba's explanation of events: 'He [General Oba] declares that he advised Semenov to recognize Kolchak, and that he has warned Volkov at Irkutsk as well as Semenov that he will permit no hostilities on the line of the Trans-Baikal railways. He affirms that he is quite neutral as regards Kolchak and Semenov.'[182] The acting US Secretary of State, Frank Polk, was not so accepting, and, on the very day of the Barrows–Oba meeting, protested via Ambassador Roland S. Morris in Japan, 'The Government of the United States believes that the present policy of Japan is fraught with possibility of dangerous consequences for Russia...It is not to be understood that this Government desires to support Admiral Kolchak as against General Semenoff, but merely [that] its purpose is to see that loyal Russians be allowed to manage their own affairs'.[183]

Soon General Oba and the Japanese staff brokered a settlement to the Kolchak–Semenov squabble, although ill feelings simmered for a year. Semenov promised to recognize Kolchak as Supreme Ruler, and Kolchak withdrew the order that branded the ataman as a traitor and relieved him of his command. Neither Semenov nor Kolchak had prevailed. But the Japanese had pried their way deeper into Russian affairs. Now – to the consternation of pro-Kolchak officers and their European allies – Japanese officers announced their intention to take control of the trains and make the railway function again.[184]

Chita had begun to wilt without the commerce–both illicit and legitimate–that the railway normally brought. 'There is barely one train a day between Manchuria and Irkutsk', reported the Associated Press in late December, 'and during the last ten days only two freight trains have come through from Manchuria because of the lack of locomotives'.[185]

Refugees and the poor and feeble faced death by starving or freezing. Only the Japanese and the Bolsheviks had benefited from the Supreme Ruler's Order No. 60.

Gloomy Omsk at its peak

Shortly after the 18 November coup Edward Heald, the young YMCA representative, had passed through Omsk. During his short stopover, Heald admired the 'well laid out city of generous proportions with big business blocks' like Petrograd. He noticed 'plentiful and fine' cheese, and bought a cheap dinner of beefsteak, soup and fried potatoes.[186] 'The sleighs are more numerous and finer than in other cities...' marveled Heald. 'The inhabitants are remarkably well dressed. I am almost reminded of Nevsky Prospect [in Petrograd]. Most of the people are big, healthy, splendid-looking specimens physically, with little of the spoiled feminism of the capital.' Heald returned to Omsk several days later for a prolonged stay that tarnished the glow on his first impressions. Newsboys still hawked papers in the streets, soldiers drilled, and 'people remained at outdoor work' – mainly hauling firewood – during days like 19 December when the top temperature reached only − 29°F. '[The Russians] are eternally bundled up, especially the women who waddle around like animated rag mountains.'[187] Many refugees, particularly Russian soldiers returning from German and Austrian prisoner-of-war camps, had few clothes to bundle in. Heald distributed tea with sugar and 'big cartwheel hard-tack biscuits' to them, but they still had to sleep in unheated boxcars.

In December 1918, the Siberian winter's gloom darkened moods more than ever before. Dusk began to blacken the city around 3 p.m., and even affluent buildings and mansions usually fell into the murky shadows with the hovels of the poor because the municipal electric system failed so often. What light there was during the long Siberian nights was usually a soft glow reflected off the endless snowdrifts. This winter's melancholy was tinged with fear from right-wing death squads, political terrorists of every stripe, and inordinate numbers of desperate, insane or villainous strangers. Even Mother Nature seemed to conspire against the citizens of Omsk. The temperature fell several degrees below normal. On 20 December Heald wrote, 'It has not gotten above 25 degrees below zero [Fahrenheit] any time during the day for the last five days.'[188] Some of Omsk's misery was attributable to Semenov's interference with the economy.

Despite these conditions, the surviving Bolsheviks in Omsk emerged from hiding to attempt a coup of their own during the night of 21–22 December – the longest of the year. They took over the jail and released all 200 political prisoners (Socialist-Revolutionaries as well as Bolsheviks) into the −50°F darkness. However, they failed to capture army headquarters or other government buildings, and soon withdrew about five miles west of Omsk to the industrial suburb of Kulomzino, a village dominated by railway workers.

'The city is under martial law this morning', wrote Edward Heald on 22 December. 'The first word we got was that all the thieves and criminals in the jail had gotten out at night. The next was that there was a general uprising of the Bolsheviki. The next that certain [army] companies of the younger Russians had mutinied.'[189] That afternoon around Kulomzino, Czechoslovak detachments destroyed the remaining Bolshevik rebels, killing 80, wounding 400 and taking 1,500 prisoners. An unknown number of Bolsheviks faded into the taiga. The well-disciplined Czechs lost one man killed and just two wounded. Everyone in Omsk tried to sleep early that night as an 8 p.m. shoot-on-sight curfew went into effect. Heald glumly noted, 'Theatres, restaurants, hotels, kinos all dark...'.[190]

Armed with the pretext of the Bolsheviks' almost suicidal coup attempt, Omsk authorities set about rounding up all remaining opposition, Bolshevik or not. Kolchak did not give Major General Ivanov-Rinov a free hand to liquidate anyone he pleased, but to observers it certainly appeared that the Supreme Ruler acquiesced while the most reactionary elements of his command went on a vengeful rampage, even shooting the 35 young soldiers who had surrendered the jail to the insurgents. Many freed prisoners – few, if any, of them Bolsheviks – willingly returned to the jail after an intimidating ultimatum from the White command. They were promptly executed, several members of the Constituent Assembly among them. Major General Graves and the American staff in Vladivostok were appalled when they heard the news.[191]

Omsk's only booming businesses seemed to be White execution squads. 'Go into the beautiful stone blocks of business buildings here, handsome, solid, columned structures that would be a credit to Chicago or New York, and what do you see?' implored Edward Heald.[192] 'Empty rooms where formerly were busy counters and throngs of purchasers and clerks. Great tiers of empty shelves...They now house investigation committees, government offices, consular offices, generals and their staffs, or refugees and soldiers.' Heald's YMCA office soon occupied one of these forlorn chambers. With the economy – and morale – in such a shambles, no wonder that a transient railway engineer noticed 'considerable drunkenness among the common people' in Omsk, even though the local government distillery sold vodka at an exorbitant 15 rubles per bottle and limited sales to one bottle per person.[193]

Though no one realized it at the time, Admiral Kolchak's luck peaked on 23 December. He had crushed all elected opposition as well as the Bolsheviks in Omsk, and worked out a grudging compromise with the upstart Semenov. On this day the supreme dictator's army captured the city of Perm, far outside of Siberia and west of the Urals. For a fleeting moment, the fantasy that Kolchak's soldiers might be able to link up with forces from the Whites' north Russian bastion around Archangel almost seemed believable. Yet, as Peter Fleming wrote, 'Things could hardly have gone much worse in Siberia if Semenov had been in power.'[194]

Attempt on the Ataman's life

By 19 December 1918 an end to Semenov's troubles with Admiral Kolchak was in sight. The ataman decided to relax at the premiere of an operetta at Chita's Mariinskii Theatre that evening. The dark throng of spectators, all needing a respite from Russia's strife as much as their leader, was brightened by the colorful bouquets brought in for the cast of 'Pupsik'. During the second act, about 10 p.m., 'a man wearing a uniform' – perhaps aided by one or more accomplices, no one seemed sure – carefully removed two bombs hidden in a bunch of flowers, then suddenly tossed the explosives toward Semenov's box. Luckily for Semenov and other theatre patrons, one of the bombs failed to detonate. Still, a single blast stunned the audience and Semenov's retinue of bodyguards. In the ensuing commotion at least one revolver blazed away in the ataman's direction as the assassin – or assassins – escaped. Miraculously no one in the crowded theatre was struck by a bullet. The bomb, on the other hand, killed a woman and child, seriously wounded a Serbian officer and his lady, and injured seven others, including Semenov and his *femme de jour*. The ataman was rushed to the hospital and treated for serious leg wounds that would keep him bed-ridden for the next three weeks.[195]

A shocked stillness fell over Chita as OMO patrols and pickets clamped down on the city. Large numbers of arrests were made in the hours after the bombing. Semenov's American friend, Lieutenant Colonel Barrows, dropped in to see him at the hospital the next day. He found him 'resting easily in bed, right elbow and ankle bandaged'. Normalcy returned briefly to the streets as the Chinese Eastern Association celebrated the Armistice and Allied victory with a parade and banquets. Yet nightfall brought anxiety and fear. Semenov sent one of his *broneviks* to Ingoda as a 'precautionary measure' against rebellion.[196]

An extraordinary court of inquiry was assembled immediately and every civilian and military investigator in the area was put on the case. Three separate investigations by the military, counterintelligence and police were launched and within a matter of days 200 people had been arrested.

In a short time, a veteran Chita detective, Aleksandr Vladimirovich Domrachev announced that he had identified the assassin, found a witness from the theatre, uncovered a document purported to be the secret order for Semenov's execution, and retrieved a grenade stashed in a log in the home of a conspirator. Just five days after the Mariinskii Theatre bombing, Domrachev took an alleged accomplice, Dmitri I. Shikunts, into custody, and within the next five days collared the bomber, Semen I. Voropaev, and another accomplice, Zasulevich. Shikunts and Voropaev were both miners from the radicalized Chernovskii mines. The industrious Domrachev coaxed further details of the crime out of the trio by beatings, and when the information was insufficient, laid Voropaev and Shikunts down at an angle and poured boiling water from a teapot into their nostrils. Domrachev's boss, Chief of Police Kamennov, was impressed. Regrettably, all three accused men were innocent.[197]

The military investigation pursued a different tack. Since the assassination of Valyaev at the Red Cross hospital weeks before, Semenov's counterintelligence had been watching the house of Ivan Grigor'ev, a member of the Socialist-Revolutionary hit squad. Apparently through that surveillance, a soldier of the 31st Regiment, Matvei Berenbaum (alias Vasilii Nerris), was identified as a suspect and an order was issued for his questioning.

New Year celebrations were more subdued than ever in Russia when the rest of the world rang in a peaceful 1919. Not only did the volatile political situation undermine the cheerfulness, but most people recognized the Julian calendar's 1 January as New Year's Day with great reluctance. To most, it was the 'Bolshevik New Year', because the Reds had converted Russia from the medieval Gregorian calendar to the modern Julian one. 'The big celebration will be according to the old date as in the past', observed Heald in Omsk. 'The Russians celebrated it very little aside from taking a day off from work.'[198]

However, neither the leftist underground nor White counterintelligence relaxed. One half-step ahead of the investigators, Berenbaum slipped onto a train for Blagoveshchensk on New Year's Day and made it as far as Priiskovaya (near Nerchinsk) before a military patrol scrutinizing all passengers recognized him, wrestled him down and hauled him back to Chita. His celebrity was acknowledged by a private cell, extra guards and special tortures.

Berenbaum valiantly denied everything at first, but soon surrendered to his torment and revealed what he knew about the assassination plot. He had volunteered to the Union of Socialist-Revolutionary-Maximalists for the Mariinskii Theatre job in order to avenge killings, beatings and humiliation by the *semenovtsy*, yet he did not know the surnames of two accomplices who accompanied him to the theatre and helped him get away. By 20 January 1919 OMO counterintelligence learned the names and picked up Ivan Grigor'ev, the Red Cross hospital killer, and the organizer of the plot, Aleksandr Pavlovich Sofronov, a 29-year-old Cossack who was none other than the former commander of the 2nd Verkhne-Udinsk Revolutionary Regiment. After a spell in Chita regional prison, the unfortunate trio was transferred to one of OMO's torture chambers at Karymskaya. There in a cold, red railway shed on a siding a short walk west from the station, their screams echoed off the iron roof and the smell of their blood mixed into the dust and odor of old machinery.[199]

5

RODOMONTADE AND GIRLS WITH DIAMONDS

January–April 1919

> A private letter from Semipalatinsk, on the Irtysh River in Western Siberia, reported that the entire population was dying of starvation. The dead were said to be lying on the streets with no one to bury them. The town has been for months, it was added, without lamps or candles.
> (*New York Times*, 26 December 1918)

Likin, diamond-studded mistresses and Jewish Cossacks

Ataman Semenov may have spent the first few days of 1919 in a Chita hospital recovering from the 19 December assassination attempt, but by the end of the first week of the year he was off to eastern Transbaikalia, then on 10 January to Harbin, pursuing multiple schemes with other Cossack hosts, various Mongol groups and the Japanese. After his convalescence he was more cautious when venturing from his lair in Chita, where he was safe among his large bodyguard of OMO cadets, Serbian mercenaries and a sizeable contingent of Japanese troops who provided tight security around his residence, staff offices and the nearby Japanese divisional headquarters.[1]

The ataman made the Chita branch of the state bank his petty cash till after 2 January 1919, when his Order No. 3 directed that all cash – 'with the exception of the deposits of private persons' – be transferred into a war ministry account to cover military expenditures 'until the availability of suitable credit', which in all likelihood would occur until after the civil war. This latter order spawned enough consternation and gossip among depositors that the ataman was compelled to issue an order one week later indignantly denying that he had stolen money from the state bank and threatening rumor-mongers with prosecution 'to the full extent of wartime laws'. In closing, he darkly warned, 'I kindly ask the peaceful population to tend to your own affairs, to disbelieve nonsensical, sniveling rumors intended to create turmoil and confusion, and remember that the security of state order and tranquility is in trustworthy hands'.[2]

Semenov created new revenue streams by collecting taxes and duties that should have be remitted to Omsk. Although the Japanese had negotiated an end to Semenov's embargo of Omsk-bound traffic in mid-December, railway traffic was barely crawling in January because the ataman had ordered Russian customs at Manchuli to begin turning over all its receipts to him during the first week in January. On 6 January Omsk instructed Manchuli customs to pass trains without collecting duties, which would be collected in Irkutsk, and for a few days pondered having duties paid in Harbin. However, there was no way to avoid Semenov on the customs issue. 'If Harbin collects, he will seize goods on arrival here [in Manchuli]', wrote US Army 1st Lieutenant Scovell, '[and] if goods are passed on to be taxed at Irkutsk, they will not get past Chita'.[3] No trains departed Vladivostok for a ten-day period because Semenov was holding up a dozen echelons in Transbaikalia so that they could be thoroughly searched for loot and 'taxed' (although a shortage of functioning locomotives may have contributed to the stoppage). On top of ordinary duty, Semenov imposed a *likin* – a super tax – of five rubles per *pood* on tea, and two rubles per *pood* on other goods, generating an estimated 20,000 rubles per day.[4] In addition, an estimated 200 tons of food were being 'impounded' each day from freight trains passing through Transbaikalia.[5] It was grand theft on an immense scale. Semenov's 'boutiques' were brimming with contraband and stolen goods again, but Chita's richness came at Omsk's expense.

Encouraged by Ataman Semenov's example, lesser officials cashed in on the bonanza. The Manchuli station commandant imposed a ten ruble surcharge on third-class tickets. Merchants had to pay him between 3,000 to 5,000 rubles per *taplushka*, or their goods would never make it out of the railyard.[6]

Again Admiral Kolchak sent Major General Volkov to yank Semenov's leash. Volkov set up a 'control gate' at Kultuk, a village of about 1,000 people on Lake Baikal, where he intended to arrest any passing OMO officers. On 17 January Volkov's men arrested Junior Captain Filippov, commander of the Machine Gun Company of the OMO 2nd Artillery Division, and allowed him to inform his division commander via telegram. Major General Verigo promptly telegraphed Volkov 'strongly requesting' that he remove the Kultuk checkpoint and addressed a copy to the Japanese Military Mission as a subtle threat.[7]

The ataman's criminal empire operated from Lake Baikal to Khabarovsk, and flourished without much interference from the White administrations in Omsk and Vladivostok, although the former surely tried to straighten out the crooked state of affairs in Transbaikalia. General Burikov, OMO's quartermaster, and all other officers connected with Semenov's Supply Corps bought and moved into some of the finest mansions in Chita. 'Some, who suddenly found they had more money than they could spend, immediately began building apartments and furnishing them with the most expensive furniture', remarked one American officer.[8] Transbaikalia was literally a gold mine for Semenov personally: rich gold fields in the Selenga valley and east of Nerchinsk on the Uryumkan river produced a constant trickle of precious ore which the ataman dispatched monthly via trusted mistresses to Japanese banks.[9]

Semenov's elite inner circle consisted of Captain Kuroki, a handful of fellow Cossack and OMO officers, a number of beautiful mistresses, and even the occasional Westerner, such as Dutch journalist Lokewijk-Hermen Grondijs or visiting Allied officers.[10] He cavorted with Chita's 'high society' – gold traders, rich merchants, generals and bon vivants of local salons. The war seemed far away, and Semenov was often on the move to meetings in Vladivostok or Manchuria and inspections inside Transbaikalia. While there may have been some truth to charges that he occasionally whiled away his days in debauchery, hosting frequent boisterous 'banquets' that began before midday and raged until midnight, he usually stayed quite busy, liberally mixing business and pleasure like a Mongol khan. During a one-month period in December 1918–January 1919, when the ataman was suffering from wounds from the Mariinski Theatre assassination attempt, Captain Moore attended a half dozen or so banquets at the Hotel Selekt.[11]

A December 1918 US intelligence report stated, 'Semenov drinks quite a bit', yet he was never reported staggering about or making drunken speeches. The following month, Nicholas Romanov, a wealthy businessman who was an informant for the AEFS intelligence office, visited the ataman on his train in Harbin, where he had come to visit a leading doctor and have x-rays made of his bomb injuries. Romanov found Semenov and Captain Kuroki sipping champagne in their dining car. As always when an outsider came around, Kuroki withdrew. 'Semenov appeared to me to be under the influence of the champagne', reported Romanov, 'unless perhaps he was under the influence of the sufferings caused by his wounds. His eyes were feverish and wandering'. He had just returned from a ceremony where he had awarded OMO versions of the St George's Cross to some of his soldiers, and, by the way, also had one pinned on himself. Romanov wondered if Semenov was drinking to kill the pain from his injuries, and studied him closely while they chatted. 'His low forehead seemed to indicate a mediocre intelligence and profound tenacity, or rather obstinacy. There was nothing to denote the leader, who, it seems, has a real ascendancy over the Cossacks of Transbaikalia.'[12]

Most foreigners who made Semenov's acquaintance remembered only his fine bearing and gentlemanly demeanor. For example, Lieutenant John Samuel Atkinson, who was detached to Red Cross service from the 259th Canadian Battalion, recalled, 'My car stood alongside of Semenov's train for ten days in Chita. I was at his house two or three times, and I never saw anything there that you would not see in any gentleman's home. I never saw any woman in his home or his train excepting the wife of one of his officers'.[13] Alas, poor Atkinson seems to have been too focused upon his work.

The ataman's appetite for women was renowned, though his first wife Zenaida – the mother of the two children he left behind in Verkhne-Udinsk in 1914 – was not on the menu. Nevertheless, it seems that Semenov put her up in Japan, where an American officer met her and wrote that she was 'a strikingly fascinating and beautiful woman, a blonde, and a typically sportsmanlike adventuress' who supposedly possessed 'a royal fortune'.[14] General Budberg sneered at an autumn 1918 visit of Semenov, 'Harbin has been honored with the presence of Ataman Grigorii Mikhailovich himself... He parades about the streets with some girl or other hung all over with diamonds... diamonds doubtlessly representing the crystallization of his love for the Motherland'.[15]

Semenov had numerous mistresses, but his favorite became Maria 'Masha' (also 'Mashka') Mikhailovna Sharaban, a beautiful cabaret artist 'with huge black eyes'. Some said she was 'the Jewish widow of a Russian merchant', and she was believed to have a 'complete mastery' of Yiddish – she could certainly sing in Yiddish. But everyone in Chita knew her as '*Tsyganka Masha*' – 'Gypsy Masha'. It was unknown when or how their relationship had begun, but a young British officer spotted her at Semenov's bedside after the Mariinskii Theatre bombing. The ataman's 40,000 ruble 'betrothal lunch' to Masha in late 1918 was the talk of the town. She loved furs, jewelry and power, and demonstrated the 'resourcefulness, unscrupulousness and greed' to acquire plenty of all three.[16] People said that she was 'good hearted, ostentatious, recklessly extravagant and often drunk', but she was able to prevail upon Semenov to issue an order forbidding pogroms against Jews in Transbaikalia.[17] Only Masha held more sway over the ataman than Captain Kuroki, or so it seemed. 'He continues to be wrapped up in Masha', wrote Nicholas Romanov in January 1919, 'whose influence over him is very great'. No one would have been surprised if she had talked him into retiring to Japan with her and a small fortune.[18]

Semenov's relationship with Masha Sharaban highlights his sympathy for the Jews and their unusual situation in Transbaikalia. Perhaps the ataman's sympathy for them sprang from his experience as a member of the Buryat minority, but also from living with them in Chita's rich cultural melange. Jewish exiles had deep roots in Transbaikalia, and while the stature of Yakov Sverdlov (first Soviet head of state) and Leon Trotsky (né Lev Davidovich Bronshtein) overstressed the presence of Jews in the Bolshevik hierarchy, devout Russian Jews certainly found little attraction in Bolshevik atheism.[19] Throughout Semenov's reign, Yiddish drama continued to enliven one of Chita's two theaters and Friday prayers echoed from the old synagogue. Semenov remembered that there had been 400 Jewish Cossacks in the ranks of the Transbaikal Host at the turn of the century, and formed a company of Transbaikal Cossack

Jews in OMO, but the experiment was short-lived and the reason for its disbanding is a mystery.[20] Regardless, in the age-old Russian tradition, White soldiers continued to single out Jews for beatings and executions, although Ataman Semenov's anti-pogrom order may have saved some lives.

Anti-Semitism was too deeply interlaced into conservative expressions of Russian patriotism for Semenov to foil it. During the first weeks of the White occupation in autumn 1918, 'Two leagues were formed in Semenov's Army', reported Lieutenant Colonel Barrows. 'First: The "Black Squadron" to fight all persons who are anti-monarchy, the Second: to massacre the Jews...The reported plot for pogroms is not a rumor.'[21] A popular piece of anti-Semitic propaganda, allegedly authored by London *Times* correspondent Robert Wilton, showed how 'the Jews and other anti-Russian races' were the standard-bearers of revolution, and that, the 384 Bolshevik commissars were made up of '2 Negroes, 13 Russians, 15 Chinamen, 22 Armenians and more than 300 Jews, [and] of the latter number, 264 had come to Russia from the United States'. Many prominent monarchists and Cossacks, such as General Baron Sergei Rozanov, bought stock in the fable of a diabolical worldwide Jewish conspiracy abetted by American Masons and the US Army.[22]

Supposedly the ataman was coerced by anti-Semitic officers in his command to dispatch Masha Sharaban to Japan during the spring of 1919.[23] She returned some time later, but was allegedly pressured to depart again. US Army Captain William S. Barrett recorded another possible reason for Masha's comings and goings. He encountered a beautiful Russian woman in Nagasaki, Japan who introduced herself as Madame Semenov. She confided that she visited Japan once a month to deposit gold in the bank.[24] Fawning Japanese journalists dubbed her the 'queen of diamonds', not realizing that her impressive jewelry collection consisted of purloined booty removed from political prisoners, victims of shakedowns, or unfortunate train travelers.[25] As late as February 1920 Masha Sharaban's Japanese journeys were still snidely mentioned in Russia's opposition press.

Semenov's British biographer and MI6 Russophile, David Footman, wrote that the ataman had nothing to do with other women after Masha Sharaban's departure.[26] If so, he had tremendous self-discipline, because he also maintained a harem in an exotically configured railway coach known as the 'Summer Car', which looked like a sultan's tent on wheels. An American railway administrator named Sayres testified, '[Semenov's] train lay alongside of mine for more than ninety days, so that I knew the gentleman [Semenov] quite well; and when you hear stories about the "nationalization" of the Russian women – all of which have been disproved – I want to tell you this – and I do not think you are going to see it reported in the newspapers – General Semenov had thirty of the most beautiful women held in his train that I ever saw'.[27] Sayres had seen the staff of the ataman's 'Summer Car'.

Semenov's pleasures may have had a darker side. Dr Burghard Breitner, an Austrian surgeon among the POWs, recorded in his diary the kind of sadistic entertainment that had Chita whispering:

> Some guests were invited into this armored car in which seventeen chained criminals were being done to death. Roundabout there stood a group of Russian officers and quite a few Russian women who observed with interest and satisfaction how the unfortunates were being beaten upon their bare bodies and genitals with iron rods. This torture took about twelve minutes and then death would mercifully come. Thereupon the ladies would all applaud. I inquired of one of the Japanese visitors who had witnessed this horror what he proposed to do when he returned to the Japanese staff at Chita. He replied 'that he intended to do nothing because the Japanese did not mix in the internal affairs of Russia'.[28]

Captain Harold V.V. Fay, AEFS intelligence officer in Harbin, found Semenov in his typical milieu on the morning of 9 February 1919. He had slept late and had the wounds from the assassination attempt dressed in his personal coach before receiving officers with urgent business in his dining car. That morning his retinue included General Verigo, another major general in charge of artillery, and a covey of OMO staff officers, while a Japanese captain and interpreter showed up to deliver a consignment of 'twelve cars with rifles, cartridges and sabers'. The omnipresent Captain Kuroki was tending to business in his own railcar. Fay waited all morning to see Semenov, and was about to give up and depart when he was called in. The ataman received him warmly, and listened to his complaint about some anti-American statements made to a Vladivostok newspaper by an OMO general named Linkov. Semenov immediately issued an order disavowing Linkov's statement, and promised to send the errant general to Fay's residence to apologize. 'General Linkov came to the apartment post haste, apparently considerably frightened, and willing to retract or apologize or anything', tittered Fay. Fay reassured the shaken general, and sent him away with 'cigars and Bureau of Public Information pamphlets'.[29]

Rodomontade, martinets and sadists

As far back as autumn 1918, the *semenovtsy* had established a vile reputation for 'laziness, rodomontade, alcohol, lucrative requisitions, dirty money and the killing of the innocent' in the words of Lieutenant General Baron Alexei Budberg, then exiled in Harbin.[30] Absent fear of tsarist (or any other) authority, lawlessness prevailed among Semenov's officers and soldiers. The military justice system had collapsed and, besides, unsanctioned 'requisitions', larceny, burglary, robbery and rape by soldiers became so commonplace that the old system never could have digested them all anyway.

In Siberian cities, where even garbage collectors and plumbers paraded about in elaborate livery, a military uniform was a license to commit abuses and crime during the civil war, particularly in the Russian Far East, far from authorities in Moscow or Omsk.[31] OMO's senior ranks attracted a number of characters whose notoriety tarnished the entire command: Colonel Sipailov, 'with his face always twitching'; Major General Skipetrov, an impulsive sadist; Colonel Shemelin, a violent Mongol–Cossack drunkard; the *razvedka* chiefs and many others who delighted in arbitrary cruelties and brazen criminal behavior. Some were polished, like General Lutzov – 'a short, clean shaven man with his hair cut close to his head' who spoke a little English. 'His personality is rather attractive', Captain Frederick F. Moore wrote, 'but I would not trust him'. Moore was welcomed into their inner circle and frequent all-night banquets. 'I observed that the officers of the lowest type seem to be the strongest in the councils of the Ataman', he noted.

'There is considerable unrest among the officers of Semenov and considerable intriguing. All are suspicious of the others. The consequence is that those being possessed with the best capacity for intrigue, which are the lowest type, seem to have the most influence with Semenov', Moore concluded. General Verigo's fate bore out this conclusion. About 4 a.m. one morning, he pulled Captain Moore aside during a drunken bash at the Hotel Selekt. 'Verigo was rather under the weather from vodka and inclined to be talkative', noted Moore, who saw General Afanas'ev take notice of Verigo and cross the room, positioning himself where he could hear what was being said. Afanas'ev was Verigo's assistant chief of staff, but Moore had come to regard him as 'the Ataman's spy'. Verigo had been telling Moore that he believed that Grand Duke Michael, then in Harbin, would soon succeed Kolchak with General Knox's assistance and exorcise Russia of her troubles. He shut up immediately as Afanas'ev drew near. When Moore woke up several hours later, he heard that Verigo was under house arrest and had been replaced by General Lutzov.[32] So went the power plays in OMO headquarters.

Semenov's officer corps came to be dominated by thieves, scoundrels and sadists. 'The intellectual level of the commanding corps is very low', an American assessment concluded. 'The average of its actions distinguishes itself by rudeness and by lack of intelligence.'[33] Officer ranks were filled by 'numerous officers of German and Austrian origin ... from the Baltic provinces, ... and by ... former war prisoners'. There seemed to be little room for officers of any moral standing. 'The true and honest Russian officers left Semenov, or were dismissed by means of violence'. As far back as November 1918, regular army officers in two infantry regiments under Semenov's control had all requested transfer 'to Irkutsk to another command'.[34] Scores of such 'unhappy cases', as they were known among Semenov's horde, were 'dismissed' with a bullet. Any dissension in the ranks was very rightly called 'suicide' by the ataman's men.

Semenov's staff was as morbidly picturesque and bloodthirsty as a pirate crew. One of the most flamboyant villains was General Skipetrov, a regular army officer who escaped Irkutsk after the aborted uprising against the Reds in December 1918. Semenov promoted him from lieutenant colonel and dispatched him to Vladivostok in autumn 1918 to round up recruits for OMO. 'Skipetrov was a thorough scoundrel', wrote Canadian Major James Bell,

> with a forceful, though brutal, character – a big, strongly built man, with a certain evil attractiveness which made him popular with the women who frequented Vladivostok's most infamous dance hall, the Aquarium... Skipetrov's already lurid reputation was not improved by his gaily pitching another Russian general from one of the curtained-off boxes in the gallery of the Aquarium to the main hall below...

Skipetrov's fellow general was merely 'badly shaken'. Major Bell arranged the escape of a junior OMO officer – 'a beautiful but worthless youth' – who feared that Skipetrov was about 'to dispatch him in a way not unusual in Semenov's army'. Skipetrov wanted the young man's mistress in Harbin. Of course, Skipetrov's violent impulses were much less restrained when the subjects were not fellow officers.[35]

Colonel Sipailov was another OMO officer notorious for his sadism. A mechanic before becoming a gendarme in pre-revolutionary days, he rose quickly in the ranks of the tsarist police. It was said that he had been imprisoned and tortured by the Bolsheviks, who, when Sipailov escaped, murdered all of his family (although it seems likely that a lieutenant by the same name in OMO's counterintelligence service was related). He was virulently anti-Semitic, short, stocky with 'cold, colorless eyes...under dense brows', a bald head shaped like a saddle, and possessed by some affliction akin to Tourette's Syndrome that compelled him to sputter, sing, babble and chortle while he killed. Sipailov was a master torturer with a criminal mind and absolute authority, who passed on his knowledge to several apprentices, instructing in such skills as removing scalps, employing different kinds of cord to achieve various effects during suffocation and hammering hot ramrods into ears. A Polish refugee, Ferdinand Ossendowski met Sipailov and wrote of him, 'He was always nervously jerking and wriggling his body and talking ceaselessly, making most unattractive sounds in his throat and sputtering with saliva all over his lips, his whole face often contracted with spasms...I heard afterwards that he himself executed the condemned people, joking and singing as he did his work'.[36]

Colonel Tierbach was a well-known brute that US intelligence reports labeled as a former German prisoner of war. However, Tierbach appears to have been a Cossack lieutenant who became a Semenov disciple early on – no later than January 1918, and helped corral the Manchuli city soviet, then served as OMO's first garrison commander in Chita. In December 1918 he was commander of a large Mongolian – Cossack detachment (broadbrushed as 'OMO' in an intelligence report) that became known as the Manchurian Ataman Semenov Division and was fighting partisans on the Argun river border region in the spring of 1919.[37] He was fanatically faithful to the ataman.[38] He zealously liquidated not only *Bolsheviki*, 'but also many [White military] officers who are not in sympathy with Ataman Semenov's views'.[39] Semenov was said to have been unaware of Tierbach's extraordinary efforts on his behalf.

With leaders like Skipetrov, Sipailov and Tierbach, the moral rot in OMO oozed down in the ranks from the top. Gratuitous sadism became commonplace. In early March 1919, a punitive detachment rounded up about 20 men from a village named Shiron and surrounding hamlets. They were said to be 'peasants, village teachers, village social men, but no Bolsheviks or anarchists'. A Lieutenant Mosalov and seven others convened a mock inquest and summoned from their prisoners Evgeni V. Borodin, 'a well-to-do peasant and founder of the Ust-Togotny Consumers and Credit Company'. They mocked him and beat him with sabers and canes till his shoulders and fingers were broken, then bound him, severed his ears and nose, and made him sing 'God Save the Tsar' before dousing him with kerosene and setting him on fire. Nineteen others were shot, and one man escaped. It was not an unusual incident.[40]

On the other hand, not every OMO officer was a villain. There was a Don Cossack named Captain Smirnov on Semenov's staff, who was noted to be 'a Russian patriot' and 'a very able man', had been a wartime commander in the Ussuri Cavalry Division and 'chief quartermaster of the All-Russian Armies'.[41] He served Semenov as chief of the Ussuri Brigade. Natsvalov, Khreshchatitskii and scores of others strove to maintain their decency in a bitter civil war that aroused the basest human impulses. Nevertheless, OMO's reputation for robbery tainted everyone in Semenov's service and undermined support for the White movement in Russia's Far East.

Crime, punishment and the Shumov–Natsvalov affair

The most egregious and scandalous robbery was covered with the bloody fingerprints of Semenov and Masha Sharaban, and, occurring early in the ataman's reign, set a sordid standard for OMO to stoop below for the next two years. General Baron Budberg noted the brazen crime in his diary on 2 November 1918, 'The Transbaikalian *hunghutzes* have distinguished themselves rather loudly: the rich Irkutsk gold trader Shumov left on a reserved train of Semenov's with a large shipment of gold, and turns up in the Selenga River with a bullet through his head'.[42] Though the exact details of the murder were well concealed, it appears that the Vasilii Konstantinovich Shumov, a junior military officer, was transferring some of his family's gold to Harbin when he was abducted by Colonel Stepanov, and delivered to a *zastenka* in Chita aboard Stepanov's armored train. There young Shumov was tortured to death in an attempt to extract information about any secret treasures his family might have. His body was deposited in an icehole in the Ingoda river.[43]

If Semenov could kill a Shumov, then no one was safe. As calendars rolled into 1919, Nicholas Romanov, the AEFS informant, wrote that while Semenov still enjoyed great popularity in the Transbaikal and Amur Cossack *stanitsas*, he was not so well-liked in Chita 'where his officers respect neither the property of the inhabitants nor the virtue of the women'.[44] There were hundreds of human skeletons and carcasses that attested to OMO's lack of respect for the lives of railwaymen, peasants and soldiers. But the Shumovs were not ordinary merchants; they were the epitome of capitalism in Transbaikalia, known far and wide beyond the province. Their home, Shumov Palace, was a Chita landmark, an architectural gem that graced the city with an air of sophistication. A pair of Shumov brothers, Konstantin Stepanovich and Aleksei Stepanovich, headed the popular clan and managed its chain of gold mines on the Kruchina river.[45] They did not flee when the Bolsheviks took over Chita in March 1918 and the Soviet of Workers', Peasants', Cossacks' and Buryats' Deputies invaded Shumov Palace. The brothers were on the verge of seeing the Reds confiscate their mines when the Czechs and Whites occupied Transbaikalia in August.[46]

Chita society did not quietly accept the murder of Vasilii, the oldest son of Konstantin Shumov. The loudest voice emanated from Zinaida Aleksandrovna Natsvalova, a friend of the victim and the wife of OMO's 35-year old chief of staff, Major General Nikolai Georgievich Natsvalov. Madame Natsvalova was an attractive actress and poetess, whose shrill protests soon provoked Masha Sharaban's feline enmity and attracted attention from Omsk.[47]

The hoopla over crime and corruption in Transbaikalia prompted Admiral Kolchak to dispatch an extraordinary commission of investigation to Chita in February 1919. The commission was chaired by the venerable Siberian Cossack, 71-year old Lieutenant General Georgii Efremovich Katanaev. Katanaev's investigation produced a gory inventory of crimes and atrocities in Semenov's territory, and may have prompted Semenov to issue an uncharacteristic order warning his officers not to interfere in police affairs, but did not result in a court of inquiry until months later when Omsk's power was waning and the danger of being overrun by the Red Army transcended concerns about house-cleaning.[48] Regardless, as Major General Volkov's aborted disciplinary campaign in December 1918 showed, there was little Omsk could do about misbehavior in Chita as long as Semenov and his Japanese partners had a stranglehold on Admiral Kolchak's railway lifeline.

Relations with Omsk and the Allies were unpleasant at best, as Semenov still refused to recognize Admiral Kolchak's authority. Indeed, Semenov even chose to bait Major General Knox, making much ado over a telegram Knox had sent to Admiral Kolchak in which the British officer lamented the admiral being caught between 'Atamanism on the right and Bolshevism on the left'. Semenov bristled about being compared on par with the Reds, and howled that in doing so Knox had committed an outrage against Cossackry. The ataman telegrammed Knox, addressing him with dripping sarcasm, 'Your Excellency!' and published his melodramatic diatribe in *Russkii Vostok* newspaper on 27 February for all to snicker.[49] Akin to a Red agitator, Semenov flaunted a cynical contempt for authority, the old regime and the upper class that garnered him the hooting favor of the unruly mob. On 4 March he announced that 'several military and civilian personages have arrived in Transbaikalia for agitation against discipline and the command structure in the billets of military units here', apparently referring to White agents from Omsk. He ordered them to surrender themselves to his field courts for execution. By March the acrimony with Omsk had so corroded the morale of Semenov's troops that he declared deserters to be Bolshevik sympathizers and ordered their home villages to round up replacements from their families.[50]

Mid-March found the young ataman in Harbin discussing matters with Lieutenant General Horvath. A report dated 12 March 1919 declared that General Horvath had refused orders from Admiral Kolchak to proceed to Omsk, and that Horvath had settled his differences with Semenov. On 13 March, the ataman was reported to be waiting at Harbin for a 'conference with General Knox' before travelling on to Vladivostok for more high level talks. With Kolchak's supply line at his mercy, the Cossack rebel was now being courted like a *debutante* in the political *milieu* of the upper-class brass that had previously brushed him off, in spite of indiscretions like the Shumov murder.

Meanwhile Masha Sharaban moved to squelch the clamor from Chita's salons by prevailing upon her powerful amour to have Major General Natsvalov transferred out of town to command the 5th Pri-Amur corps. Then, late in the night of 24 April 1919, two aides-de-camp of the ataman appeared at Madame Natsvalova's doorstep and took her away on 'urgent business'. One of the aides was Cossack Captain Vladimir Torchinov, 'a favorite' of Masha Sharaban's. Madame Natsvalova was never seen alive again. One month later her husband was shot dead while in Vladivostok on a business trip. His wife's remains were found in Sretensk in July.[51] In this manner the ataman and his courtesan laid to rest the lurid Shumov affair.

In a similarly diabolical fashion, charges of bolshevism were occasionally raised to mask robbery by military authorities in Transbaikalia. A high profile case was announced by a headline in the *Peking and Tientsin Times* on 25 January 1919, that declared 'Chinese Bolshevist Emissaries Arrested on Manchurian Frontier'. The article accused six men arrested at Dauria by 'the railway police' of being 'the first batch of Bolshevik emissaries' sent to China with a huge amount of secreted cash and an escort of 'a small party of soldiers dressed in Czecho-Slovak uniform', who fled at the first sign of trouble. In truth, the six were Chinese merchants returning from Irkutsk who, mindful of the possibility of robbery by *semenovtsy*, hired some unreliable and very conspicuous Czech legionnaires to protect them on their journey. They were arrested not by the railway police, but by Baron Ungern-Shternberg and his vehemently anti-Chinese Mongol separatists, who delightfully removed 6,500,000 rubles from the travelers' clothing. Not surprisingly, the bolshevism charge faded as the Chinese government took up the matter, whereupon Russian authorities dusted off a rarely enforced PSG regulation that prohibited more than 500 rubles from being taken out of the country.[52]

As has been seen, crime in Transbaikalia was predictably pervasive, with eager perpetrators from every strata of society – the Ataman, rapacious soldiers, railway conductors who demanded bribes in addition to a ticket, and hordes of desperate petty thieves among the refugees, indigents and riff-raff. Punishment was more fickle. Some, like Semenov and Sharaban, got away with murder, robbery and racketeering, while others, guilty of no crime, were falsely accused so that their accusers could rob or rape them. For instance, employers skirted a law requiring them to pay laid-off workers an extra month's salary by accusing them of 'supporting Soviet power', and could arbitrarily impose hefty fines upon employees for a host of petty infractions.[53] Justice had become as elusive as peace.

The moral decay that ate away at the military was rifling civil institutions as well. If Red and White police archives can be trusted, this may best be illustrated by the Chita police investigation into the attempted assassination of Semenov. A veteran Chita detective, 43-year-old Aleksandr V. Domrachev, had cracked the case in no time, arresting three suspects within a week of the Mariinskii Theatre bombing. However, his case unraveled after OMO counterintelligence apprehended the 'genuine perpetrators' of the bombing. In late January 1919, Domrachev sheepishly released from jail the unfortunate trio he had been torturing for one month, intent on eliciting confessions. Although it was alleged that Domrachev had gone to great lengths to manufacture and plant evidence against the trio, there seems to have been no suspicion that he did so to deflect suspicion from the Socialist-Revolutionaries who actually tried to kill Semenov, but rather that he fabricated the case to further his career.[54] He was a skilled detective who had risen to the top of the city's criminal investigation bureau, and had even been retained by the Bolsheviks during their period in power, presumably for his combination of crime-solving skills and either guile or integrity.

About this time, Semenov undertook a 'reassessment of values', deciding that reprisals and repression were not achieving the intended objectives, but were actually aggravating the political and military situations by driving people into the arms of the Bolsheviks. Not surprisingly this sudden realization appears to coincide with the visit of General Katanaev and his investigatory commission from Omsk. In furtherance of the resultant house-cleaning, Detective Domrachev participated in the arrests of some prominent OMO personnel – A. Mikhailov, a counterintelligence man; Major General Evseev, the chief of staff of Ungern-Shternberg's Asiatic Horse Division; Colonel Sharistanov, the chief of Dauria garrison, 'and others'.

Deep into the treacherous waters of White politics, Domrachev's career took a sudden downturn. On 15 March 1919 he was dismissed from service in the police 'for drunkenness'. Two months later he was arrested for abusing his powers and authority in the Mariinskii Theatre bombing. His case was bounced between public prosecutors in Chita and Irkutsk while he was confined in Chita's notorious regional prison, abused and threatened by criminals that he had investigated and sent there. Domrachev contracted typhus and his wife, Kseniya Dmitrievna, appealed to the civil authorities throughout the summer of 1919, to no avail. The hapless detective had become entangled in the murky, bitter squabble between Omsk and Chita; perhaps neither side wanted him released.[55]

In summer 1919 Semenov issued a number of 'warning orders' to his officers, genuinely hoping to cut the incalculable cost in popular support extracted for his army's robberies and debauchery. In one order issued on 30 June 1919 he lamented that drunkenness was causing officers to 'forget [their] duty' and become 'disgusting, rough, wild, sometimes brutal'. Like a gentle father he appealed to them, 'I ask you officers not to forget that at you looks not only poor Russia... but also our allies. On you they judge Russia and Russian people'.[56] But men like Stepanov surely scoffed at such droll entreaties issued by the architect of the Shumov–Natsvalov scandal.

White hell in Kalmykov's wild, wild east

While Ataman Semenov had, with ample help from the Japanese Army, secured a free hand for his criminal empire in Transbaikalia, his protégé Kalmykov, saw *sudbína* – Fate – dampen his avaricious aspirations in Khabarovsk. Ataman Kalmykov had not intended to remain in Khabarovsk after executing Commander Kandaurov and the other brigands of his juridical department months before. 'At one time, Kalmykov was preparing to flee with the money [which he confiscated from the unlucky Kandaurov] to America', stated a US intelligence report in early December, 'but the officers of his detachment learned of this and are watching him so well that it is hardly possible to flee'.[57]

Mistrust and paranoia permeated the ranks of Kalmykov's gang. Obedience was forced through open threats to men and their commanders, and reinforced with regular beatings and floggings. Like a band of paranoid desperados bonded only by loot and lust, every man always seemed to keep a hand on his weapon. One day four OKO men – a Lieutenant Birukov, a Sub-Lieutenant Bogdanov, a Cossack named Svetlov, and a Serb mercenary – killed a civilian named Chaika 'because he wore nice boots', then, to the surprise of scurrying bystanders, began fighting among themselves like hyenas over the corpse's coveted boots.[58]

Rich Russians were in as much danger from OKO as Bolsheviks. Ataman Kalmykov's 100-man bodyguard eagerly hunted down the rich because they received a share of the booty. Kalmykov's chief of staff, a Cossack captain named Alekseev, estimated that the bloody ataman amassed well over 2 million rubles during his reign of terror, and deposited a sizeable sum of this in a Japanese bank. A list of Kalmykov's biggest hauls and the victims who provided them read like a who's who of Khabarovsk's wealthy families: 'Brilion and Ghitilev – 168,000 rubles; Hedblum, 273,000 rubles; Levchenko, 25,000 rubles; Brandt, 32,000 rubles;... and Karpenko, 146,000 rubles'.[59] Their bodies were typically left in the street for stray dogs to disfigure, but the crimes did not go unnoticed. In accordance with the law, the military coroner, Colonel Daletzky, informed the procurator's office, to no avail.

Major General William S. Graves, commander of the American Expeditionary Force, was incensed by Kalmykov's daily atrocities against innocent people. He proposed to the Japanese command in December 1918 that they arrest the Ussuri Ataman the next time he murdered a civilian. The Japanese earnestly responded that Kalmykov had promised – on 28 November to be exact – that he would not commit murder anymore.[60] There was no doubt, however, that the Japanese knew exactly what Kalmykov and OKO were up to. In Khabarovsk, according to Graves, 'The Cossack officers of rank were quartered in the Japanese Headquarters building'.[61]

Major General Graves described one of OKO's many crimes that came to the attention of his headquarters:

> Two women came to my office from a town two or three hundred miles from Vladivostok, and told me Kalmykov had come through their village and taken their husbands. They begged me to help find out if these men were alive and if alive, where Kalmykov had taken them. I directed the [American] Commanding Officer at Khabarovsk to ask Kalmykov where these men were. Kalmykov replied that they had escaped... It later developed that when his train was passing over a lake, Kalmykov had it stop while he had stones tied to the necks of these men, and they were thrown into the lake.[62]

In rural areas where people did not know very much about the government or care about politics, they hated both Cossacks and Japanese soldiers, and Kalmykov's criminal behavior even turned many Cossacks against him.[63]

Sometime in early December 1918, a captain and 75 disgruntled OKO Cossacks tried to turn themselves over to a pro-Horvath regiment of the regular army at Nikolsk-Ussuriisk. The captain explained to Colonel Vrashtel, the regimental commander, that the Cossacks were upset because Kalmykov had murdered their commander, Shestakov. The Cossacks turned over their weapons to Colonel Vrashtel, but were soon told that 'they would not be accepted as a squadron' in the regiment. Vrashtel arrested the captain, who was 'charged with embezzlement and desertion while an officer of the Old Russian Army'. The 'real reason' the captain had turned over his men was 'to gain immunity from prosecution for his former acts'. Both Semenov and Kalmykov sent telegrams to General Horvath demanding the Cossacks' return. Vrashtel returned their weapons and released them. 'It is reported [that] only about half have started back to Khabarovsk and that the rest have scattered to their homes.'[64]

On 28 December 1918 several OKO Cossacks appeared at the US headquarters in Khabarovsk asking to enlist in the US Army to get away from Kalmykov.[65] This incident was soon overshadowed by a more explosive mutiny one month later. During the night of 27 January 1919, 398 mounted Cossacks of the 1st Khabarovsk Ussuri Cossack Regiment suddenly thundered into the US Army compound in Khabarovsk hauling four artillery pieces and three machine guns.[66] They meant no harm: they explained to the US commander that if he would guarantee their protection from Ataman Kalmykov, they would surrender their arms. If not, they would return and fight Kalmykov's remaining mercenaries and Japanese cronies to the death. About the same time, 300 other Ussuri Cossacks went into hiding in outlying towns and 30 or so begged protection from the Chinese Army.[67] The mutineers had mortally wounded one of Kalmykov's commanders, a Colonel Birukov, on their way out.[68] Nevertheless, the perplexed Americans offered them shelter and received their complaints about service in OKO: no pay, no fuel for warmth, little food, pointless atrocities, systematic robbery under the guise of Bolshevik-hunting, 'constant use of the *nagáika* (leather whip)' against Kalmykov's own soldiers and other brutalities.[69] 'While we are suffering, [our officers] lavish our money on women and get drunk from champagne, for which they pay 350 rubles a bottle', declared a statement from the mutineers.

Kalmykov's refusal to recognize or even cooperate with the Omsk government, a position dictated by his Japanese advisors to weaken Admiral Kolchak, compounded the mutineers' complaints. White patriots were surely dismayed at Kalmykov's shameless toadying to Japanese desires at the expense of the anti-Bolshevik movement. A sixth *voiskovii krug* convened in Khabarovsk from 21 February until 6 March and persuaded Kalmykov to recognize Kolchak's government, however the conscientious Ussuri officers could not compel him to cooperate. Many officers and cadets were clamoring to go to the front in the spring of 1919 but the Japanese puppet-ataman prevented them from moving.[70] In this regard he parroted Ataman Semenov, who also turned down appeals of his troops who wanted to go to the Ural Front.[71] Perhaps to silence critics, White publicists announced in late March that a detachment intended for the 'Orenburg Front' that had been held back since December would soon depart under the command of Ataman Kalmykov, upon 'receipt of Cossack pay allowances' from Omsk. Such payment was not forthcoming and, of course, Kalmykov had no intention of relinquishing his fiefdom in the Maritime Province anyway.[72]

Meanwhile the Americans confined – and fed – the Cossack mutineers in 'clean and warm' quarters at the old Krásnaya Réchka (Red River) prisoner-of-war camp. Major General Graves indignantly refused Japanese pressure to return them to Kalmykov and certain death or brutal punishment. By 6 March 248 Cossacks still remained at Krásnaya Réchka, about 150 having been released or wandered off. Delegates from the sixth Ussuri Cossack conference visited the camp in late February and were pleasantly surprised at the discipline and order that the men had assumed since their confinement.[73] All of the rebellious Cossacks were released by mid-March.[74] On the other hand, Kalmykov – bound to his ill-gotten power and booty – was thwarted from such an easy release by his own men. The young ataman remained in power through the heavy-handed presence of the Japanese Army and the threat of medieval tortures to any dissenters.

The 20 or so methods of torture employed by Kalmykov's *Jaegerski* Regiment at Nikolsk may have been typical. The officers there were specialists in several different kinds of beatings, 'with lashes, cold and hot ramrods, etc. After the beating was finished, sharp needles were pierced into the feet and nostrils', stated a Nikolsk newspaper months later. 'They poured, through a special syringe, one or two pails of water into the stomach of their victim.' The torturers often finished their work by inserting 'a detonator of a hand grenade into the anus of the victim', or by burying the victim alive. A Captain Kostovalov of the 33rd Infantry Regiment was a notorious rapist renowned among Kalmykov's sadists for dispatching his victims with his spurs.[75]

American operations along the Ussuri and Amur railways brought the US Army into conflict with Kalmykov. OKO armored trains operated in a sector patrolled by a battalion of the 27th Infantry, which spanned the tracks between the towns of Iman and Spasskoe. Kalmykov loyalists tossed dead horses off the trains as they passed through US encampments. Russian girls seen in the presence of American soldiers would be arrested later and whipped in public. Armed clashes between the doughboys and Cossacks were narrowly averted.[76] In the Khabarovsk area, the situation became so tense that General Graves' staff informed General Oi, commander of the Japanese division at Khabarovsk, that 'a clash between his [Kalmykov's] men and our troops is imminent'.[77]

Kalmykov was not the only villain in the Russian Far East. Neither the Reds nor other White factions were inclined to displays of chivalry or mercy. For instance, in early January 1919, Red partisans in Amur province captured a number of Whites who were escorting 60 prisoners; the White soldiers were 'tortured, stripped and thrown alive into an ice-hole' on the Zeya river. Likewise, General Horvath's troops tormented almost every village they entered, generously dispensing floggings and fines for not turning over clothing, arms and men of draft age. An unwelcome nine-day visit by Horvath's Whites to the village of Zinkovka, population 3,000, in early February was typical:

> One man had his ear burned with a hot iron. Another man beat so bad that he has been unable to work since...several ribs broken. His offense was that he did not halt soon enough while driving through the village street. Two other men were hung up, clear of the floor, with a rope tied around their wrists until they fainted, let down and then pulled up again...One man's wrists had the skin torn off all the way around. Two 15-year-old boys were given 40 lashes along with their fathers because they thought their parents had concealed clothes. One of the boys fainted during the flogging. Two men flogged for cutting wood on a government reserve...Another man was forced to drink a quart of vodka and nearly died. Offense: had a concealed gun. About a dozen men paid fines ranging from 250 rubles to 500 rubles, with a threat of having their houses burned if fine was not paid. Two men were drafted...[78]

The bullies who abused Zinkovka and a dozen other nearby villages that month were 400 Chinese mercenaries serving under Russian officers and non-commissioned officers. Ironically, their commander was Colonel Viktor Vrashtel, to whom Kalmykov's disillusioned Cossacks had turned for help weeks earlier. A year earlier Vrashtel's officers had fled to Manchuria when the Bolsheviks invaded. They now considered all villagers to be Red sympathizers and vengefully seized upon the slightest excuse to flog or fine the citizenry. Floggings usually entailed 15 to 40 whacks with a rattan rod. In a few cases Vrashtel's brutes confiscated all of some mens' clothing, including underwear. 'In most cases the people went around and took up collections for their friends who were fined and did not have the money', reported an American lieutenant who was sent to investigate. 'In this way considerable torturing and seizing of property was avoided.'[79]

During the past two years, the common man in Siberia had first hailed the revolution until its exhilaration was soured by Bolshevik fanaticism, then welcomed the counterrevolution until the Whites' vindictiveness showed that they were not liberators.[80] People had little faith in the deformed remnants of Russian institutions and no stomach for the incessant power struggles among White strongmen. Daily searches for food and fuel consumed the peasants' and workers' energies. Even cities surrounded by vast forests like Khabarovsk lacked sufficient firewood because of disruptions in local rail traffic. Increasingly the famished, demoralized populace pinned its hopes for salvation on foreigners.

Allies and the atamans

By March 1919 the Allied intervention force in Siberia had taken on the cosmopolitan flair of a traveling circus. Its international cast included several hundred Lithuanians, about 800 French and French colonials, 1,600 British, 2,000 Italians, 4,000 Canadians, 8,000 Americans, 12,000 Poles and more than 50,000 Japanese.[81] Several thousand Chinese soldiers were now stationed in the Chinese Eastern Railway zone in northern Manchuria and as far north as Khabarovsk in the Maritime province.[82] During a typical day at the YMCA's International Hut canteen near the Vladivostok waterfront, the visitors would include 'Americans, Canadians, English, Irish, Scotch, French, Italians, Serbians, Japanese, Ukranians, Lithuanians, Letts, Russians, Poles, Czecho-Slovakians, Siamese, Chinese, Africans, Filipinos, Indians, Romanians, Koreans, Hawaiians and German, Austrian and Hungarian war prisoners'.[83]

These foreigners were surprised to find that Siberia was not the epitome of isolation. Siberia's towns and cities had long been crossroads of Eurasian commerce before world war, revolution, counterrevolution and civil war blurred the borders and spawned an influx of refugees, adventurers, mercenaries, prostitutes and profiteers from all points of the compass. An amazed American medical officer noted, 'A brief stroll along the principal streets of any of the larger towns brings to one's notice a representative of almost any country on earth'.[84] When American First Lieutenant Ralph L. Baggs arrived in Verkhne-Udinsk in November 1918, he was surprised to encounter an African-American named Elias Walker. Walker had come to Siberia with a 'wild west show' eight years earlier, married a Russian lady and scratched out a living since as a piano player at a 'moving picture show'.

The foreign troops were concentrated at the western and eastern extremes of White territory, where they supported combat operations on the war fronts in western and central Siberia, or served guard, logistics or other support functions from quarters in Harbin or in the Maritime province around Vladivostok. Two British battalions were now supporting Kolchak's forces and a naval detachment from HMS *Suffolk* had seen action at the front, firing naval guns from an armored train. Italian military personnel were at Krasnoyarsk. Major General J.H. Elmsley and about 700 men of his Canadian Siberian Expeditionary Force (CSEF) arrived in Vladivostok on 27 October 1918 and, beginning on 9 December, moved to the front in ten echelons.[85]

The French Military Mission, *le Mission Militaire Franco-Tchecoslovaque* to be exact, was intimately woven into the command structure of the Czechoslovak Legion, which had been directed by General Maurice Janin since August 1918.[86] Janin arrived in Omsk in mid-December 1918 and promptly stirred up a political tempest by informing Kolchak that Paris had given him 'a wide measure of control over operations', including those of the Russian military. He clashed with Major General Knox as well. 'He was devious where Knox was direct', wrote Peter Fleming, 'urbane where Knox was outspoken'.[87] These poor relationships were toxic to the coordination of Allied assistance for the anti-Bolshevik movement and would have fatal results.

Few foreigners had direct sustained contact with Semenov's people. Anyone who traveled inland from the coast towards Omsk experienced the anxiety of passage through Semenov's dominion. Many memoirs record the fear created by news and rumors of Semenov's atrocities and brusque searches of railcars and baggage by unkempt Cossacks and OMO thugs. Foreigners also expressed surprise at the multi-ethnic and Asian character of Transbaikalia and at the surprising prosperity of Chita. Yet Semenov and the Japanese Army were just as anxious to keep travelers moving through — and out of — Transbaikalia as the travelers themselves were.

American military observers had taken up residence in Chita during the autumn of 1918 to be the eyes and ears of the expeditionary force headquarters in Vladivostok. A small military intelligence office in Harbin stayed in touch with the observers via telegraph and performed translation and analysis functions. In December 1918, Captain Harold V.V. Fay, supervisor of the Harbin office, employed a Russian analyst/translator, 'Captain Gregory', a former tsarist military intelligence officer (gauged to be a 'reasonable monarchist') and had at least one prolific informant, Nicholas Romanov, a wealthy businessman and stereotypical Kadet. He certainly did not need money from the Americans, but undertook investigations at substantial risk from both reactionaries and Bolsheviks because he was a believer in democracy, justice and capitalism. The small observer groups in Chita were headed by a junior army officer, who was assisted by an orderly (usually a regular army private), an interpreter (often a Russian-American Jew) and two telegraph operators.[88] They shared their lodging at the Hotel Selekt with a number of OMO officers. In the hotel's corridors and salons they listened to the Whites' horror stories of captured officers being slowly butchered to death or boiled in oil by the Bolsheviks. If the Americans ever suspected that their abode at the Hotel Selekt concealed a secret torture chamber, they never reported it to Vladivostok. However, they were successful in gleaning information from *semenovtsy* to flesh out US Army intelligence reports and even successfully cultivated some agents inside OMO, such as a homesick deserter from the Belgian Army who desired to escape Semenov's service.[89] Nevertheless, intelligence reports detailing Semenov's activities and intentions were scant. His inner circle and Japanese advisors insulated him from contact with foreigners as well as most Russians.

The American Expeditionary Force reluctantly wielded power far out of proportion with its numbers in Siberia. A constant stream of peasants flowed into the various AEFS headquarters to air complaints and report abuses by White forces. Even a White warlord, Ataman Boris Annenkov, visited the AEFS headquarters in Vladivostok to beg support for the Seven Rivers' Cossacks' crusade against the Bolsheviks. Since their arrival in August 1918, the Americans' operations had extended only 1,100 miles north and west from Vladivostok up the Ussuri and Amur railways (as far as Ushmun), and west along the Chinese Eastern Railway to Harbin. Intelligence officers were stationed at Harbin, Manchuli, Chita, Verkhne-Udinsk, Krasnoyarsk, Omsk and the Ural Front. Most of the 27th Infantry Regiment was garrisoned at Khabarovsk, while the 31st had settled into brick barracks on the edge of Vladivostok and established four strongpoints north along the railway. The first blood was shed on 29 August when partisans shot and wounded members of an American patrol at Ugol'naya.

The Suchan mines, which provided the coal that kept the Trans-Siberian Railway running in the Maritime province, fell among the 31st Infantry Regiment's responsibilities. In March 1919 the local Red commander, Yakov Ivanovich Triapitsyn, demanded that the Americans vacate the mines and his partisans and anti-Kolchak labor activists began attacking American guards and the property under their protection.[90] At about the same time, Major General Pavel Pavlovich Ivanov-Rinov, now reassigned from Omsk as the White commander in the Pri-Amur region, accused the Americans of protecting the Bolsheviks. The extremists' displeasure with the American presence seemed to confirm Major General Graves' conviction that he was toeing a neutral line as dictated by his vague instructions from the war department.[91]

Even in Vladivostok, tension often soured the air between the Allies and Russians. Major General Ivanov-Rinov had a reputation for brutality. Lieutenant Colonel Robert L. Eichelberger, General Graves' confidant and chief intelligence officer, described Ivanov-Rinov as being 'absolutely unscrupulous'.[92] The Cossack general lived and worked in an armored train in Vladivostok, always shielded by a sizeable bodyguard of a half-*sotnia* of Cossacks with four heavy machine guns and two armored cars equipped with two heavy machine guns each.[93] On the night of 2 March, a platoon of US infantry suddenly surrounded the local prison in anticipation of an imminent Bolshevik uprising. Nothing became of the rumors of the Red uprising, but the next morning Ivanov-Rinov sent a mildly indignant complaint to the Allied command about what he considered to be an overly protective move on his turf – the prison.[94]

Pompous, greedy, brutal White officers like Major General Ivanov-Rinov, Colonel Vrashtel and Ataman Kalmykov disgusted the American soldiers. YMCA worker Gail Berg Reitzel explained, 'When our boys see the corruption and atrocities practiced on the helpless peasants in the name of fighting Bolshevism, by the officers who are supposed to be upholding a better form of government, they can't stomach fighting shoulder to shoulder with them'.[95] When they arrived the previous summer, the doughboys were anxious to get into the fight. Within months, the fanatical bitterness of both Reds and Whites made the

Americans apathetic. Noted Gail Berg Reitzel,

> They put much feeling into the song which they sing whenever a big crowd gets together:
>
> I wanta go home, I wanta go home!
> The guns may shoot, the cannons may roar,
> I don't wanta go to the front anymore.
> Take me over the sea,
> Where the Bolsheviks can't get at me,
> Oh, my! I don't wanta die,
> I WANTA GO HOME![96]

Despite the hazards of the constant friction with Kalmykov, the threat of combat with the erratic ataman may have been preferable – from the American commanders' viewpoint, at least – to the moral decay that gnawed at the garrison troops' morale in Vladivostok. There incurable venereal diseases, common crime and the lure of drugs put the doughboys in constant jeopardy. Vladivostok's peacetime legion of 8,000 prostitutes had been reinforced with thousands of refugees and other desperate women. In a city of less than 100,000, these statistics made harlotry a major industry. By the end of the year, the spread of syphilis among foreign troops prompted the district commissar to call for measures to curb prostitution.[97] An October 1918 intelligence report illustrated the peril to American morale:

> Pasha, a girl in the house of prostitution at No. 19, Koréyskaya, will buy cocaine for soldiers...at a house without a number on the far side of the railway tracks on Koréyskaya...Pasha demands five rubles for one shot of cocaine and four rubles for the *droshky* which takes one there. Pasha states that she intends, with four other girls, to move to another apartment nearer the American base.[98]

Similar vices seduced the 27th Infantry garrison in Khabarovsk, including, of course, alcohol, which became dearer to the doughboys as the growing prohibition movement shut down America's breweries, distilleries and saloons. A Polish captive in a prisoner-of-war camp guarded by the 27th recalled,

> At the foot of the camp, on an elevation in the midst of the densely forested taiga on the shore of the Ussuri river, was a tiny, miserable little Chinese hamlet inhabited by practitioners of a branch of spiritualism. There you would always find the [American] soldiers who were not on duty, officers included, drinking...The Americans drank desperately, as if they wanted to be like the camel in the desert oasis, in order to store up moisture against the return home to their own 'dry' country.[99]

The Japanese Army had imported its own 'public women', or *yoshiwara* and opened large bordellos in Khabarovsk, Vladivostok and other cities. Soldiers received a monthly ration of *yoshiwara* tickets for use at these military brothels or for barter with their fellow troopers.[100] An American lady in Vladivostok recalled,

> There are...Japanese women in the city differing greatly from their modest, dainty sisters in Japan. International complications nearly followed an episode which took place recently. The American soldiers are accustomed to seeing the Japanese women who are quite apparently the typical military camp followers and one of our men made the dreadful mistake of taking the wife of the Japanese Consul for one of the other kind and playfully chucked her under the chin as she was crossing the sidewalk to her *droshky*.[101]

Some natural tension between foreign troops was to be expected, but the Japanese Army adopted the curious policy of antagonizing or bullying everyone they encountered. For instance, after watching a Japanese sentry club an unsuspecting Russian officer and then a 'well-dressed Russian lady' for no apparent reason on the platform at Nikolsk station, an outraged British colonel stormed into the Japanese commander's office. 'The [Japanese] officer seemed astonished that I should interfere on behalf of mere Russians, who he said may have been Bolsheviks for all he knew', recalled Colonel John Ward. Ward warned the Japanese commander that 'the first Japanese that touches an English officer or soldier in my presence will be a dead man'.[102] Despite similar emotional threats and outbursts from other Allied officers, the Japanese never seemed to pass up the pettiest opportunity to demonstrate their presumed superiority. For instance, an American YMCA hostess (Gail Berg Reitzel) hurrying along Vladivostok's main boulevard was deliberately shoved into the muddy street by two Japanese soldiers.[103] Such behavior defied Western logic.

The Japanese acted as if they had occupied Siberia for the long-term, if not permanently. Tokyo permeated Siberia and Manchuria with many more troops than originally agreed to in the intervention agreement. Peak estimates eventually put Japanese strength at about 72,000 men. Approximately 30,000 troops manned the Chinese Eastern Railway between Vladivostok and Manchuli; 22,000 were stationed along the Ussuri line between Vladivostok and Khabarovsk; and 20,000 guarded the *magistral* between Khabarovsk and Chita.[104] Scores of Japanese military men were funneled through a newly established school in Mukden, Manchuria to learn the Russian language and railway operations. Light draft gunboats plied all navigable rivers in the Russian Far East. Even Japanese priests were recruited from the Russian Orthodox Church in Japan.[105] Banknotes that Japan issued in Siberia illuminated Tokyo's intentions in Russia. Emblazoned in both Russian and Japanese, the bills proclaimed Siberia an 'Imperial Japanese Province', and Japanese soldiers treated refusal of their currency as a crime.[106]

The Czechoslovakians wielded power far out of proportion to the size and prestige of their home country considering that Siberia was more than 100 times the size of their infant republic. From the time in September 1918 that General Gajda's command issued the proclamation that inadvertently slighted Semenov by subordinating OMO to the Czech headquarters, relations between OMO and the Czechoslovak Legion were precarious. While some conservatives were sprinkled among the Czech staff, notably the Russian monarchist Major General M.K. Diterikhs, most Czechs were inclined toward republican and socialist parties, which created an natural source of friction with Semenov and his reactionary circles.

A handful of Czechoslovaks were counted among the 40 volunteers for the first internationalist Red Guard detachment formed in Vladivostok in spring 1918, and, in June, this catalyst led to the formation of the 1st Infantry Battalion of the Czechoslovakian Red Army, with some 200–300 men under Vaclav Mirovskii. Many Czechoslovakian internationalists were deployed at stations along the Trans-Siberian – at Penza, Samara, Petropavlosk, Chelyabinsk, Omsk and others – to proselytize revolutionary solidarity among their brethren on eastbound trains. For instance, at Penza, a small Red detachment organized in April by Junior Ensign Yaroslav Shtrombakh soon grew into the 720-man 1st Penza Czechoslovakian Revolutionary Regiment, drawing cadre from existing cells of social democrats (communists) scattered through the Czech Legion and siphoning new recruits – including Russians, Latvians and Serbs – from passing trains on the station platform at Penza. When the Czech uprising occurred in May, these units were torn by split loyalties, but many Czechoslovaks continued to fight with internationalist units and underground Red cells burrowed deep into the Czechoslovak Legion. They became the constant targets of Czech and Omsk government counterintelligence hunts.[107]

Many Whites believed that the whole Czechoslovak Legion was in cahoots with the Reds. A common accusation was that 'as soon as Vladivostok fell into the hands of the Reds [in spring 1918], the Czech "generals" began transporting groups of Soviet agents in their railway cars'.[108] Tension between Semenov and the legion increased with the number of well-armed Czech echelons crossing his territory without inspection from OMO 'customs' or counterintelligence.

Serbian mercenaries and Slavic legions

Somehow Semenov had taken control of a number of Serbian troops, former POWs from the Austro-Hungarian Army like the Czechs and Slovaks, in the spring of 1918.[109] Serbs appeared on many fronts in the fight against the Bolsheviks, as well as in Red internationalist detachments. However, when the Bolsheviks sealed the peace with Austria–Hungary via the Brest–Litovsk Treaty in March 1918, they invited the enmity of the majority of their Slavic brothers in Serbia, for whom the Tsar had originally gone to war in 1914. Serbs landed with French, Polish and Greek troops in Odessa that same month. At least one Serbian battalion was stranded by the peace on the Eastern Front and, like the Czechoslovaks, decided to head for distant France and the Western Front 'via the Arctic ports'.[110] A Serbian detachment under a Colonel Blagotich helped stormed Kazan on August 6–7, 1918.[111] A week or two later, a group of 100 or so Serb POWs on the northern front joined the shore party of the USS *Olympia* and British, French and White troops in skirmishes against the Reds along the Dvina river near Archangel.

In the early fall of 1918, an Allied account stated, 'A French officer...has had considerable success in recruiting Poles and Serbians in the region between the Urals and the Volga. It is not known with what organization these troops are connected'.[112]

Apparently, two mounted infantry companies of 190–250 Serbs fought with Semenov in his first, unsuccessful invasion of Transbaikalia in summer 1918. By the last few weeks of 1918, this number had grown to over 350 soldiers in an all-Serb cavalry regiment under a Serbian commander, Colonel Dragulich, 16 Serbian officers and one Russian adjutant.[113] The Serbs were initially devoted to the Allied cause, which championed Serbian independence and had little in common with Semenov's nefarious ambitions. No mention of Colonel Dragulich is found after December 1918, when the Serb commander 'lost faith in Semenov'.[114] Perhaps Dragulich became yet another 'suicide' in the OMO officer corps.

Apart from counterrevolutionary, pan-Slavic solidarity, the Serbian soldiers soon forgot any other ideals they might have had. Many of the Serbs became Semenov's most trusted men – 40 of them joined his personal bodyguard during 1919. An unknown number of them filled the ranks of OMO's field police service. Sometime in that same year the cavalry regiment vanished from the organizational charts, presumably after the demise or departure of the pro-Allied Colonel Dragulich. In its place appeared a Jugo-Slavian regiment of unknown quantity and quality and a 90-man Serbian detachment commanded by 'a secret Austrofil [sic]' named Piskulich.[115]

There were other detachments of east European Slavs – Rumanians, Serbs and Poles mostly – stranded in Siberia by a convoluted fate, who found themselves fighting against the Bolsheviks. Like the Czechoslovak Legion, they had begun the war as unwilling conscripts from ethnic minorities in the Austro-Hungarian Empire, been captured or deserted on the Eastern Front and formed nationalist units to fight the Central Powers.

Poles who occupied Samara with the People's Komuch Army and Czechoslovak Legion in June 1918 formed a military committee that organized the 1st Polish Infantry Battalion which subsequently fought around Ufa. This battalion formed the nucleus of the Polish Legion, formally referred to after January 1919 as the 5th Rifle Division of the Polish Army in Siberia under the command of Colonel K. Rumsha. At its peak, the division encompassed nearly 12,000 men in the 1st, 2nd and 3rd Rifle Regiments, 1st Uhlan Regiment, 5th Artillery Regiment, Storm Battalion, Engineers Battalion and a Reserve Rifle Battalion.[116]

Though not exactly interventionists, they came to be considered 'Allied' contingents. Unlike the Serbs who attached themselves to OMO, the Rumanian and Polish units spent most of their civil war service at the front and their contact with Semenov was limited to transits by military echelons through Transbaikalia.

Foreign voluntary organizations

By the spring of 1919, foreign civilians seemed to be cropping up at every desolate whistlestop on the Trans-Siberian Railway east of the Urals. Red Cross organizations from Sweden and Denmark had been in Siberia for years, providing mail service and other ministrations for Central Powers' POWs. They were now joined by an army of American do-gooders, the YMCA. Knights of Columbus, Salvation Army and American Red Cross (ARC) being the most prominent.

Charitable organizations inevitably tread into a political minefield when entering an area torn by civil war. In Siberia and the Russian Far East they would be accused of espionage, aiding the enemy and of masking commercial incursions for their host countries. On 28 July 1918 soon after the Whites occupied Irkutsk, Czechoslovak Legion Colonel Radola Gajda 'ordered all prisoners of war returned to camp and the Swedish Red Cross authorities to leave the city, giving them 12 hours to get out...on account of information to the effect that the Swedish representatives in Russia were responsible for issuing of passports to German officers'.[117] Ataman Kalmykov leveled similar accusations against the Swedish Red Cross in Khabarovsk – that they were engaged in covert dealings with German and Austro-Hungarian prisoners of war, then robbed and murdered the four people in their office. Neither charitable work nor foreign passports made civilians immune to the risks of Russia's violence.

About a dozen YMCA 'secretaries' (as field workers were known) were operating in Siberia several months before US soldiers arrived, organizing volleyball, baseball and football games among Czech Legion units, assisting American expatriates to flee Russia and selling cigarettes, chocolate and biscuits in the prisoner-of-war camps.[118] Their arrival had a positive effect on the economy: the association soon 'opened a biscuit factory, a sausage factory, and absorbed the product of two chocolate and candy factories, practically all there was in Eastern Siberia'.[119] They unwittingly affected the political scene as well. The Japanese pointed at their charitable huts, clubs and railcars as proof of a concerted American invasion, and their appearance in the Far East served as a modest restraint on the institutionalized terror of the *razvedki* around them. To the dismay of their compatriots in the AEFS, YMCA employees wore US Army officer uniforms, complete with collar insignia and Sam Browne belts. An army liaison officer in Omsk, Captain Schuyler, complained, 'A number of things done by them have been attributed to me. Russians unfortunately think they are under army orders'.[120] By June 1919 102 American secretaries were sprinkled across Siberia: 17 among the US Army units, 15 with the Czech Legion, 20 working with Russian civilians and military people, 10 in Vladivostok's famous International Hut, 12 traveling lecturers and cinema experts and the remainder in the administrative and support bureaucracy. They became synapses for an informal flow of information also, inasmuch as they worked not only with Americans, Czechs, Russians and Austro-Hungarians, but served expeditionary forces from Italy, Rumania, France, Britain, Canada, Poland, Serbia and China, too.[121]

Other foreign charitable organizations had spread along the railway line with the gloom of the preceding winter. In addition to the YMCA, zealous American volunteers from the Knights of Columbus and the ARC plied the Trans-Siberian and Chinese Eastern Railways from Vladivostok to the frontlines in the Urals, giving spiritual and educational lectures, providing medical care to those lucky enough to cross their path and donating or selling cigarettes, food and clothes.

The head of the American Red Cross mission in Siberia just happened to be Dr Raymond Teusler, cousin of Mrs Woodrow Wilson. From Vladivostok he directed a $14 million operation that employed 503 Americans and 2,164 other persons in 18 hospitals, three sanitary trains and other projects.[122] The first Red Cross units had rushed to Vladivostok in July when the Czech Legion's Major General Diterikhs had requested (via Admiral Knight aboard the USS *Brooklyn*) medical support for his wounded after the battles for Nikolsk-Ussuriisk. Secretary of State Lansing reinforced this request soon after by expressing the 'hope' of the US government that the Red Cross would see fit to send representatives to Siberia.[123] To the Japanese, the influx of ARC units, along with the YMCA and an American army of 'merchants, agricultural experts, labor advisors' and others 'hoped for' by Lansing, signaled nothing less than a 'virtual declaration of economic war'.[124] To the dismay of Major General Graves and staff, reporters and foreign diplomats attached great import to Teusler's statements and opinions because of his presidential relatives.[125]

The first ARC supply train arrived in Omsk during the first week in December 1918. It was 'the first genuine supply train' to appear in three months, so citizens were disappointed to hear that the train's cargo of 1,000 sweaters and 1,000 pairs of socks were destined for Kolchak's army, not for the countless destitute refugees shivering in constant subzero temperatures.[126] Graves complained in his memoirs, 'The American Red Cross ran hospitals exclusively for Kolchak people and acted in practice as Kolchak's supply agent as long as Dr Teusler was in Siberia'.[127] At least once Major General Graves threatened to withdraw US Army guards from Teusler's trains if the ARC continued to distribute supplies exclusively to the White military. Controversy – and peril – swirled around foreign benevolent representatives for the duration of their missions in Siberia.

Despite Major General Graves and Russian civilian protests about Dr Teusler's unabashed pro-White bent, a glimpse at a typical month of ARC operations reveals a broader base of beneficiaries than simply Kolchak troops. For instance, on 4 February 1919 a 26-car supply train – the ARC's sixth such train – departed Vladivostok carrying $38,000-worth of clothing, blankets, and medicines for 'refugees and returned Russian prisoners scattered through west Omsk'.[128] The first anti-typhus train was already treating the ill in the heart of Siberia. More than 1,000 orphans were being cared for, and $30,000 had been set aside for food and clothing for underpaid Russian railway employees. The American Red Cross was also in charge of the politically sensitive task of evacuating the Czech Legion. On 14 February 1919, the British hospital ship *Madras* departed Vladivostok with the first homeward-bound load of 453 Czechs and an ARC staff to care for them.[129] Before the winter snows began melting, the ARC opened a huge 1,000-bed hospital in Omsk. Another 200-bed hospital operated under the ARC in Vladivostok, another of 150 beds in Bukhedu, and another of 80 beds in Harbin.[130] The ARC's wealth of resources made it a powerful force in eastern Siberia.

Spring and White victory in the air

'Spring has come with a rush the past few days', exclaimed YMCA Secretary Edward Heald in Omsk on 15 April 1919. Vladivostok's sudden thawing had begun two weeks earlier.[131] 'It is warm enough during the day now to go without overcoats and it is not even freezing at ten o'clock at night. The days lengthen rapidly. It is light until 8:30 in the evening and by 4:30 in the morning it is so light that it is hard to sleep in the car where...the shades fail to keep out the light.'[132] Indeed, Siberia bursts out of winter's gloom 'so fast that the buds and leaves seem to break out with a click'.[133]

The joy of spring 1919 was amplified with new hope for Russia's anti-Bolshevik factions. 'Victory is in the air these days', wrote Edward Heald after watching a jubilant trainload of Kolchak troops depart Omsk station for the front in mid-April. 'New towns are reported captured every day. Today newspapers report the destruction of a Bolshevik army in the Caucasus with the capture of 50,000 prisoners, 13 armored trains, and 200 big guns...'.[134] Such triumphs seemed miraculous in light of the corruption and profiteering behind White lines. After Admiral Kolchak's first visit to the front two months before, he ordered an investigation to ascertain why his troops were so inadequately attired while so much Allied aid poured into Vladivostok.[135] As it turned out, much of his army's equipment was on sale in town markets behind his lines. Nevertheless, throughout March and April, his soldiers advanced against the Bolsheviks on every front and planning was afoot to move the general staff west to Ekaterinburg to be 'nearer to the actual theatre of operations' for sure, but also to interrupt the rearguard party in Omsk.[136]

A small banquet in honor of Semenov in Vladivostok reflected a similar optimism in the Far East. About 20 members of 'the Commercial Class' gathered to toast the ataman and exhort one another in speech after speech to help the Motherland. Businessman Nicholas Romanov rose, and, with a short burst of patriotic oratory, presented the ataman with '5,000 rubles as a token' of his esteem and support. Subsequently his fellow admirers coughed up 47,000 more rubles.[137]

At midnight on 20 April Russian Orthodox Easter services began throughout areas of the old empire not occupied with Reds. Peasants deposited special Easter cakes – 'wrapped in cloth, a candle stuck in the top and also a little cross' – on long benches outside country churches to await blessings by priests.[138] Ancient hymns resonated through onion-domed cathedrals in all White cities, and prayers pleaded for intervention in earthly troubles and military victory. Some churches were so mobbed that many had to stand outside in the cold. 'These Easter holidays, with all work at a standstill, stores and restaurants closed, everybody out promenading, and church bells constantly ringing, no newspapers, hardly any trains running, certainly join with the general spring air to steal away the sense of work pressure', noted Edward Heald.[139] Few would have believed that, in most places, this would be the last open celebration of Easter for two generations.

Spring also brought several annoyances. Most notably, in towns and cities, came mud, slush and filthy, hazardous streets. By day, well-traveled areas became seas of mud and the peasant sleighs that had conveyed the foreign experts and well-to-do Russians during winter months retreated to the navigable, snow-covered outskirts. By late April, as Heald explained, 'The bottoms of the streets are still covered with thick ice so capped with dirt and manure that you don't realize it is ice until you take a slide and spoil your suit or dress. The streets are full of rushing torrents which plow along in deep gullies sometimes two or three feet deep through solid ice'.[140] Pedestrians sometimes fell through the soggy, rickety wooden sidewalks common in Siberian towns to find themselves immersed in a bath of thawed sewage. Each night, as the temperature plunged, the muck in the streets and paths froze into a treacherous, glassy veneer. Intermittent snow fell through May, mixing with the mysterious ingredients already in the streets to make a hideous stew that seeped into boots and splashed onto faces. Common crime flourished with the longer daylight hours, warmer weather and proliferation of small arms.[141]

Spring stoked epidemics of typhus and spinal meningitis that were already raging throughout Ivanov-Rinov and Kalmykov's cursed domains.[142] Rats, beggars, refugees and

Red partisans also emerged in large numbers in the spring. The rats seemed to grow bolder with their increasing numbers.[143] 'The Russian beggars creep out from the protection of doorways these fine days to sit on the sunny side of the streets', noted Gail Berg Reitzel in Vladivostok. 'They pull up their ragged shirts and pursue big game in the thickly populated area between waist band and filthy skin.'[144] Refugees also arose from their winter refuges to proceed east away from the war.

Along with the mud, crime, disease, parasites and beggars emerged the notorious 'Army in the Rear', which troubled Omsk far more than all the other negatives. 'It is unwieldy and the officer class in every town from here [Omsk] to Tomsk is behaving in a manner not calculated to make for discipline', reported an American officer.

> Every club, cabaret, *chantante*, hotel and dance hall is full nightly, and the amount of cash expended by the individuals causes one to pause and wonder where they get it. Krasnoyarsk was bad, but Irkutsk worse. Captain Baron Dellingshausen [Adjutant of the 4th Eastern Siberian Army Division] and Lieutenant Baumgarten are an instance: they spend every night literally thousands of rubles, and this generally in company with General Volkov, who, it will be remembered, was the officer detailed to disarm and supplant Semenov. I saw this officer myself, very drunk, and with a couple of fast women hanging to him, in public.

The capriciousness of the rear echelon's hedonism and corruption may have been the worst byproduct of Semenov and Kalmykov's insubordination – if the Supreme Ruler could not prosecute a murdering, thieving Cossack captain, then why would he bother with mere slackers and profiteers? Yet west of Irkutsk the predominant public opinion was that Semenov and Kalmykov were traitors, Japanese collaborators and brigands whom Kolchak would soon have shot.[145]

Partisan bands, bolstered by peasants aroused by the wintertime atrocities of Semenov, Kalmykov, Ivanov-Rinov, Annenkov, Dutov, Krasilnikov and other White warlords, emerged from forests and villages throughout the Far East. They spawned faster in Kalmykov's Amur province, where, in March 1919, a marauding band of 1,000 Bolsheviks 'with many Chinese' roamed the snowy landscape between Alekseevsk and Blagoveshchensk. These peasant warriors considered themselves Reds, but few seemed to comprehend exactly what Bolshevism entailed. They simply wanted to fight back against the excesses of the Whites and their Japanese allies, loot before law and order returned or eat.

Inter-Allied Railway Agreement

Japan's expansionist aspirations in Siberia were frustrated in the spring. In early 1919, the Allies and Kolchak's Omsk government had signed an Inter-Allied Railway Agreement, which created an international committee to supervise the railways in areas where Allied troops were operating. By this time, Allied troops were operating across the breadth of Siberia, from Vladivostok to the frontlines with the Bolsheviks hundreds of miles west of Omsk. The Inter-Allied Railway Committee (IARC, consisting of one representative each from Japan, the United States, Britain, France, Italy, Czechoslovakia, China and the Omsk government) held its first meeting on 5 March 1919. John F. Stevens was named president of an Inter-Allied Technical Board (IATB), which would control day-to-day railway operations.

Also in March 1919, Allied troops were dispersed throughout eastern Siberia to guard sectors of the Trans-Siberian Railway. The Czechs were assigned the vast stretch between Omsk and Lake Baikal, and the Chinese were given responsibility for the Chinese Eastern

Railway, which was also swarming with Japanese troops. The Japanese also gladly accepted guard duties on the lengthy Amur line of the Trans-Siberian, which encompassed about 1,500 miles of track from Chita east to Nikolsk. American units were assigned two sections near Vladivostok and a distant, remote segment in western Transbaikalia.

As Major General Graves explained their mission, 'The Railway Agreement provided that the military would protect the railways, therefore, it became the duty of all military troops to see that the passengers and freight were not disturbed in passage through their respective sectors'.[146] On 17 and 18 March, two echelons departed Spasskoe carrying Lieutenant Colonel William C. Miller, most of the US 27th Infantry Regiment's 1 Battalion and one platoon of the 27th's Machine Gun Company. Their original orders directed them to Chita, but during their tedious 12-day journey west this destination was changed to Verkhne-Udinsk.

Two of Semenov's armored trains were sitting in Verkhne-Udinsk when the first Americans arrived. 'There immediately began trouble between the armored cars and Miller's command', said Colonel Charles Morrow, commanding officer of the 27th. The OMO commander claimed that he had not been advised of the American's coming and otherwise comported himself as a very rude host. Finding no quarters or camp available, Miller's doughboys made their cramped *taplushkis* home for nearly one month. Just four days after they set up a camp two *versts* east of town, seven more American echelons began arriving with the bulk of the 27th Infantry.[147] 'The 27th has a beautiful camp on rolling hills among pine timber', boasted a young American corporal. 'It is clean and cool, no flies and no dirt.'[148]

On 14 April, the Americans' sector was extended to encompass guard duties over approximately 262 miles of railway from Verkhne-Udinsk to Baikal City on the far (west) side of the lake. As if to reiterate the confusion among the Allied forces, the American sector was modified again six weeks later to stretch no further than Mysovaya on Lake Baikal's eastern shore. By this time, it was obvious that even this shortened sector overextended the 27th Infantry's resources. Nevertheless, by mid-June, despite all of the orders and counterorders emanating from confused American staff officers in Vladivostok, the 27th Infantry found itself sprawled over more than 300 miles of the Trans-Siberian Railway from Verkhne-Udinsk through the Baikal tunnels to the city of Irkutsk.[149]

Semenov was perturbed by the US intrusion into his territory. The ataman and his unruly constituency – Cossacks, opportunistic Army officers, profiteers, Harbin gangsters, Buryats and other restless nationalities – had no representation on the IARC or IATB. Although the Japanese stood up for Semenov's interests whenever possible, they could not overrule committee or board decisions agreed upon by the other Allied representatives. Regulations issued by John Stevens and the IATB to better manage traffic on the Trans-Siberian and Chinese Eastern Railways were an affront to Semenov, who was used to doing whatever he pleased in Transbaikalia and northwest Manchuria. One particular source of Semenov's ire was Circular No. 6, an IATB regulation dated 22 March that intended to restrict the 'use of special service trains' – which obviously targeted OMOs growing fleet of marauding *broneviki* – except as approved by the IATB. Even more annoying to the Japanese-Cossack cabal in Chita, Stevens' Circular No. 6 acknowledged the special needs of 'The Supreme Ruler' (Admiral Kolchak) and 'The Supreme Plenipotentiary of the Far East' (Lieutenant General Horvath), but snubbed the ataman.[150] Such mutual disrespect during the initial encounters between Americans and *semenovtsy* bode ill for the future.

6

WHITE TERROR ON THE *MAGISTRAL*

May–September 1919

'They could not have existed away from the railroads...'
(Major General William S. Graves)

War on the rails

Ataman Semenov's armored trains became the most notorious in a civil war that saw extensive action on the railways on all fronts. Red, White and nationalist forces employed armored trains in the Baltic countries, the southern front and the Caucasus as well as Siberia to control large areas and keep long lines of communication and supply open. Armored trains often 'dominated the tactical thinking of the combatants'.[1] By design, railways snaked through industrial, agricultural and population centers – strategic targets that meant victory. Across the desolate, sparsely populated expanses of Siberia, the fickle automobile quickly fell victim to the harsh climate and rough roads and even the time-honored cavalry saw seasonal limitations, requiring shelter during winter's darkest bone-chilling weeks. Flying machines (of which Semenov had eight in autumn 1918) stood on the cutting edge of technology and were still an expensive, high-maintenance novelty. The railway was the all-weather lifeline of military and political powers.

Boris Pasternak immortalized the armored train of the Russian Civil War with his portrayal of the fictional Commissar Strelnikov's *bronepoezd* streaking across the snowy steppe, zealously hunting for White Guards. Although destined to be associated with Siberia, armored trains were not a purely Russian phenomenon and, after 70 years of refinement since their use in the Crimean War, were in vogue with militaries around the world that could afford such landlocked warships. Huge British and US Navy trains lugging 15-inch howitzers and 14-inch guns (respectively) had 'added some degree of nautical color to the Western Front', while the Germans, who had operated the world's largest railway armada, terrorized Paris by hurling small (15-pound) shells up to 70 miles from their rail-mounted Lange Max gun. Every major power boasted a fleet of armored trains and even China, South Africa and Peru found reasons to deploy them.[2]

Ever since Lenin stepped off a train at Petrograd's Finland Station on 3 April 1917, trains had played a major role in bringing revolution, counterrevolution and civil war to every corner of the old empire. The Bolsheviks well understood the strategic and tactical values of railway weapons and made their rail troops an elite force in distinctive leather uniforms, established an armored school in the beginning of 1919 and standardized (to the extent possible amidst the revolutionary chaos) rail organizations, procedures, train configurations and personnel. A central base was established at Bryansk, which became known as the 'armored city', and large workshops at Moscow, Petrograd, Kharkov,

Lugansk and Kiev stamped out three main types of armored trains bristling with turrets, retractable bay windows and embrasures full of 76.2-millimeter field pieces and heavy machine guns.[3] Agitprop (agitation and propaganda) specialists enamored the public with the romanticized exploits of revolutionary trains with glorious names like 'Svoboda ili Smert'' ('Liberty or Death'), 'Smert' Parazitam' ('Death to Parasites'), 'Smert' Directorii' ('Death to the Directory'), 'Gibel' Kontrrevolyutsii' ('Ruin of the Counterrevolution'), 'Krasnaya Astrakhan'' ('Red Astrakhan'), 'Bolshevik', 'Potemkin', 'Roza Luxemburg', 'Sovietskaya Latvia', 'Yermak Timofeyevich', and several trains named after Lenin.[4] There would be more than 100 of them by October 1919.[5]

Of course, White trains commemorated counterrevolutionary heroes, such as General Yudenich's trains 'Admiral Essen' and 'Admiral Kolchak', but intimidating monikers like 'Groznyi' ('Terrible') were popular on both sides of the lines.[6]

The most famous single train of Russia's civil war became the elaborate mobile head-quarters of the *Predsedatel' Revolyutsionogo Voyenogo Soviet* (Chairman of the Revolutionary Military Council), which PREDREVVOYENSOVIET Leon Trotsky crowed was 'inseparably bound up with the life of the Red Army', though a bit more comfortable. Trotsky's 'flying apparatus of administration' contained offices, a printing-press, a telegraph station, a wireless radio center, an electric-power generator, a library, an automobile garage, his living quarters in the coach of a former railway minister and accommodations for his elite bodyguard of shock troops, hauled by two powerful locomotives.[7]

On the other side of the lines, the general commanding the 7th Division of Denikin's volunteer army took his meals with maps of the Kuban and Caucasus campaigns spread across a table in an armored dining car that was 'decorated like a church for a wedding, with bouquets on the lamps and strings of flowers festooned from the center to the corners of the ceiling – zinnias, aster, daisies and marigolds'.[8] To some White generals, trains were a status symbol and a means to maintain their standards of luxury near the fighting fronts. J.E. Hodgson, a British war correspondent on Denikin's southern front in 1919, described

> a general's train coming back from the front. It consisted of forty-four trucks and coaches and the gallant officer carried with him his own orchestra, his operatic stars and his troop of acrobats. Apart from the economic tragedy involved, it does not call for a political genius to gauge the effect of this spectacle on the minds of the starved and shivering peasants who watched the pageant from the wayside station platforms.[9]

In Siberia, the Czech uprising in May 1918 cleared the Trans-Siberian Railway of Red armored trains between Chelyabinsk and Irkutsk. Western and central Siberia saw the density of armored trains increase as Admiral Kolchak's Ural and Caucasus battle fronts expanded, then petered out and shifted east. At one time in 1919, over 130 military trains – armed echelons interspersed with armored trains – plied the rails between Chelyabinsk and Krasnoyarsk.[10]

In the Far East campaigns of summer 1918, Transbaikalia's war on rails opened with no less than eight Bolshevik armored trains operating against Semenov, while *broneviki* in the Maritime province took prominent roles fending off Allied pursuers and in the Battle of Kraevski. By early September, Japanese forces had captured at least two Red *broneviki*, while the rest retired towards Blagoveshchensk and eventual capture soon afterwards.[11]

Even the British fielded railway weapons in the Far East. In the last week of September 1918, Colonel Langtry of the RRSC watched the British Gun Train Company pass through Olovyannaya bound for the Urals Front, after enduring a baptism of fire on the Ussuri Front a few weeks earlier. The heavy train had to be cut in three sections that rumbled across the temporary wooden bridge over the Onon one at a time. The unit consisted of 47 men, and had eight 3-inch naval guns and 'one 6-inch rifled from the British cruiser *Suffolk* carried on a steel-frame American flat car; its gun carriage [rode] on another car'.[12] They stood a chance of encountering the Red Army's armored train fleet in the west, but the heavily armed echelons and *broneviki* of OMO, OKO, the Omsk government, Czechoslovak Legion and Japanese Army had the rails to themselves in Eastern Siberia and the Far East until the end of 1919.

Semenov's armored train division

Semenov's first 'armored train' was the fake *bronevik* with which he sprang his friend Roman Ungern-Shternberg from the Chinese jail at Hailar in January 1918. Armed trains with field pieces strapped down on a flatcar and a few sandbagged machine guns demonstrated the need for armored trains and Semenov was said to have taken advantage of the engineering expertise of German prisoners of war to design and construct them, although local railway metalworkers in Chinese Eastern shops had the expertise to do it. At the time of his April offensive, he had only two armored cars, one of them a wooden boxcar with 10-inch concrete-reinforced walls and gun ports, the other a platform car with a half-inch steelplate shelter for a pair of Hotchkiss guns and a pair of machine guns. The former was not used (no reason was cited), but the latter proved immensely useful, performing valuable forward reconnaissance a few miles ahead of the advance patrols and boosting the morale of OMO's cavalry spearhead. An unarmored locomotive pushed it into Red territory and a 'flatcar covered with steel rails' in front of the armored car provided a modicum of cover.[13]

By July 1918 he commanded a battalion of armored trains that provided the crucial artillery cover his beleaguered force needed to survive when it was cornered between Lazo's Red Army and the Chinese Army. His summer 1918 headquarters was aboard an armored train optimistically named 'Atamanovka' (after the first large town east of Chita).[14] Control of the railways was synonymous with political control in the Far Eastern provinces and northern Manchuria and Semenov took a special interest in building his Armored Train Division by commandeering facilities, personnel and equipment from the railways and eventually forcing soldiers into the press-gang crews and staffing his trains with a brutal cadre.

Semenov established the headquarters of his Armored Train Division at the little station of Adrianovka, 75 miles southeast of Chita on the branch of the railway that fed the Chinese Eastern. Any prying eyes interested in OMO rail activity were sure to draw unpleasant attention in Adrianovka. OMO christened its trains with colorful names: 'Ataman', 'Semenov', 'Bi-Yats', 'Groznyi', 'Khozyain' ('Master'), 'Mstitel'' ('Avenger'), 'Istrebitel' ('Destroyer'), 'Pobeditel'('Victor') and 'Bezposhchadnyi'('Merciless').[15]

Semenov employed two basic configurations of armored train: the 'strong' type, typically bearing three guns, about a dozen machine guns and 85–120 men; and a 'weak' type with two guns and proportionally fewer machine guns and crew. 'Istrebitel' was typical of Semenov's 'strong' configuration. It bore half-inch armor plate atop 18-inch concrete walls, mounted ten machine guns, two 3-inch guns and two one-pounders, and was manned by about 60 officers and men. Two or more locomotives provided power in case one of them was disabled by hostile fire. 'Whipping cars' for interrogations and sadistic recreation complemented railcars for staff offices, barracks and sometimes mobile stables. Various combinations typified the 'weak' configuration, such as 'unauthorized Train No. 106', which consisted of a single armored railcar, four coaches, six *taplushki* and Ussuri Line engine No. 3.[16]

In May 1919 an RRSC inspector reported that the Armored Train Division was made up of no less than four *broneviki*, nine locomotives, 27 passenger cars and 160 freight cars, numbers that were certainly understated, particularly considering that OMO took whatever it wanted from the railway.[17] The ataman's fleet soon grew to no less than 13 armored trains. Since his successful bluff at Manchuli in January 1918, Semenov regularly commandeered railway equipment for his holy war against the Reds and movement of stolen property. RRSC Colonel Lantry reported a typical incident on 7 July 1919: 'Semenov's armored train commandant took Chinese Eastern car 328 at Chita, moved it to Adrianovka and has repainted [it] with his standard paint color' – as simple as that![18] At one point, Semenov amassed 1,200 'impounded' passenger cars at Chita alone, where 200 of them were used as OMO barracks and others were rented out to merchants at a huge profit for the ataman. His appropriating of locomotives particularly hurt the railway, ever more so because he cannibalized them of their boiler steel for armor.[19]

Crews on Semenov's armored trains were even less fortunate than the reluctant railway workers who were forced to service his fleet. Most of the crewmen were shanghaied into service on the *broneviki* from other army units. A sadistic and often intoxicated cadre of OMO officers aboard each train oversaw their every move. Refusal to follow orders (such as an order to execute civilians) was grounds for a severe, perhaps fatal, whipping. Crewmen aboard OMO armored trains 'were killed for the least offense', lamented one of them. A surgeon forced to serve on the *bronevik* 'Istrebitel' stated that of the train's 57 or so crewmen, only six served voluntarily. He recalled one soldier who tried to slip away from the *bronevik* at Manchuli and was whipped to death.[20]

Since autumn 1918 a cutthroat named Colonel Stepanov commanded the Armored Train Division. An October 1919 US intelligence report described him as being 'well known for the collisions at Verkhne-Udinsk and...implicated in the affair of the disappearance of General Natsvalov's wife'. Stepanov directed mass executions of prisoners of war and countless innocent civilians arrested for little or no reason by Semenov's troops. Often drunk, Stepanov was known to select a rifle and board a train full of ill-fated hostages to one of OMO's many 'slaughter yards' between Chita and Manchuli. He had no conscience. Evenings found him celebrating with women, booze and orchestras. RRSC Lieutenant G.I. McNutt, a young American railway engineer who had taken a Russian wife during his tour of duty, was stationed in Stepanov's territory and visited his armored train many times. McNutt recounted that, 'He has often told me he was ashamed to eat a meal unless he had killed someone and earned that meal, that he could not sleep unless he had killed someone and earned that sleep.'[21] And he had no qualms about killing Whites either. When a junior officer and two doctors once complained about his evil deeds, he had them shot too.[22]

Stepanov disappeared for some time in November 1919; and command of the Armored Train Division went to the arrogant, hot-headed General Nikolai Bogomolets (also cited as Bogomolich) at a time when Semenov, self-conscious of his poor public image, sincerely tried to cow the division's murderers, rapists, thieves and ruffians into good behavior.[23] Semenov even trumped up a court martial and had a couple of officers shot as an example. Ironically, the executed pair, who were typical of the drunk and disorderly troublemakers in OMO's substandard officer corps, were only charged with resisting arrest, although they had led the pillaging of a Cossack village and the gang-rape of two girls.[24]

During Stepanov's absence, his fellow officers claimed that he had gone to join Denikin's White Army, while the grapevine said that he was really in Japan (the latter was true).[25] Three months later Stepanov was back in Transbaikalia, promoted to general. Semenov apparently gave up on his reforms of an officer corps in which lawlessness was indelibly ingrained.

All of the *bronevik* commanders were cold-blooded brutes in Stepanov's mold: Colonels Popov and Aparovich; Captains Sidorov and Skriabin; Lieutenant Merov; Lieutenant Colonel Freiburg, an unstable German officer captured years early in the First World War; 'Worker' Yakovenko – 'He always used to help kill and whip', said a terrorized crewman; and Colonel Zhukovski, whose subordinate OMO officers could not tell whether he was constantly soused with liquor or mentally unbalanced.[26] An RRSC lieutenant who became acquainted with these men declared,

> The officers of these trains did as they pleased and were the most feared men in this district. They were noted only for their brutality. They and their men had absolutely no respect for man, woman, child, nor anything that breathed. They took particular pains to know that people – all the people – were afraid of them. They remarked almost daily that it was necessary for them to whip, punish, or kill someone each day in order that people know who was protecting them from the Bolsheviks.[27]

An important responsibility of the division was protecting Ataman Semenov whenever he traveled. His personal train was composed of six cars armed with machine guns and containing 'the ataman, his staff, his guard of Serbs, his mistress and his servants'. Some descriptions mention a coach for his personal quarters, another for Captain Kuroki's quarters and office, and a dining car where visitors were received and meetings conducted.[28] Presumably his 'summer car' and its harem remained in Chita. He always moved in a convoy of three trains, with *broneviki* armed with cannon and machine guns preceding and trailing his special. 'One of his colonels travels about a day in advance, and makes arrangements for supplying the three trains with fresh locomotives at each terminal, and for other supplies', wrote RRSC officer C.R. Rice.

> These arrangements are no less than threats and railway men know that failure to comply means that they will be shot. On arrival of the trains at a terminal, his officers stand about with drawn revolvers until the trains are on the move again. He will not permit the three trains to be separated at meeting points, even the through passenger trains being held two to three hours until he gets by.[29]

Had the ataman made some effort to coordinate his equipment requirements with the railway, his requisitioning of precious locomotives would not have so undermined other operations and ultimately Omsk's supply line. For example, during Semenov's August 1919 visit to Vladivostok, he tied up four locomotives for the duration of his stay, clinging to three locomotives while traipsing around town for several days and even had another on an armored train at Nikolsk. When he departed Vladivostok on 28 August he gave the Nikolsk shops short notice that he would be taking their five best locomotives with him when he passed through.[30] Such demands could be devastating to railway operations on the ailing Trans-Siberian.

The ultimate mission of OMO's armored trains was to combat Red partisans, who wisely stayed clear of their path. The trains earned infamy for their 'punitive' role, but also functioned as mobile headquarters, intelligence center (complete with torture chambers) and artillery support. A portion of the crew stood ready to dismount and act as shock troops, riot suppression force or perimeter guard. Japanese infantrymen and lonely Cossack garrisons usually bore the brunt of counterpartisan operations, and Semenov's *broneviki* rarely showed up until the smoke had cleared.[31] However, when the frustrated peasantry resorted to any action that might be construed as a civil disturbance, a *bronevik* soon appeared and discharged OMO troopers who would wade into the panicked crowds, 'shooting and whipping with chains'.[32] This bloody image overshadowed all others.

Strategic railway resources

Control of railway facilities, particularly workshops, was vital to Semenov's reign. One historian states that Semenov cornered the market on boiler steel for his *broneviki* and appropriated materials and locomotives from distant Vladivostok's railway workshops.[33] However, ever since the ataman established his permanent headquarters at Chita in September 1918, the railway shops at Chita and other Transbaikal stations bore the brunt of outfitting, servicing and repairing OMO's armored trains.

About 1,400 men and women toiled in the tangle of dark, dank, contorted brick structures that comprised the Chita shops. The dilapidated buildings sprawled over a taiga swamp that was gradually swallowing them, so the warped, constantly settling sheds – shrouded in smoke, steam, noxious chemical clouds and the noise of seven electric power plants – looked like a paranoid Luddite's nightmare. The Chita shops consisted of a boiler house, with six water-tube boilers; locomotive shops, where locomotives' copper fire boxes that required patching were riveted, chipped and caulked by hand; tyre shops, which annually turned out 4,000 tyres for locomotives and cars; a brass foundry, which produced 120 tons of valves, bearings, etc. each year; an iron foundry, which recycled scrap into 400 tons of forgings each year; the machine shop, renowned for its quality of workmanship despite its lack of modern tools; the passenger shops, where both freight and passenger cars were overhauled; an under-equipped roundhouse with 27 stalls and only a few small machine tools.

After Semenov's occupation of Transbaikalia, the already impossible workload of the roundhouses and workshops at Chita, Verkhne-Udinsk, Sludyanka and other railway divisions was expanded to devote attention to the ataman's fleet, to the detriment of the Trans-Siberian's other ailing equipment. Despite abysmal salaries, dangerous working conditions and persistent revolutionary agitation, workers in railway shops persevered under daily threats of violence from Semenov's ruffians. In December 1918, American advisors were shocked to discover that railway employees had not been paid in four months but stayed on their jobs for the housing and fuel the railway provided and because they were under military control and 'do not dare to quit'.[34] Their irregular pay was hardly enough to purchase enough food to keep their families alive: a May 1919 report stated that while skilled workers earned the equivalent of two and a half to three US dollars a day and unskilled workers received up to a dollar and a half daily, railway workers made only $15 per month. Anyone who skipped worked risked a whipping or execution as a deserter.[35]

Like fellow workers on lonely stretches of the railway line, employees at railway shops were frequently whipped by OMO brutes and morale hovered near non-existent. When an OMO officer wanted something done, it seemed common practice to go right to the top and threaten the supervisor with whipping. Even the master mechanic of the Transbaikal Railway, J.K. Afanas'ev, was not immune from the *nagaika* (the traditional heavy leather whip); he was lashed by a crewmen of the *bronevik* 'Bezposhchadnyi' for some real, imagined or contrived infraction on 5 May 1919.[36]

Colonel Medi served as Semenov's transportation and railway chief from the spring of 1918, being concerned with troop movements and supply for OMO and its Cossack allies. The mainstays of these logistic operations were echelons of 35–40 tough *taplushki*, perhaps with one or two second- or third-class passenger cars or a few flatcars for artillery or wagons. A single *taplushka* could accommodate 20 men or eight horses or as many prisoners as White guards could cram aboard. The center section was dominated by a small stove during troop transport, but during horse transport was removed to make room for forage, saddles, equipment and two or three men.[37]

Semenov and his Japanese partners were unwilling to subordinate their dominion over the railway to maintain Omsk's lifeline and honor their obligations under the Interallied Railway Agreement. This became obvious as their disregard for passenger safety and the well-being of railway employees also extended to the American railway advisors. 'In the territory east of Verkhne-Udinsk [RRSC] men are in constant danger, on account of absolutely no military protection and very strong propaganda issuing from Japanese, Semenoff and Russians against Americans', Colonel Lantry wrote in September 1919, when urging John F. Stevens (and US Ambassador to Japan Roland Morris) to withdraw advisors from Semenov's lawless territory.[38] The ataman and the Japanese Army were slowly strangling Admiral Kolchak's government from behind while the Red Army pummeled it from the front.

Reign of terror on the rails

OMO *broneviki* trolled the Transbaikalian rails with the straightforward purpose of inspiring fear into everyone. Transbaikalia's scattered partisan bands were elusive but not dormant during the first nine months of White occupation and dedicated themselves to building up strength in their secluded 'forest communes'. Overt Reds and sympathizers who were foolish enough to remain in town had been liquidated soon after Semenov's arrival in autumn 1918. For a while, OMO's *broneviki* reigned supreme and their demented commanders took advantage of the lawless situation to run amok as they pleased. The visit of an armored train to a small Transbaikal town or village on the *magistral* could be a catastrophic event. Anything or anyone the OMO officers coveted was theirs. They did not even have to go through the charade of declaring their victims to be Reds, much less hold a kangaroo court. They could usually rob, rape, torture and execute without worrying about questions from any higher authority.

Mayhem was sport to the sadists commanding Semenov's armored trains. 'As a rule, when any of the *broneviks* were returning to Adrianovka from either direction, one of the officers, usually Lieutenant Colonel Freiburg, would call from one to three or four of the station commandants along the line on the telephone and order them to send him from one to ten men. One or two was what they usually asked for', recalled Colonel Morrow.[39] Normally the station commandants ordered soldiers to grab men at random – railway employees, refugees, whoever happened to be nearby. When the armored train arrived, they would be dragged inside and were usually never seen again. This pointless terror often had no purpose beyond the sadistic pleasure it brought OMO commanders.

A few sample reports of incidents during a three-month period in summer 1919 are illustrative of Semenov's reign of terror on the rails.

Armored train 'Groznyi', Karymskaya, 8 July 1919

On 12 July 1919, Lieutenant G.I. McNutt of the RRSC left Dauria in a common box car attached to a westbound freight. Nevertheless his accommodations were relatively luxurious; the car was equipped with a stove, and, unlike the overcrowded eastbound trains full of refugees, McNutt's sole travelling companion after Berzin was the Russian cook of RRSC Major Gravis.

'At Olovyannaya station, a woman perhaps about 60 years old, asked me if she could ride with me to Karymskaya', recalled Lieutenant McNutt.

> At first I refused her, but later my heart failed me and I allowed her to go with me. The train left Olovyannaya at 8:00 a.m., and arrived at Adrianovka 5:30 p.m., July 14. The lady acted peculiar, and upon investigation, she advised me [that] her husband was employed as a car inspector at Karymskaya, and that on July 8 her 19 year old daughter had been taken aboard the *bronevik* 'Groznyi' at Karymskaya and carried east from there... She followed as best she could on following trains until she found the 'Groznyi' at Olovyannaya on July 13. She went in to see the commander and asked about her daughter... The brute answered that 'he would teach her not to follow him'. He ordered her taken to the prison car and whipped...
>
> She showed me where she had been struck ten times, each blow, I believe, having [drawn] blood. I did what I could for her as far as Adrianovka, and took her to our quarters until she could get a train to Karymskaya, which she did about 9:00 p.m. that night. She was in a very bad condition. I had occasion to go to Karymskaya at different times after this time, and always inquired from the lady or her husband as to what they had learned about their daughter. They, however, never heard from her, nor about her, after she was taken away.

Armored train 'Bi-Yats', *Aga, 16 July 1919*

On Wednesday 16 July 1919, westbound train No. 55 held up the eastbound *bronevik* 'Bi-Yats' for about ten minutes at Aga station, a lonely stop about 20 miles west of Olovyannaya. Officers of the armored train were irritated by the delay and ordered No. 55's senior conductor, a man named Morosov, to be dragged off his train and into the 'Bi-Yats', where they whipped him with chains. Mr Morosov was not able to work for three months afterwards.[40]

Armored train 'Ataman', *Chita, 17 July 1919*

RRSC officers were helpless to do anything but dutifully report the comings and goings of the *broneviki* and their ill-fated human cargo. For instance, Lieutenant Waldhaus in Chita reported the departure of the 'Ataman' from there on 17 July, with no prisoners on board. At Makkaveevo the next day, Lieutenant McDonald saw 17 men and two women forced onto the 'Ataman' before it continued east. By the time the 'Ataman' left Adrianovka at 4:00 p.m. on 18 July, its prison car held 38 men and three women. A mile and a half from the station, the 41 prisoners were unloaded and promptly shot. The 'Ataman' arrived back at Adrianovka at 5:20 p.m.[41] Few if any of the victims of this mass execution were believed to have been Reds. Bolshevik activity in the area had virtually ceased months before.

Armored train 'Mstitel'' ('Avenger'), *Adrianovka, 22 July 1919*

About 7:00 p.m. on Tuesday 22 July 1919, a number of people were waiting on the station platform at Adrianovka for train No. 4 to arrive from the west. Among them was a certain Miss Lobanov from Chita. She was visiting her uncle in Adrianovka, a man who owned a team of horses and drove one of the town's many water carts. Captain Kapanov and another officer from the 'Mstitel'' approached two girls in the crowd, one of them Miss Lobanov, and told them to come with them to the *bronevik*. The girls were kept on the 'Mstitel'' until the next day, and, meanwhile, were raped or cleverly seduced.

A few hours after their release, Miss Lobanov returned to the armored train. She climbed aboard, and immediately saw Captain Kapanov. She declared that 'he had ruined her, and asked when he would marry her'. Kapanov started to bark an order for her to be taken to the prison car, when, suddenly, Miss Lobanov whipped out a revolver, killed Kapanov with one shot, then shot herself.

Miss Lobanov lingered until the next day, dying at her uncle's home. On the day after her death, 25 July, the girl's aunt and uncle were arrested and taken to the *bronevik* 'Semenov'. Mr and Mrs Lobanov were brutally whipped while they were interrogated to divulge where their niece had obtained the revolver. They did not know. On Saturday 26 July Mr Lobanov was taken out to the slaughter yard and shot on the grounds that he was a Bolshevik.[42]

Armored train 'Ataman', Adrianovka, 8 August 1919

On 8 August Colonel Stepanov, the reviled commander of the Armored Train Division, was married in the Russian Orthodox Church to 'a girl who had been living with him on his car for some time'. Shortly after the wedding, train No. 52 arrived here from Chita. Ten minutes after No. 52 pulled in, Assistant Conductor Alexandrovich was arrested for no reason, hauled into the *bronevik* 'Ataman' and whipped for Colonel Stepanov's entertainment.[43]

Armored train 'Mstitel'', Zilovo, 19 September 1919

On 10 September a band of partisans walked in and occupied Zilovo, a railway town near Nerchinsk. Of course, had any residents complained or gone off to inform the White authorities, they and their families may have been shot by the Reds. Eight days later the partisans heard of the approach of a Japanese Army patrol and withdrew into the forest. The next day, 'Mstitel'' pulled into the station. A village delegation brought the traditional welcome of bread and salt to the train commander, Colonel Popov, who shot them on the spot. Soldiers immediately rounded up a dozen more villagers at random and promptly shot them too. They then began the 'requisitions', taking any property they pleased, and making arrests. A Captain Skriabin accosted a Madame Dovgal, 'a woman of about forty, widow of a minor official', and mother of two girls. He looked at her 'with an expression of disappointment', and led the girls to a passenger car. First the officers raped them, then the non-commissioned officers, then the lower ranks. Fortunately, they were released when 'Mstitel'' departed.[44]

There the matter would have ended if not for the courage of Madame Dovgal. She prepared a deposition, and persevered in seeing that it got into the hands of Semenov, via the ataman's friend, Dutch journalist Lokewijk Grondijs. Grondijs sincerely believed that Semenov was angered by such criminal behavior against the populace. Semenov even hauled Popov and Skriabin before a court martial, where the younger Captain Grant (of the English father–son mercenary duo) served as prosecutor. Their sentence was predetermined, because Semenov hoped to make the two 'Mstitel'' officers serve as examples to motivate better behavior among armored train crews. They were shot a few hours later.[45]

Armored train 'Ataman', Eruchina, 27 September 1919

Bronevik 'Ataman' departed Chita at 10 a.m. and cruised slowly down to Adrianovka, stopping at every station in between. Just before Eruchina station, the 'Ataman' passed a slower eastbound train, No. 54. Lieutenant Colonel Freiburg, the *bronevik* commander, called ahead to the Eruchina station commandant and ordered him to pull ten people off the train, but not to delay its departure. When No. 54 arrived at Eruchina, the station commandant started to pull off the five-man crew, but RRSC Lieutenant McDonald saw what was happening and objected. The station commandant then picked ten men at random, including two railway employees who were sweeping the tracks and two water cart drivers. No one knew of the fates of 'Ataman's' unfortunate victims.[46]

Stories about atrocities even appeared in the Chita newspapers and attracted Semenov's attention. The Ataman was quite sensitive to public criticism and certainly wary of disinformation circulated by his enemies, Red, White and other:

> In various newspapers, they treat me and my forces with animosity often featuring front page items about the illegal acts of *semenovtsy*, atamans and so forth. In one newspaper, it said that, around Chita, hardly a week passes that there's not a pair of railway employees hanging from telegraph poles, strung up by Semenovtsy. In another newspaper it alleged that inhabitants of densely populated areas are – without trial – ravaged and stripped naked. A third newspaper attributed criminal acts to *Shtab-Rotmistr* (Captain) Korideev and others.

Semenov insisted that he investigated all of the published cases of abuse. For instance, regarding the regular hangings, he concluded, 'No one among the railway workers in Chita was able to recall any family hung on poles in the course of the week, and they even did not so much as suspect any corpses in their neighborhoods...' Determined to halt the propagation of false accusations and innuendo, Semenov issued an order in mid-July mandating punishment for slander in the press.[47] Presumably journalists and critics took greater care in their reporting after this.

Red partisans of Transbaikalia

During the autumn of 1918 and the succeeding winter, the paucity of Red operations in Transbaikalia gave the impression that the revolutionaries had abandoned their land to Semenov. Then, in spring 1919 the partisans emerged from their hibernation with fresh resolve, first committing skulking acts of sabotage along deserted stretches of railway, then attacking small garrisons and patrols.

In the months since the solemn convocation of Red leaders in Urul'ga station as the Whites stormed Chita on 28 August 1918, a network of 40 partisan camps – the 'forest communes' – had reconstituted a revolutionary community in the shadows of the taiga. The best known of them sprouted in the Altagachanskii, Onon-Borzinskii, Alkhanaiskii and Nizhne-Giryunskii regions of eastern Transbaikalia, and, months later on the western side of the province in the river valleys near the Mongolian border and Troitskosavsk.[48] Red Guards and soldiers from revolutionary army regiments formed the nucleus of the partisan detachments, providing leadership and training for recruits pressured in by agitators, spurred to join by some White outrage or the dreadful economic picture, or impelled by hunger and cold to seek food and a coat. Bolshevik leaders like D.S. Shilov, G.N. Aksenov and S.G. Bogomyagkov were given credit for organizing the stragglers from revolutionary Cossack regiments.

The Altagachanskii group germinated in a maze-like thicket near the town of Kurunzulaya, about 40 miles northeast of Khada-Bulak station, where 60 former cavalrymen gathered who could not return home without facing liquidation by OMO. They drew their food, fodder, animals and manpower from the surrounding population, and stayed in contact with cells of sympathizers 'in almost every village'. By the spring of 1919 the Altagachanskii partisans swelled into six irregular cavalry regiments.[49]

The partisans included Socialist-Revolutionaries, Maximalists, Anarchists and others, but they all eventually fell under Bolshevik control and Soviet histories erased the affiliations and contributions of most non-communists. Left Socialist-Revolutionaries became the exceptions to this retroactive expungement and have been blamed – perhaps rightly so – for their bent for terrorist bombings and assassinations while the Bolsheviks were commanding the underground to lay low, build strength and infiltrate White society.[50]

While much has been made of the European internationalists who formed Red Guard units, the contributions of Koreans and Chinese, who both joined the partisans in large numbers, seem to have been overlooked. Hundreds of thousands of Koreans lived between Lake Baikal and the Pacific and the hamlets and urban warrens of their communities were usually hotbeds of nationalism and anti-Japanese sentiment. In June 1918, Yi Dong Whi founded the Korean People's Socialist Party in Khabarovsk, and the formation of a Korean Red Brigade soon followed.[51] Yi was also instrumental in the growth of a Siberian Korean People's Association boasting tens of thousands of members, from whom an Independence Army was raised to attack the Japanese. In other towns in Amur and the Maritime provinces, a Bolshevik activist of Korean descent (usually a new recruit himself) would organize a local Korean society dedicated to liberating Korea from Japan – after the Red liberation of Russia was complete, of course. 'The society entered into negotiations with Red Army headquarters and signed a formal treaty, which permitted the Korean society to organize military detachments and acquire arms.'[52] Diligent Red members of the societies were steered towards membership in the Korean Communist Party, which was founded in January 1919.[53] A harsh Japanese reaction in Korea to a nationwide protest by civic leaders, students and Christians on 1 March 1919 motivated thousands of Korean settlers and refugees in Siberia to enlist in the fight against Japan during subsequent months.

In spite of the constant roundups by OMO and Japanese counterintelligence units, the nerve center of the partisan movement never strayed from Semenov's backyard in Chita. Alexander Petrovich Vagzhanov chaired the underground committee until April 1919. Vagzhanov was a 40-year-old from Tver who had been a 'professional revolutionary' since 1896 and represented his home district in the second state duma. He had been serving a hard labor sentence in the Selenginsk district of Transbaikalia when the February Revolution freed him. He returned to Tver, only to be sent back to Transbaikalia by the party central committee because of his familiarity with local 'political conditions, customs and life'. He returned with his wife and children and became well-known in his inquisitorial roles overseeing the revolutionary-military tribunal's supreme court of inquiry and serving as regional commissar for food and supplies until the White occupation in August 1918. He went underground and had survived for nearly eight months, changing location frequently, when he made the mistake of checking into the Hotel Zvezdochka on Nerchinskii Street. The owner, Okolovich, was closely associated with Chief Zaks of the Chita police criminal investigation department, who had Vagzhanov picked up and turned over to an OMO counterespionage squad. The underground committee survived, but Vagzhanov soon ascended painfully to the pantheon of revolutionary martyrs.[54]

The Chita leadership arranged periodic rural meetings for liaison between the partisan detachments and urban underground organizations in Sretensk, Nerchinsk, Aleksandrovskii Zavod and Gazimurskii Zavod. Partisan leaders gathered for a conference on the first anniversary of the Bolshevik coup near Nizhe-Goryunino, where a military revolutionary committee under a former schoolteacher, Mikhail Ivanovich Borodin, set the agenda. A March 1919 conference 'under the leadership of the Chita committee' delegated combat responsibilities and set up agitation and political departments for eastern Transbaikalia. They eventually began to publish their own newspaper, *Krasnoarmeyets*. Similar organization was occurring in western Transbaikalia under a party committee at Verkhne-Udinsk. The Reds began their campaign with railway sabotage and carefully chosen attacks.[55]

The lonesome rails begged for abuse from vandals. In March, 1st Lieutenant Ralph Baggs, the US military observer in Chita, bid adieu to a jubilant trainload of wounded Czech Legionnaires as they pulled out of the station for Vladivostok and a homebound ship. Two hours later Baggs was sickened to see the bodies of about 50 of the Czechs brought back to the depot. Partisans had sabotaged the railway line nearby by prying the spikes out of tracks and splitting the ties. Sabotage became a daily occupational hazard for railwaymen. For example, during a one-week period in May, there were four hair-raising incidents in Transbaikal province alone. One moonless night in mid-month, an alert section foreman checking the line east of Verkhne-Udinsk noticed that angle bars, spikes and tie plates had been wrested from a seven-tie span. When the foreman began to make repairs, he was fired upon twice. On 18 May five Italian soldiers were injured when their train derailed on a stretch of sabotaged track. Three nights later two bridges 30 miles west of Olovyannaya were destroyed and a *verst*-long section of tracks was blown up, causing the next train to come along to wreck. Hundreds of miles to the west (near Mysovaya) that same night, a vigilant crewman spotted several joints of track unbolted by partisans in time to avert an accident.[56]

While sabotage became almost a daily affair, the partisans planned and prepared for attacks on carefully selected targets for weeks. The first occurred against Semenov's garrison at Kurunzulaya, where a *sotnia* from Semenov's 3rd Cossack Regiment had recently arrived to reinforce a *sotnia* of garrison troops. The town sat on the home turf of the Altagachanskii partisan detachment and Red reconnaissance ascertained the locations of the Whites' machine guns and officers' quarters and rushed them in a well-coordinated attack at dawn on 29 March 1919. Owing to good intelligence, the suddenness of the partisan infiltration and takeover of the garrison's machine guns and the quick killing of four key officers (along with 22 enlisted Cossacks), 70 partisans under S.S. Kirgizov captured the town and most of the garrison at the cost of only one Red wounded.[57]

Kirgizov occupied Kurunzulaya for four nights, during which time former schoolteacher Borodin arrived to lead the 250 prisoners in a political discussion contrasting the Reds and the Whites and, in a masterful bit of indoctrination soon had the prisoners cursing Ataman Semenov and hankering to join the partisans according to Soviet histories. So complete was the Cossacks' conversion to Bolshevism that six of them sat alongside seven Reds on a hurried revolutionary tribunal that judged their surviving officers and intransigent soldiers.[58]

As White troops maneuvered to encircle Kurunzulaya during the night of 1–2 April, the Reds and their new Cossack recruits vacated the town for the nearby mountains. The Whites tracked them, moving in the direction of Klin, and came upon a scene that galvanized their resolve to eradicate the Bolshevik vermin. Not far from Kurunzulaya lay the corpses of about 20 soldiers from the 3rd Regiment. Enlisted Cossacks who refused to join Kirgizov's detachment were stripped, put in a hot bath and doused with boiling water to turn them 'Red' whether they liked it or not. Special treatment was meted out to four young lieutenants and ensigns, Borodin, Semenov and the brothers Tokmakov. One of them was fortunate enough to have been dispatched with a bullet, but the other three were the pitiful subjects of the mob's sadistic merriment. Ensign Semenov was partially skinned alive and all had endured slicing of their genitals and severing of fingers, ears and noses.[59] Thus, from the start of their campaign in Transbaikalia, the Red partisans made no effort to take the moral high ground, but avidly competed to outdo the cruelty of the Whites.

A campaign against the homegrown partisans in eastern Transbaikalia became the focus of Ataman Semenov's military efforts throughout 1919, until Omsk's collapse allowed an influx of Bolshevik advisors to form units in the western part of the province later in the year. On 22 May 1919 the ataman paid tribute to his forces fighting the Reds in the Argun river area along the Chinese border in eastern Transbaikalia, recognizing the following units:

Unit	Commander[s]
1st Transbaikal Cossack Regiment	Colonel Epova, Lieutenant Colonel Ryumkin, Lieutenant Derevtsov, *Sotnik* Yakimov
3rd Transbaikal Cossack Regiment	Colonel Voiloshnikov and Colonel Temnikov
4th Transbaikal Cossack Regiment	Lieutenant Colonel Shcheglov
29th Troitskosavsk Infantry Regiment	Staff Captain Zhukov
30th Nerchinsk Infantry Regiment	Lieutenant Colonel Manyuto
31st Chita Regiment	Captain Arset'ev
Detachment of the Aboriginal Mounted Corps	*Sotnik* Markov
Manchurian Ataman Semenov Division Mobilized Cossacks of the 2nd, 3rd and 4th Transbaikal departments	Colonel Tierbach and Colonel Nikol'sk
Priamur Mounted Regiment	Lieutenant Colonel Zhadovskii

Red sabotage and maneuvers near the Trans-Siberian line in Amur province drove rail traffic to the more secure Chinese Eastern Railway. In early March 1919, the Japanese Army forced a column of 1,000 Russian and Chinese partisans to retreat from the vicinity of Alexeievsk. But while the partisans feared the Japanese Army, they displayed little fear of the White armored trains and marched brashly over the track bed to seek refuge about 45 miles southeast of Blagoveshchensk.[60]

Red partisan campaigns in the rear areas of Kolchak's territory portended things to come in the Far East. As one moved closer to the front lines, operations were getting bigger and better organized, and partisans even engaged in pitched battles with White and Czech echelons and armored trains. On 8 May 1919, a large partisan force swarmed into the large town of Taishet, about 400 miles west of Irkutsk and well behind the frontlines. They torched the train station and several other buildings, ripped up the rails and even managed to derail a White *bronevik*. They lost 100 men before withdrawing, but proved that the partisan movement was evolving from ragtag gangs of extremists, malcontents and peasants into an army.

Ataman Kalmykov, on the other hand, was transforming White units in Khabarovsk into malcontents and rebels instead of hunting for partisan camps. He had refused a recent order from Omsk to send his artillery to the front, and, when a large number of pro-Kolchak officers protested, he arrested them. On 13 May the commander of the small American detachment in Khabarovsk, Major Charles A. Shamotulski, telegraphed Vladivostok, 'Today 50 officers in danger of execution. Everyone says Kalmykov is insane. I have requested Japanese to prevent executions.'[61] The next day the British Consul reported that Kalmykov had already executed two officers and a Japanese commander, Takashima, threatened to bombard OKO headquarters and barracks if Kalmykov carried out any more executions.[62] Takashima's threat stalled Kalmykov, but the Pri-Amur warlord had anticipated the conflict and planned around the Allied–Japanese response. Days before

Shamotulski raised the alarm, Kalmykov had sent a *bronevik* down to Ussuri to distribute 400 rifles to supporters in a nearby village.[63] The furor seemed to die down until the end of the month, when Kalmykov packed 32 of the dissenting officers aboard a train to Chita for trial. None of them made it. They were all unloaded at a station east of Chita, where 11 were thrown into prison and 16 were immediately 'stripped, beaten and executed'. The five remaining officers were sent back to Khabarovsk 'on their honor', but disappeared after they were removed from the train by Kalmykov at Station Khor.[64]

Face-off at Verkhne-Udinsk

Initially, the American soldiers assigned to Transbaikalia by the Inter-Allied Railway Agreement expected little trouble in their sector and such trouble, they thought, would come from Red partisans. But, after Colonel Morrow's 27th Infantry set up camp in western Transbaikalia in April 1919, 'The only serious friction in the sector resulted from the actions of the crews of armored trains stationed at Verkhne-Udinsk from time to time by order of Ataman Semenov.'[65] As RRSC officers fanned out across Semenov's domain in Transbaikalia and Manchuria, a constant stream of reports began flowing into Vladivostok detailing disruption of regularly scheduled rail traffic by unauthorized *broneviki* and trains commandeered by OMO officers. For example, on 26 April, two unauthorized OMO trains – 'Semenov's Specials No.'s 102 and 8' – delayed Omsk supply train No. 3158 for a very noticeable six hours.[66] The RRSC was trying hard to make the railways operate efficiently, but Semenov was determined not to submit to anyone's authority. Semenov's 'specials' not only caused lengthy delays to daily 'post trains', freights, expresses and echelons bound for the front, they also posed a major safety hazard to military and civilian traffic.[67]

Trouble began brewing in Verkhne-Udinsk on 30 April. That day, a company of Russian engineers, six officers and 105 soldiers of the 9th Siberian Division, received orders from Omsk to proceed to the front from Verkhne-Udinsk. Semenov, perhaps to spite his rival Admiral Kolchak or in hopes of extorting money out of the Omsk government, ordered OMO to prevent the engineer company from moving. The commander of the engineer company, a Colonel Tomlovskii, tried to arrange transportation with Trans-Siberian employees at Verkhne-Udinsk. On 8 May, OMO crewmen of the *bronevik* 'Bezposhchadnyi' threatened to whip any railway workers who cooperated with Tomlovskii. Five days later, Ataman Semenov ordered an embargo on most westbound commercial freight. Colonel Tomlovskii visited Lieutenant Colonel William C. Miller of the US 27th Infantry to ask for assistance, however, the Americans were still moving in and had not yet deployed. Having been sent to western Transbaikalia to simply guard trains and railway facilities against ragtag bands of partisans, the 27th Infantry was unprepared to challenge OMO. Besides that, the local OMO forces, commanded by a Major General Mezhak, outnumbered the Americans.

In addition to the 'Bezposhchadnyi', Semenov had a large military base at Beresovka, just five miles west of Verkhne-Udinsk. The town itself had only 1,200 people, 60 horses, 200 cows and 700 hogs, but the 'Park Barracks' complex housed 1,000 and 2,000 OMO troops (consisting of eight artillery pieces, an infantry regiment and some cavalry) and an equal number of Japanese soldiers, not to mention 1,000 Austro-Hungarian POWs.[68]

Semenov's embargo choked Kolchak's supply line just as the Red Army was forcing a slow retreat of the Whites after the destruction of their 4th Corps east of Orenburg.[69] In mid-May, Colonel Medi, Semenov's Superintendent of Military Transportation, issued a number of confusing orders that were supposedly intended to clarify the embargo restrictions, but which only served to muddy the waters further. For example, on 13 May Medi commanded: 'On the basis of Order No. 114, Article 2 of the Separate Eastern Siberian Army, I forbid you to accept henceforth, on the Mysovaya-Sretensk [railway] division,... any private freight for shipment except local materials and raw skins.' Two days later Medi elaborated to allow the shipment of 'horses, cattle and meat' in both directions and to make sure that freight forwarders and railway employees understood that the embargo did not affect eastbound traffic (which could be taxed and pilfered by Semenov).[70] Failure to comply with the embargo was punishable by nine months imprisonment or a 10,000-ruble fine.[71] As Medi soon made clear in a politely worded threat to the general manager of the Trans-Baikal Railway, no one in the freight business could afford to ignore the embargo orders.[72]

On 16 May, OMO troops stole an American railway car and threatened to whip the Russian caretaker if he reported the theft.[73] Several days later and hundreds of miles to the east, a 'special' transporting US Consul General Ernest L. Harris back to his post as senior US representative in Omsk was suddenly surrounded by about 500 OMO Cossacks at Dauria station. OMO officers boarded the train and demanded to inspect the Consul General's luggage – a brazen violation of diplomatic protocol. Harris refused. The OMO commander ordered soldiers into Harris' private car; crews outside trained their machine guns on it. At midnight, six hours into the standoff, OMO soldiers 'broke open the trunks, boxes and bags in possession of the American official party and made a hasty search of their contents'.[74] Surprisingly, they took nothing. An hour later, the American 'special' was allowed to proceed. American diplomats and military staff were bewildered. The incident seemed to have no purpose but to humiliate the US officials. Ironically, Consul General Harris was one of Semenov's few boosters among the Americans.

Shortly Semenov upped the ante with even more volatile provocation. On 28 May 1919 a Captain Gilleland of the RRSC was supervising a seven-car work train that was repairing telephone lines in the Verkhne-Udinsk railyard when an OMO armored train pulled up and demanded that he turn over one of his railcars to them. The *bronevik* commander informed Gilleland that he would fire on him if the car was not delivered within one hour. Gilleland asked the 27th Infantry for armed guards, who were quickly placed on his train.

Meanwhile in town, four drunken Cossacks went on the rampage in a nearby 'boarding house' (which, from later descriptions, seems to have been a bar and brothel) where US troops were present. US military police from the 27th's Company K intervened. The Cossack's Corporal Krakov pulled his sidearm but the 27th's Private Karas proved to be a faster draw. Karas dropped – and killed – Krakov with a bullet from his automatic. Karas and his two cohorts then disarmed the other inebriates and turned them over to their OMO officers.

The next day in the railyard, the *bronevik* that had threatened Captain Gilleland 'opened its ports, manned its guns and trained them' on the American train. The 27th Infantry's Report of Operations stated that, 'Captain Gilleland permitted the armored train crew to take the car they desired' (no mention of this was made in the 1922 US Senate hearings).[75]

On 1 June Colonel Tomlovskii's frustrated engineer company, now weeks overdue at the front, moved a couple of miles north up the tracks away from Verkhne-Udinsk. There they boarded the regular No. 21 train. Their trip went smoothly for about 40 miles as the No. 21 paralleled the Selenga River. When the train reached the town of Selenga, the OMO station commandant (a man named Krisco), tried to detain No. 21 until 'Bezposhchadnyi' arrived. Five officers and 12 soldiers of the engineer company commandeered No. 21's locomotive. Twenty-three miles west they entered the town of Posol'skaya, where the station commandant and OMO militiamen greeted them with bursts of artillery. The 17 engineers returned their fire with small arms, but soon had to abandon the locomotive and fled into the mountains. Back at Selenga station, six of Tomlovskii's soldiers slipped away from their now captive transport onto regular westbound trains. When they arrived in Irkutsk hours later, they informed authorities that Semenov's men had arrested 74 of their comrades at Selenga. The next day, the arrested soldiers were last seen in 'closed cars...under Japanese convoy' at Beresovka. They had been told that they would be whipped, and that their *'Praporshchik* [Ensign] Tokarev will be "transported to the Moscow district" ' – shot.[76]

That same day (2 June) an American echelon deposited 27th Infantry units throughout the US sector. One platoon (an officer, 58 soldiers and one machine gun) took up positions at Mostovoi, a village about ten miles north of Verkhne-Udinsk where a trestle spanned the Selenga River. In addition, Selenga and Posol'skaya each became hosts to an American platoon. A company of doughboys (six officers and more than 200 men) moved into Mysovaya, a large town on Lake Baikal's southeast shore and the western limit of the American sector. A few days after his troops settled in, Colonel Morrow was ready to deal with Semenov.

Colonel Morrow called for a conference at Japanese headquarters in Verkhne-Udinsk on 8 June. They met at 4:30 p.m.: Colonel Morrow; the local Japanese commander, General Yoshi; Semenov's regional chief, Major General Mezhak; and a General Panchenko, who commanded OMO's 'Park Barracks' at Beresovka. Colonel Morrow read a statement summarizing the recent aggression of the 'Bezposhchadnyi' against US troops and Trans-Siberian Railway employees. He concluded,

> The above-recited facts make it clear that the armored train does interfere with traffic and is a menace to the American sector and must therefore move out of the American sector...I request General Yoshi and General Mezhak assist me to have the armored car removed from the American sector within 24 hours. I am responsible for security of the railroad. If the armored car does not move within 24 hours from five p.m., 8 June, I will make battle on it.

Morrow's ultimatum took the Japanese and Cossack generals by surprise. General Yoshi tried to hedge, 'I understand armored car used to treat people as Colonel Morrow states – whip employees, etc. But at the same time, the armored car helps to stop the Bolsheviks and to arrest suspects'.

Colonel Morrow persisted. 'What action will the Japanese take when I open fire?' he asked General Yoshi.

General Yoshi was caught off balance by the American's frankness.

> If you open fire, of course, the Japanese Army will stand neutral, but I personally think that it is not quite right to fire on such short notice. Of course, if a battle occurs, I am under orders of Lieutenant General Oba, my divisional commander. I hope that no such trouble occurs in the vicinity of my command. I request you to ask Ataman Semenov to take the armored car away. I will ask Lieutenant General Oba to use his influence to have the armored car removed to Chita.

Colonel Morrow reminded those present, 'I asked General Yoshi three days ago to telegraph Lieutenant General Oba to use his influence to have the armored car moved'. The American commander then asserted that General Mezhak's troops 'must remain in their barracks pending disposition of the armored train...to prevent a general conflict' in Verkhne-Udinsk.

General Mezhak, who, up to this point, had insisted that OMO headquarters in Chita, not he, controlled the 'Bezposhchadnyi', now protested. He declared Colonel Morrow's plan 'unlawful', piously labeled it as 'interference in the administration of the Russian government and its guarding of law and order', and, besides, now admitted, 'I consider it necessary to have an armored train in the American sector for my needs'.

Colonel Morrow did not sit around and debate the bristling Russian and Japanese officers. He declared the conference closed and departed. Back at his Verkhne-Udinsk encampment, he telegrammed Ataman Semenov and informed him of the ultimatum and the conference.

Throughout the American sector the doughboys readied their weapons and prepared for the worst. At one point on the railway Colonel Morrow placed 'his little 37-millimeter pieces' (in General Graves' words) on each side of the tracks, piled sandbags around them and vowed not to let the 'Bezposhchadnyi' pass. In Vladivostok, General Graves noted, 'I lost some sleep over this clash and feared that Morrow, because of lack of proper weapons, could not make good.'[77] Adding to General Graves' worries were whispered messages passed from Omsk's Minister of Foreign Affairs I.I. Sukin and from Colonel Robertson, the Acting British High Commissioner in Siberia, neither of whom were boosters of AEF policy, that the Japanese were behind the whole affair, trying to incite trouble between Russia and the US.[78] The Czechoslovak Legion, whom the US Army had come to Siberia to rescue, now made secret plans to rescue the US Army at Verkhne-Udinsk from a Japanese assault, preparing a 'troop movement schedule...which would have brought 10,000 Czechs to Colonel Morrow's aid in two days'.[79]

The next day, 9 June 1919, Semenov telegrammed a hostile and sarcastic response to Colonel Morrow, 'I agree to remove immediately the armored train if you guarantee to me the full cessation of disorder and indecent acts by members of your troops...' Specifically, the ataman seemed to be referring to the indignity suffered his Cossacks on 28 May when Morrow's military police shot one and disarmed others in the 'boarding house' incident. However, Semenov's charges of 'disorder and indecent acts' by Americans were groundless; Colonel Morrow dismissed them as 'too absurd for comment'.[80]

Tensions mounted further when Colonel Kasai, a Japanese staff officer, appeared at US headquarters with a counterultimatum that read, 'The Japanese will resist by force the removal of Semenov's armored cars by American troops.' Colonel Kasai also announced that Japanese officers and troops would man the 'Bezposhchadnyi' and take it to Beresovka at 4 p.m. to protect it from the Americans. Despite all the bravado, everyone breathed a sigh of relief when, at 1:30 p.m., the 'Bezposhchadnyi' – absent any Japanese officers or soldiers – quietly left the Verkhne-Udinsk yards and steamed up to Beresovka.[81] Japanese guards were put aboard there and Colonel Morrow was assured that the *bronevik* would not budge from Beresovka without his permission. He then took time to respond to Semenov's telegram, 'As regards the conduct of my troops, their discipline and behavior will compare most favorably with that of your own troops'. The gruff American colonel noted that Semenov's train had been confined to Beresovka, then inserted a parting barb to rile the upstart Cossack captain: 'If you desire to consider my proper guarding of the railway as a challenge, you have my permission to do so.'

Semenov had the last word in a telegram he sent to Colonel Morrow on 10 June:

> Your telegram received. Looking from the point of view of not permitting foreign interference in the internal affairs of Russia, I shall ask permission only from higher Russian command and your gentle, beneficent permission sent to my headquarters I ascribe only to an incorrect translation of your thoughts by your interpreter.

John Stevens arrived in Verkhne-Udinsk on 10 June to investigate. He quickly agreed with Colonel Morrow that Semenov and his *broneviki* were a menace to the railway and reported his conclusions to the US State Department via Consul General Harris. However, Consul General Harris, even after his May run-in with OMO brigands, still believed that Ataman Semenov was Transbaikalia's only hope against the Reds. Despite the growing chorus of complaints from the Americans, Semenov smugly retained absolute control over the railway.[82]

The face-off with Colonel Morrow at Verkhne-Udinsk solidified Semenov's antipathy to the US Army. Semenov's bitterness would never subside. He railed against the doughboys in his memoirs years later, 'The Americans, by their disgraceful behavior brought disorder and caused great dissatisfaction to the inhabitants'. He piously indicted 'the low moral standards of U.S. soldiers sent to Siberia' and even asserted that 'General Graves was morally not much better than his soldiers'.[83]

Ironically, during the spring and summer of 1919, when Semenov and the Japanese ratcheted up their hostility towards the Americans, troops of the US 31st Infantry Regiment faced increasing hostility from Bolsheviks in the Suchan mine district east of Vladivostok, inaugurated by virulent threats from a young, Red guerrilla leader named Yakov Ivanovich Triapitsyn. It marked the beginning of the bloodiest period of US intervention, of small, fierce fights between American soldiers and Bolshevik partisans that continued into early August. On 25 June two companies of Triapitsyn's Reds attacked a 31st Infantry platoon, killing 24 Americans and wounding 20 in an intense three-hour combat. The next day a large partisan force attacked two US companies at Sitsa, and the uneasy, distant coexistence between the Americans and Reds dissolved into a deadly war of stalking and ambush. Several intense, isolated actions ensued around the hilly, forested peninsula east of Vladivostok, with clashes occurring at Novitskaya, Kazanka, Frolovka, Shkotovo, Litovsk and other obscure places.[84] The battle lines in the Russian Far East surely perplexed most American soldiers as the 31st Infantry fought Reds in the east, and the 27th clashed with Whites in the west.

Semenov's golden days in Chita

Chita prospered along with Semenov and became a capital befitting a renegade ataman, like a Cossack Port Royal on the Shilka river. The ataman exuded self-confidence, and his superb military bearing made a lasting impression on all he encountered, friend or foe. 'Dressed in his blue and green uniform, wearing a sable cape and highly polished leather boots, and festooned with a dagger and a sword, he had a commanding presence', remembered one émigré decades later.[85] 'The station platform was bright with the various reds, browns, yellows and greens of the Japanese and Cossack troops', recorded American traveler Edward Heald in May 1919.[86] The throngs in Chita streets that month were even more diverse than usual as delegates to the third Transbaikal Cossack Host *krug* flocked into the city.

Young Semenov addressed the convention as '*pokhodnii ataman* of [all] 71 *stanitsas*', the leading light of the host. He radiated the Cossacks' unshakable conviction that they were the moral core of the defense of Mother Russia and traditional values, and promised his brethren help in the 'continuation of the struggle against Bolshevism and armed prisoners-of-war'.[87] Accordingly, Semenov's headquarters soon announced that the next of kin of war dead would receive 300 rubles per month, while families of prisoners of war would be paid 20 rubles a month until their release or White victory.[88]

While riding high in Cossack popularity and with his embargo against Kolchak and Omsk's armies in full swing, Semenov proclaimed, by publishing a 26 May telegram to General Horvath, that he was ready to recognize Admiral Kolchak on the condition that the Supreme Ruler allow the ataman, as leader of the Far Eastern Cossack Host, to retain command and control over all forces east of Lake Baikal.[89] Perhaps mere coincidence occasioned the accidental death on the previous day of Major General Nikolai Natsvalov, newly appointed commander of the 5th Pri-Amur Corps and husband of Zinaida, the strident critic of Semenov and recently disappeared friend of the late Vasilii Shumov. While Kolchak had little choice but to accept Semenov's one-sided offer of reconciliation and cancel Order No. 60 on 27 May, the ataman's treacherous demand for control over the troops would cut off Omsk's army from reinforcements when it most needed them during the coming months. On 29 May Semenov telegrammed Admiral Kolchak, tersely pledging his allegiance to Omsk, even though OMO minions and their Japanese associates continued harassment, and sometimes outright hostilities, against westbound troops and the Americans. Likewise the embargo on supplies to Omsk was not completely lifted for four more weeks. Officially, at least, Semenov's 29 May missive ended the six-month estrangement that had left portions of Kolchak's army in rags, waiting in vain for ammunition and reinforcements, and begging for food, and was cause for jubilation and celebratory banquets in Tokyo and Chita.[90]

As the British 25th Middlesex Regiment exited Siberia in June 1919, its officer commanding, Colonel John Ward, paused in Chita for a visit with Semenov.[91] Months earlier, when Ward's soldiers were moving up to the front in the autumn of 1918, they had nearly come to blows with Semenov's men in the railyard at Manchuli. Colonel Ward expected his visit to be awkward. However, the very day the 25th Middlesex arrived in Chita Semenov's rapprochement with Supreme Ruler Kolchak was announced. Thus, the mood was unexpectedly cheerful for a 'very frank and friendly half-hour's interview' between the colonel and the ataman. In those 30 minutes, Colonel Ward's attitude towards Semenov underwent a dramatic conversion.

> Colonel Semenov is one of the most striking personalities I have met in Russia. A man of medium height, with square broad shoulders, an enormous head, the size of which is greatly enhanced by the flat, Mongol face, from which gleam two clear, brilliant eyes that rather belong to an animal than a man. The whole pose of the man is at first suspicious, alert, determined, like a tiger ready to spring, to rend and tear, but in repose the change is remarkable, and with a quiet smile upon the brown face the body relaxes. Colonel Semenov is a very pleasant personality. His great physical strength has caused the Japanese to name him 'Samurai', or 'Brave Knight of the Field', and I think that is a good description of his character. Relentless and brave, kindness nevertheless finds a part in his make-up. The princes of Mongolia have asked him to become their emperor, and should he choose this path a whirlwind will pass over the neighboring lands. Perhaps underneath he is, after all, a good Russian – time will tell.[92]

Semenov was indeed a likable and amiable young man, worthy of a prince to the few, awed foreigners admitted into his inner circle for brief encounters. He had participated little in the day-to-day administration of his kleptocratic government, although, somewhat ironically, the first order he signed as 'Representative of the Supreme Ruler and High Command for Protection of State Order and Social Tranquility in Transbaikal Region' was a decree in late July that authorized arrests of 'immoral women'.[93] Corruption and hedonism reigned, overshadowed 'by a blind conviction that things would come out right in the end', owing to the Whites' 'heroism and panache', never mind that there were not enough new recruits, ammunition, boots, clothing and victories to stem the 5th Red Army's advance. It was simply inconceivable that the grey, godless mob of Bolsheviks could ever prevail.[94] 'Intoxicated by courtiers who profit by his prodigality and abuse his name and authority', wrote Nicholas Romanov, 'he has come to believe that he is an important personage, almost a demi-god, and is called upon to become the savior of Russia'.[95]

By the summer of 1919, he was so busy attending to the pomp and circumstance of being Transbaikalia's potentate, that he had almost lost touch with affairs inside his undisciplined army. He apologetically issued an order on 31 May attributing many incidents of abuse to the inexperience of his officer corps, and, as a penalty for recent 'outrages and illegal acts... against the peaceful population', even restricted the Asiatic Horse Division to its base.[96] In subsequent weeks, he issued several more orders intended to instill discipline in his officers: No. 196, 'On the Inadmissibility of Drunkenness'; No. 21, 'On Prohibition of Illegal Requisitions'; Nos. 6 and 7, 'On Breach of Discipline by Officers'; No. 9, 'On the Talkativeness of Officers', and various others. When word reached him that two junior officers had tried to enter the first- and second-class waiting rooms at Karymskaya on horseback, he had them thrown in the guardhouse for a month.[97] After a drunken scuffle in the Chita city gardens on 14 June, he dressed down several officers of the 1st Ataman Semenov Cavalry Regiment, published their names, threw some in jail, and warned the rest of his officer corps about such disgraceful conduct in public places. Nevertheless, the ataman's actions and hedonistic example spoke louder to his men than the words of his decrees.

Insulated from much unpleasantness by his sycophantic staff, bodyguards and fawning molls, Semenov deluded himself into believing that he really was a beloved champion of the holy crusade against the Bolshevik heathens. Public demonstrations hailed him, honorary titles were bestowed upon him and Christian, Muslim and Buddhist organizations awarded him decorations.[98] The ataman began to act as if he really were king of Transbaikalia and in mid-June he even 'militarized' Transbaikalia's gold mines.[99] His performance at a June 1919 banquet attended by Sir Robert Hodgson, a high level British official, illustrates:

> The occasion was an impressive one. The Serbian representative in Siberia, Monsieur Puric, and I were guests of honor of the Ataman Scmcnov at a banquet in Chita. There were some sixty other guests, mostly Cossacks... Proceedings opened by [Ataman Semenov] reading out an edict, beautifully designed by him, appointing [Serbia's] King Peter autocrat of the Russias and handing it to Puric. He then distributed with ceremony a number of Russian decorations and medals, which, needless to say, he had no right to award. The banquet commenced shortly before noon and continued without interruption till four. Then there was an interlude. We all went into the garden and four Siberian bears were brought to wrestle with the Cossacks. Towards six o'clock the banquet recommenced. It lasted till midnight, when Puric, the Ataman and I walked to the *café chantante*.[100]

Any ideals that the daring raider and populist hero had once cherished were corrupted by the lavish wealth and power Semenov enjoyed in Chita. He whiled away the days with his court of prostitutes and brigands and his secret bank accounts in Japan and China burgeoned with bloody treasure. On the other hand, the rapprochement with Omsk lent Semenov an air of legitimacy and on 19 June his renegade command, the Separate Eastern Siberian Army, became the Sixth Eastern Siberian Army Corps. A month later Admiral Kolchak promoted Semenov from colonel to major general as part of their reconciliation deal. Shortly after this rapid elevation Semenov assumed command of all Cossack hosts in the Far East.[101] The ataman was at the pinnacle of his reign.

His appetite for power swelled with his success, and he tried to expand his influence in the Maritime province, until then General Horvath's domain. After encountering resistance to his Union of Far Eastern Cossacks from factions in the Ussuri host, Semenov had tried to build a constituency among Ukrainian migrants and sent Major General Verigo to form all-Ukrainian regiments, but the effort failed when Semenov's role was discovered. Meanwhile, Semenov tried to infiltrate every institution in the Pri-Amur with his adherents. In summer 1919, he sent a Major General Lovtsov and 'a whole staff of officers to superintend [Ussuri] Cossack affairs' to Maritime Military District Headquarters in Vladivostok, before receiving Horvath's endorsement of the assignments. Horvath had failed to capitalize on Semenov and Kolchak's rift to increase his own power, and increasingly saw the ataman muscle in on his turf. Ironically, Kolchak's appointment of General Sergei Rozanov as military commander in the Maritime province promised to further increase Semenov's growing influence there.[102]

To Semenov's dismay, a bad omen cast its shadow on these golden days when the 1st Transbaikal Cossack Regiment revolted. Two *sotnias* had fallen 'under the influence of *Fel'dsher* (Corpsman) Vasil'ev' and other Red agitators. They slew their officers and went over to the Bolsheviks during the night of 14–15 June. Semenov acknowledged this calamity publicly, and mandated the severest punishment: 'All Cossacks of the 1st Regiment who deserted to the Reds will be shot without a trial as traitors to the Motherland and their native Cossackry.' He also used the occasion to exhort his green officers to stick close to their men. While this reaction demonstrated his expertise in small unit leadership, it also laid bare his poor grasp of revolutionary politics when he threatened to take the deserters' brothers and fathers hostage and shoot them or force them into military service.[103]

OMO interference on the rails

Corralling the 'Bezposhchadnyi' in Beresovka was as much of a victory over OMO as Colonel Morrow or Major General Graves could have expected. Semenov's embargo on westbound cargo, which strangled the gasping economy of the Omsk government, was not 'loosened' until 3 July despite Admiral Kolchak and Ataman Semenov's official reconciliation in June.[104] Corrupt OMO station commandants remained in control of all rail traffic, and continued to amass princely sums in 'fees' and bribes. Open theft of train cargo and robbery of passengers was rampant. The ataman's minions continued terrorizing railway workers and committing crude provocations against individual doughboys, RRSC men and small, isolated American detachments. An Allied officer confirmed an obvious truth during a spring journey across Kolchak's realm: 'The principal request by Siberians was that the railway be properly opened up for export, as well as import trade, thereby ensuring the Economic Relief of the country.'[105] Semenov's interference with the railways severely obstructed economic recovery. However, the victims most injured by Semenov's interference on the rails were the White soldiers on the front lines hundreds of miles west, whose ammunition, warm clothing, food and other supplies were delayed or stolen outright.

Meanwhile, US intelligence sources suggested that the British government might be continuing covert arms shipments to OMO, even though it was now apparent that the weapons were as likely to be turned on other Whites (or even Americans) as on Reds. The original 14 June source of the 'positive information' concerning continuing covert British arms shipments to Semenov was probably RRSC Major Gravis. An intelligence source that was named only as 'AEP' noted that... 'Arrangements [for OMO weapons] made through one of the Allies.'[106] About this same time, however, British Colonel John Ward noted to the contrary, 'I knew that British pressure had been applied to persuade the Japanese to cease their financial and moral support – both open and secret... and it was rumored that British wishes had at last been complied with.'[107]

The US 27th Infantry brought some semblance of order to western Transbaikalia. In the weeks following the averted clash about the 'Bezposhchadnyi', only one major incident was recorded in the American sector: the killing, presumably by partisans, of three Japanese soldiers on a mapping detail in a rural area near the *magistral*. American patrols roamed the countryside looking for clues and found none. Despite their conflicts with the Japanese and OMO, most doughboys still regarded the Red partisans as bloodthirsty fanatics.

Semenov's disruption of maintenance of Trans-Siberian Railway equipment damaged the Omsk government's economy more than any partisan saboteurs. OMO had invaded railway workshops and roundhouses back in autumn 1918, redirecting their efforts to building and repairing armored trains. In January 1919, the American Captain Moore noted,

> While I was there [in Chita] 22 engines were in the local shops needing repairs. Semenov's officers had workmen in those shops engaged in building armored cars and putting boiler plate on two engines for the Ataman's private use. Considering the fact that there were only five engines available at Chita, when 20 were needed, I consider this diversion of labor for the Ataman's private interests as interference with railway traffic.

At the same time, Captain Pickens, the British railway officer at Chita, informed Moore that 48 westbound freight trains were held up in Olovyannaya for want of locomotives.[108] With Japanese connivance Semenov ran the Trans-Siberian Railway to ruin. In early July 1919, all of the Chita shops and roundhouses were still occupied performing services for Semenov, at the expense of the overworked Trans-Siberian equipment upon which the region's economy depended.[109] Semenov requisitioned nine more locomotives that month, but fortunately the region was better off than the rest of the country in terms of locomotives and rolling stock owing to the delivery of over 800 engines and other equipment from the United States via Vladivostok in 1917. Nevertheless, Siberia was hit harder than the rest of Russia by a fuel crisis in 1919, and Semenov's requisitions in Transbaikalia compounded the shortage.[110]

Along the *magistral*, daily interference by Semenov's officers and men was tying up traffic and further demoralizing railway workers. For instance, on 11 June a drunken officer named Vosnesenskii brutally beat the conductor and assistant conductor on an OMO echelon near Birka, then tossed the injured men from the train as it roared down the tracks.[111] On 20 June the regular No. 4 train was delayed for 80 minutes at Khilok station because a *bronevik* commander fancied the No. 4's locomotive so much that he just had to swap it for the one he had. An impatient British Army captain who happened to be a passenger on the No. 4 objected to the *bronevik* commander and was threatened with a knife; the *bronevik* commander was drunk.[112] East of Verkhne-Udinsk, regularly scheduled passenger, freight and troop trains were forced to stop while OMO 'specials' ferried soldiers down to the Selenga River for a swim. On 7 July the commander of Semenov's Armored Train Division stole a Chinese Eastern Railway car at Chita, moved it to Adrianovka, site of the division's headquarters and repainted it in OMO's standard color scheme.[113] This theft paled in comparison to the hold-ups at Manchuli during the three previous days, where OMO soldiers robbed more than 14,000,000 rubles from Russian and Chinese passengers entering Transbaikalia.[114] No Russian dared object.

New anti-smuggling measures were initiated at Manchuli in summer 1919, making military trains subject to searches for non-military supplies, and leading many observers to conclude that even the Japanese could no longer smuggle. However, an honest Russian customs official cried foul when he caught some Japanese soldiers loading uncleared packages onto a train that had already finished its inspection. The Russian was arrested by the Japanese, and held in confinement for ten days until the matter was cleared up and the RRSC convinced them to release him. 'It was finally established that the packages contained silk for the Japanese general.'[115]

Since Semenov's 'recognition of Kolchak', he no longer made a practice of diverting Omsk's customs proceeds into OMO coffers, but had replaced this font of revenue with tens of millions of rubles 'confiscated' from Chinese merchants returning home via Manchuli. Likewise, the ataman's underlings in the Manchuli railyard hardly made any pretense of official functions when they shook down passengers. For instance, a mid-July report related, 'One [OMO soldier] lately stopped a train, detached a Red Cross [railcar] with Americans in it to some distance where they could see the fun, and then proceeded to systematically search and collect "contributions" from the remaining passengers.'[116] Only institutions of the major Allies – Japanese, Americans, British, Canadians and French – could usually, but not always, avoid the systematic plundering of their luggage and freight by *semenovtsy* at the border. Swiss Red Cross personnel concocted fanciful epaulettes for their uniforms during visits to Chita to deter OMO hold-ups, and arranged for Japanese officers to ride shotgun on their supply trains through Transbaikalia.[117]

The continuing robberies of Chinese travelers had drawn repeated protests from officials at Manchuli to no avail. For nearly a year, OMO had trodden on Peking's sovereignty by treating a large portion of the Chinese Eastern Railway zone as if it lay within Semenov's Russian domain. OMO *broneviki* ran up and down the single track of the Chinese Eastern without fear of retribution from the Chinese Army. Their brazen behavior suggested that the Chinese generals had either been bribed, or coerced by the Japanese Army, into accepting this state of affairs. In July 1919, China even considered transferring 3,000 men of the 19th Mukden Mixed Brigade from Hailar to Manchuli to close the border, but prudently decided on a non-confrontational remedy: to deduct damages incurred by 'confiscations' from the indemnity fund (established under the railway zone agreements).[118]

RRSC officers, who enjoyed a limited measure of protection because they were Americans, were livid about the blasphemous disrespect of train schedules. These professional railway men were intent on making the trains run on time, and witnessed the sacrifices that Russian employees made to achieve that goal. Thus, every minute of delay caused by a highhanded or intoxicated OMO officer was reported up the RRSC's chain of command. Daily reports of whippings, beatings, threats and disappearances filled RRSC files in Harbin and Vladivostok.

Subtle signs hinted that Semenov wanted to cooperate with the RRSC and IATB at least enough to improve rail service, however the ataman simply would not, or could not, control his officers and troops enough to make this happen. During the early evening of 12 July, a yard engine at Manchuli suddenly latched onto a car occupied by two RRSC officers, their two interpreters, a Russian railway liaison and Chinese cook. The yard engine attached their car to a *bronevik* which promptly departed for Dauria, more than two and a half hours away. Upon arrival at Dauria, the *bronevik* commander, Colonel Zhukovski, ordered the RRSC personnel to vacate their car. No explanation was given. But this was more easily said than done, because, as in the case of thousands of other railway cars which had become home to refugees and foreigners, this car was brimming with a cornucopia of personal effects as well as RRSC documents, tools and other miscellany. One of the RRSC men, Lieutenant McNutt, was called to the telephone and informed that Ataman Semenov and Colonel Medi, OMO's superintendent of military transportation, had ordered Zhukovski not to molest the Americans. When McNutt returned to his railcar, he found an apologetic young OMO lieutenant supervising the unloading of his belongings. Zhukovski came along shortly and profanely berated everyone, including his own lieutenant, for taking so long to empty the car. They all concluded that 'Colonel Zhukovski was either drunk or crazy'. Lieutenant McNutt's appeals to the local Japanese commander for help were ignored, as usual. Under Zhukovski's orders, Russian customs officers soon began poring over all of the baggage strewn on the ground by the tracks. The inspectors found 'contraband' – some silk belonging to a Russian railway employee and 'a few yards of cotton duck' packed away by the Chinese cook. Lieutenant McNutt and his compatriot, Lieutenant B.N. Twaddle, paid a 61-ruble fine to be done with the affair. Three days later the railcar was returned – with OMO apologies – to the RRSC at Manchuli, and promptly stolen again by Zhukovski. The RRSC men noticed that Zhukovski was operating his train without any railway staff whatsoever, which would 'of course sooner or later result in a serious accident'.[119] Days later, the ataman ordered Colonel Zhukovski to report to Chita and explain. He even announced Zhukovski's 'dismissal'. However, in reality, Semenov took no action to remove, discipline or even rein in Zhukovski. When railway workers on the Chinese Eastern went on strike at the end of July 1919, paralyzing all civilian traffic, Semenov was largely unaffected, because strikers knew that to refuse an order (or request) from an OMO officer was to risk a severe whipping or death. Colonel Vrashtel's detachment, which had dished out White Terror to Blagoveshchensk in 1918, was unleashed upon the strikers in early August with authority to court-martial and shoot uncooperative railway employees.[120]

The irrational antics of Zhukovski and other OMO officers led Colonel Lantry, RRSC district inspector in Semenov's territory, to order his personnel to 'remain in their quarters' until armed guards could accompany them. On 23 July John Stevens suggested that RRSC inspectors move out of OMO's reach until 'proper protection can be given them'. By early August, Colonel Lantry warned John Stevens,

> I think our officers in that territory are in constant danger, as there is a decided feeling against them. Both the Japanese and Semenov are working against us in their usual underhanded methods of spreading propaganda against the Americans in every way possible. I do not believe we will ever be able to do anything to increase the transportation in that territory and still feel that our men are in constant jeopardy and should be moved out of there... If our men are left in the territory, it is only a question of time until some of them will be mysteriously done away with.

By this time, however, the RRSC men had developed a stubborn loyalty to the Siberian Railway and the brave Russians who made it run. Americans serving at dismal stations like Borzya and Adrianovka, where terror and random executions occurred daily, showed no inclination to desert their jobs and comrades in the hour of need.

Semenov blissfully ignored the invaluable, indirect assistance he was giving the Bolsheviks by interfering with the rail traffic that was Omsk's logistics lifeline. Horrendous management, bureaucratic inertia and the poor condition of railway equipment were enough to curse Kolchak's armies, but the greed and spitefulness of Semenov and his cronies condemned thousands of White soldiers to destitution, capture and death.

Trouble on the Chinese Eastern

Compared to bloody Transbaikalia, the Chinese Eastern Railway Zone seemed a veritable sanctuary, although it was far from untroubled. General Horvath had been named as governor of the zone in November 1918, but, in reality, no less than five separate groups jostled in constant tension, competing for power, influence, resources or, when rivalries sank to their basest form, just plain booty. The Chinese Eastern Railway Company, Provisional Siberian Government in Omsk, Allies and Czech Legion generally saw eye to eye and could be counted together as the most powerful bloc, although the company sometimes stood alone in the middle of the vicious sibling rivalry between Semenov and Kolchak. Although Semenov was nominally subordinate to the PSG and his Japanese sponsors were technically one of 'the Allies', they sailed a defiant, independent course, nurturing Pan-Mongol factions under their wings. Although the Chinese were technically Allies also, and they good-naturedly allowed a dozen foreign armies to traipse across their territory, their were understandably sensitive with all foreign parties over sovereignty issues, and especially so with the Japanese and Semenov when Pan-Mongol separatists were involved. The partisans and revolutionary workers usually restricted their aggression to the Whites and anyone associated with them, but trampled Chinese sovereignty in the process. Lastly the *hunghutze* owed no one their loyalty, were liable to prey upon all, and were disinterested in the kind of tangible political power the other parties coveted. The conflict in northern Manchuria resembled an eye-gouging, ear-biting free-for-all in a Harbin saloon, interrupted by awkward moments of insincere comradeship and exuberant back-slapping.

The *hunghutze* were the only constant in the Manchurian equation – always predatory, ruthless and unpredictable. These well-organized bands of bandits fit two general molds, the oldest being private armies of powerful land-owners who endorsed 'freebooting forays' by their tenants after the harvest around their fortified manors was collected. The second type arose in response to Chinese colonization in the late nineteenth century and the economic hardships of increased population pressure, famines and insurmountable debts to Chinese money-lenders and merchants. While these 'anti-landlord, anti-rich man, anti-provincial government' *hunghutze* assumed the mantle of rebels, their driving motive was profit, not revolution. In the years before the First World War, Togtakhu Taiji, the most famous Inner Mongolian bandit chief, became the nemesis of the up-and-coming Chinese commander at Mukden, Chang Tso-Lin, a former *hunghutze* himself. To oppressed Mongols he became a folk hero who targeted Chinese merchants, villages, soldiers and surveyors, showing no mercy, destroying usurers' accounting ledgers, and going to fight (and rob) in Khalka Mongolia in 1910 during the prelude to Outer Mongolian independence. Mongolia's Bogdo Khan showed his appreciation by bestowing the title of 'Determined Hero' upon Togtakhu, and the Russian government courted him and provided him refuge. Likewise, Bayar, another *hunghutze* leader, espoused an anti-Chinese political platform with his campaign of plunder and refused Japanese overtures during the Russo-Japanese War. Babojab, a ruthless *hunghutze* who indiscriminately raided both Mongol and Chinese settlements, lacked Bayar's qualms about foreign employers and accepted assignments and cash from both the Japanese and Russians until killed in battle by Chinese soldiers in 1916. However even the dividing lines between the Chinese Army and the *hunghutze* were not so stark as might be imagined because of a thriving exchange of military weapons for locally grown opium. *Hunghutze* also hired themselves out to the authorities as bandit-fighters and for caravan protection on the Tea Road, such as the 400-man *Pao Shang T'uan* (Mercantile Guard) formed in 1917.[121]

The line between Manchuli and Hailar saw less troubles because of the presence of proficient and disciplined Chinese troops of the 3rd Mixed Infantry Brigade from Tsitsihar. It consisted of 850 infantrymen in three battalions, a 153-man artillery battery, and a 40-man detachment with four heavy machine guns, all distributed along the Chinese Eastern in 50-man detachments. Other segments of the railway were not so fortunate.[122]

In early July 1919 *hunghutze* burned and blew up three bridges on a spur of the Chinese Eastern, marooning a locomotive and crew eight miles from the town of Vaishuhal. After various lesser acts of mischief, they demanded 100,000 rubles to refrain from further acts of sabotage, but the railway refused to pay.[123] They struck next in late July, when the railway was mired in a contentious strike, raiding Pogranichnaya and wounding several people with gunfire in the process, including an American YMCA man.

The trade union of Chinese Eastern Railway workers and masters stepped to the forefront of the revolutionary movement after the failure of Ensign Riutin's coup in December 1918. Known by its Russian acronym GLIK, the union was extremely sympathetic to the partisans, if not outright partnered to them. Thus, work stoppages were considered seditious acts by the anti-Bolsheviks. A strike called on 15 May 1919 fizzled and many GLIK leaders were arrested.[124] The workers and underground party activists organized more thoroughly for a massive strike in July. At 11 a.m. on 19 July 1919 the workers in the main shop at Tsitsihar downed their tools and walked out into the hot sun. The strike spread into the roundhouse the next day and up the tracks to the shop and roundhouse at Handaohedzy the day after that. After handicapping operations for more than a week, the company dispatched armed strike-breakers. Guards forced crews at Harbin to get five passenger trains rolling on 28 July.[125]

The first train out derailed on a stretch of sabotaged track just west of Handaohedzy, tumbling three wooden carriages down an embankment and killing two conductors, two baggage men and injuring several others. Up the line in Transbaikalia, another wreck left 65 dead. The Chinese Eastern Railway – the main artery of the anti-Red struggle – was shut down for days while the tracks were cleared and repaired. Two days after the derailments, four trains were 'shot up' in and around Harbin, two of them right in the railyard. Residents took note of an aircraft, presumably Japanese, swooping over the city at half past midnight. It appeared that the railway workers' strike was timed to correspond with a major partisan offensive.

On 5 August a train was attacked at Handaohedzy. In a flurry of more than 100 bullets, nine people aboard were killed and wounded, the fatalities including a Russian colonel, a lieutenant and three railway workers.[126] Eighteen local Russian residents were arrested and shipped to Nikolsk-Ussuriisk for trial. Two days later a formal state of emergency was declared in the Chinese Eastern Railway zone, permitting the Russian military to conduct field courts martial of strikers and shoot them expeditiously. Chinese workers were herded into the Harbin depot shops at bayonet point, and forced to work under guard. Horvath unleashed Colonel Vrashtel on the strikers and, three days and several executions later, engineers and switchmen began trudging through the rainy streets to the shops and back to work.

A number of strikers were rounded up and 'deported' from the railway zone in the days following the strike, presumably to unsavory fates in Transbaikalia or Nikolsk-Ussuriisk. On the night of 19–20 August a White armored train transporting prisoners from Harbin clashed with a Chinese echelon at Imyanpo in a furious battle that wounded 22 and killed ten. This encounter signaled Chinese willingness to combat Whites as well as Reds to end Russian domination in the railway zone.

A cholera epidemic struck the railway zone at the same time as the strike, and by 9 August was felling about 150–200 people per day in Harbin alone. Flies and a putrid stench from piles of corpses waiting to be incinerated wafted through the city. By 20 August some 2,600 people had succumbed to cholera, despite mass infusions of the ill by the American Red Cross and the hasty construction of water-purification equipment by RRSC volunteers.[127] It seemed as if Mother Nature herself was conspiring against the relative tranquility in northern Manchuria.

Refugees

OMO's constant, unwarranted interference with traffic on the *magistral* in Transbaikalia contributed to the Omsk government's worsening military and economic situation, which, as a result, pushed a swelling current of fleeing and foraging civilians further east on the Trans-Siberian. The White cavalry's spring offensive had quickly sputtered to a halt on muddy roads (the euphoric period of imminent White victory lasted from 13 March until 29 April). Their failure was largely due to bad timing (Russian spring mud), poor management (reinforcements failed to appear when the offensive's momentum faltered), spitefully envious competition among White leaders, and the ruthless win-or-die attitude of the Red commissars.[128] On 23 May Supreme Ruler Kolchak's soldiers began falling back eastward, and the Reds unleashed a determined offensive against Perm that ended with the city's occupation about six weeks later. White territory in Western Siberia gradually contracted eastward along the railway in the face of persistent Red Army advances. General Gajda's resignation was smugly accepted in Omsk after an ill-conceived retreat (ordered by the White command in May) demoralized his army. British, Canadian and French forces withdrew from western Siberia in June and went home.[129]

'All sidings at stations were filled with trains loaded with refugees from some place in Western Siberia', noted General Graves when he traveled from Vladivostok to Omsk in July. He likened the trains to 'mobile tenements'.[130] Train stations large and small were clogged not only with growing numbers of eastbound refugees fleeing war and Red Terror, but with local people traveling from town to town in search of food for their families. Throughout June and July 1919, Colonel Lantry reported that 300–600 *west*bound passengers were stranded at Irkutsk station each day due to the shortage of trains. In mid-July, in an effort to relieve pressure on the railways, Omsk's Ministry of Ways and Communications issued a ban 'on the movement of all passengers west of Irkutsk'. The senior RRSC officer in Tomsk (800 miles west of Irkutsk), Colonel G.W. Tower, expressed horror at this order in a telegram to his superiors, 'It is an unpardonable method to handle passengers and a crime against human beings...'

No one knew exactly how many refugees were pouring into the Russian Far East, but YMCA worker Gail Reitzel's description fit well in most cases, 'These people are a pitiful looking lot with their worldly goods tied in a few handkerchiefs or in a bed roll. Often whole families exist as they can, squatted in a corner or stretched on the stone floors, fortunate that they at least have a warm shelter [in the train stations]. There were many emaciated and sad faces.' Tragedy was common: 'In one group were two small children and a man with the most tragic drawn face. [Another] refugee told us that the man's wife had died a few days before. The rotten steps of a passenger coach on the railway had given way with her as she clung with a crowd while the train was bringing them from the interior. Her body swung under the wheels and both of her legs were severed.'[131]

A large number of Serbian civilians displaced by the war accumulated in a crowded barracks seven miles outside of Vladivostok. 'Whole families of these refugees live in room some twelve feet square, the partitions between them being only about eight feet high so that they can hear their neighbors very whispers', wrote Reitzel in April 1919. 'The women make very fine lace and I arranged to dispose of some of it for them. When we returned to our car, we found it surrounded by children, each with an early bud or a few green sprays or pussy willows to thrust shyly into our hands. They are wistful little things with their great, dark eyes.'[132] And they were the lucky ones who made it out of Siberia before the maelstrom.

Killing fields

Throughout the month of May 1919, Colonel Morrow, the US 27th Infantry Regiment commander, received reports of an 'enormous number of executions' performed by OMO between Chita and Manchuli.[133] Not surprisingly, all of the killing fields lay in the sector of the railway entrusted to the Japanese Army. However, before Colonel Morrow could begin investigating these atrocities hundreds of miles to the east, outrages by the OMO armored train 'Bezposhchadnyi' in the American sector demanded his full attention.

Regardless, American railwaymen, army personnel and representatives of charitable organizations frequently passed through Semenov's territory. When the YMCA's Edward Heald endured a slow ride on the post train from Chita to Manchuli on 18 May he wrote,

> We are traveling through a part of the country where the atmosphere is different than any I have been in for a long time, an atmosphere of terrorism and outlawry, where one feels like keeping as quiet and making himself as inconspicuous as possible... A village is pointed out as the place where one of the local rebels against the Semenov rule had his staff. At another place a hill is pointed out as the place where political offenders are executed. At every station are one to a half dozen *arrestantski* (jail) cars, well filled with offenders awaiting trial...

Unlike Heald and other thrifty YMCA secretaries, most doughboys and other Americans enjoyed the relative luxury of riding on fast 'specials', such as Red Cross trains bound for Omsk, or monthly supply trains bound for the 27th Infantry's camp at Verkhne-Udinsk. They all were struck by the stark beauty of Transbaikalia, which they often compared to Wyoming or west Texas, but none noticed – by sight or smell – that, in several places along the railway line, they were passing fields of fresh, shallow mass graves. Even Major General Graves himself traveled through the area in mid-July and observed no evidence of mass executions. Yet rumors persisted that Semenov's officers were conducting 'summer court' at Adrianovka, Olovyannaya, Borzya and Makkaveevo.

RRSC Lieutenant John F. McDonald regularly rode up and down the Transbaikal Railway, yet he did not believe the whispered tales of 'big killings' until an eerie encounter in a railyard one summer morning planted the seed of doubt. A prison train sat in the dusty yard with two cars filled with women. 'As I was going by', recalled McDonald, 'an old woman looked out between the bars and hailed me. Then she called a young girl up to the window – sick-looking, red-haired girl, who spoke to me in very good English. I asked her where she was going and she answered, "I only wish I knew". The train pulled out almost immediately and I could not find out more.'[134]

During the evening of 18 August 1919 John McDonald and two other RRSC lieutenants, McNutt and Griggs, decided to look for proof of the rumors around Adrianovka. There was a train of 20 or so cars in the railyard with about 400 prisoners aboard, and the Americans guessed that they would be killed during the next day or two. Early the next morning the lieutenants saw a group of OMO soldiers and prisoners trudge into town from the east carrying long-handled shovels. Then they saw soldiers loaded onto the prison train along with a machine gun which was dismounted from a *bronevik*. Not only OMO soldiers boarded, but 'Kolchak guards' as well, distinguished by their 'British uniforms'. Colonel Stepanov, commander of Semenov's Armored Train Division, selected a rifle and climbed aboard. Shortly before 10 a.m. the train pulled out, leaving about half of its cars behind. McDonald ran after it. He caught up with it just over a mile east of Adrianovka, where it idled on a curve. A sentry barred McDonald from approaching closer than 100 yards to the train. 'I pretended not to understand Russian when the guard stopped me', said McDonald, 'but he put a shell into his rifle to assist my understanding. I understood.' McDonald tramped back to Adrianovka station, and within minutes the train returned – empty. McDonald noted that the machine gun did not return with the train. Soon the train pulled the last ten cars of prisoners out of Adrianovka. When it came back two hours later, the machine gun, its work completed, came back with it.[135]

The next morning the inquisitive three RRSC lieutenants set out down the tracks in the rain. They passed a peasant woman toting an armload of boots, socks and clothing. At the place where the train stood the day before, the ground was trampled and 'littered with torn clothing, worn-out puttees, and papers of all kinds, including a Bolshevik ruble note'. Three large, fresh graves were ringed with bullet shells of various calibers. The bodies of two 'poor devils' who had tried to escape lay in the grass. One hundred yards further east the trio found three more mass graves of an older vintage, one of which had been only thinly covered with dirt. Wild dogs had unearthed a number of the corpses. 'Some had the feet cut off, one had no head, one had the genitals cut off. Of course, dogs might have done it, but it didn't look like the work of dogs.'[136]

When the rain stopped two days later, McDonald returned to the killing fields late one afternoon. Some little boys digging for loot showed him other mass graves. 'An old peasant woman that lived nearby told me that they had to give up getting in their grain because of the stench', stated McDonald. 'That same night Semenov went through on his way east. There were a number of Japanese on the train and some women. They stopped at Adrianovka and had a celebration – a big banquet. Stepanov was there. They had music and plenty of booze. Then Semenov went east to Vladivostok. I couldn't have believed it if I hadn't seen it.'[137]

Apparently the curious trio of RRSC men notified 1st Lieutenant Justis S. Davidson, the US Army intelligence officer – Chita. He walked up the railway tracks to the killing fields, knowing that he had arrived when he came upon an accumulation of rifle shells where the guards had shot prisoners that tried to flee when they were unloaded. He confirmed McDonald's observations, and added, 'The people in this district are absolutely terrorized. They do not hesitate to tell you it means death if you are found guilty of expressing your opinion regarding Semenov or his officers...' Ambassador Morris was informed of these very killings when he passed through in early September, and discussed it with Captain Raynor, the pro-Semenov British representative in Chita. Raynor was indignant that the Americans had the gall to suggest that the ataman would execute men without a fair trial.[138]

OMO stained countless locations with summary executions and torture until death, but some stood out for the sheer volume of blood spilt. According to local people, the killing fields at Adrianovka paled in comparison to the execution grounds at Makkaveevo. In sheds around a grand Cossack manor house on a terrace overlooking the Ingoda river, prisoners waited their turns for mutilation, scalding and a variety of other sadistic treatments by drunken torturers in the new wooden bathhouse. Here in April 1919, Sipailov's counterespionage squad delivered Aleksandr Vagzhanov for interrogation. An Ensign Pomigalov worked on Vagzhanov with water and pepper for several weeks until the prisoner was deemed to have nothing more to offer, at which time Semenov approved the death sentence mandated by his court martial, which was carried out by Subaltern Mikhail on 5 June 1919. The lives of 5,000 other victims were culled at Makkaveevo during the *atamanshchina*.[139] Visitors to this human slaughterhouse after the civil war recalled seeing the 'two iron rings in the ceiling from which people were suspended head over heels' and dried slices of human flesh dangling from nails. Blood had so saturated the ground under the building that the soil was discolored and befouled.[140]

Colonel Tierbach orchestrated the gory 'summer court' at Makkaveevo, employing General Baksheev and his staff for interrogations and punishment. Tierbach was so efficient that the volume of rotting corpses he threw into the Ingoda river fattened the catfish but contaminated the water, compelling Semenov to order his men not to drink from it. During the long winter months, local peasants who drew water from Ingoda ice-holes for their families and livestock complained about chunks of body parts bobbing to the surface.

As a result, Semenov directed the Makkaveevo base to burn bodies in the future rather than pollute the river with them.

The sadism that occurred at Makkaveevo inspired anti-White myths and propaganda for decades. A Soviet memoirist, Petr I. Naletov, recited the Soviet legend of an unnamed OMO torturer who lived in Makkaveevo in 1919, an alcoholic officer whose daily ritual was to put on a clean white shirt, pick a passenger at random from the station platform at Karymskaya, shoot the victim at a range close enough to spatter the shirt, then put away the shirt as a memento. When Red liberators threw open his chest in 1920, they were shocked to find 300 stained shirts, or so the story goes.[141] The most amazing part of this story is that someone could have squirreled away 300 shirts during a time when most executioners were so poorly clad that they frequently took the condemned's clothing before killing them. While Naletov's tale may have been the product of an imaginative Soviet agitprop officer, it was based on a wealth of true horrors that were certainly much more obscene.

A number of bloody killing fields were located around Karymskaya. Several small glades that dotted the birch forests around the town were blackened by large heaps of ash peppered with scorched metallic buttons, hooks, eyelets, pins and other clothing accessories. Only the executioners had any idea how many people were consumed in the flames, some of them while still alive. Just west of the main station squatted an innocuous red railway cargo shed where hundreds of lives were snuffed out after the torturers tired of their screams, pleas and curses. Some distance to the east sprawled a wide unmarked graveyard, a sandy plot where OMO allegedly buried alive two train cars of people, '...men, women and children'.[142]

A whistle stop known as 'Post 159', about four miles east of Chita, was another known killing field where 'a great many people were whipped and executed'.[143] Meanwhile, the torture chambers inside Chita were rarely idle. Ivan A. Butin, chairman of Transbaikalia's Bolshevik soviet, was apprehended in Blagoveshchensk and returned to Chita's notorious prison. According to Soviet lore, Butin survived 29 rounds of torture before he was liquidated on 16 June 1919.[144] His perseverance was rewarded by having Chita's main street named after him during the Soviet era. Bagzhanov and Butin, however, may have been exceptional cases among Semenov's victims because they were genuine Bolsheviks. OMO death squads rounded up most captives on the flimsiest pretexts. The doomed were usually accused of one of three standard charges: being a Bolshevik, aiding the Bolsheviks, or 'hindering mobilization'.

At Dauria the sadism and bloodletting took on the pall of a medieval inquisition. Baron Roman Ungern-Shternberg ruled over Dauria like a feudal lord.[145] He brooded and meditated in 'his bare quarters in that grim cluster of square brick barracks and railway sidings in the middle of the desert'. He never went to Chita to visit his old friend Semenov and drifted increasingly out of the ataman's control. A Russian expatriate in Urga, Mongolia wrote, 'I had occasion, on various pretexts, to ask the Baron's comrades in arms about his relations with the Ataman Semenov. Most of them evaded the question...Others, shrugging their shoulders, enigmatically said that the Baron did not travel along the same road as Semenov. Their roads were different...'

Surrounded by Mongol astrologers and shamans, the lanky, pale warrior with the bottomless crystal-blue eyes and drooping mustache seemed to be more of a warlock than a warlord. The baron exhibited increasingly erratic behavior, now dabbling with mystic powers and taking steps to reestablish his Order of Military Buddhists 'for an uncompromising fight against the depravity of revolution', this time prohibiting the use of alcohol (though presumably not hashish and opium). So bizarre are the authenticated accounts of Ungern-Shternberg that it is difficult to sort embellished tales, disinformation and propaganda from the surreal truth. From the autumn of 1918 onwards, the Baron held court in his torture chamber, presiding over 'medieval tortures, burnings and boilings'. Travelers through Dauria station were 'struck by the absolute quiet of the place'. One visitor observed, 'When he comes out of his quarters anyone who gets a distant glimpse of him takes care to vanish; when not in humor, a chance meeting may entail arrest, flogging and sometimes execution.' When one of the Baron's detachments encountered a senile old man wandering across the steppe, he allegedly thundered, 'Shoot that man for the collection!'[146]

His own officers were not immune from his cruelty. One Captain Popov, accused of embezzling 14,000 rubles, was whipped until he expired 'at the 300th stroke'. Invitations to drink with the Baron could prove hazardous, not only because he might whip out his revolver and shoot up the bar, but also because he might pistol-whip any guests who could not hold as much liquor as he. He single-handedly halted a typhus epidemic among his troops by shooting the ill. Like many other OMO officers, Ungern-Shternberg was accused of vehement anti-Semitism (which he denied). One tale relates that, upon seeing 'a young and very pretty Jewess' in some Transbaikal village, he offered 1,000 gold rubles to the man who would bring him her head.[147]

OKO sowed new killing fields in the Amur and Maritime provinces during their summer 1919 campaigns. The Japanese Army joined in the Khorsko-Kiinskii operation which broke up partisan groups near Khabarovsk and cast the survivors into the taiga. Simultaneous counterinsurgency operations were carried out around Iman by the OKO garrison commander, Captain A.G. Shirzhaev and in the southern Ussuri area by Lieutenant Colonel N.I. Savel'ev. The seventh Ussuri Cossack conference gathered at Grodekovo on 17 June, and was as packed with reactionaries and Kalmykov patsies as the autumn 1917 *krugs* had been with Red ideologues and slackers. Bad blood between Cossack factions had poisoned the democratic spirit of the *krug* in better, pre-civil war days. Not surprisingly, the delegates reaffirmed their approval of Kalmykov based upon OKO's recent success in the field, and quite mistakenly declared that they had halted the growth of the guerrilla bands.[148] By mid-year, the Whites had destroyed 'the Bolshevik Far East center', leaving 'only scattered organizations' living deep underground in the towns or eking out an existence by theft and banditry on the fringes of the taiga.[149]

However, the Whites and Japanese Army could not root them all out. At the end of July 1919, small groups of partisans began regularly firing on Amur river steamboats running between Khabarovsk and Nikolaevsk-on-Amur from the villages of Malmyzh and Viatsk. White machine gun crews were placed on board the boats but could not deter the attacks. The partisans still laid low, building strength for a comeback, but their sniping and fearlessness stoked anxiety in Nikolaevsk-on-Amur and 'many well-to-do families left for Vladivostok and Khabarovsk, which were considered safe'.[150]

Kalmykov's outrages against his own officers were creating a new catalyst for opposition in the Maritime province. His May 1919 purge of pro-Kolchak officers alienated many Cossacks, prompting a delegation of cavalry officers to petition Lieutenant General A.I. Dutov, Kolchak's inspector of cavalry and ataman of the Orenburg Cossacks, who met with them in Nikolsk-Ussuriisk in mid-summer. The delegation 'pointed out...the indecency of Kalmykov' and that more than 30 brave Ussuri Cossack officers were refusing to serve until Kalmykov was removed from command. Dutov sympathized with the complainants and promised to take up the question of Kalmykov when he returned to Omsk.[151]

Notwithstanding the June announcement that the Red movement was crushed, Lieutenant Colonel Savel'ev led a punitive expedition out of Grodekovo during the last week in July 1919. He collected 30 prisoners on the road to Ippolitovka, accused them of Bolshevism, burned their homes and returned to Grodekovo where his charges were interrogated and consecrated to a killing field. The executions enraged local peasants against the Cossacks, generated scores of new Red sympathizers and coincided with other efforts of Semenov to extend his control into Horvath's territory.[152]

At Iman two weeks later, two notorious Kalmykov agents, Bylkov and Lukyanov, seized 'a hunchbacked girl who had served as a clerk for the soviet during Bolshevik rule' and a telegraph operator and packed them off to Khabarovsk. A kangaroo court appointed by Kalmykov sent seven people to their deaths, while three corpses deposited at the old water station were credited to the OKO total. A nearby village, Gravskii, came out 'openly antagonistic to Kalmykov', inspiring others to raise their voices. Even the supreme council in Vladivostok was embittered by the escalating violence and began to suspect collusion between Semenov and Kalmykov to destabilize Horvath's administration. They even demanded 'all the telegraph ribbons from Khabarovsk in order to inspect all the telegrams' between the atamans.[153]

OMO and OKO's round-ups, torture and execution of suspected subversives were intended to intimidate the populace into submission, but the result was just the opposite. When the Whites occupied the Far East in the autumn of 1918, the peasantry had tired of the political experiments the revolution had wrought. Over the next several months the heavy hand of OMO and OKO oppression and crime made the ignorant masses receptive to Bolshevik agitators' entreaties, promises and goading to take from the rich. By the summer of 1919, peasants began to view the Reds as the lesser of two evils and the ranks of partisan fighters and sympathizers multiplied. Some intended to sow new killing fields with White corpses.

Dreams of a Pan-Mongolian empire

In the face of renewed Chinese efforts to hold onto traditional Mongolian territories, a Pan-Mongol movement arose in 1919 that, in its grandest form, envisioned all Mongol homelands gathered within a single border stretching from Lake Baikal to Tibet, from the Gulf of Chihli in the Yellow Sea to the Tien Shan mountains in Sinkiang, uniting Buryats in Transbaikal and Irkutsk provinces with Barguts in northwest Manchuria and Khalkhas in Outer Mongolia.[154] Rumor had it that Grigorii Semenov was also 'a Mongolian prince, referred to as the Prince of Van'.[155] For a short time, Ataman Semenov could dream of becoming King Grigorii the Unifier, when, during the first nine months of 1919, he stood on the verge of repeating what had been, perhaps, Genghis Khan's most challenging feat of all, unifying the Mongols.

Japanese expansionists shared this common dream and had long cultivated allies in the region, intending to replace Russian paternalism with control by Tokyo. During the Russo-Japanese War tsarist officials fretted over reports that Japanese agents were espousing 'Pan-Mongolism' in hopes of co-opting Buryats who were calling for self-government and linguistic freedom, and in 1911, when Outer Mongolia broke away from China, the Japanese intelligence and gun-running networks of *Kanzan So* (the Mountain of Sweat Society) were already in place to buttress the separatist forces. In 1918, the Japanese founded a Japanese–Mongol Buddhist Association that championed a Greater Mongolia. A Mongol buffer state under Japanese influence would dilute Russian and Chinese domination in the region, and be a natural extension of Japan's colony of Korea and her politico-commercial invasion of southern Manchuria.[156]

Peking recognized the danger of Mongol unification and wanted to reassert Chinese authority over the Outer Mongolian separatists now that their Russian protectors were weak and distracted by civil war. During summer 1918, while the Russians were busy fighting among themselves, a Chinese battalion appeared in Urga to reinforce the consular guard in violation of the 1915 Kyakhta agreement between Russia, China and Mongolia.[157] In that arrangement, China granted Mongolia autonomy and assented to keeping only small military escorts for Peking's *amban* in Urga, and at satellite offices of Chinese representatives in Uliassutai, Maimachen (the Tea Road bordertown adjacent to Kyakhta) and Kobdo. On the other hand, China could cry foul over Semenov's recruitment of Chinese nationals (i.e. Barguts and other Mongol minorities) during previous months. Likewise, Omsk was not pleased with Semenov's 'Greater Mongolia' schemes and in November 1918 the Siberian Provisional Government dispatched Colonel B.N. Volkov to Urga to try to undo Semenov's machinations. In the meantime, Prince Kudashev at the Russian embassy in Peking tried to assuage Chinese fears and preserve the status quo established by the 1915 Kyakhta agreement.

Urga and Outer Mongolia's seven-year-old theocratic government were in turmoil. Jebtsundamba Khutuktu had exploited his spiritual station as 'The Living Buddha' and *Bogd Gegeen*, head of the lamaist religion, to inflate his secular power as *Bogdo Khan*, the head of state. By greatly increasing the number of tax-exempt *shabins* (the Barguts' influential class of monks, shamans and Buddhist leaders), the *Bogdo Khan* built a huge power base encompassing one-quarter of the country's population, simultaneously weakening the princes to whom taxes were paid. These followers were paid out of the state treasury, which the *Bogdo Khan* continued to squander on frivolous projects, such as the long-term construction of an elaborate wooden gate at his Urga palace that cost 150,000 lan. The *Bogdo Khan*'s excesses spawned a lasting struggle between the lamas and the secular princes. The latter feared not only for their temporal authority over their communities, but for their lives as well. The lamaists were not meek, virtuous spiritualists, and earned a reputation for poisoning political opponents, even high level officials such as the minister of foreign affairs, Handa-Dorzhi, in 1915.[158]

In January 1919 rumors circulated that China was considering the cancellation of the Mongols' special status in Barga. Peking was concerned about the momentum that Mongol separatists were building up and by Semenov's enlistment of all-Bargut units in OMO and their deployment in Bargut territory along the Chinese Eastern Railway.[159] A small band of Buryats led by an OMO officer named Tsokto Badmazhanov slipped into Barga territory to arouse the peasants against the *shabins*. Pan-Mongol sentiments ran high in Inner Mongolia where, in 1912, 35 out of 49 *khoshuuns* had announced a desire to join with the new Outer Mongolian state.

About this same time, Ataman Semenov was said to have met with Outer Mongolian leaders to 'work out details for the suggested union of Mongolia and the Buryat territories as an independent state under King Grigorii I and with Japanese protection', as General Budberg's acidic pen described it.[160]

The American Captain Moore happened upon a meeting between Semenov and an Inner Mongolian leader on 2 February 1919 at Tsitsihar station. Moore was returning to Vladivostok when his train stopped at Tsitsihar for about an hour. Noticing the ataman's train nearby, he went aboard to bid him adieu since Semenov had been absent from Chita when Moore exited. He was politely sent away, being told that the ataman was taking a bath. Yet from his own car window, Moore observed 'fifteen or twenty [Russian] generals and colonels' and 'two Mongols whom I would judge to be [in] rank to mandarins' arrive for a conference on the ataman's train. One of the latter was the object of considerable deference from Mongolians and OMO staff who greeted him. 'There was considerable bustle and what I regarded as suppressed excitement.'[161]

Nonetheless, the Outer Mongolians were not so excited. The *Bogdo Khan* and his lamaist constituency refused to sign onto a plan for Pan-Mongol unification that was sure to rouse China into military action. Mongolia was virtually defenseless; years of neglect had withered the army into a poorly trained, undisciplined rabble of only 2,000 soldiers.[162]

Days later in early February 1919, Semenov convened a Pan-Mongol conference at Dauria attended by Bargut leaders, Inner Mongolian princes and lamas and representatives of the Buryat intelligencia. Lieutenant Colonel Barrows attended as an observer and politely agreed to forward a message to President Woodrow Wilson from Ataman Semenov suggesting that a Mongol delegation be received at the Versailles Peace Conference.[163] On about 7 March Barrows' favor to Semenov was emblazoned in the Peking newspapers, and the Chinese government was asking an embarrassed State Department if this implied American support for Mongolian independence or Semenov's Pan-Mongol scheme. Luckily for Barrows, he had departed for the United States and was inaccessible.[164]

Two weeks later, Semenov hosted a high profile Pan-Mongol congress in Chita on 25 February.[165] Prominent Mongols attended, including six Buryat leaders, 'several' Inner Mongolian and Barga Mongolians princes, Tibetans, Kirghiz, Kazakhs and others. Notably, no representatives from Outer Mongolia graced the proceedings. Many respected, responsible Mongols shared the young ataman's dream of a Pan-Mongol state. The attendees mapped out their vision of Greater Mongolia under the watchful eyes of Semenov's advisor, Major Suzuki and probably other Japanese observers. They even proclaimed the formation of the Pan-Mongol state and formed a provisional government under an influential Inner Mongolian lama, Neise Gegen Mendebayar. A small army began to assemble at Dauria, attracting Buryat, Bargut and Inner Mongolian recruits.[166]

Urga was consumed with speculation and worry about a recent assassination that widened the split between the lamaists and the secularists. Khan Namnan-Surena, chairman of the council of ministers, was poisoned in February by a clique of palace courtiers. The secularists began to talk openly of a cancellation of autonomy to seek China's protection – figuring that it was better to be a colony that to be slowly drained of one's property and perhaps poisoned. The return to the Chinese fold appeared so imminent that the head of government, Badam-Dorzhi, a lamaist and one of the largest feudal landlords in Mongolia, joined the movement to cancel autonomy, hoping to protect his holdings and avoid prosecution for embezzling and bribe-taking.[167]

On 12 June 1919, the *Chen' Bao* newspaper in Peking published a bellwether article describing the dangers facing Mongolia. A General Chen in Urga noted that Semenov was gathering forces for an attack, making it a foregone conclusion that China should come to her neighbor's 'rescue'. Chinese soldiers began slowly moving into Urga in early July.

The ataman was indeed preparing for a Mongolian campaign. During the summer months of 1919, Semenov siphoned off 1,800 Russian officers and Buryat Mongol soldiers from OMO and recruited a like number of Inner Mongolian warriors to form a special military expedition that would invade Mongolia via Verkhne-Udinsk and the Selenga River valley and coerce Urga's reluctant princes to cooperate. This expeditionary force included 800 Kharach'in horsemen under an Inner Mongolian warrior-prince named Fussenge (or Fushengi), who had relied on Baron Ungern-Shternberg as his military advisor for some time. The Japanese general staff financed the expedition. 'Japan has everything to gain and nothing to lose by this expedition', wrote the US intelligence officer in Chita, 1st Lieutenant Justis Davidson.[168]

Eager to ascertain the situation, in mid-July Captain Harold Fay, Davidson's counterpart in Harbin, interviewed a Scotch businessman, Mr McNutt, who had just returned from an extended trip into Mongolia. Russia's civil war had been quite lucrative for the 'Mongol village headmen' McNutt visited; they had amassed 'large stores of gold and silver bullion in bars and coffers full of Romanov money (mostly 500 ruble notes)'. McNutt recounted that Semenov had a Buryat and a Russian representative in Urga who were having no success persuading Mongolian officials to join the Pan-Mongol scheme. 'The influential Mongolian chieftains are too crafty to absorb such castles in Spain', wrote Fay. 'Semenov's sole objective is to get his fingers into their coffers, and [he] apparently underestimates their intelligence.'[169]

During the next several days, Captain Fay encountered a Mongolian conspirator in Harbin who was willing to discuss the 'future Mongolian Republic'. The plan was to capture Urga by the end of August, when the migration of Russian Buryats into Outer Mongolia would commence. With the support of the Japanese Army and OMO, China would be powerless to impede Mongolia's independence. Fay's source also confided that although Semenov had already obtained forestry concessions under the regime-to-be, Mongolians disliked his Japanese friends and preferred to do business with Americans.[170]

In late August the Pan-Mongol expedition gathered in Dauria, however the mixture of different factions proved explosive. On the afternoon of 3 September, General Fussenge and several hundred followers mutinied, murdered their Russian officer – advisors and disarmed the Buryat troops. Telegrams describing the strange situation at Dauria were more cryptic and vague than usual. The RRSC inspector for that area reported 'fifteen hundred Mongols revolted taking their arms and artillery with them. Unable to ascertain cause'.[171] An unidentified OMO *bronevik* tried to disarm them but was captured, driven out of town and ditched. From the south, a trainload of Russian troops from the OMO camp at Manchuli rushed to put down the rebellion. From the north, two *broneviki* sped down from Adrianovka. General Saito, the Japanese brigade commander in Manchuli, threw his troops into the fight against the Mongol rebels. For two days Dauria was a battleground and all rail traffic through the area was halted. Fussenge and his entire staff were killed. The rest of the rebels dispersed into Outer Mongolia, where most were cornered by the Chinese Army and executed.[172]

The fiasco at Dauria encouraged the Red partisans in Transbaikalia. During the two weeks after the mutiny, the emboldened partisans, perhaps bolstered by a few Mongol deserters, put three armored trains out of commission on the Transbaikal Railway and even attacked Sretensk in mid-September. These events were the first electrifying jolts from a fierce Red tempest that turned Semenov's attention back to Transbaikalia.

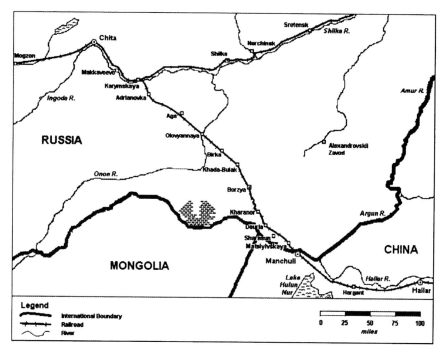

Map 1 Transbaikalia: Transbaikalia was Semenov's heartland.

Plate 1 Manchuli Station – the center of intrigue: Semenov and 7 men began the counterrevolution in Manchuli, a dusty town of 15,000 straddling the Russian–Manchurian border (*Source*: Military History Institute).

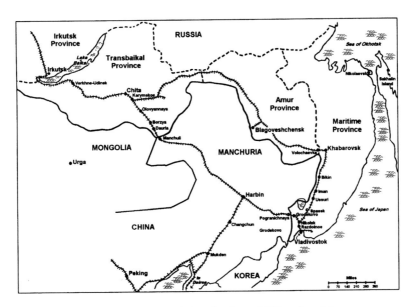

Map 2 Russian Far East: From Lake Baikal to the Seas of Okhotsk and Japan.

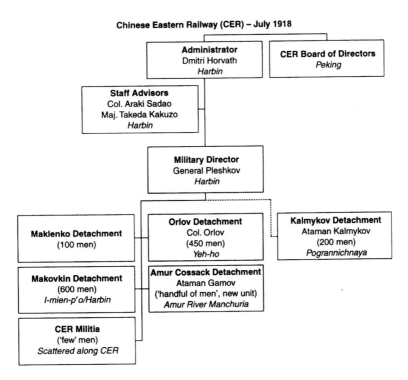

Figure 1 Order of Battle – Chinese Eastern Railway, July 1918: The Chinese Eastern Railway became a rallying point for White forces in the Far East.

Map 3 Southern portion of Russia's Maritime Province: Russia's civil war persisted in the southern Maritime Province from 1918 until 1922.

Plate 2 Vladivostok city center: Vladivostok's main artery was Svetlanskaya Street, the home of Churin's department store (left, on the corner). The city was permeated with Red sympathizers when the interventionists arrived in August 1918 (*Source*: 2nd Lieutenant William C. Jones, RRSC).

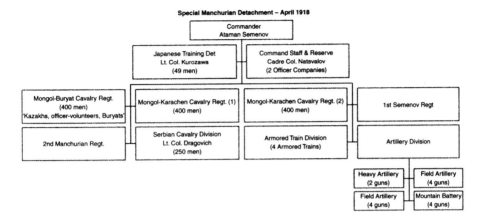

Figure 2 Order of Battle – OMO, April 1918: OMO's ranks filled with ethnic minorities, especially Mongols, Cossacks and others threatened by the Bolsheviks.

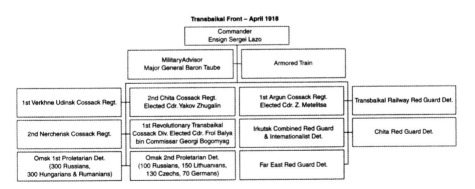

Figure 3 Order of Battle – Transbaikal Front, April 1918: Sergei Lazo's Transbaikal Front drew upon Red Guard and Internationalist detachments from all over Siberia, leaving Trans-Siberian Railway towns vulnerable to the anti-Bolshevik uprisings of May and June 1918.

Plate 3 Onon river bridge: Ataman Semenov called the Onon 'my native river', as had Genghiz Khan. The bridge over the Onon at Olovyannaya was a strategic asset that Semenov and Red commander Sergei Lazo fought over from April until August 1918. Retreating Red Guards dynamited the bridge on May 3 (*Source*: 2nd Lieutenant William C. Jones, RRSC).

Plate 4 Japanese soldiers: Japanese soldiers living in a *taplushka* at Harbin (*Source*: National Archives, Signal Corps Collection).

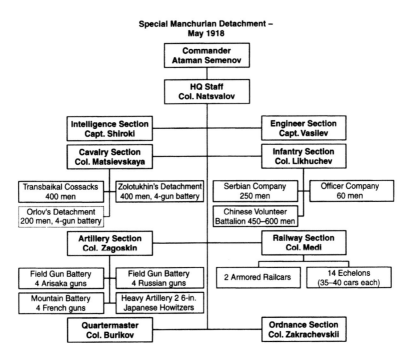

Figure 4 Order of Battle – OMO, May 1918: OMO had 2,300 men as of 1 May 1918, and volunteers increased along with the tempo of combat operations for several weeks.

Plate 5 OMO Cavalry: Buryat cavalryman typically campaigned with extra mounts (*Source*: Military History Institute).

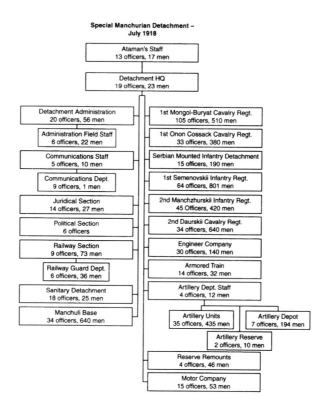

Figure 5 Order of Battle – OMO, July 1918: Semenov's anti-Bolshevik army encompassed several thousand Mongols and Cossacks by July 1918. A battalion of Japanese volunteers is not shown on this chart.

Plate 6 OMO Cavalry: OMO Cossacks and ponies take a break around a Transbaikal home (*Source*: Military History Institute).

Plate 7 Ataman Ivan P. Kalmykov: A Canadian who met him described Kalmykov as 'a little man, about five feet two inches in height, with a trim lady-like waist, small and delicate hands, and a face even more boyish than his 25 or 26 years would suggest' (*Source*: National Archives).

Plate 8 Leaders of US technical assistance: Colonel George H. Emerson, RRSC (left) and John F. Stevens, chairman of the American Railway Commission to Russia, builder of the Panama Canal and the Great Northern Railway, on the steps of Steven's railcar at Vladivostok (*Source*: National Archives, Signal Corps Collection, taken by Sgt. John G. Hammer).

Plate 9 Ataman Grigorii M. Semenov: Some say he fancied himself as the Napoleon of Russia's revolution. The cross on Ataman Semenov's chest is the Order of Saint George, 4th Class, one of two which he earned for gallantry against the Germans in the Carpathians during the winter of 1914–15 (*Source*: National Archives).

Plate 10 Dom Nikitin: Dom Nikitin, Ataman Semenov's Chita residence (1918–20), still survives (*Source*: Andrei Bukin).

Plate 11 'Death Train' and defiant peasants: Brave peasants pass bread to starving 'Death Train' prisoners at Nikolsk-Ussuriisk Station, late 1918. Such overt sympathy for Bolsheviks risked summary execution by Ataman Kalmykov and OKO (*Source*: National Archives, Signal Corps Collection).

Plate 12 Nikolsk-Ussuriisk Station: Nikolsk-Ussuriisk was a strategic railway terminus and city of 50,000 that fell under the shadow of Ataman Kalmykov and his Japanese Army allies. In this December 1918 photo, US, Japanese and Russian soldiers mill about (*Source*: National Archives, Signal Corps Collection, taken by Sgt. John G. Hammer).

Plate 13 Japanese Imperial Army staff in Siberia: 1st row (left to right): Lieutenant Colonel Takashima (who threatened Kalmykov with attack if he continued executing pro-Omsk officers in May 1919); Lieutenant Colonel Uyeda; Colonel Ameno; Lieutenant General Yuhi; General Otani, commander of Allied Forces-Siberia; Major General Inagaki (commander in Chita, winter 1918–19, later chief of staff of Japanese forces in Siberia); Colonel Sakabe (General Staff representative who ordered the 5 April 1918 landing of Japanese marines); Colonel Itoyama. 2nd row: Lieutenant Colonel Takahagi; Captain Hiro; Major Nakayama; Major Hasebe; Lieutenant Colonel Kano; Major Komoto; Captain Kawase; Captain Takahashi; Lieutenant Colonel Watanabe; Captain Watanabe. 3rd row: Lieutenant Kawakatsu; Captain Maeno; Captain Takanaka; Captain Mitome; Captain Aoyagi; Captain Oshima; Captain Tsuchiya; Captaint Egawa; Captain Nakagawa (*Source*: National Archives, Signal Corps Collection, taken by Sgt. John G. Hammer).

Plate 14 OMO armored train 'Ataman': This photo was taken 17 November 1919. 'Ataman' was in Vladivostok to crush the Gajda uprising. Three months earlier, Colonel Stepanov celebrated his wedding day by observing the whipping of Assistant Conductor Alexandrovich aboard the 'Ataman' (*Source*: Military History Institute).

Plate 15 Semenov's train with gaudy 'Summer Car': On the 'Summer Car', Semenov enjoyed a harem of 30 beautiful women, an orchestra of musically talented Austro-Hungarian prisoners and champagne (*Source*: Military History Institute).

Plate 16 Russian Naval Train, Vladivostok: White naval officers stand by an innovative gunmount aboard the armored train that defended Vladivostok, 1918 (*Source*: National Archives, Signal Corps Collection).

Plate 17 Soldiers and refugees in Vladivostok Station: Families living in Vladivostok Station, winter 1918–19 (*Source*: National Archives, Signal Corps Collection, taken by Sgt. John G. Hammer).

Plate 18 The Cossack and the Cowboy: In March 1919 the Ataman (seated at left) received a stiff reception from Major General Graves (seated at center) upon a visit to US Headquarters in Vladivostok. All US Army Signal Corps photos of the awkward event were marked 'NOT FOR DISTRIBUTION' (*Source*: National Archives, Signal Corps Collection, taken by Sgt. John G. Hammer).

Plate 19 Lieutenant Colonel Charles B. Morrow, at 27th Infantry Headquarters in Khabarovsk: Colonel Morrow was born 30 November 1877, commissioned in June 1898, and commanded the US 27th Infantry Regiment from June 1918 until August 1918, then again from April 1919 until March 1920. He returned to his native Kentucky where his brother, Edwin, was the elected governor, testified against Grigorii Semenov in Congress in 1922, and continued serving the army until 1935, finishing his career as commander of Fort Niagara, New York (*Source*: National Archives, Signal Corps Collection, taken by Sgt. John G. Hammer).

Plate 20 Bridge over the Angara river at Irkutsk: Fighting raged around this bridge as the Political Center battled OMO and PSG units for control of Irkutsk (*Source*: 2nd Lieutenant William C. Jones, RRSC).

Plate 21 Czechoslovak armored train: Czechoslovak and American soldiers (in flatbrim hats) around a turretted Czechoslovak armored car similar to the *Orlik* (*Source*: 2nd Lieutenant William C. Jones, RRSC).

Plate 22 OKO armored railcar: In Vladivostok to put down Radola Gajda's attempted uprising, 18 November 1919 (*Source*: Military History Institute).

Plate 23 Mongol caravan: Tea Road caravans connected Irkutsk, Verkhne-Udinsk and Chita to Urga and Kalgan. By early 1920, the Chinese Army under 'Little Hsu' put a stranglehold on Mongolian commerce to force the errant colony back under Peking's control, and Mongol camel drovers began avoiding Urga (*Source*: 2nd Lieutenant William C. Jones, RRSC).

7

THE WHITE COLLAPSE BEGINS

Summer 1919–January 1920

> The enemies of the country try to tempt you with peace...They will give you famine, privation, plunder and atrocities...Sooner or later a certain force will come from the East – a force that will help you to defend order in the country, and which will save you from Bolshevism and starvation. Remember that the bread we now receive comes from the East.
>
> (White handbills distributed in Irkutsk, 25 December 1919)

A black summer for Siberian Whites

Semenov had long been insulated from the main war fronts by Admiral Kolchak's territory. By the summer of 1919, this buffer was as worn-out and full of holes as the cushions in a first-class passenger coach. Kolchak's armies in western Siberia were afflicted with a terminal decay of spirit that no achievable military victory could remedy. The fervor that inspired White volunteers to rise up against the Reds in autumn 1918 had been exhausted by Omsk's disastrous spring 1919 offensive. Popular support that once cemented the fragile anti-Bolshevik alliances had crumbled in the wake of the November 1918 White militarist coup, incessant crackdowns against any political opposition to the bumbling administration of 'Supreme Dictator' Kolchak (as the opposition referred to him) and an abysmal economic climate that stifled commerce and discouraged agriculture. Instead of maturing into a hothouse for the Siberian Provisional Government's seedling democracy, Omsk became a nesting ground for profiteers, myopic militarists who could not comprehend the social changes in the empire, scores of elegant, cowardly officers who filled the cafes and purposeless staff positions and unfortunate bourgeois refugees with blind faith in Russia's old institutions.

'No matter how complicated the situation was at the front', noted Paul Dotsenko, 'Omsk continued its carefree existence'.[1] Many considered victory over the Bolshevik rabble a fait accompli, and intrigue among rival White officers was rife. Supplies meant for fighting men at the front were distributed to rear echelon slackers or evaporated into thriving blackmarkets. Despite the lack of good news from the front, Kolchak's supporters and many among the upper class seemed to enjoy an unfounded sense of security. Admiral Kolchak wisely denied himself this luxury and moved about with a bodyguard of English troops, then later (after the June 1919 British evacuation), with an elite detachment of marines to ensure his personal safety, as much from ambitious subordinates like Semenov and General Ivanov-Rinov as from Bolshevik assassins.[2]

THE WHITE COLLAPSE BEGINS

Conditions observed by RRSC Major F.A. Flanagan at Krasnoyarsk were typical:

> June 25, 1919: Usual number of beggars, filth, aimlessness. Typhus prevalent. Some cholera. Also stracoma [sic], which causes blindness. Large number of posters on the railway station which read, 'Krasnoyarsk hospitals are crowded with venereal patients and no more patients of this kind will be admitted.'... A great many of the Russian troops moving west are well-supplied with vodka.[3]

Major Flanagan was appalled by the Whites' lackadaisical treatment of their very own sick and wounded. A dismal parade of Russian 'sanitary trains' crawled east, loaded with combat casualties and typhus cases. Kolchak's supply corps, preoccupied with black-market deals and other illicit business, had failed to provide any trains with medicine, bandages or other necessities. Flanagan noted,

> Patients continually begging for bread, tea and cigarettes. Each Russian sanitary train has a Russian Officer in charge and he instructs Station Agents when to allow the train to move east. Some of these trains stand around one station (usually [in] a good town) for three or four days. In the meantime many patients die... Many of the trains have no known destination and put off a few patients along the line at various points.[4]

Daily brutality and frequent mass murders by Kolchak's army eroded what little popular support Omsk still mustered. Although Admiral Kolchak never ordered such outrages himself, his written orders directing offending officers to cease their reprehensible activities made it clear that he knew not only of the atrocities but of their instigators, as well.[5] In Omsk itself, 'four or five' secret police organizations competed with each other to cleanse the city of any perceived anti-Kolchak influences. 'People were arrested, imprisoned, judged and executed within a few hours', declared Czech writer Henry Baerlein.[6]

Loosely controlled White military commanders operated with far less restraint than the secret police. Since March 1919, White 'punitive detachments' enthusiastically carried out orders to systematically raze all buildings and execute all men in villages where detachments were met with arms. In uncooperative villages where the frightened citizenry was not forthcoming with information about local Red activity, General Sergei Rozanov instructed that 'monetary contributions' be collected and one out of every ten people be shot.[7]

Corrupt White commanders, of whom there seemed to be no shortage, loosely translated these scorched earth orders as a license to attack innocent villages to plunder, rape and pursue other sadistic pleasures. However the Omsk government did little to rein in criminal commanders, even when requested by senior military officers. For example, in May 1919, Lieutenant General Artem'ev, commander of the military region of Irkutsk, requested that Omsk do something about the excesses of Ataman Krasilnikov and his punitive detachment's frequent orgies of violence. General Artem'ev reported, 'Ataman Krasilnikov idles away his time in debauchery and disorderly behavior, and his officers are similarly occupied; the soldiers take the law into their own hands and conduct searches with the object of looting and raping...' Krasilnikov remained in command. His murderous unit was but one of 32 punitive detachments operating in Yeniseisk province alone.[8]

Major General Graves needed no convincing of the moral bankruptcy of the Omsk government and military. When the American commander was ordered to accompany Roland S. Morris, US Ambassador to Japan, to Omsk in July 1919, he gathered ample evidence to support his stand that Kolchak's military dictatorship was not only undeserving of Washington's support, but had little chance of prevailing over the Bolsheviks. Ambassador

Morris' special train left Vladivostok on 11 July – three days after the Whites evacuated Perm – and did not return from Omsk until the first week in September. Throughout the journey, General Graves jotted down notes about the attitudes of refugees and peasants, salaries of the railway workers, and the chilly receptions he met in Kolchak country. Just before the special crossed into Russian territory at Manchuli, a Chinese general confided to Graves that OMO was shaking down every Manchuria-bound train at Dauria. The special roared quickly through Transbaikalia, without any interference from OMO. They passed the spot at Dauria where, just two days earlier, a raving Colonel Zhukovski had thrown a pair of RRSC officers off their train and into the dust with their belongings. Yet, Graves had no problems until he arrived near the front several days later. There the White command and its British advisors obstructed Graves' efforts to visit the battle lines, and the American general soon deducted that there was no real 'front' anymore. While on tour near Ishim, some envious White officers tried to forcibly confiscate Graves' comfortable train, and relented only at gunpoint, when an American corporal led the train's guard detail in a stubborn defense. It was a petty incident, but it showed how ignoble the White officer corps had become.[9]

The criminality that had become so commonplace in the kleptocracies of Semenov and Kalmykov had infected all of Kolchak's territory, akin to the syphilis and typhus raging through their populations. Excesses by the White military and their Japanese allies, compounded by Omsk's profound military and economic failures, alienated much of Siberia's population from the anti-Bolshevik crusade and drove more people into the Red partisan ranks than did any propaganda or heartfelt revolutionary sentiments.

Partisan growth in the Russian Far East

The year 1919 saw partisan centers flourish in the Far East from the shores of the Pacific to the banks of Baikal, ground which was liberally seeded and fertilized with blood, corpses and despair by greedy White thugs. In Amur province a partisan subculture thrived in the Zeya river valley just north of Blagoveshchensk and in small Amur river settlements, allegedly working hand-in-hand with Chinese *hunghutze* to rob mail boats.[10] The nucleus of the Amur partisans were revolutionary veterans from Transbaikalia and the Ussuri front, who organized an aggressive sabotage campaign between January and March 1919 that damaged railway bridges and stations, derailed military trains, downed telegraph poles and detonated embankments to cause landslides atop the railbed. Declining rail transportation was already strangling the local economy. There were only three trains per day: one for passengers, one for freight and one for moving Japanese Army troops and supplies.[11] The partisans could put the Amur railway out of operation at will, and the Japanese Army reacted energetically, setting out across the countryside in pursuit of Red guerrillas, who wisely avoided pitched battles and took refuge in the hills. As 1919 wore on, the Japanese increased their presence in Amur province from 8,000 to 15,000 men (according to Red estimates) and launched punitive expeditions. Their cruelties ignited peasant uprisings that begat the Japanese burning of villages that flushed hordes of volunteers into partisan camps.[12]

Horrendous economic conditions may have created more sympathy for the Reds than the cycle of violence. During their nine-month tenure in Amur province during 1918, the Bolsheviks had churned out a pool of 80 million rubles in banknotes, to which the succeeding government had thoughtlessly contributed 14 million rubles more. Workers already afflicted with revolutionary malaise and surliness were even less inclined to labor for a dubious currency. For an extended period Blagoveshchensk's two large department stores were closed, supposed due to shortage of stock, 'but the real reason is the fact that they do not wish to accept Bolshevik money', reported an American officer. The well known

Churin's department store discretely admitted customers who were 'willing to pay in Imperial, Kerensky or foreign money'.[13]

In eastern Transbaikalia, the 'forest communes' were ripening into whole regiments of partisans, while new detachments were cropping up in western Transbaikalia around an underground center in Verkhne-Udinsk. At the opposite periphery of the White Far East, labor unions that dominated the Suchan valley coal mines grew into the rallying points for partisans in the Maritime province.

A lethargic White response to this rise in Red activism was not due to arrogance as in earlier times, but to a bleeding loss of strength and popular support. Although the Suchan valley lay in the shadow of General Sergei Rozanov's Vladivostok, the White Army quietly, timidly withdrew from it and its critical mines during the summer of 1919 (although the partisans' reckless aggression toward the Americans would prod Major General Graves into launching his 31st Infantry Regiment on a pacification campaign in June). A Red wireless dispatch on 24 September that claimed control over the Trans-Siberian Railway from Irkutsk to Blagoveshchensk was only a slight embellishment of the real situation.[14] Semenov and Kalmykov controlled the train stations and surrounding towns, but the country in between usually belonged to the partisans, if it belonged to any camp at all.

The atamans were unable to control their own men anymore, and worst of all for Semenov and company, White soldiers were going Red at an increasing rate. Individual defectors encouraged group defections that begat betrayal by whole units. During the night of 14 July 1919, Cossacks of the 1st Transbaikal Semenov Regiment had killed their officers and declared themselves the 5th Military-Revolutionary Regiment under the command of the partisan's eastern Transbaikal Front.[15]

Semenov was furious. He ordered Colonel Tierbach to remove all of the Bolsheviks from Chita prison the night of 15 July, transport them to Makkaveevo under guard of cadets from the ataman's military academy and have officers mow them down with machine guns. Four days later Semenov issued orders to all units to shoot the turncoats upon capture. He also directed that replacements be conscripted from the traitors' families, in addition to one hostage per family. To stave off future Cossack desertions, Semenov warned that henceforth the senior member of each traitor's family would be shot.[16] Thus, if men of the 5th Military-Revolutionary Regiment had any doubts about their change of allegiance, Semenov dispelled them.

On the morning of 26 September these Cossacks marched in reserve behind partisan Commander Zhuravlev when he sent his 1st, 2nd, 4th and 6th Regiments to take stanitsa Bogdat', near Nerchinsk. They faced around 2,000 Japanese soldiers and several regiments – Red memoirists say eight – of *semenovtsy*. The battle seethed uninterrupted through the day and the Reds took two machine guns, but not Bogdat'. They attacked again the next day and captured a critical mountain ridge in the evening. On the third day of combat, gunfights meandered through five miles of surrounding forest until the Whites finally withdrew to nearby Berezov with 170 dead and wounded and even two badly bruised companies of Japanese infantry. Zhuravlev showed Semenov that the partisans in eastern Transbaikalia had matured beyond simple vandalism of train tracks and clumsy headlong assaults into towns, that they could now conduct a sophisticated military operation. After Bogdat', the partisan command felt confident in orchestrating large raids and disrupting traffic on the Trans-Siberian, and began to move into new areas of Transbaikalia.[17]

A lesser event explains the popular support the partisans encountered as they expanded their operations in Transbaikalia. On the morning of 11 October 1919 the *bronevik* 'Mstitel'' stood idle in front of the Borzya train station. '...Officers and soldiers from this *bronevik* stopped and searched all passengers and baggage on Train No. 22, and appropriated all of the vodka they could find – something like 50 large bottles. The passengers appealed to the

Borzya station commandant for the return of their goods...' Miraculously, the station commandant convinced the crew of the 'Mstitel'' to return half of the confiscated vodka, but only 'after considerable argument'.

The men on the 'Mstitel'' began consuming the other half of the pilfered vodka, with tragic consequences. At 6 p.m., a switchman named Matvaenko was going about his work in the yard, carrying a lighted lantern in one hand, a whistle in the other. As he walked along the tracks towards the station – and towards 'Mstitel'' as well – a drunken sentry posted by the east end of the *bronevik* raised his rifle and fired. Matvaenko fell dead. The sentry later claimed that he had ordered Matvaenko to halt three times before shooting.

Matvaenko's co-workers were outraged. The station commandant 'made a vigorous protest to the officers of the *bronevik* against their high conduct, and reported the whole days' events to Colonel Stepanov at Adrianovka. Two days later, all of the railway workers turned out for Matvaenko's funeral. Local *nachal'niki* – station masters – acted as pallbearers. Second Lieutenant W.A. Kelley, the RRSC officer on duty at Borzya, concluded his report of the tragedy by mentioning, 'The dead man leaves a wife and four children'.[18] Trans-Siberian Railway workers, many of whom had welcomed the White 'democratic counter-revolution' in 1918, even sabotaging the Red retreat in some places, now stood firmly, but quietly, with the partisans.[19]

Another political choice between Red and White appeared after the Red advances of summer 1919, symbolized by the green and white colors that were originally worn by the New Siberian Army in the autumn of 1918. Now it fought as Kolchak's embattled Siberian Army, but some men continued to wear green and white cockades, rosettes or ribbons on their uniforms. Indeed secret cells of a Central Bureau of Military Organizations (CBMO) were being organized in White garrisons, fomenting a 'democratic and regionalist sensibility' and advocating the convocation of an all-Siberian *Zemskii sobor'* (Congregation of the Lands). Their objective was to make a truce with the Bolsheviks and establish an eastern Siberian–Far Eastern Russian state with its own Constituent Assembly. They bided their time and built up strength in Vladivostok, where the presence of Allied representatives, particularly the Americans, afforded them a subtle measure of protection.[20]

Atamans' plot against the Americans

A wealth of bad news had greeted Major General Graves upon his return to Vladivostok on 6 September 1919. From an amazing range of disparate political corners, Graves received warnings that the atamans, Semenov and his understudy Kalmykov and their Japanese Army allies were planning hostile actions against the 'ugly Americans', as Semenov referred to the US troops.[21] Warnings even came from General Horvath, who opposed Graves' 'policy of non-interference'; Colonel Butenko, the Vladivostok fortress commander; Omsk's Minister of Foreign Affairs; and a French Army colonel, who knew of Cossack attempts to buy French rifles.[22] Adding to these suspicions, Semenov and Kalmykov had departed Vladivostok together for Khabarovsk three days before Graves returned.

Prior to the atamans' departure, an American captain and corporal were abducted by a group of Kalmykov's soldiers at Iman, about 250 miles north of Vladivostok. Japanese troops witnessed the abductions and did nothing. The captain was released later the same day, however Corporal Spurling was carted off to Khabarovsk, being whipped 'unmercifully' by two Cossack officers on the train, then again for 15 minutes on the platform at Khabarovsk station.[23] The American command had to resort to open threats to force Corporal Spurling's release, but not before a tense standoff occurred between US troops and a combined Cossack and Japanese force around Iman.

General Baron Sergei Nikolaevich Rozanov, who authored the notorious March orders to loot and kill in western Siberia, was now commander of White forces in the Russian Far East (General Horvath was forcibly retired). When General Rozanov arrived in Vladivostok, the district military prosecutor, Lieutenant General Starkovskii, handed him an indictment of Ataman Kalmykov, detailing a number of the latter's crimes. Rozanov defiantly appointed Kalmykov as chief of the Khabarovsk district several days later, and informed the dismayed prosecutor that Kalmykov's 'White terror' was 'necessary for the rescue of the Motherland'.[24] In addition, Rozanov soon hosted a Kalmykov visit to Vladivostok, during which the murderous ataman threatened to execute Lieutenant General Starkovskii and several other critical White officers. Starkovskii resigned. The only restraint on General Rozanov's tyranny in the Far East came from the outrage of the American command.

Among other reports on General Graves' desk lay one detailing a horrible incident near Sviagina station on 27 July. A company of Japanese had brutally executed five Russians: two of the victims were beheaded and three were slashed and bayoneted before being buried alive in front of a group of horrified American soldiers in a sector entrusted to the American Expeditionary Force.[25] The AEFS was completely estranged from its so-called Russian and Japanese partners and sometimes from their British boosters.

The White armies of the Siberian Provisional Government began falling back in July 1919, when Perm, Yekaterinburg and Chelyabinsk were evacuated. On 30 July, two regiments of the New Siberian Army at Krasnoyarsk revolted and refused to go to the front. The Czech Legion had to quell the revolt. In August, Tyumen and Kurgan were left to the Reds. The Volga Front ceased to exist. On 21 September, the French Military Mission ominously departed Omsk, and one month later the White troops fought their last genuine battles in delaying actions against the Reds between the Tobol and Ishim rivers west of Omsk. The Bolsheviks swarmed before Kolchak's capitol, getting ready for the final kill as winter's chill fell across Siberia. On 21 October, Major General Graves cabled Washington,

> A British officer just returned from over three months service with Siberian Army describes military situation as follows: 'Stories of fighting and victories much exaggerated; there was nothing to prevent the *Bolsheviki* from taking Omsk a short time ago if their plan of campaign had so allowed; a [Russian] rabble dressed in British uniforms is sent to the front and at the first opportunity they desert to the *Bolsheviki*.'[26]

Semenov carried on as if he were immune to the Red furies approaching from the west. Instead of bolstering his defenses against the Bolsheviks in western Transbaikalia, he proceeded with the mysterious plan of attack against the Americans that he had discussed with Kalmykov in early September. In early October, Kalmykov officers set up shop at Pogranichnaya, the little Chinese Eastern Railway station on the Chinese–Russian frontier, where they commandeered the town hotel for a headquarters. The US staff surmised, 'It is believed that this incident may be considered in connection with Semenov's recent request made to the Governor of [China's] Kirin Province that he (Ataman Semenov) take over the guarding of the Chinese Eastern Railway'.[27] China did not intend to allow this. 'Mister Lou, Chinese High Commissioner, informed me that he has telegraphed to Harbin to resist with force encroachment of Semenov troops on the Chinese Eastern Railway', reported Lieutenant Colonel Eichelberger, the US intelligence officer in Vladivostok.

On 8 October, an OMO echelon cruised down the Chinese Eastern depositing soldiers at various stations before stopping at Grodekovo. Grodekovo had long been an assembly point for Kalmykov's myrmidons, having been the birthplace of his first detachment. On the morning of 10 October, an OMO echelon appeared in Pogranichnaya and began unloading troops, to the consternation of the Chinese commandant responsible for that sector of the railway. Meanwhile, the movement of a number of unscheduled military trains between Vladivostok and points north suggested that something was up. Likewise, an order published by Semenov the previous day in the Pri-Amur military region could only heighten the suspicions of US troops that some scheme was afoot. It ordered commanders not to arrest American soldiers without passports, permitting their arrests 'only in clear-cut cases of an apparent crime', and reminding Russian officers of the Americans' 'personal inviolability' and to promptly inform the nearest AEFS staff.[28] Within days, the headquarters of the Pri-Amur military district issued a press release stating that a Red prisoner had been captured with an American grenade, and confessed that his detachment had a whole box of grenades and another of Colt revolvers that had been 'supplied by the Americans'.[29]

The ataman had made amends with Admiral Kolchak back in June. As the tides turned against Omsk in October, the Supreme Ruler promoted Semenov to major general and named him governor-general and 'assistant' to General Sergei Rozanov in Vladivostok.[30] On 3 October, Rozanov's second-in-command, General Semenov-Merlin (no relation to the ataman), informed US Lieutenant Colonel Eichelberger that Rozanov was 'now following the advice of the Japanese and the hooligan element in his staff'. That same day a Japanese intelligence officer decorated Rozanov with a Japanese medal.[31] 'The [US Army's] relationship with Vladivostok cannot be considered normal', noted an 18 October US intelligence report. General Rozanov often followed orders emanating from his 'assistant' in Chita, although these orders were 'principally concerning questions of supplies and Japanese relations'.

Despite the increasing frequency of gloomy news from the front, Japan's support to Ataman Semenov did not abate. 'At the present moment', stated an October US report, 'almost all Ataman Semenov's troops are armed and clothed by the Japanese, moreover, military goods are received regularly from Japan and do not present the impression of a temporary supply'.[32] Japanese officers paid generous gratuities to any receptive Russian officers 'who occupy important positions' in Vladivostok as well as Chita.[33] The Japanese Army was betting a substantial sum that Semenov would become 'the important factor in the [Russian] Far East'.[34]

Likewise, Semenov was convinced that war between Japan and the United States was not only inevitable, but about to break out at any moment. Presumably it was Captain Kuroki who had implanted this belief in his protégé's mind some time back, along with a hearty contempt for all things American, according to a colonel who had left the ataman's staff.[35]

Chita had become 'the center of Japanese influence and propaganda' in Russia. From his vantage point near Semenov's headquarters, Lieutenant Davidson reported that,

> It is apparent that the Japanese are trying to control all the newspapers from Vladivostok to Irkutsk...I would say [that] two-thirds of the newspapers in the district are financed by the Japanese for the purpose chiefly of spreading anti-American propaganda. All the newspapers of Chita are carrying on an anti-American propaganda [campaign] and in most cases [it is] followed up by a long editorial about the assistance and good will of 'our' friends from Japan.[36]

British troops had already withdrawn from Siberia (Kolchak's loyal advisor, Major General Knox, would not slip out of Omsk until November 1919). The Czechs, Americans and other Allies were growing anxious to extract themselves from the Russian morass at the earliest opportunity. Meanwhile the Japanese general staff regularly rotated troops through arena; in September, General Oba's 3rd Division was replaced by General Suzuki's Japanese 5th Division in Transbaikalia. As shown by Tokyo's subtle support for Semenov's aborted Mongolian expedition, Japan was ardently, but clumsily trying to carve an area of influence in the Russian Far East, Manchuria, Transbaikalia and Mongolia. She was motivated not simply for political and commercial gain, but out of fear as well. The contagion of Bolshevism had crept too near Japan's shores and even her soldiers were not immune. According to historian John Albert White, 'It was reported, for example, that a whole company of Japanese troops became infected with Bolshevism and were placed aboard the warship *Mikasa* and taken out to sea and shot'.[37]

Semenov and a large retinue traveled down to Mukden in September, where the ataman could discuss sensitive matters, such as the Mongolian mutiny earlier in the month, with Japanese officials and patch up his relations with Chang Tso-Lin. A more explosive issue concerned his intention to patch up relation with his first wife, Zenaida, who journeyed from Japan to reunite with her man. The British consul recorded the scandalous scene at Mukden station when the ataman departed:

> A somewhat romantic episode occurred when the ataman was leaving his hotel for the railway station. A woman, said to be a notorious gypsy woman with whom the ataman had for some time been living in intimate relations, and who appears to have been discarded by him on the arrival in the Far East of his own wife,... suddenly ran forward and, addressing reproaches to him, swallowed some poison and immediately collapsed. She was removed to the Japanese hospital for treatment and appears to have survived.

The 'notorious gypsy' was, of course, Masha Sharaban, who was soon recovered to her previous position as the 'central figure in the [ataman's] raffish court'. Zenaida, it seems, returned to Japan.[38]

Battle of Khada-Bulak

The Red victory at Bogdat' in late September 1919 emboldened partisan commanders and signaled the beginning of a period of aggressive partisan infiltration and assaults deep inside Semenov's territory. One of the next targets was Khada-Bulak, located about 21 miles northwest of Borzya. While the Battle of Khada-Bulak was a minor event, it typified the White-versus-Red combat occurring with increasing frequency throughout Transbaikal province.

At 3:30 a.m. on the morning of 31 October 1919 the dispatcher at Borzya station tried to raise Khada-Bulak station on the telegraph. The dispatcher intended to advise Khada-Bulak of the departure of northbound train No. 21, and he was probably wondering why southbound train No. 4 was late. However, the dispatcher discovered that his communications with Khada-Bulak had been severed, and within minutes he realized that he could not even communicate with closer stations.

Soon the telegraph operator at Khada-Bulak also noticed that his communications were dead, except for the telephone line. Just as train No. 21 pulled into his station at 4 a.m., the telegraph operator managed to get *Razesd* 77 on the line. 'Raz 77', as it was known, was a small siding about six miles north of Khada-Bulak station. The old village of Khada-Bulak was situated nearby. No doubt a bit frantic, the railway man at Raz 77 said that Bolshevik partisans were swarming southeast down the track towards Khada-Bulak station and were on the verge of overrunning his little station. That was the last anyone heard from the railway man at Raz 77.[39]

This calamitous news quickly filtered back to the Borzya commandant. He ordered all rail traffic through the area halted, northbound traffic at Manchuli on the Russian–Manchurian border, southbound traffic at Olovyannaya, 41 miles north of the troubles at Khada-Bulak.

After an hour's delay, the *bronevik* 'Istrebitel' reluctantly pulled out of Borzya to investigate. A bit later, some thoughtful Bolshevik picked up the phone at Raz 77, and rang up Khada-Bulak to announce that Raz 77 was being dismantled.

For the next several hours the Borzya dispatcher's office was on tenterhooks. The thought of the Red thrust extending to Borzya was not far-fetched. After nearly two years of outrages by Semenov's unruly mercenaries, the local railway workers were surely not pro-Semenov, but they must have been apprehensive about being caught in the crossfire between Red partisans and OMO's 150-man garrison. In the dispatcher's office though, the Borzya commandant remarked to 1st Lieutenant W.A. Kelley, the American RRSC inspector, that the Cossacks on garrison duty were 'not to be depended upon'.

Shortly before 10 a.m. Borzya's defense was bolstered by the arrival of Russian echelon No. 55, which brought in 165 dependable Ussuri Cossacks and their horses.

The situation at Khada-Bulak was more tenuous, but as of mid-morning the Bolsheviks still had attempted no assault. About 10 a.m., heavy thumps of artillery were audible from the direction of Raz 77 – obviously the bark of 'Istrebitel's' guns.

'Istrebitel' had fired eight rounds. The *bronevik* commander soon reported that he fired 'into scattered groups of Bolsheviki, plainly visible on the level plain to the north [of the rail line] and that two of these shots took good effect, making direct hits into large groups of the enemy'. Actually the shots were fired at such close range and low level that the shells had skimmed through the *Bolsheviki* and off into the countryside.

'Istrebitel's' commander passed on to Borzya his estimate of Red strength at 350 partisans. Perhaps based upon this estimate, the Ussuri Cossacks detrained shortly after 11 a.m., mounted up and trotted off towards Khada-Bulak. In reality, the Bolshevik force totaled some 2,000 men, dispersed over the six miles between Khada-Bulak station and Raz 77. They whiled away the Siberian morning vandalizing the railway line. The partisans uprooted 11 telegraph poles, cut the line in four places, heaved rails away from the roadbed and burned two small bridges.

About noon the *bronevik* commander upped his estimate to 1,500 Reds, and urged the evacuation of Khada-Bulak. 'Istrebitel' stayed close to Khada-Bulak station for the next two hours. When her commander spotted two detachments of several hundred partisans lurking in the vicinity of the station, he decided to cruise back to Borzya 'to see if the line was ok'.

Meanwhile the staff and small garrison at Borzya remained nervous. Six mounted Cossacks were sent to scout for Bolshevik activity about 3 p.m. Then, to their relief, reinforcements began to pour in. A train from Dauria screeched into the station shortly before 5 p.m. and disgorged General Baron Ungern-Shternberg and 11 carloads of Cossacks. Two later trains delivered 15 more boxcars of Cossacks from Dauria and nine carloads of Japanese troops from Manchuli.

Ungern-Shternberg was not the kind of warrior to sit and wait for a partisan mob to attack him. At 10 p.m. he took his trainload of Dauria Cossacks up to Khada-Bulak to liquidate the troublesome Reds. 'Istrebitel' followed five minutes behind him, but there were no Reds to liquidate by the time they arrived.

By the next morning, 1 November, 800 Cossacks and Japanese soldiers were scouring the countryside between Borzya and Khada-Bulak, anxious to kill partisans. None was to be found. They vanished into the hills several miles northwest of Khada-Bulak. The 'Battle' of Khada-Bulak was over.

The partisans' mischievous handiwork – the sabotaged railway, burnt bridges and damage to the telegraph lines – was enough to keep two repair trains busy for the next 36 hours. Nevertheless, this destruction was almost superficial considering the size of the Bolshevik force. Even the little station at Raz 77 still stood. One telegraph set was stolen, and the other office equipment was not even damaged.

'The Bolsheviks appeared to have made the raid principally to obtain a supply of winter clothing from the villagers at Khada-Bulak', concluded Lieutenant Kelley, 'and to obtain meat and fresh horses. It is said they slaughtered and carried away 300 sheep, and ran off something like 600 horses and many cattle – all owned by Buriats'.[40]

'Normal' rail traffic (if anything in Siberia – besides the cold – could be called normal in 1919) resumed the afternoon of 2 November. 'The captain of the [Borzya] garrison who ordered the *bronevik* to return to Borzya just as things were getting interesting at Khada-Bulak, was arrested [the night of 6 November] by General Ungern', observed Lieutenant Kelley. Semenov's henchmen had no respect for the timid, even among their own ranks.[41] Major Gravis, the RRSC district inspector, told Lieutenant Kelley that he was worried about Kelley's well-being with such peril swirling around Borzya. Kelley responded, 'Please don't concern yourself about my welfare or safety. This is the life I like…'.[42]

The Ataman versus Lieutenant Ryan

Whatever plans for aggressive actions against the Americans that Semenov and his Japanese advisors had cooked up were laid aside as the fall of Omsk grew imminent. Semenov and Kalmykov would soon need all the men they could muster to resist the 5th Red Army's advance. The Cossack warlords could only depend upon Japan for support, and Japan needed the warlords to maintain her foothold in Siberia and the Russian Far East.

Mindful of the vulnerability of his dependence upon the Japanese Army, Semenov tried to rally support from other quarters. He had roving representatives and offices in Harbin, Vladivostok and Shanghai that purchased supplies, fenced pilfered goods, gathered intelligence and sought benefactors. Despite the animosity between Semenov and General Graves, the ataman was canny enough to dispatch an OMO colonel to Washington to drum up support among anti-Bolshevik politicians and bureaucrats at the US Departments of State and War. The ataman's receipt of a flattering declaration of moral support and florid adulation from the 'Supreme Arab Senate', along with a beautiful decoration, the 'Green Order of Holy Mohammed', was the work of Semenov's Baghdadi friend from the POW camp at Dauria, Prince Al-Kadir.[43]

Despite the heightening intrigue in the Russian Far East and the rapid disintegration of Kolchak's armies, Semenov's OMO still let no opportunity for larceny pass. Sometime during the autumn, the OMO supply corps seized a valuable consignment of white fox skins belonging to a US company. Armored train commanders and other OMO officers regularly appropriated locomotives, coaches and boxcars belonging to the railway companies without warning. Robbery of refugees and the looting of villages near the railway continued unabated. Trains departing Transbaikalia were regularly shaken down before they crossed into Chinese territory.

On 24 and 25 October Semenov made his most audacious attempt at grand theft in Chita. An American supply train, guarded by Lieutenant Albert E. Ryan and a small detachment from the 31st Infantry Regiment, pulled into Chita at 5 a.m. on the 24th. The train was bound for Irkutsk with a large shipment of rifles, the second consignment of US arms for 'the fighting forces of Admiral Kolchak'.[44] Soon after his arrival, Lieutenant Ryan received a demand from OMO personnel to offload 15,000 of the rifles. Ryan refused and notified US Consul Henry Fowler. Fowler was not permitted to speak with Semenov, who was throwing a banquet for Japanese General Oi. He pressed the issue with Russian officials, and 'was informed by Semenov's Chief of Staff [Colonel Zubkovskii] that if the rifles were not delivered they would use Russian tactics and get them'. By the time Fowler returned to the American supply train, a *bronevik* had pulled alongside. A short time later, Ryan and his men felt a jolt as an OMO tender tugged their train into a military area of Chita's railyards. The *bronevik* and a battalion of Cossacks shadowed them. An ultimatum was served to Lieutenant Ryan advising him that the Cossacks would take the rifles by force if he did not relinquish them by 11 a.m. the next day.[45]

Major James C. Gravis, the RRSC division inspector, located Ryan's train in the evening and assured the young lieutenant that Semenov was bluffing. That night Major Gravis and Consul Fowler haggled with the Japanese staff for the safe passage of the train. OMO's deadline passed without incident the next morning, although Ryan and his men were still sweating it out in the railyard. Semenov tried to deceive the US detachment with a forged telegram – 'a custom not infrequently resorted to by them', noted Gravis – which changed Ryan's delivery orders. By the afternoon of 25 October the situation had been defused. At 4 p.m., US Consul Fowler and Major Gravis turned out at the railway station to pay respects to General Oi, who was heading east. Semenov and his staff were also present on the platform, sulking and growling at the Americans. In what seemed to be a subtle affront to the unruly Ataman, General Oi displayed warmth and cordiality to the Americans. 'I am very pleased to state', reported Major Gravis three days later, 'that General Oi paid us marked attention and, although the subject of this incident was not mentioned, he was extremely friendly and openly expressed his gratification on my efforts to improve the railroad and the successful handling of a number of unpleasant instances'.[46]

Partisans soon reminded Semenov that his true enemies were the Reds, not the Americans. On 6 November the partisans incited a revolt in Novo-Doronino on the Ingoda river that spread like wildfire through all of the villages on the upper Ingoda. The front had dissolved with Kolchak's army and reappeared piecemeal throughout Transbaikalia and the Far East.

The fall of Omsk

When dawn broke in Omsk on 10 November 1919 the Irtysh river had finally frozen solid enough to bear the weight of pedestrian traffic. All traffic rushed east, because that morning Supreme Ruler Kolchak ordered the evacuation of Omsk. Red partisans were operating freely on Omsk's western outskirts and the main body of the Red Army was just 40 miles away. The flight from Omsk would have begun several days earlier if the city's single bridge over the Irtysh – a railway bridge – could have handled wheeled vehicles or horses.[47] Indeed, the French and Japanese missions had quit the town two days before.[48] Wealthy families fled their mansions and villas with sleds full of valuables and currency to try to bribe their way onto departing trains. RRSC Lieutenant Colonel Ben O. Johnson departed on 12 November on the last Allied train.[49] From countless rancid hovels, bored in the dirt and haphazardly sheltered with planks, emerged swarms of refugees, pitiable, starved creatures uprooted from their pasts months before and hundreds of miles west, who now fled in rags, with no food and few, if any, belongings to barter. Soldiers abandoned a rich arsenal of artillery, automobiles, ammunition and other equipment and, trudged east, deeper into a wintery Siberia, abandoning 40 cannon, 897 machine guns, 3,000 wagons, 19 million cartridges, and 50,000 cattle – 'everything that Omsk's corrupt, inefficient Procurement Office had failed to send to the front'. They also left behind several generals and at least 10,000 fellow soldiers and officers.[50]

On 14 November, just one day before the 27th Division of the Red Army marched into Omsk unopposed, a convoy of one *bronevik* and six specially outfitted trains roared east with Supreme Ruler Kolchak, his mistress Madame A.V. Timireva, assorted bodyguards, staff and 35 railcars groaning with 20,000 precious pounds of the Imperial Gold Reserve.[51] With Kolchak's retreat, the Red Army and a whimsical *sudbina* – Fate – had just made Grigorii Mikhailovich Semenov the most powerful White authority remaining east of the Urals, though no one, not even the ataman himself, realized it yet.

The panic out of Omsk sent a jolt of fear through more than 1,000 miles of railway eastward to Irkutsk. On 9 November Kolchak had declared the railway to be under a 'state of siege' and ordered all employees mobilized. However, the Supreme Ruler's enforcers were too busy trying to make their way east to monitor railway workers, many of whom were also anxious to escape the Red apocalypse. Czechoslovak Legion trains and Allied specials breezed past the hopeless mobs trudging through the snowdrifts along the *trakt*, 'now a wide ribbon of trampled snow between two and five feet deep'.[52] Sub-freezing temperatures, starvation, wolves and human predators harvested a rich daily toll from the miserable multitude of eastbound humanity. Trains overloaded with Russian refugees rolled east until exhausted for lack of fuel and water, when their supposedly lucky passengers were sent into the barren taiga to gather scrap wood, if any remained, for the engine and stoves, and snow for the locomotives' boilers. Typhus, dysentery and madness ran rampant among the desperate families.[53] Corpses, mangled and scattered by wolves and wild dogs after each dusk, littered the *magistral* and *trakt*. One source estimated more than 1 million dead in the aftermath of Omsk's hasty evacuation.[54] Peter Fleming lamented, 'Misery and squalor and cowardice, pain and fear and cold, carrion and excrement – these were the ingredients of the White migration'.[55]

Friction between the Czechoslovak Legion and the Whites poisoned an already embittered relationship. The legion dominated most of the resources – locomotives, rolling stock, fuel and facilities – along the critical 500-mile stretch of railway between Omsk and Tomsk. It had been that way since spring 1919, when the Inter-Allied Railway Board allocated that sector to the Czechs for guard duty. The Czechoslovak units had begun their orderly evacuation long before the White's panic-stricken flight from Omsk, and they were determined not to be overrun by the Reds, even if they had to run over their Russian, Polish and Rumanian allies to make it to the ships at Vladivostok. *The Times* reported, 'The Czechs are alleged to have taken engines from hospital trains, leaving the sick to perish of cold or hunger'.[56]

Omsk's sudden collapse prompted a flurry of exhortations from Ataman Semenov to rally the population and Far Eastern Cossacks against the onrushing Red horde. In a more practical vein, on 20 November the ataman belatedly laid out the stipulations for widespread requisitioning of horses, promising their return after military duty or payment in case of death.[57] A few days later he issued an appeal to Tungus men to join Russia's 'young and glorious army'.[58]

News of Omsk's capture and the catastrophic retreat thrilled the Red underground in Russia's Far East. 'An electric current ran through the entire partisan front from the Vladivostok hills to the Amur', wrote Anatoli Gutman, a Russian journalist in Japan. Partisan detachments that had been taking potshots at Amur steamboats since midsummer migrated downriver towards the mouth on the Sea of Okhotsk. One after another, villages accepted Bolshevik rule, influenced by propaganda and firing squads. In December Cossacks of the village of Kiselevka boldly voted to reject Bolshevik demands and sent a delegation to Nikolaevsk-on-Amur to request assistance. The White and Japanese garrisons there paid no heed to their petition. Soon Nikolaevsk itself was surrounded by Yakov Triapitsyn's sordid army of 'the oppressed and the insulted', thirsting to wallow in Lenin's class hatred and grab a bit of booty in the process.[59]

Gajda's plot against the Whites

In Vladivostok, the collapse of the front lines, the sudden fall of Omsk, and Kolchak's imminent Waterloo caused a great deal of uneasy shuffling among the many militarist factions. On 13 November General Semenov-Merlin, the 'principal assistant' of General Sergei

Rozanov, told the American Expeditionary Force commander that the 'Cossacks desire to let the past die...and establish friendly relations with the Americans'. He added that Ataman Semenov was dispatching a representative to discuss mutual plans for the future.[60] Major General Graves wrote, 'I told him I would see Semenov's representative, but they might just as well know that I would have nothing to do with murderers'.[61]

By mid-November, the Supreme Ruler's whereabouts were uncertain, and his future and that of his government even more so. Nevertheless, General Rozanov, Kolchak's iron-fisted commander in Vladivostok, was determined to cling to power. He poised 4,000 of Kalmykov's mercenaries on the outskirts of the city to prepare for trouble, and obtained Major General Knox's approval to mobilize 1,000 cadets then being trained by British officers on Russian Island. Knox's approval signalled the seriousness of the situation considering that the local British commander in Vladivostok, Colonel Blair, had politely refused a similar request from Rozanov in mid-September.[62]

Rumors had circulated widely since late September that democratically minded men of the Czechoslovak Legion were plotting against the Russian militarists. On 3 October General Romanovskii, a prominent White in Vladivostok, informed an American staff officer that the young Czechoslovak Legion hero General Radola Gajda had accepted 70,000 francs for travel expenses to depart Siberia, but was investing this money on 'a conspiracy against the Kolchak Government'.[63] Kolchak had given Gajda command of the Siberian Army early in 1919, but then dismissed him as White defeats multiplied. They parted with angry words on 15 July and Gajda, surrounded by a heavily armed bodyguard to prevent his seizure by Kolchak, had been sulking in Vladivostok ever since.[64] Some militarists later accused Major General Graves of financing a Czechoslovak Legion revolt against Rozanov's administration in Vladivostok, at which the Texan chuckled, 'How little they knew about the accounting system of the United States Government!'[65] However, the Americans' made no effort to hide their sympathy for local democratic forces and on occasion had even raised their weapons to defend them. For instance, on 21 September AEFS Colonel Johnston positioned a US detachment to prevent Rozanov's forces from overrunning the 'known headquarters of the CBMO at Vladivostok'.[66]

During the evening of 16 November General Gajda led a few hundred (estimates say 200 or 300) armed Russians out of the Vladivostok railyards to overthrow General Rozanov and the White militarist cliques. For these rebels, it was the last chance to establish a democratic toehold in Russia. A former chairman of the Siberian provincial duma, Pavel Yakushev, optimistically agreed to head the new administration; he declared that the uprising's goal was to establish a 'people's government'. Gajda's men wore green and white ribbons on their epaulets – the colors of autonomous Siberia – to distinguish them from General Rozanov's soldiers. They took over the cutter *Farvater* in the Bay of Bosphor, embarked 100 rebels who intended to land at the pier of the White fleet, but then ran aground and all aboard were captured. Another group of rebels overran the telegraph offices but failed to apprehend General Rozanov in his headquarters at the Great Customs House.

Both atamans, Semenov and Kalmykov, rushed men to Vladivostok to shore up General Rozanov's positions. A Kalmykov *bronevik* appeared in town on the night of 16 November, and fighting broke out around Vladivostok's railway station early the next morning. A green and white Siberian flag fluttering over Gajda's armored headquarters train in the city railyard became the center of a revolt that, at times, played out through a torrential rain. 'A feverish recruiting of volunteers as well as the delivery of arms was going on near Gajda's train', reported the *China Press*. 'The greater part of Gajda's volunteers consisted of deserters, both officers and men, of war prisoners, Chinese stevedores, workmen, some acknowledged Bolsheviks and a handful of Czechoslovaks...Altogether Gajda succeeded in recruiting some 1,500 men.'[67]

After sunset on 17 November Japanese Admiral Kawahara illuminated rebel targets for the White artillery with the searchlights of his warship *Hizen* and torpedo boats. Japanese troops also formed a ring around the city to contain the rebels and captured 'scores of Gajda's men'. The Japanese also provided guard details for the Whites' most vulnerable targets like the jail, and, according to papers later found among General Rozanov's effects, 'The families of the officers who were especially hated by Gajda's followers were taken under Japanese protection'.[68] The British shipped over the cadets from Russian Island with some artillery to boot. A steady hail of bullets and shells thundered over Vladivostok all night long. By sunrise, Gajda's rebellion had been extinguished. No less than 300 rebels lay dead, and many more were to join them shortly. Most who surrendered were executed on the spot. The British-trained cadets ambled through Gajda's field hospital, shooting the wounded like vermin. Gajda was lucky; he was only wounded in the foot and when arrested aboard the steamship *Pechanga* that morning, he was only beaten unconscious and given 24 hours to leave Siberia.

On 20 November a small notice in an obscure corner of the Vladivostok newspaper noted, 'The day before yesterday the wind drove a corpse ashore in the bay of Zolotoi Rog. The corpse was identified as former Chairman Yakushev, organizer of the mutiny'. By this time Rudolf Gajda was well on his way to a comfortable, if disconcerting, recovery at Shanghai's Palace Hotel. The public executions of Gajda's rebels and sympathizers continued into January.

Also on 20 November, partisans struck Aleksandrovskii Zavod, one of the largest towns in eastern Transbaikal province, capturing large quantities of men, weapons and other equipment. Semenov's position looked perilous to all but him.

Panic on the Trans-Siberian

To Semenov's avaricious eyes, the miserable horde of refugees and soldiers trudging in his direction from Omsk may have seemed a godsend that offered the Supreme Ruler's scepter, not to mention whatever loot they may have squirreled away to trade for their safety. As early as mid-September, Chita's police chief estimated that refugees had distended the city's population one and a half times, and the bulk of the fleeing families had not yet staggered into Transbaikalia.[69]

The refugees now looked to the ataman's Transbaikal fiefdom as a sanctuary. A few days before the evacuation, on 5 November, the ataman had received a plea for help – in the 'single voice of Cossackism' – from an Omsk conference representing the remnants of ten Cossack armies from the Caspian Sea to the Pacific.[70] After Gajda's mid-November defeat, White generals and Japanese officers in Vladivostok expected Semenov to take the reins of Supreme Ruler any day.

An eastbound shipment of two freightcars full of gold had whetted Semenov's appetite; he grabbed it in Chita on 8 November, declaring that he did not want to see Russia's treasure doled out to the Allies. This was probably a 2,000-*pood* (approximately 36-ton) consignment from the imperial gold reserve that included 550 boxes of coins and more than 800 gold ingots from the International Commerce Bank, Russo-Asiatic Bank and other financial powerhouses. To Semenov's credit, he spend a small portion of this fortune on the immediate purchase of supplies for OMO, gave about 300,000 rubles to Ungern-Shternberg for Pan-Mongolian operations, and some time later gave about 200,000 rubles to 'the Serpukhov Regiment'.[71]

Meanwhile, the dreadful conditions along the Trans-Siberian Railway between Omsk and Tomsk magnified each day. At Krasnoyarsk on 16 November, RRSC Major F.A. Flanagan noted, 'Many of the Kolchak Officers have taken off their shoulder insignia. Number of Kolchak Officers and Militiamen [i.e. policemen] trying to get space to travel east. Many posters put up in town reassuring people, etc.'[72] Krasnoyarsk's bankers and furriers quit town en masse two days later. With the avalanche of eastbound trains clogging the railway's double tracks, no trains could possibly budge west to resupply depleted fuel stocks. Regardless, the trickle of coal from nearby mines could never have satisfied the dramatic surge in demand from the wheezing gaggle of fleeing locomotives. The miners, 'having neither food nor clothing, nor their salaries having been paid', were not inclined to increase their output.[73] Doomed children aboard Russian trains pressed their noses against the windows to watch Czechoslovak Legion echelons, accused (usually unjustly) of housing brothels and being crammed full of booty, bully ahead of them. The heavy traffic and severe Siberian winter caused widespread equipment failures that the remaining railway employees were unable to repair. Breakdowns and fuel shortages stranded trains in the desolate taiga. Without food or warmth, the crowded *taplushkas* became communal coffins on wheels. Freezing passengers sometimes burned entire trains to keep warm while waiting for help that never arrived.[74] At the rear of the woeful procession, the Red Army was overtaking 10–20 refugee trains per day, dooming the wives and children of White soldiers aboard. Of 300 or so refugee trains which departed the Omsk region, only about 70 ever made it to Irkutsk.[75]

By late December, it was widely rumored that Admiral Kolchak himself had urged Semenov to blow up the Lake Baikal tunnels to force the Czech Legion to turn around, fight the Bolsheviks and protect the refugees. Heated controversy would swirl around the question of this purported order's mere existence for years.[76] Regardless, the Czechs were ready to fight to go home, but not willing to fight the Russians' war anymore.

On 18 December, the day after Supreme Ruler Kolchak's gold-laden echelons creaked through the city of Krasnoyarsk (about 150 miles east of Tomsk), the city's garrison mutinied and partisans moved in. In the Far East that same day, partisans seized a portion of the Ussuri Railway along the Khabarovsk–Vladivostok line as US troops began departing (the first outbound US transport had sailed for Manila the previous day). Throughout eastern Siberia and the Far East, partisan groups seemed to arise spontaneously out of a vengeful population. What ideologies they espoused, if any, were ambiguous, but they yearned to eliminate the White brigands that preyed upon them and to humiliate and rob the *burzhui* (bourgeoisie) that had enjoyed White protection. Yakov Ivanovich Triapitsyn, a former metalworker and army veteran, started out down the Amur river from Khabarovsk in November 1919 with ten men. Triapitsyn whipped up mobs into a bloodthirsty frenzy with his cries 'Skunks! Counterrevolutionaries! Shoot them!' leaving unspoken the commands to rob, rape, humiliate, torture and murder the oppressive *burzhui*, and then lead 'a free and easy life' under Bolshevism.[77] By the time this Red Pied Piper reached the sea, a 400-mile march from Khabarovsk through the Amur's frozen marshes and windswept valleys, 1,500 Russians, 300 Chinese and 200 Koreans had joined him.[78]

On 19 December, name day of the deceased tsar, a congregation of Cossacks and civilians heard a requiem sung in Chita's cathedral, while partisans were wiping out the 4th Semenov Regiment at Kungurovo, in eastern Transbaikalia.[79] In the western leg of the province south of Verkhne-Udinsk, General Levitskii and OMO's *Dikaya Divizia* – the Wild Division – were embarking upon a 'punitive campaign' down the Selenga River valley to hunt down and exterminate a growing infestation of partisans. While Levitskii was butchering Russians in the Selenga River valleys, more often than not innocent civilians rather than partisans, Semenov continued complaining that the Czech Legion would not protect Russians in the Trans-Siberian evacuation.

Just a few hundred miles west of Levitskii's rampage, the Red Army and partisans continued overrunning scores of exhausted and terrified White units each day. By 10 December, when the Czechoslovaks took Admiral Kolchak's locomotives, stranding him at Mariinsk for four days, the Supreme Ruler could not even muster the tangible power to keep his own train moving. When Kolchak's trains finally resumed their retreat, they were forced by the Czechoslovak Legion and General Maurice Janin to relinquish their express track to the foreigners' echelons and creep east on the parallel track which was clogged by overloaded, breakdown-prone refugee trains. The switch was enforced at gunpoint by a Czechoslovak armored train.[80] It was probably during the second week in December that Kolchak asked Semenov if he could spare troops to buttress the unreliable garrison in Irkutsk. For the next two weeks, General Syrobiarskii, Semenov's envoy on Kolchak's escape train, badgered the admiral to promote the ataman to commander-in-chief of the Far East and the Chinese Eastern Railway zone.[81] Obviously Semenov (and his associates in Japanese intelligence) grossly underestimated the fury of the approaching Red storm, and blindly considered the catastrophe unfolding all around to be merely another opportunity for promotion and enrichment. 'The Japanese were very much interested in getting Semenov and Kolchak together. Their object was to have Kolchak recognize Semenov and raise him in rank [to lieutenant general] and appoint him to some important position, thereby greatly increasing his influence in the Transbaikal District and elsewhere [i.e. Mongolia and China]', wrote 1st Lieutenant Davidson, the US intelligence officer at Chita.[82]

Even the Czechoslovaks were showing desperation now. In mid-December General Jan Syrovy, 'a bleak, plodding sort of man' with an eye-patch, ordered the takeover of the Trans-Siberian Railway east of the Ob river, replacing all Russian station commanders with Czechoslovaks who would pass legion trains ahead of the others, guaranteeing them priority on the tracks and for precious fuel. Of course, this meant death for many aboard eastbound refugee trains, and had the immediate effect of serving up 120 civilian and hospital train echelons west of Novonikolaevsk to the Red Army for looting and purging of officers, priests and '*burzhui* parasites' of all ages and genders. More accusations that the comfortable Czechoslovak Legion echelons were loaded with booty and prostitutes fueled animosity with the Russians and other evacuees.[83]

The horror along the *magistral* became so compelling that it roused indignation in Ataman Semenov, who, on 20 December, appealed publicly to General Jan Syrovy, 'in the name of Slav brotherhood and in the name of humanity', to suspend the Czechoslovak Legion's own evacuation until that of the Russian civilians and remnants of Omsk's armies was complete, and to provide security for the Russian evacuation. After several lines of histrionics, Semenov closed his appeal with a threat that he would attack if his 'Czechoslovakian brothers' did not help his old foe Kolchak.[84] A day or two later he voiced a complaint to the Inter-Allied Railway Committee on behalf of Russia's downtrodden, justly accusing the Czechoslovaks of creating 'deplorable disorder in the evacuation of numerous trains with [Russian] refugees, sick and wounded'.[85] Again he threatened 'armed force' if they did not comply. For once, the ataman could take a genuinely righteous stand, if only because no one else of any consequence spoke up for the innocent multitudes dying alongside the tracks east of Omsk. However, his vile reputation rendered his voice meaningless. A reply to Semenov's threat to the Czechoslovak Legion was telegraphed on 22 December, signed by Jan Syrovy but, in reality, drafted by French General Maurice Janin, expressing 'fraternal esteem' for the ataman's 'gallantry and military prowess' while promising 'sword in hand, to cut our way through his territory'.[86]

Finally, upon hearing that a Socialist-Revolutionary revolt was underway in Irkutsk, Admiral Kolchak issued orders Nos. 240 and 241 on 23 December, granting Semenov his precious promotion to lieutenant general and appointing him 'chief of the Irkutsk, Transbaikal and Amur military districts'.[87] For Kolchak it was a deal with the devil, bargaining away any hope of peaceful accommodation with the socialists in Irkutsk in exchange for rescue by his nemesis Semenov. However, the ataman was White Russia's last hope now that the Czechoslovaks and Allies thought only of home and evacuation. To save Russia, Semenov had to take and hold Irkutsk.

Battle of Irkutsk

A group of socialists in Irkutsk chose 23 December to stage an overthrow of the local administration. They had formed their group in November and called it *Polit-Tsentr*, the Political Center, although its carefully tended cultivation by the Czechoslovak Legion lent it an artificial air.[88] The Political Center realized that Kolchak's hated dictatorship had to be replaced as soon as possible with some semblance of democracy to regain popular support and declared its agenda to be 'the liquidation of counterrevolutionary activity in the Far East by such men as Semenov, Kalmykov and Rozanov, and the immediate conclusion of peace and the reaching of a permanent agreement with Soviet Russia'.[89] Supreme Ruler Kolchak was stranded on the congested railway west of Nizhne-Udinsk, 300 miles away. Nevertheless, his secret police rounded up about 150 personalities of the Irkutsk opposition in an effort to nip the coup in the bud.[90] Ironically, the fate of those prisoners would eventually determine the fate of the Supreme Ruler himself.

Meanwhile, railway workers chose this time to try to launch a sit-down strike to demonstrate their solidarity with the Political Center. Of course Ataman Semenov promptly made it clear that anyone foolish enough to join would pay dearly. 'I will act not only against them [the strikers]', he promised on 23 December, 'but against [their] families'.[91]

The following day the ataman declared himself commander-in-chief of all armed forces in the Far East. His telegram's distribution list showed how perilously small his command had become: Irkutsk commander; Commandant of Vladivostok Fortress and local commander; Ataman Kalmykov in Khabarovsk; Ataman Kuznetsov in Blagoveshchensk; General Levitskii in Sretensk; General Artomonov in Nerchinskii Zavod; General Missyuri at Verkhne-Udinsk (Beresovka); Colonel Lvov at Troitskosavsk and General Horvath in Harbin.[92] Semenov promptly replaced the Irkutsk garrison commander, General Artem'ev, 'who had presided over a relatively benign military regime', with General Sychev, a former Transbaikal Cossack ataman and diehard *semenovets*.[93]

During the night of 24 December the 53rd Siberian Regiment, 'smartly dressed in [new] British uniforms', proclaimed its allegiance to the Political Center.[94] Eyewitness Paul Dotsenko credited Captain N.S. Kalashnikov, 'former head of the Information Division of the Urals Army' and a leader of the secret military opposition group CBMO, with leading the 53rd's rebellion, convening a meeting at the regimental headquarters at 10:30 p.m. where Kalashnikov exhorted them to 'dispense with the bloodthirsty government of Kolchak and his Cabinet of Speculators'. Soon after the 53rd Regiment joined Kalashnikov's People's Revolutionary Army, three other units followed suit: the 1st and 3rd Irkutsk Territorial Brigades and the 38th Transbaikal Infantry.[95] The Angara river separated the southside railway district known as Glazkov, where the 53rd Regiment's barracks were located, from the heart of Irkutsk. Normally a pontoon bridge, 'held in place by strong guy ropes', spanned the Angara, but the river was churning with hunks of ice and sludge, so the fragile bridge was out of service until the river's surface solidified into a frozen plain.[96] The only opposition facing the 53rd Regiment on the south side of the Angara was an OMO *bronevik*. However, the rebels enjoyed the element of surprise, and quickly disarmed and arrested the OMO officers and men, and took over the *bronevik*, all without fighting or bloodshed.[97] Two other chance advantages favored the rebels: the Czechoslovak Legion controlled the railway station and was determined to prevent any interference with their own evacuation, and a 'special' transporting US Consul General Harris and the British, French and Japanese high commissioners from Omsk was sitting in the railyard.

THE WHITE COLLAPSE BEGINS

Despite the mutiny, Irkutsk seemed to drowse under her blanket of snow through 25 December. Only the surreal groans of the mutating Angara split the air, as the mighty river agonizingly froze in the deadly cold. After 7 p.m. streets emptied of everyone but an occasional sentry, mounted patrol, or Allied official. The Allied high commissioners, US Consul General Ernest Harris among them, shared a Christmas dinner in their train, praying, no doubt, to continue on to Vladivostok as soon as possible. That night, however, Japanese and White commanders, identified as 'Mikki and [General P.T.] Vagin', worked out plans for a joint action to subdue the rebels.[98] Accordingly, Lieutenant General Inagaki, the Japanese chief of staff in Vladivostok, had informed the American command that Japan was dispatching a battalion of infantry, an artillery section, a cavalry platoon and a team of engineers to Mysovaya and Kultuk to 'maintain communications east of Irkutsk'.[99] The acting chairman of the White council of ministers, A. Cherven-Vodali, published an appeal to the troops that implied that the ataman would soon arrive to put down the rebellion:

OFFICERS AND SOLDIERS!
The enemies of the country try to tempt you with peace. They will not give you peace. They will give you famine, privation, plunder and atrocities. Once having believed in their proclamations, you will ruin even those who, up to the present time, have honestly done their duty at the front. To whom can uprisings now be of advantage except the Bolsheviks? Is it possible that you, like Judas, betray those unfortunates who still struggle against the Bolsheviks at the front? No! You will not prove yourselves traitors! Sooner or later a certain force will come from the east – a force that will help you to defend order in the country, and which will save you from Bolshevism and starvation. Remember that the bread we now receive comes from the east...[100]

At 10 a.m. on 26 December, General Janin, the French officer overseeing the Czech evacuation, was informed of the impending Japanese–White attack against the rebels. Two batteries of light artillery had been ordered to set up on the north bank to bombard the 53rd Regiment. General Janin promptly notified the Japanese command of the presence of the Allied diplomatic missions and a 'large number of Czech troops' in the railyard. If fired upon, the Czechs would return fire. This news put Japanese Ambassador Kato in 'a very excited state', and he rushed to call upon General Janin. An afternoon conference of Japanese, French and Czechoslovak representatives 'agreed to have the Czechs take and protect the railway station and vicinity under their guard, proclaiming it a neutral zone and also to place Czech soldiers to guard the tunnels around Lake Baikal.'[101]

For the time being, the Whites in north Irkutsk seemed powerless to crush the rebellion across the river. Kolchak representatives opened negotiations with the Political Center on 26 December, even though White security forces continued arresting suspects.[102] The Whites did not negotiate in good faith. From Slyudyanka station at the west end of the Baikal tunnels came information from Czech troops and 'an American [RRSC] dispatcher' that two Semenov *broneviki* would embark for Irkutsk as soon as a Cossack echelon arrived.[103]

On 27 December, leaflets blowing in Irkutsk streets bore an ominous message from the ataman:

The mutineers hiding under the name of the much suffering Russian people have again taken up their hideous business and opened up a new civil front against the government. I herewith order to take all possible measures to hold out until the arrival of a detachment of the 'Wild Division' under the command of Major General Skipetrov, whom I have given the categorical order once and for all to put an end, mercilessly, to all those villains, who, taking advantage of Russia's desperate situation, again repeat the blunders of the past.[104]

Skipetrov's Wild Division detachment was composed of two cavalry regiments, two infantry regiments and three armored trains.[105] Irkutsk residents knew him from a 'bloody suppression of disturbances in town during December 1917 [that] had earned a place in local folklore'.[106] Behind Skipetrov trailed no less than a 'half battalion of Japanese infantry'.[107]

'In view of this', reported the Czech Legion information service, 'the Diplomatic Representatives of the Allies appealed in writing to the Commander of the Czech Troops [General Jan Syrovy] to use all necessary means, including even armed force, to prevent any of the armed forces from conducting operations against the railway station or the railway itself at Irkutsk in view of the presence of the Allied Diplomatic Missions'.[108] The city's population surely longed for an end to the standoff. Paul Dotsenko wrote,

> Paper money became worthless, essential products vanished from the markets and fuel was scarce. At this time I was living with my wife and child on the shores of the Angara river not far from the pontoon bridge leading to Glazkov station [Irkutsk's main Trans-Siberian depot]. Every second day I walked to the neighboring village for a bottle of milk for our daughter, and my wife washed diapers in the Angara's icy waters while bullets whistled overhead.[109]

During the night of 27 December, troops loyal to the Political Center stealthily crossed the Angara east of White-occupied Irkutsk, and circled the sleeping city before swarming in from the west. Sporadic rifle and machine gun fire traced their progress into the city. By midnight they held the central telegraph office and a large section of the city to the west. Two companies of Kolchak's infantry killed their officers and went over to the rebels.[110] With help from Japanese Army units, the Whites forced the rebels to retreat several blocks. According to one unconfirmed report, Political Center troops captured Major General Sychev, the Irkutsk garrison commander.[111]

On 28 December a rebel airplane circled about making observations, and light artillery fire rattled north Irkutsk. On the south side of the Angara, Political Center rebels removed segments of the railway tracks a few *versts* from Irkutsk station to slow Semenov's approach. The Czechs offered to repair the tracks and 'to clear the station of all armed forces with the exception of the station militia'. However, the stranded Allied diplomats were far from unanimous in their stance toward the Russian rebels and reactionaries. US Consul General Harris and British representatives would have been happy to see Semenov's soldiers quash the rebels, but the rest of the diplomatic corps outweighed them.[112] About this time the Czechs intercepted a telegram from the commander of Semenov's Armored Train Division at Listvenichnoe to Major General Sychev in Irkutsk: 'We are moving on Irkutsk and would have been there long ago but the Allies are energetically protesting. Yesterday they kept our trains from moving beyond Mikhailevo [15 miles east of Irkutsk].'[113]

By 10 a.m. on the morning of 29 December revolutionary forces had regained their momentum and took the bazaar and adjacent streets. The demoralized Whites were gradually losing their hold on the city, even though they enjoyed the full support of Japanese troops. That night ten OMO *broneviks* and trains and one Japanese train appeared on the tracks south of Irkutsk.

About 8:40 a.m. on 30 December an OMO *bronevik* pulled within one-quarter mile of Glazkov station and began lobbing shells haphazardly into the railyard. Twenty minutes later it began rolling towards the yard, guns blazing. The revolutionaries were ready. They powered up a light switch engine and turned it loose on the rails towards the charging *bronevik*. The two trains crashed a few hundred yards east of the switches.

After a short lull, OMO General Skipetrov sent several hundred troops charging into the railway yard, blasting away with 'dum dum and explosive bullets'.[114] They set up machine guns at the east end of the train station and on streets leading to the nearby pontoon bridge. A fierce battle ensued. Throughout the afternoon fighting raged around the station and between the railway cars lined up in the yard. In one of the few incidents where air power saw combat in eastern Siberia, the rebels' aircraft managed to drop 'a few bombs' atop the OMO onslaught. Pockets of White resistance on the north side of the Angara tried to bring their guns to bear upon rebel positions around the railway station. An OMO officer and five men burst into the station telegraph office only to be ordered out by a Czech officer. The rebel forces were never seriously threatened by Skipetrov's ill-conceived tactics. They moved into concealed positions in hills overlooking the yards and fired down upon Skipetrov's men. The railyard became a shooting gallery and the rebel snipers easily picked off the poorly trained OMO soldiers. About 3 p.m. detachments of Cheremkhovo miners and Bolshevik partisans 'loyal to Kalandarashvili and Zverev' arrived to reinforce the Political Center troops. When the badly mauled OMO force tried to withdraw, the rebels swooped down from the hills, and surrounded and captured 200 of them, as well as 300 rifles and three machine guns. A number of the captured OMO soldiers turned out to be Germans and Hungarians shanghaied from prisoner of war camps, as well as 64 Chinese and Mongols. Most of the ethnic Russians among the OMO prisoners declared that they were forced into Semenov's service.[115] About 100 OMO men lay dead in and around Glazkov station and 80 were wounded. The revolutionaries claimed to have lost only five men killed.[116] By 4 p.m. Skipetrov's assault turned into a rout, and the surviving OMO soldiers scurried east to the safety of their waiting *broneviki*.

On the night of 30 December the Bolsheviks wangled the release of Ivan Nikolaevich Brusak from the local prison. Inasmuch as the Political Center feared the arrival of the Red Army almost as much as the Whites did, it seems that the movement's leaders did not realize the extent to which Irkutsk's rebels had already been infiltrated by Bolsheviks. Brusak was a principal Bolshevik organizer, a 24-year-old Red Army commander wizened by two and a half years of intense revolutionary experience. He had been among the gray mobs of rebellious soldiers in Petrograd that stoked the February Revolution, joined the Bolshevik Party in August 1917, participated in the October Revolution, enlisted in the Red Army two months later, and commanded a unit in Siberia until his capture in May 1918. After 14 months incarcerated in Tomsk, he made a breath-taking escape from an eastbound 'death train' at Slyudyanka, and, with remarkable ease, made contact with the Bolshevik underground in Irkutsk via acquaintances from prison. Since mid-summer 1919, he had been coordinating with Bolshevik cells and preparing for the inevitable battle, gathering 'rifles, cartridges, grenades, and several times even machine guns through Czechs, Rumanians and other soldiers from interventionist units, and even through soldiers of Kolchak's army'. A Czech-speaking railway employee at Irkutsk station arranged arms purchases for Brusak, and a Socialist-Revolutionary officer serving in the White headquarters assisted with the 'difficult and dangerous' business of machine gun smuggling, once through the city center under the noses of Czechoslovak counterintelligence. Nevertheless, White counterintelligence apprehended Brusak in September 1919, but other Bolsheviks picked up where he left off and continued organizing. Finally free of the prison's dank, typhus-ridden cells on 30 December, Brusak made his way to the Irkutsk suburb or Znamenskii, where the underground Bolshevik committee headed by Aleksandr Shiryamov made its headquarters. Brusak was given command of a 250-man detachment of workers and peasants on the Ushakovka river, nominally answering to a Socialist-Revolutionary Captain Reshetin, but in fact reporting to Shiryamov.[117]

On 31 December Ataman Semenov telegrammed Lieutenant General Artem'ev, the Irkutsk military region commander, that units of Skipetrov's Wild Division were coming to the rescue.[118] After the 30 December debacle at Glazkov station, OMO had rarely ventured beyond Mikhailevo station, 15 miles east of Irkutsk. On the north side of the Angara, pockets of loyal White troops persisted as the 'Bolshevik calendar' rolled into the new year – 1920. Their situation worsened each hour, even though General Skipetrov managed to send some 200 OMO reinforcements across the Angara on 31 December. They entered the city through the Amur Gates and went to the Hotel Moderne, where they were warmly greeted by representatives of the Kolchak government. They shortly proceeded to the Japanese headquarters, 'where they were greeted by a Japanese captain who stated that he was a former *semenovets* and welcomed them to the city, hoping they would soon restore law and order in Irkutsk'.[119] 'Several trains' of Japanese troops arrived on New Year's Day, but they stated that their sole purpose was to escort foreign consular trains east and not to partake in the waning battle for the city. Also that day, OMO riflemen maliciously opened fire on a Czech Legion work detail that was clearing the tracks of the wrecked *bronevik* and rebel switch engine, killing four Czechs.

White morale and discipline were vanishing as fast as firewood and food. An RRSC major came upon 'an indifferent crew of Kolchak men' in Cathedral Square haphazardly firing a 3-inch gun. 'Gun is not anchored and turns half around when fired', observed the major, 'after which the crew point the gun "out west" and fire again in a few minutes, doing no particular damage that I know of, except one ill-directed shot did hit the American Hospital and kill five Czechs'.[120] West of Mikhailevo, General Skipetrov had wisely pulled up the tracks to hamper any Czechoslovak or Red assaults on his fainthearted force.

In past days, the 54th Regiment had gone over to the rebels and an ataman of the Irkutsk Cossacks had refused to fight.[121] An armistice went into effect at 12 p.m., on 3 January. By 10 p.m. on the 4 January, Kolchak representatives called off the armistice and further negotiations with the Political Center, and began deserting the city in automobiles, following the Angara for several miles out of town to a rendezvous with a boat that carried them across the river to Semenov's trains. Shortly after the departure of the White government that night, an OMO company began looting the state bank. They made off with 40 pounds of gold before a Czech armored car and Japanese soldiers arrived on the scene (the night before, 15 boxes of gold had allegedly been stolen from Kolchak's gold train). The Allied troops retrieved a large amount of paper currency from the OMO thieves and thwarted further looting.[122]

'The looting of the bank by Semenov troops hastened the uprising of the remainder of the city's officers and men of the Jaegerski Regiment', reported Lieutenant Colonel F.B. Parker, the RRSC's district inspector. The White soldiers may also have received word that Kolchak resigned as Supreme Ruler earlier that day. Major General Sychev, the Irkutsk garrison commander, had 'left his quarters...after removing his furniture and valuables'.[123] Large numbers of war-weary White soldiers arrested their officers.[124] Allied troops began policing the city until the new Political Center government could bring their troops under control.

Admiral Kolchak and his echelons of staff officers and treasure had been stalled 300 miles west of Irkutsk at Nizhne-Udinsk since 24 December. Their chances of escaping east diminished when Nizhne Udinsk's beleaguered White garrison agreed to a truce with the town's growing convocation of partisans on 2 January 1920, and began deserting in earnest.[125] The following night the garrison commander himself departed after failing in an attempt to empty the state bank.[126] Kolchak's echelons were whittled down as his power diminished; some

White staff officers who escaped falling into custody of the partisans set out across Mongolia's harsh steppes for the safety of China. By the time he departed Nizhne-Udinsk on 7 January even his rail caravan had gone the way of his bygone power and been reduced to a single railcar (the precious gold reserves had already gone on to Irkutsk under guard of the 6th Czech Regiment). To ensure his safe passage, Admiral Kolchak's locomotive flew the flags of the United States, Britain, Czechoslovakia, France and Japan, signifying that it traveled under the assurance of Allied protection. However, the 'queer little foreign colony' of consuls and commissioners who had grudgingly inhabited the Glaskov railyard had happily moved on to the east.[127] Chaos stilled reigned along the Trans-Siberian: many remaining railway workers were on strike, and preceding trains full of refugees and retreating soldiers had dismantled many trackside buildings for firewood. During the week it took Kolchak's train to inch its way to the outskirts of Irkutsk, the political winds in eastern Siberia shifted suddenly and the world around the admiral changed dramatically.

A treasonous White commander and murders on Baikal

Several thousand White troops were plodding east under the command of General Vladimir Oskarovich Kappel in a tragic 'ice march' that, for some, had begun weeks before and hundreds of miles west. On 6 January Kappel ordered all remaining White troops to retreat, avoiding cities and towns, which had mostly gone over to the Reds by this time. Kappel was a heroic and ultimately tragic figure among an officer corps tainted by the likes of Semenov, Kalmykov and the fiendish menagerie of OMO and OKO. Kappel had established a reputation as a 'dashing young cavalry colonel' of the Czech Legion in 1918, then served in the Samara People's Army to stave off the Reds along the Volga Front for several months.[128] When the retreat from Omsk began, General Kappel was commander of the 2nd Siberian Army, which had survived the past demoralizing months largely intact under his capable leadership. Kappel's sudden appointment to commander-in-chief of the tattered White armies occurred on 11 December 1919, two days after the young Pepelyaev brothers – Viktor, a schoolteacher who had become Kolchak's new premier just weeks before, and Anatoli, commander of the decimated 1st Siberian Army – temporarily arrested the previous commander-in-chief, General Konstantin Sakharov, at Taiga station, accusing him of being a 'bad influence' on Kolchak.[129]

The White retreat was an epic race to escape capture by the Reds and survive the trek, even for the generals on Kolchak's train. A lucky few managed to weasel onto the few passing trains evacuating Allied or Slavic legionnaires, but most White soldiers and refugees faced a long cold walk. Officers' epaulettes littered Krasnoyarsk streets like fallen leaves where 'at least 25,000' soldiers deserted to the Reds.[130] Suicide became a popular alternative. On the *magistral*, frozen limbs and torsos peppered the tracks, the remains of those who had found a moving train to throw themselves under, but to the frustration of many who wanted to kill themselves, the trains simply stopped coming.

Vladimir Kappel lived only six weeks as commander-in-chief of the White Siberian armies; he was doomed to die of frostbite on 27 January in a village west of Irkutsk. However, his legacy would live on for years in the Far East among roving bands of *kappel'evtsy* – the White outcasts he led out of the disastrous Omsk retreat.

The White strategy aimed at retreating from the Irkutsk region to regroup 'Kappel's Army' in Transbaikalia. However, a great many people in Irkutsk, including members of the Political Center, had no desire to succumb to the radical Bolsheviks and hoped that 'Kappel's Army' would turn and make a stand to defend their city. The character of the

Political Center's Irkutsk constituency tended to be democratic, and the general hope was to negotiate with the Bolsheviks for peace and autonomy. Soon after the Political Center victory in Irkutsk, the district information bureau issued a statement declaring, 'Zevereff has been appointed Minister of War in the new Government. He addressed the Soviet Government in a radio broadcast with a proposal to enter peace negotiations on condition that the Soviet Government recognizes autonomy in the territory under the authority of the new government'.[131]

By 5 January the fighting in Irkutsk had petered out. The rebels emerged to rejoice over their victory and momentary self-rule. RRSC Lieutenant Colonel Parker observed the festivities: 'About 1 p.m. the Revolutionary Army marched up the Bolshoi Ulitsa [Irkutsk's main boulevard] with Red flags flying and assembled at the Governor's mansion to celebrate their victory. Two of their leaders climbed up on the gate posts and made speeches, after which there was much cheering and some singing.'[132] Arrests of White officers and officials had already begun. Among those taken into custody were Colonel Smichnov, Irkutsk secret police chief, General Potapov, the 14th Division commander, and Acting Minister of Ways of Communication Larionov. Until the Bolsheviks arrived, the prisoners were not mistreated, and were allowed to receive blankets, pillows and food. The following day bulletins fluttered through city streets demanding the arrest of Kolchak himself.[133]

As the Whites withdrew from Irkutsk on the night of 4 January the small OMO force that plundered the state bank also took with them 'eighteen political leaders of the revolutionary party with a number of others'.[134] Interestingly, at least one Socialist-Revolutionary participant alleged that Major General Sychev, Irkutsk's White garrison commander, was also a 'Bolshevik intelligence agent', and that Sychev arranged for these hostages to be taken from prison, supposedly by replacing the Siberian Army guard at the prison with an OMO sentry.[135] The hostages included the prominent Socialist-Revolutionaries that were arrested when the Political Center revolt began. There were 30 men and one woman. 'Two former members of the Constituent Assembly, Pavel Mikhailov and Boris Markov', anti-Bolshevik leaders since 1918, were among them.[136] In the meantime, Red commander Ivan Brusak and his comrades began arresting high-ranking Whites.[137]

During the morning of 6 January OMO Lieutenant Colonel Sipailov, the sadist with the ever-twitching face, herded the hostages onto the *Angara* at Port Baikal. Generals Skipetrov and Sychev and Captain Grant, 'the renegade Englishman', also boarded her. In pre-war days, the *Angara's* first-class cabins and saloon were luxurious, second only to those of her larger sister, the *Baikal* (whose charred remains now rested on the lake's bottom). As evening fell the *Angara* pushed off from the quay and sliced through the ice in the direction of Listvenichnoye. Beneath her fang-like icicles and glistening coat of ice an agitated gang of *semenovtsy* had begun a drinking bout amid the worn velvet couches and other touches of faded elegance in her first-class saloon. A huge wooden mallet used to knock chunks of ice off the superstructure was brought inside and, one by one, the hostages were summoned up from their holding area in 3rd class, told to strip down to their underwear, then led into the saloon, where each was told that upon signing a document certifying that they received good treatment, they would be freed and given three days to leave Russia. Some were flogged for the Cossacks' amusement. All signed the document, but as each reached the top of the gangway leading from the saloon, his head was smashed in by the giant mallet wielded by a Cossack executioner. Nevertheless, many of the hostages were still alive when they were tossed over the stern into Baikal's icy black waters. Staff Captain Cherepanov, who had arrested many of the victims and one of the officers who presided over this gory amusement, recalled that *Angara* was crunching through ice five to seven inches thick, drowning the sounds of commotion and screams from the saloon.

Several days would pass before rumors of these murders floated back to Irkutsk, by which time the OMO crewmen had already sold the victims' clothing. When General Janin asked Semenov about the hostages, he could honestly say that none of them had been shot. Fairly or unfairly, this mass bludgeoning would weigh heavily against Admiral Kolchak when his day of judgment came.[138]

Meanwhile, back in Irkutsk, a railway engineer named Belotserkovyets was appointed the new minister of ways of communication. His first order of business was to prosecute dismissed White officials of his ministry for high treason. A coded telegram to RRSC headquarters on 8 January summarized the case:

> Evidence new government has found shows ministry responsible for concluding secret treaty with Japan by which Japan was to send a strong armed force to Irkutsk to assist Kolchak government and as compensation Japan was to receive Kamchatka and remaining half [of] Sakhalin Island and territory in Siberia [that] Japan troops hold at present time. Members of ministry also accepted 176,000 yen as personal bribe...[139]

The 'evidence' of such a desperate plot, if it actually existed, never seems to have been circulated. By this time, squads of Bolsheviks had arrested the chairman of the White council of ministers, A. Cherven-Vodali, Minister of Labor Shumilovskii, and General Matkovskii, former commander of the Omsk military region and a 'leader of punitive expeditions against partisan detachments'. These prisoners were sent to Novonikolaevsk for public trials.[140]

The Czechs' main concern was to evacuate some 180 Czechoslovak Legion echelons still strung out between Irkutsk and Krasnoyarsk, which was now behind the Red lines. Semenov did everything he could to impede their eastward movement. Since the uprising at Irkutsk began, OMO troops regularly cut Czech telegraph wires and prevented Czech echelons from moving into Transbaikalia. Railway employees who serviced Czechs trains at Port Baikal, Slyudyanka and other places were executed.[141]

Finally, friction between OMO and the Czechoslovak Legion sparked a shootout at Slyudyanka on 9 January. The previous day Semenov demanded that the Czechs relinquish 300 of their precious *taplushkas*, and apparently some OMO thugs at Slyudyanka tried to enforce the demand. Two Czechoslovak regiments quickly trounced a sizeable detachment of Skipetrov's Wild Division, killing 15 men, wounding 15 and capturing over 600. Nearby Japanese troops, who were also withdrawing eastward in several echelons, honored their officers' pledges to remain neutral and did not come to Semenov's rescue. The Czechs also seized four *broneviki*, a hospital train and an artillery train. The action ignited a chain of Czech assaults against every OMO position along the Lake Baikal line. When it was all over, the Czechoslovak Legion possessed all of the lakeside Trans-Siberian tracks from the town of Baikal to Mysovaya, and the danger of Semenov blowing up the tunnels, as he had often threatened to do, was finally eliminated.[142]

By this time Semenov realized that the mass evacuation into Transbaikalia was masking a large-scale infiltration by Red agents and partisans, and his tactical thinking turned from offensive measures to defensive. By the last week in December he had activated self-defense regiments in all departments of the Transbaikal Cossack Host, the last line of defense against the Red invaders and gangs of marauders that were suddenly pressing at the gates of Chita.[143]

8

RED ONSLAUGHT

January–April 1920

'I herewith announce that all the violators of the desire of the Russian people and the tools of Monsieur Bronshtein [Trotsky] will, in the future, not be shot, but that I will hang them.'

(Ivan Pavlovich Kalmykov, February 1920)

New Year in White Siberia

The year 1920 was not one to celebrate in White Siberia. The Red Army was pushing into eastern Siberia, Irkutsk had fallen to the Political Center, the Allies and Czechoslovaks were abandoning Russia, and partisans had taken over most of Amur province and predominated in rural areas of the Maritime province and eastern Transbaikal province. White Siberia had been reduced to shrinking pockets around Ataman Semenov's Chita and the Transbaikal railway line, Ataman Kalmykov's Khabarovsk, General Sergei Rozanov's Vladivostok and the Chinese Eastern Railway zone through northern Manchuria.

In Transbaikalia, the shock of the Political Center's success in Irkutsk incited a bloody backlash from nervous OMO officers, but also encouraged defiance from the Red underground and sympathetic workers and peasants anticipating a day of reckoning with the White bullies and their *burzhui* lapdogs. RRSC officers witnessed dreadful atrocities on the railway that were echoed throughout Semenov's realm of terror.

In Olovyannaya, RRSC Lieutenant H. Rattach observed the tempo of OMO violence quicken as Red pressure mounted from the west and the flow of distraught White refugees thickened. The horror commenced during the last week of December 1919, when an engineer received 25 lashes for 'dipping an engine'. Another engineer miraculously survived 200 lashes for selling a small quantity of his locomotive's firewood to buy bread (about this time, when a railway official's salary did not exceed 700 rubles, a pound of bread cost 300 'Siberian rubles' in better-supplied Manchuli).[1] The crew of *bronevik* 'Istrebitel' celebrated New Year's Day with a sadistic frenzy. 'On the night of 1 January 1920', reported Lieutenant Rattach, 'thirty men and two women were taken out of their homes at midnight, everything confiscated, taken to the armored train, without a trial taken across the [Onon River] bridge seventeen *versts*, stripped, placed on bank of river and shot...' Actually the victims were not so fortunate as to have been simply shot, but (based upon interrogations of captured 'Istrebitel' crew members shortly thereafter) were whipped, slashed with bayonets, then shoved into an icehole alive. 'On the same eve', continued Lieutenant Rattach, 'one of our staff men was given fifty lashes for delay to a train which was not his fault. Also several shop employees whipped but cannot procure any information as everyone is scared to death and in constant fear of whipping and execution'. One Olovyannaya woman was selected by 'Worker Yakovenko', raped by four or five OMO men, then murdered. Other victims surely escaped Rattach's eye that nightmarish New Year's Day. In subsequent days, 26 'railroad men' were executed and one died of a whipping administered by a 22-year-old OMO train commander.[2]

Similar roundups, executions and random whippings were occurring all along the Trans-Siberian Railway in Semenov's territory. Incidents in Adrianovka, Chita and Mogzon were documented only because RRSC officers happened to be bystanders.[3] In the cursed town of Dauria, the maniacal Baron Ungern-Shternberg orchestrated daily executions in 70–80-man batches. It seemed as if the tales of carnage from the most terrifying Buryat myths were being enacted by man.

In a discussion with Allied representatives in mid-December 1919, acting Prime Minister S.N. Tret'yakov made them shudder when he referred to Semenov as the Whites' 'last hope'.[4] However, Semenov was not rash and trod carefully when assuming power, perhaps being mindful of the need to maintain the appearance of legal continuity. On 10 January as chief of 'the Far Eastern [Transbaikal and Amur] and Irkutsk military regions', Lieutenant General Semenov took 'complete governmental authority over his entrusted territory'.[5] Three days later, Czech guards on Admiral Kolchak's railcar allowed 12 armed railwaymen adorned with red rosettes to stand watch over their high-level White prisoners. The following day the train pulled into Glaskov and as a 100-man Red Guard detachment waited and gaggles of Japanese soldiers watched, Czechoslovak officers, acting on orders of General Janin, turned over Kolchak's train to a Political Center guard. The Allies' empty promises of protection for the Supreme Ruler went no further than the colorful display of national flags fluttering gaily on his train. He and his companions were marched off to prison.[6]

Not until 20 January did Ataman Semenov take 'complete military and civil authority in all territory of the Russian eastern regions'. To the dismay of many Russians who had put stock in the democratic revolution and the Constituent Assembly, the latter pronouncement assumed inheritance of 'united Russian Supreme authority', which put Grigorii Mikhailovich Semenov at the head of Russia's White movement. It was, in effect, an assumption of the reins of the legitimate Russian government and Semenov's spokesmen prattled on with pronouncements and promises that mirrored the ataman's grand declarations when he 'liberated' Transbaikalia 18 months before. Two longtime associates, his supply chief, Lieutenant General Mikhail Afanas'ev and the manager of Transbaikal province, Sergei Afanas'evich Taskin, became the principal executives in Semenov's fragment of Russia.[7] The public and international community were shocked that a young Cossack warlord was the best that the White movement could offer Russia in her darkest moment of crisis.

By late January, however, the Allies cared little about White hopes and were simply concerned with getting out of Russia and washing their hands of the whole affair. The last Italians departed by mid-month. Allied reductions in force were measured by their decreasing occupation of railway equipment: 485 freight cars and 153 passenger cars on 20 January, down 326 cars in one month's time.[8] But while the Americans and other foreigners were anxiously boarding transports home, the Japanese prepared for an extended stay and tried various covert maneuvers to undermine the revolutionary administrations. Large numbers of Japanese reinforcements disembarked in Vladivostok each week. On 21 January 7,500 men landed to reinforce Japan's 13th Division and 'eight self-propelling armored cars' arrived later that week.[9] Two more transports disgorged 1,600 men on 5 February.[10]

Since the fall of Irkutsk, wild rumors, half-truths and wishful thinking sired numerous ominous reports trumpeting Ataman Semenov's imminent Waterloo. For instance, between 6 January and 23 January, *The Times* reported on various occasions that Semenov 'has retired from Chita and is asking for further reinforcements', that diplomatic missions were fleeing Chita, that OMO 'officers are reported as ready to throw up the sponge', and that the Buryats and other Mongols had deserted him. None of it was true.

In early January, Semenov was reported to have 'recruited' one General Hoffmann and 3,000 of Hoffmann's fellow German and Austrian prisoners of war, including 'numerous' officers from the Baltic provinces, some of whom even served on OMO's staff.[11] In mid-January, a senior Semenov staff officer, Colonel Zubkovskii, confided to a British officer that the ataman could only depend upon 'two companies and 300 cadets' in Chita, the latter serving and protecting Semenov's residence.[12] This was an understatement, but not far off the mark. 'There is an absolute deficiency of any internal unity [in OMO] whatsoever', reported American intelligence sources. 'The mobilized [conscripted] men serve most unwillingly.' OMO now comprised a total of 20,000 men, of whom 8,000 were fully equipped and only 4,000 were deemed 'reliable', mostly 'local Cossacks, Buryats [and] Kirgizes'.[13] Of these, 5,500 soldiers and 57 trains (armored and other) were available for immediate operations, including:

- the 1st and 2nd Manchurian Ataman Semenov's Regiments – about 2,700 men in six battalions;
- a 400-man Cossack detachment;
- a 100-man bodyguard, 40 of whom were Serbian mercenaries;
- the 1st and 2nd Ataman Semenov Cavalry Regiments of about 500 men in four divisions;
- a field artillery 'division' of ten 3-inch guns and 150 men;
- a heavy artillery 'division' of three 6-inch guns and three 8-inch guns and 100 men;
- Baron Ungern-Shternberg's 'Local Manchurian Division' at Dauria;
- Colonel Tierbach's 'Combined Manchurian Division' at Borzya;
- the Armored Train Division based at Adrianovka;
- a 'Field Police Service' of about 50 Serb mercenaries;
- a 120-man Yugoslavian Regiment (some estimates ranged up to 500 men);
- the Piskulich Detachment of 90 Serbian mercenaries;
- no less than eight *broneviki* in the Chita area alone.

The order of battle did not yet include the retreating units of Omsk's army, and Semenov's own army had undergone so many transformations, reorganizations and renamings that he had to issue a blanket affirmation for the proliferation of insignia, awards, decorations and orders of the Special Manchurian Detachment, 5th Priamur Corps, Separate Eastern Siberian Army, 6th Eastern Siberian Corps, Priamur Military Region, Chita Military Region, Transbaikal Military Region and High Command of the Far Eastern and Irkutsk Military Regions. In pragmatic anticipation of the casualties to come, in mid-January Semenov drafted all doctors up to the age of 55 and applauded fund-raising auctions for the Ataman Semenov Invalid Home in Chita.[14]

Chita was the destination of the pitiful multitude fleeing east from the Bolsheviks. The *magistral* was a frozen banquet for the Grim Reaper in January 1920, with Fate serving up a cornucopia of victims done in by frostbite, starvation, typhus, cholera, suicide, shells, bombs, bullets, bayonets, whipping chains and a wealth of torture utensils, among others. West of Irkutsk the Red Army swallowed up several miles of the Trans-Siberian Railway with some 10–20 refugee trains packed with hundreds of fleeing White families each day.[15] The Red 5th Army headquarters had advanced to Tomsk. The *trakt* between Irkutsk and the Red lines was an icy hell from which only walking ghosts emerged, babbling horror stories about parades of black-limbed refugees frozen in mid-stride by the fierce Siberian *buran*.[16] It was one of the coldest winters in recent memory with temperatures plunging to nearly −75°F. 'There is frost one inch thick on the bolt heads in our box car and this within two feet of a red hot stove', wrote a homeward-bound American advisor.[17] 'Piles of naked, frozen and gnawed corpses of men, women and children were stacked at every station', reported *The Times*.[18] Reds, Whites, deserters and common criminals scoured the ravished land for morsels of food, fuel, loot and revenge.

A queue of over 100 Czech echelons still inched east towards Irkutsk, and now trailed just ahead of the advancing Bolshevik spearhead.[19] Seriously wounded Czechs were reportedly shot by their fellow legionnaires rather than be left behind for the Bolsheviks.[20] Nevertheless, they sat at the top of the food chain, still in fighting shape and spurred on by the dream of a homeward-bound ship at the end of the line. Their movement through Semenov's territory loosened OMO control since the Czechs had sided with the Political Center revolutionists in Irkutsk. This leftist influence was countered somewhat by three trainloads of Japanese soldiers who withdrew from Irkutsk on 10 January.[21]

Large detachments of Rumanian, Serb and Polish soldiers, 4,000, 1,000 and 5,000 men strong, respectively, were not as fortunate as the well-organized, well-equipped Czechoslovaks. The Allies – most of them now long-gone – had determined the order of evacuation: Czechs, then Serb, Rumanian and Polish contingents, then Russians, but there was simply not enough space.[22] Around Klukvennaya, east of Krasnoyarsk, the Red Army surrounded the Polish Division during the first days of January 1920. The Poles were accompanied by their wives and children and begged the Czechoslovaks to take these innocents with them. The Czechoslovaks refused.[23] Like wolves competing for carcasses alongside the *magistral*, desperate fights broke out between the Poles, Rumanians and Serbs for possession of the few remaining locomotives that still functioned. The Poles had been trying to bring along 4,000 horses to ease their transition into agricultural lives back home, but these unfortunate creatures joined thousands of others abandoned along the *trakt*.[24] According to the Polish intelligence officer at Vladivostok, 'The Polish regiments requested that the Reds allow them to proceed home via Russia, but the Reds replied that this could not be granted and that the Poles should surrender their arms and be taken prisoners'.[25] Some Poles mutinied, killed their officers and went over to the Bolsheviks. Others, tormented by the plight of their wives and children, surrendered. All were reportedly marched off to hard labor details in the mines, except for a small band under Colonel Rumsha that was determined to fight its way east against all odds (although Polish histories state that Legion commander General Iasinskii-Stakhurek negotiated a surrender and repatriation on 8 January).[26] *The Times* reported several weeks later that they had succumbed to Siberia's frozen hell and Bolshevik bullets.[27] However, Colonel Rumsha led 120 officers and 700 soldiers on a miraculous trek to Vladivostok, from whence they returned to Poland via China.[28]

A 'tiny, straggling Rumanian contingent' marching at the tail end of the evacuation tried unsuccessfully to board Czech Legion trains and even destroyed a bridge west of Kansk when they were refused. They surrendered to the Bolsheviks around 12 January.[29] At least one Rumanian echelon, two Serbian echelons and one Yugoslav echelon at the tail end of the retreating trains survived the evacuation.[30]

Selenga River valley and Verkhne-Udinsk

Sandwiched between the front lines and Semenov's bastion at Chita lay the tranquil Selenga River valley which meandered south of Verkhne-Udinsk into Mongolia, stretching its fertile and forested tendrils in all directions through glens and hollows garnished with Bronze Age relics and mysterious *ongons*, birdhouse-sized dwellings for the nature spirits and ancestors of the shamanist Buryats, links to the invisible world. The incoming Red surf of *krasnoarmeets* and partisans was just beginning to lap at the forests from the west when it seemed as if the horsemen of the apocalypse thundered into the valleys from the north, south and east. White and Japanese punitive detachments had been marauding through the valley since mid-December on a hunt for partisans that soon became an 'orgy of murder, plunder and robbery'.[31] A three-pronged offensive stabbed into the valley like a pitchfork. General Levitskii trotted south from Verkhne-Udinsk at the head of OMO's Wild Division, a sinister legion of 2,000 Chahar Mongol mercenaries from Inner Mongolia mounted on their distinctive shaggy ponies and camels, along with 500 Cossacks, supporting artillery and machine guns. Another 600-man punitive detachment drove north out of Troitskosavsk, while 1,000 Japanese soldiers marched out of Petrovskii Zavod.[32]

The Americans would protest that it was a pointless punitive campaign with the sole objective being plunder. US Colonel Charles Morrow, commander of the 27th Infantry Regiment at Verkhne-Udinsk, recalled, 'I knew its [the valley's] population, I knew its villages, I knew its conditions thoroughly. I knew the people to be peaceful, law-abiding, hospitable Russian people, without any political ambitions or actions, wholly given to their farms and to their homes. That valley could be traveled through by anyone without being molested.'[33]

While that might have been mostly true, partisans were trying to get a foothold in the area. In November 1919, I.A. Kuznetsov's underground Bolshevik staff in Verkhne-Udinsk decided to rejuvenate and reorganize their stagnant organization in Pribaikalia – western Transbaikalia. An inexperienced partisan 'army' under E.V. Lebedev sallied forth to fight Levitskii and the Japanese in 'late December or early January', but initially did little to deter the Wild Division's rampage through the valley.[34] Levitskii's 'wanton carousal' through the Selenga valley left the local peasants little choice but to form armed bands to defend their lives and property. Many of these reluctant irregulars joined established Bolshevik partisan units that advanced into the area from the west. In the days after the fall of Irkutsk, a number of Red Army 'officers' appeared east of Lake Baikal to advise the scattered, unorganized self-defense groups.[35]

Meanwhile, Levitskii's Cossacks and Chahar mercenaries rambled through the area undaunted by the partisans. The Wild Division's riotous visit to the village of Kharashibersk was typical of their evil bacchanalia in the valley. At Kharashibersk, Levitskii's men killed 'about 30 men', robbed, raped and 'burned down 55 houses with four wives and children in them', testified Colonel Morrow.[36] 'The saleable stuff has been sent to Chita and sold from Ataman Semenov's stores', noted an American YMCA man in Verkhne-Udinsk.[37]

Throughout late December 1919 and early January 1920, small delegations of peasants from Selenga River valley villages appeared at the US 27th Infantry Regiment headquarters in Verkhne-Udinsk, appealing for help. A typical appeal, embossed with the heavy wax seal of Sheraldai village and dated 3 January 1920, read:

> Friends, Americans: The people implore your help and request you to protect them from Semenov's Wild Division, who burn villages, bread and the property of the peasants; who kill old men, women and children and who have no mercy on no one. We beg you to help us for the sake of the babies and the old men. Have mercy and help us. Upon your arrival, you can be convinced by your own eyes of the true facts, through seeing the remnants and ashes of our homes (signed by 38 peasants).

Colonel Morrow's infantrymen were neither authorized nor strong enough to challenge Levitskii's Wild Division; their explicit orders were to protect the railway. Although the Americans loathed the slovenly OMO soldiers, most of them were anxious to abandon Verkhne-Udinsk and go home. Preparations to evacuate had been underway for weeks and no one wanted to be remembered as the last man killed in Russia. A Japanese brigade under Major General Ogata (part of the 13th Division) also made Verkhne-Udinsk its base, but had no intention of leaving soon, or of helping the beleaguered villages.

The self-defense groups and partisans ambushed and wiped out a number of small, isolated White and Japanese patrols. Near Kyakhta, the ancient tea caravan crossroads near the Mongolian frontier, a 30-man Japanese detachment from Ogata's brigade at Verkhne-Udinsk was cut-off on 4 January 1920, and heard from no more.

During the first week in January, Levitskii's horde clashed with a significant partisan force near Kyakhta and turned back north. The Wild Division's retreat was hampered by 'four thousand sleigh-loads of plunder'. About 75 miles north of Kyakhta, Levitskii's Cossack and Mongol units began fighting over the booty. Levitskii and all but about 25 of his Cossacks were slain, then most of the Mongols turned south. News of the larcenous mutiny was soundly welcomed in Verkhne-Udinsk on 8 January.[38] Red histories state that the remnants of Levitskii's column were destroyed at Ganzurino, a town just south of Verkhne-Udinsk. The American garrison had learned of a large force of Bolsheviks congregating in the nearby village of Mukhino that week and Colonel Morrow expected them to attack the railway, but their purpose, as it turned out, was purely defensive for the time being.[39]

The Wild Division mutineers reportedly bolted for Mongolia with the loot, although the date of one atrocity suggests that another column lingered to run amok further. Levitskii had been dead for days when a Wild Division detachment swept into the village of Bobkina on 10 January. Five elderly survivors petitioned the Allies to see the resulting carnage for themselves. An Allied delegation went to Bobkina in mid-January to inspect the situation. The group consisted of US Consul Henry Fowler from Chita, US Army Lieutenant Davis, a Lieutenant Fujii and Captain Keda from the Japanese Army and a Major Doctor Marland and Major de Latour Dejean of the French Army. They reported:

> A dozen corpses, with the hands cut off, were lying heaped up in a pile half destroyed, all the bodies more or less cut up by saber wounds. The greater part bore many wounds made while living by saber blows, particularly on the face and back. All the corpses were burned. Many bore evident traces of having been burned while still living...[40]

The OMO column that started out from Troitskosavsk was defeated by partisans around *stanitsa* Okino-Klyuchi, where about 125 Whites were killed, 150 wounded and the rest dispersed into the hills. The partisans engaged the Japanese at Zardamoi and turned them back to Petrovskii Zavod.[41] Long a reservoir of popular support for Semenov from its Buryat communities, the Selenga River valley area now fell under partisan control.

Levitskii's death did little to relieve tensions in Verkhne-Udinsk. At night erratic potshots and the occasional concussion of an assassin's grenade echoed through winter's leaden stillness, preventing sleep but causing remarkably few, if any, casualties.[42] No one itched for an open fight in the deadly cold – thermometers dropped to $-75°F$. Avowed enemies scurried past one another in the streets and shared the same shelters. Hope was scarce and food scarcer. 'The mice were fearless and very hungry for they would run out into the lighted room and try to eat the food in the [mouse] trap the instant it was set', noted one observer.[43]

Czech and American soldiers and Russian civilians were united in their hatred toward the remaining OMO troops. On the other hand, Major General Ogata's brigade was stubbornly uncooperative with the Czechs and Americans, and showed no respect for the lives of Russian civilians.[44] Disabling Semenov was not so easy with the Japanese close by, but by 8 January, Czech and US troops had delicately begun to disarm OMO soldiers in Verkhne-Udinsk.

The following morning Semenov's *bronevik* 'Istrebitel' rumbled into Verkhne-Udinsk. General Nikolai Bogomolets, the *bronevik* commander, accused the stationmaster of being a Bolshevik and arrested him. Colonel Morrow coolly suggested to Bogomolets that he had 2,500 US soldiers at his disposal who would free the stationmaster if Morrow uttered the order. Bogomolets replied, 'I was told he was a Bolshevik and I wanted to kill him tonight, but if you insist, I shall release him. It is immaterial, if the station master is guilty we will get him sooner or later'.[45] The stationmaster walked free from the *bronevik*, although he had to 'confess' to theft as a condition of his release.

Bogomolets sulked about having lost face. That same afternoon in the village of Posol'skaya Station, 60 miles west of Verkhne-Udinsk, US Lieutenant Paul W. Kendall was informed by a sergeant's Russian girlfriend that villagers were fleeing because 'Istrebitel' was coming.[46] Kendall commanded one officer and 33 enlisted men of the 3rd Platoon, M Company, 27th Infantry, armed with only small arms and grenades, hardly a match for 60 men in an armored train bristling with field guns and machine guns. That night he ordered the men to sleep on the floor of their boxcars, to remain dressed with loaded rifles and to double the guard at the train station and nearby bridge. Kendall posted his interpreter at the telegraph office so that he would know when a train entered the area. By dusk, Posol'skaya Station's 100 or so villagers had departed and the Americans were ready for action despite six inches of snow on the ground and a temperature of −20°F. About 1 a.m., Kendall's interpreter informed him that Bogomolets' armored train was approaching and the Americans prepared for battle. 'Istrebitel' pulled alongside the American boxcars, halted and raked them with machine gun fire from one end to the other. None of the Americans was hit and several jumped out to form a skirmish line. Kendall thrust a Browning Automatic rifle into a porthole of 'Istrebitel' and fired off about 20 rounds, silencing one OMO machine gun, while the other lieutenant led a squad to the opposite side of the railway tracks to enfilade the Russian train and prevent Bogomolets' men from disembarking. Another group boarded the Russian locomotive, decoupled it, but then realized that the train had another engine. Sergeant Carl Robbins and Private Homer D. Tommie clambered onto it and were both wounded in a hail of pistol and machine gun fire, but not before Robbins, 'a tall boy from Tennessee', hurled a grenade into the cab before dropping off to die. Tommie fell onto the tracks and the train severed his leg. Bogomolets abandoned his attack and the train backed out of the station, with Lieutenant Kendall and his platoon pursuing on foot while his interpreter alerted M Company headquarters 30 miles to the east by telegraph. 'Istrebitel' soon wheezed to a halt, its boiler perforated by Robbins grenade and spewing steam. Kendall waited before reinforcements arrived before closing on the train and accepting its surrender. Bogomolets surrendered with 52 others, five of them wounded, losing five dead in the battle.[47]

The Americans took 55 prisoners, including General Bogomolets and five OMO officers. 'I was sorry that Lieutenant Kendall, who first got hold of Bogomolets, did not hang him to a telephone pole...', wrote Major General Graves of his reaction when he was apprised of events at Posol'skaya Station. A pile of 177 stolen pocketbooks and wallets attested to the 'Istrebitels' earnings during recent raids. The crew was interrogated by the US 27th Infantry. Most of Bogomolets's men declared that they served unwillingly, under constant threat of whipping, torture and execution. During the nine days prior to its capture, 'Istrebitel' killed no less than 40 civilian men. At least three or four women – no one was quite sure exactly how many – had been gang-raped and murdered.[48] Morrow's interrogators were 'frankly told how they had assaulted and tortured women and girls, killing them as fast as new victims were discovered; of flogging women with chains and hot ramrods and of tying babies to fences, abandoning them to freeze to death'.[49] Nevertheless, Bogomolets and his press-gang crew were quietly released within one week over muffled howls of protest from Major General Graves, Colonel Morrow and his doughboys.

Finally, on 13 January the Czech Legion took control of the station and town of Verkhne-Udinsk and finished disarming OMO 'Nearly a score of Semenov's men' were killed in the process and a Japanese officer was wounded by the Czechs. A local political center, headed by a recently returned émigré from Chicago, Aleksandr Mikhailovich Krasnoshchekov, took over the city administration.[50] Semenov accused the Czechs of acting on behalf of the Socialist-Revolutionaries, which was unlikely because the Czechs were having their own problems with the Socialist-Revolutionaries in Irkutsk. About this time, several Czech soldiers and officers were arrested in Irkutsk and a Czech lieutenant was 'killed in the street by the Reds'.[51] Major General Ogata mediated a settlement between Semenov and the Czechs: 'It was decided that the Russian troops disarmed by the Czechs should be armed again and resume the railway guard between Baikal City and Missovia [sic].'[52]

Levitskii's demise and the scattering of the Wild Division did not end White power in the valleys south of Verkhne-Udinsk. Indeed, White rage stoked a five-day period of bedlam in Kyakhta beginning on 17 January, during which no fewer than 800 Reds and suspects were tortured to death. 'In order to prevent the executioners from being bored', wrote Czech Henry Baerlein, 'a different process was used on each day'. Legend says that on the first day the victims were 'slaughtered by the firing of volleys', the second day they were dispatched by sword, the third by poison and asphyxiation and the fourth by burning alive.[53] Ironically, on 20 January, Semenov issued an order 'that military authorities must neither punish nor prosecute Reds who surrender to government troops', though no one seems to have set much store by it.[54]

Counter-counterrevolution in Vladivostok and Nikolsk

In the Far East, Ataman Kalmykov's soldiers, scattered between Vladivostok and Khabarovsk, were 'cut off on all sides' by mid-January. An OKO *bronevik* was wrecked and its crew captured near Shmakovka. The entire length of the Ussuri Railway, from eastern Transbaikalia to Nikolsk, began sparking with uprisings.[55] Even a powerfully armed Japanese special train, transporting an 'aide-de-camp of [the] Emperor' from Vladivostok to Chita, had to be rerouted through Manchuria, probably because of the partisans' widespread destruction of railway bridges.[56] A new wave of mass desertions and mutinies swept through remaining White units in Amur and the Maritime provinces. A large partisan detachment, swelling with eager volunteers, was gathering in the forests around Nikolaevsk-on-Amur, the thriving fishing and lumber town on the Tartary Straits near the northern head of Sakhalin Island. On 20 January the Reds laid siege to the isolated town, which was cut off from Khabarovsk and the world by the frozen Amur.

In Blagoveshchensk, Ataman Kuznetsov learned of preparations for a Red uprising, summoned his Cossacks and asked them if they would remain loyal to the Whites. They gave him no answer. Kuznetsov declared that he wanted no bloodshed, then turned over authority to the *zemstvo*. Within two weeks the area fell under Bolshevik control. Meanwhile, Japanese troops around Blagoveshchensk 'displayed a peaceful attitude', mindful, no doubt, of the long train ride through Red territory back to the Pacific coast.[57]

After a short siege, a partisan detachment under a Commander Shevchenko boldly marched into the city of Nikolsk-Ussuriisk, just 50 miles from Vladivostok, on the morning of 26 January. Upon their arrival, all but one of the local White units declared allegiance to the partisans. Even the Ussuri Cossacks, formerly the pillar of Kalmykov's power and the 3rd Transbaikal Cossack Regiment joined the rebels. The partisans began to surround the barracks of the Jaeger Cavalry Regiment. The Jaeger commander, Colonel Vrashtel and about 80 men, representing half of the understrength regiment, fled with four field guns. They lobbed three or four shells into Nikolsk from the city's outskirts, killing a handful of partisans, then 'took to the hills'. Some 500 Japanese and 1,000 Chinese troops declared their neutrality and observed the day's events from positions near the train station. Late that evening Vrashtel's group returned to Nikolsk without their officers, surrendered and offered to fight for the partisans. Vrashtel and his officers made for the Chinese border but were captured and thrown into prison.[58] The fall of Nikolsk cut off Vladivostok from Semenov's shrinking bastion in Transbaikalia.

Anti-White storm clouds had been gathering in Vladivostok since a successful day-long strike on 3 January 1920 and Sergei Lazo, among others, had been in the city plotting and organizing since November.[59] The strike organizers belonged to a shadowy Central Bureau of Professional Unions, which called for a crippling week-long strike to begin on 24 January. In contrast to local revolutionary movements elsewhere in the Far East, the Central Bureau of Professional Unions clamored as loudly against the foreign troops as it did against the White generals.[60] One week before the strike, General Sergei N. Rozanov, the White tyrant of Vladivostok, was so unnerved that he appealed to the Japanese to evacuate him, but they refused. Meanwhile, the Japanese staff tried unsuccessfully to negotiate with Vladivostok's emboldened socialists. In an attempt to win the Central Bureau's cooperation, the Japanese even offered a 'gift of a large quantity of flour and clothing', which was refused.[61] Rozanov desperately proclaimed an amnesty for political prisoners, arrested *zemstvo* leaders and tightened censorship, to no avail.[62]

The White command was split between those favoring Rozanov and the reactionaries and officers who wanted to see the introduction of democratic government, like Colonel Butenko and the notable Socialist-Revolutionary Colonel Krakovetskii. By this time, bolshevized soldiers of the Vladivostok garrison no longer obeyed the White command. In an effort to undermine anti-Rozanov officers, General Verigo, commandant of Vladivostok fortress and an associate of Rozanov and Kalmykov's, ordered Colonel Butenko's adjutant, a Captain Brochart, to report to Kalmykov for duty in late January. Had Brochart obeyed Verigo, he would have surely been liquidated after torture and interrogation to reveal any collusion between the 'progressive' officers, strikers and other revolutionaries.[63]

On 25 January a recently formed Bolshevik Military-Revolutionary Staff (*VoenRevShtab*), headed by Lazo, appealed to soldiers and officers of Vladivostok's garrison to organize revolutionary committees in each unit, arrest any uncooperative officers and to recognize a *zemstvo* board as the legitimate government. A Socialist-Revolutionary, A.S. Medvedev, headed the board to mask Bolshevik involvement and forestall objections by the Czechs and Americans.[64] Likewise, an umbrella organization formed to coordinate Vladivostok's imminent uprising, the United Operative Staff, was formed with representatives from the *zemstvo* board and several political parties, but was run by Sergei Lazo and controlled by the *VoenRevShtab*.[65]

On 27 January Vladivostok's increasingly impotent White command declared a state of siege and issued orders forbidding any public or private gatherings and publication of newspapers. The city was surrounded by towns that had now fallen into revolutionary hands. A Red delegation from Nikolsk delivered an ultimatum for Rozanov to resign by 9 a.m. on 31 January or Shevchenko's partisans and revolutionary troops from Ugol'naya would take the city by force. Rozanov was so frantic that he even asked the Americans for asylum, but was refused.[66] Finally, on 31 January, General Rozanov was overthrown with a single artillery shot that rattled the walls of his villa. No fighting occurred. In Major General Graves' words, 'That shot missed its mark, but the sound seemed sufficient for Rozanov and his supporters, the Japanese, to lose their nerve, as the Japanese clothed Rozanov in a Japanese officer's long cape and Japanese military cap and conducted him to Japanese Headquarters, which ended his crooked career in Siberia.'[67] After having endured five or six changes of government since 1917, the population was largely apathetic or fatalistic.

Vladivostok's revolutionaries launched the provisional *zemstvo* government of the Maritime province which, on the surface, seemed to sincerely strive to organize an honest, just administration, but was actually a facade for Bolshevik control. The government lacked any legislative body and was nominally led by an executive board consisting of two former teachers, a doctor and a surveyor, chaired by former educator A.S. Medvedev. Among the 500 prisoners Medvedev released from jail was a quiet, diminutive communist named Petr Mikhailovich Nikiforov, who headed the powerful Financial-Economic Council, which soon wielded more clout than the *zemstvo* board. Whites insisted that he was a former highwayman and convicted murderer whose death sentence had been commuted to hard labor years before.[68]

The new Vladivostok military commander, the mild-mannered Colonel A.A. Krakovetskii, informed the American staff that he had proof that 'the Japanese Consul gave money to a certain Russian officer, Lieutenant Greenberg, for the purpose of organizing a band of ruffians'. Greenberg's band was supposed to feign an attack under a red flag on Japanese headquarters. A similar plot in Nikolsk was revealed, where a Latvian officer had been offered 15,000 yen to stage a 'Red attack' against a Japanese position. In a similarly underhanded tactic to undermine the discipline of revolutionary troops and incite provocations, the Japanese and their Russian agents distributed free or cheap liquor to Krakovetskii's troops.[69] Meanwhile, Sergei Lazo dictated to Krakovetskii from the shadows, behind a sham military council under a Socialist-Revolutionary figurehead.[70] Nothing in Vladivostok was quite what it seemed at face value.

Semenov and the Americans

At 4 a.m. on 7 February Admiral Kolchak smoked a final cigarette, buttoned his greatcoat, refused a blindfold and, with his characteristic dignity, calmly faced a firing squad of Red executioners in Irkutsk. Beside him quivered the 'tall, paunchy' Viktor Pepelyaev, who 'had spent virtually the whole of his premiership confined in railway carriages'.[71] Ivan Brusak, an adventurous and idealistic youth from a Ukrainian town barked the order, '*Vzvcd! Po vragam revolyutsii, pli*' – 'Platoon! At enemies of the revolution, fire!' Kolchak's corpse was pushed into an icehole in the Ushakovka river like countless others before it. Shortly thereafter, Brusak's firing squad dispatched a Chinese interrogator named Cheng Ting-fan, whose abilities with torture implements had been valued in Kolchak's security service.[72] *Kappel'evtsy* troops, who had tenaciously fought their way into the Irkutsk suburbs to rescue the admiral, soon withdrew to continue their dreadful eastward retreat, deflated by news of Kolchak's death and threatened by their former Czech allies should they attack Glaskov.[73] A cruel fate mocked Russia by leaving Ataman Semenov the last White leader standing in the Far East.

That same bitterly cold morning found Colonel Charles Morrow at a nondescript railway siding a few hundred miles east of Kolchak's watery grave. A bit of drama at that desolate Transbaikal siding illuminated the deep chasms in Washington between the White House and the US State and War Departments' offices across the street and the confusion between General Graves and Red-fearing bureaucrats in Washington. The US War Department had ordered all American military personnel to begin packing for home in early January 1920. The RRSC would remain to run the railways, but the infantrymen standing guard on lonely stretches of Trans-Siberian tracks were released from their unpleasant duties. Even the American Red Cross, YMCA and Knights of Columbus abdicated their charitable missions and ordered their people to evacuate Russia by 1 March (although the ARC remained in Manchuria for quite some time afterwards).[74] Morrow began sending his 27th Infantry Regiment units east to Vladivostok on 11 January and on 29 January the old Kentucky colonel gladly bid adieu to Verkhne-Udinsk himself, then headed east on one of the last eight US Army echelons out of Transbaikalia.

Colonel Morrow was getting dressed at 7 a.m. when a visitor entered his coach to pay his respects. The caller was Lieutenant Colonel Benjamin B. McCroskey, from the Military

Intelligence Division (MID) and currently assigned to Consul General Ernest L. Harris' office. McCroskey was no naive desk jockey, but was an experienced intelligence officer who had spent 16 of his 40 years 'married to the Army', mostly in Asian service, with no dependents but his 65-year-old mother back in California. He was a dedicated Orientalist with a passion for Mandarin Chinese, who had compiled a vocabulary of Maranaw, a Moro dialect, for the US intelligence office in Mindinao. His knowledge and understanding of Asian cultures made him an under-appreciated rarity in the American military.[75] The two officers were acquainted, having both attended some 'railway meetings' in Chita about ten days prior, during which Morrow was apparently rankled by McCroskey's back-slapping fellowship with senior OMO officers.

When McCroskey strolled into Colonel Morrow's railcar on 7 February, he had no idea that he had stepped into the emotional minefield of America's vacillating Russian policy. McCroskey casually mentioned that he was heading to the Irkutsk area on an OMO supply train intended for General Voitsekhovskii's *kappel'evtsy*. Colonel Morrow bristled, 'No, you are not.'[76]

According to McCroskey, '[Morrow] asked me what I meant by associating with murderers, crooks and thieves, with people who were at open warfare with him and who had murdered his sleeping men...' McCroskey was taken aback by Morrow's bitterness, and tried to smooth things over. 'I attempted to explain to him that the [OMO] authorities at Chita regretted that incident [at Posol'skaya Station] and had assured me that punishment would be given the guilty...' McCroskey was used to dealing with the ataman and his staff officers over map tables and tea in Chita salons, not facing down drunken OMO *bronevik* commanders in God-forsaken hamlets reeking of corpses and poverty, as was Morrow. McCroskey thrust his orders from Consul General Harris towards Morrow, who refused to even look at them. Morrow knew what McCroskey's orders said: they accredited him as 'Military Observer with the Armies of Admiral Kolchak' and, like it or not, that now meant working with Semenov.[77] McCroskey told Morrow that he was proceeding on to Irkutsk and turned to leave.

'Colonel', barked Morrow, 'you are under arrest'. McCroskey coolly asked what were the charges against him. 'I don't know', growled Morrow, 'I'll tell you later'. Months later McCroskey reluctantly admitted, 'Colonel Morrow... was so thoroughly saturated with vodka as to be incapable of reasonable opinions.'[78]

About that time, Colonel Georgii Krupskii, the senior officer aboard the OMO train, made his entrance into Colonel Morrow's quarters. Krupskii was a young, urbane officer of considerable experience, having been a prosecutor in pre-war St Petersburg, assistant military attaché in Paris and 'on active service on the Archangel Front' prior to his current duties as an assistant chief of staff to Semenov.[79] McCroskey had to act as translator, interpreting into French and English Morrow's and Krupskii's brief exchanges of insincere compliments. Krupskii, sensing the tension between the American colonels, gave McCroskey a questioning glance. Colonel McCroskey bluntly summarized the ugly situation in French.

In McCroskey's words, 'Morrow then said that an officer of the United States Army, referring to me, could not associate with sons of bitches, murderers, crooks and thieves...'[80] McCroskey told Morrow that he could not interpret that to his Russian host. Krupskii muttered, in English, 'I understand, I understand', then added, '*Je ne peux pas rester ici*'. He then turned to Morrow and asked if these words represented the 'official American point of view of Ataman Semenov and inquired if relations had ceased'. Colonel Morrow responded that these were his personal views. Krupskii bade Morrow a formal goodbye, detached McCroskey's railcar from the supply train and coupled it to the American echelon, then continued west to the front.

McCroskey was fuming when he returned to his coach. He quickly churned out a message to the war department in Washington and was in the midst of encoding it when he was summoned to Morrow's car. 'I sat there for several hours listening to his tirade regarding Semenov, his antipathy to Americans, his pro-Japanism, his difficulties with Morrow, atrocities, committed, etc.', wrote McCroskey. They squabbled a little about objectionable passages in each other's message to Washington, then prisoner McCroskey lent his captor his code key. Neither message could be sent until they arrived in Chita.

During the next few days as the train crawled east, McCroskey spent most of the time confined to his coach with his interpreter and orderly, although he had occasion to point out to Morrow that 'Mr Smith of the Railway Service' had recently traveled west and that consular and Red Cross activities were continuing around Irkutsk. When the echelon finally reached Chita on 17 February McCroskey gave his word that he would not 'attempt to escape' and rushed around town to pay his local personnel, settle his bills and collect his personal baggage. Both officers fired off telegrams to MID headquarters in Washington.

McCroskey's message related, 'He refused to allow me to proceed and then placed me under arrest for my statement of alleged intentional disobedience of his orders.' In closing he insisted, 'An unprejudiced American observer in Siberia is an absolute necessity.'[81]

Colonel Morrow's message revealed the cynicism bred by 18 months of Siberian service and was not altogether honest:

> Reference to cable of Lt Col. McCroskey, my action fully warranted by situation and conditions. Not a PRISONER. Semenov is using McCroskey for political purposes to support his falling power, to whitewash his crimes and to discredit the massed testimony which I have in my possession. I have telegraphed to the Commanding General [Graves] and will report to him all the reasons for my action, that he may make his decision. This report is made to the War Department because I am unable...to communicate with General Graves at Vladivostok.[82]

The addressee of both inflammatory telegrams, Director of Military Intelligence Brigadier General Marlboro Churchill, was eager to wash his hands of the affair. The arrest of a lieutenant colonel was an unusual event in the US Army. He suggested that the army chief of staff instruct Major General Graves 'to investigate and settle the controversy'.[83] In previous days Churchill had tried to quiet the commotion by reassigning McCroskey as assistant military attaché in Peking, however, AEFS headquarters was determined to boot McCroskey from Asia altogether.[84]

By the time the echelon reached Harbin on 20 February McCroskey had been advised that no charges would be brought against him, yet Morrow immediately surrounded McCroskey's coach with sentries who had orders not to allow anyone on or off it. Several of McCroskey's friends with the consular service and Red Cross heard of his predicament and came to visit but were turned away. Meanwhile, a Lieutenant Wynne of the Army Medical Corps, who happened to be aboard Morrow's train, obligingly declared McCroskey 'mentally unsound', and a guard was stationed inside his railcar to watch him.

As the echelon slowly made its way east on the Chinese Eastern, McCroskey typed a detailed letter to Major General Graves, asking that he be permitted to report to Consul General Harris to carry out his instructions and that 'disciplinary action be taken against Colonel Morrow'.[85] He still did not realize that Graves stood solidly behind Morrow, regardless if the intemperate colonel had interfered with the orders of an MID assignment or uttered a faux pas in the presence of a Russian officer. Meanwhile Consul General Harris drew the matter to the attention of the secretary of state. Nevertheless, when the American train pulled into Vladivostok on the night of 25 February McCroskey and company remained under lock and key until mid-morning the next day.

As the days ticked by, McCroskey gradually began to realize that not only did Major General Graves stand in the way of his reassignment to Peking, but that the AEFS commander himself acquiesced to, if not approved of, McCroskey's confinement from Chita onwards. Graves heaped insult upon injury by assigning Major Slaughter to investigate McCroskey's complaints. Slaughter had been the AEFS representative at Omsk until recalled recently by the State Department and McCroskey was, in effect, the State Department's choice for Slaughter's replacement as liaison with the White command.[86] Not surprisingly, Slaughter decided that Colonel Morrow's arrest of McCroskey was justified.

The source of the controversy lay in the US government's vague and befuddled policies toward Russia, even though American troops had been deployed there for 18 months. McCroskey's orders from MID in November 1919 declared, 'The United States favors any movement in Russia striving for orderly and constitutional government. None of these movements have [sic] been granted legal recognition, though the government of Admiral Kolchak has been promised support... You will exercise the utmost care not to imply recognition by our government in any relations you may have with Russian officials...' Soon after McCroskey's arrival in Vladivostok in mid-December 1919, Major General Graves objected strongly to a key document in the newcomer's possession, the 'Siberian Monograph', a classified MID report that outlined strategic considerations and the United States' actual policy orientation. The single objectionable phrase in the monograph stated, 'American troops are in Siberia primarily to support Kolchak against the Bolsheviks by keeping his line of communication opened along the Trans-Siberian Railroad.' With the collapse of the White movement imminent, Graves interpreted the monograph as retroactively revising the AEFS mission to cast it as a scapegoat for Washington's failed Russian policies. 'The commanding general [Graves] states that the quoted extract does not accord with the instructions received by him and that if seen by others in Siberia would be used by those desirous of criticizing the American policy for not giving active military assistance to contending factions, as justifying them in the claim that the commanding general had not represented the policy of the United States.' Graves called Washington's attention to the matter and, as a result, MID ordered McCroskey 'not to show the quoted extract to any one in Siberia'.[87]

Nevertheless, no Trans-Pacific editing could shake the belief of McCroskey and his supporters in the State Department that Russia's 'only hope seems to be [White] counterrevolution'.[88] They were convinced that the AEFS had been subtly indoctrinated against Kolchak and Semenov by leftist Czech Legionnaires and Russian interpreters and by Japanese agents anxious to sow dissension among the Allies. 'The Czechoslovaks have really been one of the most pregnant causes of misunderstanding and inability to properly gauge the Russians', McCroskey asserted. 'Major Broz, Czech Intelligence Officer at Vladivostok, has evidently succeeded in absolutely molding the opinion of the American Expeditionary Forces to Czech [i.e. pro-socialist] ideas.' In addition, McCroskey suggested that Morrow's heavy reliance on his Russian interpreter, Chanan Silverman, for policy guidance was misguided, as was his intimacy with 'a Japanese named Minami (probably a high-grade man)'.[89] Silverman, a naturalized American of Russian birth, graduate of Seattle High School and 27th Infantry interpreter since October 1918, steered Morrow against the Whites, while Minami seemed to sow discord between Americans and Russians.[90]

McCroskey and the few Americans who still advocated aid for the Whites were pragmatists. He summed up US relations with the Whites and the Russian catastrophe that the Allies were abandoning:

> The representatives of the de facto Kolchak government throughout counted on sympathy and material aid from the United States. They received criticism and opposition. Their faults may have been many. The faults they possessed however

failed to make 'angels' of their opponents. Evacuation of the populace is still continuing away from Bolshevism. I know of no evacuation toward Bolshevism.[91]

Anxious to get rid of McCroskey, Major General Graves wrote to the army adjutant general on 9 March, 'I do not consider Colonel McCroskey mentally unbalanced but he is extremely nervous and to send him to [a] hospital for an examination to determine his mental condition would be detrimental to him.' Nevertheless, Graves recommended that McCroskey be returned to the United States for duty and, despite Slaughter's finding that his arrest was proper, declared, 'no disciplinary action advisable'.[92] The State Department was still clamoring for McCroskey's reinstatement, but Secretary of War Newton Baker hushed them by ordering his return home on 11 March, 'in view of the fact that the question of [his] mental condition has been raised'.[93] Initially he was slated to depart on a slow freighter via Manila, but, luckily for McCroskey, it was damaged coming into Vladivostok harbor and he was placed on the sailing list of the SS *Great Northern*, direct to San Francisco with the bulk of the AEFS on 1 April.[94]

For the next several weeks, Lieutenant Colonel McCroskey generated a flurry of messages, telegrams and letters protesting Morrow's 'illegal and humiliating actions' and insinuating that the 27th Infantry commander was himself insane, a drunkard and a Red sympathizer. The animosity between these two men epitomized the unbridgeable schism in US foreign and defense policies in Siberia and also presaged a dilemma that would face policy-makers for the next 70 years, namely, how to balance human rights and the atrocities committed by allies in the bitter fight against communism. Semenov faced the immediate challenge of drowning out the intoxicating siren songs of Bolshevik propaganda and victory. Yet the terror he employed made him so repugnant to many Americans that they preferred to abandon Russia altogether rather than gamble on a democratic revival flowering in Transbaikalia.

Although Colonel Morrow's echelon was the last American one, his train did not carry the last Americans out of western Transbaikalia. Some American troops lingered for weeks more. On 20 February, two weeks after Morrow's departure, the Vladivostok newspaper *Golos Rodini* reported, 'Semenov troops are rampant in Verkhne-Udinsk and only the presence of American troops partly controls their outbreaks.'[95] Lieutenant F.B. Byers did not depart distant Sludyanka until late February or early March and was still in Manchuria when the bulk of his regiment was disembarking in San Francisco weeks later.[96]

On his way east in mid-March, Byers and RRSC Major Colby paid a visit to the Verkhne-Udinsk home of Sergeant E.N. Davis, a deserter from 27th Infantry's headquarters company. They stopped by merely to check on the soldier's welfare, not to arrest him. Months earlier, Davis had fallen in love, married a local Russian woman and, perhaps at her urging but surely not lacking in motivation of his own, joined the partisans. His story was publicly exposed in late February 1920, when he was arrested by *kappel'evtsy* at Tataurovo (southeast of Chita on the Ingoda river) and transported back to a White headquarters at Verkhne-Udinsk.[97] The sergeant's White interrogators discovered that he 'belonged to the intelligence department of the Red Army', and separated him from the other prisoners. After interrogations by White General Konstantin Sakharov and an officer from the British mission named Captain Carroll, Davis was ordered to be executed. When he overheard his guards discussing the best way to kill him, he escaped and was hidden by villagers until Verkhne-Udinsk partisans arose against Semenov. A small number of other Americans, who either deserted or turned down return to the United States at the time of their discharges, may have joined with partisan or other revolutionary groups. By the time of Byers' and Colby's visit, Sergeant Davis had become assistant intelligence officer of the local Red Army headquarters group.[98] The Davis case lent some truth to Lieutenant

Colonel McCroskey's assertion that 'The American Army is leaving Russia now as the known friend of Bolshevism.'[99]

As a result, after the US Army evacuated, Semenov took revenge upon Russians who had 'collaborated' with the Americans by working as translators or other support positions. For example, when Major Colby left OMO territory, he wrote, 'Have the usual run of women who must get out. I am bringing one interpreter and wife as he would only be shot if left here after working for us.' Semenov may have even exacted retribution upon Americans who remained in the Russian Far East. It was later reported, but never substantiated, that OMO killed five Americans – two expatriates and three deserters in US Army uniforms – at Makkaveevo during the summer of 1920. Regardless, the US Army's experience with Semenov gave Americans a bitter aftertaste when dealing with Whites.

Kalmykov's Waterloo

Colonel Morrow was surely delighted by the dire predicament of Ivan Kalmykov, the vicious Ussuri ataman who had served the Americans their first bitter taste of civil war Russian-style on the streets of Khabarovsk in August 1918. Semenov could not raise a finger to aid his understudy in the Maritime province. Since the fall of Nikolsk-Ussuriisk on 26 January, its partisan liberators under I.G. Bulgakov-Bel'skii flowed north largely unopposed, taking Sviagino and Ussuri by 4 February, Iman shortly thereafter, then swelling around Khabarovsk as OKO's unreliable troops fled or deserted.[100] Kalmykov ranted, and addressed telegraphed tirades to the revolutionary administration in Vladivostok, the Allied commands, the foreign consuls and the Ussuri Cossacks. 'I say with resolution that I shall hang you all', he raved over the wires on 12 February.[101] He knew the end was near. That same day OKO gunmen emptied all of the gold from the state bank in Khabarovsk and Kalmykov gave his army colors to a Sub-Lieutenant Karpinskii for delivery to Chita.[102] The Japanese counted on Kalmykov to defend the city and did their part by tearing up about one mile of railway tracks leading into town. Local partisans had begun negotiating with remaining White units in Khabarovsk to convince them to mutiny and help track down Kalmykov. Suddenly, an armed force appeared from the south and the partisans took up defensive positions. A day and a half passed before they realized that the approaching force consisted of Bolsheviks and other revolutionaries from Vladivostok.[103] Meanwhile, Kalmykov and his pirates hijacked every *droshky* they could find and escaped, killing all the *droshky* drivers at the edge of town.[104]

Partisans marched into Khabarovsk unopposed on 16 February 1920.[105] People wept with joy and red flags blanketed the city. Bulgakov-Bel'skii forced a Japanese *bronevik* commander to give up eight Kalmykov officers who were hiding on his train and pressured the Japanese headquarters to agree 'not to molest Russian or foreign [i.e. Korean] residents and to abstain from entering the town' unless given permission by Vladivostok's *zemstvo* government. An increasingly Bolshevik military council in Vladivostok ordered Khabarovsk's 'liberators' to 'be firm, avoid drunkenness and theft' and maintain order.[106] However, among the 'lesser tragedies' of revolutionary vengeance which transpired, 50 White officers were forced to the center of the Amur river bridge and used for target practice by celebrating partisans.[107]

A conference of Ussuri Cossacks convened at Grodekovo on 21 February with 168 delegates present. Acting out the drab formality of revolutionary drama, they adopted a resolution that meant a death sentence for Kalmykov. 'The Cossack Conference considers Ataman Kalmykov to be a usurper of Cossack power and an organizer of civil war with the aid of foreign bayonets, a war in which Kalmykov executed and robbed the population'; so began the resolution with an eerie echo of Kalmykov's own July 1918 proclamation that had accused the Bolsheviks of the same offenses. The Cossacks divested Kalmykov of 'his title of Ataman and of all his ranks given to him by the Conference', and ordered that he be put before a Revolutionary people's court.[108]

Kalmykov's whereabouts remained a mystery. He broadcast his final diatribe to Siberia on about 26 February. Addressed to 'Soviet of the Dogs' Deputies', it raved, 'I herewith announce that all the violators of the desire of the Russian people, and the tools of Monsieur Bronshtein [Trotsky] will, in the future, not be shot, but that I will hang them.'[109] A few days later, partisans pursuing Kalmykov about 25 miles south of Khabarovsk lost him when Japanese troops burned a bridge in front of them.[110] Kalmykov and 800 diehard followers split into two groups and fled across the border into China. The Chinese Army was waiting for them. Kalmykov surrendered without a fight at a squalid, isolated village called Norti on about 5 March. His Chinese captors were then stuck with the dilemma of what to do with the ataman and his arms. For the time being there was talk of returning Kalmykov to Khabarovsk for a show trial and execution.[111]

The Ussuri ataman's mace passed to Kalmykov's assistant, Colonel Zh.A. Savitskii, who found refuge in Grodekovo. For all practical purposes however, the head of the White Ussuri Cossack movement had been severed.[112] Distant Chita remained the last island of White Cossack resistance in a swelling Red sea.

The collapse of White power spelled doom or despair for many families, not only those of OKO soldiers and White administrators. 'Mass executions of the intelligentsia, officers, students and all those unacceptable to the Soviet government' were already quietly underway in Khabarovsk, Blagoveshchensk and Nikolsk-Ussuriisk.[113] However, the newspapers that had screeched about White atrocities, like Vladivostok's *Golos Rodini*, held their tongues about Red wrongs.

On 27 February Generals Shiromidzu and Yamada at Japanese Army headquarters in Khabarovsk ordered the commander of the Nikolaevsk garrison to reach an agreement with the partisans just as they had in the city, even though during a recent attempt by the partisans to parley, the Nikolaevsk garrison had obstinately subjected the Red negotiator Orlov 'to the most excruciating tortures, from which he died'. Major Ishikawa reluctantly assembled a delegation of Nikolaevsk's Menshevik and Socialist-Revolutionary civic leaders and agreed to the surrender of the White garrison. The democratic revolutionary parties' platforms had been reduced to one simpleminded slogan, 'Down with Civil War'. That night, after a Japanese banquet in his honor, the Russian garrison commander, Colonel Medvedev, put a pistol to his temple and ended his life. His was the first of scores of suicides. At noon the next day, Commander Lapta marched his ski brigade of 300 Reds into town. The tall, handsome partisan leader Yakov Ivanovich Triapitsyn trotted behind on horseback, wearing a black bow on his arm and a smirk on his face. He was just 23 years old and far from his roots in a Simbirsk village. The 2,000 ragtag conquerors of Nikolaevsk followed, among them a number of ex-convicts, 300 Chinese laborers from rural mines hired on as mercenaries for 2,000 rubles a month and promises of 'nationalized women' and 200 Korean freedom fighters, the only disciplined soldiers in the rabble.[114]

Friction between the new revolutionary administrations in the Maritime province and the Japanese interventionists was inevitable. On the first day of March, Korean nationalists threw 'a grand [first] anniversary celebration' with three separate demonstrations around Khabarovsk, that naturally whipped up the fury of their colonial masters, but 'Japanese attempts at repression were checked by Russian troops'.[115] During the night of 7 March, the Reds discovered two fugitive Kolchak officers hiding aboard a Japanese railcar passing through Nikolsk, but Japanese soldiers spirited the pair away to their local headquarters before the partisans could arrest them. Partisan leaders were feeling defiant, having just returned from a Bolshevik pep rally at the Amur village of Viatskoe where commanders and 'all revolutionary organizations of the Khabarovsk and Nikolsk regions' demanded restoration of Soviet authority. At 2 a.m. that night, a Japanese officer killed a partisan 'in a quarrel over a woman'. This bar brawl rapidly escalated into an international incident. 'Japanese soldiers surrounded the building and later Russians arrived. Both the Japanese and Russians held themselves in readiness to fight during the night. The Russians put two locomotives on two armored trains and at noon [8 March] they were still in readiness.'[116] Another Japanese-Red standoff occurred the same day at a tunnel near Ugol'naya. Tension between Russians and Japanese presented a dangerously explosive condition.

White breakdown in Transbaikalia, Red liberation in Irkutsk

Every few days throughout the month of February 1920, rumors radiated out of Chita that Semenov and his associates had fled, despite the ataman's frequent proclamations that a transition to democratic rule was at hand.[117] Colonel Johnson, the senior RRSC man in Chita, wired his headquarters in Harbin, 'Commencement [of the] final blowup [of] Semenov Army [is] assuming very funny and panicky forms.'[118] *The Times* carried a fantasy which emanated out of Harbin on the 25th: 'Semenov has voluntarily demobilized his army and publicly begged forgiveness for the abuses and cruelties inflicted in his name. He is leaving Chita after the last Czech train has passed.'[119] Several days later, gossip from Chita erroneously asserted, 'Semenov has practically no authority and…["Kappel Army"] commander] General Voitsekhovskii decides all questions.'[120] On 29 February, Colonel Johnson added a few facts to these fantasies, wiring Harbin, 'We have been much annoyed in the past week by requests from Semenov followers to aid them in getting out.'[121] Very few OMO officers were seen roaming Chita streets, but in all probability many had gone to combat units on the nearby front lines.

Disinformation from Bolshevik propagandists added to the confusion. For example, in early March the Russian Telegraphic Agency (RTA) optimistically declared, 'Semenov and his staff [have] fled from Chita to Dauria, where the Czechs took away from him the last locomotive. The locality is surrounded by partisans. The demoralization of Semenov's troops is evident, [and] some detachments have not received any pay for the last three months.' While the last statement about pay had the ring of truth, as did coincident reports that senior OMO staff were watching Manchuli and Hailar railway stations to turn back officers as well as soldiers who tried to desert, Moscow disinformation experts understood that mixing fact and fancy produced the best results.[122]

The thousands of *kappel'evtsy* who survived the arduous Ice March across Lake Baikal infused Semenov's Transbaikal front with new blood.[123] By 14 February, the main body of Kappel's Army and accompanying refugees had reached Mysovaya on the eastern shore of Lake Baikal, where they were greeted with a trainload of provisions and grain from Ataman Semenov, the first time in many weeks that their gnawing hunger was satisfied. A hospital train soon followed to pick up the sick and wounded and regular freight trains carried the rest east as they thawed out and recovered from their horrendous ordeal.[124]

Semenov's actions behind the scenes revealed that he was not optimistic about the future, as he was busy shipping his purloined treasures out of the country. On 18 February, an RRSC inspector at Harbin came across four *taplushkas* 'under heavy guard' and full of quartz-gold loaded in Chita. Semenov was sending it to Japanese authorities at Changchun, presumably for transfer to his overseas accounts.[125] In subsequent weeks, the flow of booty out of Chita became a torrent.

On 2 March, the Japanese command in Chita called out two of its infantry battalions and a battery of artillery to prevent a Czech Legion echelon from entering the city. Semenov and the Japanese feared that they intended to take control of Chita as they had done in Verkhne-Udinsk.[126] The Japanese and Semenov had good reason to fear. On 11 February the Czechoslovak Legion and Red Army reached an agreement establishing a neutral zone between the former's rearguard and the latter's vanguard.[127] Since mid-February the Czechs had even allowed Red echelons to intermingle with theirs south of Lake Baikal and into western Transbaikalia in return for the Bolsheviks' generous assistance with fuel, maintenance and other arrangements. Additionally, since the fall of Vladivostok in late January, the Czechoslovaks facilitated Moscow's oversight of the Maritime province's new government by secretly transporting Soviet agents through Semenov's territory aboard Legion trains.[128]

For diplomatic reasons, Bolshevik regulars avoided clashes with the Japanese, but struck at Semenov's troops whenever possible. The partisans, of course, had no qualms about ambushing and slaughtering isolated Japanese patrols. The Japanese encountered many difficulties evacuating their troops out of western Transbaikalia, not least of which was the refusal of Russian train crews to man Japanese echelons out of fear of partisan and Red Army attacks.[129]

Notwithstanding the tensions between them – or perhaps because of them, the Japanese gave Colonel Medi, Semenov's transportation chief, 2 million yen in mid-February. The funds were intended to expedite the evacuation of Japanese soldiers from western Transbaikalia, which was becoming saturated with partisans and advance units of the Red Army, but also to bribe Russian railway workers to delay the Czech evacuation and, thereby, slow the Red advance.[130] The Japanese were fearful of their rearguard being slaughtered by Reds while stuck in the traffic jam on the Trans-Siberian.

On 19 and 20 February Semenov withdrew his forces ('train with motor vehicles', staff and units of unknown size) from Sludyanka and Mysovaya.[131] The withdrawal was a major reversal, as both were busy lakeside towns of about 5,000 people each with medical facilities, large railway shops and minor industries. The loss of Mysovaya was especially damaging, not only because Semenov had a recruiting and training base there, but because it was a major transportation center with more than 6,000 yards of main railway track, 27,000 yards of siding and large docks that could accommodate the largest ships on the lake. Three trainloads of Japanese soldiers followed a few days later, relocating east of Verkhne-Udinsk.[132]

To expedite evacuation of foreign troops, an agreement was hashed out between Semenov and the Allies (specifically General Janin and John Stevens' railway board) allowing mechanics from the Czechoslovak Legion to be assigned to Trans-Siberian Railway roundhouses beginning on 24 February. The Legion's machinists ploughed into a mountain of damaged equipment – some 30 worn out locomotives between Verkhne-Udinsk and Manchuli and a variety of other engineering challenges. Several days later a Czech labor battalion was put to work in a coal mine near Borzya to increase output to 15 railcars per day and to guarantee fuel for the Allied evacuation. A few days after that, a Czech railway repair battalion set up a railcar refurbishing operation in Hailar, aiming to keep enough rolling stock in service to make sure that the Czechoslovak Legion encountered no further delays on its exodus to the Vladivostok docks.[133] In the scramble to get out of the country, the noble goals of Allied railway assistance for Russians fell by the wayside.

While the front lines now inched into western Transbaikalia, eastern Transbaikalia saw an upsurge in partisan attacks and White desertions to the Reds. Semenov's Army was undertaking frequent combat operations between Nerchinsk and Sretensk against an increasingly cocky partisan army that now counted some 200 groups and detachments between Lake Baikal and the Pacific.[134] In Sretensk, for example, a Bolshevik agent, E.D. Kulikov, had been gradually infiltrating the military hospital since late 1919, employing a network of Red girlfriends to recruit sympathizers, first among the orderlies and nurses, then among the patients, most of whom came from the 29th Troitskosavsk Regiment. Most of the latter were workers, and some of them had even been Red Guards in 1918. Many were receptive to subtle Red indoctrination as the nurse-agents changed their dressings and performed other procedures. The hospital was one of the few places where all soldiers of the garrison could visit without rousing suspicion. Soon Kulikov commanded a large underground network, organized in three-, five- and ten-man cells, that was gathering detailed information about the garrison and regional military activities. In late February, the chief of staff of the eastern Transbaikal Front, S.S. Kirgizov, ordered Kulikov to prepare for an uprising in Sretensk and to coordinate the action with F.A. Podogaev, a partisan commander operating in the mountain forests outside town.[135]

On the evening of 28 February, Kulikov called in the leaders of his ten-man cells, told them that they would be revolting against the White command that night and appointed a former Red Army soldier, N. Nevolin, to coordinate the mutiny. A rhythm of rifles shots at 2 a.m. signaled for the arrests of about 20 regimental officers to begin. By dawn, all 500 men of the 29th Troitskosavsk Regiment 'except portions of 5th company' were serving under the red banner of Podogaev's 7th Partisan Cavalry Regiment. They brought with them two artillery pieces, three machine guns, a small arsenal of rifles and years of combat experience. Nevertheless, Sretensk and Nerchinsk remained under Semenov's control and several days after the aforementioned defection the ataman commended his garrison at Nerchinskii Zavod, consisting of units of the 1st Separate Transbaikal Cossack Brigade and Composite Ataman Semenov Division.[136]

In the first days of March a Japanese detachment was cut off by Reds near Verkhne-Udinsk and a Semenov *bronevik* was captured. Two Japanese echelons were stranded in Verkhne-Udinsk while fighting erupted on their eastward escape route. The town of Petrovskii Zavod and villages between the desperate Japanese echelons and Chita were falling to partisans. A strange twist occurred when the stranded Japanese disarmed OMO troops in Verkhne-Udinsk and took them prisoner, probably in a gambit to trade them for passage eastward.[137]

In a typical case of the surreal coexistence between enemies that now occurred regularly along the Siberian railway, Petrovskii Zavod's new revolutionary administrators permitted four echelons of 'Kappel's White Army' to depart their town in early March.[138] The rails of the Trans-Siberian Railway east of Verkhne-Udinsk and the parallel *trakt* were constantly pumping a desperate human current through Chita. Most *kappel'evtsy* were not so lucky as to have a warm boxcar for transportation and shelter and fled east in a monstrous column of 10,000 troikas. *The Times* reported, 'Each sleigh carried two men and was drawn by three horses. The caravan took four days to pass a given spot... The sleigh army obeyed certain unwritten rules... first, all sleighs move in sequence; second, no sleigh is permitted to overtake another; thirdly, whoever falls out on the line must expect no help.'[139] General Kappel himself had succumbed to pneumonia and gangrene in his frostbitten legs on 26 January at a village called Utai.[140] Upon arrival in Chita the *kappel'evtsy* faced the dilemma of being saved by a man they hated, Ataman Semenov. Most of Kappel's Army were pro-democracy, anti-Soviet workers from the Urals who felt compelled to redeem the White movement. Their leader, Major General S.N. Voitsekhovskii, subordinated his command to Semenov and, in exchange, became one of three corps commanders. Nevertheless, Voitsekhovskii telegraphed General Vasilii Georgievich Boldyrev in Vladivostok on 28 February, offering his men to any democratic government that would oppose Bolshevism. Boldyrev consulted the Red chiefs of Vladivostok's military council, Lazo and Nikiforov, then Medvedev. Vladivostok's 'Red–Pink coalition' wanted Voitsekhovskii to arrest Semenov as a prerequisite for the *kappel'evtsy* to be welcomed into their fold.[141]

The Czechs, who had taken up arms against Semenov during the Battle of Irkutsk, were scattered in force throughout his territory from west to east. Sixteen echelons of

Czechoslovak legionnaires had disembarked at Borzya to hold the coal mine and other critical railway assets there.[142]

The rumor that Semenov had offered to turn against the Japanese arose about this time. While many Russians and foreigners alike accused Semenov of being an unabashed Japanese puppet, a 'reliable source' of American intelligence stated that '[Semenov's] attitude towards the Japanese cannot be defined as a friendly one'. Around the end of February, Semenov was said to have telegraphed the Irkutsk Political Center and offered to turn against the Japanese in return for 'freedom for himself and soldiers'. In the same vein, the word spread in Vladivostok that Japanese diplomats in Riga were 'trying to arrange with Trotsky [an] agreeable understanding in regards their troops in Siberia'.[143] Despite these ungrateful acts of treachery – if true, the headquarters and 2,500 men of Japan's 5th ('Hiroshima') Division were stationed in Chita, guaranteeing Semenov's safety while likewise ready to take him hostage if things turned sour.[144] In the Chita area alone, three Japanese armored trains trolled the railway.[145]

The Japanese worried about the quickening Allied departure because they had no intention of leaving Russia themselves, yet they remained close-mouthed about their plans. In late February, RRSC Colonel Johnson reported, 'The Japanese have not yet said a word about evacuating.' The constant parade of evacuees could not have escaped their attention: during the third week of February 12 Czech, 2 French and 8 Russian echelons rumbled past General Hoshino's division headquarters in Chita. The Japanese command grudgingly withdrew its troops alongside the other foreigners, but only to consolidate new fronts against the Reds around Chita and in the Maritime province. Japan's evacuation from Amur province 'as decided on 2 February' was simply a transparent strategical maneuver aimed at tightening the Japanese lines by concentrating forces in the Maritime province.[146] In the meantime, General Hoshino and other Japanese commanders pulled subtle tricks to slow the evacuation, such as transporting all coal intended for the evacuees east in an effort to starve their locomotives. By late February most of the Japanese Army in Transbaikalia was sitting aboard 35 trains creeping slowing eastward between Verkhne-Udinsk and Manchuli. 'We have the Japanese absolutely bluffed', exulted Colonel Johnson from Chita, 'and [the] program from now on will be simply to entirely ignore the Japanese.' In strange contrast to the Allies strained relations with their Japanese allies, the American RRSC was amicably transferring money through the Irkutsk soviet ('for operations on the Tomsk Railway') and Reds in the Lake Baikal district were 'giving the Czechs everything possible in the way of cars, engines and coal'.[147]

Echelons of homeward-bound Czech legionnaires, Serbian and Rumanian soldiers and redeploying Japanese infantry hurtled east as fast as possible. Railway workers were paid with flour as value of the Siberian ruble plummeted with the Red Army's advance.[148] Because of partisan takeovers throughout Amur province, the busy rails around Chita and the junction at Karymskaya now had to accommodate evacuations from the east in addition to the interminable traffic from the west. The pressure on the railway workers was strong enough to drive men mad.

On 4 March, Major F.A. Flanagan, the senior RRSC officer in Manchuli, was diagnosed as having suffered a nervous breakdown.[149] However, Flanagan's associates immediately suspected a dose of Mongolian poison in revenge for his angering Baron Ungern-Shternberg. Three weeks earlier, Flanagan had called upon Japanese General Hosano (and telegraphed Ataman Semenov and Colonel Medi) to halt the execution of 40 Russians Ungern-Shternberg had arrested in Manchuli and taken to Dauria. Remarkably the prisoners were released, but a Czech friend warned Flanagan that Ungern-Shternberg was furious. Believing that he could befriend the deranged baron, Flanagan even invited him to dine with him 'in Car No. 2011', though it seems his invitation was refused.[150]

The torrent of sickly refugees brought also brought outbreaks of influenza, typhus, 'black smallpox', and scarlet fever to Transbaikalia, the Russian Far East and Manchuria. The influx of diseased refugees convinced Chinese authorities at Manchuli to begin restricting entry to curtail the epidemic.[151] The Chinese would soon realize that no quarantine was strong enough to prevent one contagion – revolution – from infecting northern Manchuria's railway zone.

On 5 March, Bolshevik radio announced that regular Red Army units had destroyed 'Semenov's Buriat Regiment', rendered heavy losses upon defending Japanese troops, and taken Verkhne-Udinsk three days earlier, although the area's strong partisan presence suggests that the Red Army did not single-handedly drive out Semenov. That same day Major Colby, the RRSC inspector living in Verkhne-Udinsk, reported that the town's liberators were 'very cordial'.[152] Ironically, Verkhne-Udinsk's Red commissar was a local revolutionary named Semenov.[153] His administration was 'composed of representatives of Socialists, workmen, peasants and Buriats', and they guaranteed safety to all White soldiers except for the worst of OMO sadists.[154] Meanwhile, 'advisors' from the Red Army began 'an attempt to bring all the [revolutionary] factions under one head and perfect some kind of organization', preferably under Bolshevik control, of course.[155]

The town's liberation from Ataman Semenov did nothing to relieve the citizens' suffering from the typhus cases that arrived with each batch of refugees. A March 1920 Red report estimated (and probably underestimated) 160,000 cases of typhus between Omsk and Irkutsk.[156] Food shortages became so dire that the arrival of 'a little flour' was cause for a mad scramble. And, despite the withdrawal of OMO, retreating Japanese echelons continued passing through Verkhne-Udinsk for several weeks more, and, as always, their troops showed little compunction about beating railway employees – or anyone else – for the slightest perceived transgression.

On 7 March 1920 the Red Army paraded into Irkutsk. Soviet histories would herald this date as the city's 'liberation' day, erasing the brave, seemingly homegrown anti-White uprising of December and January. As it turned out, a large number of the Political Center's fighters during the revolt had been under the silent control of a 'parallel Bolshevik military organization, the Workers' and Peasants' Militia'. The 53rd Siberian Regiment, catalyst of the uprising, was Bolshevized before the December fighting, and was reinforced with the arrival of the like-minded partisans of Kalandarashvili and Zverev in early January. Accordingly, Irkutsk's Political Center transferred power to a Bolshevik Revolutionary Committee on 21 January, weeks before the Red Army's arrival. 'They are disarming the people and putting them to work', according to a French officer who departed in late February. 'Workmen are ordered to work extra hours at same pay to restore normal conditions'. When the last echelon of the Czechoslovak Legion pulled out of Irkutsk on 1 March, the 5th Red Army choreographed the 'official' liberation of the city.[157]

Czech and US sources subsequently reported, 'News from Red territory west of Lake Baikal indicates great deal of unrest in Red Siberia due to harsh rule and Soviets forcing men to work a twelve-hour day.'[158] Almost immediately, eye-witness reports emerged of 'suffering in Irkutsk for want of food', 'people starving in the streets' and 'no food coming in and bread selling for 1,000 Siberian rubles per loaf'. Supposedly 'Omsk rubles' had been taken out of circulation in February, but, regardless, currency quickly became almost valueless in Irkutsk as Bolshevik rationing went into effect, and the city's grievances and protests were soon muffled by the CHEKA's blanket of repression.[159]

On 7 March, the same day that the Red Army marched into Irkutsk, 40-year-old Aleksandr Krasnoshchekov declared the establishment of the Provisional Government of Pribaikalia at Verkhne-Udinsk, also referred to during its short life as the Verkhne-Udinsk Republic. As more Red Army regulars and Bolsheviks entered town during subsequent weeks, it became apparent that they expected local revolutionary officials to relinquish their authority. For example, on 17 March, RRSC Major Colby noted 'a slight friction between the [Soviet] Commissar arriving from the west and [Verkhne-Udinsk commissar] Semenov'. The cause of the spat was a minor point concerning permission for a Czech echelon of staff officers to 'borrow' some railcars taken from the deceased Kolchak's cavalcade. However, it portended the gradual takeover of power in Verkhne-Udinsk from local revolutionaries by Bolsheviks from the west, who saw the administration as a convenient, pliable tool that could be molded into the Far Eastern Republic (FER), a transparent puppet of Lenin to rule Red territories east of Lake Baikal without stoking Japanese fear of 'Soviets'.

Vladivostok's revolutionary government laid claim to the FER title at the moment, and its facade of legitimacy was bolstered by its treatment as an equal by the Chinese government. The relatively cordial relations between China and the FER were mutually convenient, as they garnered leverage for both governments in dealings with the Japanese. Although the status of private property became murky, the FER still had the gall to declare its need for foreign capital. FER representatives in Spassk informed the retail firm of Kunst and Albers that if it tried to liquidate its business it would be nationalized, but if it continued to trade, the Soviets would assist it.[160]

On 8 March, customs officials in Harbin confiscated four 'heavy iron cases' filled with gold from the coach of 'Semenov's wife' (exactly which wife or mistress was not specified). Apparently the madam's armed escort was outgunned by the Chinese Army guards in the customs house. OMO Colonel Shadrin, the commander of the escort, telegraphed the ataman, 'All Semenov followers are searched thoroughly. Request you inform Russian Consul Mr Popov about the purpose of my traveling to China.' It is likely that the shipment was intended to buy influence in Peking, though it may have been a payment for Japanese weapons. It seems to have ended up in the coffers of General Chang Tso-Lin.[161]

The 'front' quickly receded more than 100 miles east of Verkhne-Udinsk to the outskirts of Khilok, a railway town that had long felt the whimsical lash of Semenov. By 5 March a heated battle was underway west of town, where Semenov's *broneviki* put up a fierce fight against advancing Reds. Two OMO *broneviki* were derailed, but the combat continued for several days.[162] At 4 p.m. on 14 March, Khilok fell into Red hands, and the Verkhne-Udinsk–Khilok rail line was reportedly 'quiet'.[163]

Supposedly, the Red Army would not advance east of Lake Baikal into the Far Eastern Republic. However, in mid-March ten Red Army echelons trailed right behind the Czech rear guard over the mythical Soviet-FER border. Subsequently, whether the Soviets were thumbing their nose at the February agreement not to pass the Czech rear guard, or whether they had bribed the Czechoslovak 3rd Division with fuel, food or other goodies to allow them to pass, the legion permitted three of the ten echelons to detrain at Divisionaya, and seven to continue east to Khilok. Then, as surprisingly as their decision to let the Reds barrel east, the Czechs covered their rear again, and the Czech Storm Battalion fell in just west of Mysovaya, ready to open fire if another Red echelon tried to get by.[164]

The 'front' became an abstract term referring only to the westernmost point on the Trans-Siberian where Japanese or White forces still resisted the Red tide. Partisan bands and even small detachments of Red Army regulars operated far behind them, spotting the map of eastern Siberia like a pox. On 18 March Mogzon, 75 miles east of Khilok, was predicted to fall 'within a day or so'. Although that prediction was a few weeks premature, a Red force of 3,000–5,000 men was approaching and no Kappel or OMO defenders were in sight. A Japanese armored train and infantry regiment held Mogzon; a 500-man echelon reinforced them on 20 March. Their adversaries in the 1st Irkutsk Soviet Division paused in Khilok, and nearby partisans likewise had the luxury of standing down when their food and equipment inevitably ran short. On 23 March ten echelons of Soviet regulars began advancing on Mogzon from Khilok. Red broneviki soon followed to consolidate their hold on the railway.[165]

Chita was surrounded. Father Seraphim, until July 1919 the father superior of the Alekseevskii Monastery near Perm, wisely gauged the Red threat to be serious enough to disinter eight bodies from Chita's Pokrovskii monastery and try to transport them out of Russia. They were no ordinary cadavers and included the body of Grand Princess Elizaveta Fedorovna, six other members of the royal family and a nun. Nor was Elizaveta Fedorovna any ordinary princess. Born as Princess Elizabeth of Hesse-Darmstadt in 1864, she bore her marriage to Grand Duke Sergei Aleksandrovich with dignity, despite his homosexual escapades. After he was assassinated by Social-Revolutionary terrorists in 1905, she dedicated her life to her adopted faith in the Russian Orthodox Church, and was prominent for her charity and daily work with Moscow's poor, for whom she organized clinics, a cafeteria, an orphanage, a library and a women's school at the respected monastery where she rose to become the Mother Superior. She implored her sister, Empress Aleksandra, to reject the influence of Rasputin and, when the world war erupted, she dispatched nuns to field hospitals at the front. She bravely faced mobs at the monastery gates – an anti-German mob in 1916 and a Red mob soon after the February Revolution, and remained at her post even though Kaiser Wilhelm II, Ambassador Count von Mirbach, and others made arrangements on at least two occasions for her to leave Russia. In April 1918, the CHEKA and a squad of Latvian internationalists arrested and transported her to Alapaevsk, where she was sequestered with other members of the royal family. During the night of 5 July 1918 she, her loyal assistant, Sister Varvara Yakovleva, and five royal relatives were thrown into a mine shaft, followed by several hand grenades. Elizaveta Fedorovna and a prince fell not to the bottom but onto a ledge about 15 meters down the shaft, and there they perished slowly, in the dark, of thirst and wounds. After the White counterrevolution, the bodies were recovered, but as the Red Army drew near, were boxed up and transported east in July 1919 by Father Seraphim, an old acquaintance of Princess Elizaveta. Unable to afford the exorbitant railway freight charges to ship eight coffins, Father Seraphim appealed to believers around Chita for donations, and was referred to Masha Sharaban, who bankrolled the journey with some of the gold that Semenov gave her as a parting gift. Just as important, the ataman ordered that special attention be given to Father Seraphim's boxcar as it crept south through the war-zone now raging along the Trans-Baikal Railway. The priest and his morbid cargo departed Chita on 11 March, and took several days to travel just from Chita to Manchuli, being frequently interrupted by combat operations along a fluid and unpredictable frontline that advanced 25 miles one day, and retreated 15 miles the next. The end was near.[166]

Firesales, strikes, mutinies, collaboration and a coup

White territory in Siberia shriveled to a skeletal web hugging the Transbaikal railways. The refuge that the Whites had long enjoyed in Manchuria along the Chinese Eastern Railway become increasingly inhospitable. In Harbin, White officers and Russian railway bureaucrats competed with representatives of Vladivostok's new 'Red–Pink regime' for the ears (and, no doubt, pockets) of Chinese officials.[167] In mid-February 1920, radio news announced that a certain Major General Tumbair, who seems to have been a Mongol prince of some sort, had declared himself the Supreme Ruler of a new Provisional Russian Government at Harbin, and that Ataman Semenov was subordinate to him. 'He [Tumbair] requests Semenov to continue his activities for complete restoration of a single and great Russia for the benefit of the Motherland and the people.' Days later a new report clarified the relationship of the mysterious new Supreme Ruler with Chita, stating cryptically that Prince Tumbair was 'leaving for abroad on a mission for Ataman Semenov'. Nothing more was heard of Major General Prince Tumbair.[168]

In late February, Chinese General Bao Huit-sing had ominously referred to General Horvath 'as merely the railway manager' before a group of foreign officials.[169] Soon after, General Bao assumed responsibility for law and order on the Chinese Eastern. Bao's 1st Mukden Brigade patrolled the rails, the 1st Kirin Brigade garrisoned Nikolsk-Ussuriisk and the 1st Heilong Jiang Brigade took positions along the Amur river border.

General Bao's soldiers were now bold enough to disarm and turn back Whites crossing the frontier into China at Manchuli.[170] When word of this spread up the line to echelons of *kappel'evtsy* that were trying to evacuate, the troops began deserting their trains at Dauria to attempt the border crossing on foot.[171] Sanitary trains with sick Russian soldiers were turned back at the border. The Chinese had reason to fear epidemics spawned by Russian refugees – 500 cases of typhus were reported at Mysovaya, and thousands more were estimated 'along the line'.[172] However, the Chinese were still unable to impede Semenov's powerful *broneviki*, and thus could not disarm the troops embarked inside them. The numbers were not insignificant: a couple of hundred soldiers could be squeezed onto an armored train. Semenov's uncle, an OMO general, had recently arrived in Manchuli and was making local officials nervous. To offset the OMO presence in Manchuli, Chinese military officers suggested to American RRSC men that they somehow finagle the transfer of General Horvath's *bronevik* from Harbin to Manchuli as 'moral backing for the Chinese soldiers'.[173] Though certainly sympathetic to the Chinese, the RRSC abstained from pursuing this suggestion.

Semenov's *broneviki* continued to move with relative freedom in northwestern Manchuria, whipping and torturing railway employees as always. In Harbin and Hailar, Semenov's agents and former Kolchak officers were 'selling all that was in their hands: automobiles, horses, equipment, sugar'.[174] According to Vladivostok's Red government, this firesale included 'the property of the aviation detachment, sanitary trains, river vessels of the Sungari fleet and areas of land'.[175] They also accused Semenov of looting all saleable commodities from freight on the Transbaikal *magistral* and selling 20,000 *poods* of cotton and large quantities of tungsten and gold, the latter being stockpiled and guarded by a detail of OMO officers in Hailar. Most goods were snatched up at substantial discount by Japanese and Chinese buyers.

On the third anniversary of the genuine 12 March revolution, Red factions in Vladivostok and Harbin celebrated by increasing the pressure on Semenov and the surviving Whites. A large parade of red banners choked Vladivostok's main avenues to amplify the local Socialist-Revolutionary administration's demand that Director General Horvath relinquish his authority.[176] At 11 a.m. the next day, the sirens of Harbin's mills and workshops shrieked and the workers downed their tools in a general strike to reinforce the demand.[177] Railway employees at the town of Menduchai publicly vowed to die rather than permit another White or Japanese punitive train expedition to pass over their rails.[178] General Horvath responded with a threat to replace the rebellious workers with anti-Bolshevik refugees from the Urals, who allegedly numbered 24,000 men around Chita.[179] Semenov threatened the Chinese generals that if their troops did not put down the strike, he would respond with attacks by aircraft and *broneviki*.[180] In Chita, Semenov propagandists issued a proclamation that 'Jews have ruined Russia and must be killed'. Horvath and Semenov's threats were empty. OMO desertions around Chita had grown so serious that Nikitin House, the ataman's residence, now relied on a company of Japanese infantry for protection.[181]

Sretensk was attacked on 13 March by a partisan force that now included some of the city's former White defenders from the Troitskosavsk regiment. The Japanese Army rushed in to rescue Semenov's garrison, losing three men killed and seven wounded in the process. News of the battle, although just a minor skirmish compared to others, seemed to break the camel's back of public opinion in Japan. Under the headline of 'Unfortunate Victims of the War', an article in the *Osaka Mainichi* bemoaned the Siberian quagmire on 20 March: 'Sacrificing our heroic soldiers in such absurd battles is inadmissible. We demand an answer from the Military Command.'[182]

Throughout northwest Manchuria, many Semenov's soldiers were casting their lots with the striking railway workers. At Bukhedu an OMO *bronevik* crew and all troops on board joined the strikers. Revolutionary fever spread among OMO detachments, stimulated by Chinese Eastern Railway strikers, deserting militia, retreating *kappel'evtsy* and ominous reports of Red advances from western and eastern Transbaikalia.

If not for Semenov's Japanese protectors, Chita may have fallen. On 14 March 2,000 Red cavalrymen, 'insurgents of the Yakimov Division', emerged out of the barren hills around Olovyannaya and captured the town. To placate the Czech Legion and a 300-man Japanese garrison, the Reds agreed not to occupy the train station.[183] During the next four days the Reds withdrew to the hills and returned to recapture Olovyannaya two more times. On 15 March they 'captured and dismantled' an OMO armored train. 'The railway men' – fearing forced conscription, round-ups and requisitions by the partisans – 'appealed to the Japanese colonel for protection', wrote Major Hazzard, the RRSC officer there, 'and he refused on the grounds that they [the Japanese] were not interfering with Russian affairs'.[184]

About the same time Red cavalry surrounded an OMO armored train, the 'Stanichnik', near Karymskaya junction. The *bronevik* crew wasted little time killing their officers and joining the Reds. Semenov was furious and accused the Czechs of aiding the Reds in the 'Stanichnik' capture. It so happened that the Czech Legion's commander, General Syrovy, and his headquarters train was sitting in one of the Chita railyards at the time. Three OMO trains pulled alongside, menacingly 'cleared [their] decks for action' and trained their guns on Syrovy's train. During the subsequent lull, Czech soldiers strolled back and forth between their headquarters train and the *bronveviki* 'with well-filled pockets suggesting bombs [i.e. grenades]'. A White general among the Kappel Army found out about the standoff and ordered Semenov's trains to retire. Later that night Semenov sent a letter to General Syrovy apologizing for the incident.[185]

The proximity of the impressive Czech armored train 'Orlik' may have persuaded OMO to back down. The 'Orlik' was a battlefield trophy taken from the Bolsheviks by the Czechoslovak Legion on the Volga river front in 1918, sacrificing many lives for its capture. Legion engineers and mechanics had enhanced its armor, armaments and power, and lovingly maintained it, making it the strongest armored train in Transbaikalia in 1920, the envy of every general, commissar and warlord.[186]

Even Adrianovka, the home base of OMO's Armored Train Division, was not immune from attack. Partisans raided the town the first few times in March, then returned every so often. Japanese armored trains would rush toward Adrianovka from the west, 'only to find that the Reds had made their call and departed over the hills'.[187]

Hailar, Semenov's original Manchurian springboard, fell without a fight to Socialist-Revolutionaries during the night of 15 March. When dawn broke, a revolutionary guard was in charge of the railway station, and the bulk of Semenov's Cossack garrison had switched allegiance to the Reds. General Skipetrov, former commander of the OMO Wild Division that had been trounced in Irkutsk three months before, was forced to flee with his family from his railcar headquarters to the local Japanese mission. General Bao's Chinese troops immediately established a cooperative rapport with the Socialist-Revolutionaries to prevent disorder in the city or along the rails. By dusk on 16 March, the Socialist-Revolutionaries agreed to turn over their weapons to the Chinese Army to defuse White Russian protests.[188]

That same day in Harbin, the Chinese Army occupied the offices of the Chinese Eastern Railway Board. General Bao ordered Director General Horvath to relinquish his political authority, disbanded Horvath's private army and police force, and began arresting the strikers who made these moves against Horvath possible.[189] Two days later the strike ended.

At the east end of the Chinese Eastern Railway, it seemed as if everyone in Pogranichnaya turned out to enthusiastically welcome the first Red Army men to town. A huge parade of citizens assembled at dawn and marched through town singing, waving red flags and bearing red banners emblazoned 'For the dead who were killed by the Kolchak regime.' The Red detachment arrived on a military train hauling a flatcar with a 3-inch gun, and appeared well-equipped in uniforms and arms. 'While at the station, the commander of the troops made a short speech to the people, and I saw old ladies and old men fall on their knees, tears running down their faces, and thank God that freedom had come at last', wrote an American intelligence officer.

> It is the first time since I have been in Siberia that I have seen the people and soldiers mingle together as friends in an open-hearted way and no one was afraid to talk. There were one or two minor railway officials who were openly talking against the Bolsheviks and I personally know that, if a Bolshevik under like circumstances had been talking against Semenov or Kolchak, they would immediately have been put under arrest and, no doubt, shot without trial.[190]

God and free speech would eventually be forbidden by the Bolshevik liberators, but Pogranichnaya would see Red and White rule eclipse their town several more times before that time came.

Everyone seemed to sense the shift in the winds of war. There was certainly nothing unusual in the mid-March robbery of Ivan Sovenkov and family in Olovyannaya by OMO Lieutenant Mikhailov and six Cossacks. During a supposed search for arms, the Cossacks invaded Sovenkov's home and demanded that he turn over his cash to them, whipping him and beating him with rifle butts, causing much shouting and crying from his family, which earned Sovenkov additional lashes. Mikhailov's men walked away with 10,462 rubles and 50 kopeks, a table cloth, all of Ivan's clothing and boots and all of the family's blankets, tea and leather, leaving them destitute. What distinguished this minor crime from the scores of others that day was that Sovenkov reported it, an action that, since the revolution began, would have normally been considered pointless if not a foolhardy, perhaps suicidal, provocation.[191] However, a Czechoslovak garrison had been recently established in Olovyannaya, bringing a semblance of law and order back to the town. Days later, when Japanese soldiers requisitioned – 'by means of their bayonets' – the horses of six locksmiths and machinists, the victims carried their complaint to Major Cermak, the Czech garrison commander.[192]

On 16 March the 3,000 surviving officers of Kappel's Army assembled in Chita to choose either to accept peace offers from the revolutionary governments in Verkhne-Udinsk and Vladivostok, or to accept aid from the Japanese. The latter choice implied that they would remain in Transbaikalia to fight for Semenov and alongside the Japanese. The *kappel'evtsy* chose to leave Russia altogether. As for Semenov, they sarcastically insisted that, since he had not yet fought the Reds, he should remain in Transbaikalia to have the opportunity. As they departed, they crossed paths with defeated ruffians like Ivanov-Rinov, Annenkov and Verigo (Semenov's Vladivostok commander) who were bound for OMO territory, the only Russian soil where they were still welcome.[193]

The separation between Reds and Whites grew more porous every day. There was even a railway service between Red Verkhne-Udinsk and White Chita.[194] Every faction and force but Semenov seemed to be dabbling in dialogue with the Reds. In mid-March, the commissar of Verkhne-Udinsk boldly traveled to Chita for some unknown reason (presumably incognito) and returned home alive.[195] Even the British mission in Chita now dealt regularly with the Reds to ensure the evacuation of their men still held captive behind Bolshevik lines.[196]

The Bolsheviks cultivated cordial relations with the senior RRSC representative in western Transbaikalia, Major D.S. Colby, who now was working behind the frontlines with a number of other American railway men. Aleksandr Krasnoshchekov, who gave his title as 'Soviet Representative for Far Eastern Affairs', opened a 23 March 'conversation over the direct wire' by saying, 'Greetings, Major! It is all my fault that I went away without bidding you farewell; I left for three days, but, I was delayed. But if everything that I wish for will be accomplished, we will meet again...' They discussed safe conduct passes for British Captain Carthew and a New York businessman to travel to Irkutsk, and Krasnoshchekov inquired about several freightcars of banknote paper originally destined for Kolchak's finance ministry and now stranded in the Chita railyard. As Major Colby relocated east to Chita during the last week of March, he was effusive in his praise for Bolshevik cooperation with the Americans, writing, 'I again want to thank Mr Krasnoshchekov for the splendid treatment and consideration shown our engineers.'[197] On 3 April Colby wrote, 'The supposed enemy, the Reds, are the people from who we are receiving the most assistance and they are the people who are operating the trains', referring to the predominately revolutionary inclinations of the railway workers.[198] The bitter hostility between the Reds and American interventionists in Siberia that would become a common staple of communist propaganda for the next seven decades simply did not exist.

At the end of March, the revolutionary temporary *zemstvo* of western Transbaikalia tried to reach an agreement with the Kappel Army commander, General Voitsekhovskii. This dialogue came to a quick impasse. The *zemstvo* demanded that Voitsekhovskii hand over Semenov, and Voitsekhovskii demanded that the Transbaikal partisans turn against the Bolsheviks.[199] Neither the Kappel general nor the local Reds in Transbaikal were willing to stoop so low as to betray their old treacherous partners.

Tired of Siberia's treachery and heartbreak, the last American forces happily departed Vladivostok on 1 April. Beneath a scrapbook photograph of a gaggle of senior Allied officers in dress uniforms exchanging salutes with each other on the quay, departing US Army Lieutenant Leroy Yarborough quipped, 'Everybody saluted everybody else and gave each other medals, bushwa, banana oil and apple sauce. Ain't this a great old woild?'[200] As a Japanese Army band wistfully played 'Hard Times Come Again No More', the US Army Transport (USAT) *Great Northern* steamed out of the harbor. The ship's passengers included Major General Graves, Colonel Morrow and an embittered Lieutenant Colonel McCroskey, who continued penning angry letters to his patrons in Washington to protest his humiliating extraction from the OMO *bronevik* by Morrow. Sixteen American soldiers received the Distinguished Service Cross, about 30 were killed in action and 60 wounded. An undetermined number of discharged doughboys and deserters stayed behind to tend to their Russian wives, join the partisans like Sergeant Davis, or try their hands in business or as foreign correspondents.[201] Men of the Russian Railway Service Corps also remained behind to run the Trans-Siberian Railway, report Semenov's crimes and assist bystanders swept up into the insanity.[202]

9
WHITE–JAPANESE RESURGENCE, PANIC AND DISASTER

April–December 1920

'So while the going was good he went, abandoning his little kingdom and its people to the encroaching chaos.'

(Peter Fleming)

Massacre at Nikolaevsk and the Japanese offensive

All but the Japanese Army had resigned themselves to the fact that the Red takeover was now a matter of 'when', not 'if'. The Japanese had invested too much blood and yen in Eastern Siberia to abandon their stake timidly: 40 officers killed and a like number wounded, 730 enlisted men killed and 650 wounded, 500 soldiers dead from disease and anywhere from 180 to 500 million yen.[1] In fact, in exchange for aid to the Whites, the Japanese now demanded Russian property with 'written proof of equity'.[2] Indeed, even several weeks later, the Japanese were 'purchasing...many stores, forest lands, coal mines and all other property that they can get their hands on'.[3] For 4 million yen, Japanese owners took control of the Chinese Eastern Railway's fuel supply by purchasing a huge timber concession that came with its own railway spur and saw mill.[4] However, if the Japanese Army had entertained any thoughts about departing Siberia, news of tragic events in the isolated town of Nikolaevsk-on-Amur forced them to remain to redeem their honor.

Despite Nikolaevsk's benign acceptance of Red occupation on 28 February, Yakov Triapitsyn's throng of coarse, illiterate partisans fell upon the prosperous town like stygian locusts, immediately beginning roundups and executions of White military men and class enemies against a backdrop of drunken sadism, pillaging and mass rape. Triapitsyn's scandalous chief of staff and purported mistress, Nina Pavlovna Lebedeva-Kyashko, an officious 21-year-old Moscovite, paraded about shamelessly in furs, jewelry and clothing of *burzhui* victims, and 'the wives of commissars' and 'employees of the Requisition Commission' followed suit. When not modeling the wardrobes of her victims, Kyashko reputedly strutted about 'armed to the teeth and habitually clad in dark red leather'.[5] All citizens were required to register for work assignments, to hand over 'all musical instruments, typewriters, libraries, pictures and objects of artistic value' to the Commissariat of Education; sewing machines to the Union of the Needle; and cows, pigs, poultry, paint, all items made of copper, nickel and cast-iron and 'excess' food to the Commissariat of Supply and Provisions.[6]

Several hours before dawn on 12 March, the 300-man Japanese garrison, having received an ultimatum to surrender its weapons, witnessing the on-going slaughter and realizing that it faced the same fate, attacked Triapitsyn's headquarters and a nearby partisan artillery battery. Savage fighting raged for two days, although it was quickly apparent that the greatly outnumbered Japanese were in a hopeless situation. Their strongpoints on fashionable Nevelskaya Ulitsa, in the consulate and a public meeting hall, had their backs to the Amur river where Chinese gunboats, frozen in the harbor ice, violated their neutrality to mow down escaping Japanese soldiers. Seven blocks away from the waterfront, the Japanese made a last stand in their large stone barracks after the adjacent battalion headquarters and neighboring brothels had been overrun. Long before the Reds finished off the Japanese garrison, they began slaughtering the 400 civilian men, women and children of the town's sizeable Japanese expatriate community, even Consul Ishida and family. By 16 March when 160 delegates arrived for the regional Congress of Soviets, Nikolaevsk's central business district was smoldering, frozen Japanese cadavers stripped of all saleable clothing reclined stiffly in the streets and citizens with any education or property who had not yet been crammed into the overcrowded prison were cowering in hiding.[7]

Rumors of the Nikolaevsk bloodbath soon spread to the Japanese commands in Khabarovsk and Vladivostok, then to the occupation troops and the press and by 20 March to parliamentary factions and Emperor Yoshihito's court. Nevertheless, it was inconceivable to the Japanese staff in Vladivostok that their entire Nikolaevsk garrison could be wiped out. On about 24 March Lieutenant Colonel Eichelberger, the AEFS intelligence officer, ascertained, 'Japanese Headquarters feels that two companies of infantry and one machine gun company are capable of defending themselves'.[8] Unfortunately for the people of Nikolaevsk, Japanese headquarters was wrong.

Yet the Japanese were slow to comprehend the disaster, even when confronted with evidence. In fact, several weeks after Triapitsyn's takeover, Nikolaevsk businessmen stranded in Japan encountered a Red official named Goncharev, who had 'registered in a first-class hotel [in Tokyo], hired a secretary, and began to live as becomes a man with a large amount of gold in his possession'. Indeed, Goncharev *did* have a large amount of gold, but it was only a trifle of the 70 *poods* of gold that Triapitsyn's partisans had expropriated, in addition to a wealth of lumber, furs and other commercial treasure. Behind Goncharev's ostentatious junket was an important Bolshevik mission: to cash in the property of Nikolaevsk's counterrevolutionaries and 'bourgeoisie skunks and reptiles' before anyone realized that they had been murdered. However, it is unclear if the Japanese ever made the connection between Goncharev and the silence from Nikolaevsk-on-Amur.[9] When Japan finally woke up, the Nikolaevsk massacre caused a political scandal in Tokyo that dominated newspaper headlines and publicly heaped shame upon the Ministry of War and an estranged and embittered General Headquarters.[10]

Hostility between the Japanese and new revolutionary administrations in the Maritime province was on the rise well before the gruesome news from Nikolaevsk-on-Amur ignited Japan's wrath. In recent weeks, White agents under Japanese protection had attempted to assassinate Vladivostok's Red police chief, Lazo, and a member of the Bolshevik 'counterespionage department' named Popov. The Reds complained, 'These former [White] Rozanov officers can be seen almost every day driving about in Japanese Red Cross automobiles.' On 4 March 1920 Aleksei Lutskii (alias Gubelman) addressed a 'Communist–Bolshevik Party' meeting in Vladivostok's People's Hall, telling the crowd 'that enmity of the Russians towards the Japanese is at fever height, especially since the incident when the Russian Partisans took the town of Nikolaevsk-on-Amur', seemingly referring to the killing of the Red negotiator Orlov. In retrospect, the tenor of Lutskii's speech suggested that Vladivostok unleashed Triapitsyn upon Nikolaevsk to express the fury of 'the people'.[11] He made it clear that the Reds considered the Japanese departure from Russia to be a fait accompli and even raised 'the possibility of a conflict with Japan' due to the 'grave and alarming' situation brought about by Japan's stalling. If saber rattling would hasten Japan's exit, Lutskii and his comrades were certainly willing to try. Before the end the month, hundreds of Japanese civilians from Blagoveshchensk and other towns in Amur province fled to Vladivostok with other refugees. A similar evacuation appeared likely from Nikolsk-Ussuriisk, which had become a flashpoint for Russo-Japanese tension.[12] On 26 March Japanese soldiers with fixed bayonets surrounded the railway station, roundhouse, railyards, commandant's office and telephone exchange, 'preparing for a fight', but apparently could find no one to fight with.[13]

Japan had already been gearing up for a campaign to consolidate its Siberian occupation when the other interventionists vacated, but the Nikolaevsk massacre infused Japanese soldiers with a dangerous thirst for retribution. Signs of an impending Japanese offensive became more frequent in the weeks before the departure of the SS *Great Northern*, the last official evacuation vessel of the pesky Americans, on 1 April. Japanese troop movements and infusions of reinforcements which had begun in January reached a crescendo in late March as they positioned for action. In Vladivostok, Japanese engineers wired 'the entire fortified area' with a telephone system and dug a network of trenches within 11 miles of the city, while combat units maneuvered around the suburbs and dug into overlooking hills. Troops evacuated most of the Amur province and regrouped in Khabarovsk, precipitating the embarrassing flight of Japanese émigrés in their wake.[14]

On 2 April 1920, the day after the US Army departed, Japanese troops plastered posters in train stations on the Ussuri line demanding that all Red garrisons surrender their weapons. The garrisons were small – about 1,500 Reds in Vladivostok and 2,500 in Khabarovsk, for instance and inexperienced in military duties apart from limited partisan warfare.[15] In conjunction with the poster campaign, General Takayanagi, chief of staff of the Japanese Expeditionary Force, handed the Medvedev government an ultimatum loaded with heavy-handed demands. Important Bolsheviks were recalled from a party congress at Nikolsk to sit on a hastily formed Russo-Japanese Conciliatory Commission that included Takayanagi, Zemstvo General Vasilii G. Boldyrev and a host of other luminaries of the regional political arena. The commission reached agreement on the afternoon of 4 April, so the Medvedev government lifted a state of siege and, being the Saturday before the Palm Sunday holiday, allowed its soldiers to go on short leave. The commission had been nothing but a Japanese ruse all along, intended to distract, then to reassure Medvedev's government.[16]

In the early evening of 4 April Japanese troops quietly began taking up positions and patrolling Vladivostok streets. At 9 p.m., a Japanese unit surrounded 'Edinenie Rossii', a Red armored train near the cavernous train station, demanded and received its prompt surrender just as another detachment disarmed the railyard guardhouse. Soon the main station itself, the Red headquarters across the street and the city's central business district were occupied by Japanese soldiers. Vladivostok's military council was meeting as the Japanese takeover got underway and wisely decided not to resist, but to order its men to head for the hills with their weapons. As the Japanese net drew tighter the council dispersed, except for Sergei Lazo and a few others who stayed behind to destroy secret documents. They were arrested, the first of more than 600 Reds and Pinks (as Whites now referred to Medvedev's Socialist-Revolutionaries) who were rounded up: local police, partisans and revolutionary soldiers. Council members who escaped, including Colonel Krakovetskii and Petr Nikiforov, found refuge in the Czechoslovak headquarters, as did Medvedev. Heavy gunfire shattered the air for about ten minutes shortly after midnight as the Japanese executed a gunnery display to intimidate the Russians – there were very few combat casualties. The Japanese were not so merciful in Vladivostok's Korean neighborhoods. They swooped in for a four-hour rampage to root out all traces of the Korean nationalist underground, killing 300 people, arresting 100 and beating scores of others.[17]

In Nikolsk-Ussuriisk the action began shortly before midnight on 4–5 April when a Japanese major and a large infantry detachment occupied the train station just after departure of the daily express train for Vladivostok, not allowing anyone to enter or leave the building. An American, Harold Van Vechten Fay, until recently a captain in the AEFS intelligence section who had remained in Siberia as a newspaper correspondent, witnessed the occupation and played a minor role in subsequent events by taking an automobile into town to warn the Red military command.[18] Along the way he noted Japanese sentinels posted on roads into the city, 'a strong Japanese outpost at the bridge and... several Japanese soldiers advancing stealthily along the streets in the general direction of the Russian headquarters'. At the Red headquarters, Fay informed the city commander Andreev and his staff of the Japanese movements. 'They were all taken by surprise', he noticed, 'and were at a loss [as to] what measures to take'. They received a terse message from Vladivostok stating that there was gunfire in that city, but it contained no instructions. As dawn broke over Nikolsk, no shots had been fired but Japanese and Russian units were maneuvering through the streets a few hundred yards from each other. In front of Red headquarters sat 'a two-turreted armored automobile, a number of *izvozchiks* [taxi drivers], one machine gun with crew and a small detachment of cavalry'. A few blocks away, the Japanese were beginning to round up unarmed Russian soldiers and herd them to a prisoner collection point.[19]

A company of 95 Japanese soldiers approached a hill that dominated the city with orders to occupy it, only to find that 200 Russians had beat them to it. 'The [Japanese] commander parleyed with the Russian commander and as a result, the two forces returned together to the top of the hill.' Neither unit wanted to fight.

Nikolsk's Japanese garrison normally consisted of General Adagiri's 15th Brigade of the 13th Division – four infantry battalion and a battery of 3-inch field pieces – but reinforcements on troop trains 'from the north' boosted its strength with six more infantry companies and a half-battery of artillery from the 14th Division – altogether 3,000–4,000 seasoned troops. They were assisted by a handful of Kalmykov's OKO officers 'who had been in hiding with the Japanese staff'.

Andreev had 6,000–7,000 Russians, many of dubious ability or reliability, in his command. A large number of former Whites, both officers and soldiers, had been integrated into Andreev's force but, perhaps surprisingly, showed no inclination whatsoever to throw their lot to Adagiri and his traitorous OKO collaborators. A Chinese Army unit was stationed in town to guard as part of the IATB railway guard, and an echelon transporting a part of the Czechoslovak Legion Artillery Regiment sat on the tracks between the train station and the city center. Technically the latter two detachments were neutral, but the thick fog of war in revolutionary Russia often obscured neutrality.

'The Russians did not want to start an engagement', wrote Fay, 'but the Japanese outposts kept pressing close upon the withdrawing Russians until the latter were forced back to the headquarters at the beginning of the so-called fortress or barracks area, and were forced to open fire or let the Japanese walk right in on them in force'. In this manner the Japanese could righteously claim that the Russians fired the first shot about 6 a.m. Immediately thereafter, a hailstorm of gunfire streaked in the direction of the Russian headquarters.

On the hilltop where the Japanese and Russians were only 20 yards apart, a fierce hand-to-hand fight broke out. The Russians opened up with a Maxim machine gun, killing the Japanese company commander and five other men and injuring many more. Nevertheless, most of the undisciplined revolutionary troops 'fled precipitately across the plain' towards town, abandoning a large supply of hand grenades, two 3-inch guns with an ample supply of shells and several wounded comrades. The Japanese, enraged by the death of their captain, refused to allow Russian medics onto the hill to tend to the wounded.

WHITE–JAPANESE RESURGENCE, PANIC AND DISASTER

Inside Nikolsk the battle converged on the triangular military complex fanning out from Commander Andreev's headquarters. For no apparent military reason, the Japanese wasted time and energy terrorizing the military hospital of the complex, killing six of the staff, including a doctor and bayoneting and beating nurses and patients. As the battle thickened, the Russians hunkered down to cover the orderly retreat of the bulk of their forces out of the city. The anchor of this delaying action was the barracks of a Russian engineer battalion in the triangle, 'well supplied with machine guns and protected to a certain extent by barbed wire'. Here the Japanese suffered their heaviest losses – 42 dead and 81 wounded. In contrast to the other revolutionary units, the Russian engineers were veterans of the Eastern Front, accompanied by Hungarian internationalists on the machine guns. They did not panic when the Japanese brought field artillery to bear on the barracks and breached the walls. Three times they beat off Japanese bayonet charges with hand grenades. When the engineers finally withdrew, they left behind 25 men with a machine gun to stall Adagiri's assault. Remarkably, many of this suicide team survived the battle by dispersing and hiding in surrounding houses when they were finally overrun.

As in Vladivostok, Nikolsk's Red garrison headed for the hills while their engineer battalion valiantly blocked the Japanese pursuers. The Japanese still managed to capture two entire battalions of the 33rd Infantry Regiment, composed of 1,650 recruits so raw that they had not yet been supplied with weapons. It looked as if the green troops were sacrificed into captivity to further delay the Japanese from pursuit of more valuable military units. Regardless, most of the Red garrison's materiel fell into Japanese hands, a blunder that later stirred public criticism of Red military leaders.

The Battle of Nikolsk-Ussuriisk petered out before nightfall on 5 April, leaving 200–300 Russians dead and 100–200 wounded and about 70 Japanese killed and 100 wounded. Residual casualties were relatively low, perhaps reflecting the community's increasing experience in the crossfire of civil war. 'A few civilians and two or three Chinese soldiers were killed accidentally', reported Fay, 'and some of the delegates to the Provincial Assembly staying in the barracks are reported to have been wounded'. Plundering and rape occurred 'no more than could be expected', with Japanese soldiers relieving 'captives and passers-by' of money and jewelry and pilfering among the ruins immediately after the battle.

Two days after the battle, the Japanese company on the bloody hilltop finally allowed the Russians to gather their casualties. The medics found no wounded, only 86 corpses, many with their hands clasped, others with their hands above their heads, some with bayonet wounds in the back. Chinese officers housed nearby testified to hearing the Japanese slaughter their prisoners.

The Japanese Army alienated everyone but a handful of fugitive Kalmykov officers, and turned Nikolsk into a thoroughly hostile city, whose populace considered the Japanese assault 'unwarranted and dastardly'. General Adagiri forced the operators of the local power plant back to work by threatening to evict them from their pleasant railway quarters, but could not force the railway men back to work. He turned over the city government to the 'former municipal organization' but the mayor refused to tolerate any Kalmykov officers in his administration, even though they offered to the Japanese to liquidate him. Everyone feared the ruthless OKO men who had been hiding on Japanese military bases since Kalmykov's flight in late February. The Japanese let them taunt their captives ('especially the officers, with some of whom they were personally acquainted') in the overcrowded temporary prison at the Jaeger barracks, and allowed two OKO officers to collect all the secret records from the regional *militsia* (police) office, but otherwise restrained them.

In Khabarovsk, Japanese soldiers surrounded the partisan headquarters and barracks and poured machine gun fire into them for hours, killing and wounding about 500 men.

The one-sided battle seethed from the night of 4 April until the morning of 6 April, when 'Red rule ceased to exist'. About 1,000 Reds surrendered and another 1,000 deserted or retreated towards Blagoveshchensk.[20] On the railway east of Pogranichnaya a battle erupted when the offensive interfered with the passage of Czechoslovak echelons. Had the Japanese waited two more weeks, they would not have had to contend with the Czechs at all, but in most places, the Czechs lay low and waited for the storm to pass.[21]

General Oi apologetically explained in an 5 April proclamation that his forces were simply responding to concerted Russian attacks on Japanese installations the night before, although no such attacks took place. He and his countrymen cynically painted the whole powerful offensive as a misunderstanding, just as Comrades Medvedev and Triapitsyn had shrugged off the Nikolaevsk butchery as a dreadful intercultural misunderstanding.[22] Chaos reigned throughout the Maritime province for two or three days, and, when the dust settled, Japanese flags flapped mockingly atop captured revolutionary headquarters in Nikolsk-Ussuriisk, Khabarovsk, Olga, Shkotovo, Spassk and other towns, Korean communities had been terrorized and, after a brief taste of urban comfort, Red units were settling down in the forests again. In Vladivostok former officers of Semenov, Kalmykov and Rozanov walked the streets flaunting White insignia and decorations that had been outlawed by Vladivostok's *zemstvo* government.[23]

Ninety-eight White prisoners had been en route from Nikolsk to Khabarovsk for trial when the Japanese offensive erupted. About half of the prisoners were former members of the Nikolsk garrison's Jaeger Cavalry Regiment and about 15 came from the 33rd Siberian Rifle Regiment. The group included both regimental commanders, the well-known Colonel Viktor Vrashtel and Colonel Aleksandr Evetskii and many officers. Their two railcars halted at Verino, one stop away from their destination when the Japanese pushed the Bolsheviks out of Khabarovsk. Vengeful Reds ordered the prisoners to strip and, while they shivered through the next few freezing days, withheld food as well. On 9 April an execution squad led by Comrade Orlov, the Verino station commandant, summoned Vrashtel and Evetskii from the pitiful mass. Evetskii snatched a rifle from a Red soldier and was viciously put down by dozens of bayonet thrusts. Vrashtel was more unfortunate, being subjected to a slow, agonizing death that involved whipping, bone-breaking, disjointing, castration and disembowelment before receiving a merciful shot to the head. Orlov, primped mockingly in Vrashtel's *bekesha* (greatcoat) and *papakha* (fur hat) while his men tortured and killed seven more officers that day, then left the others to tremble through the night with hypothermia, hunger and the certainty of their slaughter. On Easter Sunday, 11 April, 24 more prisoners from Spassk and Iman were trucked in. All were transported to a bridge over the River Khor where, one by one, they were called into a *taplushka*, bludgeoned with huge wooden mallets and tossed into the icy waters. Red squads tracked footprints leading from the snowy riverbank to finish off any condemned who miraculously crawled out of the Khor. The dead included the acting commander of the Transbaikal Cossack regiment of Grodekovo, *Pod'esaul'* Innokentii Pilippov, scores of other young officers and Cossacks, Khabarovsk cadets, a priest, a clerk and a few civilian 'class enemies'.[24]

On 10 April, while the Bolsheviks were in the heat of their sadistic bacchanalia at Verino and on the River Khor bridge, the Japanese began negotiating an agreement to coexist with the 'Red–Pink Vladivostok government of Medvedev'. They reached an arrangement before the end of the month.

Meanwhile, in Verkhne-Udinsk four days earlier, Aleksandr Krasnoshchekov proclaimed the creation of the Far Eastern Republic (FER), a buffer state ordered by Lenin to shield Moscow's struggling Soviet government from the wrath and voracity of the Japanese Army. In addition, the Far Eastern Bureau – the *Dal'buro* – of the Russian

Communist Party ordered its disciples to lie low and not create any new soviets until further notice to avoid antagonizing Japan, Britain and France. The buffer state was also the hope of Socialist-Revolutionaries and Irkutsk's recently deposed Political Centrists who envisioned it as a democratic model for Soviet Russia, if not the bridgehead for a democratic counterrevolution.[25] Eventually – on 14 May – the Verkhne-Udinsk government would be publicly blessed by a telegram from Soviet Commissar for Foreign Affairs Georgi Vasil'evich Chicherin informing Krasnoshchekov of the FER's recognition by Lenin's Russian Soviet Federated Socialist Republic (RSFSR). However, from the time of its inception Krasnoshchekov was pulling the financial, military and political strings of the FER at Moscow's command while administration by *zemstvos* gave his government a democratic facade. Medvedev's Vladivostok government also aspired to the helm of the FER, but was discredited by its collaboration with the Japanese, albeit forced. The Red government of the Amur province in Blagoveshchensk considered Medvedev a traitor and recognized Krasnoshchekov's administration.[26] Inasmuch as the FER claimed jurisdiction over all former Russian lands east of Lake Baikal as well as the Chinese Eastern Railway zone, little Verkhne-Udinsk suddenly became the capital of a political entity roughly the size of western Europe.[27]

Unfortunately for Red delegations wishing to travel from one side of the FER to the other, Grigorii Semenov, OMO and the Japanese 5th Division remained entrenched in Chita and along the railway line through southern Transbaikal province. The Ataman controlled both the railway and telegraph, which meant that commissars in Verkhne-Udinsk desiring to communicate with their counterparts in the Amur or Maritime provinces had to dispatch couriers through hostile territory or via a circuitous detour through Mongolia and China that took one month. Removing the 'Chita stopper' became the overriding concern of the FER and Reds in the Russian Far East.[28]

Frontline Transbaikalia

Japan's takeover was not confined to the Maritime province. OMO and Japan's 5th Division clung tenaciously to Transbaikalia, the last stronghold of anti-Bolshevism in Russia. With troops deployed around Chita and south along the Transbaikal Railway holding the Reds at bay, the Japanese command decided to tighten its grip on the critical supply line through northern Manchuria. In the vacuum of Russian imperial power and the March ouster of General Horvath, the Japanese generals aimed to take over the Chinese Eastern Railway. In the process, they would consequently be establishing a fallback position for Ataman Semenov and OMO should the strategic situation in Transbaikalia sour further, however Japan's main intent was to lay the groundwork for the puppet state of Manchukuo, not help the White Russian movement.

Since mid-March the Transbaikal Front seemed to have stabilized on the Trans-Siberian Railway in the west at Mogzon and in the east at Sretensk, roughly 100 and 200 miles from Chita, respectively. However, partisans and the *Narodno-Revolyutsionnaya Armiya* (NRA) – the People's Revolutionary Army, as the FER's regular military forces were christened, continued to envelope and press in upon Chita from the west, north and southwest. The headquarters staff and 14th and 15th Regiments of the NRA 1st Irkutsk Division arrived in Khilok on 20 March, while the division's 3rd Brigade anxiously awaited orders to push east along the *Magistral*. North of the railway line, the 2nd Brigade marched southeast from Vershino-Udinskaya and forded the Konda river to engage the Whites around a chain of six lakes 15 miles northwest of Chita. The 1st Brigade descended from the taiga north of the city. South of the railway line, partisans of the Zhartsev detachment advanced northeast up the Ingoda river, pressing upon Japanese defenses just south of Cheremkhovo. The Japanese and Reds had negotiated neutral zones between their forces that moved east with the tail-end of the evacuating Czechoslovak Legion. Both sides were getting nervous now that the evacuation was nearing the end of the line. Partisans in eastern Transbaikalia were preparing for action around Sretensk in late March, and concentrated near a railway siding at Zagarin, west of Sretensk, to be able to cut off OMO armored trains.[29]

South of Chita both OMO and Japanese troops gradually massed at Borzya throughout March 1920. The Czechs posted there were bristling at their 'host's' restrictions: 'They are not allowed to leave the zone of the railway yard to go to the city bathhouse or walk in the town', observed RRSC Major Colby. Around 1 April, the Japanese ordered the Czechoslovak Legion to move two out of three remaining echelons in the Borzya railyard 'to the east' (i.e. towards Vladivostok). The Czech depot commandant refused to comply because the movement would put his remaining troops at a numerical disadvantage to those of his supposed Japanese ally in case of trouble. The Czech's decision stirred up immediate trouble which vividly illustrated his need for more troops. 'The Semenov and Japanese forces fell in and, for a time, it looked like real action', observed Colby. Finally the Japanese backed down and insisted that their call to arms had really been just a misunderstood effort to *protect* the Czechs from OMO during yet another disagreement between the Cossacks and their Slavic brothers.[30] Ungern-Shternberg's bastion at Dauria was manned by 3,000 men. However, it was erroneously assumed that 'this last garrison will never fight and will simply straggle across into Manchuria when the Red advance reaches that far'.[31]

In Manchuli, OMO liquidated seven telegraph operators ('including one girl', noted Major Colby), presumably as a preventive counterespionage measure although it was just as likely that the shootings were for brutish intimidation or simply gratuitous entertainment.[32] Across the nearby border in Manchuria, the Japanese strengthened their garrison at Harbin by two battalions in late March. In response, the two Chinese Army divisions at Harbin reinforced themselves with machine gun companies.

When the Japanese Army unleashed its troops on the Maritime province on 4 April, the Chinese Eastern Railway zone remained calm. After all, from Manchuli on the Transbaikal border to Prograrmichnaya on the frontier with the Maritime province, the railway stations were bustling with putative Japanese allies: thousands of Chinese Army sentinels, echelons of well-armed Czechoslovak Legionnaires bound for Vladivostok and a handful of American RRSC men directing traffic.

In Transbaikalia it appeared to foreign observers that few Russians remained to fight for Semenov's White regime. On the morning of 5 April a Red airplane dropped leaflets over Chita 'advising people that they [the NRA and partisans] were coming and the only ones who need fear were Semenov and a few of his staff'.[33] Indeed, there were an estimated 60 NRA echelons strung out between Irkutsk and Verkhne-Udinsk, stuck in traffic on the Trans-Siberian.[34] When RRSC Major Merz departed Chita on 7 April, he saw so few Russian soldiers that he concluded that the defenders 'throughout the entire Chita district were Japanese alone'. On 8 April, the Japanese and *semenovtsy* were engrossed in a successful attack against positions of the Burlov partisan detachment near Shaksha, around the south end of the lakes to Chita's west. Thus the Japanese Army surprised allies and enemies alike when it commenced a large-scale campaign to dominate the Chinese Eastern Railway on 9 April. Their troops began occupying stations north of Changchun and 1,000 reinforcements were pumped into Harbin via Japan's Southern Manchuria Railway.[35]

Simultaneously, the Reds maneuvered through the taiga surrounding Chita like hungry wolves, positioning themselves for the final kill. On 10 April the partisans and NRA made their move and advanced toward the city against smaller Japanese and OMO units. On the railway west of Chita the 3rd Brigade of the Irkutsk Division pushed back Japan's 5th Regiment and a Japanese armored train about ten miles through Gongota to Sokhondo. A 2,000-man OMO unit (of whom only 200 troops were deemed 'reliable' by Allied intelligence) fought alongside the Japanese.[36] Five-hundred *kappel'evtsy* that had stood alongside the Japanese at the beginning of the month had disappeared in recent days.[37] At Shaksha, where action began two days prior, strong Red counterattacks gained about five miles. Due north of the city, the 1st Brigade emerged from the taiga at Telemba to advance within 15 miles of Chita. Heavy fighting raged for several days. The ferocity of the combat was bloodily demonstrated by the arrival of some 200 wounded Japanese in Chita (on about 13–14 April), who represented the grisly yield of one day's fighting.[38]

Japanese and OMO defenders dug in and permitted no further advances until the Reds launched a second offensive push on 25 April. Southwest of the city, the Irkutsk Division's 3rd Brigade drove ten miles further east along the Trans-Siberian to capture Kuka. On their left flank, the 2nd Brigade and the Verkhne-Udinsk Brigade advanced from the chain of lakes to Zastepnaya and Pritupovo, respectively, villages less than ten miles from Chita. The Irkutsk Division's 1st Brigade fought its way south along the Chita river, past the Orenburg Cossack Brigade at Podvolochnaya, through the Buryat Cavalry detachment and two other White units at Karlovka, until it was halted at Smolenskoe, on the very outskirts of Chita, by the Ufa Regiment of the Kappel Army. *Kappel'evtsy* also formed the backbone of the White defense to the west of town. Trenches southwest of town were manned by a detachment of General Likhachev, cadets from the Chita Military Academy and the Japanese 5th Regiment. Over the next 12 days they were forced back into the very suburbs of Chita, yet they ferociously clung to the land beneath them, knowing they were the last patches of non-communist Russia.[39]

For the time being, the White army also held against the partisans in eastern Transbaikalia. East of the railway junction at Karymskaya, the 2nd Corps of *kappel'evtsy* was deployed along the north bank of the Ingoda river and OMO units paralleled the south bank.[40] A 2,000-man Transbaikal Cossack Brigade defended Nerchinsk and a 3,000-man Transbaikal Cossack Division protected the eastern extreme of Semenov's dominion. Nerchinsk was still secure enough weeks later to host Ataman Semenov for a banquet in his honor on 2 May, where, after a stirring 'U-ra!' by the assembled Cossacks, a Colonel Umed twice compared the ataman favorably to Napoleon, apparently forgetting the latter's disastrous retreat out of Russia.[41]

The shadow of the civil war's frontline ushered new hardships into Chita. Some 25,000 Japanese soldiers occupied the city, but brought none of the prosperity or order that accompanied the occupation in 1918. Living conditions became deplorable. Food was scarce and there was no clothing, boots or other necessities except that which could be scavenged from corpses. Commerce had ceased and OMO men confiscated any merchandise they desired. A new reign of terror took hold as Japanese police augmented Semenov's counterintelligence units, arresting and disposing of 'undesirables'.[42] Relations with their former Czech allies were irreconcilable. At a garrison reunion during Easter, an OMO divisional commander collected 30 silver rubles and sent them to General Jan Syrovy, with a message that the Czechs had sold Admiral Kolchak just as Judas had sold Christ.[43] White Transbaikalia seemed to heaving its last painful gasps.

The Hailar incident

In a seemingly trivial deed far from the battle fronts, at 3 a.m. on 9 April, Japanese soldiers in Hailar arrested 11 Russians: seven members of the Regional Railway Committee, an assistant station master and three telegraphers.⁴⁴ Even though the Japanese command may have intended the arrests to be a provocation (for a devious purpose to be explained shortly), they ignited an unexpectedly fierce storm of protest from the Chinese Eastern workforce that escalated into an explosive international incident. Everyone knew of the arrest and summary execution of three railway employees by the Japanese three days prior at Imyanpo. Crowds began to gather around the Japanese headquarters, where the Hailar men were held. The workers made it known that they were willing to call a general strike to effect their comrades' release.

At first glance, Japan appeared ill-prepared for the turmoil brewing in Hailar. Only 500 Japanese troops and 500 OMO soldiers were stationed there, while three Czech Legion echelons waited in the railyard, two eastbound echelons were near enough to respond within several hours time and the headquarters train of the 3rd Czechoslovakian Division was en route from Manchuli.⁴⁵ In addition to these men, the most formidable armored train in the Russian Far East, the Czech 'Orlik', growled vigilantly among the echelons.

By the time the sun rose on 10 April, the headquarters train was trapped in the Hailar railyard and while Major Colby anxiously telegraphed RRSC officers and rail traffic managers to extricate it from the area, Chinese Eastern workers were busy ensnaring the Czech trains further by 'accidentally' derailing a decapod at the roundhouse, leaving available only a hobbled locomotive that needed a right piston packing. The Russians were not about to let a trainload of Czechoslovak leaders abandon them to face off the Japanese Army alone – or so it appeared, because the railway employees were unwittingly playing right into a carefully orchestrated Japanese plan. The workers formally protested the Japanese actions to Dr Blagosh, a senior Czechoslovak political leader passing through on the 3rd Division train.⁴⁶ Blagosh brought the arrests to the attention of Chinese authorities, who were growing increasingly frustrated by Japanese indignities, but the Chinese military commander was conveniently 'not at home'. Russian civil authorities in Hailar tried to raise the matter with the Japanese Consul in Harbin, but were ignored.

It was Easter weekend and large holiday crowds stoked the drama. 'The usual Easter crowd attended the services at the Church and there were a number of people on the streets and around the station until about 2:00 a.m.', noted Major Colby. On Easter morning, 11 April, the mail train pulled into Hailar station. 'The arrested men, with their hands bound behind their backs, were hurried into the mail coach, surrounded by a strong armed convoy who entered the coach along with the prisoners', wrote an eyewitness. 'The doors were immediately closed and bolted, and a strong Japanese guard stood outside on the platform to keep everyone at a distance.'⁴⁷ The workers spontaneously declared a strike and removed the locomotive from the mail train. From the little barred windows of the mail car, the prisoners proclaimed that 'they were quite prepared to be shot on the spot by the Japanese rather than be handed over to Semenov'.

Dr Blagosh, RRSC Major Colby and a French Colonel Loubignac called on the Japanese commander, who kept them waiting two hours in an anteroom before sending a lowly captain to inform them that the prisoners would not be released. Throughout the afternoon, bands from the Chinese Army and Czech Legion's 12th Infantry Regiment played at Hailar station before a crowd of workmen that was growing increasingly intoxicated – as was the Russian holiday tradition, but remained peaceful.⁴⁸

At 8 p.m., the Czech band played its last tune and the crowd began to disperse when a couple of Japanese platoons suddenly formed a cordon around the mail car in the railyard, then began leading the prisoners away on foot. Having realized that the workers would obstruct them every *verst* of the way by rail, the Japanese intended to transport the detainees to Manchuli by automobile. 'Among the crowd of civilians thronging after the cordon there were relatives of the railway employees, their wives and children. The crowd was convinced that the prisoners would be brought to Dauria and shot there', observed Lieutenant Colonel Kopal, the ranking Czech officer on the scene. 'The crowd shouted to the prisoners that they would not be left alone and the prisoners asked for help from the mass.'

Someone in the crowd shouted, 'Let's go!', and opened fire with a revolver as another Russian tossed a grenade at the Japanese escort trailing the prisoners, felling four or five. In rapid response a Japanese policeman tossed a grenade into the prisoners and the bedlam began. The Japanese escort quickly fell back at a run, formed a line and began firing into the gathering, sending it surging between trainloads of startled Czech and Chinese soldiers toward the station. Some Chinese soldiers on the station platform dived behind cover and began firing, presumably at the Japanese. Screams filled the air, children became separated from their parents and the nimble trampled the fallen. Japanese machine guns hammered away to cover the escort's withdrawal, slicing through the echelons in the railyard, wounding several civilians, 'including two or three women'. It was during the first terrifying minutes of madness that most casualties were struck down by the wild fusillade. 'Chinese were seen firing without aim. Several cars of the Czechoslovak trains were shot through', reported Kopal. 'One Czech officer and one soldier were killed. Seven soldiers and a Czech soldier's wife [were] wounded.' Not a shot was fired from the Czech echelons.

Lieutenant Colonel Kopal and Major Kvapil, the 3rd Division chief of staff, strode between their echelons and 'issued a strict order that nobody should interfere with anything whatever [that] may happen'. For an hour, rifle and machine gun fire thundered from the vicinity of the Chinese barracks where the Japanese had retreated, although it began to appear that there was no real fight going on. Even after the Japanese made their way back to their own barracks, they continued firing to show their displeasure and shot up the American Barracks – whose sole remaining occupant, Major Colby – escaped unharmed.

Not until the afternoon of 12 April was the Czechoslovak staff permitted to meet for an inquiry with the Chinese and Japanese commanders.[49] Lieutenant Colonel Kopal declared that the Czechoslovaks were not interested in the trouble between the Japanese and Russians, but needed to record an explanation for their casualties. To his surprise, the Japanese weaved a concocted tale of a firefight precipitated by a drunken Czech soldier and exacerbated by legionnaires who joined an attack by Russian workmen. To boot, the Japanese officers unashamedly falsely accused the 'Orlik' of having fired its artillery during the fight. This drew immediate denials from the Czechs who pointed out that the damage caused by such a 'gun projectile could not have been kept secret' in the narrow confines of the railyard. As the tone of the meeting became more confrontational between the Czechs and Japanese, the Chinese representatives sought to calm them by insisting that 'it was only a small incident [between Russians and Japanese] that was already over'. Eventually the meeting dissolved peacefully and the Czechs thought that everything was settled.

Since the Russian prisoners had made their escape from the Japanese during the mêlée, the strike was called off and the Chinese Eastern Railway began running again. The Chinese Army echelon and that of the Czechoslovak 3rd Division staff departed for the east late in the day. Hailar appeared so tranquil that no guard was posted at the train station that night. The Czechs heard unsubstantiated reports that Japan was shipping more troops up the Southern Manchuria Railway to Hailar, but naturally associated their ally's movements with the large defensive effort around Chita.

Hailar had groggily returned to normal by the morning of 13 April, when two Japanese military trains were reported a few stations to the west: an armored train and a 21-car 'mission train' that was coming to the area 'to ascertain the cause of the [recent] problems'. Just after dinner, Major Colby's interpreter, Paul Pastell, 'took a little walk' with his boss's binoculars and noticed Japanese foot soldiers west of town. He climbed a water tower for a better view and stumbled upon two railway workers on the lookout atop the structure. They watched in shock as the mission train halted some distance away and unloaded a large detachment of soldiers who formed up and advanced in skirmish order along the ridge above town. Pastell ran to tell Colby, who immediately advised the senior Czechoslovak Legion officer, a major from the 12th Regiment. The major was quite surprised, having thought that his superiors had smoothed over the Easter Day misunderstanding. Yet here before his eyes, Japanese soldiers were busily preparing offensive positions, setting up three gun positions with a breastwork overlooking town, and digging in directly opposite the two remaining Legion echelons and the 'Orlik'. About 2 p.m., Colby noticed that the Japanese had severed the telegraph lines between Hailar and the outside world. At the railway bridge east of town, Japanese soldiers pried up the rails to prevent their Czechoslovak 'allies' from escaping.[50]

An automobile with two Chinese Army officers pulled up and whisked the Czech major off to an unknown destination. Colby searched for him, and upon finding the Japanese headquarters deserted, called on the Chinese headquarters. A friendly Chinese officer plied him with tea, cigarettes and small talk and eventually informed Colby that his 'presence [at the headquarters] was not desired' by the Japanese, who, as a matter of fact, intended to disarm the Czechs. Colby emerged into panicked streets and rushed to warn his fellow RRSC officers and Russian employees. The Chinese military had warned Hailar's civilian population that the town was about to be shelled, and people were fleeing as the Czechs hurriedly prepared for battle.

The Chinese knew much more of the Japanese plans than they were sharing with their Czech and US allies. An eastbound Chinese *bronevik* refrained from entering Hailar and halted three stations to the west. Behind the scenes in Peking, the Chinese had demanded the release of the prisoners days earlier, the Japanese had refused, and the prospect of a new Sino-Japanese war had briefly loomed on the horizon.[51] 'The Chinese are passive', reported Colby to the RRSC office in Harbin.

> Through British Intelligence I learn that the Chinese Representative understands the seriousness of the situation and the position in which China is placed. Still he claims that China is not in shape to fight Japan and that this is by no means a local matter as the Japs have a well-defined policy which the Chinese are powerless to stop. He claims it is a matter for the Allies to handle.[52]

However, the Allies no longer functioned as a unified body.

In the 13 April meeting at Chinese headquarters in Hailar, the Japanese presented the bewildered Czech major with an ultimatum: turn over the armored train 'Orlik' and all of his men's hand grenades, or be attacked. Surely the major was tempted to fight, having already fought the Red Guards, Red Army, Red partisans and OMO to make it from the Volga to Hailar. However, the major chose not to spill more Czech blood for a pointless fight when his men were mere days away from returning home. He ordered his men to comply with the Japanese ultimatum. 'The Czechs feel the disgrace deeply', noted Major Colby.

Again, the Japanese cynically characterized the ugly affair as a misunderstanding, insisting that General Jan Syrovy had verbally promised General Fukuda that the legion would turn over the 'Orlik' when it reached Manchuli. However, the commander of the Czechoslovak rear guard, Colonel Prchala, was quite surprised when Japanese General Hoshino 'proposed' the transfer of the 'Orlik' at Manchuli–Syrovy had mentioned no such promise before embarking on a homebound ship from Vladivostok. In the end, Japan was willing to risk diplomatic fallout and open warfare to prevent the Czechs from bequeathing the 'Orlik' to Medvedev's 'Red-Pink government' in Vladivostok.

Forging a Japanese–Mongol buffer state

Hours after they disarmed the Czechs at Hailar on 13 April 1920 the Japanese 'forced the Chinese out of the offices of the Railway Administration at Harbin' and took over the Chinese Eastern Railway.[53] About this time an OMO representative, General Malinovskii, arrived in Mukden and put up at the Miyako Hotel in the Japanese quarter. His presence stirred suspicions and rumors, as he 'refrained from all intercourse with local Chinese officials and received numerous visits from prominent Japanese'. Malinovskii, it turned out, was laying the groundwork for the visit of Ataman Semenov to Mukden and Dairen a few days later to discuss OMO's role in Japan's Manchurian schemes. During this period the ataman was constantly accompanied by his Japanese advisor, Captain Kurizawa, 'the soul of the intervention in Chita'.

The takeover of the Chinese Eastern Railway produced immediate, tangible benefits for Ataman Semenov and his Japanese associates. In mid-April, as soon as the Japanese Army and OMO occupied the Chinese Eastern, the US Military Attaché in Peking reported, 'Gold has been shipped out of the country by the car load, and is stolen from all who are known to possess the metal. Twenty-six *poods* [939 pounds] of platinum, said to be more than the world produces in one year, were recently sent out by Semenov, and his agents are scouring the country for more'.[54] There would be no repeats of the 8 March embarrassment, when Chinese customs officers confiscated one of Semenov's shipments of treasures.

Russian, Japanese and Allied political leaders and diplomats acknowledged that a buffer state would have to be established to allow Soviet and Japanese forces to disengage, however, there was no agreement on how, when and where this buffer state would come into being. The Japanese generals aimed to cobble together a Pan-Mongol and Cossack protectorate that could eclipse the Red contender for buffer state in western Transbaikalia, Krasnoshchekov's 'Verkhne Udinsk Democratic Republic'.[55] Thus, the Japanese Army's strategic objective in spring 1920, which coincided with Ataman Semenov's ambition, was to establish White Transbaikalia as the central pillar of a buffer state that would incorporate – to the west – Outer Mongolia and – to the east – the Inner Mongolian homelands along the Chinese Eastern Railway in northern Manchuria. Fears arose among the Reds and Allies that the Japanese might even launch an offensive to reclaim western Transbaikalia to the shores of Baikal. This explained the determined Japanese defense of Chita and incursions into the Yablonovkii mountains between Chita and the Outer Mongolia border, as well as OMO deployments into Manchuria even though Transbaikalia was under siege.

As soon as the Czechoslovak echelons departed Manchuli and Hailar, OMO troops moved in, taking over small outposts in between as well. Many of their officers had preceded them aboard the Japanese mission train that checkmated the 'Orlik' days earlier. Allied agreements forbade them to enter China armed, so OMO personnel passed through Manchuli without weapons and were outfitted by the Japanese in Hailar. By mid-April, at least 200–300 hundred *semenovtsy* were stationed for the long term in Hailar and two railcars of powder and rifles had been received. This buildup was aimed more at the Chinese Army than it was at Red detachments. Before the end of April 1920, OMO troops were crossing into Manchuria fully armed, and when Chinese generals protested, 'the Japanese ... declared that the Russians were in the service of Japan'. General Pao Kwei-Ching decided that it was useless to fight against the Japanese and OMO forces that had already invaded his Manchurian military district under the guise of Allied agreements. General Pao and Chang Tso-Lin both blamed their European and US allies for China's predicament. Japanese propaganda at Hailar crowed that Semenov was 'now in control in Harbin'.[56]

Likewise, as American RRSC officers went home, droves of Japanese railway experts rushed in to replace them. In contrast to the Americans, the Japanese not only shipped in supervisors, but workers as well, and occupied many smaller stations that the Americans had not seen fit to staff. They were not interested in cultivating fraternal relationships like those that bound the Russian and American railroaders. They came to take over.[57]

From Harbin to Vladivostok, the Japanese Army increased its guards all along the line, 'there being from 200 to 300 men placed at posts where but 20 or 30 have hitherto been stationed'. They flaunted the Allied rail agreement that gave China responsibility for guarding the Chinese Eastern and sneaked in additional men each night from Korea via the Southern Manchuria Railway.

Japan signaled her expansionist intentions by quietly building out her strategic communications infrastructure. On or about 18 April Japanese military units occupied Harbin's wireless station, completing a chain of wireless stations at Chita and Manchuli. Japanese signalmen maintained dual telegraph wires between Chita and Vladivostok that they had strung in the winter of 1918. Allied agents at Pogranichnaya reported five freight cars loaded with spools of iron wire for expanding the Japanese Army communications network. In addition, Japanese businessmen were 'purchasing all electric light stations [and] what telephone stations they can'. Such preparations indicated that Japan had no intention of leaving Siberia and northern Manchuria any time soon.[58]

The evacuation of the Czechoslovak Legion was almost complete. Most of the legion was aboard some 35 echelons that were now east of Pogranichnaya, although a rear guard unit remained at Manchuli to protect the coal supply for the thinning stream of echelons traversing the Chinese Eastern Railway.

The Japanese Army made every effort to delay its day of reckoning with the Reds by impeding the evacuation. In brazen contravention of the Inter-Allied Technical Agreement, General Hoshino made everyone get written permission from the Japanese headquarters in Nikolsk for movement through that city. In late April the Japanese began holding back Czech trains at Nikolsk, claiming that Vladivostok was too congested even though the RRSC could have easily cleared the 500 freight cars clogging the railyards, if only Japan would cooperate. After an abbreviated workday, the Japanese would lock all the switches in the busy yard at Nikolsk at 5 p.m., leaving only one main track clear and freezing all traffic in place until the next morning.[59]

By the end of April, Japan and OMO exercised 'military control' over the Chinese Eastern Railway. Fear of Baron Ungern-Shternberg hushed any peep of protest from Russian railway employees and civilians. All trouble-makers were thrown into freight cars and hauled to Ungern-Shternberg's camp at Dauria, where they were exterminated. During the first two weeks in April alone, the Baron liquidated an estimated 2,000 people. 'Dauria station is described as the gallows of Siberia', noted the US Military Attaché in Peking.

The city of Harbin underwent excruciating changes that mirrored the distress in the railway zone. The city was swarming with refugees from all geographic and political corners of Russia, 'including a number of unruly characters... who kept the popular nerves strung', and became an eastern Mecca for diehard monarchists. Since the first week of April, the dynamic city's rhythm was muffled by an increasingly obnoxious Japanese occupation. For instance, Japanese troops had gradually taken control of the city's critical railway bridge over the Sungari river. Earlier in the month they had refused passage to two Russian pedestrians who carried the proper passes to cross the bridge and had tossed one into the river from the lofty span and seriously cut the other. Construction sites sprouted around the city, bringing welcome employment but producing unwelcome new Japanese barracks.[60]

In a bellwether milestone of the strategic power shift traumatizing northern Manchuria, the ruble was supplanted by the yen in financial transactions, impoverishing many of Harbin's 100,000 Russian refugees who had managed to smuggle currency past the sticky fingers of Red and OMO expropriators.[61] Currency was a powerful political weapon wielded by both Russia and Japan in their competition for Manchurian commercial dominance. The yen had been on the rise in usage and popularity since 1919, when Japanese soldiers pumped large volumes into circulation along the Chinese Eastern Railway while the ruble's credibility faded fast with the proliferation of emergency banknotes cranked out by scores of cash-hungry revolutionary and counterrevolutionary administrations. 'The Bank of Chosen [in Japanese-held Korea] has flooded the market', noted a US intelligence report, 'and the [yen] notes are being printed at Seoul as fast as possible to fill the demand'.[62] Chinese General Chang Tso-Lin, the crafty Manchurian warlord, realized that his military forces were not strong enough to expel the Japanese occupiers from the Chinese Eastern Railway, but attacked them through their soft financial underbelly by issuing a new currency, the Harbin *tayang p'iao*, which was convertible with the traditional silver tael and, more importantly, became an acceptable form of payment for Chinese Eastern fares as of 9 May 1920.[63] To the dismay of the Japanese, Chang's *tayang p'iao* soon surpassed the yen in circulation.

Harbin was the key to secret Japanese plans which the US Consul acquired in early May. Japanese authorities had agreed to furnish arms, ammunition and generous compensation to six *hunghutze* chiefs. They would cut Harbin's railway communications to the east and west and terrorize the city to demonstrate that the Chinese government was incapable of maintaining order, necessitating the recall of the Russian railway militia, who could soon leave the city in Japanese hands and join Semenov in the defense of Transbaikalia.

Japan's military control of the Chinese Eastern Railway was complemented by a firm hold on the Trans-Siberian between Nikolsk and Vladivostok, leaving only the segment between Pogranichnaya and Nikolsk to be mastered. Most employees refused to work, and the few that did refused to run a train unless it was flying the Czechoslovak flag. 'So terrified were the railway workers on the Ussuri Railway when they heard the Japanese forces were coming, that they took all the belonging they could, as well as telegraph instruments from the stations, burnt the wooden bridges on the line and fled to the forests', reported US intelligence sources. Publicly the Japanese promised to restore *zemstvo* government in the Maritime province, but few Russians believed them.[64]

The Japanese Army gave Semenov the political reins over their slowly gelling buffer state that stretched from besieged Chita through the northern Manchurian railway zone into patches of nominal control along the Ussuri Railway in the Maritime province as far north as Spassk. Medvedev's Vladivostok and Khabarovsk, where a conservative named Lokhoidov had been installed after the April offensive, operated as city-states tethered to the Japanese occupation. 'The consensus of opinion is that Semenov is a man of very little education and character', wrote an American observer in Peking, 'his chief quality being stubbornness. His thirst is for power, and he will work with the Japanese as the surest means of getting it'.[65]

Nevertheless, the ataman could feel the hungry eyes of the partisans in the woods around Chita, and made gestures of a democratic revival, allowing Cossacks and peasants to organize an All-Russian Peasant Union in Chita on 4 May and holding elections for the Regional Popular Assembly.[66] In contrast to the pro-Soviet railway workers' fear of Semenov, 'class enemies' who had been chastised by the Reds were encouraged to invigorate the torpid and gun-shy spirit of White democracy. However, Semenov's unscrupulous reputation (if not his crooked behavior) persisted and undermined his baby-steps toward democracy. Just as in the past, according to popular belief, if Semenov wanted a man's property, the owner was arrested and forced to sign over the deed or face execution as a Bolshevik.

Semenov seemed firmly entrenched in his Transbaikal bastion for the time being. The Japanese Army had deflated the NRA's momentum in its staunch defense of the Chita region in April. However, on 24 May partisans managed to set fire to the long bridge over the Onon river east of Olovyannaya. The Reds could encircle Chita, but they were still not strong enough to tighten the noose. Thus, a military stalemate prevailed on the Transbaikal Front. In a political milestone, the ataman opened the Regional Popular Assembly on 6 June, 'affirming his desire to march hand in hand with the people'. It was too late, and he could not even convince many of his own men to march with him anymore.[67]

Fearing a Japanese – OMO drive to Lake Baikal, M.S. Matiyasevich's 5th Red Army built up forces in western Transbaikalia. Evgenii Nikolaevich Freiberg, an experienced naval officer and expert artillerist with recent combat on the Caspian Sea, took command of the Red flotilla on Baikal and shipped in several light boats and 200 veteran sailors from the Baltic Fleet. He made the *Angara* his flagship, added four long-range guns and several machine guns to her armament, and installed an ultra-modern radio-telegraph station. Captain V.G. Bazilevskii, who had commanded the *Angara* against Whites and Czechoslovaks during the dark days of 1918, was shunted aside with the rest of the ice-breaker's crew as the Baltic sailors brought onboard 'an atmosphere of sharp mistrust..., indiscipline and constant *mitingovaniya*' – incessant revolutionary meetings. The *Angara* would go through three commanders and eight political commissars in one year. Meanwhile, a restless security situation prevailed along the shores of Lake Baikal in the wake of the great White retreats. Desperate bands of abandoned *kolchakovtsy* and *kappel'evtsy* raided villages to rustle cattle and steal bread, then disappear back into the taiga's shadows. In June 1920, Freiberg anchored at Nizhne Angarsk and sent a landing party of ten sailors ashore to apprehend a gang ten times its size. That same month the ship suppressed a counterrevolutionary insurrection in Barguzin, but, fortunately for her crew, the expected Japanese–OMO invasion never came. Still, the *Angara* kept busy pursuing remnants of the White armies along Baikal's northern shore until 1922 (although the greatest danger to the ship came from the sloppy seamanship of the Baltic Bolsheviks and their inept commander, J.G. Ott, until they stranded the vessel in the ice for the winter of 1920–21 and were relieved).[68]

Red panic, Lazo's fiery martyrdom and White panic

By 20 April navigation was resuming on the thawing Amur river and Japanese soldiers had occupied Aleksandrovsk on northern Sakhalin Island. In Vladivostok on 11 May General Oi issued a statement assuring the public that Japan had no territorial ambitions in Siberia, complementing statements by the chief of the Japanese diplomatic mission in Siberia, Matsudaira, that Tokyo was operating with the approval of the Allies, a claim that the United States had bluntly denied four days earlier. The avowed Allied purpose in Siberia had been the evacuation of the Czechoslovak Legion. But with that mission almost complete, General Oi amended his army's purpose, stating that his troops would stay in Siberia until 'Manchuria and Korea are freed from any menace'.[69]

Senior Bolsheviks in Nikolaevsk grew frantic and began to gather 'Kerensky and Romanov banknotes' while their printing presses cranked out piles of Soviet currency. They picked out passports for themselves from the piles of confiscated passports gathered when everyone was ordered to exchange their old ones for Soviet passports. A new CHEKA boss, Mikhail Morozov, was given lists naming about 3,500 people to be liquidated: first the

Jews (in keeping with Russian tradition it seemed), then wives and children of military families, then relatives of class enemies executed in March, then civil servants and finally artisans, workers and intelligentsia who had openly disagreed with Triapitsyn's introduction of socialism. About the third week of May, Triapitsyn paid the Chinese consul (named by Gutman as 'Dzhen Vyts-Huan') 15 *poods* of gold for all remaining Chinese merchandise in town. Mass killings began anew on 21 May when the Chinese gunboats departed, taking away the last neutral witnesses. On 28 May the partisans began torching the town, a smokey three-day process that afforded new opportunities for rape, robbery and sadism by Triapitsyn's 1st Amur Anarchist-Communist Regiment, as he christened his barbaric horde.[70] Ironically, just three days before the apocalypse at Nikolaevsk, Reds from Krasnoshchekov's Verkhne-Udinsk government began negotiating with the Japanese at Gongota, the westernmost White town on the Trans-Siberian Railway, 75 miles west of Chita.[71]

It was about this time that the Japanese Army transferred three prominent Bolsheviks to the Cossack detachment of Captain V.I. Bochkarev for liquidation. Bochkarev was a *kalmykovets* and, 'by all accounts...a scoundrel interested only in plunder,...with reckless courage and a passion for accumulating wealth'.[72] The prisoners were Sergei Lazo, Semenov's old nemesis and two other members of the Vladivostok military council, Vsevolod Sibirtsev and Aleksei Lutskii (alias Gubelman), who were apprehended during the early hours of the Japanese offensive on 4 April. Bochkarev's men thrashed the Red trio severely, then tossed them into the blazing furnace of a locomotive where, according to both Red and White legends, the fully conscious victims were 'turned over like logs with red hot iron tongs and pokers' before their earthly remains incinerated. In White lore this demise was seen as a well-deserved, hellish punishment for militant atheists, while the Reds harped upon it as proof of the evil nature of primitive, superstitious monarchists. Murav'evo-Amurskii, the place of martyrdom, was eventually renamed Lazo. In a similar fashion, a Kalmykov death squad, moving about the Maritime province inconspicuously in an innocuous railcar attached to a Japanese echelon, took Commissar Andreev, former Red commander of Nikolsk, during a stop at Evgen'evka-Spassk and did away with him.[73]

Although the Whites lagged far behind the Reds in popular support, a White recovery seemed possible and, in Vladivostok, tell-tale signs of an impending White coup appeared in late May. On 27 May General Oi suddenly returned 1,000 rifles to Medvedev's militia, distributed a number of guns to the naval headquarters, and sent Japanese patrols into the streets when evening fell, keeping pedestrians away from the *zemstvo* and government buildings. Gossip flourished the next morning that the 'Red–Pink' militia – with Japanese help – arrested 35 Kalmykov officers overnight before the latter could launch a White coup.[74] Japanese duplicity became brazen as they manipulated Whites and Reds to their own ends, helping White death squads and the Red militia at the same time.

The Medvedev government kept a lid on discontent by making Vladivostok a welfare state, doling out wages to idle workers and buying Manchurian wheat and Chinese meat to keep the hungry masses quiet. There was hardly any commerce to tax, so administrators raised funds by selling off stockpiled commodities like copper, saltpeter and sulphur. Vladivostok fell into a stupor, its cultural, economic and political dynamism stifled. 'Everything remains in the state of former indefinite activity', wrote an observer.[75]

The situation worsened as one traveled north. Between Nikolsk and Khabarovsk, the railway was damaged in several places and Russians were forced to grovel before the Japanese for written permission to travel. In Khabarovsk, rumors circulated that another reactionary coup d'état was in the works by Japanese pawns to replace Likhoidov's reactionary regime, but most people were 'greatly indifferent...to the political situation'.

A certain 'Mr Shchipin' mediated between the local government and the Japanese authorities, who wanted to involve a broader range of 'reactionary circles' in Khabarovsk's administration and even 'promised to liquidate Semenov's adventure'. West of the city, the landmark span over the Amur was closed since an abutment had been blown up at the deepest point in the river, severing the Amur province from the Maritime province.[76]

On 2 June 1920, Japanese transports landed Major General Tsuno and troops at the charred, flattened ruins of Nikolaevsk. The partisans and Red sympathizers vanished into the taiga before them, 'but the Japanese military authorities began to confiscate the store of flour, seines, barrels and means of transportation' that the survivors had salvaged out of the wasteland of bricks, roofing iron and ashes. Tsuno's soldiers evicted refugees from the few remaining structures and beat pedestrians for not showing their passes at checkpoints.[77]

The Japanese April offensive, invasion of the Manchurian Railway zone and expanding occupation of the Maritime province sparked a new solidarity between Russian socialists and non-socialists and a desire to solve domestic problems without outside interference. On 20 June, the left and right got a chance to demonstrate this newfound unity when Vladivostok's first Popular Assembly opened with 109 elected representatives from the Maritime province, Sakhalin Island and Kamchatka. During the next few weeks a moderate coalition cabinet formed in which communists (Nikiforov and Kushnarev) headed only two out of seven departments. For a fleeting moment, it looked as if Vladivostok was becoming the model for a buffer state in which Reds and Whites could coexist and flourish together. In reality, prominent Whites, such as Vladimir Anichkov of the Russo-Asiatic Bank in Harbin, still hoped with unrealistic optimism to undermine the FER and communist organizations in the Far East while similarly the Reds underestimated their opponents' strength and popularity. Whites in the Maritime province were encouraged when a conference of local Reds convened in early July and acrimonious personal differences emerged between party leaders in Vladivostok and Krasnoshchekov's Verkhne-Udinsk government. Boris Shumyatskii, Moscow's prelate in Verkhne-Udinsk, demanded that Vladivostok subordinate itself to Krasnoshchekov and threatened to excommunicate Nikiforov and Kushnarev from the party when they refused.[78]

Likewise, Semenov began to feel vulnerable as his Japanese sponsors discussed his future in private with the Reds at Gongota and in June 1920 he suddenly realized the desperation of his situation. The ataman became willing to do almost anything to remain in Transbaikalia, even bargain with the Reds. Up to this point, he had tried to impede the Czechoslovak evacuation, implored the Japanese (with some success) to delay the evacuation, negotiated unsuccessfully with the Kappel Army to convince them to stay in Transbaikalia and tried to win over the conservatives in Vladivostok. He created popular organs of governance with which he hoped he could make arrangements to stay on as military chief and even communicated with Bolsheviks from Vladivostok and Verkhne-Udinsk. When all else failed, he would eventually recognize General Baron Vrangl as the sole power in the Russian Far East, even though Vrangl was thousands of miles away.[79]

On 3 July 1920, the Japanese government issued an official statement committing its army to withdrawal from Siberia. Twelve days later General Takayanagi signed the Treaty of Gongota with the Verkhne-Udinsk government establishing a neutral zone between Semenov's forces and the NRA that would allow the Japanese Army to disengage. This agreement spelled the end of Semenov's fiefdom in Transbaikalia.

About the same time that Japan announced its intention to abandon Transbaikalia, partisans burst through the door of a cabin near Kerbi, a frontier town on the Amgun river about 300 miles west of the ruins of Nikolaevsk, arrested Yakov Triapitsyn and Nina Lebedeva-Kiashko and charged them with the murders of an unruly Red commander and his associates several weeks prior. Their baggage train included 35 *poods* of gold and other loot. The butchers of Nikolaevsk had become an embarrassment to the party and perhaps it was no coincidence that their arrest and trial coincided with the agreement between Japan and the FER at Gongota. Survivors from Nikolaevsk were dredged from the taiga to 'perform the comedy of a People's Court' that convened on 9 July and that very night sentenced and shot Triapitsyn, Kiashko, Chekist Morozov and three others to death. Many others, whose hands were no less bloody, were acquitted.[80] A period of horse-trading and betrayal had dawned on the war-weary Far East.

After two and a half years of combat and merciless crusade against the Reds, Ataman Semenov was now anxious to cut a deal with them. In late July 1920, he sent a delegation led by General Khreshchatitskii and General Afanas'ev to a conference of oblast governments that was convening in Vladivostok, while in Chita the ataman reorganized the regional government to resemble a democracy. The Verkhne-Udinsk government ignored the conference altogether and delegates from the Amur province refused to negotiate with Semenov's delegates, although the Vladivostok delegation met with the generals from Chita. On the bright side, Semenov's retinue was not even the most reactionary participant at the conference. That dubious honor fell to the Khabarovsk representatives of Likhoidov, with whom neither the Amur nor Vladivostok delegations would meet. Behind the scenes, General Oi and his diplomatic counterpart Matsudaira campaigned for an agreement favorable to the ataman. However, Semenov's waning power could not buttress his unrealistic demands – at first, to be recognized as Kolchak's successor as head of state in the Russian Far East and, failing that, to be appointed commander-in-chief and Cossack leader of the buffer state.[81] Additionally, while the bitterness between Whites and Reds was not as irreconcilable as it seemed, mysterious hands always sabotaged efforts to achieve harmony. About the time of the oblast conference, the Medvedev government's extraordinary commission investigating the River Khor massacre returned to find that its' voluminous report had been stolen during the train ride from Nikolsk. To the thieving party's delight, no doubt, the Whites' kneejerk reaction was to blame a Jewish–Masonic cabal that pulled the strings of Medvedev's administration.[82]

As the conference fruitlessly ground on in Vladivostok, Medvedev dispatched a seven-man delegation to Verkhne-Udinsk via Chita. During the first days of August, Semenov himself welcomed the delegates, who included two communists, a Menshevik, two peasants and two *tsenzoviki* (as the bourgeois businessmen were referred to). He was eager to reach an understanding with the communists – Nikiforov and Kushnarev and assured them that he had no binding agreements with Japan and would readily cooperate with a new buffer state government. The sight of Japanese troops packing and leaving Chita certainly fueled the ataman's spirit of cooperation, as did the fact that Japanese Colonel Isome was again negotiating privately with Krasnoshchekov's representatives at Gongota station. When the Vladivostok delegation passed through Gongota, Red politicos from Verkhne-Udinsk and Moscow began haranguing them unremittingly to reject any compromise with Semenov, and kept up the pressure for the duration of their unpleasant trip to and from Verkhne-Udinsk.[83]

The fall of White Transbaikalia

Before late summer 1920, the Reds considered Semenov's demise a fait accompli, simply awaiting someone to hammer the nails in his coffin. On 13 August, Lenin impudently proclaimed ('in the form of a resolution of the Central Committee of the Russian Communist Party') that the buffer state must be a bourgeois-democratic government with its capital at

Chita, never mind that Grigorii Semenov and several thousand diehard Whites still resided there. From Chita, that same day, emanated a surreal plea from Ataman Semenov to Red Army soldiers to convince their leaders to call a halt to the civil war. 'You are tired of the three-year civil war', it hypnotically cajoled. 'All of you want to return to your native homes, to your native villages, where you will again lead a peaceful life with your families.' Indeed, the ataman's prospects looked bleak and within the next few days his government relocated its offices to Dauria.[84] Also within days of Lenin's pronouncement, Kappel Army General Mikhail K. Diterikhs left Chita for Vladivostok to negotiate the entry of his army into the Maritime province. The *kappel'evtsy* had given up on collaboration with Semenov, who conversely tried to sabotage their talks with Medvedev – anything to keep them in Transbaikalia.

The mounting suspense even transformed Ataman Semenov himself, who traded his hedonistic lifestyle for marriage, taking 17-year-old Helen V. Manstein as his wife in an evening ceremony on 16 August. She was a lovely, doe-eyed brunette of German parentage, originally from the province of Rinburg near the Turkestan border, who had been living with her aunt and refugee mother, Maria, in Chita and working on the secretarial staff of Semenov's executive officer, General Afanas'ev. Months later, opponents would accuse Semenov of bigamy based upon his pre-war marriage to Zenaida, although in his own defense he stated that he was granted a de facto divorce under a Kerensky-era law that stipulated, in Semenov's words, 'Any woman who leaves her husband and doesn't live with him for two years and three months... is free automatically'. Under this law, a spouse need only make an entry in the 'parochial book' to formalize the divorce, and Helen insisted, 'I went to the consistory in the parish and the register shows that he was divorced before I was married'. In addition, it seems that Semenov did not send Zenaida (and their son) away from Chita to Japan until October 1920.[85]

A general peasant revolt began spreading through the remnants of White Transbaikalia on 19 August but could hardly have heightened the atmosphere of lawlessness with ruthless OMO gangs and runaways from both Red and White armies plundering as they retreated. An OMO colonel named Mikhailov adorned his men in Red insignia and robbed a Chinese pay office in Manchuria.[86] In the areas surrounding Nerchinsk and Sretensk, the looting became so bad that peasants formed a self-defense detachment, *Otryad Sokol*.[87]

One of the more unusual events as White Transbaikalia disintegrated was Semenov's 20 August decoration as a Knight of the Sacred Tomb of Christ by Patriarch Damian of Jerusalem.[88] While his life since 1918 had been the epitome of vanity, self-indulgence, hypocrisy and depravity, the ataman received the decoration for helping Father Seraphim and two novice monks transfer the body of Grand Princess Elizaveta Fedorovna out of Red Siberia (along with the corpses of a murdered nun and at least three Romanovs). Near Manchuli the priest sweated through a brief captivity by partisans who wanted to throw the coffins out of the boxcar and an armed rescue by the Chinese Army. Father Seraphim reached Harbin in April 1920 with his reeking cargo of royal cadavers intact after a harrowing three-week rail journey through the combat zone in southern Transbaikalia and northwest Manchuria. Prince Kudashev opened the coffins to identify the remains as best he could and make a consular report and was amazed to find that, in comparison to the other, rotten corpses, the bodies of Elizaveta and her assistant, nun Varvara Yakovleva, had not decayed and, in the case of the former, actually emitted a fragrance. He forwarded their coffins on to Peking, then to Shanghai, for shipment to Palestine for burial in accordance with the Grand Princess' wishes.[89]

On 24 August 1920, Grigorii Semenov returned all civil powers to the Regional Popular Assembly, retaining only military command. By this time, the Japanese Army had already withdrawn from Chita and the last Czechoslovak Legion echelon had departed for the east.

As the delegation of Vladivostok Popular Assemblymen passed back through Transbaikalia on its way home from Verkhne-Udinsk, Semenov signed an agreement with a *tsenzovik* delegate named Rudnev, submitting to Medvedev's provisional *zemstvo* government in exchange for the titles of commander-in-chief of the Transbaikal region and field ataman of Cossack troops.[90] Red histories would accuse the Menshevik and Socialist-Revolutionary delegates of going along with this eleventh-hour pact, but the deal was meaningless anyway without the approval of Vladivostok's communist delegates, Nikiforov and Kushnarev. Apparently many Whites put little stock in Semenov's overdue political reforms and began the exodus out of Chita. On 2 September about 1,000 Whites from Transbaikalia arrived in Grodekovo on a Japanese echelon.[91]

Trotsky snickered, 'General Semenov is petitioning the Soviet power for an amnesty', but few Reds were in a forgiving mood. In Irkutsk, a revolutionary tribunal convicted and shot three perpetrators of the brutal January murders on the *Angara*.[92] Even the usually tolerant Chinese seemed to be losing patience. On 9 September Ataman Ivan P. Kalmykov was killed while trying to escape from a Chinese convoy escorting him to Peking from the Kirin prison where he had spent the past six months.[93]

Semenov's political maneuvers took on an air of desperation. Medvedev dispatched another Vladivostok delegation to Verkhne-Udinsk in mid-September, this one consisting of the communist leader, Nikiforov, a Menshevik, Kabtsan and a Socialist-Revolutionary, Trupp. Semenov detained them for four days at Manchuli while General Khreshchatitskii implored them to negotiate. They refused and Semenov allowed them to pass. When they reached Dauria, Semenov detained them again and went cap-in-hand to plead with the Red trio to speak with him. Not so long before he would have sent uncooperative Reds to a torture chamber to loosen their tongues, but, again, Nikiforov and company refused to parley and the ataman allowed them to continue their journey west. Meanwhile, General Voitsekhovskii approached the communist Nikiforov about placing the Kappel Army under the Vladivostok *zemstvo* government. Nikiforov received permission for the discussion from Krasnoshchekov over the 'direct wire' from Verkhne-Udinsk, making it obvious that the Russian Far East had already fallen into the Red shadows, even if several thousand White troops remained in Transbaikalia and the Maritime province. On the other hand, the FER and NRA refused to negotiate directly with the *kappel'evtsy*.[94]

On 23 September, a congress in Nerchinsk elected a regional people's revolutionary committee for eastern Transbaikalia and began setting up justice, finance, labor and other departments of a civil administration. The staff of the 2nd Amur Rifle Division set up headquarters in the town while a partisan detachment pushed the frontlines just west of Shilka. Some 7,600 local partisans of the Transbaikal Cavalry Division now controlled most of the territory north of the Chita–Manchuli railway line from the Onon river to Kharanor. Partisan camps dotted the taiga northeast and south of Chita, as the Reds drew nearer to pinching Karymskaya from east and west in the hope of cutting off Semenov's retreat. The NRA's plan for capturing Chita was approved on 27 September and so confident was the NRA that, on 1 October the FER audaciously called for a conference to meet in Chita 14 days later, never mind that several thousand White troops still barred their travel. Semenov's forces were estimated at 18,000–20,000 men, nine armored trains and 175 artillery pieces.[95]

White Chita went down fighting in late October. On 11 October, citizens of Burgen', a town on the Ingoda river, 35 miles north of Chita, formed an armed detachment and revolted, fighting a tenacious battle against Semenov's troops who occupied the hamlet but were pressured out by the NRA on the 12th.[96] Three days later the Japanese Army completed its pull-out from Transbaikalia, leaving Semenov to his own devices. Sometime during OMO's last days in Chita, about 50 men and women were thrown down a well beside Semenov's headquarters and horses and cattle were then driven in to crush them.[97] On 19 October, the NRA launched a new offensive to take the city and White soldiers, fearing encirclement and annihilation, began evacuating in earnest. Red workers inside Chita disarmed Semenov's police the following day and the day after that they seized telegraph facilities, the train station, arsenal and military warehouses with help from the NRA.

It is unclear exactly when Semenov departed Chita and his orders and communications in early October bore a confusing pattern of datelines from Chita, Borzya and Dauria.[98] Semenov later claimed, 'The evacuation from Transbaikalia was conducted in an organized and calm manner', but his detractors accused him of flying out of Chita for Harbin in a rickety aircraft, abandoning his remaining men to fight their way through the surrounding partisan armies. Peter Fleming recorded the impression of Semenov's departure that, true or not, was to be his legacy: 'So while the going was good he went, abandoning his little kingdom and its people to the encroaching chaos. Before his aircraft took off from Chita, his great hoard of bullion and other loot had already been transported, by courtesy of the Japanese, to Manchuria.'[99] At 10 a.m. on 22 October 1920, NRA soldiers marched into Chita.[100]

Greater military and political significance attended the liberation of Makkaveevo and Adrianovka two days later. Not only did Red forces overrun Semenov's largest military bases, but they captured '150 boxcars, locomotives and many other war trophies'. The greatest prize, however, was the Trans-Siberian Railway junction at Karymskaya, which, once all the burnt bridges and sabotaged tracks were fixed, would restore Moscow's direct transportation and communications links with the Pacific coast for the first time since the Czechoslovak Legion rebelled almost two and a half years before. The 'Chita stopper' had been unplugged.[101]

Chita transformed rapidly from being the Babylon of reactionary Cossackdom to the Mecca of Far Eastern bolshevism. Just six days after the Red liberation, a Conference of United Provinces of the East convened and proclaimed its host city the new capitol of the FER. Military-political specialists from the NRA and Red Army occupied the upper floor of the Hotel Dauria. The four-story complex encompassing the Hotel Selekt, Cafe Modern and store became the primary residence of high-ranking FER commissars, including Krasnoshchekov himself. They soon discovered that while Semenov had retreated, he certainly had not capitulated. Shortly after the Reds checked in, some OMO officers disguised as waiters torched the Hotel Selekt with carefully planted incendiaries, killing a number of senior FER executives. The gaping, charred facade of Chita's premier hotel and office space loomed over the city center for years to come, like a gangrenous scar that refused to heal.[102]

Diehard Whites fought tooth and nail to keep a toehold in southern Transbaikalia, but throughout the first three weeks of November 1920 the partisans and NRA herded them toward the Chinese border at Manchuli. Surprisingly the *kappel'evtsy* even beat back the NRA's 1st Transbaikal Corps at Borzya on 11 November and Khada-Bulak on 13 November.[103] But, at Soktui siding on 16 November partisans repelled last-ditch attacks by the *broneviki* 'Spravedlivyi', 'Khrabryi' and 'Istrebitel', then drove on to capture Borzya and 340 freightcars full of booty. Three days later, Semenov's men suffered a conclusive defeat at Matsievskaya and on 20 November the remnants of OMO and the Kappel Army withdrew from Transbaikalia altogether.[104]

They pooled on the strip of Russian territory abutting Manchuli, waiting for permission from Chinese authorities to proceed into Manchuria until 24 November when NRA advances pressured them across the border. Echelons of OMO soldiers and refugees, whose passage Semenov paid from his treasury of gold, began traversing the Chinese Eastern Railway to the chagrin of the Chinese, who were assured that the transients would not detrain in Manchuria. Within days, Semenov's loyal forces set up camp under Japanese protection at Grodekovo, just inside the Maritime province. The ataman visited for several days near the end of November, then proceeded to Vladivostok where he met with General Oi and started scheming to take power. His presence drew protests from the consular corps and the city's Popular Assembly and his plotting alienated the Cossacks from the *kappel'evtsy*. Lacking Semenov's Japanese connections, the latter could not begin evacuating Manchuli until 29 November, and were halted at Pogranichnaya, the last stop in Manchuria. For several days the Kappel Army and accompanying families, estimated at between 25,000 and 30,000 people, lived on freightcars lined up outside Pogranichnaya, prohibited by the Chinese from detraining. On 2 December General Boldyrev, then the senior military officer in Vladivostok, took pity upon the refugees and gave permission for the sick, wounded and children to enter the Maritime province. Subsequently all of the *kappel'evtsy* gradually mobbed the border, and fights broke out between them and *semenovtsy* as they passed Grodekovo. A few days later, FER President Krasnoshchekov and his military chief, Eikhe, suddenly realized just how many White refugees there were and issued a 'full amnesty' in the hope of defusing any bellicose intentions among them. Kappel General Verzhbitskii had recently been quoted in Harbin discussing preparations for new battles, however most of his men were anxious to resume their civilian lives. For administrative purposes the White settlements were divided into three corps: the first corps of Semenov's men at Grodekovo, and the second and third corps of *kappel'evtsy* centered around Razdolnoe and Nikolsk, where they turned to trades and agriculture. The 12 December resignation of the Maritime *zemstvo* board in favor of the FER at Chita caused the shutdown of Medvedev's bureaucracy in Vladivostok, and spurred an exodus of Reds to Transbaikalia and an influx of Whites into the Maritime province.[105]

The Japanese whisked Ataman Semenov out of Vladivostok and off to Port Arthur on 5 December 1920, though it was surely not his choice to leave Russia. They set him up to live a comfortable life in Port Arthur, where he held court with other disgruntled émigrés and continued conspiring and plotting to take over his homeland. Within weeks he was engrossed in a variety of negotiations with various parties of Russians, Chinese and Japanese. General Savel'ev took over direct command of the Cossack encampment at Grodekovo, where Semenov's followers lived in boxcars and ramshackle dwellings, drilled in their faded uniforms and remained openly hostile to the Reds in Chita and Pinks in Vladivostok. Only 5,000 people lived in the camp, but Savel'ev claimed that he could raise 10,000 more men from nearby Ussuri Cossack villages. Semenov bankrolled the settlement with his fund of gold and the Japanese Army shielded it from any attempt of armed putdown by Vladivostok. In addition, a clause in the agreement that was forced upon Medvedev's government by Japan shortly after the April offensive prohibited revolutionary troops from operating within 30 *versts* of the railway.[106] Semenov and his people bided their time, waiting for a time to pounce and liberate their homeland.

10

GÖTTERDÄMMERUNG

October 1920–November 1922

'Without Ataman Semenov and his detachment, Russia would be obliged to burn for a long time in the flame of Bolshevism's yoke and violence.'

(Semenov propaganda tract, 1919)

Ungern-Shternberg's liberation of Mongolia (October 1920–January 1921)

As Transbaikalia was being overrun by Red partisans and the NRA in October 1920, Baron Roman Fedorovich Ungern-Shternberg was busy positioning his troops for an assault on the Mongolian capitol, Urga, some 400 miles away from the front. Until this time, Baron Ungern-Shternberg was just another face in the crowd of high-ranking OMO killers, notorious primarily for transforming Dauria station into a showcase of medieval torture. However, his winter campaign in Mongolia indelibly etched his name in the bloody legends of twentieth-century warfare.

At first glance, Urga hardly seemed worth fighting for. West Urga, the heart of the city, had the impermanent and aromatic air of a nomad camping ground inhabited by about 30,000 people, a 'felt city' of *gers* squatting in a valley of the Tola river, the city's generous 100-meter-wide water source. Mountains stripped of their forests for fuel and building materials rose 1,500 feet above the encampment, cupping the smoke from thousands of hearths, many of which crackled with *argol*, dried animal droppings. Streets were crisscrossed by tributaries of the Tola, always deep in dust or mud and pitch-black after sunset, there being no effort to light them in any way. West Urga encompassed three distinct quarters: the *kuren* (monastery) complex of temples, towers, shrines, altars, schools, libraries and inns; Bogdo-ol, the sacred quarter of the Living Buddha's palace, set among groves linked to the city by a long wooden bridge across the Tola; and finally the sprawling city proper, where the bazaar and homes of foreigners mixed among the *gers* and animal pens.

Although Urga lay 165 miles from the Russian frontier at Kyakhta and a three-day drive from Kalgan, the city emitted the transient buzz of a bustling border town. Trade and commerce revolved around the grey-walled Chinese business district, Maimachen, which was insulated from west Urga by a two-mile thoroughfare plied by camels, camel carts, bullock wagons, horses and gaily attired pedestrians. Maimachen boasted orderly streets lined with substantial houses and buildings, amongst which Chinese, Russian and Central Asian merchants haggled over cattle, camels, horses, sheep, milk and piece-goods. A short distance beyond Maimachen sprouted 'a long row of Russian private houses, a hospital, church, prison and...the awkward four-storied red brick building that was formerly the Russian

Consulate'.¹ There was scant evidence that the twentieth century had arrived. Modern firearms, of course, were popular. Electric lighting was a novelty enjoyed by a handful of the elite with connections to 'private Delco plants'. Another sign of the times was a growing foreign population that included about 400 Russian businessmen, settlers and refugees and 'two Americans, one Britisher, a few Scandinavians and several Austrians'. Hoofed stock milling around in the streets was terrorized by the city's 20 automobiles, most of which were owned by the Khutuktu, the living god, head of state and embodiment of nationhood, lechery, decadence and feudal backwardness.²

Semenov took credit for planning this Mongolian expedition in his memoirs, even though he was consumed with evacuating the remnants of OMO and the White armies from his home province at the time. He also insisted that Ungern's Asiatic Horse Division was not an invading force, but the 'cadre of a [new] Mongolian Army' which had been training at Dauria under strict secrecy for months to liberate Outer Mongolia from 'Marshal Chang Tso-Lin's Chinese imperialism'.³

Semenov's allegation against the Chinese were absolutely true. The seeds of Ungern's 1920 campaign had been planted in September 1919, as soon as OMO and Japanese soldiers slaughtered the last of General Fussenge's Mongol mutineers after they refused to march on Urga. Semenov promptly assembled a civilian delegation of 10–20 Russians to go to Urga, but it was uncertain if they ever made it while the ataman's attention was drawn to the collapse of Omsk and a series of other disasters in the meantime.⁴ Anyway, the time had passed for negotiations to resolve Mongolia's political crisis.

The Chinese were not so reticent about reclaiming their lost Mongolian colony now that a weakened Russia was increasingly preoccupied with her civil war. Since Russia's revolutionary troubles began, China had gradually increased her consular guards in excess of 200, as limited by the 1915 Treaty of Kyakhta. When 'the Semenov scare' gripped Mongolia during the summer of 1919, China infused more troops to defend against an OMO–Buryat invasion, and, at the time, the Mongols considered them the lesser of two evils, though they were far from welcome visitors. The Mongolians were justifiably wary of visitors who arrived with so much baggage. On 1 September 1919, 300 more Chinese cavalrymen entered the city with six machine guns and 'a lot of camels with supplies'. In the wake of Semenov's aborted expedition days later, a full-fledged Chinese invasion appeared imminent and was loudly promised in China's newspapers. 'The movement of Chinese troops towards Urga has been going on for some time', reported a US naval intelligence informant. In early autumn a large number set out across the Gobi Desert in 'motor busses' – normally a four-day drive from Peking, but most of the urban vehicles 'died a natural death' in the wasteland and for an extended period soldiers straggled into Urga on camels and ponies.⁵

In October 1919, China's President Hsü Shih-chang dispatched General Hsui Shu-cheng, commonly known as 'Little Hsu' to distinguish him from the president, to Urga to straighten out the Mongolian separatists once and for all. Little Hsu arrived in Urga bearing gifts on 29 October, and whipped up a parade in the Khydzhir-Bulune suburb to intimidate on-looking Mongolian ministers and princes with China's martial power, followed by dinner and a theatrical presentation.⁶ He made lavish promises – improvements in government administration, representation, commercial, mining and agricultural development and the right to live in peace, which, after eight years of misrule by the Khutuktu, certainly sounded enticing to many Mongols.⁷ However, the promises were blatant lies meant to sugar-coat Peking's invasion, because Little Hsu intended to apply whatever means necessary to bring Mongolia back into Peking's fold, dispel any notions of independence and make a profit.

From Peking Prince Kudashev warned Omsk on 2 November that China was maneuvering to destroy Mongolian autonomy and breach long-standing agreements with the

Russian government despite the fact that the 'danger of pan-Mongol armies and Semenov's independent enterprises have disappeared'. However, Mongolia's traditional protector, the Russian government, was on the verge of extinction itself and could hardly concern itself with a Chinese brigade in Urga when the 5th Red Army was in Omsk's suburbs. Smugly aware of Russia's predicament, on 8 November Little Hsu insisted that Mongolia officially petition Peking for the return of Chinese rule and an end to the autonomy experiment. Bogdo Khan pushed this shameful task onto Mongolia's parliamentary bodies, which were not representative anyway: an upper chamber of five leading ministers (internal affairs, foreign affairs, finance, justice and war) and their 11 assistants and a lower chamber composed of leading ministry bureaucrats. However, when the two chambers assembled under the presidency of Badam-Dorzhi, the lower chamber refused to do away with autonomy, not out of any deep patriotic feeling, but because they would be legislating the demise of the bureaucracies which employed them. Six days later, his patience exhausted, Little Hsu gave the Mongolian government an ultimatum: call an end to autonomy by 8 p.m. on 15 November, or he would take the Khutuktu to Peking. When the assembly met the next day at noon, the roads leading from the city center to the Khutuktu's palace were lined with Chinese soldiers. Nevertheless, only the upper chamber agreed to renounce autonomy and signed Little Hsu's petition, which the Bogdo Khan subsequently refused to endorse but was sent to Peking anyway. On 22 November the President of China declared the transfer of Mongolian state authority back to Peking and unilaterally cancelled all agreements between Russia and Mongolia.[8]

According to the A.A. Orlov, the Russian Diplomatic Agent in Urga, Little Hsu had only 2,300 Chinese soldiers in the city, most quartered in temples, barracks and rented houses in Maimachen, to ensure the smooth transition of power from the Bogdo Khan to the *amban*. Yet other estimates of the strength of China's occupation force, the 3rd Mixed Brigade, ranged no higher than 4,000 men. Whatever their number, they were sufficient to take over the city from the demoralized Mongolians. In December the Chinese Army seized Urga's telegraph and telephone stations.

A schism divided Mongolia's feudal elite between pro-autonomy and pro-Chinese factions, who squabbled among themselves, while the Mongolian Army, modern descendent of Genghiz Khan's great horde, passively watched the invaders take charge of their capitol. 'The Mongols have so entirely lost their martial spirit that their army amounts to very little for practical purposes', noted the US Navy's informant. In fact, the Chinese demobilized what was left of the 2,000-man army in December, leaving only small units to guard the Khutuktu and Russian Consulate, and requisitioned most of its arsenal (consisting of 5,776 relatively new Russian or Japanese rifles with 874,362 cartridges; 2,456 old Berdan rifles and 714,779 cartridges; seven artillery pieces with 5,410 shells; 10 machine guns and 12 pistols).[9]

Among the demobilized troops was a 27-year-old senior non-commissioned officer (NCO) named Namdini Sukhe Bator who, anticipating a long Chinese occupation; had formed a group of army friends to plan a revolt. Sukhe Bator had been among the poor peasants shoved into military service in 1912, but stood out from the other recruits, was bright and energetic and eventually selected for the Mongolian Army's elite machine gun company. Working with machine guns was prestigious, afforded valuable exposure to technology and mechanics, and allowed the company's soldiers to learn the Russian language and to hear tales of modern combat from Russo-Japanese war veterans. Sukhe Bator proved himself a natural leader, technically proficient and showed courage and good judgment in skirmishes on the Chinese border during the early years of autonomy. He was quickly promoted and served until December 1919 in an army that was constantly short-changed in men and materiel, shriveling up altogether in the hour of its nation's greatest need. Unbeknownst to Sukhe Bator, another secret revolutionary group had been formed in Urga, led by Khorloogin Choibalsan. Both groups had recently sent emissaries to Russia to seek assistance from the soviets.[10]

In spring 1920, marauding OMO units gave the Chinese a *raison d'être* in Mongolia. 'There was a gang of pirates on the Kyakhta Up Road two weeks ago', reported a US intelligence source in Urga in mid-April when some of Semenov's Chahar mercenaries wandered into Khalka territory from the Selenga Valley. 'They were Semenov Men who had been cleaning up Troitskosavsk and after having finished that job went crazy and came over here.' Chinese troops justified their presence by chasing them into the hills.[11]

Of course, the Chinese were not sincerely interested in protecting Mongolia. After they disbanded the autonomous government, they proceeded to execute numerous nationalists, loot and commit a variety of brutal atrocities. 'It is no uncommon sight to see a Chinese policeman-soldier beating a Mongol child on the streets here, although you can bet that they let the grown ones alone unless they are in force', wrote an American merchant in Urga. China's most debilitating measure was to demand that Mongolians pay all back taxes that had accrued since the declaration of autonomy eight years before.[12] Coupled with other requisitions, theft and corruption, the Chinese embarked on a systematic campaign to subjugate Mongolia by first destroying her economy. An Urga merchant explained:

> Last year the camel freights were around 12 to 15 dollars per animal from here to Kalgan at this season [spring]. Today they are up to 35 dollars and it is almost impossible to get transport at that price. This is because the Mongol camel drovers will not bring their animals into Urga. The instant they come in they are commandeered and lugged off to Kyakhta to join Little Hsu's great expedition against the Bolsheviks... Again, a Russian [camel] caravan was held up a few miles from here the other day, its cargo dumped in the mud and the animals carried in here by troops to transport more Chinese coolies with guns in their hands to Russia.[13]

Throughout 1920, Chinese warlordism sank its roots into Mongolian soil. 'Little Hsu is a number one grafter with a good deal of ability', opined the American merchant in Urga. 'He is in the pay of the Japanese and himself is making a fortune by selling valuable mining concessions in Mongolia to the Japanese.' He took over and corrupted a relatively honest system of customs administration and payments, ran Chinese mercenaries up to the Transbaikal Front to support Japanese military operations against the Reds, issued his own visas and lived the high life with 20 Russian women catering to the staff of his Urga headquarters. Only American and Japanese merchants were exempted from forking out a 'special concession' fee on all exports, although Little Hsu had no love for the former and treated only the latter as 'privileged characters'. Even most Chinese merchants of Maimachen grew fed up with their army's constant affronts and disruption of business. Chinese Army outposts sprouted on roads in and around Urga. 'These make themselves obnoxious to travelers whenever the occasion presents itself, calling for passports and searching baggage, which they are not authorized to do, except to the Russians who no longer enjoy the prestige of other white foreigners.'[14]

China's abuse and oppression wore Mongolian patience thin by spring 1920. The Chinese Army was not so engrossed in its bacchanalia that it overlooked the furor rising around it, but responded to the growing public anger by inflicting further indignities. Prominent Mongolian nobles were arrested on the flimsiest pretexts and the Khutuktu was not allowed to drive among his flock during religious festivals, as was the custom, imposing upon him the indignity of having to walk. 'The Chinese military show no respect for the religious customs of the Mongols and often interfere with them, a dangerous imposition on any deeply religious people', observed a visiting American. The Khutuktu ordered his people to boycott the Chinese, and the Chinese imposed a 9 p.m. curfew on all Mongolians. In early May, the American trader wrote, 'I have been approached by certain important lama officials re supplying them with machine guns and rifles, with ammunition for same, and as you know, the gun business is about as sure a weathercock of revolutions as there is anywhere.' Tensions simmered throughout the summer, and the Chinese Army reinforced its Mongolian task force with a full battalion.[15]

Russian emissaries, both Red and White, skulked between the yurts plotting with Mongol leaders. Soviet agents in Urga had engineered the merger of Sukhe Bator and Choibalsan's secret groups and sent them and 50 Mongolian volunteers to Russia to train for the revolution. The American merchant in Urga predicted,

> If the Russians help the Mongols it will mean the entering of many Bolsheviks into Mongolia. Urga's municipal council is now run by them and once they get in here they will go ahead and try to extend their influence into China, across to Tibet, and thence to India. This has all been publicly announced here in Urga by a Bolshevik leader. The Mongols are not Bolsheviks, but in their present frame of mind, they will take help where they can get it ...

Likewise, Semenov had been sending agents to organize resistance and gather intelligence in Mongolia, but the Chinese aggressively pursued any Russian suspected of working for him and had jailed over 100 *semenovtsy* before summer 1920 arrived.[16]

On 23 September 1920 China withdrew recognition from Russian diplomatic and consular officials on her territory, and during the next week took control of the Russian concessions in Tientsin and Hankow, practically canceling all extraterritorial rights in the former, and instituting a financial and regulatory framework that favored Chinese over foreigners. Peking was gleefully retaliating for two decades of indignities that had begun with the Cassini Convention. Chinese officials smirked while Russian settlements in Mongolia polarized into warring Red and White factions. White officers among refugees who had fled to Mongolia began forming detachments to help the Mongols break free of the Chinese yoke.[17]

Little Hsu had departed Mongolia a short time before after his ouster by Chinese political rivals, temporarily leaving Urga in the hands of the old Qing *amban*, Sando, an 'utterly incapable' Chahar who had no control over the boisterous troops.[18] On 30 September the Chinese government created a Pacification Commission of Mongolia, named Ch'en Yi commissioner and, at his request, assigned General Chang Ching-hui, described as 'Tartar General of Chahar', as his military deputy. A week later, President Hsu also designated Ch'en Yi as director general of Mongolian gold mines, a move aimed to obstruct Japanese claims based on concessions received from the deposed autonomous government in exchange for loans from Mitsui and Lungkou banks.

China's gamble on Mongolia seemed a safe bet as the cold weather began to set in during the autumn of 1920 and the Russians and Mongols were still fighting among themselves. On high ground between Maimachen and west Urga soared three 300-foot tall masts, supporting the antenna of a newly installed Marconi radio that linked Mongolia to Peking (via Ti Hua Fu, 1,000 miles to the southeast). Looming over three modern buildings and the curious passers-by on Urga's main road, the site was a costly investment signaling Peking's intent to stay and a fitting metaphor for Mongolia's future as China's colony, a wonderful and imposing piece of construction built around out-of-date transmitting equipment and manned by 'pitifully incompetent' Chinese bureaucrats according to Major Dockray, the retired British Army officer who was Urga's Marconi radio representative.[19]

As soldiers had been deployed to other locales in Mongolia, Urga's Chinese garrison decreased to the point that one intelligence report in early October 1920 underestimated it to contain only about 1,000 soldiers. There were surely more than this, although they were dispersed around town, deployed to separate sites east and south of Maimachen, at another around General Tsu's residence, another south of west Urga and at four outposts along the Kalgan–Urga road within 15 miles of the city. About half of them were cavalry – 'well paid and as loyal as Chinese soldiers can be', under General Kao Tsai-ting. The other half was General Tsu Jui Fu's infantry, who had not received any pay in seven months and were on the verge of mutiny. 'That their discipline is gone is beyond question', stated an American intelligence report. While some Chinese officials and foreign military observers scoffed at the baron's ragtag horde as being incapable of serious martial endeavor, General Tsu's unpaid men had degenerated into a robbing and raping rabble. There was a complete breakdown of law and order in the city and even the Chinese Chamber of Commerce grew so worried that it organized and armed a self-defense group of 200 civilians 'to protect Chinese property against the possible and very probable outbreak of mutiny of the Chinese soldiers'. One expatriate businessman wrote, 'Today no one dares venture on the streets of Urga in the daytime without being armed to the teeth.'[20]

The core of Ungern's army were the predominantly Cossack, Buryat and Chahar OMO units of the Dauria garrison, around which he had accumulated survivors and stragglers from the disintegrated White armies, thousands of Mongolian patriots, several dozen sympathetic Tibetans, and a smattering of 'other peoples of the East – from Bashkirs to Koreans'. They were the 'nucleus of a continental counterrevolutionary army, the instrument for the realization of a pan-Asian vision'.[21] Estimates of Ungern's peak strength ranged between 6,000 and 8,000 men, although these figures did not include a Semenov force of 4,000 reported between Kyakhta and Verkhne-Udinsk and other detachments of stragglers and refugees.[22] White detachments that were previously roaming Mongolia, such as that of Colonel Kazagrandi, joined the baron's march. The Dalai Lama sent a Tibetan detachment, including 'seventy of his finest warriors to act as bodyguards', in fulfillment of a 1913 mutual aid treaty between Tibet and Mongolia. A small Japanese Army contingent, described as a *sotnia* of 50–70 artillery officers and a 40-man bodyguard also accompanied the baron, although sources differ as to whether they were commanded by a Colonel Hiroyama or Captain Suzuki. Local troops were raised by 'the great prince of the Buryats, Dzham Bolon', who welcomed Ungern-Shternberg into Mongolia, though as Chinese outrages multiplied, many ordinary Mongols flocked to the Baron's standard. Togtokh-gun, a Bargut Mongol guerrilla leader from Hailar who had fought the Chinese for years before being forced to take refuge in Chita, mobilized Inner Mongolian warriors. Most of the baron's regulars were issued Japanese weapons, his elite machine gunners were outfitted with Italian equipment, and the rest carried a rich cornucopia of killing instruments – hunting rifles and every bladed weapon imaginable, even medieval lances and pikes. For the moment, Ungern's campaign was the only substantial anti-Chinese movement in Mongolia, and the rainbow of uniforms in his encampments attested to the diversity of his supporters: Ungern's own men 'in long blue coats, Mongols and Tibetans in red coats with yellow epaulets bearing the swastika of Genghis Khan and the initials of the Living Buddha', the Japanese in yellow-khaki and columns of raggedy White officers 'with pieces of leather tied to the soles of their feet', alienated from the world, desperate men who had lost their homes, families and country, and had nothing more to lose.[23]

Although the Japanese approved of Baron Ungern's expedition, they could not control him like they did Semenov. Ungern may have even held a grudge against the Japanese for stopping him from executing 40 Russian prisoners at Dauria back in February. Indeed the ataman wielded only limited influence over the flighty baron. Ferdinand Ossendowski, a Polish scientist and former POW became acquainted with the baron and left the richest portrait:

> A small head on wide shoulders; blonde hair in disorder; a reddish bristling mustache; a skinny, exhausted face, like those on the old Byzantine icons. Then everything else faded from view save a big protruding forehead overhanging steely sharp eyes. These eyes were fixed upon me like those of an animal from a cave.[24]

The wiry, shrill Ungern believed that he was leading a divine mission, or at least convinced observers that he believed it and encouraged rumors that he was the reincarnation of Mahagala, the god of northern Buddhism. His wardrobe left a lasting impression. In battle, he sometimes dressed in a 'bright silk gown' so as to be visible to his men. Alioshin described him, *nagaika* (a heavy leather whip) in hand, wearing a red Chinese jacket and blue breeches of the tsar's army. His entourage traveled in 'barbaric luxury and glory', and included a number of fortune-telling shamans and his wife, who was by some accounts a Mongolian princess, by others the daughter of China's former president Yuan Shih-Kai or a 'Manchurian princess of dynastic blood'. His August 1919 marriage had strengthened his authority in the eyes of his Asian admirers and gained him the Mongolian title of *vana*, a prince of the second degree.[25]

Sensationalist memoirs published in the 1920s painted Ungern's approach on Urga as a scourge that sowed horrors upon the land akin to the supernatural violence of Mongol mythology. However, intelligence reports from Urga in the several weeks before and during the siege project popular support for Baron Ungern-Shternberg and buoyant anticipation of the city's liberation. His detractors insist that he allowed his soldiers to indulge freely in indiscriminate mayhem, exterminating anyone who objected, even his own officers. Dmitri Alioshin cataloged atrocities within the Baron's own retinue: the whipping to death of Captain Vishnevskii, the strangling of Colonel Likhachev and Colonel Yakhontov, the burning at the stake of Dr Engelgard-Eserskii and the slow roasting of deserters. When a Captain Ruzhanskii and his 68 men deserted, they were hunted down, killed and mutilated by a Chahar detachment and Ruzhanskii's young wife was tossed to the Chahars.[26]

On 26 October 1920, Baron Ungern launched his attack on Urga 'after his Mongol soothsayers had declared it a propitious day'. The Chinese easily beat Ungern off, and his division retreated to the hills, then attacked five days later, again without success. Inside the city, martial law was declared, the Khutuktu and other leading nobles were placed under arrest by General Chu and Chinese troops subjected Russian and other European residents to 'barbarous treatment' in revenge for Ungern's assaults. Ch'en Yi, the new *amban*, arrived in Urga at this inopportune time, as did some Chinese reinforcements who hurried in from Kalgan, however Urga's continued requests for additional reinforcements fell victim to political deviousness in Peking and Mukden.[27]

Extremely concerned by the situation, the US embassy in Peking organized a rescue mission across the Gobi Desert to retrieve the two-man American community in Urga, a mining engineer named Edwin W. Mills, and a Mr McLaughlin of the Mongolian Trading Company. The owner of the latter, Charles L. Coltman, provided the automobiles and the assistant military attaché, Major John Magruder, led 16 American citizens into Urga on 13 November. Chinese authorities in Peking vigorously opposed the expedition, and after their arrival in Urga, the Americans narrowly averted many 'armed clashes' with the Chinese. Nevertheless, Magruder rescued his two countrymen, and the stubborn American interest in Mongolian affairs compelled China to reconsider – if not soften – its iron-fisted approach. The

Urga garrison was 'rewarded' for the city's defense by payment of 'full arrears of salary', and Peking guaranteed protection for foreigners.[28]

Baron Ungern withdrew along the Kerulen river in the direction of China and made camp at Zum Kuren, 160 miles east of Urga, but returned to launch at least two more unsuccessful attacks in subsequent weeks. Grisly punishments discouraged desertion, as Mother Nature tortured the undernourished, underclothed Whites with gnawing hunger and arctic cold. To call upon supernatural powers to release the Khutuktu, a lama among Ungern's following obtained the hair of some Chinese soldiers, constructed puppets of the Chinese commander and troops, and ritually burned them in an exorcism ceremony. In the meantime Mongol volunteers flocked to enlist at Zum Kuren.[29]

Meanwhile, Sukhe Bator finished his military training in Irkutsk and relocated to Troitskosavsk on 22 November, preparing to launch Mongolia's Red revolution. A Mongolian delegation that had just returned from Moscow remained in Irkutsk to maintain liaison with the Comintern. However, leery of the welcome Ungern-Shternberg was receiving, the Soviets hesitated to contribute generously to Sukhe Bator, but soon seconded a number of Red military advisors to his lair. Nevertheless, six weeks would pass before Sukhe Bator began recruiting in earnest.[30]

Mr McLaughlin, the American representative of the Mongolian Trading Company who had been rescued in November, returned to Urga on 24 December. The tension was thicker than the dust as 'strange patrols of Cossacks and Mongols' were frequently sighted and the telegraph lines kept getting cut near town. 'The Chinese military commander, General Chu Chi-hsiang, circulated a verbal report among the foreign population to the effect that in case of an attack upon the city, he would kill every white man, woman and child in town', reported McLaughlin. And despite Peking's earlier pronouncement that it would 'reward' its troops by giving them their back pay, the Urga garrison had still not received a single *lan*, so Chu gave his troops carte blanche to rob Russians. At first, they entered houses on the pretext of searching for arms and simply helped themselves to whatever struck their fancy. Shortly they were looting Chinese and foreign shops alike without even bothering to conjure up a pretext. 'Scarcely a day passed without one or more cases of rape by Chinese soldiers upon white women and girls', continued McLaughlin. 'It was during this reign of terror that a Greek subject was crucified and horribly tortured with red hot irons and candles by the troops.'[31]

In early January 1921 Semenov met Chang Tso-Lin for a 'mysterious interview' in Mukden, following which a 'general conference' with Japanese officials convened. In the aftermath, about 30 OMO officers went to Peking 'to intrigue, amply supplied with yen', presumably to act as an intelligence network to verify Chang's compliance with some secret agreement forged at Mukden. Political pundits noted how Chang was maneuvering cleverly to take advantage of Peking's troubles with Urga to expand his power. Chang's rival, Little Hsu, had suffered a political downfall in the summer and the Manchurian warlord had been scheming to weaken his strongest adversary, General Tsao Kun, by sending the mixed brigade of a Tsao associate to Urga. In the end, however, *amban* Ch'en Yi and General Chu never received the reinforcements that they asked for, even though the central government ordered General Chang Ching-hui, a subordinate of Chang Tso-Lin, to dispatch reinforcements to Urga in December 1920. At the time, most observers predicted that while Chang Tso-Lin could manipulate Semenov and the Khutuktu, Japan would end up controlling all of them and a Mongolian buffer state. Few imagined that the Far Eastern Republic would eventually play a strong hand in the Mongolian outcome. China had even declined the FER's offer of 'disciplined troops... to cooperate with Chinese forces', with a crucial public promise to withdraw from Mongolia when the Whites were beaten.[32]

White Götterdämmerung in Mongolia
(January–September 1921)

On 18 January, Ungern-Shternberg moved his camp to a site on the Tola river just 26 miles from Urga, a fact which was common knowledge to everyone in town but the Chinese. Apparently the French Caudron biplanes that they had employed against Mongol separatists earlier were unavailable for reconnaissance at this critical time. While critics later alleged that Ungern was waiting for his soothsayers to give the signal for the attack, current day reports stated that he was awaiting the delivery of more munitions. His ranks included 2,500 Russian Cossacks and 1,500 Buryat Cossacks from OMO and 5,000 Mongolians under 'Se Ven Kung'. About this time, General Chu's outposts reported Cossack activities north of town on the Urga–Kyakhta road. To prevent Urga from being enveloped, he obligingly withdrew from the city's defense force General Kao and his 1,500 cavalrymen, 'considerable bodies of infantry and a few light guns' and sent them towards Barota in pursuit. General Chu also deployed 250 men around the Bogdo Khan's palace, where he had been under house arrest but unguarded for weeks.[33]

During the night of 31 January 1921 Ungern's men crept through the hills above Urga starting camp fires to give the illusion that a vast horde was about to fall upon the city.[34] At daybreak on 1 February his Japanese artillerists orchestrated a heavy artillery fire from the hills northeast of Maimachen that roared throughout the morning. The Chinese made no serious attempt to answer the fire, and hunkered down in their positions. About 10 a.m., merchant A.M. Guptill witnessed the spectacular rescue of the Bogdo Khan:

> I was watching his palace expecting something of the sort. Suddenly, at full gallop, a force of 70 Mongols, Russians, Buryats and Tibetans under a Buryat colonel, appeared in the mouth of the ravine leading out of Bogda-ol directly behind Bogdo Khan's palace, rushed his Chinese guard, killed 150 of them and routed the rest. They put Bogdo Khan on a horse and retired as rapidly as they came. The entire action consumed exactly one-half hour and was the prettiest piece of cavalry work that one could desire to witness.[35]

The daring rescue heightened the panic seizing the Chinese command. Gunfire ceased around noon, 'except for desultory shooting now and them to keep the Chinese unhappy'. In the afternoon, General Chu ordered that cars be prepared for his escape. Chinese troops rode madly through the city, but were too afraid to pause for looting. The main body of the garrison, some 4,000 men now, was concentrated in Maimachen, with about 1,000 others scattered throughout town. It was evident that Ungern was only awaiting nightfall and the cover of darkness to make his attack. Guptill noted with amazement, 'The Chinese sent out no patrols and evidently made no contact with the attacking force during the entire day and were quite in ignorance of the strength and position of [Ungern's] main force.'[36]

The day of 2 February opened with a bad omen for the Chinese soldiers, as they witnessed General Chu, Chen Yi and 'the rest of the higher officers' roar out of town in eight motor cars aimed for Kyakhta. City residents and A.M. Guptill sneered, 'They left at daybreak, just in time to save their skins in the most approved Chinese military manner and will probably be made Field Marshals for their skill and bravery in retreating.'[37] A mass of Chinese soldiery attempted to flee west out of Maimachen for west Urga, but were cut down by machine guns concealed on both sides of the highway east of the old Russian Consulate. Ungern then allowed the survivors of this strafing to flee north on horses, camels, carts and on foot in a terrified cavalcade that would be intercepted by White-Mongol ambushers up the Kyakhta road. Mindless of their imminent doom, many Chinese soldiers remained after the general flight to loot the Russian community, then discarded their uniforms and rifles and hid in houses. The White-Mongol army attacked heavily from the east pass and the south, complemented by field artillery on the Han mountain, reported Major Dockray, whose wireless station 'engine room' was struck by a shell. 'A strong Chinese force holding the pass was thrown into a panic at the first cavalry charge', stated Dockray and ran for Maimachen 'under a double machine gun enfilade'. They suffered very heavy casualties. 'No prisoners were taken on either side', noted Dockray, at least not in combat situations.[38] At night the flames of saboteurs' fires in Maimachen licked the sky.

The next day, 3 February, the city capitulated without resistance, although lone Chinese soldiers continued to take potshots at foreign civilians. About half of General Chu's garrison had perished and the other half was fleeing north, abandoning artillery and large quantities of munitions.[39] Most people in Urga welcomed the several thousand Mongols and 2,500 Cossacks of Ungern's army. Political prisoners crammed into the crowded Chinese penitentiary were liberated, including scores of battered Russians shackled with huge iron collars; Urga's richest Buryat merchant, Sulionanov, and several prominent Mongols.[40] Most foreigners were well-treated, but no one was allowed to evacuate to Kalgan. Baron Ungern-Shternberg entered Urga in the afternoon, accompanied by '40 Japanese bodyguards and [a] Tartar regiment'.[41]

Meanwhile, in the Tola river valley west of Urga, Ungern's Tibetans fell upon the fleeing Chinese baggage train, leaving the road 'strewn with overcoats, shirts, boots, caps and kettles' and marked with piles of dead men, horses and camels. A column of 6,000 Chinese from Kyakhta marching to save Urga were defeated and about half of them surrendered, but they foolishly tried to escape, provoking a unit of Transbaikal Cossacks to butcher them with their *shashki*, a traditional Cossack saber.[42] Two large columns of Chinese reinforcements approached the city from the south unaware of the garrison's capitulation. One group was ambushed and 'slaughtered in the snow twenty-five miles outside Urga', and the second group was scattered into the Gobi Desert.[43] These actions settled the Urga campaign decisively in Ungern-Shternberg's favor. In Washington and other capitals that followed Far Eastern affairs, the intelligence clerks scratched the 3rd Mixed Brigade from China's order of battle.[44]

About 60 Chinese soldiers were dragged from hiding places in Urga houses and executed, but Baron Ungern-Shternberg, being as practical as he was magnanimous, enlisted about 2,000 former Chinese soldiers of the Urga garrison into his horde, organizing them into two regiments which were entitled to wear the 'old Chinese silver dragons on their caps and shoulders'. Apparently these were garrison units that had deserted, were refused entry into the FER and returned to Urga, where the Cossacks executed their officers and convinced them to join up. Ungern ordered Chinese civilians to bury the 2,500 dead, most of whom bore saber wounds. When this gory three-day task would be completed, all Chinese received a blanket amnesty, as the Mongols were anxious to resume trade with China.[45]

From Urga, Guptill reported, 'They did not plunder the town and the property of both the foreign and Chinese merchants was saved.'[46] Dockray's reports agreed, stating, 'Baron Ungern is strictly prohibiting looting and is heavily punishing the slightest disobedience'. Memoirs published later portrayed three hellish days immediately after the liberation in which the Cossacks and Mongols were allowed to run amok, raping, assaulting, killing and looting as they pleased. Alioshin and others graphically described the cooking alive of a baker's boy suspected of Red sympathies, a Cossack strangler who sought old maids, an outraged Dane named Olsen dragged through the streets behind a horse, women 'raped to death by whole squadrons of Mongol cavalry', wild drunken shootings, hackings, bayonettings, disembowelings, castrations, skinnings, crucifictions, roastings and myriad other atrocities unleashed upon 'men, women and children of all ages, races and creeds'.[47]

'Jews, Germans and known Bolsheviks' seem to have been the targets of this violence, and were summarily executed unless their tormenters decided to toy with them first.[48] This Mongolian pogrom had begun a few weeks before when Ungern's men had lynched two carloads of Russian Jews fleeing along the Kalgan road from Urga's Chinese terror. Yet Ossendowski wrote that Ungern claimed no ill feelings toward Jews, and as proof declared that 'one Jewish officer, Vulfovich... commands my right flank' and that all of the baron's agents in Chita, Irkutsk, Harbin and Vladivostok were Jews.[49] At least one order published by Baron Ungern (if it was not Red disinformation) mandated that all Jews, Communists and commissars be killed along with their families and their property confiscated.[50]

One Bolshevik prisoner supplied Ungern's counterintelligence with the names of 28 comrades, then was 'cut in pieces'.[51] Armed with this information, the White inquisition rounded up approximately 120 Russians and Mongolians accused of collaboration with the Reds. Forty Jews were killed during this witchhunt, even though only one was said to have been genuinely Red, Doctor Sheinman, the president of the Urga soviet who was executed with his entire family. The victims' homes were dispersed throughout west Urga, there being no concentrated foreign settlement, and the whole city became aware of Ungern's pogrom as raucous death squads charged through the quarter, invaded and plundered a home and raped, tortured and butchered whole families in the street. A mysterious night fire in Zkhadyr, the Urga market, was linked somehow to the pogrom, which took on a festive, sadistic air. There were moments of high drama, as a White officer gave a young girl the 'privilege of committing suicide' before her gang rape, and bravery, as a Mongolian nanny saved a baby by sprinting to the church for a hasty baptism. The Bargut leader, Togtokh-gun, who had raised a 200-man bodyguard for the Khutuktu, provided a covert refuge for many Jews in his compound, but was discovered after several days, and this last pocket of innocents was tortured in the streets and slaughtered.[52] This old fashioned, wanton pogrom, which manifested all the despicable savagery of the old order that had ignited Russia's revolution in 1917, seemed to be an unwitting curtain call for the reactionaries.

Ungern stationed some Buryat officers and 200 Cossacks in Urga to train new Mongol recruits and dispatched detachments throughout Mongolia, while he led the main body of the army up the Kyakhta road in pursuit of Chinese.[53] Colonel Kazagrandi's detachment was sent to Van-Khure, where it cleared out the Chinese and apprehended a Korean internationalist 'on his way from Moscow with gold and propaganda to work in Korea and America'.[54] A 300-man detachment under Buryat Captain Vandalov and Russian Captain Bezrodnov was sent to restore order to points west of Urga and Uliastai. Ossendowski encountered their column of Mongols, Buryats and Tibetans with Bezrodnov at its head wearing 'a huge black Astrakhan [hat] and black felt cape with red Caucasian cowl on his shoulders'. Empowered as a military judge by Ungern-Shternberg, Bezrodnov roamed the countryside rounding up and shooting suspicious wanderers. Another White Buryat detachment took Menza, 130 miles northeast of Urga.[55]

Mongolia's small core of Reds began to act one week after Ungern liberated Urga. On 10 February a revolutionary council appointed Sukhe Bator as military commander, Choibalsan as political officer and ordered that recruitment of soldiers be expedited. During the second half of February, Sukhe Bator and his lieutenants began to enlist partisans in the Kyakhta area, and signed on 'the banner of Sumiya beise', a Chahar leader from Sinkiang who had migrated to Mongolia during the 1911 revolution. Another nucleus was a detachment of 50 former soldiers from Kyakhta under Puntsag, an old friend of Sukhe Bator's. By the end of February, the Mongolian Reds mustered some 400 men in four brigades, although they were mostly unarmed and some were unwilling conscripts. They ambushed larger, unsuspecting Chinese units to capture weapons, build morale and lay claim to territory, assisted by advisors from the FER. The Mongolian People's Party held its first party congress during the first three days in March, overseen by Comintern representatives and attended by 26 so-called representatives drawn from the new army and the surrounding area, the Tushetu Khan *aimag* around Kyakhta. Of the five-member general staff established during the congress, two were Russians 'invited' from the Red Army.[56]

On 10 March A.M. Guptill arrived in Manchuli by automobile. He excitedly informed an American friend connected to the legation in Peking that Mongolia was now independent and the United States should send a consular officer to Urga 'to seize the great opportunities for seizing business'.[57] The Khutuktu was proclaimed emperor of Mongolia and conferred extravagant titles on Ungern, lauding him as 'invincible general [and] incarnation of the fierce divinity Jamsarang' (a god of war and horses).[58] Awe and fear had already engendered myths that blurred truth and embellishment about Ungern-Shternberg. Cossack veterans told Ossendowski, 'At one fight seventy-four bullets entered his overcoat, saddle and the boxes by his side and again left him untouched.'[59] Mongolians immersed in the lamaist superstitions similarly revered him.

The baron began a three-month respite in Urga, lounging in his *ger*, trying to divine which visitors were traitors and spies, praying and meditating in old temples and roaring around the region in his chauffeured Fiat, saluted by fearful soldiers and civilians alike. In the meantime he cleaned up and modernized the city, 'making the trains run on time', so to speak, as only totalitarian governments can. He illuminated Urga with 'splendid great arc lights from the electric station', ordered a modern telephone system and bus service and directed Major Dockray to repair the wireless radio station. 'He also ordered his men to clean and disinfect the city which had probably not felt the broom since the days of Genghis Khan', noted Ossendowski and 'built bridges over the Tola and Orkhon Rivers; published a newspaper; arranged a veterinary laboratory and hospitals; [and] reopened the schools'. Law and order, as defined by Baron Ungern, settled upon Urga.[60]

Discipline and security were responsibilities of the baron's frequent companions, Major General B.P. Rezukhin and Captain Veselovskii. Rezukhin was a regimental commander in the drive on Urga and was 'the watchdog of Baron Ungern...a small dapper man with soft voice and courteous manners' who wore 'an old green Cossack cap with a visor, [and] a torn grey Mongol overcoat', and was 'distinguished for his absolute bravery and boundless cruelty'. Veselovskii was Ungern's personal executioner, tall, young, with long red curls falling onto his ivory visage, 'large, steel-cold eyes and...beautiful, tender, almost girlish lips'. The minutiae of day-to-day affairs and counterintelligence fell to the notorious Colonel Sipailov, 'the darkest person on the canvas of Mongolian events', whom Ungern-Shternberg appointed Commandant of Urga. Even the baron was wary of him and his assistants, the executioners Shestyakov and Zhdanov. Other senior officers included Colonel Ostrovskii as chief of staff, regimental commanders at various times: Colonel V.I. Shaiditskii, Cossack Lieutenant Colonels Tsirkulinskii and Markov, Colonel Likhachev, Captain Zabiyakin and, recently promoted from subalterns, Colonels Parygin, Khobotov and Achairov; and battery commanders: Captains Dmitriev and Popov.[61]

As the threat from Russian Whites mounted after the fall of Urga, China hedged its bets in Mongolia by 'entering into secret relations with the *Bolsheviki*'. Before Ungern's invasion the Chinese had turned a blind eye to the Russian Reds' takeover of the Urga municipality. In the aftermath of the Urga disaster, they went so far as to hand over White refugees to Reds at Kyakhta and Ulaangom, and allowed the NRA to conduct cross-border operations in the Selenga valley and near Lake Kosogol.[62] However, the relationship between Soviet Russia and its FER proxy and China changed as the Reds realized how weak was the Chinese resolve to hang onto Mongolia.

Thus, Sukhe Bator and his Red Army advisors planned the first major attack of the Mongolian People's Revolutionary Army not against Ungern, but against the 10,000-man

Chinese garrison at Maimachen (present day Altan Bulag), the Mongolian border town with Kyakhta. Ch'en Yi, the fugitive *amban*, had fled to Maimachen, and in early March appealed to FER authorities for the military assistance against the Whites that they had offered weeks before. On 15 March, Sukhe Bator, backed by his four inexperienced, poorly armed, understrength brigades, called upon General Ko to surrender and, upon receiving no reply by the morning of 18 March, attacked from three sides in a miserable wet snow at 10 a.m., withholding a thin 90-man reserve in case things went wrong. By noon the Red Mongols had occupied the town, but the Chinese counterattacked and fighting continued until midnight, when General Ko's force fled. While Sukhe Bator's victory was hailed as an incredible triumph, it was backed up by the thinly veiled power of the Red Army and Chita's NRA. He renamed the town Altan Bulag and made it the temporary capital of a Mongolian Provisional Government proclaimed in Russia two days before the battle. On 23 March, Mongolia's new Red government published a letter to nobles and lamas warning them against helping Ungern-Shternberg. The Khutuktu's Ministry of the Interior ordered Sukhe Bator to come to Urga and surrender and warned that the Bolsheviks who were so generously helping him intended to plunder the property of farmers, merchants and nobles, destroy temples, monasteries and other shrines and kill tens of thousands of people.[63]

Reports of collusion between the Chinese and Bolsheviks encouraged Whites to keep up the fight. Ferdinand Ossendowski, the former Polish prisoner of war and scientist who was trekking through Mongolia to escape the Reds, encountered a detachment of White socialists from Irkutsk and Yakutsk districts under a Captain Vasil'ev who had been defeated around Lake Baikal and were trying to link up with Kazagrandi. In the valley of Tesiyn Gol he found another ten-man detachment from Irkutsk under a Lieutenant Ivanov that was working for Lieutenant Colonel Mikhailov's independent White headquarters at Uliastai.[64]

The whole country was in ferment, but the Chinese could not comprehend that their centuries-old colonial rule could possibly collapse. At Uliastai, Kobdo and elsewhere in western Mongolia, Chinese merchants distributed rifles to their fellow colonists and planned preemptive pogroms against Russian and Mongol communities. At Kobdo, they succeeded in pulling off a bloody purge but when they made for the Sinkiang border with their booty they were overtaken and annihilated by Kaigorodov. A detachment of Chahar mercenaries under a 'notorious one-eyed *hunghutze* leader' tried in vain to pacify the Kobdo and Urianhai areas, but the populace was too agitated to submit to Peking's iron-fisted bumbling.[65]

In late March, the Chinese grip on western Mongolia was still strong enough to black out news of their defeats at Urga, Maimachen and on the roads between Urga and Ude, where approximately 15,000 soldiers had been destroyed or dispersed in the past two months' battles. In Uliastai, the Chinese commissioner, a 'young and inexperienced man' named Wang Tsao-tsun, had dismissed the Mongolian *sait* (governor appointed by Bogdo Khan), Prince Chultun Beyle, and was arresting and beating any Mongolians who dared protest and Whites. Russian officers formed a self-defense detachment under Lieutenant Colonel M.M. Mikhailov, but it soon broke down into squabbling factions.[66] The peace depended upon a capable Chinese Army commander and his 80-man garrison to keep 'three thousand coolies, one thousand armed merchants and two hundred gamins' apart from the self-defense squads of Whites and Mongols.[67] Into this milieu entered three Bolshevik agents from Irkutsk, Saltikov, Freimann and Novak, who tried to convince the Chinese Chamber of Commerce to petition the Irkutsk soviet to send a detachment and distributed Red leaflets in Mongolian. When news spread that Colonel Kazagrandi's detachment had captured Van-Khure and the large monastery of Dzain, then formed three Russian–Mongol cavalry brigades, patrols of White officers and Mongolian nationalists organized under Lieutenant Colonel Mikhailov ventured into the streets of Uliastai to take over. Mikhailov soon discovered that he had acted prematurely because the three new brigades were fictional, and the Chinese still held a fortress and four machine guns.[68]

On 31 March Pacification Commissioner Ch'en Yi arrived back in Peking, via an undignified retreat through Manchuli to find himself 'deprived by Presidential mandate of his ranks and offices'. In subsequent weeks, Chinese refugees and wounded soldiers straggled into China bearing news of their 'disastrous and inglorious campaign against Ungern'. Now faced with invasion from the FER, an envoy from the Khutuktu also appeared in Peking with a peace proposal based upon Mongolian autonomy under the Chinese Republic.[69]

Mongolia's Red Provisional Government announced the mobilization of all men 19 years of age or more, but their battles were increasingly fought by Red Army units. The wandering refugee Ossendowski found the town of Karaul Khathyl in a panic in late April or early May 1921. 'The Russian detachment of Colonel Kazagrandi', he wrote, 'after having twice defeated the Bolsheviki and well on its march against Irkutsk, was suddenly rendered impotent and scattered through internal strife among the officers'.[70] Not so far away in Chita, the FER was entertaining former White allies, the assistant military attaché and commercial attaché from the US embassy in Tokyo, who naively reported to Washington on the democratic and independent nature of Krasnoshchekov's puppet government.[71]

Rumors circulated of the return of Ataman Boris P. Annenkov, however the Chinese had bottled up his 600-man detachment somewhere in 'the depths of Turkestan'. A Tartar officer, Captain A.P. Kaigorodov, led 1,000 White followers on a trek from Kosh Agach (just inside the Russian border) through the Altai mountains and penetrated the loose Chinese cordon around western Mongolia in April 1921. Other small White bands – of Smol'yannikov, Shishkin and Vanyagin – that had consolidated at Oralgo under Colonel V.Yu. Sokol'nitskii, joined Kaigorodov's column, as did many angry Mongols from Kobdo and Ulaangom, where the Chinese Army continued to thrash men to death with bamboo poles if they tried to defend their womenfolk against rape.[72]

On 22 May Ungern-Shternberg led his army north out of Urga with about eight field guns and no fewer than 20 machine guns. Estimates of his army's size range from 3,500 to 8,000. His horde poised like a dagger at the Selenga River valley and the main artery of Soviet Siberia, the Trans-Siberian Railway. His objective was to cut the rail line between Verkhne-Udinsk and Chita and liberate the Buryat homeland of his OMO troops. After a five-day march they crossed the border into Soviet territory.[73] He could expect little additional help from Japan, apart from the small detachments he already had, as the Japanese Army was even evacuating Blagoveshchensk again. Sukhe Bator and his little army, on the other hand, could expect the support of a division-sized task force from the 5th Red Army.[74]

Still trying to 'grasp the Mongolian nettle', Peking appointed Chang Tso-lin the high commissioner for Mongolia on 30 May, 'with plenipotentiary powers over Inner Mongolia and control over the Special Administrative Districts of Chahar, Jehol and Suiyuan'. The Chinese government expected Chang to expeditiously mount a campaign to recapture Urga and 'to retrieve Chinese military honor'. However, noted an analyst at the American Legation in Peking, 'This [promotion] was the great opportunity so long planned for by Chang. By this he acquired his coveted and absolute control of all of China and Mongolia north of Peking'. Chang dallied and avoided launching the campaign while he sought to find out the critical attitude of the Japanese toward Mongolia. Chang's main concern was Manchuria, where he was gaining ground against both Russia and Japan. China had even begun to create a special judicial district in the Chinese Eastern Railway zone with Chinese courts (*Shun P'an T'ing*) that would, for the first time in two decades, exercise jurisdiction over Russian nationals. Thus, for the time being he left the Russian Reds, Whites and Mongols to scrap over the Mongolian backwater.[75]

Early in the morning of 5 June 1921, a secondary column of 1,500 followers of Ungern-Shternberg fell upon the Transbaikal settlement of Basiiskii, where the school of 106th Sakhalin Regiment happened to be located. The Whites' field pieces repelled the handful of Red cadets who were present, but within an hour the regimental commander Lysov arrived with a small force that managed to chase Ungern's column back into the knolls. Eighty peasants from surrounding villages 'armed with hunting rifles, pitchforks and boar-spears' joined Lysov in pursuit of the invaders as far as the Mongolian border.[76]

On the following day Ungern's main force attacked Altan Bulag, but was initially repulsed by Red Mongolian and Soviet defenders. Within days the White-Mongol horde occupied Troitskosavsk, then on 11 June suffered a stinging defeat by the NRA. Ungern-Shternberg's Asiatic Horse Division ceased to exist as two-thirds of its force were destroyed and the survivors splintered into a handful of diehard detachments. A Red Army task force entered Mongolia on 2 July, defeated Ungern about ten miles east of Dulaanhaan on the Orkhon river, and quickly marched south 100 miles towards Urga. A small detachment of Ungern's soldiers and police fled on 5 July, after anti-Bolshevik exorcisms and the placing of a *dui*, 'a magical structure for repelling demons and evil influences', failed to turn back the Reds. The first Red Mongol and Soviet soldiers entered Urga on the afternoon of 6 July, completed their occupation of the city by the morning of 8 July, then turned to hunting down and eradicating the 'White Guard bandits'.[77] Among the hunters were several Rumanian soldiers of the 1st Chita Internationalist Detachment, which had begun the fight against Ungern in spring 1918, and had fought its way through Siberia from the Urals. On 11 July 1921 Sukhe Bator's compatriots proclaimed the Bogdo Khan as titular head of state and 27-year-old Dogsomyn Bodoo as prime minister of a provisional parliamentary government. Togtokh-gun, who had tried in vain to protect a group of Urga Jews, was named minister of justice.[78]

That same day, Chang Tso-Lin, who was suddenly showing renewed interest in Mongolia, concluded a conference with the governors of Kirin and Heilungjiang provinces in Mukden to the accompaniment of loud saber-rattling about a Chinese invasion. Chang announced that he would 'assume personal command of the Mongolian expedition', and dispatched General Chi of the 28th Division to plan an approach on Urga from Manchuli. A recruiting drive throughout Manchuria clamored to raise 40,000 men by promising double pay ('about $20 per man per month'). Behind the scenes however, Chang did not exert much effort to adequately fund the campaign and the central government was surely concerned about 'Manchurian troops [that] may become rebellious and a distinct menace to Peking'. In addition, Chang began to make use of new aircraft he received for the expedition by sending 'one or two aeroplanes...[on] almost daily flights' over Peking.[79]

Sometime during the summer a Cossack and Buryat column under Cossack Captain Maketno set out from Urga with a 200-camel caravan laden with a treasure of gold, jewelry and plunder from the Irkutsk state bank. They unloaded and buried it at Lake Buyr Nur on the Mongolian–Chinese border, just 120 miles southwest of Hailar, in a convenient location should Ungern-Shternberg's evacuation become necessary. Like the bearers of Genghis Khan's treasure centuries before, Maketno and his men were slain by Colonel Sipailov, supposedly under orders of Ungern-Shternberg.[80]

In the meantime the remnants of Baron Ungern-Shternberg's army had been reinforced with two Mongolian regiments from Urga and White units that had been held in reserve. They thundered west and crossed the Selenga River to Akai-Gun-Khure, where they clashed with the Red Army's 104th Brigade on 18 July. Defying logic, as he had been wont to do in less desperate times, Ungern struck north into Soviet Russia again, passing through the town of Tsezheiskii on 24 July, where he turned east and bore down upon the Selenga River valley once again. At Novo-Dmitrievka he murdered two families, children as well as parents, fended off the Reds' 7th Special Detachment on 29 July, flogged a group of lamas at Gusinoozersk, made Novo-Selengensk by 1 August and stabbed within 37 miles of Verkhne-Udinsk before being turned back by the Red Army. By mid-August, his tattered column was slogging back into the Mongolian badlands like fugitives, and rumors suggested that the baron might flee to Tibet to place himself at the Dalai Lama's disposal and rekindle his militant Buddhist order, if only he could break free of the Red Army detachments that shadowed them across the border.[81]

However, the greatest immediate danger to Ungern arose from his own war-weary, demoralized men. On the evening of 21 August a machine gun unit opened fire on the baron in an assassination attempt planned with the connivance of one of his own Russian regimental commanders. The baron's loyal assistant Major General Rezukhin fell dead, but Ungern miraculously escaped, although badly wounded and fell unconscious from his horse near a Mongolian battalion about two miles away. Also mutinous but fearful of divine wrath should they kill him, the Mongols bound him and left him in a yurt for the Reds.[82] 'His end came when his own Mongolian troops betrayed him to the Bolsheviks', wrote Baerlein. 'They sold him as one sells a horse.'[83] A Captain Makeev (and subsequently Colonel Ostrovskii) led the remaining Whites out of Mongolia to Manchuli.

On 27 August 1921 Ungern-Shternberg was interrogated by a number of high-ranking Reds, to whom it seems he responded concisely and with pride. He was transported through Verkhne-Udinsk and Irkutsk to Novonikolaevsk for a quick trial on 15 September. Baerlein wrote, 'We are told that this expert in death scenes managed his own very finely. He impressed the Red officers by whom he was tried and executed.' Though most accounts state that the baron was executed by a firing squad, one version says that Chairman Pavlunovskii of the Siberian CHEKA dispatched Ungern-Shternberg with a shot through the nape of his neck.[84]

Ungern-Shternberg's demise did not entirely finish off the White threat in Mongolia. Colonel Kazagrandi's detachment of about 350 men withdrew through the Gobi Desert in June 1921, where 42 surrendered to the Chinese and were taken to Peking. The majority of the detachment fell in combat against the Chinese Army and the last 35 men surrendered at Tsitsihar on 5 October and were taken to the Maritime province. In western Mongolia, all of the men of a Buryat detachment under a Colonel Vangdanov had been clubbed to death by their Mongol comrades during the evening prayer time near Uliastai in midsummer. Similar treachery neutralized other White Mongol and Buryat units.[85] Captain A.P. Kaigorodov's detachment continued to grow during summer 1921, gaining three *sotnias* of cavalry, a machine gun team and an artillery platoon.[86] They engaged the Reds in battles around Lake Tulba that spilled across the border into Russian territory and were defeated in September. Kaigorodov and four other officers remained in Soviet Russia to carry on a futile partisan campaign, while most of the detachment returned to Kobdo under a Colonel Sokol'nitskii. In late October, Sokol'nitskii departed Kobdo, leading a column of 488 soldiers (including 50 officers) and just under 200 dependents. They fought several skirmishes with the Mongols before wandering into Chinese Turkestan in December, where they camped along the River Bulgun.[87] Like many other White refugees in the Far East, they became pariahs with no state or safe haven.

Mongolia wriggled free of Chinese colonialism only to become the guinea pig for a new brand of Red imperialism. The advisors that Moscow consigned to her Mongolian apprentice were often bilingual Buryats who would insure that Sukhe Bator's new state was cast in the Red Russian mold. With the loss of Mongolia, the Chinese Republic lost suzerainty over a territory two-thirds the size of the original 18 provinces of China, and one-quarter the size of all Chinese territory.

Ataman's exile and White Russia's last spasms (October 1920–November 1922)

The flight of OMO and other Semenov loyalists into the Maritime province added a tumultuous ingredient to a region that was spiraling deeper into turmoil. The economy was in a shambles, dominated by barter transactions or payment in yen, and the port of Vladivostok slumped as Dairen soaked off all regional maritime traffic that was unwilling to bear the high risks and costs of operations in the Maritime province. *Hunghutze* activity was on the rise. Some bands of *hunghutze* operated covertly in the employ of the Japanese Army to destabilize Pink authority, while other freelance gangs grew bold enough to enter Vladivostok to kidnap and rob. As if manmade pestilence was not enough, the plague drifted into the area from Manchuria in March, killing several hundred people, mostly in the province's Chinese communities. Similar instability racked the north end of the province, where the Japanese had evacuated their military and civilian population from Khabarovsk on 23 October 1920, taking with them six Russian steamboats brimming with loot.[88]

Since December, when Medvedev disbanded the provisional *zemstvo* government and the province was absorbed into the FER, a local administration under Bolshevik V.G. Antonov governed the area, although with so many Whites now living in his jurisdiction, his days were numbered. A 'veritable pilgrimage' wound its way to Semenov's villa at Port Arthur, as White émigrés and conspirators appeared to plead for money and support for sundry plots. A congress of non-Socialists gathered in Vladivostok in early March 1921 under Japanese protection, but delayed its opening until 20 March while it awaited a pledge of support from the ataman. That same month Nikolai Merkulov visited Port Arthur asking to borrow Semenov's Grodekovo army and some gold to install his brother in power. Spiridon Dionis'evich Merkulov was 'the son of an Amur peasant' who had become a lawyer at the Agriculture Ministry in St Petersburg. Semenov agreed to aid them as long as he could be the leader, however, after an uproar from conservative opponents, a Harbin businessman, Vasilii Ivanov, convinced Semenov to lower his ambition to military chief.

On 31 March 1921 a pro-Semenov officer in the Kappel Army, Colonel Gludkin, attempted a coup against Antonov, but it was unclear if the ataman had a hand in the planning or if Gludkin acted independently. Regardless, Antonov got wind of the rebellion and quietly suppressed it. A few days later Antonov tried and failed to disarm Savel'ev's army at Grodekovo. Encouraged by news of Ungern-Shternberg's resurgence in Mongolia, the Kronstadt uprising and anti-Moscow insurrections in western and central Siberia and even inside Russia, White plotting intensified. On May Day in Chita the Reds put on a potent display of military strength to discourage any ideas of rebellion, parading infantry, artillery and sailors by the thousands across *Ploshchad' Svobody* – Liberty Square – formerly Atamanovskii Square, while military aircraft circled overhead.[89] Krasnoshchekov wired Moscow on 6 May begging for diplomatic, materiel and military support, but the Soviets were busy fighting fires closer to home.

On 23 and 24 May 1921 the long-awaited White coup d'état began materializing at Razdolnoe and Nikolsk-Ussuriisk, where *kappel'evtsy* disarmed the revolutionary militias and captured the train stations. Savel'ev led the Cossacks at Grodekovo into the fray, assured by the Merkulovs that Semenov was a patron of the coup, even though they had wired him to stay put in Port Arthur. Ugol'naya fell on 26 May and the next day Spiridon and Nikolai Merkulov took over Vladivostok, establishing a White enclave that they named the Provisional Priamur Government, even though it only extended from the southern tip of the Maritime province to Spassk, 125 miles north. Moscow finally had to take notice of the threat from the Far East and immediately ordered a formidable rescue expedition into the FER: a Siberian division of the Red Army, 100 military-political zealots, a number of armored trains and General Vasilii Blyukher.[90]

Given a new lease on life by fate, the White movement deteriorated under the Merkulov brothers until few could deny its moral bankruptcy. They inherited a disastrous financial situation from the spendthrift Red–Pink administrations, cursed by insufficient income and deep-rooted corruption. The Merkulovs raised money by selling timber concessions to the Japanese and promoting opium trade, licensing its cultivating and smoking. Heavy-handed press censorship returned with threats against major newspapers *Vecher* and *Golos Rodiny*. Their counter-intelligence units and military sweeps quickly smashed the overt communist organization, igniting a second partisan struggle in rural areas under Commanders Il'yukhov and Vladivostokov at the old Red headquarters in Anuchino. Yet the Merkulovs encountered more threatening trouble from a new antagonist – the *semenovtsy*.[91]

Since the Merkulovs maintained power behind the bayonets of the *kappel'evtsy*, who despised the *semenovtsy* for shaming and weakening the anti-Bolshevik movement with their corruption, Ataman Semenov was not invited out of his forced retirement at Port Arthur. Even the Japanese could not force the Merkulovs to accept Semenov. Thus, Semenov, driven by his insatiable personal ambition and blindly manipulated by his Japanese sponsors, undermined the Merkulovs just as he had undermined Admiral Kolchak. He distracted them from their struggle with the Red enemy and sapped the energy of their government in negotiations to prevent a Cossack rebellion.[92]

Semenov strained at the leash to rush to Vladivostok and claim the titles promised him by Nikolai Merkulov in March, but the Japanese refused to give him permission to depart Port Arthur. They tried to prevent him from chartering a ship, but the obstinate Semenov hired a rusting tramp steamer named *Kiodo Maru*, rode out a storm and appeared in Vladivostok harbor on 3 June 1921. The ataman was surprised to find his political position much weaker than expected, and was not allowed to disembark in Vladivostok. The head of government himself, Spiridon Merkulov, came to negotiate with Semenov on 5 June and the ataman subsequently issued a statement declaring that he 'did not desire to interfere with the policies and work of the local government'.[93]

Meanwhile, the Merkulovs had appointed Kappelist General Verzhbitskii as their military commander-in-chief. It was the position that Semenov coveted, and the spurned warlord cried foul and rightly asserted that OMO had been critical to the coup's success. On the other hand, the *kappel'evtsy* threatened to go over to the partisans or move to Khabarovsk before they would serve under Semenov. As was expected, the consular corps and city duma came out against Semenov's intrusion, and, not passing up an opportunity to kick the Whites while they were down, on 10 June the chairman of the regional revolutionary committee (ObRevKom), Bolshevik V.P. Shishkin, ordered a sabotage campaign against the provinces tattered mining and railway resources. That same day, to everyone's surprise a Cossack conference in Grodekovo declared opposition to Grigorii Semenov's presence in the Maritime province. Semenov stubbornly, blindly refused to budge, even though his Japanese friends were also maneuvering to stymie him. On 15 June Spiridon Merkulov again came aboard the *Kiodo Maru* for five hours of negotiations with the ataman. Talks continued the next day when the exasperated government offered Semenov 'a large sum' to leave. Semenov demanded an even larger sum – 400,000 gold rubles – and other preposterous conditions. When the Second Non-Socialist Congress opened on 17 June, many delegates supported the defiant Cossack maverick.

Eight days later, in what appeared to be a well executed escape 'with Japanese assistance', Semenov slipped out of the tight security net around the *Kiodo Maru* and made his way to Grodekovo. Perhaps not coincidentally, the Merkulovs' police quickly rounded up Semenov's supporters in Vladivostok that same day. A firefight occurred between OMO and *kappel'evtsy* militia and military supplies and reinforcements slated for Baron Ungern-Shternberg were held up. In the northern part of Merkulov territory around Spassk and Ussuri stations, the renegade Cossack Bochkarev took advantage of the disorder to lead his detachment on a spree of murder, rape, robbery and assault.[94]

In July 1921, Semenov fell out of favor with his Cossack constituency. He tried in vain to persuade Chang Tso-lin to let him transport his remaining OMO troops across Manchuria, presumably to reinforce Ungern-Shternberg in Mongolia, but was refused under pressure from the United States. A gathering at Grodekovo stripped Semenov of his position of field ataman for not acting in Cossack interests. On 2 September Semenov dispatched his chief of staff Lieutenant General Ivanov-Rinov to Vladivostok to negotiate his departure from the Maritime Province. Eleven days later, OMO subordinated itself to the Provisional Priamur Government and the Ataman paid a final visit to his men at Grodekovo. He left Grodekovo on 14 September 1921 and later wrote, 'On this day finished my armed struggle against Bolshevism on the native soil.' Grigorii Semenov quietly exited Russia, boarding a steamship in Vladivostok to a new emigrant life.[95]

Semenov's tenacity inspired rumors of plots and coups for years to come. Just days after he departed, 900 refugees from Baron Vrangl's camp in European Russia disembarked in Vladivostok, their passage paid for by the British government. Immediately their arrival spawned tales of a secret agreement between the French and Japanese to rekindle the civil war under Semenov's banner. The Merkulovs faced opposition from *semenovtsy* for the remainder of their short reign, but more formidable foes rapidly appeared.[96]

Grim months unfolded for both the Merkulov regime and Russia's White movement, which looked on mute and uninvited as foreign diplomats discussed the future of the Russian Far East in international conferences at Dairen (August 1921–April 1922) and Washington, DC (November 1921–February 1922). In early October 1921, the Merkulovs bought time with a counterintelligence triumph that unraveled an impending coup by disillusioned *kappel'evtsy* collaborating with the FER *Dal'buro*. Armed with intelligence gleaned through a double agent or a loquacious high-level prisoner, the Provisional Priamur Government rolled up the Reds' urban organization. Yet *hunghutze* and partisans freely roamed the countryside, the latter dynamiting the Ussuri Railway about six times a week.[97] Corruption reached new heights during the Merkulov administration, as even Nikolai Merkulov's 16-year-old son ran a lucrative racket buying *assignats* for government debts far below face value and cashing them in; a Merkulov decree required his father's signature to redeem an *assignat*.[98]

The Whites carried out a successful winter 1921–22 offensive, storming the Red port of Olga from land and sea, capturing the partisan headquarters at Anuchino and sweeping the guerrillas out of the Suchan valley.[99] The army of 10,000–15,000 men included former OMO soldiers, though now they were under strict discipline, and the freebooting requisitions of the past were forbidden. Many *semenovtsy* were largely uncooperative, refusing to go to the front and in November 1921 the Kappel leadership arrested four OMO generals for their defiance. As in previous campaigns, the Whites were banking on the population behind enemy lines to rise up against the FER For instance, OMO General Shil'nikov reported widespread disaffection in Transbaikalia, but did not realize how war-weary the population had become. However, the popular uprisings simply did not occur and likewise no volunteers rushed to enlist in the army and the Japanese continued to refuse to turn over the vast stockpile of war materiel at Vladivostok.[100]

In January 1922, the *kappel'evtsy* tried to force the Merkulovs to resign but discovered that the brothers had new sources of support: the OMO encampment at Grodekovo and the White navy, Admiral I.K. Stark's Siberian flotilla. At the same time the government sent V.I. Bochkarev on an expedition to invade the Kamchatka peninsula that month to stake out a last bastion in case of a Soviet overrun, but Bochkarev's excesses soon had the population up in arms. In a familiar ploy in April, the government even adopted the tired slogan, 'Long live the All-Russia Constituent Assembly!'[101] The succeeding months' decline was vividly personified by Spiridon Merkulov himself during the May festivities to commemorate his first year in power. Staggering drunk, he pushed himself in front of a conference of non-Socialists and verbally attacked his audience, drawing hisses and jeers before he ordered the police to disperse the meeting. Five days later, on 31 May, the Merkulovs dissolved the Popular Assembly, replaced General Verzhbitskii with the pro-Semenov Colonel Glebov, and tried to fire and replace other Kappel officers in a similar fashion.

A new crisis fell upon Vladivostok and after much in-fighting including several shootings and a *perevorot* – a near coup d'état, the Popular Assembly reconvened and General Mikhail K. Diterikhs was appointed military chieftain – *voevod*, although White political turmoil dragged on throughout the summer.[102] Diterikhs was 'a deeply religious man, the walls of whose private railway coach were plastered with icons', and who believed that he was waging a holy war against the Bolshevik heathens. He had been at the forefront of the fight since May 1918, and was now being called upon to preside over the apocalypse.

On 15 August 1922 General Tachibana announced that the Japanese Army would begin a phased withdrawal from the Maritime province starting in 11 days. Japan also began new negotiations at Changchun to normalize relations with the FER, although the bitterness between the two parties was still fresh and the talks broke off on 26 September. By that time a new White offensive was underway with new urgency to clear out the partisans once and for all, since soon the White army would not be able to seek protection behind Japanese lines. On 28 September, the government even mobilized children and teenagers and actually sent many of them to the front to fight the experienced Red soldiers.[103] The NRA broke through the fortifications of Spassk on 9 October and 'the last White stand, a useless shedding of blood', occurred midway between Spassk and Nikolsk during 10–14 October. The White survivors of these battles fled in two directions, about half to Pogranichnaya and the other half to the coast to seek vessels to foreign shores.[104]

General Diterikhs issued an order to end the struggle and evacuate Vladivostok on 15 October. Communists fanned the flames of panic by declaring a general strike that cut off electricity and shut down transportation and the Cossacks ran amok in a final spasm of terror and pillage. The last White refugees – somewhere between 9,000 and 15,000 of them – departed during the night of 24 October, filing numbly past the great stockpiles of weapons that their allies, even the Japanese, had denied to them, and boarding a motley fleet of rusty freighters, gunboats, trawlers, scows and rafts to the nearest foreign port, Wonsan, Korea. By noon the next day the Japanese Army had vacated Vladivostok.[105]

People joyously threw flowers and unfurled banners as NRA troops marched triumphantly into Vladivostok hours later singing revolutionary tunes. On 14 and 15 November, the FER abolished itself and rejoined Soviet Russia, yet bands of former Whites roamed the forests for years, playing cat and mouse with the Red Army and militia. In the cities and towns, the CHEKA resumed its round-ups of class enemies and added *belogvardeitsy* – White Guards – to the list of public menaces. At the first congress of Maritime province soviets in March 1923, the *Gospolokhrana* boasted of liquidating 200 monarchists and 5,000 former officers in recent months.[106] It was a modest beginning for the communists' ambitious and brutal program of *sovietizatsiya* – sovietization.

11

DIASPORA, MANCHURIAN REVIVAL AND LEGACY

June 1921 to the present day

'Yes...poor deceived Russians, shout your "Banzais" today! Tomorrow you will curse yourselves for having thus acclaimed these beings.'
(Amleto Vespa, Manchurian intelligence officer, 1938)

White diaspora and ambush by New York lawyers (January 1921–June 1922)

Ataman Semenov was the only Cossack warlord who survived to join the diaspora of Whites from the Russian Far East. The remnants of OMO languished in Grodekovo while most of their comrades had been scattered by the winds of war across the Far Eastern taiga, Mongolia and China, into squalid refugee camps, desperate bands of White fugitives, detachments of Merkulov's army, Red prison camps, foreign armies or on the wings of fate. Some were among the 16,000 mostly destitute Russians who crossed the Chinese frontier at Hunchun in search of refuge in Manchuria in autumn 1922. In comparison, Cossack émigrés from southern Russia and the western Siberian front were already settling down to new lives in dozens of organized, though usually impoverished, *stanitsas* in Bulgaria (18), Serbia (4), Greece (4), Rumania (2), Hungary and Tunisia and eventually Germany, Poland, Czechoslovakia, Luxembourg and farther flung environs. Manchuria's Marshal Chang Tso-Lin was hospitable to the incoming refugees in spite of his occasional differences during the Russian Civil War era with Semenov and other Whites, and allowed them to find employment, buy and sell land and start new lives.[1]

Many of the OMO sadists and criminals who had so disgraced the White movement and Cossackry managed to disappear into exile without a reckoning of justice. In one rare instance, Colonel Stepanov was arrested and prosecuted by the Chinese in 1921 for the 1918 murder and robbery of the Shumov boy.[2] However, Stepanov's accomplice Masha Sharaban made it to Port Said, Egypt in January 1921, then escorted Princess Elizaveta's body on to Jerusalem before settling in Lebanon.[3] Lieutenant General Georgii Katanaev, the Siberian Cossack who began cataloging Semenov's crimes and atrocities in spring 1919, died in 1921, his evidence unused. He had been arrested with Admiral Kolchak in Irkutsk, and sent back to Omsk for trial in 1920. However, the Reds found no 'serious accusations' against him and, owing to his 'decrepitude' – he was 72 years old – released him.[4]

Grigorii Semenov quietly exited Russia, boarding a steamship in Vladivostok to a new emigrant life in the third week of September, 1921. However, the ataman's emigrant experience contrasts sharply with that of most of his countrymen, who tasted humility immediately upon losing their wealth and titles, both of which Semenov never relinquished. General Tachibana, commander of the Japanese expeditionary force, visited Semenov's ship in Vladivostok harbor to bid him adieu before the vessel carried him to the little northern Korean port of Genzan. It was there, the ataman later lamented, that he had endured the humiliation of exile, having to ride to Seoul in a second-class carriage. Upon arrival in Seoul, the migrant ataman enjoyed the hospitality of his old friend General Oba, former commander of the Japanese 3rd Division in Chita, now governor-general of Korea. After a few days in Seoul, he traveled to Japan where, for the first time in his adult life, he faced the traumatic fashion ordeal of donning civilian clothing.[5]

On 24 September 1921 Semenov left Kobe, Japan for Shanghai, where he put up in a hotel for about two weeks before moving into a small apartment in a quiet neighborhood off Rue Observatoire in the French concession. Soon he was forced to move again after a Bolshevik assassination team led by one Nekii Nakhabov made an attempt on his life on 4 November. Police of the French concession arrested Nakhabov and three or four fellow conspirators, but informed Semenov that they could not guarantee his safety. The French were not thrilled to be hosting Semenov in light of his challenging General Janin to a duel after the latter's betrayal of Kolchak at Irkutsk, and, in addition, the allied consular corps was convinced that the White movement was washed up and that any further assistance to Semenov would only impede discourse with Soviet representatives. On the other hand, the ataman could not return to Chinese Shanghai while Ungern-Shternberg and his OMO–Mongol army were slaying Chinese troops in Mongolia. Semenov slipped into Tientsin and found refuge for a while in the home of Lieutenant Colonel Compatangelo, who had befriended the ataman during Siberian service with the Italian battalion. Nevertheless, Semenov's presence endangered all around him as he was still stalked by persistent Red assassins.[6]

In late February 1922, Semenov and wife set out for France, traveling from Tientsin to Shanghai to Japan, where they left their eight-month old baby, Elena, with Helen's family and boarded a trans-Pacific ocean liner. They held visas from the French consul in Tientsin, and, according to Semenov, even had a telegraphic invitation from outgoing President Raymond-Nicolas-Landry Poincaré. The purpose of his journey was to seek medical treatment for his wife and perhaps to confer with Grand Duke Nicholas in Paris about 'arranging a counterrevolution' in Russia, though it is uncertain if the grand duke was actually expecting the ataman.[7] The Semenovs sailed from Yokohama aboard the Canadian Pacific luxury liner *Empress of Russia* on 4 March.

US newspapers immediately carried a terse blurb distributed by the Associated Press announcing that Semenov was sailing to the United States under the false name of 'H. Victorne'. Five weeks earlier the US military intelligence division had encouraged immigration authorities (then under the Department of Labor) to issue a 'lookout' for Semenov should the ataman appear at an American port of entry. 'It is the Bureau's belief', stated an MID letter dated 24 January, 'that a questioning of Semenov by immigration authorities should he arrive at a port of this country, will develop ample ground for excluding him under the immigration law'.[8]

The *Empress of Russia* slid into Vancouver harbor on 14 March 1922 and the ataman received a taste of things to come when US immigration officers confiscated his revolver, then returned it at the behest of their Canadian counterparts when he disembarked. Semenov was met 'with the splendor of an eastern Prince' by Misak E. Aivazov, the suave president of Aivazov & Penklo Ltd. manufacturers' agents and 'one of the richest men in Vancouver', who would serve as his escort across North America.[9] He was also met by a writ charging that he had wrongfully deprived C.B. Richard & Company of $150,000 worth of furs, skins and hides which OMO confiscated from a Trans-Siberian freight train several months before. The ataman paid no heed to the latter.

March 1922 found Major General Graves back in the United States commanding the 1st Brigade of the 1st Division. For his service in Siberia, he had been awarded Chinese Order of the *Wen Hu* (Striped Tiger), the Czechoslovakian War Cross, America's Distinguished Service Cross and even the Order of the Rising Sun (2nd Class) from his Japanese enemies. Colonel Charles Morrow had returned home to become an instructor for the Kentucky National Guard at Frankfort, not far from his brother's office at the state capitol where he presided as governor.[10] His former prisoner, Benjamin B. McCroskey, was about to complete a nine-month stint in Columbia University's Chinese language program. Upon his return to the United States in 1920, the war department had been on the verge of muzzling him with an assignment to Eagle Pass, Texas, however, McCroskey protested to his California congressman, Hugh S. Hersman, who brought his constituent's predicament to the attention of Secretary of War Newton D. Baker. McCroskey, who had reverted to his peacetime rank of major, continued to serve as a China specialist for military intelligence.[11] His old friend, OMO Colonel Krupskii, now lived in New York city, and was eagerly awaiting a visit from his former commanding officer.

Semenov's original plan seemed to have been to traverse Canada and depart for France by way of Halifax, however blissfully unaware of the controversy that his arrival had aroused, he charted a new course through the United States. In his memoirs, he mentioned an 'invitation' from the chief of the immigration service in Washington and another from the University of California, where his old friend Lieutenant Colonel Barrows was now president. Inspector John L. Zurbrick ran a branch office of the US immigration service in Vancouver and was saddled with admitting or denying Semenov, fully appreciative of the building public furor after a flurry of anxious telegrams and bureau memoranda from Washington since the Associated Press reports hit the newspapers. On the day following Semenov's arrival, Zurbrick convened a special board of inquiry in the hope of turning Semenov away, asking tough questions (through a translator) about the killing of civilians, theft of rifles intended for Omsk and his relationship with the Japanese. With an eye on the American Legion's accusations of bigamy, Zurbrick asked several questions about Semenov's first marriage and his present wife, Helen, even inquiring if she was a Jew (apparently because her last name was Manstein). Even Mrs Semenov was also called to testify, in the hope of finding discrepancies in her answers. Finally, the immigration bureaucrats declared Semenov and wife 'debarred from admission to the United States as persons likely to become public charges', an unlikely prospect since Semenov was carrying at least $4,000 in US currency and gold.[12]

Semenov suggested that this $4,000 represented his net worth at the time. When asked where it had come from, he said, 'I had some estate left me by my mother and I sold everything to raise this money'.[13] He surely needed no money during his stay in Vancouver.

Five days after the immigration office thought it had laid the Semenov case to rest, it was faced with subtle diplomatic pressure in the form of testimony from J.W. Warden of the British Military Commission. Then a Canadian major general, R.G. Leckie, added Ottawa's weight to the argument by testifying, 'General Semenov has a pleasing personality which does not in the least indicate a despotic or autocratic character'.[14] Finally the US State Department added its voice to the clamor for admitting Semenov, noting positively that the Japanese consul in Vancouver strongly opposed their former minion's trek to the United States. On 21 March Zurbrick reluctantly issued Semenov a transit visa, good for two weeks, to proceed through the United States to Paris.[15] Before he left Vancouver, however, he was feted by former officers from BritMis and welcomed into the banks and best clubs in the city. The ataman, accompanied by his wife and Aivazov, departed on a transcontinental journey, curiously giving their destination (on their visas) as 'Columbus Circle, Washington, DC', opposite the Union Station railway depot. Little did he know that they were also discreetly accompanied by private investigators.[16]

Semenov paused for two uneventful days in Chicago, home of many of the AEFS veterans opposed to his US visit. Perhaps lulled into a false sense of security, he continued on to Washington, where he was greeted by several State Department functionaries at Union Station. The following day he met with A.A. Bakhmet'ev, the last Russian representative to the United States.[17]

When the 'Washington Express' pulled into New York's Pennsylvania Station at 6:10 p.m. on 6 April 1922, a pair of private detective alighted and signaled to a cluster of waiting men in suits, indicating the chair car from which the Semenovs would disembark. Aivazov pushed his way through the crowd and scurried off to get porters for his master's luggage. The ataman and his bride emerged onto the platform, bewildered by the reception committee. 'Despite his military mustache, his mild, light blue eyes gave one anything but the picture of a bloodthirsty guerrilla', wrote the *New York Times* reporter on the scene. 'In civilian clothes, with a light gray fedora hat, plain blue overcoat and stiff collar and tie, he looked the picture of peace'. Of young Mrs Semenov he gushed, 'In a trim turban and sables, with big blue eyes and a fresh complexion, she made a pretty picture beside the General'. She was frightened by the commotion, and earned the fawning sympathy of the pack. John K. Murphy stepped forward and thrust an arrest warrant and a writ of attachment into Semenov's hand. Before the ataman could gather his thoughts, two more documents were shoved into his hands: one, a subpoena to appear as a witness in bankruptcy proceedings, the other, a summons and civil complaint. Semenov looked blankly at the crowd of deputies, lawyers, process servers, reporters and photographers, trying to comprehend this novel American welcome. Aivazov came running back and Murphy pulled back his coat to flash a badge, then explained, 'I'm a deputy sheriff, this is a warrant for arrest. The General is my prisoner.' After a quick negotiation between Aivazov and Murphy's boss, Sheriff Percival E. Nagle, the deputy sheriff led the Semenovs to a car and escorted them to the Waldorf-Astoria Hotel, where they took a suite on the eleventh floor and scrambled to come up with $25,000 cash bail so that Semenov could avoid a stay in the Ludlow Street jail. Sheriff Nagle refused to accept for collateral Madame Semenov's necklace of 432 matched pearls with a 4.5 carat diamond clasp, valued at $60,000, which she claimed was 'an heirloom handed down by her grandmother'. She 'broke down under the strain and had to be treated by a hotel physician'. Aivazov spent nearly five hours telephoning a network of White boosters before he was able to arrange a bond. In the meantime, Semenov answered reporters' questions through an interpreter, denying that he was a criminal, emphasizing Britain, France and Japan's support for OMO and pointing out that he had court-martialed the officers responsible for killing Colonel Morrow's men at Posol'skaya.[18]

Among the crowd at the Waldorf-Astoria that night was one Moses Fainberg, secretary of the Youroveta Home and Foreign Trading Company, a New York corporation.[19] It is uncertain if he met Semenov, but the ataman's misfortune was tied to that of Youroveta's. Fainberg told the press that Youroveta could have paid 100 cents on the dollar to its investors had OMO not robbed them, 'embarrassing the company financially' and causing its bankruptcy in July 1920. The property at issue was a mundane shipment of 'woolens and other merchandise' which Youroveta had shipped to Vladivostok from the United States, and tried unsuccessfully to recall as conditions became chaotic in 1920. According to Semenov, the controversial garments were seized by Ungern-Shternberg's Asiatic Horse Division at Dauria. On 1 December 1921 a Chinese–Russian judicial commission in Harbin entered a judgment against Semenov demanding payment of 930,000 gold rubles or $478,578 for the Youroveta merchandise.[20]

On Semenov's first morning in Manhattan, his portrait graced the front page of the *New York Times*, looking decidedly warlike in his Transbaikal Cossack uniform with cloak and *papakha*. The news of his presence stirred up a hornets' nest of opposition. The story related sworn statements by Major General Graves and Charles H. Smith, an IATB representative until 1921, that Semenov was 'only a bandit and brigand' and thus not entitled to the legal protections that a legitimate military commander enjoyed. The American Legion, the largest veterans' organization in the United States, had already made a formal protest to the Department of Labor that Semenov was also a bigamist and, as such, had illegally entered the country. A Siberian veteran's association added its voice to the chorus, claiming to represent 18,000 American soldiers and sailors who had seen service in the Russian Far East.[21]

On Saturday morning, 8 April 1922, Semenov fidgeted for two hours during the Youroveta bankruptcy proceedings at the offices of Greenbaum & Kahn on Broadway. 'The Ataman of the Cossacks', reported the *New York Times*, 'a chunky man with heavy brown mustache turned up at the ends, appeared calm throughout the hearing and answered questions promptly. He wore a blue serge suit, low shoes, striped shirt and a gold bracelet watch. He twirled his mustache occasionally or stroked the grey beaver hat in his hand.' When an FER propaganda tract was presented as evidence, lawyer Greenbaum asked Semenov's opinion of charges contained within against him and Kalmykov, and the ataman responded, 'One would have to take a special course in lying to think of lies like that'. Semenov never lost his calm, cool composure. Madame Semenov had remained at the Waldorf, but Colonel Krupskii attended the hearing. As it concluded, Krupskii loudly charged that the proceedings were a Bolshevik plot and engaged one of the lawyers in a heated argument until silenced by counsel Kahn. The lawyers chuckled at Krupskii as he withdrew with Semenov, the former still muttering about Red plots. Thus put off guard, Semenov was ambushed outside by yet another process server who stuffed more complaints into his hand, one from a banker demanding $19,510, another from a merchant claiming $180,000 for stolen property.[22]

The brewing legal battles forced Semenov and wife to cancel their 11 April departure for France aboard the Cunard Line's opulent RMS *Aquitania*. The previous day, Colonel Krupskii nearly came to blows with another lawyer and the bankruptcy proceedings were thrown up to a federal district court after Semenov refused to answer whether OMO had robbed the state bank in Chita of 1,250,000 rubles (the federal judge upheld Semenov's refusal to answer). By this time the ataman had retained two law firms to protect him against the flurry of lawsuits swirling around him.[23]

On 12 April 1922, amid much public fanfare, the US Senate Committee on Education and Labor convened a hearing to consider whether new legislation was required to keep out 'undesirable aliens', specifically people like Grigorii Semenov. The committee chairman, Idaho Republican William E. Borah, announced that he had subpoenaed Major General Graves, Colonel Morrow and a former British Army captain, Edwin Earle, to testify about the 'butchery' of US soldiers in Semenov's territory. The ataman was now national news, and newspapers around the country repeated the insults of his old enemy, Colonel Morrow, to the tune of, 'He was known by all people of Siberia to be a murderer, robber and his crimes were unspeakable, unprintable and beyond the conception of mankind. He is the greatest monster of modern times.'[24] The American public seemed inclined to scapegoat Semenov for the incomprehensible Russian tempest.

Semenov stayed put in New York while his lawyers faced the committee. The day that the Washington hearings began, New York deputies almost took Semenov into custody after some unknown party spread rumors that his bail collateral was insufficient. As Semenov's notoriety grew, so did the demands of the surety company guaranteeing his bail bond. That company, the Fidelity and Deposit Company of Maryland, forced Semenov to surrender his tickets for the RMS *Aquitania*, his wife's pearl necklace, a platinum watch and 'diamond earrings weighing 3.5 carats'. It was quite a jewelry collection for a soldier who claimed to have earned only 100 rubles per month and a 19- or 20-year-old stenographer, both unemployed.[25] When Colonel Krupskii went to negotiate Semenov's bond, he was frisked by New York police who were informed that he was carrying a concealed weapon. They found a revolver, but also found a permit to carry concealed weapons signed by a deputy police commissioner.[26]

Semenov's treasure was not enough to override public revulsion when, on 13 April, newspapers carried accounts of the OMO atrocities being described by witnesses to Senator Borah's committee in Washington. Readers were disgusted by tales of Colonel Stepanov's mass executions along the railway, General Skipetrov's malleting of Political Centrists on Lake Baikal, the wholesale liquidation of prisoners and the terrorizing of the civilian population. Colonel Morrow and other officers told reporters that 'Semenov carried on a deliberate campaign of murder, rape and pillage and the lives of 100,000 men, women and children were sacrificed as a result of his ravages.' No one questioned the numbers nor the balance of the reporting, particularly since the FER was portrayed as a struggling democracy, not a Red puppet. Wire reports from Chita that day added that an NRA unit pursuing White bandits near a village named Brussifka was attacked by Japanese artillery, infantry and aircraft, losing 30 men killed and wounded and that a renewed Japanese offensive had rekindled a state of chaos in the Maritime and Amur provinces.[27]

In the face of such notoriety, the Maryland surety company cancelled Semenov's bond 'for patriotic reasons' and Sheriff Nagle took him into custody in the sheriff's office on 13 April, allowing Helen to kiss him goodbye and return shortly thereafter to arrange for his meals to be delivered from a neighborhood restaurant. Word spread through New York's Lower East Side of his arrest 'through underground channels' and by the time he was transported to Ludlow Street jail at 4:30 p.m. a crowd of men, women and children were waiting to catch a glimpse of him. 'Yes, that's Semenov', spat a Russian shopkeeper who peered in the police station window as Semenov was being booked. 'They ought to shoot him on the street like a mad dog.' It was the second night of Passover in a neighborhood full of Russian Jews. They gathered in the streets around the jail, even though no one could see the ataman's cell (No. 8, on an upper tier) and 'Semenov was the main topic of conversation in the cafes and restaurants on East Broadway and Grand Street [that] night'.[28]

Ataman Semenov spent one week in the Ludlow Street jail. Mrs Semenov nervously paced her suite at the Waldorf-Astoria Hotel, but was soon whisked to a private hiding place as the testimony continued against the ataman and her safety became an issue. Finally, two local White organizations, the Russian National Society and Association of Unity of Russia, put up $20,000 cash and $5,000 in Liberty Bonds to free Semenov.[29] He was smiling when he emerged from jail on the afternoon of 20 April, but not for long. A frenzied mob of 3,000 men, women and children fought a detail of 30 police to get close enough to the Cossack leader to curse him in Russian, Yiddish and broken English. Reported the *New York Times*, 'Taunts were hurled at him from fire escapes, roofs and windows filled with people.' They called him 'Bandit', 'Murderer', 'Cut-throat' and 'Killer of children' and the air was filled with jeers, catcalls and threatening fists. As he was hustled into a taxi, an ominous roar rose from the on-lookers, who pressed forward as the police beat them back to clear an avenue for Semenov's escape. Two members of the police bomb squad jumped into the taxi with Semenov and another patrolman hopped onto the running board as the taxi screeched away, followed closely by two taxis, one of bomb squad detectives, the other of newspapermen.[30]

The next day the front page of the *New York Times* accused the ataman of bigamy, based upon an article dated 19 March in the *Japan Advertiser* newspaper in which his first wife, Zenaida, 'took the first steps in an attempt to expose the Cossack chief'. Zenaida Semenov – or, at least, a woman *claiming* to be Zenaida – declared that 'the woman now traveling with him is Mademoiselle Tersitskaya, formerly the Ataman's stenographer at Chita'. In a statement published by the Japanese newspaper, Zenaida stated, 'I am the first and only legal wife of Ataman Semenov. I have been residing in Japan since October 1920. I came to Japan at his instructions and at his expense with our son Vyacheslav.'[31]

For the remainder of his visit to the United States, Semenov remained in hiding in fear of process servers bearing more subpoenas and, to a lesser degree, vengeful émigrés. On 9 June he suddenly appeared in Toronto, though it was unclear if he had jumped bail or not, because the Youroveta bankruptcy proceedings were still plodding along. The plethora of other civil suits against him had not even begun yet. US immigration officials discovered his flight upon reading new dispatches from Toronto, yet 'heaved a sigh of relief', as did Senator Borah – they were glad to be rid of him. And likewise, Semenov and wife were surely glad to be rid of the American lawyers, politicians, reporters and emigrant rabble as they made their way to Vancouver and, on 18 June 1922, headed back west across the Pacific to search for a home.[32]

Red dawn (1922–1930s)

Red Mongolians inaugurated 1922 with a bloody purge, orchestrated by their Buryat Comintern advisor, Elbek-Dorzhi Rinchino. Dogsomyn Bodoo, one of Choibalsan and Sukhe Bator's original revolutionary recruits and party chairman, was ousted under the cloud of 'counterrevolutionary activity' along with 12 associates including the new Minister of Justice Togtokh-gun, the bold Bargut leader who had given refuge to several Russian Jews. Choibalsan's state security agents concocted the Bodoo conspiracy to remove the strongest advocates of democracy, warn less powerful supporters of parliamentary government, and clear the way for the implantation of soviet dictatorship. Bodoo and his accused colleagues were tortured to confess and shot without trial.[33] Throughout the first half of the year, Russia returned an estimated 20,000 Chinese and Mongolian refugees – 'wounded soldiers, merchants with Russian wives and Eurasian children, coolies and an occasional European', on long echelons creeping along the dilapidated Trans-Siberian. War raged on in the Mongolian countryside. A spring 1922 traveler reported, 'Nearly every morning a stern-wheeler would come down the Selenga River carrying the wounded from the fighting with Ungern's bandits while I was at Verkhne-Udinsk. Frequently 300 would be crowded on the little boat, with only a couple of nurses to care for them during the three-days voyage'.[34]

As people in Chita emerged into the warm spring sun, Semenov's 'boutiques' and markets brimming with OMO's plentiful booty were faint memories. The city's weak economic heart was now the *barakholka*, the 'market of heartbreaks' where 'class enemies' and proletariat congregated to barter family heirlooms and household treasures for basic subsistence. The hapless vendors sprawled across two blocks in the center of a soft, sandy street, selling their precious belongings, described by US correspondent Junius B. Wood:

> All had been used and some of it so long used that it had passed the useful stage – carts, pianos, music-boxes, furniture of all descriptions, clothes for every size and sex, soiled collars and cuffs, shaving sets, tooth-brushes, family albums with photographs of bewhiskered men and old-fashioned women, unknown and

valueless except to the owners, mouse-traps, lamps books, paintings, candlesticks, soldering irons, tools in many varieties, silverware, jewelry enough to stock a loan bank, and locks off cabin doors. When everything is sold, a lock is no longer needed... An old lady had a basket of family keepsakes – a once gaily gilded icon, odd spoons, photographs in frames, half a dozen Russian books, a pair of earrings in a plush case, and the knickknacks which are dear to motherly hearts.[35]

Chita's commerce revolved around several blocks of cubical frame sheds resembling a careworn street fair, dominated by cheap Chinese merchandise, harsh *papirosy*, pressed chunks of tea and few potential customers. Wood summarized his impressions of Chita business: 'Buriat peasants, fat and greasy, with carts of flour and fresh meat; swarthy Georgians, with putty-like soap and desperate home-made candy; Russian shops for tea and cakes, with unkempt waiters and all the hawkers and traders habitual to where commerce is primitive and unlicensed.' Foreign trade conditions favored only barter deals, for which few firms had the patience or facilities. A representative of a Canadian trading company was trying to swap each of his 10,000 German scythe blades for '60 pounds of butter or some equivalent farm product'. Semenov banknotes were used for cigarette paper, and a Caucasian money-changer could not get three silver rubles (about 42 US cents) for a 10,000-rouble 'Moscow bill'.[36] Gold and silver were the only real currencies and the FER had abolished paper currency to squeeze precious metals from their hiding places. Hundreds of refugees still made their homes in box cars, there was no work and government rations were as meager as hope. Yet, a mix-matched military band blared revolutionary and popular American tunes in daily concerts, and even a circus – 'mostly clowns with racy songs' – revived the smiles of Chita's survivors.[37]

Wood spoke with a pretty teenage girl in the *barakholka*, wearing mended, faded clothes, white slippers that scooped sand with every step and white stockings generously patched and darned. 'She was a good girl and came from a good home', explained an old woman peddler, when Wood inquired about the girl's absence several days later.

Her father and mother died and her brother was killed by Semenov's men... She sold her jewelry, then her furs, her clothes and everything except what she wore... She had nothing more to sell except herself. A few nights ago she was at a dance. She did not go home, but went alone to the river. The next morning, when the other girls were swimming, they found her body. She is not the first and there will be many more.[38]

Forsaken White bands continued to clash with the Reds in the Russian Far East throughout 1922. In May, a senior NRA commissar and *Dal'buro* secretary, Petr F. Anokhin, was killed in an ambush 22 miles west of Chita.[39] Sizeable gangs of old Kalmykov veterans still terrorized the Maritime province and the Red flotilla on Lake Baikal continued counterrevolutionary operations through the year.[40] Nevertheless, a semblance of peace settled over the region, enough so that Red officials in Chita organized a river cruise for orphans of fallen comrades living at the *Tsentral'nyi Detskii Dom* (Central Children's Home). As their motley fleet of three flat-bottomed boats meandered down the Ingoda and Shilka rivers, many saw the places where their fathers and mothers had been drained of life by OMO torturers – the sheds at Makkaveevo, the red railway barn at Karymskaya, the switching yard at Adrianovka and the rivers themselves, where iceholes had swallowed prisoners alive and dead.[41]

In October 1922, communist prosecutors reconsidered the case of former Chita detective, Aleksandr Domrachev, who had tortured and tried to frame several innocents for the attempted assassination of Ataman Semenov at the Mariinskii Theatre. Domrachev held a glimmer of hope that Red prosecutors might release him from prison, having proven himself an enemy of their Semenovist enemies. He appeared before a revolutionary appeals court, was remorseful in his closing remarks to the judge and, 'being guided by his revolutionary conscience', confessed his wrong-doing. On 27 October 1922 the court issued its decision: it found Domrachev guilty of beating Andrei Andreev and of torturing mine-workers Shikunts and Voropaev and sentenced him to 20 years' hard labor in Chita regional prison, a sentence to slow death. Red justice was no kinder than White justice.[42]

In 1923, OGPU agents arrested Bishop Safron (former priest Sergei Starkov) and Anatoli Popov, secretary of the provincial eparchial council, cutting off the head of the Russian Orthodox Church in Transbaikalia.[43] These regional 'princes of the church' had overtly cooperated with Ataman Semenov and other counterrevolutionary authorities, and mobilized local priests and other church functionaries to gather and feed information on local events and attitudes into the White counterintelligence network. Regardless of the Church's wartime role, it was a 'resilient and dangerous intermediary body' that posed a threat to the Communist Party since 'all non-proletarian institutions...were counter-revolutionary by their very nature'. Thus, in early 1922, the party had launched 'a carefully orchestrated, minutely regulated and astutely presented [anti-church] campaign' aimed to confiscate the valuables of individual churches, ostensibly to raise money for famine relief, promote a schism between 'progressive' (i.e. cooperating) clergy and 'reactionaries', violently suppress public demonstrations in defense of churches, and bring the church to heel.[44] Although Mongolian communists would prevent Buddhists from seeking the reincarnation of the Khutuktu upon his death in May 1924, some monastic leaders and scholars 'tried to reconcile Buddhism with Communist theory'. However, many Buryat Buddhists recognized the futility of trying to coexist with militant atheists in the Soviet Union and sought refuge in the slightly less repressive environment in Mongolia in the post-civil war years.[45]

On 3 October 1923 V.V. Kuibyshev, head of the Russian Communist Party's Central Control Commission and the People's Commissariat of Worker-Peasant Inspection, announced the arrest of Aleksandr M. Krasnoshchekov for corruption.

Months before, Mongolia's revolutionary hero Sukhe Bator died of a mysterious illness on 22 February 1923 at the age of 30 (Choibalsan later claimed that he was poisoned). On 20 May 1924 the Khutuktu died and Mongolia's new leadership prevented the search for his reincarnated successor, thus interrupting the theocratic lineage. Eleven days later a Soviet treaty with China set forth the withdrawal of the Red Army from Mongolia, though Comintern advisors increasingly muscled their way into the country's decision-making process. This was glaringly obvious when the Third Party Congress of the Mongolian People's Party met from 4–24 August 1924, and El'bek-Dorzhi Rinchino, a Soviet Buryat who pulled the strings of the Mongolian government through his seat on the Mongolian People's Party Central Committee and the country's military council, engineered a sweeping purge on behalf of Moscow. He denounced party chairman S. Danzan, an old comrade of Sukhe Bator and critic of the growing Soviet control, as a Chinese spy and capitalist, had him dragged out of the meeting by thugs of Choibalsan's Revolutionary Youth League and executed. Danzan's associates and anyone else who disagreed with Moscow's plans for Mongolia were also liquidated. By November, a Soviet-style constitution and government were in place and Urga was renamed Ulaanbaatar – Red Hero – in memory of Sukhe Bator.[46]

In 1925, with the stroke of a pen, Japan and the Soviet Union signed a treaty that dispelled the cloud of the Nikolaevsk massacre and Japan's invasion of the Russian Far East.[47]

On 30 October 1926 a Japanese investigator looking into the Semenov's plunder in Japanese banks ended up dead beneath a train, supposedly a suicide. Subsequent investigations were much less diligent.[48]

In 1929 Stalin's violent collectivization of Russia's economy sent many Buryats fleeing into Mongolia. However, Comintern lackeys in Ulaanbaatar, who had earlier abandoned use of Mongolia's ancient alphabet for Cyrillic, followed Moscow's lead in collectivizing all livestock and agriculture and confiscating all religious property. Widespread dissidence required that the Mongolian party invite the Red Army back in to enforce this accelerated socialist evolution at bayonet point.[49]

Chita's Hotel Selekt was finally reconstructed in 1931, the same year that Prince Kudashev died in exile. Also that year, Major General Graves published a popular memoir, *America's Siberian Adventure*, and when it reached Vienna in 1933, former Lieutenant General Konstantin Sakharov was so outraged that he challenged Graves to a duel (by mail). Graves ignored the challenge.[50]

The dictatorship of the proletariat trod coarsely over traditional values and individual freedoms, but large-scale unrest was infrequent owing to the unvarying response from state security and the party – economic privation for the community, arrest and liquidation for the individual. For those people who could not or would not hide or discard their religious beliefs, clashes with the zealous Red atheists were inevitable. An armed rebellion by Buddhist clerics and lamas in Arhangai *aimag*, suppressed in May 1932 by Mongolian *Gosudarstvennaya Vnutrennaya Okhrana* (GVO, State Internal Security) troops and Soviet NKVD advisors, was said to have been Japanese-inspired. However, the uprising occurred after a two-year campaign of confiscations and repression begun by the 1929 Seventh Mongolian Party Congress which forbade the installation of the ninth Living Buddha, then found in Tibet. Indeed, the 'Shambala War', as it became known in Buddhist circles, received as much encouragement from China as it did from Japan, but attracted Stalin's stern attention because Japan, from its base in Manchukuo, was 'making common cause with Buddhists in Buryatia and Outer Mongolia'.[51] The senior Soviet advisor to the GVO, Viktor Stanislavovich Kiyakovskii, was killed in the fighting, a fact which indicates the intensity of the hostilities.[52] Nevertheless, fearing alienation of his Buddhist population, Stalin ordered the Mongolian Party to adopt a 'New Turn' policy from 1932–34, relaxing repressive measures and even allowing some monasteries to reopen. Buddhists in the Soviet Union were not so fortunate. By 1935, there were no functioning monasteries and less than 1,300 surviving monks.[53]

General Horvath worked as a consultant on railway management for the Chinese government until his death in 1937. That same year, Josef Stalin unleashed his diabolical campaign to eradicate religion. Mongolian *chekisti* destroyed monasteries and executed approximately 27,000 people (about 3 per cent of the population) and the NKVD accused Buryat high lamas of spreading Japanese propaganda. Bishop Safron's magnificent cathedral in Chita was demolished and the bricks were used to construct School No. 4.[54]

Semenov in Dairen (1922–39)

After Semenov's traumatic trip across the United States and through the American legal and media ordeal, he arrived in Yokohama on 28 June 1922 and required three weeks to recuperate in a Nagasaki hospital. He returned to Tientsin the following month, checked into the Tokyo Hotel and soon dodged another attempt on his life. This time he was targeted by a five-man assassination team made up of three Russians, a Russian–American and a Korean employee of the hotel, who failed their mission despite a small arsenal of grenades and revolvers. Four of the conspirators were arrested (all but the Korean), then released. At the end of August Semenov rambled on to Tsinanfu, where he again saw one of the Russian assassins from Tientsin, a man named Silinskii, prompting Semenov to relocate to Tsing Tao. It became obvious that he would not be able to settle in China without constantly looking over his shoulder for more Silinskiis or Chinese police, who might arrest him for his complicity in Ungern-Shternberg's Mongolian expedition. Thus he decided to resettle in Japan in autumn 1922, arriving there under the surname Erden, which was part of his Mongolian title. Nevertheless he was swarmed with journalists until he could slip away on an express train to Nagasaki, where he lingered a month, trying to make himself useful to his old sponsors.[55]

Semenov eventually settled in Dairen, where he raised his growing family. In addition to Elena, born during the ataman's wanderings in 1921, he fathered Mikhail in 1922, Tatyana in 1925 and Elizaveta in 1929.[56] Wealth that he accumulated as ataman spared him the humiliation of having to beg or seek civilian employment, unlike most of the White refugees from Siberia. He also had family in Manchuria, being related to 'Prince De-wan...a power among the Buryats and Kirghizes north of Tsitsihar'.[57] Dairen was a Japanese-controlled enclave with a large Russian community on Chinese territory. Russians had laid out Dalny (as the city was known until 1905) at the turn of the century and spent over 20 million rubles on its construction before the Russo-Japanese War. In the painful aftermath of the war, the Treaty of Portsmouth forced Russia to give Japan its lease of the Liaotung Peninsula – including Dalny, as well as the southern branch of the Chinese Eastern Railway (from Port Arthur north to Kwang Cheng Tzu, near Changchun). The Japanese changed the city's name to Dairen, rebuilt the war-damaged railway as the Southern Manchurian Railway and tenaciously maneuvered to increase Dairen port traffic (at the expense of Vladivostok) and to expand their economic influence through Manchuria. They invested a large sum in major port improvements during the 1920s, and amplified the Russians' elaborate city plans, paving macadam roads, laying tramways, stringing electric lines and telephone systems and constructing modern public works. The trademark three green domes of the Yokohama Specie Bank had risen over Dairen in 1909 and the building became as important as any governmental decision-making edifice in the city and, if the stories about his secret fortune were true, a place of regular pilgrimage for Semenov.

Most of Semenov's Transbaikal Cossack brethren congregated in Manchuria's Trekhrech'e (Three Rivers) region about 45 miles from Hailar, whence they could gaze longingly across the Argun river to the collective farms that had taken over their old homeland. Their Manchurian homesteads revolved around a dozen villages – Verkh Urga, Ust' Urga, Pokrovka, Dragotsenka and a few others – where chapels, religious processions, Cossack administrative institutions and other old traditions persevered. Another rural center of Russian emigration was the Toogenskii region north of Tsitsihar. Most Cossacks returned to tilling the soil, although a few turned to skills they had honed in OMO, kidnapping, extortion, banditry and conversely, the bodyguard business. Many became mercenaries in the armies of warlords Chang Tso-Lin, Feng Yu-xiang and others. As years went by, refugees who fled from collective farms across the river came to outnumber the civil war exiles.[58]

Harbin absorbed tens of thousands of destitute refugees who nourished a post-revolutionary rejuvenation of Russian culture and provided a boon to the Manchurian economy. The Russian community adapted to living in China, but did not assimilate much beyond bilingualism and business: there were several Russian–Chinese newspapers, Chinese language classes in most schools and Chinese law replaced Russian in legal institutes. The city blossomed as a bountiful oasis of non-Soviet Russian culture, with a vast range of organizations representing every shade of Russian thought: from elementary schools (including at least one 'for the children of deprived emigrants') to theological, pedagogical, legal and scientific institutes, including the first-rate Harbin Polytechnic Institute, financed by the Chinese Eastern Railway, and a number of internationally renowned music conservatories and ballet schools; about 20 large magazines, more than 50 newspapers from the monarchist *Tsvet* (Light) to the communist *Den'* (Day); publishing houses, more than a dozen libraries, trade unions, national clubs of Jews, Georgians and others; six literary and art circles; a touring symphony (conducted by S.I. Shvaikovskii) and covert and overt political cells spanning all hues of the Red, Pink, Green and White movements, including the old Black Hundreds and, no doubt, new combinations.[59] New Russian Orthodox steeples rose over the neighborhoods of villas, the rabbinical school flourished, new immigrants swelled congregations of the Ukrainian Catholic church and Tatar mosque, and a colony of Volga German Mennonites sprouted. I.I. Churin & Company's department store embodied Harbin's relative wealth and capitalist spirit: 'There it was possible to buy everything – from cars and tractors to sewing needles', in contrast to the stark workers' paradise across the Soviet frontier. Businesses were typically overstaffed as sympathetic managers employed as many refugees as possible.[60]

In 1924, the Chinese government recognized the Soviet government and on 31 May Russia formally repudiated the gains of the Cassini Convention and surrendered extraterritorial rights. In return, China agreed to joint administration of the Chinese Eastern Railway. A separate, similar agreement had to be signed with Chang Tso-Lin's autonomous provincial government of Three Eastern Provinces on 24 September 1924. Moscow acknowledged Chinese sovereignty over the railway zone and assented to China's desire to purchase the railway as soon as she could raise enough capital to buy out the shareholders. In the meantime, the Soviet Union retained control over the railway and replaced senior managers of the Chinese Eastern with obedient, unknowledgeable communists, starting at the top by ousting the experienced B.V. Ostroumov and bringing in A.N. Ivanov. Predictably the quality of service plummeted. The rest of the workforce had to choose between Soviet or Chinese citizenship by 1 June 1925, although a few managed to remain stateless citizens holding a special émigré passport.[61] 'During this period', wrote railway historian Peter Crush, 'passengers on the CER had every likelihood of being robbed on their trains by bandits, even if they managed to complete a journey on the CER. without derailment on the poorly maintained track.'[62]

Armed conflict between China's warlords broke out in November 1924 and created job opportunities for *semenovtsy* as mercenaries for the next three years. In the early months of China's civil war, some 800 officers and 2,000 men joined the Nechaev Division, commanded by Lieutenant General Konstantin P. Nechaev in the service of Chang Tso-Lin. Their fight against the central government, controlled by Wu P'ei-Fu's Chihli clique, transformed into a continuation of the holy war against Bolshevism as Chinese communists came into the fight and the Cossacks found themselves pitted against Soviet military advisors like 'General Galina', the *nom de guerre* of their old enemy and former partisan commander Vasilii Konstantinovich Blyukher. In 1925 the unit suffered a major defeat at Suichzhou, where Chinese adversaries pulled up the rails and trapped and slaughtered a *bronevik* full of Nechaev's soldiers of fortune. Nechaev lost part of his leg, but returned to the field the following year. Somewhere between 4,000 and 12,000 veterans of Semenov's and Kolchak's armies eventually enlisted in Chang Tso-Lin's mercenary corps during the mid-1920s.[63]

In 1927 a 'major political scandal' erupted in Japan over the misuse of 500 million yen in 'secret military funds' during the Russian Civil War. 'The allegations...were not refuted', observed Peter Fleming.[64]

At 8 a.m. on 10 July 1929 Chinese police stormed the Chinese Eastern Railway's central telegraph office in Harbin, arrested and deported the Soviet railway manager and his assistant, then clamped down on other Soviet establishments and authorities throughout

Manchuria. Ten days later the Soviet foreign ministry closed its consulates in China and broke off diplomatic relations. Two days after that a Chinese Army echelon unloaded 2,000 soldiers and eight artillery pieces in Manchuli, authorities issued arms to 'White Guards' in Harbin, while Whites working for the Chinese police arrested 20 Soviet railway employees at Pogranichnaya. General Vasilii K. Blyukher arrived in Khabarovsk to take command of a hurriedly mobilized Special Far Eastern Army, which began positioning units along the frontier in Transbaikalia in early August. Soviet propaganda trumpeted that 70,000 'White Guards' – meaning *semenovtsy*, *kalmykovtsy* and *kappel'evtsy* – were arrayed against the Motherland. While this number was greatly exaggerated, many White veterans joined the Chinese military and police and eagerly engaged their Red foes by sniping, ambushes and attacks on isolated outposts and freight trains. For example, a White regiment and 200-man Nazarov detachment were reported at Sochintszy, 10-man infiltration teams of the 'Dutov-Pozdnikov White Guard band' near Blagoveshchensk and White specialists manned four Chinese *broneviki* at Pogranichnaya and one near Manchuli. Red border guards heard 'drunken revelry and the singing of Russian songs' by White guerrillas on the eastern end of Menkuseli Island in the Argun river, and a White platoon under one Mokhov gathered Korean residents in the Maritime province village of Lefinka and exhorted them to rebel. The nastiness accelerated through August and September and, while the Soviet and Chinese armies massed for war, White outfits from Manchuria stole across the Argun and Amur rivers, to terrorize the rural population of the Soviet Far East, torching houses, scattering cattle, stealing horses and robbing farmers, sometimes disguised in NKVD or Red Army uniforms. Invaders repelled from the village of Ivanovka supposedly left behind 'forms and signed documents [imprinted] with dies and presses of Harbin White Guard organizations'. Finally, on 17 November, General Blyukher launched a massive strike at Manchuli and along the Argun river front, throwing 3 *broneviki*, 9 tanks, 32 aircraft and 8,000 men, including a Buryat cavalry division, against the entrenched Chinese. Within four days the Manchuli garrison surrendered, Chinese and White forces suffered 5,000 casualties and China sued for peace.[65] The Whites hobbled back to their Trekhrech'e and Toogenskii settlements to await another chance to liberate their homeland from the Bolsheviks.

Semenov's inter-war years present a murky image. It has been presumed that he submerged himself into the organized crime rackets of Cossack émigrés in Manchuria, enterprises that would have come natural to an unemployed, albeit skilled and experienced warlord. As the 1920s matured, these rackets evolved into a mercenary arm of Japan's state-sponsored terrorism campaign to conquer Manchuria, and in this capacity Semenov became a minion of Colonel Doihara Kenji, the Japanese Army intelligence officer who was generously dubbed the 'Lawrence of Manchuria' by international correspondents. Doihara's flattering sobriquet was misapplied however, because he fought to oppress, not to liberate like T.E. Lawrence, and, contrary to the image he cultivated, he excelled in his nefarious profession not by dubious feats of espionage in deep disguise as a master linguist – as sensationalist accounts claimed, but by gangster-like ruthlessness and deceit backed by the generous, enthusiastic financial and political support of Japanese Emperor Hirohito himself. Additionally, Doihara lacked Lawrence's physical charm, being 'a short, round-faced, stoutish man with a little black mustache', and looking more like a shopkeeper than a spymaster.[66] However, he mastered the use of sex, drugs and money to blackmail, bribe and extort and by the mid-1920s employed several thousand émigré women in a prolific chain of brothels and opium dens.[67] Doihara built and controlled a vast network of White Russian agents, couriers and informants by supplying them narcotics to satisfy addictions that he had nurtured.[68] Semenov was involved with a Manchurian network of OMO veterans who provided intelligence, sabotage, reconnaissance and security for Doihara's operations.

In 1931 the ataman's network allegedly assisted in laying the groundwork for the Kwantung Army's gradual invasion of Manchuria, which was engineered by many Japanese officers and NCOs who had participated in the 1918–22 Siberian expedition. It began with the infamous 18 September 'Manchurian Incident' in the Mukden suburbs, when the Kawamoto Platoon of the Japanese 2nd Division's Shimamoto Battalion provoked a firefight with Chinese troops of the Peitaying camp, commanded by General Wang I-cheh, in what was arguably the first battle of the conflagration that ultimately evolved into the Second World War. Whether premeditated or not, this provocation led to the takeover of the Kirin province within three days, and the creeping occupation of the rest of Manchuria by February 1932. Japan cemented its colonization of Manchuria by proclaiming it the independent puppet state of Manchukuo on 2 February 1932 and marched into Harbin three days later, welcomed by a 10,000-strong procession of flower-throwing, pro-Japanese Russians. Spymaster Doihara named himself mayor of Mukden and Semenov placed himself at the disposal of the invaders. The ataman allegedly organized pro-Japanese groups of Russian emigrants which were armed with weapons confiscated from the Chinese Army under the supervision of a Colonel Isimure of the Kwantung Army staff. Meanwhile, Japanese agents hoodwinked 26-year-old Henry Pu-Yi, deposed child emperor of China, into coming to Changchun (soon renamed Xinjing) into becoming Manchukuo's chief executive.[69] On 15 September Tokyo beneficently declared a protectorate over its Frankenstein state and, at the invitation of the Manchukuo government, implanted the country with omnipresent Japanese 'advisors': 150,000 soldiers, 18,000 gendarmes and 4,000 secret police. Hailar, Manchuli and areas along the Amur river held out against the Japanese invasion until December 1932.[70]

The Japanese occupiers ran Manchukuo like a vast criminal enterprise and began settling their new real estate with fanatical patriots and contingents of land-hungry poor from Japan. Rape, child molestation, sexual humiliation, sadism, assault and murder became institutionalized means of terror and control over Manchuria's Chinese and Russian populations. Robbery by soldiers and gendarmes, arbitrary confiscation of property and unabashed extortion by Japanese officials – even judges, magistrates and senior police officials, became commonplace. Underground brothels, opium dens, gambling houses and narcotics shops run by Japanese gendarmes competed with the state monopoly syndicate, sometimes stooping to gang warfare to settle disputes.[71] Conscientious Japanese officers were silenced and the emperor ignored the noble self-sacrifice of Field Marshal Muto Nobuyoshi, commander of the Kwantung Army, who committed ritual suicide on 27 July 1933, allegedly leaving a note to Hirohito pleading for mercy for the people of Manchuria.[72]

While forced labor and threat of bodily harm numbed most of the 30 million Chinese inhabitants into abject submission, the Japanese cleverly wangled to coopt the Russian and Mongol minorities to help control the Chinese majority and share in their exploitation. White émigrés in Manchuria became an essential prop for Tokyo's puppet kingdom of Manchukuo. Political parties were disbanded and Russians were pushed into the chocolate-colored uniforms of the state's only official political organization, *Manchu Teikoku Kyowakai* – the Manchuria Imperial Concordia Society. Many Russian immigrants took positions in Manchukuo's new national army and the Peace Protection Army, thought it seems that the Japanese and Manchukuo gendarmeries and intelligence services harbored the most hardcore White quislings.[73] For example, the Hengtao gendarmerie employed 23 Russian 'auxiliaries'. Russian collaborators were drawn into a variety of internal security agencies: the Japanese intelligence service (which answered only to Tokyo), the Japanese gendarmerie (subordinate to the Kwantung Army), the Manchukuo gendarmerie (subordinate to the Manchukuo military command), the Manchukuo state police (commanded by the Interior Ministry), city police and criminal police (independent of each other but controlled by puppet municipal governments), Japanese consular police (answering to Japan's consulate); the state intelligence service (under the Manchukuo War Office) and the railway police (under the railway administration).[74]

These collaborators were usually opportunists motivated by greed, criminals who sometimes paid for their lucrative positions with the proceeds of extortion, or victims of Japanese coercion or blackmail who were forced to serve the invaders 'or else'. There were some genuinely pro-Japanese émigrés, although, according to a later intelligence analysis, 'This feeling was not the result of any great admiration or feeling of friendship for the Japanese, but rather the result of an intense hatred for the USSR.' One effusive font of sympathetic Russians was the Russian Fascist Union, founded in Harbin in 1925 and modeled after Benito Mussolini's organization. In May 1931, the union reorganized itself as the Russian Fascist Party under 24-year-old Secretary General Konstantin V. Rodzaevskii, with guidance from former generals V.D. Kos'min and V.V. Rychkov and a Merkulov government minister, V.F. Ivanov.[75]

However, most of the émigré community looked askance at their fellow Russians who collaborated with the Japanese. 'Not a single self-respecting Russian wanted to have anything to do with the Japanese', wrote Amleto Vespa, who had served Marshal Chang Tso-Lin for eight years as an intelligence officer and was forced into Japanese service in 1932. Even in the Cossack villages of Trekhrech'e, the Japanese eventually resorted to coercion to enlist Russians into Manchukuo cavalry and commando units, who were instructed in the use of portable radios, demolitions and mapping, and then assigned perilous missions on Soviet soil.[76]

Ataman Semenov was still popular among the Cossacks and retained General Afanas'ev as his office manager, but did not appear to live lavishly, as might have been expected of a man with vaults full of gold and booty. Indeed, the former Russian Consul in Dairen, Pavel Yur'evich Vaskevich became acquainted with Semenov during the late 1920s and early 1930s and was convinced that the widespread rumors of Semenov's vast civil war treasure trove were untrue. Vaskevich rented rooms at his pleasant dairy farm outside Dairen and one of his regular summertime tenants was Ataman Semenov 'who took two rooms for 200 yen per month and was one of the most careless payers'.[77]

Semenov became deeply involved with the Refugees' Bureau that resettled several hundred families of Russian colonists in the Trekhrech'e area during the first two years of the Japanese occupation. These refugees had been enticed with 'financial aid, farm implements, horses, cattle and homes', but found themselves 'compelled to work like slaves under the guard of Japanese soldiers'. According to Vespa, 'the Bureau' assigned as overseer of the colony 'a certain Tirbash', who almost certainly was the notorious OMO Colonel Tierbach, perpetrator of the gruesome 'summer court' at Makkaveevo in 1919 and diehard follower of the ataman since his first capture of Manchuli. Apparently the years had not mellowed Tierbach at all, who 'assassinated dozens of Russians [at Trekhrech'e] on the pretext that they were Communists'. Tierbach's savagery coupled with rapes and constant abuses by Japanese soldiers ignited a rebellion in August 1935 that resulted in a massacre of Tierbach, his assistants and several Japanese officers and soldiers.[78]

Despite Japan's heavy military presence, traditional Manchurian banditry continued, though now it was fueled by nationalist sentiment in addition to poverty. Bands of genuine partisans – 'the irregulars' – materialized in the forests. Some of them were communist, but most were self-defense groups of both Chinese and Russians with no political agenda beyond the common struggle to resist or avenge Japanese ravages. Eventually the irregulars were augmented by disaffected Russian auxiliaries who had been originally recruited by Semenov and other collaborators with the promise of 'sixty dollars a month plus uniform, lodgings and the promise of European food', little of which they received once they took the field for the Japanese. As early as 16 August 1933 a gang of 22 Russian auxiliaries rebelled at Tungpei station (on the Harbin–Lungmenchen line), killed two Japanese officers and five soldiers, torched the station and fled into the hills with five machine guns. By 1935, the irregulars' effectiveness could be gauged by partisan activities along Manchukuo's railways: '73 wrecks of international trains, 131 armed attacks on trains, 74 railway stations burned, 340 railway employees killed, 650 wounded and 451 kidnapped'.[79]

Indeed, the Japanese made themselves so obnoxious that few Russian generals would work with them. Even some OMO veterans were not inclined to cooperate with the Japanese invaders. Nikolai Medi, the son of Semenov's transportation chief, had to be forced into working for Japan, probably by threats to his family.[80] When the Japanese hunted for a willing Russian to serve as a leader of one of their booster societies, they had to resort to former OMO General Salnikov, now 'tubercular and syphilitic...a poor sick fellow who for years had been begging in front of Churin's department store'.[81]

Other OMO alumni were more industrious. In the early years of the Japanese occupation, a group of 16 Russians and Japanese drove from Hailar in two new trucks, secretly crossed into Mongolia, set up a clandestine camp near the shore of Lake Buyr Nur and began excavations using the most modern drilling equipment. The mysterious group was detected by Mongolian border guards and Vyacheslav V. Gridnev, a Soviet NKVD officer and advisor to the Mongolian GVO, was given a Mongolian cavalry squadron and ordered to pick up the intruders. The secretive excavators were headed by none other than Colonel Sipailov, who was trying to find the treasure buried by the unfortunate *sotnia* Commander Maketno in summer 1921. Unfortunately for Sipailov, the water level of the lake had fallen drastically since then, and he could not find the site. When CHEKA agent Gridnev and his Mongolian horsemen thundered over the treeless horizon, the treasure-hunters scampered out of their tents and drove away, abandoning all of their expensive gear and a couple of snoring Japanese. When Gridnev's men roused them, they claimed to be businessmen although NKVD headquarters felt sure they were Japanese intelligence officers working under cover in the research bureau of the Southern Manchuria Railway. Nevertheless, they were handed over to the Japanese military mission in Kalgan.[82]

As the Japanese solidified their foothold on Manchukuo, they realized that while Semenov did not command broad authority among White emigrants, he was also not in contact with – or under the control of – White organizations in the West, such as the Paris-based *Russkii Obshche-voinskii Soyuz* (ROVS, Russian All-Military Union). The Japanese assumed that ROVS and similar organizations had been penetrated by foreign intelligence services. On his part, Semenov had enjoyed long, mutually beneficial relationships with many influential Japanese officers, but even more compelling was the fact that 'Semenov's personal fortune [was] entirely under Japanese control'.[83] Thus Japan promoted Semenov in establishing and recruiting for the *Soyuz Kazakov na Dal'nem Vostoke* (SKDV) – the Union of Cossacks in the Far East (also later known as the Union of Cossacks in East Asia). They also endorsed his overtures to Russian fascist organizations and the *kirillovtsami* – monarchists wanting to see Prince Cyril take the throne. Japanese authorities exerted pressure on other White émigré organizations to subordinate themselves to Semenov and even threatened to dissolve local branches of ROVS, the largest international veterans organization.[84] In Manchukuo, the ROVS organization was known as *Dal'nevostochnyi Soyuz Voennykh* (DVSV, the Far Eastern Union of Servicemen) and at the outbreak of the Second World War counted at least 4,000 members forming a naval department, military youth group and societies of young officers, cadets and alumni of the Irkutsk, Alekseev, Orenburg and other military academies. 'The most counterrevolutionary active elements were concentrated' in the alumni society of the Ataman Semenov Military Academy, according to Soviet intelligence.[85]

In 1934, Dairen was visited by Anastasi Andreievich Vonsiatskii, a Russian–American dandy and sensationalist who had had the good fortune to marry a rich American heiress 20 years his senior when he fled to the West in 1922. Vonsiatskii had made the heiress' Thompsen, Connecticut estate the headquarters and training ground of his Russian National Fascist Revolutionary Party in 1933 and made regular world cruises to recruit among the Russian diaspora and strut about in his brown shirt and swastika. In February–March 1934, he had met Konstantin Rodzaevskii in Japan and agreed upon the creation of an international organization to unite all Russian fascist groups worldwide. Upon arrival in Harbin, Vonsiatskii was feted by the local Russian Fascist Party and, at the end of April 1934, he attended the party's second congress where the All-Russian Fascist Party, the international umbrella, was proclaimed. Semenov and his Japanese sponsors were suspicious of this North American contender for the post-Soviet throne, and Whites in Manchukuo were warned to avoid Vonsiatskii. The goodwill between Rodzaevskii and Vonsiatskii was short-lived anyway, because an ideological schism split the international union in December. Vonsiatskii found the extreme anti-Semitism of the Manchukuo fascists unacceptable and disdained Rodzaevskii's association with Semenov, because the ataman's dastardly reputation from civil war days discredited the fascists among émigré communities.[86]

Amazingly, several thousand Soviet citizens still lived and worked on the Chinese Eastern Railway in 1935, inasmuch as the Chinese government had never been able to raise enough capital to buy it. However, as Japan sank her claws into Manchukuo, the Kwantung Army brazenly cheated the railway of freight payments and Japanese intelligence underwrote *hunghutze* raids and sabotage to discourage use of the railway. Finally, the Russians resigned themselves to Japan's conquest of Manchuria and, on 23 March 1935, sold the Chinese Eastern Railway to Tokyo for ¥140,000,000, one-third paid in cash upon signing the transfer agreement, with the balance due in instalments from future revenues. This Japanese victory was all the sweeter because of the Soviet snub of the Chinese government, which was not even consulted about the sale.[87]

Despite the sale, tension along the Soviet–Manchukuo border continued to rise and armed clashes broke out between the Kwantung Army and the Red Army.[88] Russian detachments of the Manchukuo Army refused to fight their Soviet countrymen and were disarmed and executed by the Japanese.[89] After the Red Air Force launched strikes into Manchukuo, the Japanese summarily shot many Soviet workers who had missed the hurried mass evacuation of Chinese Eastern Railway personnel.[90] Many of the seemingly fortunate repatriates who did made it back to Soviet territory were forced to return to Manchukuo to spy for Red intelligence services, or were accused of being Japanese spies themselves and sent to the gulag or executed.

The reactionary Whites of Manchukuo were ascending to new heights of power in league with the Japanese military. Despite the rupture between Russian fascists in Manchukuo and Vonsiatskii's Russian–American clique, Konstantin Rodzaevskii was able to assemble 104 delegates for an international Russian fascist congress in summer 1935. Delegates came from Russian communities in Japan and China, and from as far away as Syria, Morocco, Bulgaria, Poland, Finland and Germany. General Minami Jiro, commander of the Kwantung Army, and Colonel Ando, commander of the Japanese Military Mission in Harbin, were honorary chairmen of the congress.[91]

Just as the Japanese entangled the Russian minority in the rule of Manchukuo, they also gave Mongols a special role in the new state.[92] In neighboring Inner Mongolia, the Kwantung Army established an 'autonomous council' government in 1934, then a military government in 1936 that later became the Mongolian Alliance League autonomous government, alongside other Inner Mongolian puppet states (e.g. South Chahar and North Shansi) and the quasi-autonomous Mongolian Hsingan province. The Hsingan Bureau oversaw

Mongols in Manchukuo (who occupied about one-third of the territory) and tried to foster Mongol cultural autonomy. For a while, the Japanese even allowed these entities to combine into a new Mongol state of Mongokuo under a western Sunnid prince, Teh Wang, in a short-lived resurrection of the Mongol strategic buffer concept. The Mongokuo scheme unraveled when the Japanese accused a prominent Mongolian from Manchukuo, Ling Sheng, of passing secrets to Red Mongolians and executed him in 1936. Subsequently the Hsingan office lost its special status and Tokyo became suspicious of Mongol secession, yet Mongol–Japanese relations persevered. Prince Teh Wang established a capital at Chan Pei, near Kalgan and raised a Mongol force that joined the Kwantung Army in the 1937 invasion of China.[93] Yet Pan-Mongol aspirations paled into insignificance in the shadow of the superpower competition between Japan, China and the Soviet Union.

The lengthy Mongolia–Manchukuo border was a short fuse of potential conflict and Stalin pledged in 1936 to fight any Japanese encroachment upon Red Mongolia, particularly since a 1932 uprising by Buddhist clerics and lamas in Arhangai *aimag* had been encouraged by the Japanese.[94] Here in Mongolia, despite nearly two decades of Red police state oppression, Grigorii Semenov was still associated with Mongol nationalism, and, as in Buryatia, Transbaikalia and Cossack villages of the Soviet Far East, the ataman was a bogeyman whose name was whispered and still inspired fear, fury and defiance.[95]

Foreigners departed Manchuria for friendlier environs, transforming the demographics of her formerly cosmopolitan cities. By the late 1930s in Dairen, for example, there were fewer than 500 *gaijin* (including Americans, British, Dutch, Finns, French, Germans, Swedes and a few remaining Russians), and of the city's population of 300,000, about one-third were Japanese. At the time of the Japanese invasion in 1932, nearly 200,000 Chinese and 100,000 Russians called Harbin home, and the latter number dropped drastically as the occupation continued.[96]

Protected by Japanese police, White criminal gangs extorted money from Harbin's thriving community of Russian Jews. 'Dr. [Abraham] Kaufman, president of the Hebrew Association of Manchuria, a most cultured scholar, beloved by Gentiles and Hebrews alike, was attacked daily for months in the two Japanese-owned newspapers', wrote Amleto Vespa. Russian thugs in Japanese employ complemented the verbal attacks with occasional physical assaults and repeatedly smashed the windows of Harbin's two synagogues until the congregation gave up on repairing them and just shivered through wintertime services.[97] Although kidnapping and the occasional murder of Jewish businessmen and family members quickly became a cottage industry under the Japanese occupation, one particular murder had shocked decent Russians into realizing that Manchuria was no longer safe. Simeon Kaspe, a handsome, 24-year-old concert pianist, was taken from his car about at midnight on 24 August 1933. He was no ordinary Jewish victim. His father, Joseph Kaspe, was a self-made tycoon and one of Harbin's leading citizens, 'owner of the finest jewelry business in the Far East', Harbin's Hotel Moderne and a chain of theaters and cinemas. To thwart a Japanese takeover of his businesses, the elder Kaspe had cleverly taken advantage of China's extraterritoriality agreements and transferred ownership to his sons, who were now French citizens. Kaspe's self-confidence rankled the Japanese gendarmerie, who enlisted police inspector N. Martinov and 'a gang of about fifteen criminals, picked with the help of [fascist leader] Rodzaevskii', to kidnap young Kaspe. The father refused to pay but 10 per cent of the exorbitant ransom demanded, and not until his son was released. One month later he received his son's ears in a package. The case made international headlines and embarrassed the Japanese, who finally ordered the hostage killed after 95 days of torture. International attention resulted in the arrest of Martinov and five accomplices. The inspector and three others were sentenced to death, but, when the foreign correspondents forgot about them six months later, they were released.[98]

Such relentless outrages drove most of Harbin's Jewish community south into nationalist China by 1935, with commensurate negative effects upon the economy. Some sources suggest that the Japanese realized their error, and tried to convince Manchukuo's remaining Jews that it was in their best interests to collaborate, even curbing fascist organizations and closing down *Nash Put'* (*Our Journey*), the Russian fascist newspaper, on behalf of the Jews. However, these actions occurred several years later (in 1943) and were intended to check European fascist influence, not to succor the Jewish community. Various historians also suggest that some Japanese schemes actually persuaded Dr Kaufman that Japan meant well, however this seems most unlikely considering that Kaufman delivered Simeon Kaspe's funeral oration and was a regular target of Rodzaevskii's state-protected fascists.[99]

Two years after Manchukuo's creation, the Japanese foreign office had actually proposed to bring in 50,000 German Jews in a scheme cooked up by Colonel Yasue Norihiro, who even visited the United States to promote the plan and arranged for Abraham Kaufman to visit Tokyo. Yasue had developed his interest in Judaism while a young captain and language expert on Semenov's OMO staff. When he returned to Japan in the early 1920s, his fascination led to a formal study (along with with a naval officer, Inuzuke Koreshige) of world Jewry, White anti-Semitism and the Zionist movement, even interviewing David Ben Gurion and Chaim Weizmann. They were impressed not only by Jewish achievements in science and business, but also by Chiang Kai-Shek's chief intelligence officer, a London-born Jew named Morris Cohen.[100] The Japanese foreign office boasted that Kaufman was so impressed with Japan's warmth towards the Jews that, in 1936 and 1937, he asked to set up a Far Eastern Jewish Council to unite Jewish organizations in the Far East and to propagandize on Japan's behalf, particularly against communism. The Japanese even allowed Harbin to host three conferences of Far Eastern Jewish communities, the first of which occurred in December 1937.[101] Meanwhile, the Japanese were facilitating publicity and financing for the National Order of Russian Fascists, and *Nash Put'* still appeared in the streets laden with anti-Jewish slogans. Although some individual Japanese like Yasue may have taken the Jews' plight to heart, any friendly gestures from the Japanese militarist regime were merely cynical attempts to take advantage of the Jews' predicament and harness their talents and resources.[102]

Japanese patronage gave Semenov a chance to attempt a Cossack revival. In May 1938, former General A.P. Baksheev chaired a Harbin conference of Transbaikal, Amur and Ussuri Cossacks during which SKDV leaders were selected and pledged their loyalty to *Pokhodnyi Ataman* Semenov. Their goal was the establishment of a Cossack state in the Russian Far East, under Japanese guardianship akin to Manchukuo, built upon *rossizm*, a simplistic nationalist 'ideology' conjured up by Semenov and promoted by his recently published memoirs, *O Sebe – About Myself*. *Rossizm* advocated that White emigrant organizations should reject aims to establish any particular form of government in post-communist Russia, since such goals bred divisiveness among the Whites. The SKDV came to include many fascists, but most Cossacks who joined were motivated by dreams of reclaiming their lost property and privileges.

Ataman Semenov relished this second chance to fulfill his destiny and 1938 was rich in promises. In his staff headquarters he pored over military maps of Transbaikalia with his adjutants and discussed tactical maneuvers under a large portrait of Tsar Nicholas II, 'drinking mai-tais with strong Chinese vodka'. He mustered some 12,000–15,000 White cavalrymen, anxious to charge into Siberia behind a number of 700-man shock detachments that were already poised on the banks of the Argun river, their diversionary targets ripe for the kill. In Tokyo, a German correspondent and Red spy named Richard Sorge got wind of the short deadlines for Japanese topographic teams surveying the Manchukuo–Mongolia border, the dispatch to Dairen of a general staff officer, Major Yamasaki, to meet with

Semenov and Semenov's visit to Tokyo to meet with General Araki Sadao, a leading ideologue of radical Japanese militarism. Sorge passed the information on to Moscow. Semenov maintained close contact with General Hata Shunroku and the Japanese military mission in Harbin as he prepared to deploy Russian scouts along with the Kwantung Army's 'reconnaissance in force' around Mongolia's Lake Khasan.[103] These were heady days for the ataman, reminiscent of that hopeful summer 20 years before when he faced Sergei Lazo on the Transbaikalian steppe, only this time, he was backed by two whole armies – the Manchukuo Army and Japan's Kwantung Army, not just a ragtag detachment of irregulars and a handful of advisors.

Émigré youths recruited through Concordia Society sports and cultural activities and the fascist party were trained and dispatched into Transbaikalia, Amur and Maritime regions to gather intelligence or commit sabotage. These were extremely dangerous tasks not only because of the danger of capture and torture by the NKVD, but also because Japanese counterintelligence often interrogated survivors of these suicidal missions as if they had been recruited by the NKVD.[104] As early as 1936, the NKVD intercepted and destroyed a 40-man team of such saboteurs near Amazar station.[105]

Soviet fear of Semenov and the popular discontent that such a renegade could arouse was felt far from the Russian Far East's sensitive border areas. A standard accusation during Stalin's 1938 purges was that of being a Japanese agent or in cahoots with Semenov. In addition to repatriated Soviet workers from the Chinese Eastern Railway, many Russians had departed Harbin and other Manchurian émigré settlements after the Japanese occupation to return to Russia, and all of these unfortunate returnees became grist for Stalin's paranoia mill. For example, on 26 October 1938 a roundup of accused Japanese and Semenovist spies in Omsk netted 178 suspects, 112 of whom were sentenced to death by firing squad – an unlikely band of suspects encompassing several accountants, mechanics, plumbers, veterinarians, a promiscuous hotel clerk and her waiter husband, a driver, a high school teacher, a shoe-shiner, a jobless man, a kindergarten nurse, a seamstress, a bread inspector, a medical student, a photographer, men, women, Koreans, Chinese, a Greek, a Lithuanian, party members and managers of a collective farm advertising agency, a nursery and a fishery, among many others just as diverse and random.[106]

Despite the animosity between Tokyo and Moscow, Soviet defectors could not count on safe sanctuary in Manchukuo. Defectors joined Soviet prisoners of war, captured irregulars and émigrés accused of being communists or criminals in the pool of guinea pigs for horrific biological warfare experiments conducted by the Japanese Army's Unit 731 at Pingfan station, 12 miles from Harbin, and other sites. In the late 1930s, for instance, Japanese scientists demanded more Caucasian subjects for their anthrax and plague experiments. When the NKVD chief for the Soviet Far East, Commissar Genrikh Lyuskov, defected, 300 of his subordinates fled to Manchukuo fearing an imminent house-cleaning by Stalin, only to perish at the hands of Unit 731's cruel doctors.[107]

Manchuria became one of the world's hotspots of international tension, the hairpin trigger of war between a predatory Japan, radical Russia and struggling China. In the years leading up to the Second World War, the 3,200-mile Soviet–Manchukuo border was a powderkeg that produced more explosive incidents than any region in the world. 'About 2,000 of them have been officially recorded in ten years', wrote political analyst John Gunther in 1939, 'ranging from catcalls across the border to pitched battles'.[108] Semenov's extensive contacts in and knowledge of the communities across the Amur and Ussuri river borders made him a vital asset to Japanese military and intelligence ambitions. He played a hand in recruiting men for special operations, such as the bands of Manchukuo Whites who donned Soviet uniforms and attacked Chinese villages, then withdrew towards Soviet territory to feign border incidents.[109]

In April 1939, Semenov's men joined the 60,000 men of the Kwantung Army's 23rd Division on the march into Outer Mongolia to occupy a deserted and disputed sector on the Manchukuo–Mongolian border near the Khalkin Gol river in the vicinity of a village called Nomonhan. Mongolian and Soviet forces resisted and for the next three months Japanese tanks, infantry and cavalry launched fierce attacks to take this desolate real estate, but were repulsed by an unexpectedly determined Red Army. General Georgii Zhukov took over the Russian defense in June and by August amassed 550 combat aircraft, 500 ultra-modern T-34 tanks, 20 cavalry squadrons and 35 infantry battalions against the overconfident Japanese–Manchukuoan invasion force. Whether compromised by Soviet counterintelligence or just simply inept, Semenov's intelligence network failed to alert the Japanese commanders to the Red buildup. On 20 August Zhukov thrust into western Manchukuo on a blitzkrieg that virtually annihilated the 23rd Division. The Soviets humiliated the Japanese, and Hirohito's imperial family was mortified by the desertion of Prince Higashikuni's son, a 23-year-old lieutenant.[110]

Semenov's 16-year-old godson, Igor Vladimirovich Slutskii, who was working at Anta railway station between Harbin and Tsitsihar, watched a cavalcade of trains rumble east full of dead and wounded Japanese. He was shocked by 'the callous and inconsiderate treatment given to the wounded Japanese, who were returned from the border in cattle cars, while the dead were returned in the comparative luxury of passenger trains'. The Japanese explained that the wounded had lost face and become a burden on the empire while 'failing to achieve perpetual glory by dying in battle for the Emporer'. Zhukov's men helped no less than 18,000 Japanese troops achieve perpetual glory on the battlefield, and several disgraced officers joined their number by ritual suicide shortly after the defeat. White soldiers in the Manchukuo Army informed Slutskii of Zhukov's 'complete victory'.[111]

The Nomonhan debacle (remembered as the Battle of Khalkin Gol in Soviet and Mongolian lore) had a profound effect on the White émigré community in Manchukuo. The superiority of Soviet military power over the previously invincible Japanese stirred a growing national pride among Russian-Manchukuoans, particularly among the younger, post-civil war generations. Japanese military leaders recoiled from provoking the powerful Red giant. A new Japanese policy substituted anti-British activity for the former anti-Soviet attitude, and the Whites suddenly realized that Japan had little further interest in Siberia or the anti-communist crusade.

Semenov, godfather of Manchukuo's Reactionary Whites (1939–45)

The defeat at Nomonhan put a damper on Semenov's ambitions, but he continued his work with the Japanese authorities, running operations from his Dairen compound and collecting a ¥1,000 per month 'pension' from Japan.[112] About 1939, Semenov relocated his household to a seaside compound where his old acquaintance Pavel Vaskevich happened to be a neighbor. Semenov's house was 'inferior' to Vaskevich's, which reinforced the old diplomat's conviction that his neighbor could not possibly be in possession of the 'tsarist gold'.[113] Indeed, it seems that the Japanese did not give Semenov access to the estimated 33.7 tons of gold – 172 boxes of golden nuggets and 550 boxes of golden coins worth 43.5 million rubles – that he had entrusted to Yokohama Specie Bank and Chosen Bank during Russia's civil war.[114] In contrast to Vaskevich's account, a US Office of Strategic Services (OSS) report described Semenov's estate in palatial terms:

> Semenov now resides at Kaka-Kashi (Hsia-chia-hotzi), a few miles southwest of Dairen, in a 90,000-yen villa which contains offices, residential quarters, an air

raid shelter and a small arsenal, including stores of ammunition. The residence is carefully guarded by Japanese secret agents and every precaution has been taken to insure the safety of his person. Semenov, himself, wears a bulletproof vest when out of his home and is always armed.[115]

In 1940, Semenov looked older than his 50 years, with a smaller mustache and a larger paunch that reflected a rich diet, his thinning brown hair crowning a puffier face that accentuated the Asian lines of his eyes and made his face look more Buryat than Russian. 'He limps slightly on his right leg, does not use drugs, but is a heavy drinker', stated an OSS report.[116] The ataman attended a Russian Orthodox church in Dairen, standing among a congregation that included Churin, the owner of the famous department store, and his Kaka-Kashi neighbor Vaskevich.[117] Yet the OSS noted his Cossack machismo: 'His chief interests are horse-racing and women.' Helen had divorced him in 1932 and he was now on his fourth marriage, although he strived to be a good father as much as a Cossack warlord's many other responsibilities permitted.

He had taken custody of his two oldest children by Helen, Elena and Mikhail, welcomed Zenaida's son Vyacheslav from Paris in 1935, and took in his 14-year-old godson, Igor Slutskii, after Igor's father, an agent of Semenov's, was reported 'accidentally killed' by Japanese police near Shanghai in October 1937.[118] Elena had been educated in Roman Catholic boarding schools at Chefu and Tientsin, and Mikhail, whose right leg was shorter than his left as a result of a childhood infirmity, was taught at home by a private tutor. He overcame his handicap with rigorous physical training and exhibited a sharp mind. 'He always dresses in a Cossack-type uniform and spends most of his time hunting, riding and yachting', said his boyhood companion, Igor Slutskii. 'Despite a somewhat anti-social attitude, probably because of his lameness, Mikhail is General Semenov's favorite because of his soldierly qualities.' Vyacheslav, on the other hand, had been raised in France, and was 'a suave, diplomatic young man and a sharp contrast to his militaristic father'. In 1935, Semenov had arranged for Vyacheslav and Prince De-wan's sons, Singa Rinchin and Singa Dorzhi, to attend the Imperial University of Meiji in Japan. He sent his godson Slutskii to the Harbin Railway Institute for about a year before he became an interpreter at Anta station, then an exchange student at the University of Waseda, Japan.[119]

He continued to oversee the activities of the Cossack union (the SKDV), which counted about 18,400 members in 1940, mostly in Manchukuo's Trekhrech'e region. As would be expected, the union had paramilitary leadership and organization:[120]

Chief	Major General A.V. Zuev
Assistant to the Chief	Lieutenant Colonel M.N. Gordeev
Chief of Staff	Lieutenant Colonel L.L. Chernykh
Chief of Staff Administration Department	Major General V.V. Kruchinin
Chief of Economic Department	Colonel M.F. Ryumkin
Chief of Military Instruction	Colonel S.F. Starikov
Manager of Publishing Department	Lieutenant M.N. Darwin
Clerk of Staff	P.L. Firsov

All Russian emigrant, military and veteran's organizations in Manchukuo fell under the aegis of the *Byuro po Delam Rossiiskikh Emigrantov* (popularly known as BREM, the Bureau for the Affairs of Russian Emigrants). BREM registered new emigrants and refugees from the Soviet Union, screened them for Red intelligence operatives, doled out prized jobs on the Chinese Eastern Railway, conducted propaganda activities, organized youth sports leagues and coordinated the political and economic direction of Manchukuo's

Russian community. 'All banks, firms, corporations, factories, business houses, restaurants, etc., etc., must be "registered" with "the Bureau"', wrote Amleto Vespa. 'No one can employ anyone, much less seek employment, unless he or she be inscribed on the register of "the Bureau"'. In this way, BREM got a cut from every European business and every worker therein, which flowed straight into the coffers of the Japanese military mission. 'The Bureau' also ran a lucrative national lottery. Semenov, the godfather of Manchukuo's reactionary Whites, always loomed large behind the scenes, but BREM was nominally led by other former 'respectable ex-generals': former Imperial Army general and fascist organizer V.V. Rychkov until his death in 1935, General A.P. Baksheev until 1938 and General V.A. Kislitsyn until 1943, when L.F. Blas'evski took the helm.[121]

BREM consisted of six departments and all of its employees were Russian, even though 'the Bureau' exercised authority over every European in Manchukuo, not only Russians. Vespa stated that BREM employed only 'criminals, crooks and adventurers of the worst kind'. K.V. Rodzaevskii, head of the Russian Fascist Union, played a major role in BREM, heading its second department from 1934 until 1943, which was responsible for cultural activities and interface with Japanese intelligence. All BREM departments cooperated with Japanese intelligence, however BREM's third department – ostensibly responsible for administration – played a predominant role. Commanded by M.A. Matkovskii (during the Second World War), the department fielded a Russian cadre of intelligence and sabotage specialists called the Asano Detachment. Matkovskii also ran a network of some 20 paid agents and roughly 100 informants, presumably behind enemy lines.[122] 'The Bureau' also operated branch offices in Peking, Tientsin, Hankow and Shanghai 'which are nothing but nests of Japanese spies', according to former Japanese operative Vespa.

The Nomonhan defeat convinced Japan that Siberia and Mongolia lay outside the achievable boundaries of the Great East Asian Co-Prosperity Sphere, and the Japanese military machine turned towards south Asia and the Pacific. On 13 April 1941 Japan and the Soviet Union signed a five-year neutrality pact in Moscow that included a joint declaration regarding the frontiers of Manchukuo. 'Assisted by Russian and Japanese advisers', Manchukuo and Outer Mongolia amicably concluded border talks in Harbin in mid-October.[123] These settlements brought relative tranquility to the turbulent junctions of the Soviet and Japanese empires while the rest of the world plunged into the Second World War. The Japanese were so fearful of the Soviet Union that they even banned a special edition of *Nash Put'* on 25 July 1941 that celebrated the opening of Operation Barbarosa.[124]

The day of the attack on Pearl Harbor, a speech by a General Yanogita of the Japanese Military Mission in Harbin highlighted the Russian contribution to the war effort and called for a 'fast and decisive victory...over England and America'.[125] A best-selling American book, *Sabotage! The Secret War Against America*, painted a hostile picture of Manchukuo's Russian population, declaring that they were 'headed by saboteur-spy Lieutenant General Gregory Semenoff', who had led several thousand to 'join the Japanese Army under the command of [a Japanese] Major Batase' one week before Pearl Harbor.[126] The book linked him to the eccentric Connecticut fascist Anastasi Vonsiatskii, whom Semenov disdained and who was soon arrested in June 1942. However, in contrast to the Manchurian Whites' hatred and distrust of the British – a product of successful Japanese propaganda and perceptions of British arrogance – there was a general fondness for Americans among non-Japanese in Manchukuo attributed to the pre-war work of American missionaries and schools, such as those operated by the Maryknoll Sisters. This explains how the declaration of war on 8 December 1941 found Igor Slutskii, the ataman's godson, attending Seattle's Garfield High School. He had arrived on a visa one year before, and after graduating in June 1942, was employed as an interpreter for Russian vessels entering Seattle. In spring 1943, he became a Japanese language instructor for an Army Specialized Training (AST) unit at the University of Washington. AST was a new program begun by the US war department in collaboration with universities to accelerate the flow of high-grade technicians and specialists into the army.[127]

K.V. Rodzaevskii's Russian Fascist Union (referred to in OSS reports as the National Order of Russian Fascists) burgeoned to over 20,000 members after the Japanese defeat at Nomonhan, as Manchukuo's Whites turned to Nazi Germany as the only power capable of dislodging Stalin from Russia. 'Pictures of Hitler were displayed in meeting halls and members of the organization paraded in flashy uniforms with the German Brown Shirts and Italian Black Shirts while giving the Nazi salute and wearing the swastika on the sleeves of their uniforms', stated an OSS report. Several Manchukuo chapters had traveled to Berlin in 1939 for extensive indoctrination in fascist ideals and training 'to handle the administration of Russian territory which might be occupied by Germany'. The fascist newspaper *Nash Put'* continued its 'frequent discussion of the impending war between Germany and Russia' even after Joachim von Ribbentrop and Vyacheslav Molotov signed the Nazi–Soviet non-aggression pact on 23 August 1939. In spite of the fascist union's anti-Red vitriol, the majority of Manchukuo Whites frowned upon it 'because it was a complete departure from all Russian tradition' that advocated a type of rule no less foreign or radical than communism. 'Several leading White Russians were openly anti-fascist and denounced the National Order of Russian Fascists as an unacceptable alternative for restoration of the Imperial Russian Government', continued the OSS report. 'Prominent among these persons was General Semenov, who represented the group advocating a semi-democratic monarchy'. Analysts surmised that the Japanese encouraged the rift among the Whites to ensure a disunified Russian community.[128]

In spring 1943, a captured Soviet officer, General Andrei Andreievich Vlasov, received German permission to form the *Russkaya Osvoditel'naya Armiya* (ROA, Russian Liberation Army), an anti-Soviet military unit under Wehrmacht control. Vlasov appealed to all Russian patriots to join his movement for the liberation of Russia from Bolshevism. Semenov answered this appeal with a declaration of friendship published in the émigré newspaper *Harbinskoye Vremya* in Manchukuo. His endorsement may have even enticed an old Cossack or two to volunteer for ROA.[129]

Ironically, the Ataman's 20-year-old godson, Igor Slutskii, volunteered for the US Army the following spring. 'For reasons of personal security his name was recently changed to Gene Mitchell', indicated an OSS report a few months later. On 10 July 1944, Private Gene Mitchell of Company C, 86th Infantry Training Battalion, proudly took the oath to become a US citizen at Camp Roberts, California.[130]

On 8 August 1945, two days after a single American B-29 bomber destroyed the city of Hiroshima with an atomic bomb, Josef Stalin unleashed a massive simultaneous attack upon Japanese forces in Manchukuo, Korea, Sakhalin and the Kurile Islands. Manchukuo was penetrated on seven major axes from the east, west and north by nearly 80 divisions of Red air, land and naval power. The Mongolian Army and several units of internationalists joined in, such as the Red Army's 88th Special Independent Guerrilla Brigade which was made up of several hundred Korean, Chinese and Russian survivors of the Manchukuo irregulars.[131] Tanks of the Transbaikal Front's five armies darted across the Mongolian deserts and between the 6,000-foot peaks of the Greater Khingan Mountains, covering 600 miles in 11 days to liberate Changchun, Mukden and Tsitsihar.[132] Many Russians in detachments of the Manchukuo and Japanese armies refused to fight. Some Kwantung Army units acknowledged the futility of resisting the overwhelming Red invasion and surrendered, while others fought furiously, desperately trying to defy fate's promise of slow death in the gulag.[133] Regardless the Soviet vanguard simply bypassed Japanese strongpoints and sliced quickly through Manchukuo in a flawless, textbook invasion.

Soviet paratroopers descended into Harbin and were shortly joined by naval infantry of the Pacific Fleet's 1st and 2nd Amur Flotilla Brigades, who accepted the capitulation of

Japan's Sungari Flotilla on 20 August.[134] Russian residents lined the streets to greet their liberators enthusiastically and toss bouquets, just as they had greeted the Kwantung Army in 1932. However, they soon discovered that the first wave of Red occupation troops sent to Harbin were 'not disciplined combat troops but units of former criminals' who raped, robbed and murdered just as the Japanese had before them (they were eventually replaced by regular army forces who grew enamored of Harbin life).[135]

Despite the warm assurances of Soviet radio propagandists that their émigré 'brothers and sisters' were all forgiven by the Motherland and Comrade Stalin, SMERSH and NKVD detachments arrived in Manchuria with hit lists of about 10,000 Russians who had served in OMO, other White armies, or the Japanese–Manchukuo military or police. The fugitives were promptly packed off to the gulag.[136]

On 23 or 24 August seven huge Consolidated PBY Catalinas rose into the air near Vladivostok carrying 90 paratroopers recruited from warships and coastal units of the Soviet Pacific Fleet. Five hours later they swooped down into Dairen's Victoria Bay just as ten other Catalinas were depositing 135 naval infantrymen in Port Arthur. Japanese garrisons in both cities meekly laid down their arms, and Russian sailors hoisted the Soviet naval ensign up the flagpole of the Port Arthur fortress.[137] Russian historian Leonid Petrov writes that a 'pardon was promised to General Semenov... in case of his voluntary surrender', however the crafty ataman would have surely seen through such an obviously insincere pledge from the Bolsheviks.

Russian writer Vadim Sotskov discovered three versions of the story of the ataman's apprehension, each backed up by various witnesses. In the first version, Semenov attempted to flee to China by plane, and while en route made a routine landing at Changchun, where the passengers were surprised to find that the city had already been taken by the Red Army and they were under arrest. In the second version, Semenov awaited his arrest in his Kaka-Kashi villa, where he had an elegant dinner set for his Soviet captors when they arrived. They accepted his invitation, and at the conclusion of the banquet a Soviet colonel arose and placed Semenov under arrest. A third version has Semenov decked out in full dress uniform adorned with all his regalia and cartridges, meeting Soviet troops at the railway station, where he was taken into custody.[138] However his arrest happened, Grigorii Semenov returned to Russia just as he had left – in a hurried flight aboard an aircraft. His favorite son Mikhail and three daughters, Elena, Tatyana and Elizaveta, were also placed under arrest but the girls, at least, remained at Dairen eight months longer. Fascist leader Konstantin Rodzaevskii had deserted his wife and two children and successfully escaped to China where he was convinced by a journalist – actually a Soviet agent – to return to his Fatherland, where he was led straight to Lubyanka prison.

In April 1946, a Soviet freighter transported Semenov's daughters, wooden-legged brother and several Japanese prisoners from Dairen to Vladivostok. Elizaveta recalled seeing at least one Japanese prisoner dive overboard during the voyage. The guards held their fire and let the sea settle accounts with the escapee. A Soviet court judged the girls, none of whom had ever set foot on Russian soil before, and sentenced them each to 25 years in the gulag.[139]

Also in spring 1946, Semenov's custody was transferred to the recently formed Ministry of State Security (MGB) along with his SMERSH jailers, who were incorporated into the new bureaucracy's 3rd Directorate (Military Counterintelligence). Semenov's prosecution was packaged with that of Fascist Union leader Konstantin V. Rodzaevskii, former OMO Sotnik Lev Fillipovich Vlas'evskii, General Aleksei P. Baksheev, L.P. Okhotin, Prince N.A. Ukhtomskii and other lesser defendants, all accused of being *semenovtsy*. Trials of the ROA collaborator, General Andrei A. Vlasov, and other anti-Communist Russians who had cast their lots with the Nazis (such as P.N. Krasnov and A.G. Shkuro) preceded Semenov's trial, accompanied by 'meager reports' in the Soviet press. In contrast, newspapers filled columns with details about the trial of the *semenovtsy* when it opened in Khabarovsk on 26 August 1946. There was little doubt about the trial's outcome. Rodzaevskii, Vlas'evskii and Baksheev were sentenced to death with Semenov for being 'enemies of the Soviet people' and 'active accomplices of the Japanese aggressors'. Prince Ukhtomskii and Okhotin received sentences of 20 and 15 years hard labor, respectively, which amounted to virtual death sentences.[140]

Details of Semenov's execution were published in an obscure article by a former Transbaikal Cossack under the byline A. Kaigorodov, presumably the Tartar captain who fought to the end of Ungern-Shternberg's Mongolian campaign and took to the hills as an anti-Bolshevik partisan. He wrote that when the time arrived for the ataman's execution, 11 p.m. on 30 August 1946, Semenov requested a priest, although he knew that the Communists had no tolerance for religious superstition. Kaigorodov wrote of the 'loud idiotic laughter of the hangmen', who strung up the ataman in a 'long forbidden manner' and taunted him with shouts of 'Repent, reptile!' while he danced his final convulsive jig in the basement air. His greatest punishment would have been knowing that his son Mikhail had already been shot by the Bolsheviks.[141]

Epilogue

The ataman outlived most of his contemporaries. Lieutenant General Aleksandr I. Dutov, Ataman of the Orenburg Cossacks, was murdered by Bolshevik assassins in China in February 1921, and Semirech'e Cossack Ataman Boris V. Annenkov was lured back to the Soviet Union and shot in August 1927.[142] General Mikhail M. Pleshkov, former chief of staff of Russian forces in the Chinese Eastern Railway zone, died that same year in Harbin.[143] General Boris Khreshchatitskii, the young Ussuri division commander who was the first senior officer to subordinate himself to Semenov's command, joined the French Foreign Legion, rose to command a Chechen cavalry squadron in Syria, where he distinguished himself in combat and died in France in 1940.[144] Semenov's first vocal critic, General Baron Aleksei P. Budberg, had served as the North American chief of ROVS until 1939 and died in San Francisco in 1945, having mellowed his condemnation of the ataman demonstrably in light of the arbitrary brutality of the Soviet police state. As proof that mercy is more mysterious than vengeance, the brutal White general Pavel Ivanov-Rinov 'returned to the Soviet Union and found work in the Red Army'. General Konstantin Sakharov found a job as a steel worker in San Francisco, wrote his memoirs in Europe and died as a farmer in Shanghai in 1955.[145]

FER leader Aleksandr Krasnoshchekov became chair of the directorate of the Bank of Industry and Trade when his sham state was incorporated into the Soviet Union, and in March 1924 was arrested and subjected to a show trial that was widely publicized, even in the Western press.[146] Mikhail Frunze, who oversaw Trotsky's 1920 campaign into the Russian Far East, was rewarded with appointment as chairman of the Revolutionary Military Council in January 1925, a position that brought him into awkward conflict with Comrade Stalin, but died mysteriously ten months later during surgery for a stomach ulcer. Krasnoshchekov and scores of other Reds who had been on Semenov's death lists were executed by Stalin during the great purges of 1937–38. Meier A. Trilisser, lifelong Bolshevik, member of the Irkutsk soviet and *Tsentrosibir*, commander of the Red's makeshift fleet on Lake Baikal in summer 1918, and principal figure of Blagoveshchensk's Red underground during Semenov's reign, so efficiently guided the Red Terror in the Russian Far East during the post-civil war era that Stalin made him chief of foreign intelligence for OGPU from 1926–29. He rose to the highest ranks of the party before being arrested in 1938 and executed in 1941.[147] Many Red partisan veterans of the war against Semenov were called upon to apply their extensive knowledge of behind-the-lines operations during the Great Patriotic War. For example, Commissar A.K. Flegontov, who rose to become the partisan commander in the Maritime province in 1921, was dispatched behind Nazi lines in Belorussia in autumn 1942.[148]

The last concentration of Cossack warlord detachments disintegrated with Manchukuo in 1945. Most White emigrants who managed to avoid reprisals from both the Japanese and the Soviets moved on to third countries after the war. Still, some were inveigled to accept Soviet passports and return to the Motherland such as two steamships of 3,000 returnees who departed Tientsin for Nakhodka in 1947. 'Instead of the promised red carpet and orchestra', wrote historian Leonid Petrov, 'they were met with barbed wire and rifle shots; some were executed on arrival, the rest were sent to the gulags'. Konstantin Nechaev, former commander of Chang Tso-Lin's Nechaev Division, was hung in Chita in 1946.

In 1948, former Czechoslovak Legion General Radola Gajda died at the age of 56. Ironically the bold young general who had revolted against the White reactionaries in Vladivostok in November 1919 became a shrill advocate of fascism in his homeland during the 1930s, after having been driven out of the Czechoslovakian Army in 1926 for plotting against his own democratic government. His fellow legionnaire General Jan Syrovy was Czechoslovakia's Minister of War at the time of the 1938 Munich Agreement, was imprisoned for collaborating with the Nazis after the war and died in 1953.[149] In contrast, most other legionnaires became key figures in the Czechoslovakian republic until Britain and France betrayed them to the Nazis with the 1938 Munich Pact. Many were executed by the Germans in 1939 in Poland, where they had gone to establish a national liberation movement, and others were executed after the Communists took power in 1948. Their Austro-Hungarian adversaries among the internationalists in Siberia probably suffered the majority of the 11,000 deaths cited for Austrian subjects during the Russian Civil War.[150]

On 14 February 1950, the governments of the Soviet Union and the Peoples' Republic of China signed a treaty that transferred to China all Russian rights to common management of the Chinese Changchun rail line (formerly the Chinese Eastern Railway).[151]

Masha Sharaban had made a new life in Beirut with her stash of gold. She married a wealthy man, Khan Nakhichevan and bore him two sons who became officers in the Egyptian Army. They apparently were blessed with their mother's sense of survival, because they managed to weather Gamel Abdel Nasser's purge of the officer corps in 1952, and were still serving the Republic of Egypt as of 1956.[152] That same year saw the natural death of former POW Burghard Breitner, head of the Austrian Red Cross and 1951 presidential candidate, who had witnessed a number of comrades tortured to death by OMO specialists in an exhibition of sadism in Chita.

During the honeymoon of Soviet–Chinese relations in the late 1950s, Premier Nikita Khrushchev convinced large numbers of the remaining Russian *Kharbintsy* to return to Russia to cultivate the 'virgin lands' of Kazakhstan. Trainloads of sophisticated, highly educated settlers from Harbin were dumped onto the central Asian steppes in their suits, high heels and nylons, their boxes full of books and records soaking up the pouring rain. They would never be forgiven for their parents' decisions to flee Russia 30 years before. Nevertheless, they were more fortunate than their neighbors who remained in China to be assaulted, terrified and humiliated by Mao's violent Red Guards during the xenophobic Cultural Revolution from 1966–76. The towering Cathedral of St Nikolai and scores of other Russian churches were reduced to kindling by the Red Guards.[153]

Former Czech Legion Lieutenant Ludvik Svoboda fought the Wehrmacht as a battalion commander, rose to the rank of general, became the pro-Communist Minister of Defense in Prague after the Nazi defeat and played an active part in the overthrow of Czechoslovakian democracy in 1948. Stalin demoted him, Khrushchev rehabilitated him, and Svoboda became president of Czechoslovakia after Antonin Novotny's fall in 1968. He helped usher in the 'Prague Spring' reforms and challenged Soviet bullying until the Red Army flooded into Czechoslovakia in August 1968. He died in 1979.

In 1973, the US Congress finally recognized men of the Russian Railway Service Corps as military veterans and accorded them the corresponding medical and financial benefits. Only 25 RRSC veterans were still alive at the time.[154] RRSC Lieutenant Colonel Benjamin O. Johnson returned home to Minnesota to become an executive for the Northern Pacific Railroad, and turned down a lucrative offer from *Colliers Magazine* for two albums of about 800 photographs given to him by the Czechoslovak Legion in 1922, which included several photos of gruesome atrocities committed by the Bolsheviks. Having witnessed many OMO atrocities, Johnson believed that the photographs would paint a distorted, one-sided view of the civil war. Johnson acknowledged having pro-Soviet sympathies and was chastised as a result. Nevertheless, he visited the Soviet Union in 1930, where he gratefully refused a three-year contract as a senior railway advisor because of lingering health problems from his Siberian service. He died two years later.[155]

Major General William S. Graves had served as governor of the Panama Canal Zone after his retirement from the army in the late 1920s, died in 1940 and was buried in Arlington National Cemetery, never having regretted his refusal to assist the Whites, despite the legacy of Stalinist terror and accusations from political opponents that he was pro-Red. Senator William E. Borah died that same year, 12 years after the passage of his crowning achievement, the Pact of Paris Treaty, also known as the Kellogg–Briand Peace Pact, which was signed by the United States, France, Britain, Japan and Germany and outlawed war as an instrument of national policy. Paul 'Bull' W. Kendall, the young American lieutenant who captured the OMO *bronevik* at Posol'skaya in January 1920, commanded the 88th Infantry Division against the Nazi 'Gothic Line' in Italy in 1943, and led an army corps against the Red Chinese onslaught in Korea eight years later.

The regional KGB office in Chita, which resides in Shumovskii Palace, was perplexed by a number of secret compartments found during renovations of the mansion during the 1970s. They surmised that the Shumov family had used the compartments to conceal gold and other treasures from Red revolutionaries, then from OMO officers, during the civil war. All of the compartments were reported empty upon discovery.

Even after General Secretary Mikhail Gorbachev set in motion the processes of glasnost and perestroika in 1986, the Soviet press continued to parrot the old propaganda that the RRSC and General Graves' American Expeditionary Force were the vanguard of a US invasion aimed at Moscow and in cahoots with Ataman Semenov and Admiral Kolchak.[156] Compounding this gross distortion of history was its general acceptance and recirculation by the American public, press and academia.

The fall of communism found Elena and Tatyana Semenova living in a clean, two-room apartment on the 7th floor of a Novorossiiisk apartment block. They had no savings and only a pittance of a pension, and earned food money by doing occasional translations, a talent they had learned from their father.[157]

On 4 April 1994, the military board of the Supreme Court of the Russian Federation reexamined the criminal case of Grigorii M. Semenov, rehabilitated him on the anti-Communist charges but concluded that his pro-Japanese activities were treasonous.[158]

Russia's lost treasures remain a sensitive domestic and international political issue. Accusations against the Japanese, Czechs and even Americans are frequently aired in print and broadcast media pieces in Russia. Semenov's millions in the Yokohama Specie Bank, Chosen Bank and elsewhere were never recovered. To this day, vague tales circulate of the occasional godsend when little stashes of civil war treasure are uncovered in the Russian Far East, Manchuria and Mongolia, the loot of Perezhogin, Semenov, Kalmykov, Ungern-Shternberg and others. The fabled cache of Sotnik Maketno and countless other lost treasure troves are the last legacy of the Cossack warlords.

Appendix 1

THE *MAGISTRAL*

On 12 June 1917, at the same time that Captain Grigorii Semenov was reporting to the All-Russia Revolutionary Committee for the Formation of the Volunteer Army, the US State Department's Advisory Commission of Railway Experts arrived in Petrograd to help the Russian Provisional Government solve its railway problems.[1] One of America's greatest engineers, John F. Stevens, builder of the Panama Canal and the Great Northern Railroad, headed the five-member commission. Stevens was already in Petrograd overseeing Russia's purchase of 1,500 locomotives and 30,000 railway cars on generous ($325 million) US credits which had been extended to Alexander Kerensky's new regime in April 1917. The commission expeditiously inspected the railway and recommended substantial operational improvements, which Russian officialdom was reluctant to digest.[2] For several weeks, Stevens, Henry Miller and other commission members languished through continuous negotiations through interpreters, first with minor bureaucrats of the Ministry of Ways of Communication (as the Russian rail ministry was known), then with the Ministry's Council of Engineers, and then with Comrade Minister Boris Vasil'evich' Ostroumov. Finally, on 10 August, the commission gained an audience with head of government Alexander Kerensky, who ordered that the American Commission's recommendations be implemented at once.[3]

The 4,700-mile long Trans-Siberian Railway – the *Magistral* – was the crowning achievement of Russian civil engineering and, since the outbreak of the First World War in 1914, a critical umbilical cord upon which rested Russia's very survival. The empire's Baltic and Black Sea ports were blockaded, and supplies and exports could only pass through the ports of Archangel and Vladivostok. Archangel lay in the shadow of the Arctic circle on the temperamental White Sea, and connected to the Russian heartland via an inadequate, narrow-gauge railway. Vladivostok, though 12 days ride from the frontlines under optimal conditions, had to sustain Russia's lifeline to her allies in western Europe and North America.[4] The war's insatiable appetite for men, food and material from Siberia herself was enough to disrupt timetables and regular maintenance schedules on the Trans-Siberian. On top of this, tons of military supplies from Russia's allies poured into Vladivostok. Wartime demands put a tremendous strain on the railway as its equipment and employees were pushed to the limit to haul supplies from the docks of Vladivostok to the fighting fronts.

The inept railway administrators in Petrograd seemed oblivious to a disastrous situation that was brewing with their slapdash management, inefficient operations, neglected infrastructure, worn out equipment and abused workforce. Soldiers on the fighting fronts were outraged when their comrades were maimed or killed because of shortages of arms, ammunition and other equipment. Morale plunged, desertions soared. Meanwhile, 700,000 tons of military materiel piled up around the piers and railyards in Vladivostok.

Russia's vast rail network was controlled by an 'elaborate centralized technical department at Petrograd without [any] practical experience'.[5] This government railway bureaucracy was

APPENDIX 1

universally regarded as 'extravagant, inefficient and unpopular'. Unlike American railways, the 42,000-mile Russian system lacked any operating department. 'Imagine the Baltimore and Ohio [Railway] operated by only the General Manager and Station Masters, eliminating all other officials and you have a picture of the method here', reported Henry Miller of the US State Department's Advisory Commission of Railway Experts. 'Trains are not dispatched, but handled by station masters [from] station to station', continued Miller. 'Trains [are] operated by tape telegraph block signal system on double track and staff block system on single track'.[6] This piecemeal management method slowed traffic.

Railway operations were conducted by divisions based in cities and large towns on the line. Each division was responsible for running and maintaining the trains on stretches that varied from about 50 miles long in congested European Russia to 80 miles long in Siberia. Thus, on the Trans-Siberian, the daily engine run from principal depot to turn-around point and back averaged 160 miles. Much like the baton in a relay race, passengers and freight moving from the Baltic to the Pacific would be passed off through 70 divisions of the Russian railway system.[7]

Russia's antiquated railway infrastructure showed signs of long neglect. 'They have ample sidings', noted Henry Miller, 'but poor telegraph and an entire absence of any coal chutes, modern boiler washing plants, or other time-saving facilities for handling locomotives... Shops, tools and machinery [are] 40–60 years old, of poor design and generally inefficient'.[8] The brunt of the hauling fell upon four-axle coupled locomotives ('0-4-0's') that averaged 24 years old. About 17,000 locomotives (including 3,500 passenger locomotives) plied the Russian rails, but more than one-third of them were old nags that had been in use before 1890. Also, because so many skilled mechanics and other resources had been diverted into military service, the frantic pace of wartime operations had put more than one-quarter of Russia's locomotives on the 'bad order' list.[9] *Taplushki*, hardy, two-axled wooden boxcars, were as common as mice and used to haul everything except upper class Russians. Over 10,000 American four-axled boxcars and gondola cars shared the loads of peasants, livestock, agricultural products, coal and other freight. Siberia was better off than the rest of country for rolling stock and locomotives, the latter thanks to several hundred American locomotives that rolled into Vladivostok in 1917.[10]

Workers aboard Trans-Siberian trains and switchmen and others along the line had to contend with frostbite, outlaws, wild animals and a cornucopia of malevolent natural forces lurking in the dark forests. The constant peril of derailment loomed as the ground froze and defrosted, shifting beneath the tracks, which also perched precariously over many of the world's most immense rivers. Mechanics and laborers in the 'small, rambling and badly lighted' shops were hardly more secure. 'Everything is done by hand and, during the war, by women', observed Henry Miller.[11] They lifted huge locomotive engines with 'jacks having long vertical screws, operated by a hand spur-gear reduction mechanism'. It was hard, dirty, dangerous work, but the clever workforce surprised foreign observers with their ingenuity and simple solutions to complex problems despite the lack of modern tools and machinery.

After Tsar Nicholas II abdicated on 15 March 1917, imperial authority collapsed and standards of service on the Trans-Siberian Railway plummeted. Union agitators and political firebrands found receptive audiences in the underpaid, over-worked labor force. 'The labor conditions are as bad as they can be', grumbled Henry Miller in the summer of 1917:

> All branches [of workers] including even the guards on the track who are enlisted as soldiers, are in one [union] organization and the first demand was that the hours be reduced from 12 to 8 and that wages be doubled. They compromised

temporarily on an 8-hour day with a 40-to-60 per cent increase in wages, the railways furnishing food and wearing apparel, board and lodging and allowing full-time [pay] and expenses while on [political] committee work. They are now agitating for a 6-hour day and further increase in pay and in the meantime efficiency is almost nil, as they are either laying off or spending their time while on duty in discussing their own affairs. There is no discipline and they do just about what they please regardless of orders and instructions. They also demand the removal of any officials who are objectionable to them.

At Kerensky's request, the US government established a Russian Railway Service Corps (RRSC). The RRSC would be made up of experienced American railway men – superintendents, trainmasters, dispatchers, auditors and other specialists – who would be paid from the credits to the Russian government. The US government quickly circulated appeals for recruits 'over railway wires and roundhouse bulletin boards' in the north central states where long cold winters approximated Siberian conditions.[12]

Even two years after Russia's revolutionary trauma began in 1917, an American traveler remarked that Trans-Siberian express trains remained 'much more comfortable than Pullmans'.[13] Most travelers on the Trans-Siberian Railway enjoyed much simpler accommodations, which nonetheless offered a far safer alternative to the Great Post Road that roughly paralleled the tracks. Tales abounded of the hazards awaiting travelers on the Great Post Road, the ancient route treaded by Mongol warriors, Cossack frontiersmen, convicts, exiles, adventurers and settlers. Wolves, bears, bandits and bitter cold prematurely ended many a journey on the lonely *trakt*, before Red and White military columns, punitive squads, pressgang 'recruiters', deserters, cutthroats and desperate vagabonds populated the route. East of Irkutsk, life revolved around the Trans-Siberian.

Appendix 2

CADRE AND STAFF

Semenov's Original Cadre and Volunteers, December 1917

Name	Rank and/or Notes
Al-Kadir	Prince, POW, Captain of Turkish General Staff, native of Baghdad
Batuev	Private
Baturin	Private
Berezovskii	Member of Chita Soviet and Commandant of Dauria, December 1917
Burdukovskii	Private
Firsov	Senior NCO
Madtsievskii	Ensign
Oparin	Staff Captain, Commander, Dauria Garrison, December 1917
Shvalov	Junior Ensign
Stepanov	Captain, Chief of Manchuli Police
Ungern-Shternberg	Baron Roman F.
unknown – Couriers	Three couriers 'transmitting [Semenov's] letters to Barga to the government of knight Gui-Fu'
unknown – Horsemen	Three privates tending horses in Dauria
unknown – Assistant	One assistant to Lieutenant Zhevchenko in Harbin
Usikov	Staff Captain, Second-in-Command, Dauria Garrison, December 1917
Zhevchenko	Lieutenant, Semenov's negotiator and courier, December 1917

Semenov's Staff, May 1918

Position	Name
Commander	Ataman Semenov
Chief of Staff	Colonel Natsvalov
Intelligence Officer	Captain Shiroki
Engineer Officer	Captain Vasil'ev
Chief of Cavalry Section	Colonel Matseevskaya
Chief of Infantry Section	Colonel Likhuchev
Chief of Artillery Section	Colonel Zagoskin
Chief of Transportation	Captain Medi
Chief Quartermaster	Captain Berinkov
Ordnance Officer	Colonel Zakhrachevski
Advisor	Captain Kuroki

Composition of Semenov's Detachment, 4th July 1918

Unit	Officers	Men
Staff of Ataman	13	17
Staff of Detachment	19	23
Staff of Intendant of Detachment	20	56
Staff of Intendant in the Field	6	22
Staff of Officer Commanding Line of Communications	5	10
Juridical Section	14	27
Political Section	6	—
Railway Section	9	73
Department of Artillery Depot	7	194
Department of Communications	9	1
Department of Railway Guard	6	36
Department of Artillery Reserve, 1st Line	2	10
Department of Commander of the Artillery	4	12
Sanitary Department	18	25
Artillery Units	35	485
Motor Company	15	53
Armored Train	14	32
1st Mongol–Buryat Mounted Regiment	105	510
1st Onon Mounted Regiment	33	380
Serb Mounted Double-Company	15	190
1st Semenovskii Infantry Regiment	64	801
2nd Manchzhurskii Infantry Regiment	45	420
2nd Daurskii Mounted Regiment	34	640
Engineer Company	30	140
Reserve Remounts	4	45
Administration of Commandant at Manchuli	34	640
Totals	537	4,232

Appendix 3

PROCLAMATIONS OF THE ATAMANS

Proclamation of the Temporary Government of Transbaikal Territory, May 1918

In view of the magnitude of the responsibilities it is undertaking, the Temporary Government of the Transbaikal Territory feels it essential at the outset to announce to the general public its policies and procedures in the present situation. First of all, we must express our gratitude to the Allied powers for having several times declared their respect for the territorial integrity of Siberia. Moreover, we are confident in anticipating close relations with the Allied powers in the difficult path that lies ahead for our government. The territorial government, wielding all military power, will be the sole organ to lead the Siberian people forward toward the securing of democratic rights, development of the economy and the establishment of Siberian self-government, on the basis of equality, justice and equity. We shall establish the fundamental conditions for quickly calling a Siberian legislative assembly, which will be the proper organ of authority of a self-governing Siberia. A Siberian government will be set up by the Siberian assembly.

The government will gradually restore the organs of republican self-government which existed before the invasion by Bolshevik power; and we are confident that these organs will not interfere with the objectives or obstruct the attainment of these objectives, announced by the detachment.

In view of the extreme importance placed by all civilized countries on the establishment of a system of justice to protect the people's rights, lives and property, the government intends to restore by degrees the laws relating to justice established during the period of the Russian Provisional Government. When it becomes necessary to revise them, they will be referred to the Siberian legislative assembly or to the body which has authority to revise them according to the laws of the Russian Provisional Government.

The government will also take particular care to select suitable persons to restore banking facilities which have been disrupted and to readjust agriculture, which has been devastated.

Proclamation of Ataman Kalmykov in Grodekovo District, July 1918

Citizens of Russia! On 27 February 1917 [old style], the Emperor's government fell and the power of the state passed into the hands of the provisional government elected by the executive committee of the 4th Duma. The provisional revolutionary government promised the people:

1. Full and immediate pardon to all who, under the old government, struggled against the wrongs committed by an autocratic power and fought for the church and for the betterment of the life of the people.
2. Freedom of speech of the press and at public meetings.
3. Repeal of all class and national restrictions, that is, all Russian citizens without distinction by faith, tongue or race will have equal rights before the law.
4. To summon the Constituent Assembly which was to determine the form of government and the fundamental laws of the country.
5. Election to self-governmental organs on a basis of general, direct, equal and secret voting, that is, to the people's *zemstvos* and to the people's municipalities.

The Russian people breathed freely. The provisional government, in spite of tremendous difficulties, endeavored to fulfill the promises made to the people. Some were indeed fulfilled. For example, there came into existence provincial, district and village self-governing organs elected by general, direct, equal and secret voting, that is by the whole people. These self-governing organs were to have settled Russian public life on principles of democracy; they were to have protected the interests of the laboring classes. The great day was approaching – 28 November 1917 [old style] – when deputies of the whole of Russia were to have arrived in Petrograd to meet in the Constituent Assembly. This assembly was to have determined and settled the life of all Russia, just as the local self-governing organs were to have settled local life in villages and towns. This assembly of the best elements of the Russian people was to have settled the question of war or no war.

But our enemies, the Germans, were not asleep. They could not defeat our glorious army in the field of battle. They then planned an evil deed. Lenin and his colleagues were sent off to Russia with special honors from Germany. With gold received from the German emperor, Lenin and his colleagues raised an insurrection in Petrograd on 4 June [old style]. The aim of this insurrection was to overthrow the provisional government and to seize power for themselves. The attempt did not succeed. On 26 October [old style] the Bolsheviks promised the people the following:

1. Immediate termination of the war and the conclusion of peace on the basis of the self-determination of nations.
2. To hasten the date of the meeting of the Constituent Assembly.
3. To feed the starving Russian people.
4. To hand over factories and workshops to the working men.

By these promises they secured the support of the army and with its help they seized power. The ignorant people also believed the Bolsheviks. Citizens! What did the Bolsheviks do during these eight months of domination? They did much, but it was all to the detriment of the Russian people and to the profit of the Germans. Their guilt before the people is great, but their chief ill deeds are the following:

1. They concluded peace with the Germans, but a shameful peace, not an honorable one. The whole of the Russian people became slaves to Germany. Many of the most fertile provinces with a population of over 40 million people were given to the Germans.

APPENDIX 3

2   The Bolsheviks endeavored by all means to block the convocation of the Constituent Assembly and when it met in January 1918, they dispersed it before it had sat a few hours. They thus destroyed the last hope of the salvation of Russia.
3   The famine-stricken people were not relieved by the Bolsheviks. On the contrary, in many towns hungry mobs were fired on, millions of *poods* of bread were exported by the Germans from the Ukraine into Germany for their army. And now there is a dreadful famine in Russia. If there is bread anywhere it cannot be transported to the famine-stricken provinces, owing to the fact that the railways have been destroyed by the Bolsheviks.
4   The workmen received the factories and workshops but neither factories nor workshops are in operation. Thousands of unemployed are suffering from lack of food.

Citizens! Who could inflict so much ill and grief on the mother country! Only enemies and traitors to Russia. The Germans wanted in some way to remove Russia from the ranks of her opponents and thus to weaken our brave Allies. They succeeded in this by bribery and treason. This evil work was done by the Bolsheviks under the guidance of Lenin and his friends, the Germans. In order to strengthen their power, the Bolsheviks destroyed the regular army and organized the Red Army. Soldiers belonging to this army, which was joined by a number of criminals, ne'er-do-wells and emigrants, received high pay. The Jew Trotsky was placed at the head of it. In addition to this, the Red Army was joined by many German and Magyar prisoners and this mixed lot had to defend the Soviet power, or in other words, the power of Lenin, Germans, Jews and criminals of various degrees. The Bolsheviks declared that they did not want to fight the Germans, but they began a war against our brothers! How many people have fallen in this civil war? Who could have invented such a war? Only traitors and their name is 'Bolshevik'. Citizens! Where are the liberties that were promised by the Bolsheviks? Instead of freedom, there have appeared bare-faced commissars consisting of emigrants and criminals who began to dispose of the people and of their property.

Citizens! It is impossible to live like this any longer. We have taken up arms in order to drive the Bolsheviks and Germans out of the province. They have been driven out of the whole of Siberia. By force of arms we shall resuscitate the *zemstvos* and municipalities, self-governing organs and drive away the commissars. We are fighting for universal, equal, direct and secret voting. Let the people, in the persons of their chosen representatives, settle their own lives. Down with commissars and violators. Citizens! We are not the enemies of the laboring classes, but their friends. Join our ranks and fight alongside us for your freedom and that of your children. Only by combined efforts can we give back the Constituent Assembly to the country. It alone can settle the fate of Russia. Citizens! In your hands lies the salvation of the mother country and the people. Let us bravely go into battle to the better the lives of our children.

Brother Cossacks I address a strong appeal to you. Mobilize your regiments and hurry to join me. You are the free sons of free Cossacks and must settle your lives yourselves. I call you to a bitter fight with our enemies and with traitors to the Motherland. If we shall perish, Russia will perish. No, Cossacks! We shall conquer and mighty Russia will rise again with us.

Long live general, direct, equal and secret voting! Long live the Siberian Constituent Assembly! Long live the All-Russian Constituent Assembly! Long live Russia!

[signed] Kalmykov
Ataman of the Ussuri Cossacks and of the Special Cossack Force

GLOSSARY

Term	Language	Definition or description
aimag	Mongolian	Mongolian province
amban	Chinese	Chinese imperial representative in frontier states (e.g. Tibet and Mongolia)
arban	Mongolian	Mongol 10-man squad, building block of Genghiz Khan's military organization
ard	Mongolian	Mongolian peasant herdsman
argol	Mongolian	dried animal droppings
assignat	French	notes, bills or bonds, issed as currency by a revolutionary government (initially by France, 1790–96)
ataman	Russian	Cossack chief
atamanshchina	Russian	Cossack warlordism
bagatur	Mongolian	Mongol squad leader of 10-man *arban*
barakholka	Russian	flea-market
Barguzin Tukum	Buriat	ancient Buryat name for Mongol heartland around Lake Baikal basin
bekesha	Russian	fur-lined, military greatcoat
belogvardeitsy	Russian	literally White Guards, but during Stalin's reign came to imply a broad range of vile Russian enemies of Soviet power
'Besposhchadnyi'	Russian	'Merciless', OMO armored train
Bogd Gegeen	Mongolian	head of Mongolia's Buddhist-Lamaist religion
Bogdo Khan	Mongolian	Holy Ruler
Bogoroditsa	Russian	'female who couples with God' among Siberian sex cults, literally 'the Virgin Mary'
bronepoezd	Russian	armored train
bronevik	Russian	armored train (slang)
buran	Russian	fierce Siberian blizzard
burzhui	Russian	derogatory term for bourgeoisie
Burte Chino	Mongolian	Blue Wolf People, predecessors of modern Buryats in mythology
Changchun	Chinese	Xinjing, Manchukuo capital 1932–45
Chernosotentsy	Russian	Black Hundreds. Anti-revolutionary, anti-Semitic groups formed in Russia during and after 1905 Revolution. Most

Glossary Continued

Term	Language	Definition or description
		prominent groups were the League of Russian People (*Soyuz Russkogo Naroda*), League of Archangel Michael (*Soyuz Mikhaila Arkhangela*) and Council of United Nobility (*Soviet Obedinennogo Dvoryanstva*)
Chernovitz	English	Austro-Hungarian city on Russian frontier, now Ukrainian city of Chernivtsi, also formerly known as Czernowitz
chekist	Russian	CHEKA agent, secret policeman
Dairen	Japanese	Dalian, Manchuria
Dalny	Russian	Dalian, Manchuria
datsan	Buryat	Buddhist spiritual center
delovoi kabinet	Russian	Business Cabinet, sobriquet of Dmitri L. Horvath's conservative 'government' proclaimed in the Maritime province 9 July 1918
dessiatin	Russian	Russian unit of land area measurement. 1 *dessiatin* = 2.6997 acre
Dikaya Divizia	Russian	Wild Division
dom	Russian	house
droshky	Russian	traditional Siberian conveyance; a low carriage with a high seat in front for the driver
dugan	Mongolian	prayer house or small temple
duma	Russian	national parliament allowed by Nicholas II's October Manifesto in 1905; also local and regional legislative and/or administrative bodies
echelon	Russian	military or troop transport train, usually armed but not armored, from Russian railway jargon for an 80-axle train, usually made up of 40 double-axle railcars
'Edinenie Rossii'	Russian	'Russian Unity', Red armored train in Vladivostok, April 1920
esaul	Russian	Cossack captain
fel'dsher	Russian	corpsman
feng shui	Chinese	Chinese geomantic practice in which a structure or site is chosen or configured to harmonize with spiritual forces inhabiting it
furazhka	Russian	traditional peaked military cap with brim
gaijin	Japanese	foreigner, a contraction of the word *gaikokujin*
gamin	French	street urchin
genro	Japanese	Japanese elder statesmen

(*Glossary continued*)

Glossary Continued

Term	Language	Definition or description
Genyosha	Japanese	Black Ocean Society, an ultra-nationalist Japanese terrorist organization active throughout East Asia
ger	Buryat Mongolian	literally 'home'; either a portable felt and woodframe dwelling with central smokehole common to Central Asia, a 'yurt' in Russian; or a permanent Buryat cabin shaped like a yurt
gimnasterka	Russian	traditional high-collared military blouse
gimnazia	Russian	secondary school (Russian)
Gospolokhrana	Russian	FER state political police
Gosudarstvennaya Vnutrennaya Okhrana	Russian	Mongolian State Internal Security, counterpart of the Soviet NKVD in the early 1930s
'Groznyi'	Russian	'Terrible', OMO armored train
guberniya	Russian	province
hunghutze	Chinese	Manchurian bandits
internatsionalisty	Russian	internationalists
'Istrebitel'	Russian	'Destroyer', OMO armored train
izba	Russian	cottage, hut (Russian)
Jebtsundamba	Mongolian	Holy Venerable Lord; the most prominent reincarnation in Mongolian Buddhism and the third most important in Tibetan Buddhism after the Dalai Lama and Panchan Lama
jihad	Arabic	Muslim holy war
Kadet	Russian	constitutional democrat, conservative party
Kalgan	Mongolian	Mongolian name for Chiang-ja-kuo, China
kalmykovets	Russian	member of Ataman Kalmykov's Detachments or OKO
Kang Teh	Chinese	title of Henry Pu-Yi as Emperor of Manchukuo
Kanzan So	Japanese	Mountain of Sweat Society (Japanese), a secret organization which aimed to set up a Manchurian–Mongol state, formed 1911
kappel'evtsy	Russian	survivors of the Provisional Siberian Government army, December 1919
karatélnie otryádi	Russian	punitive detachments
katorga	Russian	hard labor
Kempei tai	Japanese	Japanese military police, with broad intelligence and internal security functions
Kharbintsy	Russian	resident of Harbin
khlisti	Russian	Russian Orthodox cult in Siberian villages known for sexual orgies in rituals, literally 'whippers'
Khorunzhi	Russian	sub-lieutenant

Glossary Continued

Term	Language	Definition or description
khoshuun	Mongolian	Traditional Mongol administrative unit for management of pastures and resources for herding
khuriltai	Mongolian	assembly of Mongol tribal leaders
Khutuktu	Mongolian	reincarnate lama
kirillovtsami	Russian	Monarchists supporting Prince Cyril in the 1930s
Kobdo	Mongolian	city and/or *aimag* of Hovd
kontr-razvyedka	Russian	counterintelligence
Krasnoarmeets	Russian	Red Army Man, one of the two ranks in the Red Army after 10 November 1917
Krasnyi Komandir	Russian	Red Commander, one of the two ranks in the Red Army after 10 November 1917
krug	Russian	traditional spring assembly of Cossacks, literally 'circle'
kuren	Mongolian	monastery
Kyakhta	Mongolian	Siberian trading center on Tea Road near Mongolian border, officially known as Troitskosavsk until 1935
lan	Chinese	Chinese currency, equal to 2 US dollars (1910)
lesnaya kommuna	Russian	forest commune, Red partisan camp concealed in the forest
likin	Russian	'super tax' imposed by *semenovtsy* on goods at Manchuli
Magistral	Russian	Trans-Siberian Railway
Maimachen	Chinese	Two locales in Mongolia: 1) Mongolian border town (present day Altan Bulag) opposite Kyakhta, Russia, and 2) Chinese commercial quarter of Urga
Manchu Teikoku Kyowakai	Japanese	Manchuria Imperial Concordia Society, Manchukuo's 'nation-building' organization
Manchuria	English	Region covered by present-day Heilongjiang, Jilin and Liaoning provinces in People's Republic of China
mangathai	Mongolian	fierce, multi-headed beasts in Buryat mythology
Maritime province	English	*Primorskii Oblast'*
militsiya	Russian	police
Mongokuo	Japanese	Conceptual strategic buffer state in Inner Mongolia, late 1930s
'Mstitel''	Russian	'Avenger', OMO armored train
Mukden	Russian	Feng T'ien, China
Murav'evo-Amurskii	Russian	Railway town in Maritime province, present-day Lazo
Mysovaya	Russian	Railway town on southeast shore of Lake Baikal, present-day Babushkin

(*Glossary continued*)

Glossary Continued

Term	Language	Definition or description
nachal'nik	Russian	station-master
nachal'nik militsii	Russian	chief of police
nagaika	Russian	heavy leather whip
Nash Put'	Russian	*Our Journey*, Russian fascist newspaper in Manchukuo, late 1930s
nedovorot	Russian	a near coup d'état
Novonikolaevsk	Russian	present-day Novosibirsk
noyon	Mongolian	Mongol prince
ongon	Buryat	small boxes mounted on posts that contain spirits that guard property, according to Buryat Buddhist belief
orlovtsy	Russian	Soldiers of Colonel Orlov's Detachment, known for their loyalty to Admiral Kolchak, 1918–19
Osobii Kazach'ii Otryad	Russian	Special Cossack Detachment, formed by Ivan Kalmykov in March 1918
Osoboi Manchzhurskii Otryad	Russian	Special Manchurian Detachment, name of Semenov's core unit formed in January 1918, often applied to all forces
ostrog	Russian	Cossack fort
osvedomitel'nii otdel	Russian	information department, performing agitation-propaganda functions
Otdel'naya Vostochno-Sibirskaya Armiya	Russian	Separate Eastern Siberian Army, Semenov's command 19 November 1918 until mid-June 1919
otryad	Russian	detachment of roughly 100 men (army), or a flight of 4–6 aircraft (air force)
Pao Shang T'uan	Chinese	Mercantile Guard for Inner Mongolian caravans formed in 1917
papakha	Russian	tall fur hat
papirosy	Russian	Russian cigarettes
perevorot	Russian	failed coup d'état
Petrovskii Zavod	Russian	Town in western Transbaikalia, present-day Petrovsk-Zabaikal'skii
plastun	Russian	Cossack infantryman
pod'esaul	Russian	junior captain(Cossacks)
pokhodnii ataman	Russian	expedition chief of a Cossack Host or group of hosts
pood	Russian	standard unit of mass, 1 *pood* = 36.11 pounds
Port Arthur	English/ Russian	Lushunkow (also Liu Shun-k'ou), Manchuria; modern Lüshun; also formerly Ryo-Jun
poruchik	Russian	subaltern (Army)
praporshchik	Russian	ensign (Army)
Predsedatel' Revolyutsionogo Voenogo Soviet	Russian	Chairman of the Revolutionary Military Council

Glossary Continued

Term	Language	Definition or description
Pri-Amur	Russian	Primorskaya (Maritime) and Amur provinces
Pribaikalia	Russian	western Transbaikalia
prikaz	Russian	decree
Rabochaya Marseleza	Russian	The Workers' *Marseillaise*
raskol	Russian	schism
raskolniki	Russian	Old Believers
razvedka	Russian	intelligence unit
Revel	Russian	Talinn
rossizm	Russian	deology of 'Russianism' conjured up by Semenov in the 1930s
sait	Mongolian	governor
Samara	Russian	renamed Kuibyshev during the Soviet era, but is now called Samara again
semeiskie	Russian	Old Believers, literally 'the family ones'
semenovtsy	Russian	followers of Ataman Semenov
Semirech'e	Russian	Seven Rivers, referring to area of Kazakhstan bounded by Zailiyskii Alatau and Dzhungarskii Alatau mountains to south and Lake Balkhash to north
shabin	Mongolian	influential class of monks, shamans and Buddhist leaders
shalmo	Mongolian	invisible evil spirits in Buryat mythology
shashka	Russian	traditional Cossack sabre
shtab-rotmistr	Russian	staff captain, army
Shun P'an T'ing	Chinese	Chinese court of law
Sibiryak	Russian	A Siberian citizen
Smert' Shpioni!	Russian	literally 'Death to spies!', Soviet counterintelligence detachments during the Second World War
sotnia	Russian	traditional 100-man Cossack detachments
sotnik	Russian	lieutenant, or commander of a *sotnia*
sovietizatsiya	Russian	sovietization
stanitsa	Russian	Cossack village
staroveri	Russian	Old Believers
tael	Chinese	Chinese weight unit of account. 1 silver *tael* (34 to 38 grams) was the standard monetary unit, nominally equivalent to 1000 copper cash. Never used as an actual coin, but rather to weigh silver ingots.
taiga	Russian	Boreal forests of needleleaf evergreen with extreme range of temperatures
taisha	Mongolian	Buryat chief
taplushka	Russian	standard Russian railway freight car
tarantass	Russian	Four-wheeled, cradle-shaped wagon pulled by three horses on the *trakt*
tarasun	Mongolian	fermented mare's milk, popular among Buryats and other Mongols

(*Glossary continued*)

Glossary Continued

Term	Language	Definition or description
tayang p'iao	Chinese	Chinese currency successfully introduced in northern Manchuria in 1919 to counter dominance of yen after disappearance of rubles
Tenyukyo	Japanese	Society of the Celestial Salvation of the Oppressed, 15-man Genyosha cell that undermined Korean government
toll	Russian	Red Army's explosive, 'gun-cotton soaked in nitro-glycerin'
Tonghak	Korean	Eastern Learning, Korean xenophobic movement in late nineteenth century
tovarishch	Russian	comrade
trakt	Russian	Great Siberian Post Road
Trekhrech'e	Russian	Three Rivers region of Manchuria along Soviet border settled by Transbaikal Cossacks
Troitskosavsk	Russian	formal name of Kyakhta until 1935
Tsentral'nyi Detskii Dom	Russian	Central Children's Home, Chita orphanage for offspring of Red fighters
Tsentrosibir'	Russian	Central Executive Committee of Siberian Soviets in Irkutsk
tsenzovik	Russian	bourgeois businessman
tsibik	Russian	traditional unit of tea commerce, as baled, inspected, marked and sewn into raw bull hide at Kyakhta
Urga	Mongolian	Ulan Baator, also referred to as Yihe Huree, Ikh Kuree and similar variations by Mongolians and as K'ulun by Chinese
vana	Mongolian	Title of prince of the 2nd degree
Verkhne-Udinsk	Russian	Ulan Ude
verst	Russian	Russian unit of distance measurement, = 1.0668 kilometers or 0.6629 mile
voevod	Russian	military chief
voisko	Russian	A host, the largest Cossack unit of administration, roughly equivalent to a tribe or indigenous nation
voenno-polevoi sud	Russian	field court martial
voenspets	Russian	*Voennii spetsialist*, military specialist, tsarist officer in Red Army service
voiskovoi starshina	Russian	Cossack lieutenant colonel
vrag naroda	Russian	enemy of the people
vyborni komandir	Russian	elected commander
Yakuza	Japanese	Japanese organized crime organization
yasak	Mongolian	Traditional tribute paid in furs
Zabaikal	Russian	Transbaikal
zaibatsu	Japanese	Great family-controlled banking and industrial combines of modern Japan (leading *zaibatsu* called *keiretsu* after the Second World War)
zakuski	Russian	hors d'oeuvres

Glossary Continued

Term	Language	Definition or description
zastenka	Russian	torture chamber
zemstvo	Russian	elected county assembly empowered to administer local government under tight supervision of central government 1864–1917
zheleznaya doroga	Russian	Iron Road
zimov'e	Russian	winter cabin

NOTES

1 PRELUDE TO TERROR: CREATION – NOVEMBER 1917

1 Jeremiah Curtin, *A Journey in Southern Siberia*, Arno Press, New York, 1909, pp. 121–310.
2 Edward J. Vajda, 'The Ewenki', Western Washington University, Bellingham, WA, 2001.
3 Sarangerel Odigon, 'History of Buryatia', n.p., 1997, and Eric Newby, *The Big Red Train Ride*, Weidenfeld & Nicolson, London, 1978, p. 194.
4 Chinggis is the more accurate transliteration but Ghengis remains the most common and is used here.
5 Curtin, *A Journey in Southern Siberia*, pp. 14–17.
6 At the same time that Russia was moving in from the West, the Manchus were expanding their empire from the east, and the Inner and Outer Mongolian principalities gradually succumbed to them, becoming administrative units of the Manchus' military-feudal hierarchy. Academy of Sciences–Mongolian People's Republic (ASMPR), *Information Mongolia: The Comprehensive Reference Source of the People's Republic of Mongolia*, Pergamon Press, Oxford, 1990, p. 115.
7 Curtin, *A Journey in Southern Siberia*, p. 16.
8 Philip Longworth, *The Cossacks: Five Centuries of Turbulent Life on the Russian Steppes*, Holt Rinehart & Winston, New York, 1970, p. 72.
9 Vasilii Valerianovich Belikov, *Evenki Buryatii*, Ulan-Ude, 1994.
10 Charles Wenyon, *Across Siberia on the Great Post-Road*, C.H. Kelly, London, 1896, p. 164. 'If a merchant travelling by sledge in winter missed his stopping point, he ran the risk of being irretrievably buried beneath the snow with his retinue, animals and merchandise.' Fernand Braudel, *The Structures of Everyday Life: The Limits of the Possible; Civilization and Capitalism, 15th–18th Century, vol. 1*, Harper & Row, New York, 1979, p. 100.
11 City hall and a lower court of justice began operating in 1722, and a magistrate appeared in Irkutsk the following year.
12 Stefan P. Krasheninnkov, *The History of Kamatschataka, and the Kurilski Islands, with the Countries Adjacent*, printed by Robert Raikes for T. Jeffroys, Gloucestor, 1764; reprinted by Quadrangle Books, Chicago, IL, 1962.
13 Longworth, *The Cossacks*, pp. 154ff.
14 Belikov, *Evenki Buryatii*.
15 Longworth, *The Cossacks*, p. 159; and V. Aprelkov, 'Zabaikal'skoe kazach'e voisko', *Ekstra*, Chita, No. 79, 25 July 2001. Aprelkov elaborates on the initial membership of 51,000 Cossacks as including the Evenk-Tungus Regiment of Prince Gantimur, the Buryat-Cossack Regiment of Atamans Ashebagetov, Tsongolov, Ataganov and Sortolov and the Tsurukhaituevskii and Kharatsaiskii border guards.
16 Annette Meakin, *A Ribbon of Iron*, Arno Press, New York, 1901, p. 178.
17 Longworth, *The Cossacks*, p. 261. Nikolai Nikolayevich Murav'ev-Amurski was the scion of an ancient noble family, born in St Petersburg in 1809, who distinguished himself in battle against the Turks as a young man, and rose to the rank of major general by the time he

NOTES

was 32. Tsar Nicholas I considered him a liberal democrat, and appointed him governor general of eastern Siberia in 1847. He died in Paris in 1881.
18 Prince Peter Kropotkin, *In Russian and French Prisons*, Ward & Downey, London, 1887.
19 Curtin, *A Journey in Southern Siberia*, p. 13. When Tsar Fyodor's half-brother, the Tsarevich Dmitri, died in 1593 in Uglich, townspeople became the first exiles to be punished by banishment to Siberia. Even the church bell which tolled over Uglich to announce the royal death was packed off to Tobolsk.
20 Andrew Gentes, 'Review: Iakutiia v sisteme politicheskoi ssylki Rossii 1826–1917 [and] Politicheskaia ssylka v Sibiri: Nerchinskaia katorga', *Kritika: Explorations in Russian and Eurasian History*, vol. 3.1, 2002, pp. 140–51.
21 Paul J. Wigowsky, *Collection of Old Believer's History and Tradition*, Hubbard, OR, 1978.
22 Old Believers are called Kerzhaks in the Urals, Lipovans in Romania and Nekrasov Cossacks in Turkey.
23 Longworth, *The Cossacks*, p. 161.
24 Russell E. Snow, *The Bolsheviks in Siberia 1917–1918*, Fairleigh Dickinson University Press, Madison, NJ, 1977, p. 23.
25 Kropotkin, *In Russian and French Prisons*, p. 181.
26 Wenyon, *Across Siberia*, p. 170 and Kropotkin. In Russian and French Prisons. Wives and children sometimes accompanied convicts, though the latter suffered particularly high mortality. George Kennan's *Siberia and the Exile System* (1891) remains the classic non-Russian muckraking description of Siberian exile.
27 Meakin, A *Ribbon of Iron*, p. 185.
28 Wenyon, *Across Siberia*, p. 170.
29 Ibid., p. 183. Wenyon wrote that 'not less than 20,000' escapees roamed Transbaikalia in the 1890s.
30 Gentes, 'Review', p. 149.
31 Leon Trotsky, *My Life*, Charles Scribner's Sons, New York, 1930, ch. 9.
32 Among exiles, for example, the ratio of woman to men was one to six in 1887. Kropotkin, *In Russian and French Prisons*, p. 180.
33 Longworth, *The Cossacks*, pp. 43–4.
34 Wenyon, *Across Siberia*, p. 173.
35 Maria Rasputin, *Rasputin: The Man Behind the Myth*, Warner Books, New York, 1977, pp. 98–108. *Khlisti* engaged in frenzied ritual dancing that climaxed in group copulation with a female selected to be *Bogoroditsa*, literally the Virgin Mary but in this context meaning one who couples with God.
36 Eva-Maria Stolberg, 'Siberia and the Russian Far East in Japanese Strategic and Economic Conceptions, 1890s–1920s', Institute of Russian History, University of Bonn. Milkito Hane explores the mechanics and impetus for Japan's overseas prostitution rings in *Peasants, Rebels & Outcastes: The Underside of Modern Japan*, Panthean Books, New York, 1982, pp. 207–25.
37 John Murray, *A Memoir of the Life of Peter the Great*, William Clowes, London, 1832, p. 319.
38 George Bassett Digby, *Tigers, Gold and Witch-Doctors*, Harcourt Brace. New York, 1928, p. 113.
39 Wenyon, *Across Siberia*, p. 137.
40 Trotsky, *My Life*, ch. 9.
41 Vladimir Dinets, 'Brown Bears of Russia', n.p., 2001.
42 Wenyon, *Across Siberia*, p. 167.
43 Ibid., p. 166 and Trotsky, *My Life*, ch. 9.
44 US Army, *Medical History of the Siberian Expedition*, n.d. (c.1920), NARA RG165, Microfilm 917.
45 Wenyon, *Across Siberia*, p. 187.
46 Henry Michelson, 'The Trans-Siberian Railroad', *Scientific American*, 26 August 1899, and Edward W. Pearlstein (ed.), *Revolution in Russia! As Reported by the* New York Tribune *and the* New York Herald, *1894–1921*, Viking Press, New York, 1967, p. 22. Engineers bridged 301 miles of water crossings between Cheliabinsk and Vladivostok.

47 Sergei G. Sigachov, 'Transsiberian Historical Background 1857–1891', 1998.
48 'The Cost of Transsib', *Trans-Siberian Web Encyclopedia*, 1998.
49 Edward Thornton Heald, in James Gidney (Ed.), *Witness to Revolution: Letters from Russia 1916–1919*, Kent State University Press, OH, 1972, p. 339.
50 *Baikal* began operation between Baikal and Mysovaya in April 1900. In 1903, Tankhoi replaced Mysovaya as the eastside port.
51 Meakin, *A Ribbon of Iron*, p. 20. Traveler Annette M.B. Meakin avowed that the Trans-Siberian's *Train de Luxe* surpassed comparable amenities on the much vaunted Canadian Pacific Railway in 1901. 'An electric bell on one side of your door summons a serving-man to make your bed or sweep your floor, as the case may be, while a bell on the other side summons a waiter from the buffet. Besides the ordinary electric lights, you are provided with an electric reading lamp by which you may read all night if you choose. Time passes very pleasantly on such a train...'
52 Pearlstein, *Revolution in Russia!*, p. 22.
53 Michelson, 'The Trans-Siberian Railroad'.
54 Richard Deacon, *Kempei Tai: The Japanese Secret Service Then and Now*, Charles E. Tuttle, Tokyo, 1990, pp. 45–6. Deacon cites a statement by General Kuropatkin to Count Sergei Witte from *Krasnii Arkhiv*, vol. 2, to describe the geographical extent of the Tsar's 'grandiose plans'.
55 Burton Holmes, 'A Trip Across Russia by Railroad'.
56 Manchuria consisted of China's 'three eastern provinces': Fengtien, Heilong Jiang and Kirin provinces.
57 Deacon, *Kempei Tai*, p. 46, who cites British Minister Sir Reginald Johnston, *Twilight in the Forbidden City*, East Asia Printers, Shanghai, 1934.
58 Deacon, *Kempei Tai*, pp. 67–79.
59 Ibid., pp. 36–41. *Genyosha*, the Black Ocean Society (named for the strait between Kyushu and Korea), was a secret nationalist society founded in 1881 that cultivated close ties to Japan's Army Intelligence Service and *Kempei tai*. Its membership consisted of 'ultranationalists from the samurai and merchant classes, a large number of *Yakuza*, thugs and petty criminals'. Penetration of the Tonghak was accomplished by a specially selected 15-man Genyosha cell that called itself Tenyukyo, Society of the Celestial Salvation of the Oppressed.
60 Korean Overseas Information Service (KOIS), *Facts about Korea*, Samhwa Printing Company, Seoul, 1984, pp. 46–50.
61 Richard Storry, *A History of Modern Japan*, Pelican Books, Baltimore, MD, 1960, pp. 127–8.
62 Deacon, *Kempei Tai*, p. 41 and KOIS, *Facts about Korea*, pp. 48–51.
63 *New York Tribune*, 29 July 1901, cited by Pearlstein, *Revolution in Russia!*, p. 40.
64 Storry, *A History of Modern Japan*, p. 144.
65 200 million taels was roughly equivalent to US$130,000,000. A tael of silver was China's standard monetary unit, nominally equivalent to 1,000 copper cash. The tael was never used as an actual coin, only to weigh silver ingots; 400,000,000 francs was roughly equivalent to US$50,000,000 in 1896.
66 Kainichi Asakawa, *The Russo-Japanese Conflict: Its Causes and Issues*, Houghton Mifflin, Boston, MA, 1904, pp. 83–100. The statutes of the Russo-Chinese Bank were published on 8 December 1895.
67 Arthur Judson Brown, *New Forces in Old China; An Unwelcome but Inevitable Awakening*, F.H. Revell, New York, 1904. By 14 December, Germany's Admiral Diedrich had landed marines at Kiao-chou Bay, and in a matter of weeks the German occupation evolved into a forced 99-year lease. Within four years, the 'few straggling, poverty-stricken Chinese villages at the foot of the barren hills bordering the bay' had been leveled and transformed into a modern German 'boom city'.
68 Peter Fleming, *The Siege at Peking*, Oxford University Press, Oxford, 1959, p. 30.
69 Fleming, *The Siege at Peking*, p. 43.
70 Ibid., pp. 43–4, 61.

NOTES

71 Burkova, *Dal'nevostochnaya*, who states that 80 percent of railway cor destroyed by the Boxers. Other sources place the damage at about 66 perce
72 Meakin, *A Ribbon of Iron*, pp. 185–6.
73 John Foster Fraser, *The Real Siberia*, Cassell, London, April 1902, ch. 15. subsequently demoted and sent to a minor post near Archangel.
74 Asakawa, *The Russo-Japanese Conflict*, p. 87.
75 Storry, *A History of Modern Japan*, pp. 139–40.
76 'Assassin's Bomb Kills Tsar's Chief Minister in St Petersburg', *New York Tribune*, 29 July 1904. To add insult to injury, a mob stoned the Minister of Justice as he made his way through the city to inform the emperor of von Plehve's killing.
77 Pearlstein, *Revolution in Russia!*, p. 82.
78 Digby, *Tigers, Gold and Witch-Doctors*, p. 86.
79 Ibid., p. 87.
80 Deacon, *Kempei Tai*, pp. 72–9.
81 Digby, *Tigers, Gold and Witch-Doctors*, p. 88.
82 Storry, *A History of Modern Japan*, pp. 141–2.
83 Ibid., p. 143.
84 Ibid., p. 144. The alleged assassin, An Joong-Gun, was a 31-year-old schoolteacher from Korea's Hwang-Hae province who had taken up arms against the Japanese well before Ito's killing.
85 Pearlstein, *Revolution in Russia*, pp. 57–8.
86 Alan Woods, *Bolshevism: The Road to Revolution*, Wellred Books, London, n.d. Woods notes that among the political prisoners freed were a number of mutinous Black Sea sailors.
87 Nadezhda K. Krupskaya, *Reminiscences of Lenin*, International Publishers, New York, 1970. Kurnatovsky was a graduate of Zurich University and had worked in a sugar refinery near Minusinsk before his revolutionary career.
88 S. Savin and G. Tarasov, *Za Baikalom*, Izdatyelstvo Sovyetskaya Rossiya, Moscow, 1963, p. 185.
89 Though Kurnatovsky was sentenced to death, he was 'taken by train to see the revolutionaries shot', then his sentence was surprisingly relaxed to exile-for-life at Nerchinsk. He escaped exile in 1906, and wandered to Japan, Australia and France before his death in 1912. Meller-Zakomelsky was a staunch monarchist and tsarist troubleshooter – called a 'hangman' by Trotsky – who put down the *Potemkin* mutiny and served as Governor-General of the restless Baltics after 1905. Rennenkampf was a cavalry commander during the Boxer Rebellion who retook Tsitsihar and Kirin, but was criticized for poor leadership in northeast Korea during the Russo-Japanese War. He was executed by the Bolsheviks in 1918.
90 Tim Severin, *In Search of Genghis Khan*, Atheneum, New York, 1992, pp. 192–4. Mongolia's arid climate and large population of marmots and other burrowing rodents provide ideal conditions for incubating the plague. The 'Black Death' that harvested an estimated 25 million Europeans was launched into the West by the Kipchak khan's army in 1347, when his catapults flung infected corpses into the besieged Black Sea city of Kaffa.
91 Brian Lafferty, 'Going Back to the Future in Tibet', *Columbia East Asian Review*, Spring 1998.
92 'China turns Battlefield into Tourist Resort', *People's Daily* (Beijing), 9 May 2001.
93 Younghusband overreached his orders in 1904 and originally coerced the intimidated Tibetans into signing a document that gave Britain colonial powers, to the great consternation of ministers in Beijing, St Petersburg and even London. A 1906 agreement toned down Younghusband's faux pas.
94 ASMPR, *Information Mongolia*, pp. 114–17. One silver lan equalled two US dollars.
95 Ibid.
96 'History of the Temple of Kalachakra', St Petersburg Temple of Kalachakra, 2000. Ukhtomsky was an orientalist, publisher of the *St Petersburg News*, and close personal friend of Tsar Nicholas II who published a three-volume album of his 1890–1891 Siberian journey with the Tsarevich.

97 The temple's August 1915 consecration was attended by representatives of King Rama VI Vajiravudh of Siam and of Mongolia's Khutuktu. Agvan Dorzhiev performed the invocation and benediction ceremony. The temple was looted in 1919, but remained open until Stalin's antireligious campaign. Dorzhiev died in a prison hospital in Ulan Ude on 29 January 1938. The temple reopened in 1990.
 98 Robert L. Worden and Andrea Matles Savada (Eds), *Mongolia: A Country Study*, Federal Research Division, Library of Congress, Washington, DC, 1989. The 1911 delegation was headed by Ching Wang Handdorj. Urga was also referred to as Yihe Huree.
 99 ASMPR, *Information Mongolia*, p. 117. Jebtsundamba Khutuktu is referred to as Bogd Gegeen, 'head of the Lamaist religion'.
100 Charles R. Bawden, *The Modern History of Mongolia*, Weidenfeld & Nicolson, London, 1968, pp. 146–7.
101 ASMPR, *Information Mongolia*, p. 116.
102 Deacon, *Kempei Tai*, p. 89.
103 Ibid., p. 104. Kawashima was 'an excellent linguist...and [former] chief of police in the Japanese section of Peking'.
104 Ibid., pp. 102 and 107.
105 ASMPR, *Information Mongolia*, p. 118.
106 Don Croner, 'Avenger Lama: The Life and Death of Dambijantsan', Ulaan Baatar, n.d.; and Ferdinand Ossendowski, *Beasts, Men and Gods*, E.F. Dutton & Co., New York, 1922, pp. 118–21. Ossendowski states that Hun Baldon liberated Kobdo (Khovd), then moved on to capture Uliastai. Warden and Savala state that Uliastai fell in 'early 1912' and Khovd in August.
107 Worden and Savada, *Mongolia*.
108 Worden and Savada, *Mongolia*.
109 Pradyumna P. Karan, *The Changing Face of Tibet*, University Press of Kentucky, Lexington, KY, 1976, pp. 87–8. The Tibetan–Mongolian treaty was signed at Urga in January 1913. Relations between Mongolian princedoms and the tsarist government had existed since an exchange of embassies in 1608.
110 US Senate Committee on Education and Labor, *Deportation of Gregorie Semenoff: Hearings Relative to the Deporting of Undesirable Aliens, April 12–18, 1922*, Government Printing Office, Washington, DC, 1922 (reprint by Beamur International Hong Kong, 1972), pp. 57ff. Semenov's US visa application, which contained his physical description, was read aloud at the Senate hearings.
111 *Deyatelnost' Osobago Man'chshurskago Otryada, Atamana Semenova*, Tip. Kharbininsatsusho, Harbin, 1919, p. 6 (hereafter cited to as *Deyatelnost'*); B. Borisov, *Dalnii Vostok*, Izdaniye Novoi Rossii, Vienna, 1921, p. 34; B.M. Shereshevskii, *Razgrom Semenovshchiny*, USSR Academy of Science, Siberian Division, Novosibirsk State University, Science Publishing House, Novosibirsk, 1966, p. 13; *Pravda Buryatii*, 'Velikii Knyaz Mongolii, Kavaler Ordena Proroka Magomeda', 25 July 1992, p. 3 (hereafter referred to as 'Velikii Knyaz Mongolii'), courtesy of Dr Chingis Andreev.
112 Vadim Sotskov, 'General i Ataman: Sud'ba generala Semenova po materialam Tsentralnogo Arkhiva FSB', *Zavtra* (Moscow), 2, 371, 1 September 2001. Sotskov was allowed access to the 29 volumes of information about Semenov in the central archives of Russia's *Federal'naya Sluzhba Bezopasti* (FSB).
113 Borisov, *Dalnii Vostok*, pp. 34–5, and David John Footman, 'Ataman Semenov', *St Antony's Papers on Soviet Affairs*, St Antony's College, Oxford, February 1955, p. 1. Footman (1914–83) was a British foreign service officer in the Balkans during the 1920s (e.g. Vice Consul at Skopje, Macedonia in 1925), chief of MI6's political section for central Europe during the Second World War, fellow of St Antony's College, Oxford (1953–63) and author of several books on modern Russian history.
114 Sotskov, *General i Ataman*. C.H. McCormick Brothers was an early innovator and international marketer of farm machinery and merged with the Deering Harvester Company in 1902 to become International Harvester Company.
115 Semenov, G.M., *O Sebe*, Harbin, 1938; Izdatyelstvo AST, Moscow, reprinted 2002, p. 66.

NOTES

116 Semenov, *O Sebe*, pp. 10–11; Borisov, *Dalnii Vostok*, pp. 33–7; Footman, 'Ataman Semenov', p. 1.
117 Borisov, *Dalnii Vostok*, pp. 34–5.
118 Orenburg was the venue for Kazakh nationalist congresses in April, July and December 1917.
119 Semenov, *O Sebe*, pp. 13–16, and Footman, 'Ataman Semenov', p. 2.
120 Semenov, *O Sebe*, p. 17.
121 *Deyatelnost'*, p. 6.
122 Footman, 'Ataman Semenov', p. 2.
123 Longworth, *The Cossacks*, p. 263.
124 Benkendorff, pp. 14–16.
125 Semenov, *O Sebe*, pp. 17–18. Borisov, *Dalnii Vostok*, p. 36. Although Chinese, Mongolian, Manchurian and Japanese languages were taught in the Irkutsk public school, linguists of Asiatic languages were few, particularly among military men. Sotskov writes that Semenov also translated Pushkin, Lermontov and the works of other Russian literary luminaries for the Bogdo Gegen.
126 Semenov, *O Sebe*, p. 19 and James William Morley, *The Japanese Thrust into Siberia, 1918*, Columbia University Press, New York, 1954, p. 43.
127 Semenov refers to the area as Maimachen in his memoirs, which causes confusion with the distant Tea Road emporium across the border from Kyakhta.
128 Semenov, *O Sebe*, pp. 19–20.
129 Ibid., pp. 17 and 21–2 and Borisov, *Dalnii Vostok*, p. 36. Keller became commander of the Astrakhan Cossack Brigade in the world war. Ossendowski's *Beasts, Men and Gods* describes the Mongolian post relay system on pp. 110–11.
130 *Deyatelnost'*, p. 7.
131 Semenov, *O Sebe*, pp. 25–7, Morley, *The Japanese Thrust into Siberia*, p. 43; Footman, 'Ataman Semenov', p. 3; and 'Semenoff, Freed, Called Bigamist', *New York Times*, 20 April 1922, pp. 1 and 2. Semenov describes his artillery unit as the 2nd Transbaikal Battery. Footman alleges that Semenov jumped from one assignment to another because he was falling foul of superior officers and getting bounced from unit to unit, however, that does not seem to have been the case. Semenov's commander at Grodekovo, Major General Perfil'ev, was a longtime family friend. Some sources state that Semenov fathered two children before the Great War.
132 Semenov, *O Sebe*, pp. 27–30; and US Senate Committee on Education and Labor, *Deportation of Gregorie Semenoff*, p. 60. Semenov claimed that, at the start of the Great War, his wife was 'in south Russia... in the province of Shironskii'.
133 Novo Georgievsk was originally constructed in the 1830s to solidify Russia's hold on Poland, and constantly strengthened over the years. It is still in use today.
134 Semenov, *O Sebe*.
135 Semenov, *O Sebe* and Borisov, *Dalnii Vostok*, p. 36. Semenov names the place of his first action as Sakhotsin, near the 'city of Pekhanov'. The overrun of the Bavarian outpost occurred near Mlave, Poland.
136 Borisov, *Dalnii Vostok*, pp. 36–7. Borisov identified the pass as lying 'over the Zhupani valley' and the attacking unit as the 9th Bavarian Division, but no such unit appears on the orders of battle. The unit may have been the 9th Bavarian Infantry Regiment.
137 Petr N. Vrangel, *The Memoirs of General Wrangel*, Duffield, New York, 1930, p. 6.
138 Ossendowski, *Beasts, Men and Gods*, pp. 238–40; and Henry Baerlein, *The March of the Seventy Thousand*, Leonard Passons, London, 1926, p. 263. Baerlein wrote that this exiled pirate lured ships to their destruction with false lights on the 'island of Dagen', which seems to have been the handiwork of Baron Peter Ungern, not Count O.R.L. von Ungern-Shternberg (1744–1811).
139 Stanislav Vital'evich Khatuntsev, 'Ungern fon Shternberg: Buddist s Mechom', Voronezh State University, Historical Faculty, 2003.
140 Vrangel, *Memoirs of General Wrangel*, pp. 6–7.
141 Khatuntsev, 'Ungem for Shternberg', p. 2.

142 Ossendowski, *Beasts, Men and Gods*, pp. 245–6.
143 Vrangel, *Memoirs of General Wrangel*, pp. 6–7.
144 Morley, *The Japanese Thrust into Siberia*, p. 43.
145 The first echelon (troop train) of the British expeditionary force, the 16th Infantry Brigade and two Indian mountain batteries under Brigadier-General Delamain, landed at Fao in early November 1914.
146 Viscount Bryce, *The Treatment of Armenians in the Ottoman Empire 1915–16: Documents presented to Viscount Grey of Fallodon, Secretary of State for Foreign Affairs*, Sir Joseph Causton & Sons, Eastcheap, 1916, ch. 6; Bryce's book contains several lengthy first-hand descriptions of the barbarous jihad around Lake Urmia. Fourteen thousand sympathizers and refugees tried to follow the Russian retreat in January 1915. A letter dated 20 May 1915 from Mrs J.P. Cochran in Urmia to friends in the United States mentions the Russian arms and conscription in Christian communities.
147 E.W. McDowell, letter dated 6 March 1916 from Urmia Mission Station, Salmas. This is one of a number of letters reproduced by Bryce that describes helpful Kurds during the genocide and Ottoman government threats against them.
148 Rugo A. Mueller, letter dated 20 August 1915 from Tabriz, reproduced in Bryce's book.
149 See Ronald Millar, *Death of an Army: The Siege of Kut, 1915–1916*. Boston, MA, Houghton Mifflin, 1970. Some 2,070 British and approximately 6,000 Indian troops surrendered at Kut.
150 Gulpashan was one of the last Urmia villages attacked. Bryce records accounts of the initial attack on 1 February 1915, when the 51 elders were killed, another assault that killed 45 men one night, and the mass execution of '79 men and boys [who] were tied hand to hand, taken to a hill outside the village and shot'. Wives and daughters 'were distributed among the Turks, Kurds and Persian Mohammedans', according to Dr Jacob Sargis, an American medical missionary who worked in Gulpashan.
151 Footman, 'Ataman Semenov', pp. 4–5.
152 Maurice Paléologue, *An Ambassador's Memoirs*, vol. 3, ch. 10, 6 April 1917 entry. 'While the troops at the front are melting away at an increasing rate, as the result of socialist propaganda, the little army which is fighting under the orders of General Baratov on the borders of Kurdistan is valiantly persevering in its stiff task. After occupying Kirmanshah and Kizilraba, it has just entered Mesopotamia and effected its junction with the English to the north-east of Bagdad.'
153 Geoffrey Jukes, *Carpathian Disaster: Death of an Army*, Ballantine Books, New York, 1971, pp. 91, 144, 159.
154 Leon Trotsky, '*The History of the Russian Revolution*,' vol. 1, ch. 7, Sphere Books, London, 1967. The February Revolution occurred on the old (Julian) calendar dates of 23–27 February, 8–12 March on the new (Gregorian) calendar instituted by the Bolsheviks in late 1917.
155 Kerensky subsequently endorsed Military Order Number 1 in his 22 May 'Declaration of Soldiers' Rights'.
156 Jukes, *Carpathian Disaster*, p. 155. Jukes declares that more than 2 million men deserted during the months of March and April 1917.
157 Semenov, *O Sebe*, pp. 70–1.
158 Footman, 'Ataman Semenov', p. 4.
159 Borisov, *Dalnii Vostok*, p. 37.
160 Jukes, *Carpathian Disaster*, p. 155. The January 1914 order of battle did include two Caucasian and six Turkestan rifle brigades (David Woodward, *Armies of the World 1854–1914*, G.P. Putnam's Sons, New York, 1978, p. 75).
161 Robert N. North, *Transport in Western Siberia: Tsarist and Soviet Development*, University of British Columbia Press/Centre for Transportation Studies, Vancouver, n.d., p. 104.
162 Semenov, *O Sebe*, pp. 76–9.
163 Borisov, *Dalnii Vostok*, pp. 40–1 and Morley, *The Japanese Thrust into Siberia*, p. 44. Morley identifies the committee as the General Staff's All-Russian Revolutionary Committee for Forming a Volunteer Army.

NOTES

164 Bruce Lincoln, *Red Victory: A History of the Russian Civil War 1918–1921*, Da Capo, New York, 1989, pp. 54–5.
165 Semenov, *O Sebe*, p. 81.
166 'Velikii Knyaz Mongolii', p. 3; Footman, 'Ataman Semenov', p. 5 and Morley, *The Japanese Thrust into Siberia*, p. 44. Footman and Soviet writers suggest that Semenov actually met Kerensky, but Semenov does not mention any such meeting.
167 Borisov, *Dalnii Vostok*, p. 38.
168 Semenov, *O Sebe*, pp. 76–7.
169 The Russian Army lost 170,000 men killed and 213,000 captured in the July offensive.
170 In Vladivostok in May, 1918, American YMCA Secretary Edward Heald wrote, 'The Russian soldiers are scarce around here, and what few there are don't salute.' *Witness to Revolution: Letters From Russia 1916–1919*, Kent State University Press, OH, 1972 (ed. by James Sidney).
171 Semenov, *O Sebe*, pp. 90–1.
172 V. Aprelkov, 'Zabaikal'skoe kazach'e voisko', *Ekstra*, Chita, No. 79, 25 July 2001.
173 Semenov, *O Sebe*, pp. 92–3.
174 Aprelkov, 'Zabaikal'skoe kazach'e voisko'.
175 US Senate Committee on Education and Labour, *Deportation of Gregorie Semenoff*, p. 60.
176 Letter from W.H. Blaine to US Consul, Vladivostok, 3 June 1919 (MID 1766-1107).
177 Verkhne-Udinsk Report, 11 May 1919, 1st Lieutenant Ralph L. Baggs, US 27th Infantry Regt, USAT Sherman (RG395, File 095, Box 29).
178 Major General William Sidney Graves, *America's Siberian Adventure 1918–1920*, Jonathan Cape & Harrison Smith, New York, 1971 (reprint), p. 212.
179 Jonathan D. Smele, *Civil War in Siberia: The Anti-Bolshevik Government of Admiral Kolchak, 1918–1920*, Cambridge University Press, Cambridge, 1996, p. 19.
180 Since mid-April, 1917, buying or selling land was forbidden, and landed estates, monasteries and private monopoly property had been confiscated. However, Siberia's Socialist-Revolutionaries had not attempted to appropriate small businesses, or even large family farms and factories.
181 Peter Fleming, *The Fate of Admiral Kolchak*, Harcourt, Brace & World, New York, 1963, p. 145.
182 Semenov, *O Sebe*, pp. 96–8. Semenov recalled the names of the Buryat nationalist leaders: 'Rynchino, Vampilon, Dr. Tsibiktarov, Professor Tsybikov, Tsampilun and others'.
183 V.I. Vasilevskii, *Ataman Semenov, Voprosy gosudarstvennogo stroitel'stva: Sbornik dokumentov i materialov*, Knizhnoe Izdatel'stvo Poisk, Chita, 2002, p. 120.
184 Semenov, *O Sebe*, p. 99.
185 Footman, 'Ataman Semenov', p. 6.
186 Russell E. Snow, *The Bolsheviks in Siberia 1917–1918*, Fairleigh Dickinson University Press, Madison, NJ, 1977, pp. 87 and 216.
187 Morley, *The Japanese Thrust into Siberia*, p. 44.
188 Paul Dotsenko, *The Struggle for Democracy in Siberia 1917–1920*, Hoover Institution Press, Stanford, CA, 1983, p. 13. The Red Army was not formally established by SOVNARKOM (the Council of People's Commissars) until 23 February 1918.
189 Nikolai Egorovich Dvornichenko, *Putyevodityel' po Chitye*, Vostochno-Sibirskoye Knizhnoye Izd-vo, Irkutsk, 1981, pp. 121–2.
190 Andrei Bukin, 'Sokol-Nomokonov V.M.', Project ZAO-EKT, Chita, 2002.
191 'Proclamation issued by Ataman Kalmykov in Grodekovo District', July 1918, Enclosure No. 3 to Barrows report XV, July 1981.
192 Dotsenko, *The Struggle for Democracy*, p. 14.
193 Snow, *The Bolsheviks in Siberia*, p. 215.
194 Dotsenko, *The Struggle for Democracy*, p. 16.
195 Semenov, *O Sebe*, p. 103. Semenov marked the 'official inception' of the Mongol–Buryat Regiment as 15 November (*Deyatelnost'*, p. 9).
196 Ibid., p. 104; Borisov, *Dalnii Vostok*, p. 42; and Footman, 'Ataman Semenov', p. 6.

197 A. Ya. Manusevich, M.A. Birman, A. Kh. Klevanskii and I.A. Khrenov, *Internatsionalisti: trudyashchiyesya zarubyezhnykh stran – uchastniki borbi za vlast sovietov*, Izdatyelstvo Nauka, Moscow, 1967, pp. 123–4.
198 Semenov, *O Sebe*, pp. 105–8. The telegram to Semenov from the General Staff shows how porous Bolshevik control was over a critical centralized resource like the telegraph lines more than ten days after the October Revolution.
199 Letter from F.M. Tilus (Vladivostok) to C.M. Muchnic, (American Locomotive Sales Corporation New York City), 6 January 1918.
200 Roman Dyboski, *Seven Years in Russia and Siberia (1914–1921)*, Warsaw, 1922, pp. 44–6. Krasnoshchekov was born in 1880 and died in 1937.
201 Morley, *The Japanese Thrust into Siberia*, pp. 150 and 160.
202 Letter from F.M. Tilus (Vladivostok) to C.M. Muchnic (American Locomotive Sales Corporation, New York City), 6 January 1918.
203 Manusevich *et al.*, *Internatsionalisti*, pp. 122–3. Rydzinski had been a Social Democrat since 1906.
204 M. Sergeyev, *Irkutsk: Putyevodityel*, Raduga Publishers, Moscow, 1986, pp. 24–5. The memorial plaque on the White House wall names the Bolshevik party leaders as Postyshev, Zoto, Chuzhak, Trillsser, Blumenfeld, Raikher 'and others'.
205 Ibid. Other leaders of the POW Red Guard detachments in Irkutsk were named as F. Omasta, Schwabengauzen and Shebeko.
206 Manusevich *et al.*, *Internatsionalisti*, p. 123 and Dotsenko, *The Struggle for Democracy*, p. 14.
207 G.J.A. O'Toole, *Honorable Treachery: A History of U.S. Intelligence, Espionage and Covert Action from the American Revolution to the CIA*, Atlantic Monthly Press, New York, 1991. O'Toole cites the 1.6 million POWs in writing about US intelligence agent Xenophon Kalamatiano in Petrograd, but does not cite any further source.
208 Morley, *The Japanese Thrust into Siberia*, p. 37. The majority of prisoners in the Russian Far East were Austro-Hungarians.
209 Manusevich *et al.*, *Internatsionalisti*, p. 125. The first commissar for POW affairs, M.A. Faerman, was replaced in late December 1917 by a Bolshevik, A.L. Mentsikovski.
210 Dotsenko, *The Struggle for Democracy*, pp. 16–17.
211 Morley, *The Japanese Thrust into Siberia*, p. 74.
212 Joseph Naayem, *Shall This Nation Die?*, Chaldean Rescue, New York, 1920. The commanders of the Assyro-Chaldean Army were Agha Petrus Elie and Malik Khochaba from Tiari. The Russian withdrawal was not complete until spring 1918, but military operations ceased the previous November.
213 According to Peter Fleming, 'a small but stout-hearted Russian contingent in North Persia which had refused to recognize the Brest Litovsk armistice' would remain to try to cooperate with a British Military Mission under General Dunsterville. Fleming, *The Fate of Admiral Kolchak*, p. 34.

2 REVOLUTION AND RED TERROR: NOVEMBER 1917–MAY 1918

1 Anton Yur'ev, '*Chto prines "veter peremen"?*', Zabaikal'skii Rabochii, Chita, No. 242 (23524), 2001.
2 Semenov, *O Sebe*, pp. 108–11; Footman, 'Ataman Semenov', p. 7 and Morley, *The Japanese Thrust into Siberia*, p. 45.
3 Stanislav Vital'evich Khatuntsev, 'Ungern fon Shternberg: Buddist s Mechom', Voronezh State University, Historical Faculty, 2003. Ungern allegedly assaulted the aide de camp when he was refused an apartment.
4 Footman, 'Ataman Semenov', p. 7.
5 Semenov, *O Sebe*, pp. 112–13. According to Semenov, Berezovskii survived the civil war to become a missionary in northern China.
6 Ibid., p. 114.

NOTES

7 Semenov, *O Sebe*, pp. 110–12, Footman, 'Ataman Semenov', p. 7 and Morley, *The Japanese Thrust into Siberia*, pp. 45 and 86. Footman transcribes the Turk's name as Elhadin; Morley writes it as Alhadin.
8 Semenov, *O Sebe*, p. 111.
9 Ibid., p. 114.
10 Kainichi Asakawa, *The Russo-Japanese Conflict: Its Causes and Issues*, Irish Academic Press, Dublin, 1972, pp. 88–99.
11 Joseph L. Wieczynski (ed.), *The Modern Encyclopedia of Russian and Soviet History*, Academic International Press, Gulf Breeze, FL, 1990, vol. 7, pp. 50–1.
12 R.K.I. Quested, *Sino-Russian Relations: A Short History*, George Allen & Unwin, Sydney, 1984, pp. 86–9.
13 Nadezhda E. Ablova, 'Politicheskaya Situatsia na K.B.Zh.D. nosle Krusheniya Rossiiskoi Imperii', *Belorusski Zhurnal*, 98, 4, Minsk. Riutin had been a Menshevik until July 1917, when he organized a Bolshevik committee in Harbin.
14 Ye. Kh. Nilus (ed.), *Istorícheskii Obzor' – Kitaiskii Vostochnii Zheleznoi Dorogi 1896–1923*, Tipografii Kit. Vost. Zhel. Dor. & T-va Ozo, Harbin, 1923, pp. 523–4 and Morley, *The Japanese Thurst into Siberia*, pp. 46–7. A Japanese source placed the number of rebellious railway guards at only two companies: the 559th and the 618th. Ayakawa Takeharu, *Waga Tairiku Keiei Shippai no Shinso*, Heisho Suppansha, Tokyo, 1935, pp. 586–7.
15 Semenov, *O Sebe*, p. 115; Footman, 'Ataman Semenov', p. 7 and Morley, *The Japanese Thrust into Siberia*, p. 46.
16 Vladimir N. Brovkin (ed.), *The Bolsheviks in Russian Society: The Revolution and the Civil Wars*, Yale University Press, New Haven, CT, 1997.
17 Semenov, *O Sebe*, p. 115.
18 Heald, *Witness to Revolution*, pp. 345 and 347.
19 Semenov, *O Sebe*, pp. 115–16.
20 Ibid., pp. 117 and 120.
21 Ibid., pp. 117–18.
22 Ibid., pp. 118–19.
23 Ibid., pp. 120–1. Semenov regarded 19 December as the official birthdate of his movement (Vasilevskii, *Ataman Semenov*, 'Telegramma atamana Semenova generaly Khorvatu', Chita, 26 May 1919), p. 22.
24 Semenov, *O Sebe*, pp. 120–3.
25 Ibid., pp. 119 and 122.
26 Semenov, *O Sebe*, pp. 122–3. Sotskov names the escort of the 37-car prisoner train as Master Sergeant Shuvalov, 'General i Ataman'.
27 Morley, *The Japanese Thrust into Siberia*, pp. 46–7 and Footman, 'Ataman Semenov', p. 8. Footman erroneously states that Semenov arrived in Manchuli on 20 December.
28 Nilus, *Istorícheskii Obzor'* pp. 523–4.
29 Letter from F.M. Tilus (Vladivostok) to C.M. Muchnic (New York City) dated 6 January 1918.
30 Quested, *Sino-Russian Relations*, p. 92.
31 Wieczynski, *Encyclopedia*, vol. 7, pp. 50–1.
32 Nicolas Ventugol, '*Les officiers à titre Etrangers*', n.d. General Khreshchatitskii left Semenov several months later to join the staff of Admiral Kolchak's Army of the Provisional Siberian Government in Omsk, but would return to the ataman's service in late 1919.
33 Semenov, *O Sebe*, pp. 67–77, and Footman, 'Ataman Semenov', pp. 9 and 13.
34 Snow, *The Bolsheviks in Siberia*, p. 218.
35 Vasilevskii, *Ataman Semenov*, p. 6.
36 Many different dates have been cited for the starting date of Semenov's 'offensive'. The earliest: R.E. Snow writes that Semenov was joined by officers forced out of Irkutsk after the anti-Bolshevik uprising there failed in mid-December and that they began 'raids into Transbaikalia' in late December 1917 (Snow, *The Bolsheviks in Siberia*, p. 216). The latest: N.E. Dvornichenko states that Semenov 'occupied the railway stations of Matsiyevskaya,

Sharasun and Dauria' with 600 men on 29 January (Dvornichenko, *Putyevodityel' po Chitye*, p. 31).
37 Semenov, *O Sebe*, pp. 123–6; Morley, *The Japanese Thrust into Siberia*, p. 46 and Footman, 'Ataman Semenov', p. 8. It is unclear whether they were beaten or executed, but one way or another the members of the Manchuli soviet rolled into Chita in early January. A Soviet account describes 'their *bodies* arriving in sealed railway cars in Chita' on 3 January.
38 Footman, 'Ataman Semenov', p. 13.
39 *Deyatelnost'*, p. 12.
40 Fleming, *The Fate of Admiral Kolchak*, p. 48.
41 Vasilevskii, *Ataman Semenov*, p. 7.
42 *Deyatelnost'*, p. 11.
43 Report dated 9 May 1918, 'Memorandum for General Evans: Advance of Ataman Semenoff's Forces, April 20th to May 5th', Peking, MID File 2070-505 (RG395).
44 Morley, *The Japanese Thrust into Siberia*, p. 76 and Footman, 'Ataman Semenov', p. 14. Morley says OMO captured 175 rifles at Olovyannaya, Footman says 236.
45 Snow, *The Bolsheviks in Siberia*, p. 217, Dvornichenko, *Putyevodityel' po Chitye*, p. 30, and Footman, 'Ataman Semenov', p. 14.
46 Morley, *The Japanese Thrust into Siberia*, p. 77, citing Soviet memoirs and archival documents.
47 Oliver Henry Radkey, *The Election to the Russian Constituent Assembly of 1917*, Harvard University Press, Cambridge, MA, 1950, Appendix pp. 77–80.
48 Bruce Lincoln, *Red Victory: A History of the Russian Civil War 1918–1921*, Da Capo Press, New York, 1989, pp. 121–3.
49 Translation of 'Semienoff and the Special Manchurian Detachment', *Primorskaya Zhizn*, 10 November 1918, No. 54, AEFS intelligence office, Vladivostok (RG395, File 095 Semenoff, Box 29).
50 Semenov, *O Sebe*, p. 132.
51 Ibid., pp. 132–3. Semenov named his old acquaintance in the Kharachen camp as Talama.
52 Ibid., pp. 133–6.
53 Ibid., pp. 136–8.
54 Ibid. and Footman,'Ataman Semenov' p. 9.
55 Snow, *The Bolsheviks in Siberia*, pp. 220–1. CHEKA was the Soviet acronym for *Vse-Rossiiskaya Chrezvichainaya Komissiya po Bor'be s Kontr-revolutsiei i Sabotazhem*, the All-Russian Extraordinary Commission for Combating Counter-Revolution and Sabotage, predecessor of the Soviet KGB and the modern Russian Ministry of Security, officially created on 20 December 1917, and placed under Feliks Edmundovich Dzerzhinsky, who established his headquarters in the building of the All-Russian Insurance Company on Moscow's Lubyanka Square. Presumably the units Lenin ordered to Siberia to expedite grain shipments were 'functional CHEKAs' formed to oversee transport and communication (John Barron, KGB: The Secret Work of Soviet Secret Agents, Bantam Book, New York, 1974, pp. 457–8).
56 John J. Dziak, *Chekisty: A History of the KGB*, Lexington Books, Lexington, MA, 1988, p. 28. Dzerzhinsky's statement 'We stand for organized terror' was published in an interview by newspaper *Novaya Zhizn* on 14 July 1918.
57 Dotsenko, *The Struggle for Democracy*, pp. 76–7.
58 Tamara Komissarova, 'A Library Legend', *We/Myi – The Women's Dialogue*, 4, 20, 1999.
59 David E. Powell, *Antireligious Propaganda in the Soviet Union*, MIT Press, Cambridge, MA, London, 1975, pp. 24–6. Patriarch Tikhon died on 7 April 1925, allegedly from poison administered by a *chekist* doctor.
60 Vasilevskii, *Ataman Semenov*, p. 8. Semenov mentioned the January telegram in his telegram dated 10 September 1918 to the government of autonomous Siberia.
61 Snow, *The Bolsheviks in Siberia*, pp. 214 and 226; Dotsenko, *The Struggle for Democracy*, p. 22.
62 Smele, *Civil War in Siberia*, p. 20. Novonikolaevsk is present-day Novosibirsk.

63 Semion Lyandres and Dietmar Wulff (eds), *A Chronicle of the Civil War in Siberia and Exile in China: The Diaries of Petr Vasil'evich Vologodskii, 1918–1925*, Hoover Institution Press, Stanford, CA, 2002, p. 19.
64 *Deyatelnost' Osobago Mančhshurskago otryada, Atamana semenova*, Tip. Kharbininsatsu-sho, Harbin, 1919, pp. 19–20. The PGAS cells were known as *Voennye Organizatsii*, Military Organizations.
65 Fleming, *The Fate of Admiral Kolchak*, p. 49.
66 Morley, *The Japanese Thrust into Siberia*, p. 80.
67 On 10 November 1917 all but two ranks were abolished in the army: *Krasnoarmeyets* – Red Army Man, and *Krasny Komandir (KrasKom)* – Red Commander.
68 Dotsenko, *The Struggle for Democracy*, p. 17 and 'Velikii Knyaz Mongolii'. Dotsenko and Morley give the date as 16 February, and *Pravda Buryatii* cites 26 February.
69 Dvornichenko, *Putyevodityel' po Chitye*, p. 31.
70 Andrei G. Bukin, 'Ivan Afanasevich Butin', Project ZAO-EKT, Chita, 2002.
71 US Senate Committee on Education and Labor, *Deportation of Gregorie Semenoff*, pp. 80–1.
72 Dziak, *Chekisty*, p. 28, and US Senate Committee on Education and Labour, *Deportation of Gregorie Semenoff*, pp. 80–1.
73 Colonel John Ward, *With the 'Die-Hards' in Siberia*, Cassell, London, 1920, p. 85.
74 Intelligence Summary No. 15, AEFS intelligence section (RG395, File 095 Semenoff, Box 29) 27 September 1918.
75 Vladimir Ilyich Lenin, *Collected Works*, vol. 28, Progress Publishers, Moscow, 1965, pp. 53–7. Lenin spewed this inflammatory entymological denigration in his August 1918 work 'Comrade Workers, Forward To The Last, Decisive Fight!'
76 *Pravda Buryatii*, 'Velikii Knyaz Mongolii'.
77 Vasilevskii, *Ataman Semenov*, p. 7. From Manchuli in January 1918, Semenov published a 'Proclamation to the Population of Transbaikal Province Explaining the Purpose of Our Struggle' which referred to traitors 'in service of Germany and the self-seeking interests of the flag of the International'.
78 Vladimir I. Shishkin, 'State Administration of Siberia from the End of the Nineteenth Through the First Third of the Twentieth Century', Proceedings of Summer 1998 Symposium: *Regions: A Prism to View the Slavic-Eurasian World*, Slavic Research Center, Hokkaido University, Sapporo, 2000, pp. 108–9.
79 Dvornichenko, *Putyevodityel' po Chitye*, p. 32.
80 Petr Ivanovich Naletov, 'Pedagogicheskoi Eksperiment: Vospominaniya Uchastnika Splava 1923 goda', Irkutsk, 1985. Naletov met Lazo in Chita in September 1918.
81 Snow, *The Bolsheviks in Siberia*, p. 225.
82 Dvornichenko, *Putyevodityel' po Chitye*, p. 32; Dotsenko, *The Struggle for Democracy*, p. 17; Morley, *The Japanese Thrust into Siberia*, p. 196; Manusevich et al., *Internatsionalisti*, p. 124; B.M. Shereshevskii, *Razgrom Semenovshchiny*, USSR Academy of Science, Siberian Division, Novosibirsk State University, Science Publishing House, Novosibirsk, 1966, p. 15; and Fleming, *The Fate of Admiral Kolchak*, p. 48.
83 *Deyatelnost'*, pp. 27–9.
84 Morley, *The Japanese Thrust into Siberia*, p. 111.
85 Ibid., pp. 111 and 180.
86 Vrangel, *The Memoirs of General Wrangel*.
87 Footman, 'Ataman Semenov', p. 16. 'When it [Semenov's army] was first formed... it represented a small partisan division unsupported by anyone', stated a report by the American Expeditionary Force intelligence section, 18 October 1919.
88 Shereshevskii, *Razgoom Semenovshchimg*, p. 15, and Footman, 'Ataman Semenov', p. 15. David Footman writes that 'Ten days after launching their [OMO] offensive [21 January 1918] the OMO were back in Manchuria station' (p. 15). However, Soviet historians seem unanimous in stating that Lazo took Dauria on 1 March, the first significant victory of his campaign.
89 Dvornichenko, *Putyevodityel' po Chite*.

90 Report on Northern Manchuria in General and Harbin in Particular, Captain Harold V.V. Fay, AEFS (RG395, File 095, Box 29) 1 March 1919; and Graves, *America's Siberian Adventure*, p. 210. The Sungari at Harbin was about twice the width of the Thames at London.
91 James Mackintosh Bell, *Side Lights on the Siberian Campaign*, Ryerson Press, Toronto, 1922, p. 61.
92 Anatoli Gan Gutman, *The Destruction of Nikolaevsk-on-Amur: An Episode in the Russian Civil War in the Far East*, 1920, Limestone Press, Fairbanks, 1993, p. 69.
93 Bell, *Side Lights on the Siberian Campaign*, pp. 59–60 and 66. 'Never did I see anything described as sanitary appliances which were a more flagrant travesty on the name', declared Major Bell.
94 Alla Crone, *East Lies the Sun*, Dell, New York, 1982, pp. 238–9.
95 Amleto Vespa, *Secret Agent of Japan*, Little, Brown & Company, New York, 1938, pp. 15–18. Chang Tso-Lin is also transcribed Zhang Zuolin, among other variations.
96 Bell, *Side Lights on the Siberian Campaign*, p. 65.
97 Footman, 'Ataman Semenov', p. 20; and Fleming, *The Fate of Admiral Kolchak*, p. 68.
98 Fleming, p. 50. Peter Fleming (1907–71) was born in Britain, the son of a Member of Parliament and hero killed during the First World War. He excelled at Eton and Oxford, served as a foreign correspondent for *The Times* and British intelligence, married renowned actress Celia Johnson, and was a prolific writer and historian, eventually overshadowed by his younger novelist brother, Ian. Peter Fleming was called 'the epitome of the enlightened English gentleman adventurer and explorer'.
99 Bell, *Side Lights on the Siberian Campaign*, pp. 57–8.
100 Richard Luckett, *The White Generals*, Viking Press, New York, 1971, p. 212.
101 Footman, 'Ataman Semenov', p. 16 (citing from Baron Budberg's *Dnevnik Byelogvardeista*, Leningrad Priboi, Leningrad, 1929).
102 Bell, *Side Lights on the Siberian Campaign*, p. 61.
103 Ibid., p. 59.
104 Neville Hilditch, *Battle Sketches 1914–1915*, Clarendon Press, Oxford, 1915.
105 Roy Alexander, *The Cruise of the Raider Wolf*, Yale University Press, New Haven, CT, 1939, pp. 182–7 and 268. The *Hitachi Maru*, bound for London from Yokohama, was not sunk until 7 November 1917. Alexander, a prisoner on the *Wolf*, says that up to 30 Japanese seamen died during their ship's capture.
106 Juergen Schmidt, 'The Diversionary Operation of a German Military Attaché in China in 1915', *Arbeitskreis Geschichte der Nachrichtendienste e. V. Newsletter*, 7, 2, Winter 1999, pp. 25–7. Shadrin and Berkovitz were each awarded 'a silver medal attached to the Stanislaus Ribbon' and a 200–300 ruble reward.
107 China sent labor units to Europe and the Middle East, revoked the Central Powers' extraterritoriality and Boxer Rebellion indemnity payments and revoked their concessions at Tientsin and Hankow. The Allies postponed Boxer payments due to them for five years.
108 US Ambassador to Russia, David Rowland Francis, wrote to Secretary of State Lansing from Vologda, '[German Ambassdor] Mirbach is dominating Soviet government and is practically dictator in Moscow.' 2 May 1918, letter (telegram), State Dept. File No. 861.00/1955.
109 Morley, *The Japanese Thrust into Siberia*, p. 277. Oshima's estimate was stated in a 16 July 1918 meeting of Japan's high level Advisory Council on Foreign Relations.
110 Leon Trotsky, 'Order Concerning Prisoners of War', *Izvestia*, 21 April 1918. On the other hand, Japanese and Allied intelligence may have underestimated the number of POWs in Siberia, which Soviet sources state in January 1917 as (by region) 199,000 in Omsk, 136,000 in Irkutsk, and 47,000 in Priamur (Manusevich *et al*., *Internatsionalisti*, p. 16). Red Cross figures obtained by the British Foreign Office indicate that there were still 161,000 POWs in Siberian camps in 1919 (Smele, *Civil War in Siberia*, p. 350).
111 V.I. Lenin, 'Speech At A Meeting Of The Warsaw Revolutionary Regiment', *Vecherniye Izvesta Moskorskovo Soveto*, 15, 3 August 1918. Lenin was speaking to and lauding several thousand Polish volunteers for serving with 'Germans, Austrians and Magyars'.

NOTES

112 Jane Degras (ed.), *Soviet Documents on Foreign Policy*, Oxford University Press, New York, 1951, vol. 1, p. 137.
113 Storry, *A History of Modern Japan*, pp. 147–8, and Eva-Maria Stolberg, 'Siberia and the Russian Far East in Japanese Strategic and Economic Conceptions, 1890s–1920s', Institute of Russian History, University of Bonn. Socialist Saiwa Tokuta and 11 compatriots were executed.
114 Li Narangoa, p. 4 'Japanese Geopolitics, Manchuria and the Mongol Lands 1905–1945', Nordic Institute of Asian Studies, Copenhagen, 2001. The term 'Man-Mo' first appeared in the Japanese press in 1915 at the time of the '21 Demands' on China for special rights in eastern Inner Mongolia.
115 Quested, *Sino-Russian Relations*, p. 36.
116 Deacon, *Kempei Tai*, pp. 100, 104 and 106.
117 Ibid., p. 111.
118 Ibid., pp. 112 and 114.
119 Morley, *The Japanese Thrust into Siberia*, pp. 68, 70 and 80; and Fleming, *The Fate of Admiral Kolchak*, p. 73.
120 Deacon, *Kempei Tai*, p. 114 and Morley, *The Japanese Thrust into Siberia*, p. 69.
121 Morley, *The Japanese Thrust into Siberia*, pp. 172–3 and 189–90. Prince Kudashev agreed that a Russian government formed on Chinese soil was not proper.
122 Ibid., pp. 84, 93 and 174.
123 Ibid., p. 88. Prince Kudashev asked Chargé d'Affaires Yoshizawa Kenkichi for 30–40 machine guns, 3,000 rifles and ammunition. Colonel Tanaka Kunishige received the same request in London from the British military.
124 Sato was one of at least 24 intelligence officers in Manchuria and the Russian Far East managed by the Japanese army headquarters in Korea, Ibid., p. 68. Tanaka had served in Russia prior to the Russo-Japanese War and knew the Russian language. He became Prime Minister of Japan in 1927.
125 Ibid., pp. 91–3.
126 Ibid., pp. 88–9, 94–5 and 98.
127 'Velikii Knyaz Mongolii'.
128 Fleming, *The Fate of Admiral Kolchak*, p. 41. In addition to French colonials, 'this ludicrous proposal' would have drawn in British, American, Japanese and Chinese troops from the Peking legation guards, with a French naval officer to guide them overland across Asia.
129 Morley, *The Japanese Thrust into Siberia*, pp. 86 and 90–1 and Footman, 'Ataman Semenov', p. 17.
130 Fleming, *The Fate of Admiral Kolchak*, pp. 48–9. The British Consulate in Harbin made the actual disbursements.
131 Ibid., p. 51.
132 28 October 1918, AEFS intelligence section newspaper summary for 27 October 1918. The newspaper that described Knox's 'loan' to Semenov was cited as *Dalekaya Okraina*. The original Japanese article complained that Japan could not compete with British and French largesse.
133 Fleming, *The Fate of Admiral Kolchak*, p. 50; Footman, 'Ataman Semenov', p. 17 and Morley, *The Japanese Thrust into Siberia*, p. 99. Footman cites an unpublished manuscript by a British Colonel Stevens regarding the gift of howitzers.
134 Footman, 'Ataman Semenov', pp. 17–18.
135 Letter from Lieutenant Colonel Barrows, AEFS Vladivostok, to AEFS intelligence officer, Harbin, 21 February 1919, and attached report, 'Ataman Semenoff', by Nicholas Romanoff.
136 Deacon, *Kempei Tai*, p. 117.
137 Report No. 15 by Lieutenant Colonel David P. Barrows, US Military Attaché, Peking, 'Notes on the Situation in Manchuria and Eastern Siberia, July 1918', (RG395, File 095, Box 29) (hereafter referred to as Barrows report, 28 July 1918).
138 Morley, *The Japanese Thrust into Siberia*, pp. 180–1.
139 Ibid., p. 169. Morley cites a letter dated 26 March 1918 from Sato to Motono in which the former stated, 'It is clear from their declaration, printed in the newspapers here on

March 23, that they [Derber government] are extreme socialists, for, before the assembly meets, they would seize authority, make the land common property, and nationalize mining and industry.'
140 Barrows report, 28 July 1918.
141 Footman, 'Ataman Semenov', pp. 21 and 24; Morley, *The Japanese Thrust into Siberia*, p. 174. Orlov became a colonel about this time.
142 Elena Varneck and H.H. Fisher (eds), *The Testimony of Kolchak and Other Siberian Materials*, Hoover War Library Publications, No. 10, Stanford University, CA, 1935, p. 223.
143 Morley, *The Japanese Thrust into Siberia*, pp. 177–8. Kanai's statement was made on 30 April.
144 Manusevich *et al.*, *Internatsionalisti*, p. 172. The Omsk 1st Proletarian detachment arrived on 19 March and the 2nd arrived 'shortly' thereafter.
145 In recent years Shumov Palace (Ulitsa Bolshaya 84) housed the regional office of the KGB and currently shelters its successor, FSB.
146 Bukin, 'Ivan Afanasevich Butin'.
147 Morley, *The Japanese Thrust into Siberia*, pp. 155–6. Motono submitted his resignation 'due to illness' on 10 April; it was accepted on 23 April.
148 Degras, *Soviet Documents on Foreign Policy*, vol. 1, p. 137. Gutman states that the a Japanese landing party of 400–500 troops landed in Nikolaevsk-on-Amur in 'spring of 1918' and 'saved the intelligentsia from a cruel death and the entire population from ruin' (*The Destruction of Nikolaevsk-on-Amur*, p. 1). The town would not be so fortunate two years later.
149 Morley, *The Japanese Thrust into Siberia*, pp. 146–54; Francis A. March, *History of the World War: An Authentic Narrative of the World's Greatest War*, United Publishers of the US and Canada, Chicago, IL, 1919, p. 735.
150 'Reports Korniloff and Semenoff Dead', *New York Times*, 22 April 1918, p. 1:2; and Smele, *Civil War in Siberia*, p. 73.
151 Morley, *The Japanese Thrust into Siberia*, p. 178. A Japanese engineer and two technicians borrowed from the Kwantung government took over until a 9-man Japanese army communications team arrived in June.
152 Report 'Advance of Ataman Semenoff's Forces', MID File No. 2070-505, 9 May 1918.
153 Morley, *The Japanese Thrust into Siberia*, p. 198. Morley cites correspondence from Major General Saito Kijiro, Military Attache in Peking, to Army chief Baron Uehara, dated 24 April 1918. Barrows report, 28 July 1918. Barrows noted the reason for Semenov's haste and desire to keep his cadre together.
154 Fleming, *The Fate at Admiral Kolchak*, p. 52.
155 Footman, 'Ataman Semenov', p. 27, who cites Budberg, *Arkhiv Russkoi Revoliutsii*, 13, 1921, p. 226.
156 Semenov, *O Sebe*, ch. 1. Born in 1869, Budberg rose to become chief of staff of the 10th Army and a corps commander during the First World War.
157 Morley, *The Japanese Thrust into Siberia*, p. 198, and Footman, 'Ataman Semenov', pp. 21 and 24. Orlov had been rapidly promoted to colonel from the rank of captain during the past month.
158 *Deyatelnost'*, p. 19; and 9 May 1918 report 'Advance of Ataman Semenoff's Forces', MID File No. 2070-505.
159 Varneck and Fisher, *The Testimony of Kolchak*, pp. 115–16; and Footman, 'Ataman Semenov', pp. 21 and 24. Bitter feelings between OMO and the Orlov Detachment persisted throughout the civil war. Kolchak stated that the rift between Orlov and Semenov occurred 'before my arrival there [in Harbin]', although in Major Barrows' firsthand account, the American accompanied the *orlovtsy* to the Daurskii Front on 30 April and mentioned no 'serious strife'.
160 Semenov, *O Sebe*, ch. 1.
161 9 May 1918 report 'Advance of Ataman Semenoff's Forces', MID File No. 2070-505. The chief quartermaster was named as Captain 'Berinkov' (also known as Burikov) at Harbin.

NOTES

162 Barrows report, 9 May 1918, 'Memorandum for General Evans: Advance of Ataman Semenoff's Forces, April 20th to May 5th', Peking, MID File No. 2070-505 (RG165, Microfilm M1443, Roll 3) (hereafter Barrows report, 9 May 1918).
163 27 April 1918, telegram from Summers, US legation Moscow, to Secretary of State Lansing, Dept. of State File No. 861.00/1810.
164 'Reports Korniloff and Semenoff Dead', *New York Times*; and Footman, 'Ataman Semenov', p. 23.
165 Gibson Bell Smith, 'Guarding the Railway, Taming the Cossacks: The US Army in Russia, 1918–1920', *NARA Prologue*, 34, 4, Winter 2002. Smith cites Barrows report, 9 May 1918.
166 Barrows report, 9 May 1918.
167 Ibid.
168 Ibid.
169 Ibid.
170 Ibid.
171 Ibid.
172 Ibid and Morley, *The Japanese Thrust into Siberia*, pp. 193–7. Barrows says the Buryats referred to their swinging pontoon as a *ploslkot*. Morley's coherent account of 'the Onon offensive' is based upon correspondence and memoirs of the Japanese participants, Soviet histories, Budberg's *Dnevnik* and Semenov's *O Sebe*, however Morley states that Lazo blew the bridge and retreated across the Onon on 30 April.
173 Barrows report, 9 May 1918.
174 Ibid. and Semenov, *O Sebe*, ch. 1.
175 Barrows report, 9 May 1918.
176 Barrows report, 28 July 1918. Capatain Vrashtel informed Barrows of Cossack resistance to Semenov's mobilization order in the Nerchinsk-Sretensk region.
177 Varneck and Fisher, *The Testimony of Kolchak*, pp. 9–12 and 18; Luckett, *The White Generals*, p. 213; Smele, *Civil War in Siberia*, pp. 61–6; and Sotskov, *'General i Ataman'*. Kolchak was a captive of the Japanese from December 1904 until April 1905 and received the Black Sea Fleet command in June 1916.His memory placed his arrival in Harbin during 'early April'.
178 Varneck and Fisher, *The Testimony of Kolchak*, pp. 107–8.
179 Morley, *The Japanese Thrust into Siberia*, pp. 87, 191 and 198. Also, according to some sources, Semenov's emissary Zhevchenko approached Kolchak in Shanghai in December 1917.
180 Fleming, *The Fate of Admiral Kolchak*, pp. 35–6.
181 Ibid., Kolchak explained the board position:'One member of the railway board had always been appointed by the [Russian] General Staff who handled the military strategic matters pertaining to the railway and its protection' (Varneck and Fisher, *The Testimony of Kolchak*, p. 111).
182 Smele, *Civil War in Siberia*, p. 72; *Papers Relating to the Foreign Relations of the United States (FRUS)*, Government Printing Office, Washington, DC, 1918, *Russia*, vol. 2, pp. 155–6; and Morley, *The Japanese Thrust into Siberia*, pp. 87, 191 and 198. Other notable railway board appointments included former Consul General A.I. Putilov for finance and former provisional government Minister of Ways and Communications Ustrugov for technical matters.
183 Bell, *Side Lights on the Siberia Campaign*, p. 88.
184 Footman, 'Ataman Semenov', pp. 19–21.
185 Varneck and Fisher, *The Testimony of Kolchak*, p. 120.
186 Ibid., p. 110.
187 Fleming, *The Fate of Admiral Kolchak*, p. 157, citing French General Maurice Janin.
188 Brovkin, *The Bolsheviks in Russian Society*, p. 126. Historian Norman Pereira wrote, 'The magnifying factor was personality, which...assumed a disproporationate significance. In Russia's "wild east" of the civil war period, idiosyncratic whims and prejudices became historical fissures.'
189 Varneck and Fisher, *The Testimony of Kolchak*, p. 114.

190 Morley, *The Japanese Thrust into Siberia*, p. 198.
191 Varneck and Fisher, *The Testimony of Kolchak*, p. 120.
192 Letter dated 8 May 1918 from US Consul Charles Moser/Harbin to Secretary of State Lansing, US Department of State, *FRUS, 1918, Russia*, vol. 2, p. 156; 'Semenoff Sets Up Independent State', *New York Times*, 24 May 1918, p. 5:1; and Semenov, *O Sebe*, p. 109. See the appendices for the text of Semenov's proclamation.
193 Morley, *The Japanese Thrust into Siberia*, p. 194. Morley states that the earliest reference to Semenov's government in reports from Japanese army agents occurs in a letter dated 20 May from General Nakajima to Lieutenant General Tanaka Gi'ichi, vice chief of the General Staff.
194 Ibid., p. 200. Morley cited Major General Muto's donation of 100,000 rubles to destitute Buryat refugees at Manchuli as another example of 'Asia First' solidarity.
195 *Deyatelnost'*, p. 15.
196 Morley, *The Japanese Thrust into Siberia* pp. 189–91.When Kudashev returned to Peking in early May, he left two agents in Harbin, Cole and Romanov, the former to create maps and the latter to monitor Semenov, Kalmykov and 'political agitations in Harbin'.
197 Proclamation of the Temporary Government of Transbaikal Territory, May 1918.
198 Semenov, *O Sebe*, ch.1. Semenov does not state that Shilnikov was tasked with Cossack affairs, but Morley's Japanese records do.
199 Barrows report, 9 May 1918.
200 Morley, *The Japanese Thrust into Siberia*, p. 195 and Semenov, *O Sebe*, ch. 1. In his memoirs, Semenov insisted that Taube was a veteran of the German General Staff; Soviet historians say that he was Russian. Both agree that Taube had been director of communications of the Irkutsk military district staff. Prince Vasilii A. Dolgorukii, who accompanied the royal family to Yekaterinburg had a brother-in-law who was a General Baron Taube, who seems an unlikely, but not altogether impossible, candidate for Red strategist.
201 Manusevich et al., *Internatsionalisti*, pp. 169–73.
202 Morley, *The Japanese Thrust into Siberia*, p. 196. The agent, Sasaki, reported to Consul General Sato in Harbin.
203 Vasilevskii, *Ataman Semenov*, p. 121, which cites the 8 May 1918 *Dekret Tsentrosibiri ob ob'yavlenii Semenova vne zakona*, signed by *Tsentrosibir'* chairman N. Yakovlev and secretary N. Krylosov.
204 Fleming, *The Fate of Admiral Kolchak*, pp. 73–4; and Varneck and Fisher, *The Testimony of Kolchak*, pp. 120–1.
205 'Semenoff Sets Up Independent State', *New York Times*, 24 May 1918, p. 5:1.
206 Fleming, *The Fate of Admiral Kolchak* p. 74; and Varneck and Fisher, *The Tesimony of Kolchak*, p. 121.
207 Varneck and Fisher, *The Testimony of Kolchak*, pp. 121–2.
208 Ibid., pp. 9 and 120–1; and J. Silverlight, *The Victor's Dilemma: Allied Intervention in the Russian Civil War*, Weybright & Talley, New York, 1971, p. 221. Kolchak testified about his meeting with Semenov to the Extraordinary Investigating Commission of the Irkutsk Cheka during the last days of January 1920, shortly after handing over his command and White Russia's last hopes to Ataman Semenov.
209 Barrows report, 28 July 1918.
210 Morley, *The Japanese Thrust into Siberia*, p. 201.
211 Ibid., p. 203. On 14 May Japan's cabinet approved a proposal by War Minister Lieutenant General Oshima Ken'ichi to 'fulfill the previous agreements with the Semenov Detachment and continue aid'.
212 Ibid., p. 200.
213 Ibid., p. 204.
214 Footman, 'Ataman Semenov', p. 21; and Morley, *The Japanese Thrust into Siberia*, p. 199.
215 Morley, *The Japanese Thrust ino Siberia*, p. 197.
216 'General Semenoff Reported in Flight', *New York Times*, 8 June 1918, p. 5:1. The 'Austrians' were probably Hungarian POWs from the Austro-Hungarian Army.

NOTES

217 Ibid. and Footman, 'Ataman Semenov', p. 24.
218 Vasilevskii, *Ataman Semenov*, p. 7. Order No. 132, one of the first that was signed 'Ataman Semenov', was issued on 12 June 1918 in Manchuli.
219 Fleming, *The Fate of Admiral Kolchak*, pp. 50 and 52. Fleming also made the contested statement that 'by the middle of 1918, he [Semenov] had ceased to be a charge on the British taxpayer'.
220 Morley, *The Japanese Thrust into Siberia*, p. 206. The diplomatic community could not understand Kolchak's action. US Secretary of State Lansing cryptically informed Ambassador Francis in Vologda, 'Admiral Kolchak began movement towards... Vladivostok but without tangible success and reported to have resigned'. 6 July 1918, letter (telegram), State Dept. File No. 861.00/2096.
221 Morley, *The Japanese Thrust into Siberia*, p. 208. The Heilung Jiang Province Military Governor was named Pao.
222 Ibid., p. 212.
223 'Bolsheviki Can't Get Siberian Grain; Gen. Semenoff Defeated', *New York Times*, 22 June 1918, p. 3:3.
224 'Semenoff Advances Again', *New York Times*, 28 June 1918, p. 3:5.
225 Sabin, Burritt, 'The Pianos Fall Silent: The Tragic End of the Yokohama Colony of the Russian Diaspora', *The East*, 37, 4, November/December 2001.
226 Morley, *The Japanese Thrust into Siberia*, pp. 204–5.

3 COUNTERREVOLUTION: MAY–OCTOBER 1918

1 Jonathan Allen, 'A Long Road Home: The Czechoslovak Legion in Russia', *Command Magazine*, 24, September–October 1993, p. 38. For example, on the Carpathian Front, 'the entire Austro-Hungarian 28th Infantry Regiment, originally mustered in Prague, went over to the Russians, complete with heavy equipment, band instruments, and regimental colors'.
2 Heald, *Witness to Revolution*, p. 210.
3 Barrows report, 28 July 1918.
4 March, *History of the World War*, p. 456.
5 Fleming, *The Fate of Admiral Kolchak*, p. 24; and Lyandres and Wulff, *A Chronicle of the Civil War in Siberia*, p. 21.
6 *Deyatelnost'*, pp. 21–4. An article dated 10 November 1918 in Vladivostok's *Primorskaya Zhizn*, 'Semienoff and the Special Manchurian Detachment', restated the number of Red adversaries at 15,000 (RG395, File 095 Semenoff, Box 29).
7 Dotsenko, *The Struggle for Democracy*, pp. 27 and 29.
8 *New York Times*, 28 June 1918.
9 Robert B. Shaw, 'The Railroad War', Veterans AEFS So. Western Div. No. 1 (reprinted by permission of Federation for Railway Progess), n.d., Jos. B. Longuevan Papers, Box 1, Shaw Folder, MHI Carlisle Barracks, PA, p. 2.
10 Dotsenko, *The Struggle for Democracy*, p. 147.
11 Snow, *The Bolsheviks in Siberia*, pp. 225–8, Dotsenko, *The Struggle for Democracy*, pp. 38–9. These right-wing organizations, dominated by ex-officers, included the White Legion in Omsk, formed by one Captain Kirilov right after the Bolshevik coup in November, 1917, and at least three other underground groups in Omsk, Tomsk and the Russian Far East. The groups had begun collaborating with each other by March 1918.
12 Dotsenko, *The Struggle for Democracy*, pp. 36–7, and Smele, *Civil War in Siberia*, p. 22. Grishin-Almazov and other officers were drawn to the new army by a 'shared indignation' with the Brest–Litovsk Treaty.
13 Lyandres and Wulff, *A Chronicle of the Civil War in Siberia*, pp. 25 and 27.
14 6 July 1918, letter (telegram), State Dept. File No. 861.00/2096. 'Semenov's movement has been defeated for the time and he has retreated...', US Secretary of State advised US Ambassador Francis.
15 *Deyatelnost'*, pp. 22 and 27–8.

16 Dvornichenko, *Putyevodityel' po Chitye*, pp. 137 and 122, and Andrei G. Bukin, 'Sergei Lazo', Project ZAO-EKT, 2002.
17 Morley, *The Japanese Thrust into Siberia*, p. 209; Semenov, *O Sebe*, ch.2, and Fleming, *The Fate of Admiral Kolchak*, p. 49. Fleming contributed the details about the brawling rejects.
18 Barrows report, 28 July 1918.
19 11 October 1918, AEFS memorandum from intelligence section to chief of staff; and AEFS Engineer Office, 1918 Annual Report, p. 70 (hereafter referred to as Engineer Report, 1918) (NARA RG165, microfilm M917). This 70-page after-action report was completed by Colonel Emerson on September 28, and contains his detailed firstand accounts of events in the forward echelons of the eastward advance of the Czech Legion.
20 Budberg, *Dnevnik Byelogvardeitsa*, and Footman, 'Ataman Semenov', p. 27.
21 Bell, *Side Lights on the Siberian Campaign*, pp. 55–7.
22 *Deyatelnost'*, pp. 23–4.
23 Barrows report, 28 July 1918.
24 Semenov, *O Sebe*, ch.2, Semenov named the Chinese general as 'Chzhan Kuyu'.
25 Barrows report, 28 July 1918. At this time, General Kreshchatitski was commander of the officer corps.
26 Semenov, *O sebe*, ch.2 (pp. 111ff.), Dvornichenko, *Putyevodityel' po Chitye*, p. 30 and Footman, 'Ataman Semenov', p. 24. While Semenov praised Okumura, Kuroki and Takeda in his memoirs, Japanese records cited by Morley apparently did not suggest any outstanding performance by the volunteer battalion.
27 Barrows report, 28 July 1918.
28 Footman, 'Ataman Semenov', p. 24. 'The Japanese were firm in their support of their Ally', adds Footman of the negotiations.
29 Semenov, *O Sebe*, ch. 2.
30 *Deyatelnost'*, p. 16.
31 Deacon, *Kempei Tai*, pp. 118–20.
32 Iva Spector, *An Introduction to Russian History and Culture*, D. Van Nostrand, New York, 1949, p. 285.
33 Ibid., p. 282.
34 Betty Miller Unterberger, *America's Siberian Expedition 1918–1920: A Study of National Policy*, Greenwood Press, New York, p. 95.
35 2 September 1918, telegram from Associated Press (AP) correspondent Simpson at Ataman Semenov's Headquarters, Borzya (RG395, File 095 Semenoff, Box 29). Simpson wrote, 'The Japanese volunteers, some hundreds of who were with Semenov, all resigned here two days ago; whether instructed to do so or not by the Japanese Government I leave it to you to judge.'
36 Morley, *The Japanese Thrust into Siberia*, p. 209. Morley wrote that the Japanese volunteer battalion was 'quite ineffective'.
37 Barrows report, 28 July 1918.
38 Dyboski, *Seven Years in Russia and Siberia*, p. 47.
39 G. Guins, *Sibir', Soyuzniki i Kolchak: Povorotnyi moment russkoi istorii, 1918–1920 g.g.; vpechatlieniya i mysli chlena Omskago pravitel'stva*, vol. I, Peking, Tipo-lit. Russkoi dukhovnoi missii, 1921, pp. 84–5.
40 Lincoln, *Red Victory*, pp. 120–3.
41 Spector, *An Introduction to Russian History and Culture*, pp. 275 and 281.
42 Dziak, *Chekisty*, p. 26.
43 Ibid., p. 27.
44 *Deyatelnost'*, pp. 25–6.
45 Shaw, 'The Railroad War', p. 2, and Dotsenko, *The Struggle for Democracy*, p. 33.
46 11 October 1918, AEFS Memorandum from intelligence Section to Chief of Staff and AEFS Engineer Office, 1918 Annual Report, p. 70. One core unit was identified as the 1st Tomsk Regiment under Colonel Shuman.

NOTES

47 Engineer Report, 1918, p. 70.
48 Newby, *The Big Red Train Ride*, p. 183 and *Lloyd's Register of Shipping*, The Register, London, 1918. *Baikal*, the largest of the two ferries, was a 'huge, slab-sided, gleaming white' vessel with luxurious saloons, staterooms, restaurant and chapel. Her keel was laid in Britain, and she inaugurated the lake service in April 1900, soon becoming a popular site for weddings. She drew 20 feet, and displaced 4,250 tons.
49 Newby, *The Big Red Train Ride*, pp. 61 and 63.
50 Trilliser was destined for high rank in Red Russia. Having joined the Social Democratic Party in 1901 at the age of 18, Trilliser was arrested numerous times, partook of the 1905 Revolution in Finland, became a member of the Irkutsk Bolshevik committee in 1917 and *Tsentrosibir'* in 1918. K.A. Zalesskii, *Imperiya Stalina: Biograficheskii entsikolopedicheskii slovar'*, Beche, Moscow, 2000.
51 V.V. Vertyankin, *Istoriya Ledokola 'Angara'*, Irkutsk, 1991.
52 Ibid. Shevtsov was killed in November 1918 on the Olekma river.
53 Shaw, 'The Railroad War', p. 2. An undated AEFS 'Report on Section between Myssovaya & Irkutsk' stated 'We counted 56 tunnels.'
54 Engineer Report, 1918, p. 61.
55 Gajda would cross paths often with Semenov during the next two years. He had begun the war as an unwilling enlisted corpsman in the Austro-Hungarian Army. After he cast his lot with the Russians, he was promoted to captain and distinguished himself as a battalion commander in the Battle of Zborow on 2 July 1917. When the battle was joined, Gajda's regimental commander (Colonel Zembalevski) was drunk, and the other regimental commander of the Czech Brigade was ill. Gajda and two green lieutenants broke their men into small groups, defying conventional tactics of fighting in line, and defeated the Austro-Hungarian 19th Infantry Division.
56 Vertyankin, *Istoriya Ledokale 'Angara'*
57 Engineer Report, 1918, p. 63.
58 An undated AEFS 'Report on Section between Myssovaya & Irkutsk' describes Tankhoe as a town of 'about 500' with no doctors and a power plant and water works operated by the railway. A small garrison of Czechoslovak troops 'quartered in box cars' soon took up residence until early 1920.
59 Engineer Report, 1918, and Vertyankin, *storiya Ledokala 'Angara'*.
60 One *verst* equals approximately two-thirds of a mile.
61 Engineer Report, 1918, p. 65.
62 9 September 1918, AEFS intelligence summary (NARA RG165, microfilm M917).
63 Engineer Report, 1918, p. 65.
64 Ibid. The retreating Red Army's explosive of choice was 'gun-cotton soaked in nitroglycerine', called *toll* in Russian, pyroxylin in English.
65 Dotsenko, *The Struggle for Democracy*, p. 148.
66 Engineer Report, 1918, p. 67.
67 Artem Vlasov, *Kuda Ischezlo Chitinskoe Zoloto?*, Provintsiya, Moscow, 2000. Other Anarchist detachments were led by Karaev and Lavrov.
68 Butin's remark was, '*K Sovetskom vlasti primazalis' merzavtsy* …'.
69 24 August 1918, AEFS intelligence diary for 18–24 August (RG395, File 095 Semenoff, Box 29). 'Lieutenant Shirek' may have actually been the OMO intelligence officer, Captain Shiroki. Much of this information came from OMO intelligence reports. The author of this AEFS report, Frank Brezina, was so new to the campaign that he still signed his name 'Captain, Phillipine Scouts'.
70 24 August 1918, AEFS intelligence diary for 18–24 August and 31 August 1918, AEFS intelligence diary for 25–31 August (RG395, File 095 Semenoff, Box 29). OMO reports stated that the Red field staff at Borzya included one Naumov, a staff commander Podgurski and Artillery Chief Tuanikov. The Zargol detachment seems to have been the 'Zargomsk unit' referred to in other intelligence reports.
71 Semenov, *O Sebe*, p. 44. Semenov wrote that the request came from Colonel Ushakov.
72 Bell, *Side Lights on the Siberian Campaign*, p. 75 and Semenov, *O Sebe*, ch. 3.

73 4 December 1918, letter from Captain Harold V. Fay, AEFS intelligence officer – Harbin, to AEFS intelligence officer, Vladivostok.
74 Fleming, *The Fate of Admiral Kolchak*, p. 69. The terms of the agreement were so vaguely defined as to give Japan 'the right to deploy her troops on Chinese territory whenever she cared to concoct a pretext for doing so'.
75 An account of the AEF in Siberia, August 1918 to March 1919, Office of the AEF Chief of Staff, Vladivostok, April 1919, p. 48 (hereafter referred to as 'Account of AEFS'). Japanese communiqués, which were not published until 30 August, boasted that their cavalry led the advance from Manchuli up the railway line into Russian territory, falsely suggesting that Semenov's forces played only a supporting role.
76 Semenov, *O Sebe*, ch. 3; and 31 August 1918, AEFS intelligence diary for 25–31 August.
77 Semenov, *O Sebe*, ch. 3.
78 Dvornichenko, *Putyevodityel' po Chitye*, p. 122.
79 Annual report, Engineer Office AEFS, 1918, p. 67; and 2 September 1918, telegram from AP correspondent Simpson at Ataman Semenov's headquarters, Borzya.
80 *Deyatelnost'*, p. 28.
81 31 August 1918, AEFS intelligence diary for 25–31 August.
82 Annual Report, Engineer Office AEFS, 1918, p. 68.
83 Artem Vlasov, *Kuda Ischezlo Chitinskoe Zoloto?*, Provintsiya, Moscow, 2000; Dotsenko, *The Struggle for Democracy*, p. 149; and Dvornichenko, *Putyevodityel' po Chitye*, p. 30. Vlasov reveals that the first topic at Urul'ga station was the looting of the Chita state bank by Efrem Perezhogin's anarchist detachment and a mob of Red Guards and Hungarian internationalists.
84 Ward, *With the 'Die-Hards' in Siberia*, p. 240.
85 Communiqué No. 14, General Nakajima, Japanese General HQ, Bureau of Information, Vladivostok, 3 September 1918; and 31 August 1918 AEFS intelligence diary for 25–31 August.
86 2 September 1918, telegram from AP correspondent Simpson at Ataman Semenov's Headquarters, Borzya; Dvornichenko, *Putyevodityel' po Chitye*, p. 30 and Footman, 'Ataman Semenov', p. 30. Bukin and others state that OMO did not appear in Chita until 6 September. The 'Irkutsk Czechs' beat OMO to the left bank (northwest side) of the Onon.
87 Fedor N. Petrov, *Geroicheskiye godi borbi i pobed*, Izdatelstvo Nauka, Moscow, 1968, p. 158. The most famous 'forest communes' in eastern Transbaikalia were Altaganskaya, Onon-Borzinskaya, Alkhanaiskaya and Nizhne Giryunsksaya.
88 9 September 1918, AEFS intelligence summary.
89 2 and 3 September 1918, AEFS communiques Nos. 14 and 16.
90 9 September 1918, AEFS intelligence summary.
91 22 January 1920 Report No. 2344 of US Military Attache to China, 'Forces of Ataman Semenov'.
92 Lokewijk-Hermen Grondijs, *La Guerre en Russie et en Siberie*, Editions Bossard, Paris, 1922, p. 469. Semenov feigned outrage at Grondijs' question and declared that he had assigned various committees to look into such crimes.
93 Vasilevskii, *Ataman Semenov*, p. 8.
94 6 September 1918, '*Vsem russkym grazhdanam, lyubyashchim svoyu rodinu*', Glavnokomanduyushchii Soyuznymi Voiskami.
95 2 and 7 September 1918, telegrams from AP correspondent Simpson at Ataman Semenov's Headquarters, Borzya and Bukhedu.
96 3 and 7 (2) September 1918, telegrams from AP correspondent Simpson at Borzya, Hailar and Bukhedu.
97 An account of the AEFS, August 1918–March 1919, p. 54 (RG165, M917). Ushuman was an important crossroads on the Tigda River with a branch railway line to Chernyaevskaya *stanitsa* and a major road to Ovsyanka, a gateway village into the Zeya river goldmining district (5 June 1919, memorandum, RG395, Box 95).
98 September 27, 1918, intelligence summary No. 15, AEFS intelligence section (RG395, File 095 Semenoff, Box 29). Lefrovo was cited as 'Lefrobo' in this report, which also states

NOTES

that eastbound and westbound Japanese columns met on the Amur river at Reinova, but omits the date.
99 Morley, *The Japanese Thrust into Siberia*, p. 247.
100 The Soviet met in the former military governor's house at Ulitsa Svetlanskaya 25. Diterikhs was a monarchist and mystic who would cling to Russian soil until the bitter end in 1922.
101 Bell, *Side Lights on the Siberian Campaign*, p. 73, Morley, *The Japanese Thrist into Siberia*, pp. 247–9 and Edward L. Ginzton, *Times to Remember: The Life of Edward L. Ginzton*, Blackberry Creek Press, Berkeley, CA, 1995. The author was a boy whose father was chief health officer for the Reds' Ussuri Front command.
102 Bell, *Side Lights on the Siberian Campaign*, p. 72, Morley, *The Japanese Thrust into Siberia*, pp. 248 and 251.
103 Bell, *Side Lights on the Siberian Campaign*, p. 75.
104 Ibid., p. 73.
105 Ibid., pp. 75 and 99.
106 Morley, *The Japanese Thrust into Siberia*, pp. 255–7.
107 Fleming, *The Fate of Admiral Kolchak*, p. 68. Apart from its socialist bent, another strike against the Derber government with conservatives arose from the fact that Petr Derber was 'an Odessa Jew'.
108 Bell, *Side Lights on the Siberian Campaign*, p. 79.
109 Ibid., p. 80.
110 Ginzton, *Times to Remember*, August 15 entry.
111 Bell, *Side Lights on the Siberian Campaign*, p. 77.
112 Ibid., pp. 78–9.
113 Communiqué No. 14, General Nakajima, Japanese General HQ, Bureau of Information, Vladivostok 2 September 1918 (RG165, M917). It was the *Magdeburg's* captured code book, which happened to contain a key to the cipher system, that ultimately allowed British naval intelligence analysts to crack the German ciphers Barbara W. Tuchman, *The Zimmerman Telegram*, Ballantine, New York, 1958, pp. 12–13.
114 Heald, *Witness to Revolution*, pp. 222–3. Veterans of the Western Front seemed to gauge every army by the quality of its trenches. Major Bell noted, 'The trenches were simple affairs compared with those I had known in France...' (Bell, *Side Lights on the Siberian Campaign*, p. 80).
115 Ibid.
116 Fleming, *The Fate of Admiral Kolchak*, pp. 58–9.
117 Heald, *Witness to Revolution*, p. 223.
118 In the final analysis, based upon casualty figures that circulated in Vladivostok in November 1918, the Austro-German-Hungarian threat was exaggerated, but certainly not insignificant. Some 848 Germans and Hungarians were killed in action in Siberia, some 17 percent of the Red total in the August–October 1918 campaign. Nearly 2,100 Germans and Hungarians were taken prisoner while serving with the Reds. Fred M. Roberts, *Assignment Siberia 1917–1919: Russian Railway Service Corps*, FMRoberts Enterprises, Dana Point, CA, 2000, Diary entry for 8 November 1918.
119 A. Deriabin and P. Palacios-Fernandes, *Grazhdanskaya Voina v Rossii 1917–1922: Natsionalniye Armii*, Izdatelstvo AST, Moscow, 2000, pp. 42–44. The Polish Legion reached its peak strength in June 1919, comprising three Rifle (1st, 2nd and 3rd), an Engineer and Reserve Rifle, 1st Ulhan and 5th Artillery Regiments.
120 Bell, *Side Lights on the Siberian Campaign*, pp. 75–6; Ward, *With the 'Die-Hards' in Siberia*, p. 4; and Barrows report, 28 July 1918. Tolstov's force consisted of cadres of the 1st Siberian Infantry Regiment and a battery at Vladivostok and cadres of the 3rd Siberian Infantry Regiment at Nikolsk.
121 Medical history of the Siberian expedition, RG165, Microfilm M917, c.1919, p. 17. Support of the prostitutes and barkeepers accounted for approximately 10 percent of Vladivostok's population in autumn 1918.
122 Bell, *Side Lights on the Siberian Campaign*, p. 75.
123 Canfield Ferch Smith, *Vladivostok Under Red and White Rule 1920–1922*, University of Virginia, VA, 1972, p. 4.

124 24 August 1918, AEFS intelligence diary for 18–24 August (RG395, File 095 Semenoff, Box 29).
125 The 27th Infantry Regiment consisted of 53 officers and 1,537 enlisted men and the 31st had 46 officers and 1,375 enlisted men.
126 Dyboski, *Seven Years in Russia and Siberia*, p. 59.
127 Dyboski noticed an Austrian officer-prisoner who managed to communicate quite well with the Americans: 'He would strike up a discussion of the Jeffries–Johnson fight, or the various methods of playing baseball in America. With this they [the American officers] would all start talking at once, each trying to get in a word ahead of the other' (Ibid., p. 61).
128 Graves (1865–1940) was a Texan and a graduate of the US Military Academy (Class of 1889) who saw combat in the Phillipines in 1899 and was commander of the US Border Patrol 1913–14.
129 Graves, *America's Siberian Adventure*, pp. 4 and 354.
130 Stevens' commission was created in March 1917 by Daniel Willard, a railway executive who was chairman of the US Council of National Defense, an advisory panel that steered military-industrial decisions during the First World War. Stanley Washburn, a correspondent for *The Times* and the *Chicago Daily News*, stirred Willard's interest by telling him of Vladivostok's huge stockpiles of Allied military material, stranded by a dysfunctional railway system.
131 11 August 1917, letter from Henry Miller to Daniel Willard. Also, National Archives description of Record Group (RG) 43, Records of the Advisory Commission of Railway Experts to Russia, the Russian Railway Service Corps (RRSC) and the Interallied Railway Committee, 1917–22.
132 Tom Mahoney, 'When Yanks Fought in Russia', *American Legion Magazine*, April 1978, p. 22.
133 Frederick C. Griffin, 'An American Railway Man East of the Urals, 1918–1922', *The Historian*, 22 June 1998, 60, 4, p. 812.
134 Mahoney, 'When Yanks Fought in Russia', p. 22.
135 John Reed, 'Liar or Just Doesn't Know', *The Revolutionary Age*, 19 August 1919.
136 8 May 1918, letter (telegram), from Secretary of State Lansing to Ambassador David R. Francis, File No. 861.00/1729.
137 Lane R. Earns, 'Where Do We Go From Here: The Russian Railway Service Corps in Nagasaki', *Crossroads: A Journal of Nagasaki History and Culture*, 6, Showado Printing Co., Nagasaki, 1999.
138 Bell, *Side Lights on the Siberian Campaign*, p. 81.
139 V.D. Ivanov, and O.I. Sergeev, '*Ussuriiskoye Kazachestvo b Revolyutsiyakh 1917 goda u Grazhdanskoi Voine na Dal'nem Vostoke*', Institute of History, Archaeology and Ethnography of the People of the Far East, DVO RAN, 1999.
140 Graves, *America' Siberian Adventure*, p. 128.
141 AEFS intelligence section newspaper summary, 28 October, 1919 (RG165, M917).
142 Morley, *The Japanese Thrust into Siberia*, p. 95. The plan to occupy Iman's railway station allegedly originated with British Major Dunlop.
143 Ibid. Morley and AEFS sources state that the *krug* assembled in February.
144 AEFS intelligence section newspaper summary, 23 October 1918 (RG165, M917), and Morley, *The Japanese Thrust into Siberia*, pp. 79–80.
145 Ivanov and Sergeev, 'Ussuriiskoye Kazachestvo'.
146 Morley, *The Japanese Thrust into Siberian*, pp. 96–7, and Ivanov and Sergeev, 'Ussuriiskoye Kazachestvo'.
147 Morley, *The Japanese Thrust into Siberia*, p. 166. Their leader was an engineer, Major Samura Masao.
148 AEFS intelligence section newspaper summary, 28 October 1919 (RG165, M917).
149 Graves, *America's Siberian Adventure*, p. 128.
150 Ivanov and Sergeev, 'Ussuriiskoye Kazachestvo'. A Cossack Host soviet elected S.V. Korenev chief at this *krug*.
151 Bell, *Side Lights on the Siberian Campaign*, p. 74.
152 Major Barrows report, 28 July 1918.

NOTES

153 Ibid. Morley, *The Japanese Thrust into Siberia*, pp. 254 and 256, and Bell, *Side Lights on the Siberian Campaign*, pp. 98–9. Major General Saito expressed his concerns about Czech weakness and democracy in early July.
154 Barrows report, 28 July 1918.
155 Ibid.
156 Communiqué No. 14, General Nakajima, Japanese General HQ, Bureau of Information, Vladivostok, 2 September 1918 (RG165, M917); and
157 Communiqué No. 16, General Nakajima, Japanese General HQ, Bureau of Information, Vladivostok, 3 September 1918 (RG165, M917).
158 Ginzton, *Times to Remember*, August 15 diary entry; Communiqué No. 14, General Nakajima, Japanese General HQ, Bureau of Information, Vladivostok, 2 September 1918; and 31 August 1918 intelligence diary for 25–31 August. A newspaper at Iman, behind the Red lines, claimed that Bolshevik forces numbered 15,000.
159 24 August 1918, AEFS intelligence diary for 18–24 August.
160 Bell, *Side Lights on the Siberian Campaign*, p. 82; and 31 August, 1918, intelligence diary for 25–31 August.
161 Ward, *With the 'Die-Hards' in Siberia*, p. 22.
162 31 August 1918 intelligence diary for 25–31 August.
163 Barrows was AEFS intelligence officer from 16 August 1918–10 March 1919. Prior to that he was a military attaché in the American Legation in Peking. At least one source states that he had been chief of the US military intelligence office in Manila.
164 Heald, *Witness to Revolution*, pp. 222–3.
165 'In Siberia they take the shape of big, ugly winged spiders, which will suck your blood through a thick blanket as easily as if you had nothing on', averred Colonel Ward of the 25th Middlesex.
166 31 August 1918, intelligence diary for 25–31 August.
167 Dyboski, *Seven Years in Russia and Siberia*, p. 47.
168 Bell, *Side Lights on the Siberian Campaign*, p. 83. American participation in the August–September campaign carried them as far as Ushman.
169 7 September 1918, intelligence summary No. 2, AEFS intelligence office (RG395, File 095 Semenoff, Box 29).
170 Gutman, *the Restruction of Nikolaevsk-on-Amur*, pp. 1, 3 and 394.
171 Jaanus Paal, *Kamchatka Story*, Tartumaa Muusemumi Toimetised, Tartu (Estonia), 1993. Paal claims that there were only two Bolsheviks on Kamchatka at the time of the October Revolution.
172 Bell, *Side Lights on the Siberian Campaign*, p. 82.
173 Dyboski, *Seven Years in Russia and Siberia*, pp. 47–8.
174 US Senate Committee on Education and Labor, *Deportation of Gregorie Semenoff*, p. 10.
175 Dyboski, *Seven Years in Russia and Siberia*, p. 48.
176 Young Sik Kim, 'The Sacrificial Lamb of the Cold War: The Nationalists of Korea', Seattle, WA, 2000. Kim was born 22 Februrary 1885 in a Korean village in Ussuriisk, daughter of a nationalist fighter, Kim Du Suh, and attended a girls' school in Vladivostok. She was executed by firing squad on 16 September 1918.
177 Engineer Report, 1918, p. 61. Kalmykov accused the Swedish Red Cross of covert dealings with German and Austro-Hungarian prisoners of war.
178 General Otani had previously been commander of the Japanese garrison at Tsingtao, China (*The Story of the Great War,* vol. 15, P.F. Collier & Son, New York, p. 517).
179 US Senate Committee on Education and Labour, *Deportation of Gregorie Semenoff*, pp. 10–11.
180 'English–Japanese Alliance in Siberia', *Osaka Mainichi*, 18 October 1918, translated in AEFS intelligence section newspaper summary, 26 October 1918 (RG165, M917).
181 US Senate Committee on Education and Labor, *Deportation of Gregorie Semenoff*, pp. 10–11.
182 AEFS intelligence section newspaper summary, 26 October 1918 (RG165, M917).
183 AEFS intelligence summary No. 44, 10 December 1918 (RG165, M917).
184 Ivanov and Sergeev 'Ussuriiskoye Kazachestvo'. The Fifth *Krug* convened in Khabarovsk on 21–31 October.

185 Morley, *The Japanese Thrust into Siberia*, pp. 35, 75 and 80. Forsyth writes that a Republic of Great Siberia was declared at Blagoveshchensk on 22 December 1917, but was disposed of by Red Guards the next day. Nakajima's Russian agent's name was transliterated as 'Randouishefu' in Japanese records. James Forsyth, *A History of the Peoples of Siberia: Russia's North Asian Colony 1581–1990*, Cambridge University Press, New York, 1992, pp. 230–1.
186 Smele, *Civil War in Siberia*, p. 25.
187 Morley, *The Japanese Thrust into Siberia*, pp. 108–9.
188 21 September 1918, weekly intelligence summary, AEFS intelligence office (RG395, File 095 Semenoff, Box 29).
189 3 October 1918, Communiqué No. 46, Japanese General H.Q. Vladivostok, Bureau of Information (RG395, File 095 Semenoff, Box 29); An Account of the AEFS, April 1919 (RG165, M917); 21 September 1918, Weekly Intelligence summary and 27 September 1918 weekly intelligence summary No. 19, AEFS intelligence office. Some post-war historians, apparently not aware that the internationalist threat turned out to be greatly overblown, wrote that 2,000 Germans and Austro-Hungarians 'laid down their arms' at Blagoveshchensk and Alexeievsk.
190 27 September 1918, intelligence summary No. 15, AEFS intelligence section (RG395, File 095 Semenoff, Box 29). This report details the Japanese–US campaign in the Blagoveshchensk area.
191 Ginzton, *Times to Remember*. Ginzton was Red Army's chief health officer on the Ussuri front in the summer of 1918.
192 Artem Vlasov, 'Kuda Ischezlo Chitinskoe Zoloto?' *Provintsiya*, Moscow, 2000. N. Yakovlev, a principal figure of *Tsentrosibir'*, was among those who perished on the road to Yakutsk.

4 THE WHITE TERROR BEGINS: OCTOBER 1918–DECEMBER 1918

1 *Deyatelnost'*, pp. 24 and 26–7.
2 Fleming, *The Fate of Admiral Kolchak*, p. 142. This observer was unique in considering Semenov to be small in stature.
3 Unterberger, *America's Siberian Expedition*, p. 119.
4 AEFS intelligence section newspaper summary, 23 October 1918 (RG165, M917).
5 Semenov, *O Sebe*, pp.196–210. Semenov had also loaned Horvath another 'skilled manager' by the name of A.V. Volgina in July.
6 11 May 1919, Verkhne-Udinsk Report, 1st Lieutenant Ralph L. Baggs, US 27th Infantry Regt, USAT Sherman. Mayor A. Kortov returned to office in Verkhne-Udinsk.
7 Dotsenko, *The Struggle for Democracy*, p. 34 and Footman, 'Ataman Semenov', p. 33. 'The Provisional Government [of Kerensky] had failed to organize an effective system of administration in the provinces', wrote historian Leonard Schapiro (The Russian Revolutions of 1917: The Origins of Communism, Basic Books, New York, 1942, p. 154.
8 AEFS intelligence summary No. 37, 1 December 1918 (RG165, M917). Alexeievsky was 'a doctor of law in Paris', and fluent in French and English.
9 Vasilevskii, *Ataman Semenov*, p. 9. Semenov's Order No. 2 as Commander of the 5th Pri-Amur Independent Corps, promulgated 11 October 1918, continued the existence of the *voenno-polevyi sud* (military field court) begun by White forces during the summer, but added the possibility of appeal to the Supreme Siberian Court in Omsk.
10 Artem Vlasov, 'Kuda Ischezlo Chitinskoe Zoloto?', Provintsiya BG, Moscow, 2000.
11 Alexander Barinov, 'Zabytyi Pisatel' ili 'Piarshchik' Atamana', *Zabaikal'skii Pabochii*, 65 (23593), 9 April 2002.
12 Ibid.
13 Vasilevskii, *Ataman Semenov*, pp. 6–9, Semenov, *O Sebe*, pp. 196–210; Footman, 'Ataman Semenov', p. 25; and *Deyatelnost'*, p. 12.
14 AEFS intelligence summary (App. No. 61), 9 September 1918 (RG165, M917).

NOTES

15 Semenov, *O Sebe*, pp. 196–210. Semenov wrote that Gajda was 'a very sociable person and interesting interlocutor'.
16 Footman, 'Ataman Semenov', p. 29.
17 Smele, *Civil War in Siberia*, p. 189.
18 Vasilevskii, *Ataman Semenov*, pp. 8–9. Semenov issued Order No. 1 as corps commander on 8 October at Borzya.
19 24 September 1918, memorandum from Major David P. Barrows, AEFS intelligence officer, for General Graves, interview between Ambassador Morris and the Ataman Simeonof (RG395, File 095 Semenoff, Box 29).
20 Dvornichenko, *Putevodityel' po Chitye*, p. 23.
21 In March 1919, water cost 1 ruble 50 kopeks per barrel, and delivery cost an extra 8 rubles per barrell.
22 V. Kuranov, *The Trans-Siberian Express*, Sphinx Press, New York, 1980, p. 266; and 20 March 1919, extract from engineers. Office report on Chita (RG395, File 095, Box 29). At the time, Chita also had 177 horse-drawn taxicabs, 233 freight wagons, 43 watercarts and 30 manure carts.
23 Bishop Safron would be arrested by the Bolsheviks in January 1923 and charged with conducting espionage for Semenov during the Ataman's reign.
24 Footman, 'Ataman Semenov', p. 30.
25 Semenov, *O Sebe*, pp. 171–83. In the next breath, Semenov accused the socialist governor of Irkutsk and PSG Director N.D. Avksent'ev of collusion with the Bolsheviks.
26 Smele, *Civil War in Siberia*, pp. 21, 555 and 564.
27 AEFS intelligence section newspaper summary, 29 October 1918 (RG165, M917), and Vasilevskii, *Ataman Semenov*, p. 8.
28 Ibid.
29 AEFS intelligence section newspaper summary, October 1918, which cited the 22 October edition of *Novisti Zhizni*. Flegontov may have been the same A.K. Flegontov who later commanded partisan forces in Primorye in 1921–22, and survived to lead partisans against the Germans in Byelorussia in 1942.
30 Interview of Semenov by *Primorskaya Zhizn* appeared in 28 October issue. Chita political report was published in *Moya Gazeta*. AEFS intelligence section newspaper summary, 29 October 1918 (RG165, M917).
31 Norman Pereira, 'Siberian Atamanshchina: Warlordism in the Russian Civil War', in Vladimis Brovkin's *The Bolsheviks in Russian Society*, p. 125.
32 Andrei Bukin, 'Pokushenie na Atamana Semenova', Chita, 2002.
33 Dvornichenko, *Putevodityel' po Chitye*, p. 32, and Snow, *The Bolsheviks in Siberia*, p. 215. During the Soviet era a Chita street was named for Vasilii M. Serov, a Bolshevik since 1902 and deputy to the second State duma (congress). Another early apprehension and execution was of Commissar Kazachkov, a local teacher who became a Red military commander for a short time. (Naletov 'Pedagogicheskoi Eksperiment').
34 Footman, 'Ataman Semenov', pp. 43–44.
35 US Senate Committee on Education and Labor, *Deportation of Gregorie Semenoff*, p. 81.
36 Andrei Bukin, 'Zabaikal'skaya Militsiya na Sluzhbe Boennogo Rezhima', Chita, 2002.
37 AEFS intelligence summary No. 37, 1 December 1918 (RG165, M917).
38 10 February 1919, Report 'Ataman Semenoff and his officers', Captain F.F. Moore, AEFS, Vladivostok (RG395, File 095, Box 29).
39 9 February 1919, Report, Captain Harold V.V. Fay, AEFS intelligence officer, Harbin (RG395, File 095 Semenoff, Box 29). A Russian 'reliable source' stated that Verigo had been a *esaul* – a captain – until his promotion to major general by Semenov (5 August 1919, Report on Semenov (RG395, File 095, Box 29).
40 Barinov, *Zabytyi Pisatel'*. Data gathered and provided by churches concerning attitudes of the population formed the basis for counterespionage charges against the church after the communists took over. Oliger lived from 1882–1919.
41 Memorandum from AEFS intelligence section to AEFS chief of staff, 'Friendly Russian Forces in Eastern European Russian and Siberia', 11 October 1918 (RG165, M917).

42 AEFS intelligence summary No. 37, 1 December 1918 (RG165, M917).
43 Ibid.
44 5 August 1919, translation from Russian of report on Semenoff.
45 21 February 1919, letter from Lieutenant Colonel Barrows, AEFS Vladivostok, to AEFS intelligence officer, Harbin, and attached report, 'Ataman Semenoff', by Nicholas Romanoff. The Belgians worked on the Ataman's personal staff, but eventually became desparate to depart, even offering to serve in Omsk's army to make amends for their desertion from the Belgian Army. One Belgian became Romanov's prolific informant on Semenov's inner circle.
46 9 October 1919, report on interview with Mr Braude, Assistant Chief of the Russian Information Bureau (RG395, File 095, Box 29).
47 Pereira, 'Siberian Atamanshchina', p. 123.
48 Vasilevskii, *Ataman Semenov*, pp. 11–12. 18 December 1918, 'Appeal to Transbaikal Tungus On Induction into the White Army', Chita, signed by Colonel Semenov, Expedition Ataman of the Far Eastern Host.
49 Stanislav Vital'evich Khatuntsev, 'Ungern fon Shternberg: Buddist s Mechom', Voronezh State University, Historical Faculty, 2003.
50 9 June 1919, letter from Captain Montgomery Schuyler to AEFS chief of staff, general report on Omsk (RG395, File 095, Box 29).
51 Sergei Volkov, 'Tragediya Russkogo Ofitserstva', ch. 4 (*Ofitserstvo v Belom Dvishenii*), n.p., 2002. The school staff: chief of the school was Colonel M.M. Likhachev, assistant chief was Colonel Dmitriev, and inspector of classes was Colonel Khilovskii.
52 10 December 1918, telegram (RG43).
53 11 January 1919, extracts from report of Captain Conrad Skladal (RG395, File 095, Box 29).
54 20 July 1919, report on Manchuria station, Captain. H.V.V. Fay, Hailar (RG395, File 095, Box 29).
55 Semenov, *O Sebe*, pp. 171–82. Likewise, although the Bolsheviks inherited several hundred aircraft, these machines are not cited in any action against Semenov or his armored trains. Few pilots, observers or mechanics voluntarily opted to stay on with the new regime, and large numbers of the neglected air fleet were captured by the Germans in Ukraine in the spring of 1918, and by British, French and White armies on the southern fronts around the Volga, Crimea and Baku. The only notable large-scale employment of Red aircraft in the east occurred in August 1918, when 30 aircraft showered leaflets over the White armies and Czech Legion near Samara. In 1919, 17 *otryady* (flights) totaling about 100 aircraft were committed against Admiral Kolchak's army. The Red air fleet depended heavily on special trains that served as mobile maintenance and refueling bases and provided long-range transportation (Alexander Boyd, *The Soviet Air Force Since 1918*, Stein & Day, New York, 1977, pp. 2–5).
56 Vice Consul-General Edward Thomas to Consul-General Ernest Harris, 'Political Conditions in Chita up to December 15, 1918', State Dept. 861.00/4345 (Microfilm M316, roll 21); 24 September 1918, David Barrows/Vladivostok memorandom for Major General Graves, 'Interview between Ambassador [Roland] Morris and Ataman Semenoff' (AEFS 21-21.3, M917, roll 1).
57 1 December 1918, telegram from Captain Skladal/AEFS Chita to Colonel Barrows/AEFS Vladivostok (RG165, Microfilm M917).
58 10 December 1918, intelligence summary No. 44, AEFS intelligence section (RG165, Microfilm M917).
59 *Deyatelnost'*, p. 12.
60 B. Kandidov, 'Tserkovnye shpiony yaponskogo imperializma', *Sputnik Agitatora*, 14, 1937, pp. 24–7.
61 Dotsenko, *The Struggle for Democracy*, p. 42.
62 Memorandum from AEFS intelligence officer to AEFS chief of staff, 23 October 1918 (RG165, M917).
63 Smele, *Civil War in Siberia*, p. 41.

NOTES

64 Alexander Kerensky, *Russia and History's Turning Point*, Duell, Sloan & Pearce, New York, 1965, p. 361. Kerensky accused the 'Army and Navy Officers' Union' of seeding many reactionary groups; it began within two months of the Tsar's abdication to defend officers' interests and counter the influence of the vociferous soldiers' soviets.
65 9 June 1919 letter from Captain Montgomery Schuyler, Vladivostok, to AEFS chief of staff, general report on Omsk (RG395, File 095, Box 29).
66 Dotsenko, *The Struggle for Democracy*, p. 44.
67 Ibid., p. 43.
68 AEFS intelligence section newspaper summary, 23 October 1918 (RG165, M917).
69 Mikhail Khvostov, *The Russian Civil War: The Red Army*, Osprey Military, Oxford, 1996 and Schapiro, *The Russian Revolutions of 1917*, p. 172.
70 Footman, 'Ataman Semenov', p. 30.
71 Semenov, *O Sebe*, pp. 211–13.
72 Smele, *Civil War in Siberia*, pp. 74–5. Knox was born in Ulster in 1870 and died in 1964.
73 Footman, 'Ataman Semenov', p. 17.
74 US Senate Committee on Education and Labor, Deportation of Gregorie Semenoff, p. 38.
75 Footman, 'Ataman Semenov', p. 25.
76 Fleming, *The Fate of Admiral Kolchak*, p. 137, citing Grondijs, *La guerre en Russie et Siberie*.
77 10 February 1919, report 'Ataman Semenoff and his Officers', Captain F.F. Moore, AEFS, Vladivostok.
78 Budberg *Inevnile Byelogvardeitsa* and Footman, 'Ataman Semenov', p. 34.
79 10 February 1919, report 'Ataman Semenoff and his Officers', Captain F.F. Moore, AEFS, Vladivostok.
80 AEFS intelligence summary No. 45, 12 December 1918 (RG165, M917). Various sources refer to Semenov's supply officer as Colonel 'Birzokov' or 'Borisov'.
81 'Report of the Situation in the Trans-Baikal District', AEFS 1st Lieutenant Justis S. Davidson, 6 October 1919 (RG165, M917).
82 AEFS intelligence summary No. 45, 12 December 1918 (RG165, M917).
83 Morley, *The Japanese Thrust into Siberia*, p. 210.
84 4 June 1919, letter, from US Consul, Vladivostok, to US Secretary of State (RG165, File No. 1766-1107/1).
85 6 October 1919, letter/report from 1st Lieutenant Justis S. Davidson, chief intelligence officer/AEFS intelligence section (Classified 'Confidential') (RG165, Microfilm M917). Davidson noted, 'The Japanese brought goods into the Trans-Baikal District without paying duty – this was accomplished chiefly through the aid of General Burikoff who was Chief of Supplies...'.
86 Smele, *Civil War in Siberia*, p. 458.
87 Report from Captain V.V. Fay, intelligence officer – Harbin, to AEFS intelligence officer, 4 December 1918 (RG165, M917). After the 1932 invasion of Manchukuo, the Japanese Army repeated this profitable smuggling scheme. Since merchandise marked as 'Japanese Army military supplies' was shipped free on the Russian-owned Chinese Eastern Railway, Japanese army and gendarmerie officers made deals with merchants in Manchuria to ship at discount rates and pocketed all of the proceeds (Vespa, *Secret Agent of Japan*, pp. 82–3).
88 4 January 1919, letter from 1st Lieutenant Robert J. Scovell, AEFS, Manchuli, to Lieutenant Colonel Barrows, Vladivostok (RG395, File 095, Box 29).
89 Memorandum of Major Johnson, 27 December 1918 (RG43, New Entry 844, Index 2, Box 8, File 224A).
90 AEFS intelligence section newspaper summary, 29 October 1918 (RG165, M917).
91 Footman, 'Ataman Semenov', p. 33.
92 AEFS intelligence section newspaper summary, 23 October 1918 (RG165, M917).
93 Schapiro, *The Russian Revolutions of 1917*, p. 172.
94 Smele, *Civil War in Siberia*, pp. 87–9. The directory was a coalition of right Socialist-Revolutionaries, Constitutional Democrats (Kadets) and the 'bear-like' General Vasilii Georgevich Boldyrev, wartime commander of the Riga front.

95 Dotsenko, *The Struggle for Democracy*, p. 149.
 96 Ibid.
 97 Smele, *Civil War in Siberia*, pp. 82–4.
 98 27 December 1918, memorandum of conversation Major Johnson had with Mr Alex Osheroff (RG43 RRSC, New Entry 844, Index 2, Box 8, File 224a). Samara (Kuibyshev during the Soviet era) had been liberated from the Bolsheviks by the Czech Legion on 8 June 1918, but soon fell back into Bolshevik hands.
 99 October 1918 report 'Habarovsk', Major Malcom Wheeler Nicholson, AEFS, Khabarovsk (RG395, Box 095, File 29).
100 *Golos Primorya*, 25 October 1918, No. 321, in AEFS intelligence section newspaper summary, 25 October 1918 (RG165, M917); and Volkov, 'Tragediya Russkogo', ch. 4.
101 AEFS intelligence summary No. 44, 10 December 1918 (RG165, M917).
102 *Golos Primorya*, 26 October 1918, No. 322, in AEFS intelligence section newspaper summary, 28 October 1918 (RG165, M917).
103 Ibid.
104 Volkov, 'Tragediya Russkogo', ch. 4.
105 AEFS intelligence summary No. 44, 10 December 1918 (RG165, M917).
106 'A Conflict', *Dalekaya Okraia*, 22 October 1918, No. 3661, in AEFS intelligence section newspaper summary, 23 October 1918 (RG165, M917).
107 Ibid.
108 Just days later, on 27 October. Atamans Semenov and Kalmykov were brash enough to visit Vladivostok, where they had an audience with the 'temporary governor' of Primorsky province, General Horvath 'on the question of the organization of authority and of the relations of the Ussuri Cossack Army with the All-Russian Government'. The two young uncompromising warlords departed on 29 October, having resolved nothing with Horvath. [10/29/18 NS]
109 'English-Japanese Alliance in Siberia', *Osaka Mainichi*, 18 October 1918, in AEFS intelligence section newspaper summary, 26 October 1918 (RG165, M917).
110 Dyboski, *Seven Years in Russia and Siberia*, p. 55.
111 October 1918 report 'Habarovsk', Major Malcom Wheeler Nicholson, AEFS, Khabarovsk. Nicholson reported three Chinese officers and 116 men arrived on 5 October, with about 500 more due.
112 AEFS intelligence summary No. 44, 10 December 1918 (RG165, M917).
113 7 December 1918, extracts from Lieutenant Yates' Report on Nikolsk (RG395, File 095, Box 29). The city administration consisted of Mayor Prokofiev, Council Chairman Maksimenko and Police Chief Kotzubinskii.
114 14 December 1918, intelligence summary No. 46, AEFS intelligence office and 4 December 1918, letter from Captain Harold V.V. Fay/intelligence officer – Harbin, to intelligence officer/AEFS – Vladivostok. Major General Gao Fin Tonen allegedly smuggled the opium from Pogrannichnaya to Harbin in his own automobile.
115 10 February 1919 report 'Ataman Semenoff and his officers', Captain F.F. Moore, AEFS, Vladivostok (RG395, File 095, Box 29).
116 *Dalekaya Okraina*, 13 December 1918, in AEFS intelligence section newspaper summary, 17 December 1918 (RG165, M917).
117 19 November 1918, report from Captain Roger W. Straus to AEFS intelligence officer, 'Military Clique of the Amur Province' (RG165, M917).
118 Ibid.
119 Ibid.
120 AEFS intelligence summary No. 34, 26 November 1918 (RG165, M917).
121 AEFS intelligence summary No. 44, 10 December 1918 (RG165, M917).
122 AEFS intelligence section newspaper summary, 17 December 1918 (RG165, M917).
123 11 February 1919, telegram from Lieutenant Baggs, Chita, to Colonel Barrows, Vladivostok (RG395, File 095, Box 29). Baggs advised Barrows: 'General Schemmelin permanently replaces Afanassief.'
124 AEFS intelligence summary No. 42, 7 December 1918 (RG165, M917).

NOTES

125 AEFS intelligence summary No. 44, 10 December 1918 (RG165, M917). The town under siege was named as Alexandro.
126 7 October 1918, intelligence summary No. 19, AEFS intelligence office (RG395, File 095 Semenoff, Box 29).
127 6 October 1919, letter/report from 1st Lieutenant Justis S. Davidson, Chief Intelligence Officer/AEFS intelligence section (Classified 'Confidential') (RG165, Microfilm M917).
128 Henry Baerlein, *The March of the Seventy Thousand*, Leonard Parsons, London, p. 261.
129 Heald, *Witness to Revolution*, p. 252.
130 AEFS intelligence section newspaper summary, 28 October 1918 (RG165, M917).
131 AEFS intelligence section newspaper summary, 25 October 1918 (RG165, M917).
132 *Moya Gazeta*, 28 October 1918, in AEFS intelligence section newspaper summary, 28 October 1918 (RG165, M917).
133 Dyboski, *Seven Years in Russia and Siberia*, p. 52.
134 3 June 1919, letter from W.H. Blaine to US Consul, Vladivostok (RG165, MID 1766–1107).
135 *Moya Gazeta*, 28 October 1918, in AEFS intelligence section newspaper summary, 29 October 1918 (RG165, M917).
136 AEFS intelligence section newspaper summary, 28 October 1918 (RG165, M917).
137 Heald, *Witness to Revolution*, p. 342. Heald made these observations in May 1919.
138 4 January 1919 Letter from 1st Lieutenant Robert J. Scovell, AEFS, Manchuli, to Lieutenant Colonel Barrows, Vladivostok (RG395, File 095, Box 29).
139 18 March 1919, report No. 1945 from HA, Conditions between Harbin and Omsk (RG395, File 095, Box, 29). 'The situation from Irkutsk to Tomsk is distinctly good, there is absolutely no shortage of commodities of any kind except matches.' When the author declared for a payment of duty on five cars of goods, he 'aroused astonished, but favorable comment'.
140 June 3 1919, letter from W.H. Blaine, Vladivostok, to US Consul, Vladivostok (RG165, File No. 1766-1107/2). Blaine documented his experiences in Verkhne-Udinsk for the US Consul on the eve of his departure, adding, 'Had I known that this information was of any value I could have substantiated it with actual figures and dates'.
141 22 February 1919, letter from Lieutenant Colonel Barrows, AEFS Vladivostok, to AEFS intelligence officer, Harbin, and attached report, 'Ataman Semenoff', by Nicholas Romanoff.
142 Changchun was a major Japanese railway terminus and border town to the Japanese colony of Korea. Like many towns in Manchuria, Changchun was divided into Chinese, Japanese and Russian sectors.
143 *Primorskaya Zhizn*, 25 October 1918, in AEFS intelligence section newspaper summary, 25 October 1918 (RG165, M917).
144 Bell, *Side Lights a the Siberia Campaign*, p. 61.
145 Ward, With the 'Die-Hards' in Siberia, pp. 80–1.
146 Bukin, 'Pokushenie', Chita, 2002.
147 Trotsky's order No. 92 on 1 May 1919 read: 'Arbitrary shooting of men who come over from the enemy, as also of prisoners of war, will be punished ruthlessly in accordance with military law. Let Kolchak's executioners shoot prisoners. The workers' and peasants' army will turn repentant enemies into friends.'
148 Roberts, *Assignment Siberia 1917–1919*, RRSC diary entry, 13 November 1918.
149 26 November 1918, 'Semenoff Defies Siberian Dictator', *New York Times*, p. 2:4.
150 AEFS intelligence summary No. 34, 26 November 1918 (RG165, M917).
151 Heald, *Witness to Revolution*, p. 252.
152 Ibid., p. 254.
153 2 December 1918, telegram from Captain Skladal/AEFS Chita to Colonel Barrows/AEFS Vladivostok, (RG165, M917).
154 9 December 1918, 'Semenoff's Arrest Ordered by Kolchak', *New York Times*, pp. 3ff.
155 Parkin, *Razgrom Kolchaka*, Boennoe Izdatel' stuo Ministerstva Oborony' Moscow, 1969, p. 266. Ivan Brusak escaped from a 'death train' at Slyudyanka in July 1919.
156 Dotsenko, *The Struggle for Democracy*, p. 142, and 'Semenoff Defies Siberian Dictator', *New York Times*, 26 November 1918, p. 2:4.

157 Smele, *Civil War in Siberia*, p. 190.
158 Vasilevskii, *Ataman Semenov*, p. 11. Semenov's Order No. 23 on 19 November declared his sole command over Transbaikal and Amur provinces and the Ussuri Cossack Host.
159 Ibid., pp. 12–29. Semenov's breakaway command referred to itself as the *Otdel'naya Vostochno-Sibirskaya Armiya*, from late November or December 1918 until mid-June 1919.
160 AEFS intelligence summary No. 34, 26 November 1918 (RG165, M917).
161 AEFS intelligence section, 'Japanese Opinions', 18 December 1918 (RG165, M917).
162 Smele, *Civil War in Siberia*, pp. 188–92. Despite the animosity between Omsk and Chita, Semenov's chief of staff (as of 26 November) was Colonel Zubkovskii, who was also indicated (in a reliable US intelligence report) as the 'Kolchak representative' on the OMO staff.
163 Vasilevskii, *Ataman Semenov*, p. 122; and Pereira, 'Siberian Atamanshcina', p. 130.
164 1 December 1918, telegram from Captain Schuyler/AEFS Omsk, 'Conversation with Captain Skladal, Chita' (RG395, File 095 Semenoff, Box 29).
165 Telegram from AEFS Captain Skladal, Chita, to AEFS Colonel Barrows, Vladivostok, 2 December 1918 (RG165, M917).
166 Undated telegram (and translation) from Colonel Semenov, Chita, to Major General Lebedev, Omsk (RG395, File 095, Box 29).
167 AEFS intelligence summary No. 41, 6 December 1918 (RG165, M917).
168 Footman, 'Ataman Semenov', p. 32.
169 AEFS intelligence summary No. 41, 6 December 1918 (RG165, M917). The identity of 'Tieverhor' is unknown. Volkov had been chief of the Omsk garrison.
170 AEFS intelligence summary No. 42, 7 December 1918 (RG165, M917).
171 13 December 1918, 'Semenoff Finding Enemies in Front and Rear', *Osaka Mainichi*, AEFS intelligence section newspaper summaries, 17 and 18 December 1918 (RG165, M917), and US Department of State, *FRUS*, 1918, vol. 2, p. 458.
172 AEFS intelligence summary No. 45, 12 December 1918 (RG165, M917).
173 AEFS intelligence summary No. 42, 7 December 1918 and AEFS intelligence section, Japanese Opinions, 18 December 1918 (RG165, M917).
174 AEFS intelligence summary No. 44, 10 December 1918 (RG165, M917).
175 *Dalekaya Okraina*, 17 December 1918, in AEFS intelligence section newspaper summary, 17 December 1918 (RG165, M917).
176 11 January 1919, telegram No. 7 from Captain Frederick F. Moore, AEFS, Chita, to Lieutenant Colonel Barrows, Vladivostok (RG395, File 095, Box 29).
177 Report from Captain V.V. Fay, Intelligence Officer-Harbin, to AEFS intelligence officer, 4 December 1918, and AEFS intelligence summary No. 45, 12 December 1918 (RG165, M917).
178 11 December 1918, telegram from Captain Scovell, Manchuli, to Lieutenant Colonel Barrows, Vladivostok (RG395, File 095, Box 29).
179 *Golos Primorya*, 17 December 1918, in AEFS intelligence section newspaper summary, 17 December 1918 (RG165, M917). The Japanese mission in Vladivostok denied that Fujii issued Volkov an ultimatum.
180 'Arrest of Ataman Semenoff', *Dalekaya Okraina*, 17 December 1918, in AEFS intelligence section newspaper summary, December 17, 1918 (RG165, M917). 'The newspaper Manchuria (in Harbin) states (from an American source) that Ataman Semenov has been arrested by the French Command.'
181 17 December 1918, telegram from Captain C. Skladal, Chita, to AEFS intelligence officer, Vladivostok, and 18 December 1918, telegram from Lieutenant R. Baggs, Verkhne-Udinsk, to Major Eichelberger, AEFS HQ (RG395, File 095, Box 29).
182 Letter from AEFS Lieutenant Colonel. Barrows, Chita, to AEFS Major Eichelberger, Vladivostok, 19 December 1918 (RG165, M917). Barrows concluded his letter, 'The trouble lies entirely in the shortage of railway income and in the railway administration'. He failed to see that Semenov was raking off all the railway income for his personal coffers.

NOTES

183 18 December 1918, letter from Frank Polk to US Ambassador to Japan Roland Morris, Washington, No. 861.00/3430 (Microfilm 316, roll 18). Roland Sletor Morris was an accomplished Philadelphia lawyer and 'progressive' Democratic party leader when he was appointed ambassador by Woodrow Wilson. He served in Tokyo from 30 October 1917 until 15 May 1920.

184 AEFS intelligence section newspaper summary, 17 December 1918 (RG165, M917).

185 'Semenoff Now Offers to Recognize Kolchak', *New York Times*, 26 December 1918, p. 3. Only 12 of the 58 locomotives sitting in Chita's railyard were fit for service, but they lay idle because there were no funds to pay the crews.

186 Heald, *Witness to Revolution*, p. 260.

187 Ibid., p. 275.

188 Ibid.

189 Ibid., p. 276.

190 Ibid., p. 277.

191 Dotsenko, *The Struggle for Democracy*, pp. 38 and 74; Graves, *America's Siberia Adventue*, p. 245, and Fleming, *The Fate of Admiral Kolchak*, pp. 121–2. N.V. Fomin, a Socialist-Revolutionary member of the Constituent Assembly and Siberian Provisional Government official, was brutally beaten, slashed, stabbed and shot. His corpse bore 17 different wounds from firearms, bayonets and sabres. Ironically, when the moderate Socialist-Revolutionary and right-wing military alliance had begun coalescing in July 1918, Fomin remarked, 'Among the military there are some who say, "First we will take care of the Bolsheviks, and then we will begin hanging the Socialist-Revolutionaries." ' Fomin's observation erred only in the method of liquidation.

192 Heald, *Witness to Revolution*, p. 289.

193 Memorandum of conversation between Major Johnson and Mr Alex Osheroff, 27 December 1918 (RG43, New Entry 844, Index 2, Box 8, File 224A).

194 Fleming, *The Fate of Admiral Kolchak*, p. 121.

195 'Bomb Wounds Semenoff', *New York Times*, p. 6:7, 27 December 1918; Footman, 'Ataman Semenov', p. 35, and Bukin, 'Pokushenie', A Mr and Mrs Shafzher, Lieutenant Torchilov and military public prosecutor Lieutenant Sharaburin were listed among the lightly wounded.

196 21 December 1918, telegrams from Chita to AEFS HQ, Vladivostok (RG395, File 095, Box 29).

197 Bukin, 'Pokushenie'.

198 Heald, *Witness to Revolution*, p. 284. The council of ministers in Omsk did not issue a decree declaring the Julian calender New Year's Day as a holiday until 19 days before (AEFS intelligence section 17 December 1918, newspaper summary No. 439).

199 Petr Ivanovich Naletov, 'Pedagogicheskoi Eksperiment: Vospominaniya Uchastnika Splava 1923 goda', Irkutsk, 1985. Other writers say that Bernbaum/Nerris was taken to Makkaveevo, Naletov visited the shed at Karymskaya in 1923, which had become an informal place of pilgrimage to the next of kin of the hundreds of victims said to have been executed there.

5 RODOMONTADE AND GIRLS WITH DIAMONDS: JANUARY–APRIL 1919

1 Vasilevskii, *Ataman Semenov*, p. 14. Semenov mentioned his short trip to eastern Transbaikalia in his 9 January Order No. 9.

2 Ibid., pp. 13–14. Semenov's Order No. 9 of the Separate Eastern Siberian Army, 'On the Propagation of False Rumors', was issued 9 January 1919 and published in Chita newspaper *Russkii Vostok* two days later.

3 13 January 1919, letter from 1st Lieutenant Robert J. Scovell, AEFS, Manchuli, to Lieutenant Colonel Barrows, Vladivostok (RG395, File 095, Box 29). General Ivanov-Rinov and three officers from Ataman Annenkov's detachment called on Semenov around 10–11 January, but it is unclear if they came to pressure Semenov or to offer him support.

4 18 March 1919, Report No. 1945. Semenov also charged 3 rubles to validate a traveler's passport.

5 Smele, *Civil War in Siberia*, p. 456, citing a report by Colonel Jack of the British Railway mission.
6 18 March 1919, Report No. 1945, p. 6.
7 17 January 1919, telegram (and AEFS translation) from Junior Captain Filippoff, Kultuk, to Division Commander; and undated telegram (and AEFS translation) from Major General Verigo, Chita, to Major General Volkov, Irkutsk (RG395, File 095, Box 29).
8 Report from AEFS 1st Lieutenant Justis Davidson, Chita, to AEFS chief intelligence officer, 6 October 1919 (RG165, M917).
9 AEFS intelligence section newspaper summary, 18 December 1918 (RG165, M917); *The Story of the Great War*, p. 4574; and Goldhurst, Richard, *The Midnight War: The American Intervention in Russia, 1918–1920*, McGraw-Hill, New York, p. 130.
10 Grondijs, *La Guerre en Russie et en Siberie*.
11 10 February 1919, report 'Ataman Semenoff and his officers', Captain F.F. Moore, AEFS, Vladivostok.
12 21 February 1919, letter from Lieutenant Colonel Barrows, AEFS Vladivostok, to AEFS intelligence officer, Harbin, and attached report, 'Ataman Semenoff', by Nicholas Romanoff (RG395, File 095 Semenoff, Box 29).
13 US Senate Committee an Education and Labor, *Deportation of Gregorie Semenoff*, pp. 100–1.
14 Fleming, *The Fate of Admiral Kolchak*, p. 53.
15 Footman, 'Ataman Semenov' p. 27, citing Budberg, *Arkhiv Russkoi Revolyutsii*, vol. 13, pp. 204–5.
16 9 April 2002, Barinov, Aleksandr, '*Tsyganka Masha*', *Zabaikal'skim Rabochii*, Chita, No. 65 (23593)/No. 239 (23521), and Fleming, *The Fate of Admiral Kolchak*, pp. 52–4.
17 Footman, 'Ataman Semenov' pp. 27 and 41.
18 21 February 1919, letter from Lieutenant Colonel Barrows, AEFS Vladivostok, to AEFS intelligence officer, Harbin, and attached report, 'Ataman Semenoff', by Nicholas Romanoff.
19 The most prominent Bolsheviks of Jewish heritage were Yakov Sverdlov, first head of the Soviet state, and War Commissar Leon Trotsky (born Lev Davidovich Bronshtain in 1879).
20 Leonid Iouzéfovitch, 'Il ne doit rester graine ni d'homme ni de femme', *Bulletin de l'Association Anda*, Paris, No. 40, January 2001.
21 Intelligence summary No. 41, 6 December 1918. Presumably the Black Squadron was an offshoot of the *Chernotsenty*, the Black Hundreds, Russia's foremost anti-Semitic league.
22 AEFS intelligence section newspaper summary, 20 February 1920 (RG165, M917); and 9 June 1919, letter from Captain Montgomery Schuyler to AEFS chief of staff, General Report on Omsk (RG395, File 095, Box 29). Schuyler also believed in the Jewish–Bolshevik conspiracy and submitted Wilton's table as evidence.
23 Footman, 'Ataman Semenov', p. 41.
24 Goldhurst, *The Midnight War*, p. 130.
25 'Kalmykov's Cell of Tortures', *Golos Rodini*, 3 February 1920, in AEFS intelligence section newspaper summary, 3 February 1920 (RG165, M917). This article described Mashka as a gypsy.
26 Footman, 'Ataman Semenov', p. 41.
27 US Senate Committee an Education and Labor, *Deportation of Gregorie Semenoff*, pp. 100–1.
28 Dr Magnus Hirschfeld (ed.), *The Sexual History Of The World War*, Panurge Press, New York, 1934. Dr Breitner, the witness to this horror, later became president of the Austrian Red Cross (1950–56) and a candidate of the Independent Party (VdU) in the 1951 presidential elections. He recorded the event in his diary under the date of 1 December 1919 (Österreich Lexikon).
29 9 February 1919, report 'A Visit to the Train of Semenoff', Captain Harold V.V. Fay, Harbin (RG395, File 095, Box 29).
30 Footman, 'Ataman Semenov', p. 27.
31 Goldhurst, 'The Midnight War', p. 131. Gail Berg Reitzel and Raymond J. Reitzel, *Shifting Scenes in Siberia* (Bk 2 of biography of Raymond J. Reitzel), privately-published (Library

NOTES

of Congress Call No. D639.Y7 R44), p. II-34. 'An ornate old gentleman in purple uniform, trimmed with gold braid, looking no less than a general, turned out to be head of the Plumbers' Union!' exclaimed Gail Reitzel, a YMCA hostess at the International Hut in Vladivostok.
32 Footman, pp. 43–4; 10 February 1919, report 'Ataman Semenoff and his officers', Captain F.F. Moore, AEFS, Vladivostok. Verigo left for Harbin shortly thereafter. 'Lutzov' may have been the same officer later referred to in other reports at 'Lovtsov' (5 August 1919, translation from Russian of report on Semenoff, RG395, File 095, Box 29).
33 'Forces of Ataman Semionov', report of US Military Attaché – China, 22 January 1920 (RG165, M1444, MID 2009-82).
34 AEFS intelligence summary No. 37, 1 December 1918 (RG165, M917).
35 Bell, *Side Lights on the Siberian Campaign*, pp. 95–6.
36 Aleksandr Fridman, 'Evreiskie Pogromy... v. Mongolii', *IJC*, Nizhne Novgorod, 2002 and Ossendowski, *Beasts, Men and Gods*, pp. 233–4 and 267–8, and Bukin, 'Pokushenie'. In January 1919, Lieutenant Sipailov arrested the organizer of the attempt on the Ataman's life, Alexander Sofronov.
37 Vasilevskii, *Ataman Semenov*, p. 21, 'Prikaz No. 166 voiskam Otedel'noi Vostochno-Sibirskoi armii o vyrazshenii blagodarnocti voinskim chastyam', Chita, 22 May 1919.
38 Semenov, *O Sebe*, p. 124.
39 2 December 1918, telegram from Captain Skladal/AEFS Chita to Colonel Barrows/AEFS Vladivostok (RG165, Microfilm M917).
40 10 March 1919, AEFS translation, 'A Not Unusual Incident' (RG395, File 095, Box 29).
41 AEFS intelligence summary No. 45, 12 December 1918 (RG165, M917).
42 Budberg, *Dnevnik Byelogvardeitsa*.
43 Aleksandra Barinova, 'Taina Shumovskogo Dvortsa', Chita, 2001.
44 21 February 1919, letter from Lieutenant Colonel Barrows, AEFS Vladivostok, to AEFS intelligence officer, Harbin, and attached report, 'Ataman Semenoff', by Nicholas Romanoff.
45 The Shumovs' holdings included the Voznesenskii and Kruchininskii gold mine.
46 Barinova, 'Taina Shumovskogo Dvortsa'.
47 Barinov, 'Tsyganka Masha'.
48 Omsk State Archive, Description of Personal Collection of G.E. Katanaev, f.366, op.1, 488 d.; and Vasilevskii, *Ataman Semenov*, p. 15, citing 'Prikaz No. 49 komanduyushchego po Otdel'noi Vostochno-Sibirskoi armii o vmeshatel'stve ofitserov v dela militsii', Chita, 11 February 1919.
49 Vasilevskii, *Ataman Semenov*, pp. 17–18, citing 27 February 1919, telegram from Semenov to Knox.
50 Ibid., pp. 18–19, 'Uvedomlenie G.M. Semenova', *Russkii Vostok*, 4 March 1919; and Prikaz No. 88 voiskam Vostochno-Sibirskoi armii o bor'be s sabotazhem pri mobilizatsii v armiyu, Chita, 17 March 1919.
51 Vasilevskii, *Ataman Semenov*, p. 25, 'Prikaz No. 179 voiskam Otdel'noi Vostochno-Sibirskoi Armii', Chita, 2 June 1919; and Barinov, 'Tsyganka Masha'.
52 18 March 1919, report No. 1945, pp. 6–7. The author cited Ungern-Shternberg as 'a German, Captain Unger von Steinburg'.
53 Smele, *Civil War in Siberia*, p. 351.
54 Bukin, 'Pokushenie'.
55 Ibid.
56 Barinov, 'Zabytyi pisatel'.
57 AEFS intelligence summary No. 46, 14 December 1918 (RG165, M917).
58 'Materials from Kalmykov's Time', *Golos Rodini*, 3 February 1920, in AEFS intelligence section newspaper summary, 3 February 1920 (RG165, M917).
59 'Kalmykov's Cell of Tortures', *Golos Rodini*, 3 February 1920, in AEFS intelligence section newspaper summary, 3 February 1920 (RG165, M917).
60 Graves, *America's Siberian Adventure*, p. 127.
61 Ibid., p. 133.
62 Ibid., p. 128.

63 22 January 1919, letter from Captain I.C. Nicholas, AEFS 27th Infantry Regiment, Khabarovsk, to AEFS intelligence officer, Vladivostok (RG395, File 095, Box 29).
64 AEFS intelligence summary No. 46, 14 December 1918 (RG165, M917).
65 Graves, *America's Siberian Adventure*, p. 129.
66 Volkov, 'Tragediya Russkogo Ofitserstva', ch. 4.
67 Graves, *America's Siberian Adventure*, p. 130.
68 US Senate Committee on Education and Labor, *Deportation of Gregorie Semenoff*, p. 11.
69 Ibid.
70 Volkov, '*Tragediya Russkogo Ofitserstva*', ch. 4. Kalmykov's reluctant recognition of Kolchak may have been forced more by prominent Cossacks in Omsk, such as Lieutenant General A.I. Dutov, *pokhodnii ataman* of all Cossack armies, than by the votes of his Ussuri *krug*.
71 Vasilevskii, *Ataman Semenov*, p. 18, 'Uvedomlenie G.M. Semenova o narushenii zakonnosti komandirami ryada voinskikh chastei v Irkutske', Chita, 4 March 1919.
72 Vailevskii, *Ataman Semenov*, p. 19, 'Ob otpravlenii na Orenburgskii front', Chita, 26 March 1919. The unnamed detachment was supposedly 'about division-strength' and included three machine gun companies.
73 'The Cossack Conference in Khabarovsk', *Dalny Vostok*, in AEFS intelligence section newspaper summary, 8 March 1919 (RG165, M917).
74 Graves, *America's Siberian Adventure*, p. 135.
75 *Nachálo*, AEFS intelligence section newspaper summary, 20 February 1920. *Nachálo* was the 'official organ of the Revolutionary Staff at Nikolsk' (RG165, M917).
76 Shaw, 'The Railroad War', p. 2.
77 Graves, *America's Siberian Adventure*, p. 135.
78 Report from AEFS 1st Lieutenant H.F. Cauthard, US 27th Inf., to CO 27th Inf–Spasskoe, 21 February 1919 (RG165, M917).
79 Ibid.
80 The main concern of most people at the time of the White counterrevolution was money: during the Bolsheviks' first turn in power, imperial rubles had been hoarded by banks and merchants, and change was always given in Bolshevik paper money. When the Whites took over, Bolshevik currency became valueless. People who had accumulated large sums of Bolshevik money were impoverished by the Red retreat. AEF intelligence section memorandum of 20 October 1918.
81 The numbers varied widely by date and definition (e.g. whether to take into account troops in Manchuria or other parts of China or forces at sea). For example, in January 1919, the Canadian Siberian Expeditionary Force (CSEF) consisted of 1,100 men in Siberia, 2,700 at sea and 1,200 in Canada still waiting to deploy (8 January 1919, telegram 7B from Canadian Chief of Staff to War Office). At one point approximately 72,000 Japanese military personnel were in eastern Siberia, the Russian Far East and Manchuria.
82 The Poles and Serbians were former prisoners of war from the Austro-Hungarian army; the Italians were transferred from Tientsin, China, the French from Saigon, the British from Hong Kong.
83 Reitzel and Reitzel, *Shifting Scenes*, p. II-34.
84 Medical History of the Siberian Expedition (hereafter referred to as Medical History), p. 17 (RG165, M917).
85 P. Whitney Lackenbauer, 'Why Siberia? Canadian Foreign Policy and Siberian Intervention 1918–19', University of Waterloo, April 1998; 'Canadians Go to the Front', *Sibirsky Put*, 17 December 1918, in AEFS newspaper summary, 18 December 1918; and Fleming, *The Fate of Admiral Kolchak*, p. 122. CSEF consisted of 259th and 260th Battalions, No. 6 Signal Section, 16 Field Company (engineers), 20th Machine Gun Company, 'B' Squadron of the Royal Canadian Mounted Police and a field battery. Some references state that the *Suffolk* gun train was equipped with 'a pair of 12-pounder guns'.
86 Miloslav Caplovic, 'French Military Mission in Czechoslovakia 1919–1938', *Slovak Army Review*, Bratislava, Autumn 2001. Janin had been commander of the 'Czechoslovak Army abroad' since 27 February 1918.

NOTES

87 Fleming, *The Fate of Admiral Kolchak*, p. 128.
88 AEFS intelligence summary No. 46, 14 December 1918. See the appendices for a list of field assignments of AEF intelligence officers to Semenov's territory.
89 21 February 1919, letter from Lieutenant Colonel Barrows, AEFS Vladivostok, to AEFS intelligence officer, Harbin and attached report, 'Ataman Semenoff', by Nicholas Romanoff.
90 *From the Past*, Newsletter of the 31st Regiment Association, No. 9, February 1998.
91 Graves, *America's Siberian Adventure*, p. 188.
92 Unterberger, *America's Siberian Expedition*, p. 119.
93 At Ivanov-Rinov's disposal for the defense of Vladivostok were: a platoon of Marine Guards, a naval company, six companies of cadets, a battalion of 'Fortress Artillery', and a *sotnia* of mounted Cossacks.
94 Letter from Major General Ivanov-Rinov to CINC Allied Forces, Far East, 3 March 1919 (RG165, M917).
95 Reitzel and Reitzel, *Shifting Scenes*, p. II-42.
96 Ibid., p. II-90.
97 'Growth of Prostitution', *Sibirsky Put*, 17 December 1918, in AEFS newspaper summary, 18 December 1918.
98 18 October 1918 AEFS intelligence report, Vladivostok. 'A *droshky* is a low carriage with a high seat in front for the driver, who is so padded with clothes and thick coats as to appear monstrous. He yells, grunts, whistles at his horses and flicks them with a whip unceasingly. There are two horses driven: the larger in the shafts and the other, sometimes little more than a colt, is driven at one side and not in the shafts, but harnessed so that he also helps pull. There is a low, narrow seat for two where the lady always sits on the right side, directly back of the driver and the gentlemen on the left, back of the little horse where he gets mud in the face' (Reitzel and Reitzel, *Shifting Scenes*, p. II-22).
99 Dyboski, *Seven Years in Russia and Sikena*, pp. 54 and 60.
100 Goldhurst, *The Midnight War*, p. 130.
101 Reitzel and Reitzel, *Shifting Scenes*, p. II-38.
102 Ward, *With the 'Die-Hards' in Siberia*, pp. 54–5.
103 Reitzel and Reitzel, *Shifting Scenes*, p. II-37.
104 Goldhurst, *The Midnight War*, p. 79. Estimates vary widely, but also are a function of time since troops were being shifted around often. Smele states that two-thirds of the Japanese Army in Siberia (approximately 45,000 men) was stationed on the Chinese Eastern Railway.
105 The Russian Orthodox Church had 37,000 adherents in Japan.
106 AEFS intelligence section memorandum, 20 October 1918 (RG165, M917); and Goldhurst, *The Midnight War*, p. 79.
107 Manusevich *et al.*, *Internatsionalisti*, pp. 305–12 and 318–23.
108 Gutman, *The Destruction of Nikolaevsk-on-Amur*, pp. 374–5. Gutman cites 'Krasnoshchekov's helper Vilensky' as an example of a Soviet agent transported into the Far East on a Czech Legion train. Gutman alleges that Vilensky 'directed the work of Red partisans and agents' in Amur and Maritime provinces.
109 Fleming, *The Fate of Admiral Kolchak*, p. 49.
110 Reitzel and Reitzel, *Shifting Scenes*, p. I-197.
111 The Serbs stormed Kazan along with Colonel Kappel's 'People's Army', the 1st Regiment of the Czech Legion and the White Volga River Flotilla.
112 11 November 1918, AEFS intelligence report (RG165, M917).
113 1 December 1918, telegram from Captain Skladal/AEFS-Chita to Colonel Barrows/AEFS–Vladivostok.
114 10 December 1918, intelligence summary No. 44, AEFS intelligence section, attached report, 'Semenoff's Troops'.
115 'Forces of Ataman Semionov', US Military Attaché-China, 22 January 1920 (RG165, M1444, MID 2009-82).
116 A. Deriabin and P. Palacios-Fernandes, *Grazhdanskaya Voina v Rossii 1917–1922: Natsionalniye Armii*, Izdatelstvo ACT, Moscow, 2000, pp. 42–4.

117 Engineer Report, 1918, p. 61 (RG165, M917).
118 Heald, *Witness to Revolution*, pp. 210–11 and 222–3, and William Howard Taft, Chairman of Editorial Board, *Service with Fighting Men: An Account of the Work of the American Young Men's Christian Associations in the World War*, vol. 2, Association Press, New York, 1922, pp. 314–31 and 419–58.
119 Taft, *Service with Fighting Men*, p. 441.
120 12 February 1919, telegram from Captain Schuyler, Omsk, to AEFS intelligence officer, Vladivostok (RG395, File 095, Box 29).
121 Taft, *Service with Fighting Men*, pp. 442–3.
122 *American Legion Magazine*, April 1978, p. 56.
123 17 July 1918 aide-memoire from US Secretary of State Lansing to Allied ambassadors, US Department of State, *FRUS*, 1918, *Russia*, vol. 2, pp. 287–90.
124 Ibid., and Morley, *The Japanese Thrust into Siberian*, p. 294. Antony C. Sutton, *Wall Street and the Bolshevik Revolution*, n.p., 2001, provides modern, libertarian support for the Japanese view.
125 Goldhurst, *The Midnight War*, p. 82.
126 *New York Times*, 9 December 1918, p. 3:1.
127 Graves, *America's Siberian Adventure*, p. 206.
128 *Red Cross Magazine*, April 1919, 14, 4. An example of Russian civilian protests against the ARC's pro-Kolchak activities is cited in AEFS intelligence summary No. 318, 10 October 1919 (RG165, M917).
129 *Red Cross Magazine*, May 1919.
130 *Red Cross Magazine*, May and June 1919.
131 Reitzel and Reitzel, *Shifting Scenes*, p. 38.
132 Heald, *Witness to Revolution*, p. 312.
133 Ibid., p. 338.
134 Ibid., p. 312.
135 Baerlein, *The March of the Seventy Thousand*, p. 260.
136 9 June 1919. letter from Captain Montgomery Schuyler to AEFS chief of staff, General Report on Omsk.
137 3 April 1919, Memorandum from Dobrovidoff to Montgomery F. Schuyler, AEFS (RG395, File 095, Box 29).
138 Heald, *Witness to Revolution*, p. 318.
139 Ibid., p. 320.
140 Ibid., p. 316.
141 Robberies, such as the 6 March hold-up of Engineer Moiseyev and family in the official railroad car where they lived near Vladivostok railroad station of 50,000 rubles, did little to inspire senior railway personnel to stay on.
142 AEFS intelligence section newspaper summary, 8 March 1919 (RG165, M917) and *From the Past*, Newsletter of the 31st Regiment Association, 9, February 1998.
143 'Music is furnished free at night by rats. It takes two or three nights to get used to them. Rat poison from the American Red Cross doesn't seem to phase them. My mattress is spread on a high table. After the lights are out, I feel the rats approach from all angles, level with my head on the shelves, under me by the floor, over me by the projections. It gives the sensation of the incoming tide.' Edward Heald, Omsk, 6 April, *Witness to Revolution*, p. 312.
144 Reitzel and Reitzel, *Shifting Scenes*, p. II-45.
145 18 March 1919 Report No. 1945.
146 Graves, *America's Siberian Adventure*, p. 184.
147 By 15 May 1919, US 27th Infantry strength at Verkhne-Udinsk consisted of: Regimental Headquarters, Headquarters Company, Supply Company, Machine Gun Company (less one platoon), Field Hospital No. 4, the 1 Battalion (less Companies C and D) and Companies I, K, L and M.
148 Jesse A. Anderson, *A Doughboy in the American Expeditionary Force Siberia*, J.A. Anderson, CA, 1983, p. 56.

NOTES

149 Anderson, *A Doughboy*, p. 28.
150 12 June 1919 [Circular] No. 6, 'Kantselyariya Mezhdusoyuznogo Tekhnicheskogo Sovieta Kit. Vost. i Sibirsk. zh. d.', Harbin (RG43, New Entry 844). The Allies deference to General Dmitri Horvath is peculiar in light of his constant insolence to the Omsk government. On 12 March 1919, General Horvath met with Ataman Semenov at Harbin, where they reportedly settled all their previous squabbles. The same day, 'Supreme Plenipotentiary' Horvath refused orders from Kolchak to proceed to Omsk. He then traveled to Vladivostok with Semenov the next day.

6 WHITE TERROR ON THE *MAGISTRAL*: MAY–SEPTEMBER 1919

1 G. Balfour, *The Armoured Train: Its Development and Usage*, B.T. Batsford, London, 1981.
2 John Batchelor, *Rail Gun*, John Batchelor, Broadstone, Dorset, 1973, pp. 1–2.
3 Wilfried Kopenhagen, *Armored Trains of the Soviet Union 1917–1945*, Schiffer Military History, Atglen, PA, 1996, pp. 7–9; Steven J. Zaloga, 'Soviet Armoured Trains', n.p., 2001; and Athol Yates and Ilya Karachevtsev, 'The History of Russian and Soviet Armored Trains', Academic International Press, Gulf Breeze, FL, 1997.
4 V.A. Potseluyev, *Bronenostsi Zheleznikh Dorog*, Molodaya Gvardiya, Moscow, 1982, pp. 19–23, 26, 35, 41, 67, 74, 75, 79 and 82.
5 Zaloga, 'Soviet Armored Trains'.
6 Ibid., pp. 69 and 74. Admiral Nikolai Essen was a brilliant Russian naval officer whose quick thinking in the first months of the First World War denied the Gulf of Finland to a much larger and modern German Fleet and captured the *Magdeburg* and her precious signal logs and code tables. Trains named *'Groznyi'* operated in Semenov's army and in the Red Army under S.M. Lepetenko against Denikin in summer 1919.
7 Trotsky, *My Life*, ch. 34, and Albert Seaton, *The Soviet Army*, Osprey Publishing, Reading, 1972, p. 10.
8 American Red Cross Photograph No. 07207, 14 October 1919, Kuban Command of American Red Cross, Library of Congress Still Picture Division, ARC Lot 2918 F.
9 J. Silverlight, *The Victor's Dilemma: Allied Intervention in the Russian Civil War*, Weybright & Talley, NY, 1971, p. 336.
10 Robert N. North, *Transport in Western Siberia: Tsarist and Soviet Development*, University of British Columbia Press/Centre for Transportation Studies, Vancouver, p. 105.
11 Communiqué No. 19, 5 September 1918, General Headquarters Vladivostok, Bureau of Information (National Archives microfilm M917, Roll 2, Frame 210).
12 7 October 1918, intelligence summary No. 19, AEFS intelligence office (RG395, File 095 Semenoff, Box 29).
13 Barrows report, 9 May 1918, Appendix C: 'Notes on Armored Car'.
14 Semenov, *O Sebe*, ch. 2. The 'defection' of Captain Shelkov and OMO's armored trains to General Pleshkov in Harbin in July is discussed elsewhere.
15 US Senate Committee on Education and Labor, *Deportation of Gregorie Semenoff*, pp. 16 and 21–23, and compilation of reports.
16 15 January 1920, letter from M.K. Jones, District Inspector/Harbin, to J.F. Stevens, Harbin (RG43, New Entry 844). No. 106 was charging eastbound to Vladivostok via Harbin without authorization from railway traffic managers.
17 RRSC memorandum from Irkutsk to Mr Thompson, 16 June 1919 (RG43).
18 Telegram No. 167 from RRSC Colonel Lantry, Irkutsk, to Colonel Emerson, Omsk (RG43).
19 Smele, *Civil War in Siberia*, pp. 456 and 457.
20 US Senate Committee on Education and Labor, *Deportation of Gregorie Semenoff*, pp. 17–18.
21 Ibid., p. 4. Ms Natsvalov was the wife of one of Semenov's staff officers. Stepanov's outrageous statement to McNutt is often misattributed to Semenov.
22 Grondijs, *La Guerre en Russia et Siberie*, pp. 449–50.

23 Footman, 'Ataman Semenov', p. 49.
24 Grondijs, *La Guerre en Russia et Siberie*, pp. 451–8 and 467–71, and Footman, 'Ataman Semenov', pp. 46–9.
25 20 November 1919, letter from Lieutenant Colonel S.T. Cantrell/District Inspector Transbaikal Railway, Adrianovka, to Colonel G.H. Emerson/Chief Inspector, Irkutsk (RG43 RRSC, Entry 848, File 526, District Inspector Records).
26 Footman, 'Ataman Semenov', p. 44, US Senate Committee on Education and Labor, *Deportation of Gregorie Semenoff*, pp. 23–4. AEFS veterans testified that Semenov eventually promoted Freiburg to the rank of general. Freiburg told RRSC Lieutenant McDonald that he had been captured early in the First World War.
27 US Senate Committee on Education and Labor, *Deportation of Gregorie Semenoff*, pp. 21–2.
28 9 February 1919, report and Captain Harold V.V. Fay, AEFS intelligence officer, Harbin; and 21 February 1919, letter from Lieutenant Colonel Barrows, AEFS Vladivostok, to AEFS intelligence officer, Harbin and attached report, 'Ataman Semenoff', by Nicholas Romanoff (RG395, File 095 Semenoff, Box 29).
29 C.R. Rice, 'Pravda', RRSC Reunion, 11 November 1932.
30 28 August 1919, telegram from Blunt, Vladivostok to Colonel Jones, Harbin (RG43, New Entry 844, File 226).
31 Footman, 'Ataman Semenov', p. 45.
32 John A. White, *The Siberian Intervention*, Greenwood Press, New York, 1950.
33 Luckett, *The White Generals*, pp. 226–7.
34 Telegram from RRSC Colonel Lantry to RRSC Colonel Emerson, 4 July 1919 (RG43, New Entry 844).
35 11 May 1919, Verkhne-Udinsk Report, 1st Lieutenant Ralph L. Baggs, US 27th Infantry Regiment, USAT Sherman (RG395, File 095, Box 29).
36 US Senate Committee on Education and Labor, *Deportation of Gregorie Semenoff*, p. 12.
37 Barrows report, 9 May 1918, Appendix D: 'Observations on the use of railroad trains in handling troops'.
38 2 September 1919, telegram from RRSC Colonel Lantry, Irkutsk to J.F. Stevens, Harbin. 'All over entire [Transbaikal] railway we have no authority whatever, none of our instructions are complied with...' (RG43, New Entry 844, File 226).
39 US Senate Committee on Education and Labor, *Deportation of Gregorie Semenoff*, p. 23.
40 Ibid., p. 23.
41 Ibid., p. 21.
42 Ibid., p. 22.
43 Ibid., p. 23.
44 Grondijs, *La Guerre en Russia et Siberie*, pp. 447–8.
45 Ibid., pp. 470–1. Grondijs attended the court martial at Semenov's invitation.
46 Ibid.
47 Vasilevskii, *Ataman Semenov*, p. 33, 'Prikaz No. 16 voiskam Shestogo Vostochno-Sibirskogo armeiskogo korpusa o nakazaniyakh za klevetu v presse', Chita, 12 July 1919.
48 Petrov, *Seroicheskye godi bodi i pobed*, pp. 158 and 168.
49 Ibid., pp. 159–60. Petrov does not define the size or structure of these partisan cavalry units.
50 Anatolii Kulikov, 'Mnogo sdelal ya dobra...', *Zabaikal'skii Rabochii*, Chita, No. 12 (23539), August 2001.
51 Young Sik Kim 'The Sacrificial Lamb of the Cold War: The Nationalists of Korea', Seattle, WA, 2000. The author stated that 300,000 Koreans lived in Siberia during the Civil War.
52 Gutman, *The Destruction of Nikolaevsk-on-Amur*, pp. 118–24.
53 Young Sik Kim, 'The Sacrificial Lamb of the Cold War'. Young states that the party was founded in Irkutsk.
54 Kulikov, 'Mnogo sdelal ya dobra...'. Vagzhanov was arrested by Chita police inspector Myl'nikov. Dvornichenko writes that Vagzhanov escaped to Omsk when OMO occupied Chita and was arrested when he returned to visit his family.
55 Petrov, *Geroicheskye godi bodi i pubed*, pp. 159–60.

NOTES

56 Telegram from RRSC Lieutenant Colonel Lantry, Irkutsk, to RRSC Colonel Emerson, Harbin, 25 May 1919 (RG43).
57 Petrov, *Geroicheskye godi bodi i pubed*, pp. 160–6. Petrov cited from the memoirs of Kurunzulaya participant, M.M. Yakimov.
58 Ibid., Petrov writes that ten surviving officers and six enlisted men went before the tribunal.
59 9 April 2002, Aleksandr Barinov, 'Zabytyi pisatel', ili 'piarshchik' atamana', *Zabaikal'skim Rabochii*, Chita, No. 65 (23593)/No. 54 (23582).
60 'On Information from Japanese Hdqrs.', *Echo*, 8 March 1919, in AEFS intelligence section newspaper summary, 8 March 1919 (RG165, M917).
61 13 May 1919, telegram No. 32 from Major Shamotulski, Khabarovsk, to AEFS Vladivostok (RG395, File 095, Box 29).
62 14 May 1919, telegram No. 33 from Major Shamotulski, Khabarovsk, to AEFS Vladivostok (RG395, File 095, Box 29).
63 17 May 1919, telegram No. 139 from Allderdice, Spasskoe, to AEFS chief of staff, Vladivostok (RG395, File 095, Box 29).
64 1 June 1919, telegram No. 55 from Major Shamotulski, Khabarovsk, to AEFS, Vladivostok (RG395, File 095, Box 29).
65 Report of Operations of the 27th Infantry, 1 January–30 June 1919 (RG165, Roll 10, Frame 305). Hereafter referred to as January–June 1919 report of 27th Infantry Operations.
66 29 April 1919, wire, from RRSC Major Egber, Hailar, to Colonel Emerson, Harbin (RG43, New Entry 844).
67 28 April 1919, letter from Chief Inspector (unidentified) to D.P. Kasekavitch, Assistant General Manager/Chinese Eastern Railway, Harbin RRSC; 28 April, wire from Colonel Emerson/Harbin to Major Egber/Hailar; 6 May 1919, letter from Chief Inspector (unidentified) to John F. Stevens, President/Technical Board; and 20 June 1919, letter from Colonel George H. Emerson/Verkhne-Udinsk to Colonel C.H. Morrow/Commanding Officer, 27th Infantry, Verkhne Udinsk. RRSC Files contain scores of messages documenting Semenov's interference with military and civilian rail traffic between Lake Baikal and Manchuli during spring and summer 1919.
68 Undated extracts from the report of Lieutenant Byrnes concerning the town of Beresovka (RG395, File 095, Box 29). Park Barracks consisted of about 200 buildings, and the train station had 3,800 yards of siding. The town of Beresovka had two churches, two schools, two doctors, a hospital, 20 stores and plentiful water and forage.
69 Leon Trotsky, 1919, 'The Eastern Front: Kolchak's offensive (March–April 1919)', *Military Writings*, vol. 2, Merit Publishers, New York, 1969.
70 Semenov and his associates were not the only White authorities to shake down merchants who shipped on the railroad. 'Station masters [and] their military cohorts' in Kolchak's territory 'would all demand their cut from goods in transit', sometimes exceeding the cost of the goods, despite laws threatening death for speculation. Smele, *Civil War in Siberia*, pp. 462–4.
71 As of August 1919, 20 'old rubles' would buy US$1 gold. Roberts, 'Fred Martin Roberts' RRSC Diary' (August 21, 1919 entry), *Assignment Siberia*.
72 16 June 1919, memorandum from author unknown in Irkutsk to Mr Thompson/RRSC (RG43, New Entry 844).
73 US Senate Committee on Education and Labor, *Deportation of Gregorie Semenoff*, p. 12.
74 'US Consul Train Held Up in Siberia,' *New York Times*, 31 May 1919, p. 2:5.
75 January–June 1919 report of 27th Infantry Operations.
76 US Senate Committee on Education and Labor, *Deportation of Gregorie Semenoff*, p. 13.
77 Graves, *America's Siberian Adventure*, p. 184.
78 Ibid., p. 206.
79 Robert James Maddox, *The Unknown War with Russia: Wilson's Siberian Intervention*, Presidio Press, San Francisco, CA, p. 73. Maddox cites a paper read at the US Army War College by Lieutenant Colonel H.H. Slaughter, the AEFS liaison at Omsk. A member of the Czech staff told Slaughter about the Legion's plans after the incident.

80 15 June 1919, paraphrase of cipher to Consul General Harris and American Legation Peking (RG43, New Entry 844, Box 8, File 226).
81 15 June 1919, paraphrase of cipher [from Colonel Morrow] to Consul General Harris and to American Legation Peking for Department of State, Irkutsk (RG43, New Entry 844, Box 8, File 226).
82 Letter from RRSC Colonel G.H. Emerson, Verkhne Udinsk, to AEFS Colonel C.H. Morrow, 27th Inf. Regiment, Verkhne Udinsk, 20 June 1919 (RG43, New Entry 844, Box 8, File 226).
83 Semenov, *O Sebe*, pp. 122–3.
84 Newsletter of the 31st Regiment Association, 'From the Past', No. 9, February 1998, Pro Patria Press.
85 Crone, *East Lies the Sun*, p. 206 and 21 June 2002 letter from Alla Crone-Hayden to Jamie Bisher. Alla Crone was born and raised in Harbin.
86 Heald, *Witness to Revolution*, p. 342.
87 Vasilevskii, *Ataman Semenov*, pp. 20–1, 'Obrashchenie atamana Semenova k zabaikal'skim kazakam' and 'Vystuplenie G.M. Semenova pri otkrytii Tret'ego Voiskovogo Kruga Zabaikal'skogo kazach'ego voiska', Chita, 4 and 21 May 1919.
88 Vasilevskii, *Ataman Semenov* p. 23, 'Prikaz No. 173 voiskam Otdel'noi Vostochno-Sibirskoi armii ob ustanovlenii posobii sem'yam progibshikh i voennoplennym', Chita, 30 May 1919.
89 Vasilevskii, *Ataman Semenov*, p. 22, 'Telegramma atamana Semenova generalu Khorvatu o gotovnosti priznat' vlast' Kolchaka', Chita, 26 May 1919, published in *Russkii Vostok*, 29 May 1919.
90 Vasilevksii, *Ataman Semenov*, p. 23, 'Telegramma G.M. Semenova admiralu Kolchaku o priznanii ego vlasti', Chita, May 29; and telegram No. 55 from Baldwin, Tokyo, to Major General Graves, AEFS, Vladivostok (RG395, File 095, Box 29).
91 Colonel Ward returned to Britain and was elected to parliament where he became an outspoken proponent of Admiral Kolchak's government. The 18 November 1919 London *Times* reported, 'He [Colonel Ward] insisted on his old argument that, having gone to Russia for our own war purposes, we thereby acquired solemn responsibilities to the loyalists, which we could not repudiate when they had served our purposes and danger no longer threatened us.'
92 Ward, p. 238.
93 Vasilevskii, *Ataman Semenov*, p. 34, 'Prikaz No. 1 upolnomochennogo Verkhovnogo pravitelya i Verkhovnogo glavokomanduyushchego po okhrane gosudarstvennogo poryadka i obshchestvennogo spokoistviya v Zabaikal'skoi oblasti o beznravstvennykh zhenshchinakh', Chita, 23 July 1919.
94 Fleming, *The Fate of Admiral Kolchak*, pp. 132–3.
95 21 February 1919, letter from Lieutenant Colonel Barrows, AEFS Vladivostok, to AEFS intelligence officer, Harbin, and attached report, 'Ataman Semenoff', by Nicholas Romanoff.
96 Vasilevskii, *Ataman Semenov*, p. 24, 'Prikaz No. 176 voiskam Otdel'noi Vostochno-Sibirskoi armii o bespechnosti ofitserov i beschinstvakh karatel'nykh otryad Aziatskogo konnogo korpusa', Chita, 31 May 1919.
97 Vasilevskii, *Ataman Semenov*, pp. 28–32. The offending officers at Karymskaya were *Poruchik* (Subaltern) Tsukanov and *Praporshchik* (Ensign) Gibner of the Composite Artillery Battalion of the Composite Manchurian Ataman Semenov Division.
98 *Pravda Buryatii* and Footman, 'Ataman Semenov', p. 51.
99 Vasilevskii, *Ataman Semenov*, p. 29, 'Prikaz No. 197 voiskam Otdel'noi Vostochno-Sibirskoi armii', Chita, June 18, 1919. In the militarization order, Semenov specifically named the Uda river system of mines, Gazimuro-Borzinskii mines, Mogocha river mines and Gornyi Zerentui-Kadaya-Kutomara assets.
100 Footman, 'Ataman Semenov', p. 40, citing a manuscript 'privately communicated by Sir Robert Hodgson'.
101 Vasilevskii, *Ataman Semenov*, pp. 30, 34 and 37.

NOTES

102 5 August 1919, translation from Russian of report on Semenoff (RG395, File 095, Box 29). Rozanov passed through Chita on his way to Vladivostok during the first days of August, and was said to be 'highly pleased with the situation in Transbaikalia'. In addition to Lovtsov, an Ataman Magomaev was another prominent Semenov representative in Vladivostok. On 5 August Horvath was absent from a meeting in his office about Semenov's inroads into the Far East.
103 Vasilevskii, *Ataman Semenov*, p. 34, 'Prikas No. 630 Zabaikal'skomu kazach'emu voisku o vosstanii v Pervom imeni atamana Semenova kazach'em polku', Chita, 19 July 1919. 'Unfortunately', declared Semenov, 'the officers were not in their places, [and] they stood apart from their Cossacks'.
104 Footman, 'Ataman Semenov', p. 38.
105 18 March 1919, Report No. 1945.
106 16 June 1919, telegram No. 142 from Lieutenant Colonel Lantry to Colonel Emerson, Harbin (RG43, New Entry 844).
107 Ward, *With the 'Die-Hards' in Siberia*, p. 237.
108 10 February 1919, report 'Ataman Semenoff and his officers', Captain F.F. Moore, AEFS, Vladivostok.
109 4 July 1919, telegram from Colonel Lantry, Irkutsk, to Colonel Emerson, Omsk 1919 (RG43, New Entry 844).
110 North, Transport in Western Siberia, p. 106.
111 Memorandum from Irkutsk to Mr Thompson, 16 June 1919 (RG43).
112 Telegram from RRSC Colonel Lantry to RRSC Colonel Emerson, 4 July 1919 (RG43, New Entry 844).
113 Telegram from RRSC Colonel Lantry, Irkutsk, to Colonel Emerson, Omsk, 11 July 1919 (RG43, New Entry 844, Box 8, File 226).
114 US Senate Committee on Education and Labor, *Deportation of Gregorie Semenoff*, p. 3.
115 20 July 1919, report on Manchuria Station, Captain H.V.V. Fay, Hailar (RG395, File 095, Box 29).
116 Ibid.
117 Footman, 'Ataman Semenov', p. 43.
118 Ibid.
119 15 July 1919, telegram from RRSC Colonel Lantry/Irkutsk, to J.F. Stevens/Harbin (RG43).
120 Ablova, 'Politicheskaya Situatsia na K.B.Zh.D'.
121 Timothy M. May, 'Banditry in Inner Mongolia', University of Wisconsin, Madison, WI, 1998.
122 20 July 1919, report on Manchuria Station, Captain H.V.V. Fay, Hailar (RG395, File 095, Box 29).
123 11 July 1919, letter from Marley, Handaohedzy, to Major Winter (RG43).
124 Ablova, 'Politicheskaya Situatsia na K.B.Zh.D'.
125 Roberts, *Assignment Siberia 1917–1919*, RRSC diary.
126 Ibid.
127 Ibid. The dead from cholera included 2,499 Chinese, 150 Russians and 30 Japanese.
128 After the retreat began, according to Paul Dotsenko, 'General Kappel asked for permission to make a break in the front and go behind the enemy lines, but permission was not granted because of the fear that "he will get behind the Bolshevik lines, take Moscow, form a Kappel government there – and won't even let us in".' (Dotsenko, *The Struggle for Democracy*, p. 97)
129 Lackenbauer, 'Why Siberia?', p. 5, and US Senate Committee on Education and Labor, *Deportation of Gregorie Semenoff*, p. 32.
130 Graves, *America's Siberian Adventure*, p. 209.
131 Reitzel and Reitzel, *Shifting Scenes* p. II–27.
132 Ibid., p. II–48.
133 US Senate Committee on Education and Labor, *Deportation of Gregorie Semenoff*, p. 12.
134 Ibid., p. 3.

135 3 September 1919, report, AEFS intelligence office – Chita to AEFS chief intelligence officer (RG165), and US Senate Committee on Education and Labor, *Deportation of Gregorie Semenoff*, p. 4.
136 US Senate Committee on Education and Labor, *Deportation of Gregorie Semenoff*, p. 4.
137 Ibid.
138 3 September 1919, report, AEFS intelligence office – Chita to AEFS chief intelligence officer (RG165, Microfilm M917). Davidson's report was classified 'secret' and not declassified until 1963.
139 Anatolii Kulikov, '*Mnogo sdelal ya dobra*...', Zabaikal'skii Rabochii, Chita, No. 12 (23539), August 2001. A touching farewell letter purportedly written by Vagzhanov to his wife and children and smuggled out of the sheds at Makkaveevo has become part of local civil war lore.
140 Naletov, 'Pedagogicheskoi Eksperiment'. Naletov visited the infamous bathhouse in 1923.
141 Ibid.
142 Ibid.
143 US Senate Committee on Education and Labor, *Deportation of Gregorie Semenoff*, p. 23.
144 Dvornichenko, *Putevodityel' po Chitye* pp. 122 and 143.
145 An 18 October 1919, US intelligence report stated, 'The Chief of the Division and Garrison at the Station Dauria is Colonel Jukovski...' However, other reports name Jukovski as a *bronevik* commander.
146 Baerlein, *The March of the Seventy Thousand*, pp. 262–5; Ossendowski, *Beasts, Men and Gods*, p. 246; Footman, 'Ataman Semenov' pp. 42–3, and various RRSC reports (RG43).
147 Baerlein, *The March of the Seventy Thousand*, p. 263, Ossendowski, *Beasts, Men and Gods*, p. 246.
148 Ivanov and Sergeev, 'Ussuriiskoye Kazachestvo'.
149 Gutman, *The Destruction of Nikolaevsk-on Amur*, p. 3.
150 Ibid., pp. 4–5.
151 5 August 1919, translation from Russian of report on Semenoff.
152 Ibid.
153 Ibid., and 14 August 1919, AEFS translation (RG395, File 095, Box 29). The telegraph operator's name was Fedoruk.
154 Footman, 'Ataman Semenov', p. 36. The rough geographic boundaries of the Pan-Mongolian state were outlined during the March 1919 Pan-Mongol conference in Chita.
155 10 February 1919, report 'Ataman Semenoff and his officers', Captain F.F. Moore, AEFS, Vladivostok.
156 ASMPR, *Information Mongolia* p. 116; Deacon, *Kempei Tai*, p. 52 and Alexander Berzin, 'Exploitation of the Shambala Legend for Control of Mongolia', Berlin, 2003.
157 Worden and Savada, (eds), *Mongolia*.
158 E. Belov, 'Kak Byla Likvidirovana Avtonomiya Vneshnei Mongolii', Aziatskaya Biblioteka, 2001. In 1912, the Bogdo Khan's agents poisoned Khan Tszasaktukhan of *aimag* Agvan-Tserena and Khan Tushetukhan of *aimag* Dashi-Nimu.
159 Semenov, *O Sebe*, pp. 132–6. Bargut territory extended from Manchuli to Khingan on the Chinese Eastern.
160 Budberg, *Dnevnik*.
161 10 February 1919, report 'Ataman Semenoff and his officers', Captain F.F. Moore, AEFS, Vladivostok.
162 Belov, 'Kale Byla', p. 11.
163 7 February 1919, telegrams from Ataman Semenov to President Wilson and the President of the League of Nations, sent from Vladivostok (RG395, File 095, Box 29).
164 13 March 1919, telegram from Major General S. Graves, Vladivostok, to US Military Attaché, Peking (RG395, File 095, Box29).
165 White, *The Siberian Intervention*, p. 202. The Mongolian delegation to Versailles never made it further than Tokyo because the Allies, suspicious of Japan's ill-concealed intentions, refused them visas.

NOTES

166 Belov, 'Kale Byla', p. 3, Footman, 'Ataman Semenov', p. 36 and Worden and Savada. (eds), *Mongolia*.
167 Belov, 'Kale Byla', pp. 5–6.
168 6 October 1919, letter/report from 1st Lieutenant Justis S. Davidson, chief intelligence officer/AEFS intelligence section (classified 'Confidential') (RG165, Microfilm M917); and Volkov, '*Tragediya Russkogo Ofitserstva*', ch. 7.
169 20 July 1919, report on Manchuria Station, Captain H.V.V. Fay, Hailar (RG395, File 095, Box 29).
170 3 August 1919, telegram from Captain Fay, Harbin, to AEFS intelligence officer, Vladivostok (RG395, File 095, Box 29).
171 6 September 1919, telegram No. 239 from Colonel Lantry, Irkutsk to Colonel Emerson, Omsk (RG43, New Entry 844, File 226). Lantry was passing on to Omsk the sketchy information he received from Major Gravis in Transbaikalia.
172 5 and 6 September 1919, telegrams No. 234 and 239 from RRSC Colonel Lantry, Irkutsk to Colonel Emerson, Omsk (RG43). Saito's headquarters in Manchuli's Rossiya Hotel commanded a brigade of the 3rd Division that was responsible for the area all the way to Nerchinsk.

7 THE WHITE COLLAPSE BEGINS: SUMMER 1919–JANUARY 1920

1 Dotsenko, *The Struggle for Democracy*, p. 98.
2 Ibid., pp. 95 and 98.
3 Letter from RRSC Major F.A. Flanagan to Colonel B.B. McCroskey, 7 January 1920 (RG43, New Entry 844, File 215-D).
4 Ibid.
5 Dotsenko, *The Struggle for Democracy*, p. 86.
6 'A hole in the ice and all was finished', wrote Baerlein of the long winter months.
7 Graves, *America's Siberian Adventure*, p. 214.
8 Dotsenko, *The Struggle for Democracy*, pp. 86–7.
9 Graves, *America's Siberian Adventure*, p. 229.
10 Bell, *Side Lights on the Siberian Campaign*, p. 128, and White, *The Siberian Intervention*, pp. 279–80.
11 Undated (probably December 1918) extracts from report on the Amur province, Captain Straus, AEFS (RG395, Files 095, Box 29).
12 Ginzton, *Times to Remember*. In December 1918 US Army Captain Straus reported 2,500 Japanese troops in Blagoveshchensk and 4,000 in the rest of the province.
13 Undated (probably December 1918) extracts from report on the Amur province, Captain Straus, AEFS.
14 White, *The Siberian Intervention*, p. 285.
15 Vasilevskii, *Ataman Semenov*, p. 34 and Petrov, *Geroicheskiye godi borbi i pobed*, pp. 165–6.
16 A. Barinov, 'Zabytyi pisatel', ili 'piarshchik' atamana'.
17 Petrov, *Geroicheskye godi borbi i pobed*, p. 167.
18 14 October 1919, letter from 2nd Lieutenant W.A. Kelley/RRSC–BorzYa to Major J.C. Gravis/RRSC–Adrianovka (RG43, Entry 848, File 526, District Inspector Records).
19 Beloborodov describes the popular excitement in an Irkutsk province village to join the march on Irkutsk city in autumn 1919. A.P. Beloborodov, *Proryv na Kharbin*, VoenIzdat Ministerstva Oborony SSSR, Moscow, 1982, ch. 1.
20 Smele, *Civil War in Siberia*, pp. 552–3 and 558.
21 Semenov, *O Sebe*, ch. 3.
22 3 October 1919, intelligence summary No. 311, AEFS intelligence section and 6 October 1919, letter/report from 1st Lieutenant Justis S. Davidson, chief intelligence officer/AEFS intelligence section (RG165) and Graves, *America's Siberian Adventure*, pp. 251–2.
23 Graves, *America's Siberian Adventure*, pp. 248–50.
24 AEFS intelligence section newspaper summary, 20 February 1920 (RG165, M917).

25 Graves, *America's Siberian Adventure*, p. 253.
26 Ibid., pp. 268–9.
27 Telegram from RRSC Major Colby, Verkhne Udinsk, to Lieutenant Colonel Cantrell, 3 October 1919 (RG43, New Entry 848, File 526).
28 Vasilevskii, *Ataman Semenov*, p. 39.
29 6 October 1919, translation from the summary of information No. 1116 issued by Offices of Commander of the Pri-Amur Military District (RG395, File 095, Box 29).
30 AEFS intelligence section, untitled report, 18 October 1919 (RG165, M917). Footman, 'Ataman Semenov', p. 38, states that Semenov was promoted to major general 'following a request [to Kolchak] from a Transbaikal Cossack Conference'.
31 Intelligence summary No. 311, AEFS intelligence section, untitled report, 3 October 1919 (RG165, M917).
32 AEFS intelligence section, untitled report, 18 October 1919 (RG165, M917).
33 Ibid.
34 Report of the situation in the Trans-Baikal district, AEFS 1st Lieutenant Justis Davidson, 6 October 1919 (RG165, M917).
35 8 January 1919, translation of letter from Colonel Katanaief to Captain K. Skladal (RG395, File 095, Box 29).
36 Ibid. and AEFS intelligence section, untitled report, 18 October 1919 (RG165, M917).
37 White, *The Siberian Intervention*, p. 284.
38 Fleming, *The Fate of Admiral Kolchak*, pp. 52–3, citing *Documents on British Foreign Policy, 1919–1939*, vol. 3.
39 1 November 1919, letter from 1st Lieutenant W.A. Kelley/RRSC–Borzya, to Major J.C. Gravis/RRSC–Adrianovka (RG43, Entry 848, File 526, District Inspector Records).
40 Ibid.
41 7 November 1919, letter from RRSC District Inspector, Transbaikal Railway, to Colonel G.H. Emerson/RRSC Chief Inspector, Irkutsk (RG43, Entry 848, File 526/District Inspector Records).
42 1 November 1919, letter from 1st Lieutenant Kelley to Major Gravis (RG43).
43 Borisov, *Dalnii Vostok*, pp. 47–8.
44 Graves, *America's Siberian Adventure*, p. 261.
45 18 October 1919, letter from Major J.C. Gravis/RRSC–Adrianovka, to Major General W.S. Graves/AEF–Vladivostok (RG165).
46 28 October 1919, letter from RRSC Major J.C. Gravis, to Major General W.S. Graves (RG43, New Entry 844, File 226).
47 Silverlight, *The Victor's Dilemma*, p. 340.
48 Grondijs, *La Guerre en Russie et en Siberie*, ch. 12, p. 1.
49 Frederick C. Giffin, 'An American Railroad Man East of the Urals, 1918–1922', *Historian*, 22 June 1998, 60, 4, p. 812.
50 Dotsenko, *The Struggle for Democracy*, p. 106; Graves, *America's Siberian Adventure*, p. 287; and Fleming, 'Ataman Semenov', p. 160. Major General Graves cited information forwarded by the British in late November: 'Bolshevik radio intercept reported capture ten generals, 110 guns and 30,000 prisoners at Omsk.' The Red Army enjoyed a similar windfall on the Southern Front when Novocherkask, 'capital of the Don Cossacks', fell in early January and Moscow boasted of capturing '400 guns, 1,000 machine guns, 11,000 rifles, 18 armored trains, 37 motor machine-guns, about 200 locomotives...' in addition to 35,000 prisoners (The *Times*, 10 January 1920, p. 10f).
51 Fleming, *The Fate of Admiral Kolchak*, pp. 159–60 and 163–4. Goldhurst, *The Midnight War*, writes that the treasure consisted of '5,143 boxes and 1,680 bags of gold.' *The Times* estimated the value of the gold at £65,000,000.
52 Fleming, *The Fate of Admiral Kolchak*, p. 166.
53 Among the Czech Legion soldiers, who were at least fortunate enough to enjoy the legion's relatively rich resources of food, trains and security, 'about 300 soldiers had become insane', according to Henry Baerlein and, '...only four of them leaped overboard on the way back [via ship to Europe]'. (Baerlein, *The March of the Seventy Thousand*, p. 275)

NOTES

54 Shaw, *'The Railway War'*, p. 3.
55 Fleming, *The Fate of Admiral Kolchak*, p. 170.
56 'Red Menace to the Far East, Horrors of Siberian Retreat', *The Times*, 8 March 1920, p. 13.
57 Vasilevskii, *Ataman Semenov*, p. 43.
58 Ibid., p. 44, 'Bozzvanie k tungusam Zabaikal'skoi oblasti o vstuplenii v beluyu armiyu', *Kazach'e Ekho*, Chita, 23 November 1919. Semenov aimed the appeal at men between 22 and 30 years of age.
59 Gutman, *The Destruction of Nikolaevsk-on-Amur*, pp. 6–7.
60 The representative was likely one Colonel Magomayev, who records show was 'Ataman Semenov's liaison officer at Vladivostok'. (Minutes entitled 'Discussion of the Meeting of the Inter-Allied Railway Committee Held on December 22nd, 1919', p. 6, RG43)
61 Graves, *America's Siberian Adventure*, p. 290.
62 Goldhurst, *The Midnight War*, p. 238; and Smele, *Civil War in Siberia*, p. 559.
63 3 October 1919, AEFS intelligence summary No. 311, AEFS intelligence section, Vladivostok (RG165).
64 Fleming, *The Fate of Admiral Kolchak*, pp. 158–9.
65 Graves, *America's Siberian Adventure*, p. 286.
66 Smele, *Civil War in Siberia*, p. 559.
67 *China Press*, 3 December 1919 (RG165, MID 2657-I-19); and Fleming, *The Fate of Admiral Kolchak*, pp. 171–2.
68 5 March 1920, AEFS intelligence section report, which cites that day's issue of *Dalnivostochnoye Obozreniye*.
69 Barinov, 'Zabytyi pisatel', ili 'piarshchik' atamana'.
70 Borisov, *Dalnii Uostok*, p. 44.
71 Vadim Sotskov, 'Zoloto Imperii: obespechit li protsvetanie Rossii eë byvshii Verkhovnyi Pravitel'?', *Ekonomist*, Moscow, January–February 2001. Presumably the Serpukhov Regiment was a unit of Kolchak's army that survived the retreat into Transbaikalia.
72 Letter from RRSC Major F.A. Flanagan, Verkhne Udinsk, to Colonel B.B. McCroskey, 7 January 1920 (RG43, New Entry 844).
73 Discussion of the meeting of the Inter-Allied Railway Committee held on 22 December 1919, p. 1 (RG43, New Entry 844).
74 'A Federal Siberia, Changes Forced by Omsk Disaster', *The Times*, 29 December 1919, p. 7e.
75 Silverlight, *The Victor's Dilemma*, pp. 344–5.
76 Smele, *Civil War in Siberia*, pp. 605–8. Smele examines this issue surrounding the lake tunnels' demolition order from every reasonable angle, and concludes that the order was a myth, possibly 'a piece of calumnious propaganda against Kolchak on the part of the Czechoslovaks'. Fleming called the purported telegram with Kolchak's order 'virtually a declaration of war' on the Czechoslovaks (*The Fate of Admiral Kolchak*, pp. 178–9).
77 Gutman, *The Destruction of Nikolaevsk-on-Amur*, p. 5.
78 White, *The Siberian Intervention*, pp. 286–8.
79 *The Times*, 29 December 1919 and Petrov, *Geroicheskye godi borki i pobed*, p. 167.
80 Fleming, *The Fate of Admiral Kolchak*, pp. 171–3.
81 Smele, *Civil War in Siberia*, pp. 600–4.
82 6 October 1919, letter/report from 1st Lieutenant Justis S. Davidson, chief intelligence officer/AEFS intelligence section (classified 'Confidential') (RG165, Microfilm M917).
83 Smele, *Civil War in Siberia*, pp. 600–1; and Fleming, *The Fate of Admiral Kolchak*, pp. 177 and 179.
84 Vasilevskii, *Ataman Semenov*, pp. 57–8. Semenov's appeal to General Syrovy seems to have been published in Chita newspaper *Zabaikal'skaya Nov'* on 4 January.
85 Discussion of the meeting of the Inter-Allied Railway Committee, 22 December 1919, p. 1 (RG43, New Entry 844).
86 Fleming, *The Fate of Admiral Kolchak*, pp. 180–1.
87 'To Save Siberia from Chaos', *The Times*, 1 January 1920, p. 12f; Smele, *Civil War in Siberia*, pp. 602–5 and Vasilevskii, *Ataman Semenov*, p. 51. An AEFS translation of a

24 December telegram of Semenov's shows his signature as 'Major General Ataman Semenov'.
88 Smele, *Civil War in Siberia*, pp. 648–9.
89 Memorandum, opening meeting of the Siberian Soviet of national government, Irkutsk, 12 January 1920 (RG43, New Entry 844, File 238).
90 Silverlight, *The Victor's Dilemma*, p. 346; Dotsenko, *The Struggle for Democracy* p. 112; and Smele, *Civil War in Siberia*, pp. 612–13. Silverlight states that 17 Socialist Revolutionaries were arrested, and Dotsenko says that 31 'members of the Political Center' were arrested. Dotsenko further states, 'Among those arrested were [Boris] Markov and [Pavel] Mikhailov, leaders in the preparatory work of spring 1918 for the uprising against the Bolsheviks'. Smele adds that a Captain Cherepanov led the counterintelligence sweeps on 23 December and updated the arrest figure to 150.
91 Vasilevskii, *Ataman Semenov*, p. 50, 'Telegramma atamana Semenova ob ital'yanskoi zabastovke na zheleznoi doroge', Chita, 23 December 1919.
92 24 December 1919, telegram from Major General Ataman Semenoff (translation), Order of the Commander-in-Chief of All the Armed Forces in the Far East, Chita No. 2 (RG395, File 095, Box 29).
93 Smele, *Civil War in Siberia*, p. 613.
94 Fleming, *The Fate of Admiral Kolchak*, p. 184; and Smele, *Civil War in Siberia*, p. 615. Smele adds that the 53rd's defection was 'led in many cases by British-trained NCOs'.
95 Dotsenko, *The Struggle for Democracy*, p. 111; and Smele, *Civil War in Siberia*, pp. 554, 608 and 614. Smele identified Kalashnikov as 'Head of the Information Section of the Staff of the Siberian Army'.
96 Graves, *America's Siberian Adventures*, p. 213; Smele, *Civil War in Siberia*, p. 613. Glazkov is now known as Sverdlovsk.
97 Telegram from Lieutenant Colone F.B. Parker, RRSC, to John F. Stevens, 25 December 1919.
98 Report from Lieutenant Colonel, F.B. Parker, RRSC, to Colonel, B.O. Johnson, RRSC, 26 December 1919.
99 25 December 1919, letter from Lieutenant General Inagaki, chief of staff, Japanese forces in Siberia, Vladivostok, to Major General Graves, AEFS (RG395, File 095, Box 29).
100 AEFS intelligence section newspaper summary, January 1920.
101 Ibid. French General Maurice Janin had been in nominal command of the Czechoslovak Legion since August 1918. For more about the Legion's French command structure, see Miloslav Caplovic, 'French Military Mission in Czechoslovakia 1919–1938', *Slovak Army Review*, Bratislava, Autumn 2001.
102 Silverlight, *The Victor's Dilemma*, p. 346.
103 Report from Lieutenant Colonel, F.B. Parker, RRSC, to Colonel, B.O. Johnson, RRSC, 26 December 1919.
104 'Prikaz, General-Leitenanta Atamana Semenova Kommanduyushchemy Voiskami Irkutskovo Voyennovo Okruga, Russkoe Byuro Pechati' (Russian Printing Bureau), Irkutsk, 26 December 1919.
105 Smele, *Civil War in Siberia*, p. 605.
106 Ibid., p. 618.
107 Fleming, *The Fate of Admiral Kolchak*, p. 185. The Japanese restrained themselves from fighting and by 5–6 January 'were enigmatically ensconced in a siding' near Glaskov.
108 Summary of telegrams of the Czech *Dennik*, 31 December 1919 (RG43).
109 Dotsenko, *The Struggle for Democracy*, p. 112.
110 Ibid.
111 Coded telegram from Captain Sundheimer, RRSC, to John F. Stevens, Irkutsk, 29 December 1919 (RG43).
112 On 1 January 1920, *The Times* stated, '... it is understood that the State Department officials have made clear that the attitude of the [Wilson] Administration towards the Siberian question is that the Bolshevist forces are getting too close to Manchuria and Japan for comfort'.

NOTES

113 Telegrams of the Czech *Dennik*, Irkutsk, 31 December 1919 (RG43). Vertyankin adds that the *semenovtsy* approach was obstructed by railway workers at Kuz'mikh and Titovo, but gives no further details.
114 Letter from RRSC Lieutenant Colonel, F.B. Parker, Irkutsk, to Colonel B.O. Johnson, 8 January 1920.
115 Letter from RRSC Major F.A. Flanagan, Verkhne Udinsk, to Colonel B.B. McCroskey, 7 January 1920; Fleming, *The Fate of Admiral Kolchak*, p. 185; and Smele, *Civil War in Siberia*, p. 619. Fleming states that a total of 168 of Skipetrov's men were captured.
116 Letter from RRSC Lieutenant Colonel F.B. Parker, Irkutsk, to Colonel B.O. Johnson, 8 January 1920, pp. 1–2.
117 Parkin, *Razgrom Kolchaka*, pp. 266–80 and 294. Brusak was born in Chernyi Ostrov, Kamenets-Podol'skaya *guberniya* in 1895, and was taken into the Imperial Army in 1915. His agent at Irkutsk station was named Pol'dyaev and the SR officer agent was Kudryashov.
118 Vasilevskii, *Ataman Semenov*, p. 55.
119 Letter from RRSC Lieutenant Colonel F.B. Parker, Irkutsk, to Colonel, B.O. Johnson, 8 January 1920, p. 2.
120 Letter from RRSC Major F.A. Flanagan, Verkhne Udinsk, to Colonel B.B. McCroskey, 7 January 1920, p. 4.
121 Dotsenko, *The Struggle for Democracy*, p. 112.
122 Smele, *Civil War in Siberia*, p. 640. Smele states that a joint Czech Legion–Political Center patrol under a Captain Malyshev interrupted the *semenovtsy* trying to load 400 *poods* of gold onto a truck outside the state bank.
123 Letter from RRSC Lieutenant Colonel F.B. Parker, Irkutsk, to Colonel B.O. Johnson, 8 January 1920, p. 3.
124 Telegram from Captain Sundheim, RRSC, to John F. Stevens, Irkutsk, 6 January 1920 (RG43, New Entry 844).
125 Silverlight, *The Victor's Dilemma*, p. 347; and Fleming, *The Fate of Admiral Kolchak*, pp. 181, 184 and 188–9.
126 Silverlight, *The Victor's Dilemma*, p. 347.
127 Fleming, *The Fate of Admiral Kolchak*, p. 191.
128 Silverlight, *The Victor's Dilemma*, p. 349.
129 Fleming, *The Fate of Admiral Kolchak*, p. 172.
130 Ibid., p. 190.
131 AEFS intelligence section newspaper summary, January, 1920.
132 Letter from RRSC Lieutenant Colonel F.B. Parker, Irkutsk, to Colonel B.O. Johnson, 8 January 1920, p. 3.
133 Telegram from Captain Sundheimer, Irkutsk, to John F. Stevens, 6 January 1920.
134 Ibid., p. 3.
135 Dotsenko, *The Struggle for Democracy*, p. 115, declares that Sychov was a Bolshevik agent. White, *The Siberian Intervention*, p. 344, states that an OMO sentry was substituted for a 'sentry posted by Kolchak's officers'.
136 White, *The Siberian Intervention*, p. 344.
137 Parkin, *Razgrom Kolchaka*, p. 271.
138 Vertyankin, 'Istoriya Ledokola "Angara",'; Bell, *Side Lights on the Siberian Campaign*, p. 97; Fleming, *The Fate of Admiral Kolchak*, pp. 194–5; and Smele, *Civil War in Siberia*, pp. 612–13 and 641. Vertyankin named the executioner as Lukin. Fleming names him as Godlevski. The *Angara* stayed in service on Lake Baikal into the 1970s (Newby, *The Big Red Train Ride*, p. 183), and has been a floating museum in Irkutsk since 1990.
139 Coded telegram from RRSC Captain Sundheimer, Irkutsk, to John F. Stevens, 8 January 1920.
140 Parkin and Spirin, *Razgrom Kolchaka*, p. 271.
141 Smele, *Civil War in Siberia*, p. 640. The mutilated bodies of 18 railwaymen were found at Slyudyanka.

142 10 January 1920, letter from RRSC Lieutenant Colonel F.B. Parker, Irkutsk, to Colonel B.O. Johnson; and 24 March 1920, 'The Japanese and the Czechs', *Golos Rodini* (RG43).
143 Vasilevskii, *Ataman Semenov*, pp. 53–5.

8 RED ONSLAUGHT: JANUARY–APRIL 1920

1 Letter from RRSC Lieutenant H. Rattach, Olovyannaya, to RRSC Major A.S. Merz, 5 January 1920 (RG43, New Entry 844, File 226).
2 Ibid. and US Senate Committee on Education and Labor, *Deportation of Gregorie Semenoff*, pp. 17–18.
3 2 January 1920, letter from 1st Lieutenant C.G. Grigg, Adrianovka to Major A.S. Merz, 'Armored train "The Punisher" whipped station masters Goshkov and Nevitsky, December 31, [on] account of armored train being delayed 20 minutes...' (RG43, New Entry 844, File 226).
4 Smele, *Civil War in Siberia*, p. 603.
5 Vasilevskii, *Ataman Semenov*, p. 58, 'Prikaz No. 31/a Glavnokomanduyushchego voiskami Dal'nevostochnogo I Irkutskogo voennikh okrugov o vzyatii vlasti', Chita, 10 January 1920.
6 Fleming, *The Fate of Admiral Kolchak*, pp. 198–9. To their credit, the Reds treated Kolchak 'with a consideration for which the annals of either side in the Civil War can provide few precedents'.
7 Vasilevskii, *Ataman Semenov*, pp. 61–2, 70, 'Prikaz No. 56 Glavnokomanduyushchego voiskami Dal'nevostochnogo i Irkutskogo voennykh okrugov s ob'yavleniem ukaza Kolchaka ot 4 yanvarya 1920 goda', Chita, 20 January 1920. Semenov named his government the Russian supreme authority on 5 February.
8 21 January 1920, weekly report, Inter-Allied Railway Committee, prepared by Captain R.A. Grammes, Vladivostok (RG43).
9 Weekly report, Inter-Allied Railway Committee, 21 January 1920, p. 4 (RG43).
10 AEFS intelligence summary No. 37, 6 February 1920, p. 2 (RG165).
11 'Semenoff's Activities', *The Times*, 13 January 1920, p. 12b.
12 AEFS intelligence summary No. 18, 18 January 1920.
13 22 January 1920, Military Attaché China (HA) Report, 'Forces of Ataman Semionov', MID 2009-82 (Microfilm M1444, Roll 6).
14 Vasilevskii, *Ataman Semenov*, pp. 60 and 63–4.
15 Smele, *Civil War in Siberia*, p. 600. The rate of 10–20 trains per day comes from a December 1919 British Military Mission report.
16 Ibid., p. 594.
17 C.R. Rice, 'Pravda', RRSC Reunion, 11 November 1932.
18 'Red Menace to the Far East', *The Times*, 8 March 1920, p. 13.
19 *The Times*, 30 January 1920.
20 AEFS intelligence section report, 28 January 1920 (RG165).
21 10 January 1920, letter from Lieutenant Colonel F.B. Parker, Irkutsk to Colonel B.O. Johnson, Harbin (RG43).
22 Smele, *Civil War in Siberia*, pp. 598 and 600. N. Khudiakov 'witnessed one old [Russian] colonel, who had been refused a berth on a Polish train, shooting his wife and daughter before committing suicide on a station platform'. Fleming, *The Fate of Admiral Kolchak*, pp. 170–1. Fleming states that the Polish contingent numbered 12,000. Another handicap to the Polish Division was that '[General] Janin had a low opinion of them', even though he had supposedly spent five days in mid-November at Novonikolaevsk trying to expedite their evacuation.
23 'Story of Siberian Retreat', *The Times*, 24 March 1920, p. 15.
24 Fleming, *The Fate of Admiral Kolchak*, p. 170.
25 AEFS intelligence section report, 28 January 1920.
26 'Koltchak to the Wolves', *The Times*, 30 January 1920, p. 12c; AEFS intelligence summary No. 18, 18 January 1920 and Smele, *Civil War in Siberia*, p. 655.

27 *The Times*, 24 March 1920.
28 Deriabin and Palacios-Fernandes, *Grazhdanskaya Voina v Rossii 1917–1922: Natsionalniye Armii*, p. 44. In July 1920, Rumsha and the survivors of the Polish Legion formed the cadre of the Polish Army's Independent Siberian Infantry Brigade, 1st and 2nd Siberian Infantry Regiments.
29 Smele, *Civil War in Siberia*, p. 655.
30 13 March 1920, letter from RRSC Major D.S. Colby, Verkhne Udinsk, to RRSC Colonel B.O. Johnson, p. 16a (RG43, File 238). In mid-March Colby reported that the echelons of the Slavic volunteers were east of Divisionaya (on Lake Baikal).
31 US Senate Committee on Education and Labor, *Deportation of Gregorie Semenoff*, p. 27.
32 Petrov, *Geroicheskiye godi borbi i pobed*, p. 168.
33 US Senate Committee on Education and Labor, *Deportation of Gregorie Semenoff*, p. 19.
34 Petrov, *Geroicheskiye godi borbi i pobed*, p. 168. Other members of the western Transbaikal military-revolutionary staff were G.T. Petrov, N. Izakov, N. Turyshev and S. Marakulin.
35 Letter from RRSC Major D.S. Colby, Verkhne Udinsk, to RRSC Colonel B.O. Johnson, 17 March 1920 (RG43, New Entry 844, File 238).
36 US Senate Committee on Education and Labor, *Deportation of Gregorie Semenoff*, p. 19.
37 Reitzel and Reitzel, *Shifting Scenes*, p. 192.
38 Ibid.
39 Petrov, *Geroicheskiye godi borbi i pobed*, p. 168; US Senate Committee on Education and Labor, *Deportation of Gregorie Semenoff*, pp. 19 and 34; and Virginia Westall Taylor, 'Bull Kendall in Siberia', *The Blue Devil*, 38, 2, Havertown, PA. May 1987.
40 US Senate Committee on Education and Labor, *Deportation of Gregorie Semenoff*, p. 20, which cites an eyewitness report compiled in Verkhne Udinsk by US, Japanese and French observers dated 18 January 1920.
41 Petrov, *Geroicheskiye godi borbi i pobed*, p. 168.
42 Reitzel and Reitzel, *Shifting Scenes* p. 193.
43 Ibid., p. 194.
44 US Senate Committee on Education and Labor, *Deportation of Gregorie Semenoff*, p. 26.
45 Graves, *America's Siberian Adventure*, p. 311.
46 Posol'skaya Station was situated on Lake Baikal a few miles from Posol'skaya proper, a quiet village of about 900 people, 780 horses, 1,000 cows, 1,500 pigs, a church-monastery and a small fish cannery. Undated extracts from the report of Lieutenant Byrnes re the town of Posol'skaya Station (RG395, File 095, Box 29).
47 Taylor, 'Bull Kendall in Siberia'; and Tom Mahoney, 'When Yanks Fought in Russia', *American Legion Magazine*, April 1978.
48 AEFS intelligence summary No. 18, 18 January 1920.
49 7 April 1922, *New York Times*, 'Semenoff, Cossack Chief, is Arrested on Arrival Here', pp. 1 and 3; and US Senate Committee an Education and Labor, *Deportation of Gregorie Semenoff*, pp. 3, 16 and 70. The *bronevik* commander was allegedly named Moscolev, but he was fortunate in being absent the night of his train's capture.
50 White, *The Siberian Intervention*, p. 285.
51 AEFS intelligence section newspaper summary, 28 January 1920. Also, *Menace to Manchuria*, *The Times*, 16 January 1920, p. 12b. A telegram dated 8 January from RRSC Captain Sundheimer in Irkutsk stated, 'It is reported that Social Revolutionaries have taken Verkhne-Udinsk, Shilka and Petrosky Zavod, but uprisings at Chita were suppressed' (RG43, New Entry 844), however this appears to be just rumor, at least as far as Verkhne-Udinsk was concerned.
52 AEFS intelligence summary No. 17, 17 January 1920. 'Missovia' should read Mysovaya.
53 Baerlein, *The March of the Seventy Thousand*, p. 261 and Newby, *The Big Red Train Ride*, p. 190.
54 'Order by Ataman Semenov', *Dalnyvostochnoe Obozrenie*, reported in AEFS intelligence section newspaper summary, 28 January 1920 (RG165).
55 'The Russian Muddle', *The Times*, 17 January 1920, p. 12.

56 16 January 1920, telegram from RRSC Captain R.A. Grammes, Vladivostok, to John Stevens (RG43, New Entry 844). This unusual 'special' consisted of '*Dynamo* car 1710, Diner, First, Second and Third Class Coach, as well as several Armoured Cars'. An article in the 24 February issue of Vladivostok newspaper *Golos Rodini* swaggeringly avered that the partisans destroyed 300 bridges in Amur province in a single day.
57 24 February 1920, Narod (Vladivostok), 'The Situation in Amur Province', undated AEFS newspaper summary (excerpt), AEFS intelligence section (RG165).
58 28 January 1920, Russian Railway Service Corps report on the taking of Nikolsk, AEFS intelligence Section.
59 Smith, *Vladivostok Under Red and White Rule*, p. 25.
60 'To All Who Work', Central Bureau of Professional Unions of Vladivostok, 3 January 1920 (RG43, New Entry 844, File 238).
61 17 January 1920, AEFS intelligence summary No. 17 (RG165).
62 Smith, *Vladivostok Under Red and White Rule*, p. 27.
63 6 February 1920, AEFS intelligence summary No. 37 (RG165). Captain Brochart showed the author of this summary, Lieutenant Colonel Eichelberger, the original order No. 38 dated 22 January and signed by General Verigo. Verigo had denied knowledge of the order, but Brochart found it in 'the secret files of the Fortress'.
64 Smith, *Vladivostok Under Red and White Rule*, pp. 24–5.
65 Ibid., p. 26.
66 Ibid., p. 28, citing a 30 January 1920 communication from MacGowan to Lansing, US State Department No. 861.00/6274.
67 Graves, *America's Siberian Adventure*, p. 317. Rozanov and his fellow high-ranking Whites were either put aboard the steamer *Orel* and shipped to Japan on or before 4 February (according to Smith) or secluded in the Japanese headquarters until mid-February and shipped to Japan aboard a transport that ominously deposited 500 new Japanese troops in Vladivostok.
68 Smith, *Vladivostok Under Red and White Rule*, p. 32. Nikiforov was said to have influenced Lenin's new economic policy but faded from the political scene, became a metal worker and carpenter and was not recognized for his revolutionary contributions until his 90th birthday in 1972 when he was awarded the Order of the October Revolution. He died in 1974.
69 AEFS intelligence summary No. 37, 6 February 1920 (RG165).
70 Smith, *Vladivostok Under Red and White Rule*, p. 32. The head of the military council was M. Ya. Lindberg.
71 Fleming, *The Fate of Admiral Kolchak*, p. 216.
72 Ibid.
73 Smele, *Civil War in Siberia*, p. 666. Czech Colonel Krejci delivered the ultimatum to General Voitsekhovskii on 8 February warning him not to violate the neutrality of the railwaay zone at Glaskovo station.
74 Weekly report, Inter-Allied Railway Committee, 21 January 1920, p. 4.
75 18 February 1921 and 22 March 1922, questionnaires for Oriental Language Detail, Major B.B. McCroskey (RG165, MID 2663-45 & 2663-59). In addition to French and Spanish, McCroskey spoke Mandarin Chinese of which he could read 1,500 characters and write 1,000.
76 22 February 1920, letter from Lieutenant Colonel B.B. McCroskey, military observer, en route to Vladivostok, to commanding officer, AEF Vladivostok (RG165, MID File 2663-23).
77 6 November 1919, instructions from DMI to Lieutenant Colonel B.B. McCroskey (RG165, MID File 2663-2).
78 3 May 1920, letter from Lieutenant Colonel B.B. McCroskey, Hotel Stewart, San Francisco to Brigadier General Marlboro Churchill, DMI (RG165, MID File 2663-24). McCroskey covered for his brother officer for months, until he realized that his AEFS compatriots were hardly concerned about minimizing damage to McCroskey's career.
79 31 March 1920, US Military Attaché China (HA) Report No. 2484, 'Semenoff's Agents in Peking' (RG165, Microfilm M1444 Roll 6, MID 2657-I-101). A Semenov order in January 1920 referred to Krupskii as 'chief of [Semenov's] military department'.

NOTES

80 Letter from Lieutenant Colonel B.B. McCroskey to Major General Graves, 22 February 1920 (MID 2663-23/1).
81 17 February 1920, telegram from Lieutenant Colonel B.B. McCroskey, military observer, Chita, to Milstaff, Washington (RG165, MID File 2663-13). Dated upon receipt.
82 9 February 1920, telegram from Colonel C. Morrow and 1st Lieutenant John James, Acting Adjutant, 27th Infantry, Chita, to Milstaff, Washington (RG165, MID File 2663-13). Received in Washington 18 February.
83 20 February 1920, memorandum for Chief of Staff, from Brigadier General M. Churchill, Director of Military Intelligence (RG165, File 2663-13).
84 18 February 1920, memorandum for Chief, Personnel Branch of Operations Division, from DMI (RG165, MID File 2663-12).
85 22 February 1920, letter from Lieutenant Colonel B.B. McCroskey, military observer, en route to Vladivostok, to Commanding Officer, AEF Vladivostok (RG165, MID File 2663-23).
86 9 March 1920, letter from Lieutenant Colonel B.B. McCroskey, Vladivostok, to DMI (RG165, MID File 2663-23).
87 16 December 1919, letter from Brigadier General Marlboro Churchill, DMI, to the army Chief of Staff, Washington (RG165, MID File 2663-8).
88 22 April 1920, telegram (encoded) from Lieutenant Colonel B.B. McCroskey, SS Great Northern, to DMI (RG165, MID File 2663-21).
89 9 March 1920, letter from Lieutenant Colonel B.B. McCroskey, Vladivostok, to DMI (RG165, MID File 2663-23). Silverman was also named as Silberman in McCroskey's letter of 22 February. Morrow considered Silverman 'absolutely loyal and trustworthy' and increased his pay to $100 per month in June 1919 for 'performing work of great value' (6 June 1919, memorandum for AEFS chief of staff from Lieutenant Colonel Eichelberger, AEFS intelligence officer, RG395 File 095, Box 29).
90 US Senate Committee on Education and Labor, *Deportation of Gregorie Semenoff*, p. 75. Actually Colonel Morrow employed a pair of Silverman brothers as interpreters. They had lived in the United States for 10–12 years before their deployment to Siberia.
91 9 March 1920, letter from Lieutenant Colonel B.B. McCroskey, Vladivostok, to DMI, p. 2 (RG165, MID File 2663-23).
92 9 March 1920, cablegram from Major General Graves, Vladivostok, to the Adjutant General (RG165, MID File 2663-28).
93 11 March 1920, letter from Secretary of War Newton D. Baker to Secretary of State (RG165, MID File 2663-20).
94 5 May 1920, letter from Lieutenant Colonel B.B. McCroskey, San Francisco, to DMI (RG165, MID File 2663-23).
95 20 February 1920, Golos Rodini (Vladivostok), 'The Situation in Transbaikal', *Golos Rodini* (Vladivostok), in AEFS intelligence section newspaper summary, 20 February (RG165, M917).
96 14 April 1920, letter from Major D.S. Colby, Hailar to Colonel. B.O. Johnson, Harbin (RG43, New Entry 844, File 238) and 23 April 1920 Military Attaché China (HA) Report No. 2531 (RG165, Microfilm M1444 Roll 6).
97 26 February 1920, telegram from RRSC Colonel Johnson, Chita to RRSC Captain Sundheimer, Harbin (RG43, New Entry 844, File 238).
98 13 March 1920, letter from RRSC Major D.S. Colby, Verkhne Udinsk, to RRSC Colonel. B.O. Johnson, pp. 3a–4a (RG43, File 238).
99 9 March 1920, letter from Lieutenant Colonel B.B. McCroskey, Vladivostok, to DMI (RG165, MID File 2663-23).
100 4 February 1920, Eko (Vladivostok), in undated AEFS intelligence section newspaper summary (RG165, M917).
101 'Kalmykov is Getting Angry', *Krasnoe Znamya*, 14 February 1920 in AEFS intelligence section newspaper summary 14 February (RG165, M917).
102 27 February 1920, AEFS intelligence section newspaper summary (RG165, M917) and Ivanov and Sergei, 'Ussuriiskoye Kazachestvo'. Karpinskii was also given a St George's award banner of the Ussuri Division to pass on to Semenov.

103 27 February 1920, AEFS intelligence summary No. 58 (RG165, M917).
104 27 February 1920, interview between Lieutenant Colonel R.L. Eichelberger and Mr Loots, AEFS intelligence section (RG165, M917).
105 17 February 1920, AEFS intelligence summary No. 48 (RG165, M917).
106 27 February 1920, AEFS intelligence summary No. 58 (RG165, M917) and 'Red Menace to the Far East', *The Times*, 8 March 1920.
107 Bell, *Side Lights on the Siberian Campaign*, p. 131. The Bolsheviks 'shot at the legs of their victims till one by one they fell off the narrow bridge into the river', including Bell's 'dear friend, Captain Galyavin'.
108 23 February 1920, intelligence summary, AEFS HQ (RG395, File 095 Semenoff, Box 29).
109 27 February 1920, AEFS intelligence section newspaper summary (RG165, M917).
110 2 March 1920, AEFS intelligence summary No. 62 (RG165, M917).
111 6 and 8 March 1920, AEFS intelligence summaries Nos. 66 and 68 (RG165, M917). No. 68 cited a telegram sent to the Chinese consul in Vladivostok and the governor of Kirin province from Lu Lu Cheo, town chief of Sopki and 'Iochosyan, Adjutant Assistant Commander of Troops-Spassk-Iman Semenov', stating, '[Kalmykov's] arms dispatched to Fugdin... Tumanov arrived at Norti, demands arms. Request you [consul] ask Kirin if arms may be surrendered or not. Reply urgently.' An 8 March report in *The Times* of Kalmykov's capture (datelined 25 February in Harbin) 'on the Manchurian border' seems to have been premature.
112 Ivanov and Sergei, 'Ussuriiskoye Kazachestvo'.
113 Gutman, *The Destruction of Nikolaevsk-on-Amur*, p. 45.
114 Untitled report of 4 March Communist-Bolshevik Party meeting under Mr Gubelman at People's Hall, AEFS HQ, Gubelman informed the meeting that 'Citizens of the town had his [Orlov's] grave dug up and photographs taken of the mutilations unpon the deceased's body.' (RG395, File 095 Semenoff, Box 29). Gutman, *The Destruction of Nikolaevsk-on-Amur*, pp. 19–22, 41, 61, 142 and 299. Ishikawa's delegation included Mayor Karpenko, Engineer Komarovskii and Chairman Shelkovnikov of the *Zemstvo* Executive Branch. Triapitsyn was from Simbirsk province, Kurmyzhsk district, Svosteika village.
115 4 March 1920, 'From the Russian Telegraphic Agency', AEFS HQ (RG395, File 095 Semenoff, Box 29). The celebration marked the 1 March 1919 reading of Choi Nam-seon's Korean Declaration of Independence at Tapgol Park in Seoul, which was followed by nationwide demonstrations of support by the populace and violent suppression by Japanese police and military.
116 8 March 1920, AEFS intelligence summary (RG165).
117 20 February 1920, letter from Sundheimer forwards message from Colonel Johnson, Chita to J.F. Stevens, Harbin (RG43) and Borisov, *Dalnii Vostok*, pp. 22–5. On 15 February Semenov officially promised a Regional Popular Assembly.
118 23 February 1920, telegram from RRSC Colonel Johnson, Chita to RRSC Captain Sundheimer, Harbin (RG43, New Entry 844, File 238).
119 'Red Menace to the Far East', *The Times*, 8 March 1920, p. 13.
120 11 March 1920, intelligence summary No. 71, AEFS intelligence section (RG165).
121 29 February 1920, telegram from RRSC Colonel Johnson, Chita to RRSC Captain Sundheimer, Harbin (RG43, New Entry 844, File 238).
122 6 March 1920, from the Russian Telegraphic Agency, AEFS HQ (RG395, File 095 Semenoff, Box 29).
123 Vasilevskii, *Ataman Semenov*, p. 73. An article in *Zabaikal'skaya Nov'* newspaper on 19 February 1920 estimated the *kappel'evtsy* numbers at 50,000.
124 Crone, *East Lies the Sun*, pp. 171–3.
125 17 February 1920, excerpt from RTA bulletin No. 53 (RG395, File 095 Semenoff, Box 29); 18 February 1920, letter from RRSC Division Inspector James E. Hood to Lieutenant Colonel M.K. Jones (RG43, New Entry 844). Hood reported: '... Left Harbin on train 21 this morning under heavy guard: [car no.'s] 634643 (Waybill 19301), 452508 (Waybill 19304), 485317 (Waybill 19303), [and] 347041 (Waybill 19302)... It looks irregular to me, as I have always understood that gold could not be shipped out of Russia.'

NOTES

126 2 March 1920, telegram from RRSC Colonel Johnson, Chita, to RRSC Captain Sundheimer, Harbin (RG43).
127 Translation of untitled 14 February 1920 article in *Dalnyvostochnoe Obozrenie*, citing 11 February 'Bolshevik Radio' report from Irkutsk, undated AEFS intelligence section newspaper summary (RG165, M917). Fleming (*The Fate of Admiral Kolchak*, p. 208) states that the truce was arranged on 7 February at Kuitin.
128 Gutman, *The Destruction of Nilolaevsk-on-Amur*, pp. 374–5 and Smith, *Vladivostok Under Red and White Rule*, pp. 38–9. Soviet passengers aboard legion trains included high ranking Bolsheviks Kushnarev and Vilenskii.
129 2 March 1920, telegram from RRSC Colonel B.O. Johnson, Chita, to RRSC Captain Sundheimer, Harbin (RG43).
130 20 February 1920, telegram from RRSC representative Smith, Chita, to RRSC Captain Sundheimer, Harbin (RG43, New Entry 844). This encoded communication, full of detailed current intelligence, was intended for Major General Graves and the Czechoslovakian leader Dr Girsa.
131 20 February 1920, telegram from RRSC representative Smith, Chita, to RRSC Captain Sundheimer, Harbin (RG43, New Entry 844).
132 23 February 1920, telegram from RRSC Colonel Johnson, Chita to RRSC Captain Sundheimer, Harbin (RG43, New Entry 844, File 238); and undated AEFS reports on each town. Mysovaya had 4,500 inhabitants, a 100-bed hospital, 2 doctors, 2 stores, 2 schools, 2 churches, a synagogue and large herds of cattle. Sludyanka had a glass factory and two hospitals and had been a training camp for 450 Czechoslovak Legion officer-candidates.
133 7 March 1920, telegram from Johnson, Chita to S.F. Stevens, Harbin (RG43).
134 *Geroicheskiye godi borbi i pobed*, Petrov, p. 172. As of January 1920, Petrov stated that there were 200 partisan 'groups or detachments' in the Russian Far East.
135 Petrov, *Geroicheskiye godi borbi i pobed*, pp. 162–3.
136 Vasilevskii, *Attaman Semenov*, p. 93. Semenov specifically commended the chief of garrison, Colonel Malaken, Captain Kolmogorov and 'officers, dear fellow Cossacks, [and] soldiers'.
137 2 March 1920, transcript of telegram from RRSC Colonel B.O. Johnson, Chita (RG43).
138 6 March 1920, letter from Czech Lieutenant Kotrba, Inter-Allied Technical Board, Harbin (RG43).
139 'Story of Siberian Retreat', *The Times*, 24 March 1920, p. 15.
140 Smele, *Civil War in Siberia*, p. 656. Kappel fell through the ice on the River Kan on 11 December 1919 and refused a 'berth on a warm Czech train' because of the legion's disloyalty to Kolchak.
141 Smith, *Vladivostok Under Red and White Rule*, pp. 42–45. Voitsekhovskii exaggerated slightly when he told Boldyrev that he had 30,000 men. *The Times* estimated 24,000 men as of mid-March.
142 7 March 1920, telegram from Colonel Johnson to J.F. Stevens, Harbin (RG43).
143 3 March 1920, telegram from Major Clarke, Vladivostok, to RRSC Harbin (RG43, New Entry 844, File 238).
144 22 January 1920, 'Forces of Ataman Semionov', US Military Attaché China (RG65, MID File 2009-82).
145 19 February 1920, transcript of 17 February 1920, telegram from RRSC Colonel B.O. Johnson, Chita (RG43, New Entry 844, File 238).
146 'The Evacuation of the Japanese', *Dalnyvostochnoe Obozrenie* (Vladivostok), 23 February 1920, in undated AEFS newspaper summary (RG165, M917).
147 23, 26 and 27 February 1920, telegrams from RRSC Colonel Johnson, Chita to RRSC Captain Sundheimer, Harbin (RG43, New Entry 844, File 238).
148 4 March 1920, telegram from RRSC Colonel B.O. Johnson, Chita, to John Stevens, Harbin (RG43, New Entry 844, File 238). Bolshevik radio declared in mid-March that Semyonov 'appropriated' 2,000,000 yen provided by the Japanese to pay railroad wages (AEFS intelligence summary No. 81, 21 March 1920, RG 917).
149 5 March 1920, telegram from RRSC Captain Sundheimer, Harbin, to RRSC Colonel B.O. Johnson, Chita (RG43).

150 18 February 1920, letter from Major F.A. Flanagan, Manchuli to Lieutenant Colonel M.K. Jones, Harbin (RG43, New Entry 844, File 226).
151 10 March 1920, report from Lieutenant Colonel F.B. Parker, Manchuli, to Colonel B.O. Johnson (RG43).
152 5 March 1920, telegram from Colonel Johnson, Chita, to John Stevens (RG43).
153 13 March 1920, letter from RRSC Major D.S. Colby, Verkhne Udinsk, to RRSC Colonel B.O. Johnson, p. 23A. The administration was led by a Temporary *zemstvo* of Transbaikal province, headed by 'President Pyatidesyátnikov' and his 'associate' Romm (RG43).
154 15 March 1920, telegram from Captain Sundheimer to Major Clarke (RG43).
155 17 March 1920, letter from RRSC Major D.S. Colby, Verkhne Udinsk, to RRSC Colonel B.O. Johnson (RG43).
156 15 March 1920, telegram from Captain Sundheimer to Major Clarke (RG43).
157 Smele, *Civil War in Siberia*, pp. 649–53. The Workers' and Peasants' Militia, under Red Commander Mironov, maintained its own underground staff at Glaskovo. Fleming (*The Fate of Admiral Kolchak*, p. 195) states that Bolshevik leader Aleksandr Krasnoshchekov left Irkutsk on 11 January and was discussing establishment of a semi-autonomous Siberian entity with Moscow (using 5th Red Army communications) when the Revkom displaced the Political Center. The information from 'a French officer' was recorded in a 5 March 1920 report, telegram received from Mr Smith, AEFS HQ (RG395, File 095 Semenoff, Box 29).
158 Telegram from RRSC Colonel B.O. Johnson, Chita, to RRSC Harbin, 8 March 1920 (RG43, New Entry 844, File 238).
159 13 March 1920, letter from RRSC Major D.S. Colby, Verkhne Udinsk, to RRSC Colonel B.O. Johnson, Chita, p. 3A (RG43, New Entry 844, File 238). A recent arrival from Irkutsk, YMCA secretary Warren, reported that there was great unrest over the Reds' refusal to honor Siberian rubles.
160 AEFS intelligence summary No. 68, 8 March 1920 (RG165, M917). Kunst and Albers operated a chain of successful and stylish department stores throughout the Russian Far East.
161 'Detention of Gold by Ataman Semenov', *Dalnyvostochnoe Obozrenie*, 10 March, reported in 10 March 1920 AEFS intelligence section newspaper summary (RG43, Entry 843/338, Index 1, 73/Press).
162 Telegram from RRSC Colonel B.O. Johnson, Chita, to John Stevens, Harbin, 7 March 1920 (RG44, New Entry 238).
163 13 March 1920, letter from RRSC Major D.S. Colby, Verkhne Udinsk, to RRSC Colonel B.O. Johnson, Chita, p. 3A (RG43, New Entry 844, File 238).
164 17 March 1920, letter from Major D.S. Colby, Verkhne-Udinsk, to Colonel Johnson, Chita (RG43, New Entry 844, File 238).
165 25 March 1920, intelligence summary No. 85, AEFS intelligence section (RG165).
166 Barinov, 'Tsyganka Masha'; Nun Seraphima, 'Bury Me Like a Christian', *Orthodox Life, Brotherhood of Saint Job of Pochaev at Holy Trinity Monastery*, 47, 6, November– December 1997, pp. 29-31 (originally published in Paris in a Russian periodical *Renaissance*, 151, 1964); and Lyubov Miller and Irina Nabatova-Barrett, trans., 'Holy Martyr of Russia, Grand Princess Elizaveta Fedorovna', n.p.
167 Gutman referred to Medvedev's coalition government of Socialist-Revolutionaries and Bolsheviks as the 'Red-Pink regime' (pp. 75ff.). American reports also infrequently referred to 'Pinks' in 1920, usually meaning non-Bolshevik revolutionaries.
168 17 February 1920, excerpt from RTA bulletin No. 53, AEFS HQ; and February 1920 excerpt from weekly intelligence summary, AEFS (RG395, File 095 Semenoff, Box 29). The latter referred to 'Prince Tumbaef'.
169 'Red Menace to the Far East', *The Times*, 8 March 1920, p. 13.
170 10 March 1920, letter from RRSC Lieutenant Colonel F.B. Parker, Manchuli to RRSC Colonel Johnson, Chita (RG43, New Entry 844, File 238).
171 14 March 1920, telegram from RRSC representative Smith, Chita, to RRSC Major Clarke, Vladivostok, via RRSC Captain Sundheimer, Harbin (RG43).

NOTES

172 13 March 1920, record of daily events, from Major D.S. Colby, Verkhne-Udinsk, to Colonel B.O. Johnson (RG43, File 238).
173 10 March 1920, letter from Lieutenant Colonel F.B. Parker, RRSC–Manchuli, to Colonel B.O. Johnson, RRSC–Chita. 'They [the Chinese] stated that they, of course, could not ask for it but would be glad to have it here as moral backing for the Chinese soldiers. Perhaps you could give the hint to Mr Stevens.'
174 15 March 1920, memorandum No. 259 from the provisional government Maritime Provincial Zemstvo Board Administration of Foreign Affairs, Vladivostok, to the High Commissioner of the Chinese Republic in Siberia (RG43, New Entry 844, File 238).
175 Ibid.
176 11 March 1920, intelligence summary No. 71, AEFS intelligence section, Vladivostok (RG165).
177 *The Times*, 23 March 1920, p. 13d.
178 17 March 1920, reports from the Russian telegraph agency regarding the program of the strike of the Chinese Eastern Railway, AEFS intelligence section, Vladivostok (RG165, Microfilm M917).
179 'Forgotten Koltchak Force', *The Times*, 23 March 1920, p. 13d. The replacement workers were cited as being 'men from the Izhevsky factories who are as skillful with tools as with the rifle'.
180 15 March 1920, memorandum No. 259 from the provisional government Maritime Provincial Zemstvo Board Administration of Foreign Affairs, Vladivostok, to the High Commissioner of the Chinese Republic in Siberia (15 March 1920, memorandum No. 259 from the provisional government Maritime Provincial Zemstvo Board Administration of Foreign Affairs, Vladivostok, to the High Commissioner of the Chinese Republic in Siberia (RG43, New Entry 844, File 238).
181 14 March 1920, telegram from RRSC representative Smith, Chita, to RRSC Major Clarke, Vladivostok, via RRSC Captain Sundheimer, Harbin (RG43).
182 26 March 1920, intelligence summary No. 86, AEFS intelligence section, Vladivostok (RG165).
183 21 March 1920, intelligence summary No. 81, AEFS intelligence section, Vladivostok (RG165).
184 16 March, telegram from Smith, Chita to John Stevens, Vladivostok and 26 March 1920, letter from Major C.H. Hazzard, Olovyannaya to Colonel B.O. Johnson, Chita (RG43, New Entry 844, File 238).
185 18 March 1920, telegram from Chita to Sundheimer, Harbin (RG43, New Entry 844, File 238).
186 15 April 1920, letter from Lieutenant Colonel Kopal, chief, military mission of the Czechoslovak Ministery of National Defense, Harbin, to Lieutenant Colonel Engineer Clupek, Czechoslovak Legion, Harbin (RG43).
187 13 March 1920, record of daily events, from Major D.S. Colby, Verkhne-Udinsk, to Colonel B.O. Johnson, RG43, File 238, p. 26A. Though dated 13 March, this detailed log of events ran until 10 April.
188 16 and 18 March 1920, telegrams from RRSC Lieutenant Colonel F.B. Parker, Hailar, to RRSC Colonel B.O. Johnson, Harbin (RG43).
189 'Russians Ousted by Chinese', *The Times*, 24 March 1920, p. 15c. Many, if not most, of the Chinese Eastern militiamen continued their employment under the new Chinese management.
190 23 April 1920, Military Attaché China (HA) report No. 2531, p. 8 (RG165, Microfilm M1444, Roll 6).
191 Undated (March 1920) protocol of a citizen of the village Olovyannaya, Ivan Gerasinov-Sovenkov (RG43, New Entry 844, File 238).
192 26 March 1920, letter from Major C.H. Hazzard, Olovyannaya to Colonel B.O. Johnson, Chita (RG43, New Entry 844, File 238). Johnson had been recently decorated by the Czechoslovak Legion in a public ceremony on 23 March.
193 21 March 1920, telegram from Smith, Chita, to Major Clarke, Vladivostok (RG43, New Entry 844, File 238). Verigo traveled to Olovyannaya on 18 March. Ivanov-Rinov and Annenkov arrived in chita from the west on 20 March.

194 13 March 1920, record of daily events, from Major D.S. Colby, Verkhne-Udinsk, to Colonel B.O. Johnson, p. 26A (RG43, File 238). Though dated 13 March, this detailed log of events ran until 10 April.
195 Ibid., p. 3A. Commissar Semenov was the bold traveler from Verkhne-Udinsk.
196 Ibid., pp. 1A and 26A.ff. As of 12 March, the Reds' inventory of British prisoners included one major, five captains, five lieutenants, two sergeants and two privates, all army engineers being held at Krasnoyarsk. The Bolsheviks allowed the British military mission at Chita to send an officer, Captain Carthew, with money and a freightcar full of supplies. He departed Chita the night of 1 April.
197 30 March 1920, telegram from RRSC Major D.S. Colby, Chita to Mr Krasnoshchekov, Verkhne-Udinsk, contained in Colby's 13 March log.
198 Ibid., pp. 22A–24A and 27A. Krasnoshchekov provided the numbers of freightcars, waybills and baggage checks, apparently gleaned from documents captured at Omsk, for the banknote cargo.
199 Ibid., p. 25A.
200 Scrapbook, Leroy W. Yarborough Collection, RG505S, US Military History Institute, Carlisle, PA.
201 US Senate Committee on Education and Labor, *Deportation of Gregorie Semenoff*, p. 5. Major General Graves informed the Committee of the killings of five former doughboys in Siberia by OMO.
202 For example, two days before the Great Northern steamed away, RRSC Colonel Johnson in Chita telegraphed Major Colby in Verkhne-Udinsk, 'Will you please find out from Commissar of Khilok why Mrs Clayman was arrested at that point and where she is at present?' 13 March 1920, record of daily events, from Major D.S. Colby to Colonel B.O. Johnson.

9 WHITE–JAPANESE RESURGENCE, PANIC AND DISASTER: APRIL–DECEMBER 1920

1 24 November 1919, letter No. 44 from Captain Yano, Headquarters-Japanese Forces, Beresovka (Transbaikal province) to General Mezhak, OMO Commander, Verkhne-Udinsk, translation contained in 9 April 1920, letter from Colonel. B.O. Johnson, Harbin to J.F. Stevens, Harbin (RG43, New Entry 844, File 226). Yano cited the 180 million yen figure. *The Times* estimated in November 1920 that Japan had spent 600 million yen 'on the Siberian intervention' (30 November 1920 *The Times*).
2 19 March 1920, telegram from Parker, Hailar via Sundheimer, Harbin to Stevens, Harbin (RG43).
3 23 April 1920, Military Attaché China (HA) report: 'Conditions in Siberia and Manchuria', (RG165, Microfilm M1444 Roll 6, MID 2657-I-130).
4 23 April 1920, Military Attaché China (HA) Report No. 2531, p. 7 (RG165, Microfilm M1444 Roll 6). The timber concession was between Imyanpo and Hilene, where the saw mill was located. It was previously owned by an Englishman, W. Jones.
5 Fleming, *The Fate of Admiral Kolchak*, p. 232.
6 Gutman, *The Destruction of Nikolaevsk-on-Amur*, pp. 53–7 and 142.
7 Ibid., pp. 37–9, Bell, *Side Lights on the Siberian Campanign*, pp. 128–30. According to another version of Ishida's death, he shot his wife and children, then turned his gun on himself shortly before the consul building was captured.
8 25 March 1920, intelligence summary No. 85, AEFS intelligence section, Vladivostok (RG165). Eichelberger points out that the Japanese headquarters realized that the wireless radio station at Nikolaevsk was 'in the hands of the partisans'.
9 Gutman, *The Destruction of Nikolaevsk-on-Amur*, pp. 77–8.
10 Ibid., pp. 153–5.
11 Untitled report of 4 March Communist-Bolshevik Party meeting under Mr Gubelman at People's Hall, AEFS HQ, P. Utkin, 'president of the party', was present at the meeting. (RG395, File 095 Semenoff, Box 29).

NOTES

12 21 March 1920, intelligence summary No. 81, AEFS intelligence section, Vladivostok (RG165).
13 26 March 1920, intelligence summary No. 86, AEFS intelligence section, Vladivostok (RG165).
14 Gutman, *The Destruction of Nikolaevsk-on-Amur*, p. 91.
15 Ibid.
16 Smith, *Vladivostok Under Red and White Rule*, pp. 52–5.
17 Ibid., pp. 57–60.
18 Linda Fay Kaufman, 'Harold Van Vechten Fay', Fay Family [Genealogy] Page, www.fayfamily.org, April 2003. Fay was born in June 1890 to a wealthy family in the small city of Auburn, a prosperous, socially conscious community in central New York. Harold Fay returned to New York three days before Christmas 1920, got married there in 1923 and apparently moved to Switzerland shortly thereafter. He attended a 'great world conference' at Geneva in May 1927 where Cordell Hull and other visionaries tried in vain to steer postwar commercial policy towards a reduction in trade restrictions and, later that year, Fay co-authored a book about the conference with Allyn Abbot Young, one of America's most renowned monetary economists. By 1930, Fay was living in the Washington, DC, suburb of Bethesda, MD, where he had given up his journalism aspirations and become an investor with a trust company to better support his wife and daughter. During the Second Word War Fay served the OSS as a 'Russia expert'.
19 H. Van Vechten Fay, 'The Taking of Nikolsk by the Japanese', 5 April 1920 (RG43, New Entry 844, File 238). Fay had served as US Army intelligence officer in Nikolsk until his recent discharge. He was acquainted with Commander Andreev, got along well with the Czechoslovaks and also had amicable relations with the Japanese Army.
20 Gutman, *The Destruction of Nikolaevsk-on-Amur*, pp. 95–8.
21 13 March 1920, record of daily events, Major D.S. Colby, p. 27A (RG43, File 238).
22 Gutman, *The Destruction of Nikolaevsk-on-Amur*, pp. 96–8.
23 Smith, *Vladivostok Under Red and White Rule*, p. 127.
24 A.P. Bragin, 'Vozrozhdenie russkoi gosudarstvennosti', Vladivostok, 1997 and ibid., 'Krovavoe prestuplenie zhido-bol'shevikov na rekov Khor', *Nashe Otechestvo*, St Petersburg, 73–74, August–September 2001. Nashe Otechestvo is a post-Soviet, anti-Semitic publication.
25 Dvornichenko, *Putevodityel'po Chitye*, pp. 33–4 and Smele, *Civil War in Siberia*, p. 652.
26 Smith, *Vladivostok Under Red and White Rule*, p. 71. The Amur government was under Seryshev, Postyshev and Flegontov.
27 23 April 1920, Military Attaché China (HA) report: 'Conditions in Siberia and Manchuria', (RG165, Microfilm M1444 Roll 6, MID 2657-I-130); Smith, *Vladivostok Under Red and White Rule*, p. 69 and J.B. Wood, 'The Far Eastern Republic', *National Geographic*, 41, 6, June 1922, pp. 565–92. Technically the FER encompassed Transbaikal, Amur and Maritime provinces and Sakhalin Island.
28 Smith, *Vladivostok Under Red and White Rule*, pp. 70 and 86. Boris Shumyatskii, leader of the FER and Comintern, referred to Semenov's territory as the 'Chita stopper'.
29 26 March 1920, intelligence summary No. 86, AEFS intelligence section, Vladivostok (RG165) and S.N. Shishkin, Grazhdanskaia voina na Dal'nem Vostoke 1918–1922, Moscow, 1957.
30 13 March 1920, record of daily events, Major D.S. Colby, p. 27A (RG43, File 238).
31 11 March 1920, intelligence summary No. 71, AEFS intelligence section (RG165, M917).
32 13 March 1920, letter from RRSC Major D.S. Colby, Verkhne-Udinsk, to RRSC Colonel B.O. Johnson, pp. 3a–4a (RG43, File 238).
33 6 April 1920, telegram from Major Merz, Chita via Sundheimer to J.F. Stevens, Harbin (RG43).
34 23 April 1920, Military Attaché China (HA) report No. 2531 (RG165, Microfilm M1444 Roll 6).
35 14 April 1920, Military Attaché China (HA) report: 'General Situation in Manchuria and Eastern Siberia', (RG165, Microfilm M1444 Roll 6, MID 2657-I-125). When Japan

finally carved Manchukuo out of China's hide in 1932, Changchun was renamed Xinjing and became Emporer Pu-Yi's capital.
36 23 April 1920, Military Attaché China (HA) report: 'Conditions in Siberia and Manchuria', (RG165, Microfilm M1444 Roll 6, MID 2657-I-130).
37 16 April 1920, memorandum from Colonel. B.O. Johnson, Harbin to J.F. Stevens (RG43, New Entry 844, File 226).
38 Ibid. RRSC Major Merz remained in Chita until mid-April and witnessed events in the city.
39 Shishkin, *Grazhdanskaya voina na Dal'nem Vostoke*, figs. 13ff.
40 RRSC Colonel B.O. Johnson estimated that there were 'possibly 1,000 [Kappel Army soldiers] on the Sretensk front' in early April although many of them had 'disappeared' by 7 April. 16 April 1920, memorandum from Colonel. Johnson, Harbin, to J.F. Stevens (RG43, New Entry 844, File 238).
41 Vasilevskii, *Ataman Semenov*, p. 126, '*Iz rechi polkovnika Umeda na bankete v chest' atamana Semenova*', Vostochnaya Okraina, Nerchinsk, 19 May 1920.
42 23 April 1920, Military Attaché China (HA) report: 'Conditions in Siberia and Manchuria', (RG165, Microfilm M1444 Roll 6, MID 2657-I-130).
43 N.P. Daurets, *Semenovskie Zastenki*, Harbin, 1921, p. 53.
44 16 April 1920, translation of 9 April letter from Prosecutive Attorney Sotchin, Russian Vice Consul, Hailar to Chief of Military Mission, Japanese Consul, Certified by Lieutenant Colonel Klupek, Harbin (RG43, New Entry 844, File 238). The arrested were named as 'Judge Gramskovskii, Post Officials Vidotich, Ramsh and Burtasovskii and Hailar residents Vasilii and Ivan Kuznetzov and Psarevskii'.
45 13 March 1920, letter from RRSC Major D.S. Colby, Verkhne-Udinsk, to RRSC Colonel B.O. Johnson, p. 30a (RG43, File 238).
46 10 April 1920, letter from Dr Blagosh, representative of Czechoslovak Republic, Hailar to Commander of Chinese Troops, Hailar (RG43, New Entry 844, File 226). Blagosh distributed copies of this letter to the RRSC and to Czech Legion Lieutenant Colonel Clupek in Harbin. A Lieutenant Petak served as Blagosh's assistant.
47 22 April 1920, 'The Hailar Incident: Eyewitness's Account', *Peking and Tientsin Times*. Some accounts refer to the mail car as a prison car, which it resembled. After a few years of Soviet rule, 'every passenger train inevitably had a prison car, painted dark green, with small barred windows', wrote Bulat Okudzhava in *Unexpected Joy*, trans. S. Melnikova, Rosen Publishing, New York, 1992.
48 15 April 1920, report No. 19/0 from Lieutenant Colonel Kopal, Chief military mission of the Czechoslovak Ministry of National Defense, Harbin, to Lieutenant Colonel Clupek, Harbin, 'Short explanation of events at Hailar from April 11–13' (RG43). Kopal refers to Dr Blagosh as Balhosh.
49 According to Lieutenant Colonel Kopal, the Chinese representatives included 'Tum Yi, Governor of the Kulombirs District, General Chan-Kui-U, Colonel Chi-Shin, Military Governor, Lieutenant Colonel Tsan-Ui-Do in the capacity of the Chief of Military Governor's Staff; for the Japanese: Lieutenant Colonel Tsidheu, commander of Japanese battalion garrisoned at Hailar, Major Taido, Japanese Attaché at the military governor's office at Tsitsihar and Captain Uhda'.
50 14 April 1920, letter from Major D.S. Colby, Hailar to Colonel B.O. Johnson, Harbin (RG43, New Entry 844, File 238).
51 14 April 1920, Military Attaché China (HA) report: 'General Situation in Manchuria and Eastern Siberia', (RG165, Microfilm M1444 Roll 6, MID 2657-I-125).
52 14 April 1920, letter from RRSC Major, D.S. Colby, Hailar, to RRSC Colonel B.O. Johnson, Harbin (RG43, File 238). Colby wrote this detailed description of events as the Hailar incident unfolded.
53 14 April 1920, Military Attaché China (HA) report: 'General Situation in Manchuria and Eastern Siberia', (RG165, Microfilm M1444 Roll 6, MID 2657-I-125).
54 23 April 1920, Military Attaché China (HA) report: 'Conditions in Siberia and Manchuria' (RG165, Microfilm M1444 Roll 6, MID 2657-I-130).

NOTES

55 23 April 1920, Military Attaché China (HA) report: 'Conditions in Siberia and Manchuria'. This detailed seventh-page report contains insightful analysis substantiated with ample intelligence, although it refers to Krasnoshchekov as 'Krasnorkoff'. Gutman, *The Destruction of Nileolaevsk-on-Amur*, p. 67, refers to the Verkhne-Udinsk Democratic Republic, which assumed many names during its short, eventful life.
56 21 April 1920, letter from RRSC Colonel B.O. Johnson, Harbin, to John Stevens (RG43, File 238).
57 23 April 1920, Military Attaché China (HA) reports No. 2531 and 'Conditions in Siberia and Manchuria' (RG165, Microfilm M1444 Roll 6).
58 23 April 1920, Military Attaché China (HA) reports No. 2531 and 'Conditions in Siberia and Manchuria' (RG165, Microfilm M1444 Roll 6).
59 21 April 1920, letter from RRSC Colonel B.O. Johnson, Harbin, to John Stevens (RG43, File 238).
60 23 April 1920, Military Attaché China (HA) reports No. 2531 and 'Conditions in Siberia and Manchuria', (RG165, Microfilm M1444 Roll 6).
61 23 April 1920, Military Attaché China (HA) report: 'Conditions in Siberia and Manchuria', (RG165, Microfilm M1444 Roll 6, MID 2657-I-130).
62 Ibid.
63 Ayumu Yasutomi, 'Money and Finance in Manchuria 1895–1945', Nagoya University, 1998.
64 23 April 1920, Military Attaché China (HA) report No. 2531 and 'Conditions in Siberia and Manchuria', (RG165, Microfilm M1444 Roll 6).
65 Ibid.
66 Borisov, *Dalnii Vostok*, pp. 22–5 and 28.
67 Ibid. and Footman, 'Ataman Semenov', pp. 55–6.
68 Vertyankin, 'Istoriya Ledokola "Angara"', p. 13. The other *Angara* commanders were I.I. Karlov and, after his sudden death in summer 1920, J.G. Ott, both former naval officers.
69 Smith, *Vladivostok Under Red and White Rule*, p. 68.
70 Gutman, *The Destruction of Nileolaevsk-on-Amur*, pp. 99–110, 118 and 121; and Varneck and Fisher, *The Testimony of Kolchak*, pp. 304 and 308–9. Morozov was from the village of Dermidovka. Triapitsyn's regiment 'wore black and red ribbons on their chests and red-on-black five-point stars on their caps'. His staff was 'all smartly dressed in suits of high-grade brown leather, cut on a military pattern. Their boots and caps were of the same color... They wore revolvers on their sides on belts of the army officer pattern'. Anton Z. Ovchennikov, commander of the Red detachment from Sakhalin, stated that 'fire started in the city' on 1 June.
71 Smith, *Vladivostok Under Red and White Rule*, pp. 78 and 80.
72 Ibid., p. 186.
73 White, *The Siberian Intervention*, p. 295 and Bragin, A.P., 'Krovavoe prestuplenie zhido-bol' shevikov na rekov Khor', *Nashe Otechestvo*; 73–4, August–September 2001, Sankt Peterburg, *Nashe Otechestvo* is a post-Soviet, anti-Semitic publication.
74 28 May 1920, memorandom from Lieutenant F.B. Byers, Harbin, to J. Stevens, [record of] conversation with Lieutenant Webster – Vladivostok this a.m. (RG43, New Entry 844, File 238).
75 24 May 1920, report, 'The Local Situation', Vladivostok (RG43, File 238).
76 Ibid., p. 2.
77 Gutman, *The Destruction of Nikolaevsk-on-Amur*, pp. 160–163; and Varneck and Fisher, *The Testimony of Kolchak*, pp. 311–12.
78 Smith, *Vladivostok Under Red and White Rule*, pp. 77, 78–79 and 88.
79 Vasilevskii, *Ataman Semenov*, p. 119 and Smith, *Vladivostok Under Red and White Rule*, pp. 90–1. Semenov's recognition of Vrangel also seems to have been an attempt to safeguard a legal continuity of White authority.
80 Gutman, *The Destruction of Nikolaevsk-on-Amur*, pp. 138–45.
81 Borisov, *Dalnii Vostok*, p. 28 and Smith, *Vladivostok Under Red and White Rule*, pp. 83–4.
82 Bragin, *'Kravavoe, prestuplenie'*, pp. 8–9.

83 Smith, *Vladivostok Under Red and White Rule*, pp. 85–6.
84 Vasilevskii, *Ataman Semenov*, pp. 106–7.
85 US Senate Committee on Education and Labor, *Deportation of Gregorie Semenoff*, pp. 61–2; and 'Semenoff, Freed, Called Bigamist', *New York Times*, 20 April 1922, pp. 1 and 2. In testimony to a special board of inquiry of the Vancouver branch of the US immigration service on 15 March 1922, Mrs Semenov stated that she had been living with a 'Colonel Firdesi' in Chita. The wedding was formally witnessed by 'Torchinov and Seborovskii'.
86 Daurets, *Semenovskie Zastenki*, pp. 60–2.
87 S. Tsypkin, *Oktiabrskaya Revolutsia i Grazhdanskaya voina na Dal'nem Vostokye: Khronika Sobitii 1917–1922*, Dal'giz, Moscow and Khabarovsk, 1933, pp. 200–1.
88 Borisov, *Dalnii Vostok*, p. 48. The decoration included a 'large gold cross with an original particle of the life-giving tree of the Master with Aleksandrovski ribbon'.
89 Nabatova-Barrett Miller and Nun Seraphima. Nun Seraphima wrote (based on her conversation with Prince Kudashev), 'The coffins were opened and put in the Russian Church [in Harbin]'. The only apparent injuries on the grand princess were a broken nose and bruise on her face. Elizaveta Fedorovna and her husband had sponsored the construction and, as representatives of the emporer, presided over the consecration of the Church of Saint Mary Magdelene on the slope of the Mount of Olives in the Garden of Gethsemane in Jerusalem.
90 Smith, *Vladivostok Under Red and White Rule*, p. 87. The last Czechoslovak transport sailed out of Vladivostok on 10 September 1920.
91 Tsypkin, *Oktiabrskaya Revolutsia*, p. 201.
92 Borisov, *Dalnii Vostok*, p. 29 and Vertyankin, 'Istoriya Ledokola "Angara" '.
93 Tsypkin, *Oktiabrskaya Revolutsia*, p. 202. Tsypkin cited the Harbin *Novosti Zhizni*.
94 Smith, *Vladivostok Under Red and White Rule*, pp. 89–91 and 95.
95 Vasilii Evgen'evich Shambarov, *Belogvardeishchina*, Moscow, EKSMO-Press, 2002, p. 539. Shambarov states that the Reds 'demonstrated peaceful aspirations' and tried to lull Semenov into a sense of false security.
96 Tsypkin, *Oktiabrskaya Revolutsia*, p. 203 and Shishkin, *Grazhdanskaya voina na Dal'em Vostoke*, map 15. Shishkin depicts White forces as the 2nd Ufa Brigade in Chita, Molchanov's 3rd Corps with about 7,000 men between Darasun and Adrianovka, the 2nd Corps with 4,700 men between Olovyannaya and Khada-Bulok and the 1st Corps between Kharanor and Manchuli with 6,300 men, two armored trains and eight aircraft.
97 Junius B. Wood, 'The Far Eastern Republic', *National Geographic*, 41, 6 June 1922, pp. 565–92.
98 Vasilevskii, *Ataman Semenov*, pp. 118–19.
99 Fleming, *The Fate of Admiral Kolchak*, p. 233.
100 Dvornichenko, *Putevodityel' po Chitye*, pp. 160–1; Semenov, *O Sebe*, p. 257; Footman, 'Ataman Semenov', p. 57 and Tsypkin, *Oktiabrskaya Revolutsia*, p. 203.
101 Tsypkin, *Oktiabrskaya Revolutsia*, p. 204.
102 Ibid. and Smith, *Vladivostok Under Red and White Rule*, pp. 95–7.
103 Shambarov, *Belogvardeishchina*, p. 260.
104 Semenov, *O Sebe*, p. 255.
105 Tsypkin, *Oktiabrskaya Revolutsia*, p. 205; Smith, *Vladivostok Under Red and White Rule*, pp. 102, 104, 110–11, 114–16 and 118; Semenov, *O Sebe*, pp. 257–9. The ataman left Harbin on 24 November arrived in Grodekovo on 27 November and stayed about a week.
106 Smith, *Vladivostok Under Red and White Rule*, pp. 116, 120 and 132. Thirty *versts* is just under 20 miles.

10 GÖTTERDÄMMERUNG: OCTOBER 1920–NOVEMBER 1922

1 Ossendowski, *Beasts, Men and Gods*, pp. 232–3.
2 9 February 1921, intelligence report on Urga, Mongolia; Source: Marine Detachment, American Legation, Peking, Office of Naval Intelligence (ONI). The report was originally

NOTES

prepared 7 October 1920. A regular source of US intelligence was Mr A.M. Guptill, a manager with the American-owned Mongolian Trading Company.

3 Semenov, *O Sebe*, pp. 246–7 and 249–50.
4 6 September 1919, telegram No. 239 from Colonel Lantry, Irkutsk, to Colonel Emerson, Omsk (RG43).
5 25 November 1919, report 'Conditions in Mongolia', ONI (RG165, MID File 156-130/1). All of the text of the ONI report was raw intelligence provided by 'a reliable source in Mongolia'. The referred-to Treaty of Kyakhta was the 2nd Tripartite Agreement of 25 May 1915.
6 E. Belov, 'Kak Byla Likvidirovana Avtonomiya Vneshnei Mongolii', Aziatskaya Biblioteka, 2001, p. 8; and 25 November 1919, Report 'Conditions in Mongolia', Captain F.F. Rogers, ONI (RG165, MID File 156-130/1). Other transliterations of Little Hsu's name are Syui Shuchzhen, Xu Shucheng and Hsu Shu-cheng; and of President Hsü Shih-chang: Hsu Shih-chang, Syui Shichan and Xu Shichang.
7 12 May 1920, MID report No. 312, 'Conditions in Urga' (RG165, File No. 156-130/3).
8 Belov, 'Kak Byla', pp. 8–9 and 11–12.
9 25 November 1919, report 'Conditions in Mongolia', ONI (RG165, MID File No. 156-130/1) and Belov, 'Kak Byla', pp. 12–13.
10 E. Belov, 'Kak Byla Likvidirovana Avtonomiya Vneshnei Mongolii', Aziatskaya Biblioteka, 2001; Embassy of Mongolia, 'About Mongolia', Seoul, 2002.
11 27 April 1920, report 'Conditions in Urga', ONI (RG165, MID File No. 156-130/2). All of the text of this report was raw intelligence provided by 'a reliable source in Peking'.
12 Ossendowski, *Beasts, Men and Gods*, pp. 104 and 107.
13 12 May 1920, MID report No. 312, 'Conditions in Urga' (RG165. File No. 156-130/3).
14 Ibid. and 9 February 1921, intelligence report on Urga, Mongolia; Source: Marine Detachment, American Legation, Peking, ONI. The report was originally prepared on 7 October 1920.
15 12 May 1920, MID report No. 312, 'Conditions in Urga' (RG165, File No. 156-130/3), 9 February 1921, ONI Report and Belov, 'Kak Byla'.
16 Worden and Savada, *Mongolia*; and 12 May 1920, MID report No. 312, 'Conditions in Urga' (RG165, File No. 156-130/3). The revolutionary group included other Mongolians who would soon rise to prominence including S. Danzan and D. Bodoo.
17 Ossendowski, *Beasts, Men and Gods*, pp. 104–5.
18 Bawden, *Modern Histroy of Mongolia*, p. 215. Little Hsu was recalled from Urga as a result of 'the An-fu clique's loss of power'. US reports mistakenly identified Sando as 'Sambo'.
19 9 February 1921, intelligence report on Urga, Mongolia; Source: Marine Detachment, American Legation, Peking, ONI. The report was originally prepared 7 October 1920. The transmitter was a '25 kilowatt continuous arc set with a guaranteed sending radius of 1,000 miles. The permanent wave length is 4,000 meters, but can be cut down to 2,000 meters, or stepped up to 10,000 meters.' A 50-horsepower gasoline engine ran the plant. The three buildings consisted of a single transmitting and engine house, living quarters and a sound-proof receiving house with 'supplementary aerial and apparatus for determining the location of aeroplanes'.
20 9 February 1921, ONI intelligence report and 30 March 1921, MID report No. 212, File No. 810-200, 'The Capture of Urga by the Troops of Baron Ungern and Mongols' (RG165, MID File No. 2657-I-158/3). The February report named the cavalry commander as 'Kao Ssu Ling'.
21 Stanislav Vital'evich Khatuntsev, 'Ungern fon Shternberg: Buddist s Mechom', Voronezh State University, Historical Faculty, 2003; and Volkov, *Tragediya Russkugo Ofitserstva*, ch. 7. Volkov estimates Ungern's original Dauria garrison nucleus at '400 Russians and up to 2,000 Asians'.
22 'Intrigue and Force in Siberia: Semenoff's Aspirations', *The Times*, 11 November 1919, p. 13. Volkov states the lowest estimate for Ungern's core force from Dauria at 2,400 consisting of 400 Russians and 2,000 Asians.

23 Peter Hopkirk, *Setting the East Ablaze: Lenin's Dream of an Empire in Asia*, Kodansha Globe, New York, 1984, pp. 127 and 129–30; Ossendowski, *Beasts, Men and Gods*, pp. 108, 219 and 236; Irina Yu Morozova, 'Japan and its Influence on Pan-Mongolism and Pan-Buddhism', Nordic Institute of Asian Studies, Copenhagen, 1999; undated extracts from MID China monographs (RG59, Microfilm M1444, pp. 795–8 and 846–58), Bawden, *Modern Histroy of Mongolia*, p. 216; 17 March 1921, report No 180, ONI File No. 810-200; Karan, *Changing Face of Tibet*, pp. 87–8; Leonid Iouzéfovitch, 'Il ne doit rester graine ni d'homme ni de femme', *Bulletin de l'Association Anda*, 40, January 2001, Paris; and S.K. Stierlin, 'Mysteries Surrounding the Fall of Urga', *Milton's Review*, 5 March 1921. Hopkirk relies heavily on the memoirs of White officer Dmitri Alioshin (*Asian Odyssey*, 1941), whose recollections sometimes differ from other eye-witness reports that were published earlier. Kazagrandi was, according to Ossendowski, 'a man of good family, an experience engineer and a splendid officer who had distinguished himself in the war at the defense of the Island of Moon in the Baltic and afterwards in the fight with the Bolsheviki on the Volga'.

24 Ossendowski, *Beasts, Men and Gods*, p. 223.

25 Hopkirk, *Setting the East Ablaze*, pp. 127–8; Morozova, 'Japan and its Influence'; Apollinaria Tumina, 'Trup Pyatiletiya: Aktual'noe Interv'yu', n.p., n.d.; Baerlein, *The March of the Seventy Thousand*, p. 263; and Khatuntsev, 'Ungern fon Shternberg'. Tumina transcribes much of Ungern's 27 August 1921 interrogation. Baerlein wrote that Ungern-Shternberg married the daughter of Yuan Shih-Kai when the Baron 'joined Semenov in eastern Siberia'. Yuan had died in 1916. Khatuntsev wrote that Ungern married in August 1919.

26 Hopkirk, *Setting the East Ablaze*, p. 128.

27 Ibid., p. 129, and December 1920, China monograph, MID, p. 18 (RG59, Microfilm M1444).

28 December 1920, China monograph, MID, pp. 18–19 (RG59, Microfilm M1444).

29 Bawden, *Modern History of Mongolia*, p. 147.

30 Ibid., pp. 216–18.

31 30 March 1921, MID report No. 212, File No. 810-200, 'The Capture of Urga by the Troops of Baron Ungern and Mongols' (RG165, MID File No. 2657-I-158/3).

32 Stierlin, 'Mysteries Surrounding the Fall of Urga', and 17 March 1921, report No. 180, ONI File No. 810-200 (RG59).

33 30 March 1921, MID report No. 212; and Hopkirk, *Setting the East Ablaze*, pp. 130–2.

34 Hopkirk, *Setting the East Ablaze*, p. 131.

35 30 March 1921, MID report No. 212 (RG59). Major Dockray, in an interview shortly after the attack, refined the Chinese casualty figure at Bogdo-ol to 96 dead.

36 30 March 1921, MID report No. 212 (RG59).

37 30 March 1921, MID report No. 212 (RG59).

38 17 March 1921, report No. 180, ONI File No. 810-200 (RG59).

39 Ibid.

40 9 February 1921, ONI report on Urga. The 'well-known Duke Lebsenjensen' was one of the prominent prisoners.

41 17 March 1921, report No 180, ONI File No. 810-200 (RG59).

42 Ossendowski, *Beasts Men and Gods*, p. 229.

43 Hopkirk, *Setting the East Ablaze*, p. 135.

44 16 April 1921, memorandum from Major W.S. Drysdale, Office of Military Attaché, Peking, to DMI (RG165, MID File No. 156-130/8).

45 June 1921, China monograph, MID, p. 26 (RG59, Microfilm M1444); Ossendowski, *Beasts Men and Gods*, p. 236 and Hopkirk, *Setting the East Ablaze*, p. 135.

46 10 March 1921, MID report (marked 'Di-JT/BMM-SS') (RG165, MID File No. 2657-I-159/1).

47 Hopkirk, *Setting the East Ablaze*, pp. 132–4. Another source was Captain Makeev's 1926 book *Bog Voini*, published in Shanghai.

NOTES

48 17 March 1921, report No. 180, ONI File No. 810-200 (RG59).
49 Hopkirk, *Setting the East Ablaze*, p. 130; and Ossendowski, *Beasts Men and Gods*, p. 246.
50 R.F. Ungern-Shternberg, 'Prikaz No. 15: Prikaz russkim otryadam na territorii sovetskoi Sibirii', 15 May 1921, Urga; State Archives of the Russian Federation, F. Varia, d. 392, l. 1-6; reproduced by Radio Islam, 2002.
51 17 March 1921, report No. 180, ONI File No. 810-200 (RG59).
52 Aleksandr, Fridman, 'Evreiskie pogromy...v Mongolii', *IJC*, Nizhne Novgorod, 2002; and Iouzéfovitch, 'Il ne doit rester graine ni d'homme ni de femme'. The discovery of the Jewish refuge resulted from the macabre tragedy of a Korean dentist, Dr Li, who informed the Whites to protect the mummified corpse of his three-year old daughter, a typhus victim, at a roadblock on the Kalgan road. Li was executed anyway.
53 17 March 1921, report No. 180, ONI File No. 810-200; and 30 March 1921, MID report No. 212 (RG59). Leonid Petrov estimated the size of Ungern's expedition as '11,000 horsemen'.
54 Ossendowski, *Beasts, Men and Gods*, pp. 168 and 219.
55 Ibid., pp. 208–9.
56 Bawden, *Modern History of Mongolia*, pp. 218–25.
57 30 March 1921, MID report No. 212 (RG59).
58 Bawden, *Modern History of Mongolia*, p. 216.
59 Ossendowski, *Beasts, Men and Gods*, p. 228.
60 Ibid., pp. 243 and 245–6.
61 Volkov, *Tragediya Russkogo Ofitserstva*, ch. 7, and Ossendowski, *Beasts, Men and Gods*, pp. 219–21 and 233–4.
62 Ossendowski, *Beasts, Men and Gods*, pp. 104–5.
63 Bawden, *Modern History of Mongolia*, pp. 230–3.
64 Ossendowski, *Beasts, Men and Gods*, pp. 151–5. Ossendowski referred to Tesiyn Gol as 'Tisangol'.
65 Ibid., pp. 112, 114–15 and 160–7.
66 Ibid., p. 109; and Volkov, *Tragediya Russkogo Ofitserstva*, ch. 7. Fu Hsiang was advisor to the Chinese commissioner in Uliastai. Ossendowski says that the self-defense detachment had 60 men before it fractured; Volkov states that Mikhailov had 'up to 300 Russians' in a 'secret organization'.
67 Ossendowski, *Beasts, Men and Gods*, pp. 160–2 and 166–7.
68 Ibid., pp. 166–9.
69 June 1921, China monograph, MID, p. 22 (RG59, Microfilm M1444).
70 Ossendowski, *Beasts, Men and Gods*, p. 150.
71 June 1921, China monograph, MID, p. 28 (RG59, Microfilm M1444). Mr Yourin, president of the mission of the FER to China, had prompted the visit when he asked the American Legation in Peking to exchange diplomatic representatives in early May.
72 Volkov, *Tragediya Russkogo Ofitserstva*, ch. 7. Ossendowski referred to Kaigorodov as 'Kaigordov, an Altai Tartar officer'.
73 17 March 1921, report No. 180, ONI File No. 810-200; 30 March 1921, MID report No. 212 (RG59); Hopkirk, *Setting the East Ablaze*, p. 146; Tumina, 'Trup Pyatiletiya'; and Volkov, *Tragediya Russkogo Ofitserstva*, ch. 7. US and allied intelligence estimated Ungern's strength at 8,000 and Volkov gave it at 3,500, citing I.I. Serebrennikov, *Velikii Otkhod*, n.p., 1936, pp. 35–40.
74 June 1921, China monograph, MID, p. 27 (RG59, Microfilm M1444); Worden and Savada, *Mongolia*; and Shishkin *Grazhdanskaya voina na Dal'nem Vostoke*. According to MID sources, the Japanese withdrawal from Blagoveshchensk was followed, not by 'the reign of communistic terror forecasted by Japanese propagandists', but by a Red regime perceived as 'corrupt and unable to maintain order' and beyond the control of Chita. Peasants and miners purportedly formed an independent militia 40,000 strong opposed to the Reds, but were 'quashed' after the communists declared a state of siege in June.
75 June 1921, China monograph, MID, pp. 23, 26 and 28–9; and December 1920, China monograph, MID, p. 20 (RG59, Microfilm M1444).

76 Ivan Ivanovich Fedyuninskii, *Na Vostoke*, VoenIzdat, Moscow, 1985, ch. 1.
77 Bawden, *Modern History of Mongolia*, p. 234.
78 Worden and Savada, *Mongolia*; June 1921 China monograph, MID, p. 26 (RG59, Microfilm M1444); Fridman, 'Evreiske pogromy...v Mongolii', p. 13; Manusevich *et al.*, *Internatsionalist*, p. 435; and Volkov, *Tragediya Russkogo Ofitserstva*, ch. 7. Urga/Yihe Huree was renamed Niyslel Huree.
79 19 July 1921, Naval Attaché–Peking, report No. 427, 'Mukden Political Conditions', ONI File No. 103-100 (MID 2657-I-189) (Microfilm M1444, Roll 6).
80 E.K. Kolbenev, 'Drug Mongol'skogo Naroda Chekist Gridnev', *Ocherki Istorii Rossiiskoi Vneshnei Razvedki*, 4, 1999. Kolbenev mistransliterated Lake Buyr Nur as Vuir Nur.
81 Hopkirk, *Setting the East Ablaze*, pp. 147–8; Fridman, 'Evreiske pogromy...v Mongolii'; Tumina, 'Trup Pyatiletiya'; Shishkin, *Grazhdanskaya voina na Dal'nem Vostoke*, map 18; and Khatuntsev 'Ungern fon Shternberg'. Gusinoozersk is 68 miles south-south-east of Verkhne-Udinsk on Lake Gusin.
82 Fridman, 'Evreiske pogromy...v Mongolii'; Khatuntsev, 'Ungern fon Shternberg' p. 10; Volkov, *Tragediya Russkogo Ofitserstva*, ch. 7; Hopkirk, *Setting the East Ablaze* p. 149; and Brovkin, *The Bolsheviks in Russian Society*, p. 138. In the latter, Norman Pereira states that Ungern-Shternberg was captured by partisans under P.E. Shchetinkin, citing a 23 September 1921 *Izvestiya* article.
83 Fridman, 'Evreiske pogromy...v Mongolii'; Tumina, 'Trup Pyatiletiya'; and Baerlein, *The March of the Seventy Thousand*, p. 265.
84 Baerlein, *The March of the Seventy Thousand*, p. 265; Fridman, 'Evreiske pogromy...v Mongolii'; Anatolii Dorbnya, 'Klady samozvanykh atamanov', Kladoiskatel'stvo, 2001, p. 3. A corps commander Gailit led the interrogation.
85 Bawden, *Modern History of Mongolia*, pp. 236–7.
86 Volkov, *Tragediya Russkogo Ofitserstva*, ch. 7. Ossendowski referred to Kaigorodov as 'Kaigordov, an Altai Tartar officer'.
87 Ibid. Volkov writes that Sokol'nitskii's detachment was 'eliminated as a fighting unit' on 26 November 1922 and dispersed around northern China in February 1923.
88 Smith, *Vladivostok Under Red and White Rule*, pp. 120–1, and Tsypkin, *Oktiabrskaya Revolutsia*, pp. 202–3.
89 Dvornichenko, *Putevodityel po Chitye*, pp. 106–7.
90 Smith, *Vladivostok Under Red and White Rule*, pp. 132–8, 141, 143, 149, 151 and 162; Dvornichenko, *Putevodityel po Chitye*, pp. 106–7; and Bragin, 'Vozrozhdenie nisskoi gosudarstvennosti', p. 3. Vasilii Antonov's administration lasted from 11 December 1920 until May 1921. In anticommunist lore, the longshot Merkulov coup was remembered as being 12 rifles versus 2,000 Reds.
91 Smith, *Vladivostok Under Red and White Rule*, pp. 152–6 and 159.
92 Ibid., pp. 141 and 149–50.
93 Undated extracts from MID China Monographs (RG165, Microfilm M1444, pp. 854–5).
94 Smith, *Vladivostok Under Red and White Rule*, pp. 128, 153, 156–7, 160, 163 and 165. Bochkarev killed a prominent member of the former *zemstvo* government, Utkin, during his June 1921 rampage.
95 Semenov, *O Sebe*, pp. 285–91; and Smith, *Vladivostok Under Red and White Rule*, pp. 168–9.
96 Smith, *Vladivostok Under Red and White Rule*, p. 183. The Vrangelites arrived in Vladivostok on 23 September 1921.
97 Ibid., pp. 180–2. In July 1921, the *Dal'buro* had ordered that a 'spontaneous uprising' among *kappel'evtsy* be prepared for mid-October.
98 Ibid., p. 204.
99 Ibid., pp. 184 and 188–9.
100 Ibid., pp. 199–202.
101 Bragin, 'Vozrozhdenie nisskoi gosudarstvennosti', p. 5.
102 Smith, *Vladivostok Under Red and White Rule*, pp. 207–8, 218–19, 221 and 233.
103 Ibid., pp. 233–41.

NOTES

104 Ibid., p. 241.
105 Petrov, 'Out of the Frying Pan, Into the Fine: Russian Immigrants in China', Asian Studies Association of Australia, Hobart, 2002. L.A. Petrov states that 8,870 people evacuation Vladivostok with Admiral Stark. Stark and 800 refugees and soldiers reached Manila in January 1923. US President Warren G. Harding approved the transport of 500 emigres to the United States aboard transport USS *Merritt*, which reached San Francisco on 3 July 1923. Gutman believed that Japan's Siberian expedition cost 6,000 men killed, wounded and dead from disease and 1 billion gold yen (*The Destruction of Nikolaevsk-on Amur*, p. 84).
106 Bragin, Vozrozhdenie nisskoi gosudarstvennosti', p. 15, Wood, 'The Far Eastern Republic'; and Zalesskii, *Imperiya Stalina, Gospolokhrana – Gosudarstvenaya Politicheskaya Okhrana*, the state political police, was the FER's equivalent of the CHEKA. Meier A. Trilisser was one of the *Gospolokhrana* leaders who steered the post-civil war Red Terror in the Russian Far East.

11 DIASPORA, MANCHURIAN REVIVAL AND LEGACY: JUNE 1921 TO THE PRESENT DAY

1 Petrov, 'Out of the Frying Pan, Into the Fire'; and S.V. Karpenko, 'Kazach'i Stanitsy v emigratsii (1921–1930s)', Rossiiskii Gosudarstvennyi Gumanitarnyi Universitet, Istoriko-Arkhivnyi Institut, 2002.
2 V.G. Lobanov, Staraya Chita, Chita, 2001, p. 50. Prosecutors said that Stepanov killed V.K. Shumov for 16 kilograms of gold dust.
3 Lyubov Miller, trans. Irina Nabatova-Barrett, 'Holy Martyr of Russia', Grand Princess Elizaveta Fedorouna', n.p.; and Aleksandt Barinor, 'Tsyganka Masha'.
4 Omsk State Archive, Description of Personal Collection of G.E. Katanaev, f.366, op.1, 488 d.
5 Semenov, *O Sebe*, pp. 285–91; and Smith, *Vladivostok Under Red and White Rule*, pp. 168–9. Genzan is also known as Wonsan.
6 Semenov, *O Sebe*, pp. 300–3.
7 US Senate Committee on Education and Labor, *Deportation of Gregorie Semenoff*, pp. 61–2; Semenov, *O Sebe*, p. 302. Semenov also mentioned an anticommunist gathering in Genoa about this time. It was the US State Department that suggested that he was going to meet Grand Duke Nicholas. Helen Semenov was quoted as saying that her parents resided in 'Chindall, Japan'.
8 US Senate Committee on Education and Labor, *Deportation of Gregorie Semenoff*, pp. 52–3. The MID letter was read aloud at the Senate hearing.
9 Semenov, *O Sebe*, pp. 303 and 306; and 'Semenoff, Cossack Chief, is Arrested on Arrival Here', *New York Times*, 7 April 1922, pp. 1 and 3.
10 'New Bail Bond or Jail for Semenoff', *New York Times*, 13 April 1922, p. 21. The Colonel accompanied Governor Edwin P. Morrow to the Republican Party National Convention in Chicago in June 1920, then returned to Camp Zachary Taylor for duty. He continued serving until 1935, commanding Fort Niagara, New York during his last five years in uniform, overseeing daily training of the 28th Infantry, parades, band concerts and restoration of the historic bastion by Civilian Conservation Corps workers (27th Infantry Regimental Historical Society, 'Colonel Charles H. Morrow', Schofield Barracks, HI, 2003; and Old Fort Niagara Association, 'Old Fort Niagara', Youngstown, NY, 2004.
11 22 March 1922, questionnaire for Oriental Language Detail, Major B.B. McCroskey (RG165, MID 2663-59).
12 US Senate Committee on Education and Labor, *Deportation of Gregorie Semenoff*, pp. 56–62; Semenov, *O Sebe*, p. 304. Anti-Semitic suspicions and prejudice were common in US military intelligence circles and, apparently, in customs and immigration as well.
13 Ibid., p. 60.
14 Leckie's written testimony was inscribed on stationary of the Vancouver Club, dated 20 March 1922. Though Leckie claimed to have known Semenov in Russia, Colonel Morrow testified in April 1922 that he never heard of Leckie during his tour of duty in Siberia.

15 US Senate Committee on Education and Labor, *Deportation of Gregorie Semenoff,* pp. 62–3.
16 Aivazov's office was in Vancouver's Standard Bank building. He claimed to be a naturalized British subject, and represented several companies in trade with Russia, including the Remington Typewriter Company, Martin Senour Company and the World Harvester Company.
17 Semenov, *O Sebe*, pp. 303–4.
18 'Semenoff, Cossack Chief, is Arrested on Arrival Here', *New York Times*, 7 April 1922, pp. 1 and 3.
19 Fainberg, the secretary of Youroveta, lived at 500 West 114th Street. The president was named as Leon M. Wourgraft, a Russian banker living in Paris.
20 'Semenoff, Cossack Chief, is Arrested on Arrival Here', *New York Times*, 7 April 1922, pp. 1 and 3; 'Move to Deport Semenoff Begun', *New York Times*, 9 April 1922, p. 13; and Semenov, *O Sebe*, p. 305.
21 'Semenoff, Cossack Chief, is Arrested on Arrival Here', *New York Times*, 7 April 1922, pp. 1 and 3; and 'New Bail Bond or Jail for Semenoff', *New York Times*, 13 April 1922, p. 21.
22 'Move to Deport Semenoff Begun', *New York Times*, 9 April 1922, p. 13.
23 'Semenoff Silent as to Bank Theft', *New York Times*, 11 April 1922, p. 9; Semenov, *O Sebe*, pp. 307–8. Semenov retained Clark, Prentice and Roulston (61 Broadway) for international issues and deportation proceedings, and Glaze & Fine (271 Broadway) for bankruptcy issues.
24 US Senate Committee on Education and Labor, *Deportation of Gregorie Semenoff,* p. 1; and 'Semenoff Silent as to Bank Theft', *New York Times*, 11 April 1922, p. 9.
25 'Seek Allies' Part in Semenoff Case', *New York Times*, 14 April 1922, p. 4; and 'More to Deport Semenoff Begun', *The Times*, 9 April 1922.
26 Krupskii's permit was signed by Deputy Police Commissioner John J. Cray.
27 'Japanese Attack Chita Forces', *New York Times*, 13 April 1922, p. 24; and 'Japanese Prevent Chita Army Advance', *New York Times*, 14 April 1922, p. 3.
28 'Semenoff in Jail; East Side Throngs Hiss Cossack Chief', *New York Times*, 14 April 1922, pp. 1 and 4; and 'Seek Allies' Part in Semenoff Case', *New York Times*, 14 April 1922, p. 4.
29 Apparently both émigré organizations shared the same address, 5 Columbus Circle, in Manhattan.
30 'Semenoff, Freed, Called Bigamist', *New York Times*, 20 April 1922, pp. 1 and 2.
31 Ibid.
32 'Semenoff Departs to Rejoin His Army', *New York Times*, 10 June 1922, p. 12; and 'Semenoff's Departure a Relief to Officials', *New York Times*, 11 June 1922, p. 24; and Semenov, *O Sebe*, p. 309. The Youroveta case had bogged down in debate about US jurisdiction over thefts that occurred on Russian territory. Years later, Semenov tried to recast events in his memoirs, and declared of the US Senate hearings and their revelations of his atrocities, 'I easily refuted all of the insinuations of Graves and proved them false, calling in question the discordant performance of a few eminent officers of the American Army who discredited themselves by false witness.'
33 Iouzéfovitch, Leonid, 'Il ne doit rester graine ni d'homme ni de femme'. Rinchino seems to have answered to the Oriental People's Section of the Communist International (Comintern) in Irkutsk.
34 Wood, 'The Far Eastern Republic', pp. 565–92. Wood, a 1900 graduate of the University of Michigan, was an experienced foreign correspondent for the *Chicago Daily News* who had covered the US occupation of Vera Cruz, Mexico in 1914, Cuban unrest in 1917, the European front with the AEF. He traveled extensively in Asia and interviewed Ataman Semenov.
35 Ibid.
36 Most Semenov banknotes appear to have been 1,000- and 500-ruble 'pigeon' notes, so called because of the squabbish resemblance of their Russian eagle. The 'Moscow bills' were gorgeous notes bearing the stirring admonition, 'Workers of the world, unite!' in several languages. A new depreciated silver coinage of 5, 10, 15 and 20 kopek pieces, minted in Japan, traded at about 28 per cent of face value.

NOTES

37 Wood, 'The Far Eastern Republic'.
38 Ibid.
39 Dvornichenko, *Putevodityel'po Chitye*, pp. 100–1. Anokhin had been a Red party member since 1908.
40 Vertyankin, 'Istoriya Ledokala *'Angara'*, p. 13; and Ivanov and Sergei, 'Ussuriiskoye Kazachestvo'.
41 Naletov, 'Pedagogicheskoi Eksperiment' The author was one of the children on the 1922 orphans' cruise.
42 Bukin, 'Pokushenie na Atamana Semenova'.
43 B. Kandidov, 'Tserkovnye shpiony yaponskogo imperializma', *Sputnik Agitatora*, 14, 1937, pp. 24–7. Kandidov cited 'Epickoi zabaikal'skii eparkhial'nyi sovet-semenovkie kontrrazvedchiki', *Dal'nevostochnyi krai* 11, 1923.
44 Jonathan W. Daly, ' "Storming the Last Citadel": The Bolshevik Assault on the Church, 1922', in V.N. Brovkin, *The Bolsheviks in Russian Society*, pp. 235–68.
45 Alexander Berzin, 'Exploitation of the Shambala Legend for Control of Mongolia', Berlin, 2003. Berzin writes that Mongolian monastic leader Darva Bandida 'advocated a return to early Buddhist principles of simplicity…[that was] similar to the Revival of Faith Movement led by the Buryats in the Soviet Union'. Buryat scholar Jamsaranov supported Bandida and their efforts led to the rise of a Pure Buddhism and Renewal Movements in Mongolia from 1926 until its condemnation by the 7th Mongolian Party Congress in 1929.
46 Worden and Savada, *Mongolia* Prime Minister Bodoo was among the executed. He had hammered out the July 1921 Oath of Accord that provided for a parliamentary regime under a limited monarchy.
47 Smith, *Vladivostok Under Red and White Rule*, p. 49.
48 V. Aprelkov, 'Zoloto Atamana', *Ekstra (Chitinskaya Oblastnaya Gazeta)*, 4 October 2000, Chita.
49 For details about Mongolia's first decades of nominal independence and Choibalsan's bloody rise to power, refer to Shagdariin Sandag and Harry H. Kendall, *Poisoned Arrows: The Stalin-Choibalsan Mongolian Massacres, 1921–1941*, Westview Press, Boulder, CO, 2000.
50 'Gen. W.S. Graves Dead, AEF Leader', *New York Herald-Tribune*, 28 February 1940.
51 Berzin, 'Exploitation of the Shambala Legend'.
52 E.K. Kolbenev, *'Drug Mongol'skogo Naroda, Chekist Gridnev'*, *Ocherki Istorii Rossiiskoi Vneshnei Razvedki*, 4, n.p., 1992. A monument was erected to Kiyakovskii on the spot in 1982.
53 Victor M. Fic, 'Book Review: *Tibetský buddhismus v Burjatsku*', *Journal of Global Buddhism*, 4, 2003. Fic, citing from Luboš Bělka's book, states that, in 1916, 'Buryatia had almost fifty monasteries, temples and shrines and about sixteen thousand monks'.
54 Ablova, *Istoriya KVZhD*; Berzin, 'Exploitation of the Shambala Legend'.
55 Semenov, *O Sebe*, pp. 316–22.
56 Anatolii Dovbnya, 'Klady samozvanykh atamanov', *Kladoiskatel'stvo*, 2001.
57 26 October 1944, intelligence report No. 604, Headquarters 9th SC, Fort Douglas, UT. 'Who's Who – Dairen', OSS File XL-2139 (RG226, Entry 19).
58 Petrov, 'Out of the Frying Pan'; and V. Grigoryan, 'Chelovek s poslednego parokhoda: Dve sud'by pevchego 'Man'chzhurtsa' Vasiliya Nikolaevicha Molchanova', *Vera: Khristianskaya Gazeta Severa Rossii*, 409, March 2002.
59 Oleg K. Antropov, 'Kharbin kak Kul'turnyi Tsentr Zarubezhnoi Rossii (1920–1930s)', Rossiiskii Gosudarstvennyi Gumanitarnyi Universitet, Istoriko-Arkhivnyi Institut, 2002.
60 Grigoryan, 'Chelovek s poslednego parokhoda'; and Vespa, *Secret Agent of Japan*.
61 Petrov, 'Out of the Frying Pan'; Fedyuninskii, *Na Vostoke*, ch. 1; and Lyandres and Wulff, *A Chronicle of Civil War*, agreement of pp. 48–9. The 31 May 1924 also officially repudiated tsarist concessions at Tientsin and Hankow and returned the remainder of the Boxer Indemnity for educational purposes to China. On 4 June 1925 Ivanov purged the CER of about 200 Russians with White backgrounds.
62 Peter Crush, 'The Chinese Eastern Railway: A Glimpse of History', Hong Kong Railway Society, 2002.

63 Michael Blinoff, 'Civil War in China. Russian Division of Armored Trains 1924–28', Tank Museum of Kubinka, 2003; and Shambarov, *Belogvardeishchina*. China's civil war erupted on 5 November 1924. Nechaev's Armored Train Division was commanded by a General Chekhov and Colonel Popov and included *broneviki* 'Shandong', 'Hunan', 'Pekin', 'Chan-Dian', 'Tai-Shan', 'Chzili' and 'Hubei'. In 1930 Nechaev became chairman of an émigré organisation that called itself *Russkaya Natsional'naya Obshchina*, the Russian National Community.
64 Fleming, *The Fate of Admiral Kolchak*, p. 69.
65 Sergei Piskunov, '*Sovetsko-kitaiskii vooruzhennyi conflict na KVZhD 1929 g.*', in Vyacheslav Rumyantsev (ed.), 'Khronos', www.hrono.ru, Moscow, 2003; and Fedyuninskii, *Na Vostoke*.
66 Vespa, *Secret Agent of Japan*, p. 41.
67 Deacon, *Kempei Tai*, pp. 141–8.
68 11 September 1944, interview report No. 324 from M.A. ID CSD 9SC, Fort Douglas, UT. 'Political Situation in Manchoukuo as of 1941', OSS File XL-1674, RG226, Entry 19, Box 21.
69 Henry Pu-Yi was declared Emperor K'ang The of Manchuria on 1 March 1934.
70 Vespa, *Secret Agent of Japan*, pp. 27–8; Aprelkov, 'Zabaikal'skoe Kazach'e Voisko' and US. Department of the Army, US Army Forces Far East, Military History Section, 'Political Strategy Prior To Outbreak Of War', Pt I, Japanese Monograph No. 144, 1952.
71 Vespa, *Secret Agent of Japan*, pp. 29–30, 34 and 38–9. 269,000 Japanese lived along the Southern Manchuria Railway and Japanese-controlled Kwantung Province before the 1931 invasion. By 1945, some 320,000 Japanese emigrated to Manchukuo.
72 Ibid., pp. 100–3 and 108–9. According to Vespa, in 1936 there were 172 brothels, 56 opium dens and 194 narcotics shops in Harbin alone.
73 Petrov 'Out of the Frying Pan'; and Gunther, *Inside Asia*, pp. 122–34. On the other hand, Vespa, *Secret Agent of Japan*, cites many White Russians who joined anti-Japanese partisans to fight against the occupation.
74 Vespa, *Secret Agent of Japan*, p. 139.
75 Nadezhda E. Ablova, 'Rossiiskaya Fashistskaya Partiya v Man'chzhurii', *Belorusski Zhurnal*, 99, 2, Minsk, 1999 and Vespa, *Secret Agent of Japan*, p. 64. General Kos'min was president of the fascist organization in 1932.
76 V. Grigoryan, 'Chelovek s poslednego parokhoda: Dve sud'by pevchego 'Man'chzhurtsa' Vasiliya Nikolaevicha Molchanova', *Vera: Khristianskaya Gazeta Severa Rossii*, 409, March 2002.
77 Petr E. Podalko, 'Pavel Vaskevich: Uchenyi, Diplomat, Puteshestvennik: k 125-letiyu co dnya rozhdeniya', Hokkaido University, Slavic Research Center, Sapporo, 2001, p. 283.
78 Vespa, *Secret Agent of Japan*, p. 265.
79 Ibid., pp. 186–98 and 264–5. Vespa cited the annual report of the railway administration.
80 Ibid., p. 66.
81 11 September 1944, interview report No. 324 from M.A. ID CSD 9SC, Fort Douglas, UT, 'Political Situation in Manchoukuo as of 1941', OSS File XL-1674, RG226, Entry 19, Box 21; and Vespa, *Secret Agent of Japan*, p. 67.
82 Kolbenev, E.K., 'Drug Mongol'skogo Naroda, Chekist Gridnev', *Ocherki Istorii Rossiiskoi Vneshnei Razvedki*, 4, n.p., 1992. It was said that Sipailov had drilled some exploratory chinks, but had apparently lost the reference points.
83 26 October 1944, intelligence report No. 604, Headquarters 9th SC, Fort Douglas, UT. 'Who's Who – Dairen', OSS File XL-2139, RG226, Entry 19.
84 *Ob'edinenie Kazakov, Razdel V, No. 26, Spravka sostavlennaya v UMVD Khabarovskogo kraya, o Soyuze kazakov na Dal'nem Vostoke*, 15 August 1953, Rossiiskii gosudarstvennyi istoricheskii Arkhiv Dal'nego Vostoka, Vladivostok.
85 *Dal'nevostochnyi Soyuz Voennykh, Razdel III, No. 9, Spravka sostavlennaya v UMVD Khabarovskogo kraya, na osnovanii materialov sbornika 'Belaya emigratsiya v Man'chzhurii' (razvedotdel UNKVD po Chitinskoi oblasti, 1942 g.) Rossiiskii gosudarstvennyi istoricheskii arkhiv Dal'nego Vostoka*, Vladivostok.

NOTES

86 US Department of Justice, Federal Bureau of Investigation, 'Famous Cases: Vonsiatsky Espionage', 2002; Michael Sayers and Albert E. Kahn, *Sabotage! The Secret War against America*, Harper & Brothers, New York, 1942; and Ablova, *'Rossiiskaya'*. In the years preceding US entry into the Second World War, Vonsiatsky visited Dairen again, as well as Tokyo and Berlin, where he met with Alfred Rosenberg, Dr Josef Goebbels and representatives of German military intelligence. In the United States he met with German American Bund leader G. Wilhelm Kunze and other American Nazis, as well as Ukrainian nationalists and helped finance Nazi agents in the United States in the hope that Berlin would guarantee him a high post in Russia when the Germans invaded. He was arrested by the FBI in June 1942 and incarcerated.

87 Crush, 'The Chinese Eastern Railway' and US House of Representatives, *Events Leading Up to World War II: Chronological History of Certain Major International Events Leading Up to and During World War II with the Ostensible Reasons Advanced for Their Occurrence*, 78th Congress, House Document No. 541, Government Printing Office, Washington, DC, 1944.

88 Vespa, *Secret Agent of Japan*, p. 60. Vespa wrote than more than 60,000 Soviet citizens lived in Manchukuo and about 22,000 worked on the Chinese Eastern Railway.

89 Grigoryan, Chelovek s poslednego', Vasilii N. Molchanov, a Russian conscript in the Manchukuo Army, recalled how his 40-man unit under commander Ivan Peshkov threw down their carbines, refused to fight and were shot by the Japanese.

90 UKGB, *Byuro po delam rossiiskikh emigrantov*, Razdel, 7, 29.

91 Ablova, *'Rossiiskaya Fashistskaya Partiya v Man'chzhurii'*. The 61-year-old Minami later served as the iron-fisted governor-general of Korea from 1936 until 1942. He was convicted as a war criminal in 1947 and was paroled in 1954.

92 Li Narangoa, 'Educating Mongols and Making "Citizens" of Manchukuo', *Inner Asia*, 3, 2001, pp. 101–26.

93 Gunther, *Inside Asia*, pp. 144–6 and Li Narangoa, 'Japanese Geopolitics, Manchuria and the Mongol Lands 1905–1945', Nordic Institute of Asian Studies, Copenhagen, 2001.

94 Kolbenev, 'Drug Mongol'skogo Naroda'.

95 The Mongol Cossack bogeyman inspired verse as well, such as this 1935 piece by Dem'yan Bednyi:

> Vot Semenov, ataman, Tozhe pomnil svoi karman. Krepko grabil Zabaikal'e. Udalos' bezhat' kanal'e. Utverdilsya on v nravah Na yaponskih ostrovah. Stav otpetym samuraem, Zamenil 'ura' 'banzaem' I, kak istyi samurai, Glaz kosit na russkii krai. Hod syskal k yaponcam v shtaby: 'Eh, voina by! Uh, voina by! Ai, ura! Ur...zai! Banzai! Poskoree nalezai!' Zayavlen'ya. Pis'ma. Vstrechi. Soblaznitel'nye rechi. 'Ai, horosh sovetskii med!' Vidit oko - zub neimet! Kogo my bili.

96 Grigoryan, 'Cheloveks poslednego parokhoda', and Vespa, *Secret Agent of Japan*.
97 Vespa, *Secret Agent of Japan*, p. 241.
98 Ibid., pp. 204–40.
99 Lenni Brenner, *Zionism in the Age of the Dictators*, L. Hill, Westport, CT, 1983.
100 Deacon, *Kempei Tai*, pp. 144–5.
101 Brenner, *Zionism in the Age of Dictators*.
102 11 September 1944, OSS interview report No. 324.
103 Yurii Mikhailovich Korol'kov, *Sovershenno Sekretno: Pri Opasnosti Czhech'!*, Izd-vo Belarus', Minsk, 1986. Araki was a major player in the expansion of militarism and had been Minister of War 1931–34, member of the Supreme War Council 1934–36, and Minister of Education 1938–39. Semenov's old acquaintance Doihara was Kwantung Army commander from 1938–40. Doihara was hung as a war criminal and Araki was paroled in 1955.
104 Petrov, 'Out of the Frying Pan'.
105 Ablova, 'Rossiiskaya Fashistskaya Partiya v Man'chzhurii'.

106 Omsk Troika Protocol 75 dated 26 October 1938.
107 Petrov, 'Out of the Frying Pan'.
108 Gunther, *Inside Asia*, p. 140.
109 Vespa, *Secret Agent of Japan*, pp. 262–3.
110 Laurie Barber, 'Checkmate at the Russian Border: Russia–Japanese Conflict before Pearl Harbour', University of Waikato, 1997.
111 11 September 1944, OSS interview report No. 324.
112 Sotskov, 'General i Ataman'.
113 Podalko, 'Pavel Vaskevich', p. 284. Podalko transliterates the location as Kaka-khasi.
114 Petrov, 'Out of the Frying Pan'.
115 11 September 1944, OSS interview report No. 324, p. 3. Presumably Kaka-Kashi was Semenov's summer residence near Dairen, referred to by Knyazev.
116 Ibid.
117 Podalko, 'Pavel Vaskevich', p. 284.
118 Details of Vladimir Slutskii's 'accidental death' were never forthcoming from the Japanese police, although they did pay his son 1,000 yen in 'damages'.
119 11 September 1944, OSS interview report No. 324; and 26 October 1944, OSS intelligence report No. 604.
120 The 1953 MVD report named the SKDV leaders as M. I. Vaulin, I.I. Pochekunin, S.I. Firsov, N.M. Shalygin, P.N. Sotnikov, I.F. Korenev, I.F. Surikov, K.M. Biryukov and one Aslamov.
121 1942 Chita UNKVD report on BREM, and Vespa, *Secret Agent of Japan*, pp. 260–1.
122 1942 Chita UNKVD report on BREM.
123 *The Times*, 14 April 1941, p. 8; and *The Times*, 3 November 1941, p. 6.
124 Ablova, 'Rossiiskaya Fashistskaya Partiya v Man'chzhurii'.
125 1942 Khabarovsk UMVD report on the DVSV, The report cited the 26 December 1941 issue of *Kharbinskoe Vremya*.
126 Sayers and Kahn, *Sabotage!*, ch. 4.
127 11 September 1944, OSS interview report No. 324; and 12th Armored Division Memorial Museum and Abilene Christian University, 'Organization of the ASTP', Abilene, TX, n.d.
128 11 September 1944, OSS interview report No. 324.
129 10 June 1943, reference card: 'Siemeonov', OSS File OB-1344 (RG226, Entry 14, Box 18, NM54).
130 11 September 1944, OSS interview report No. 324.
131 Andrew L. Hallman, 'Battlefield Operational Functions and the Soviet Campaign Against Japan in 1945', US Marine Corps Command and Staff College, Quantico, VA, 1995.
132 Ibid.
133 Aprelkov, 'Zoloto Atamana'.
134 A.V. Borodin, *History of Russia's Pacific Fleet*, Institute of History, Archaeology and Ethnography of the Peoples of the Far East, Vladivostok, 1998.
135 'Reminders of Russian Legacy Linger in Harbin', *St Petersburg Times*, 658, 3 April 2001.
136 Petrov, 'Out of the Frying Pan'.
137 Borodin, *History of Russia's Pacific Fleet*; and Marc Commandeur, 'Red Star Cats II', *Catalina Chronicles*, vol. 2, PBY Catalina Foundation, 2002.
138 Sotskov, 'General i Ataman'.
139 Lev Knyazev, 'Doch' Atamana', in *Morekhody 3: Skazaniya o Moryakakh Rossiiskikh*, Dal'nevostochnaya Gosudarstvennaya Morskaya Akademiya, Vladivostok, 1999.
140 Okhotin died in 1948. Prince Ukhtomskii died on 18 August 1953.
141 Sotskov, 'General i Ataman'.
142 S.V. Denisov, 'General-Leutenant A.I. Dutov', n.p., 2001. Dutov's supporters call him the 'founder of the White movement in the east'.
143 Varneck and Fisher, *The Testimony of Kolchak*, p. 234.
144 Ventugol, Nicolas, 'Les officiers à titre Etrangers', n.d.
145 Smele, *Civil War in Siberia*, pp. 625–6.
146 Krasnoshchekov survived the show trial and lived until Stalin's 1937 purges.

NOTES

147 Zalesskii, *Imperiya Stalina*. Trilisser used the pseudonym Mikhail Moskvin during the Spanish Civil War.
148 F.L. Kurlat and L.A. Studnikov, translated by James F. Gebhardt, 'OMSBON: Independent Special Purpose Motorized Brigade', *Voprosy istorii*, 10, 1982.
149 Fleming, *The Fate of Admiral Kolchak*, p. 233.
150 Ibid., p. 58, citing Gustav Krist's *Prisoner in the Forbidden Land*, trans. E.O. Lorimer, Faber & Faber, London 1938.
151 Burkova, *Dal'nevostochnaya*.
152 Aleksandr Barinov, 'Tsyganka Masha', *Zabaikal'skii Rabochii*, 9 April 2002, 65 (23593)/ 239 (23521), Chita.
153 'Reminders of Russian Legacy Linger in Harbin', *St Petersburg Times*, 658, 3 April 2001.
154 Mahoney, 'When Yanks Fought in Russia'.
155 Giffin, 'An American Railway Man East of the Urals'. According to Johnson's sister, Colliers offered him $35,000 for the albums. Entitled 'Views of Siberia, Russia and China, 1917–1922', they reside at the Department of History, Arizona State University.
156 Balkarei, Boris, 'Svidetel'stvo podpolkovnika Eikhel'bergera', *Novoe Vremya*, 34, 19 August 1988, pp. 34–7.
157 Dovbnya, 'Klady samozvanykh atamanov'.
158 Vadim Sotskov, 'General i Ataman'.

APPENDIX 1 THE *MAGISTRAL*

1 Originally known as St Petersburg, the capital's name was russified to Petrograd when Russia went to war with Germany in 1914. Renamed Leningrad after the death of Vladimir I. Lenin in 1924, the city was rechristened St Petersburg again in 1991.
2 Giffin, 'An American Railroad Man East of the Urals'.
3 11 August 1917, letter from Henry Miller to Daniel Willard. Also, National Archives description of RG43, Records of the Advisory Commission of Railway Experts to Russia, the Russian Railway Service Corps and the Interallied Railway Committee, 1917–1922. Miller wrote Ostroumov's name as 'Oustrougoff'.
4 Victor Louis and Jennifer Louis, *The Complete Guide to the Soviet Union*, St Martin's Press, NY, 1976, pp. 351–3.
5 11 August 1917 letter from Henry Miller, Department of State Advisory Commission of Railway Experts to Russia, to Daniel Willard, Council of National Defense.
6 Ibid.
7 Ibid.
8 Ibid.
9 Ibid.
10 North, *Transport in Western Siberia*, p. 106.
11 11 August 1917, letter from Henry Miller to Daniel Willard.
12 Mahoney, 'When Yanks Fought in Russia'.
13 Heald, *Witness to Revolution*, pp. 311–12.

SELECT BIBLIOGRAPHY

Relevant page numbers are included when available, however note that many electronic texts do not include page numbers.

Archival documents

The following Record Groups (RGs) at the US National Archives and Records Administration (NARA) were explored:

RG	Title
43	International Conferences, Commissions and Expositions, Records of the Advisory Commission of Railway Experts to Russia, Russian Railway Service Corps (RRSC) and Inter-Allied Railway Committee, 1917–22
59	General Records of the Department of State
165	War Department General and Special Staffs
395	US Army Overseas Operations and Commands, 1898–1942, general correspondence of intelligence officers, AEFS

Documents are sorted chronologically by date. Names and places are recorded as they appear on the documents.

Date	Document
undated	Tables of Distances, Engineer Office AEFS Source: RG165, Microfilm M917
undated	Report of Operations of the Quartermaster (QM) Corps, AEFS 1 January–30 June 1918 Source: RG165, Microfilm M917
undated	Reports of Operations of AEFS intelligence office Source: RG165, Microfilm M917
undated	Medical History of the Siberian Expedition Source: RG165, Microfilm M917
undated	Scrapbook of Lieutenant Leroy W. Yarborough, AEFS Source: Leroy W. Yarborough Collection, RG505S, US Military History Institute, Carlisle, PA
6 June 1917	Report Subject: Chita Shops – personnel, buildings, capabilities, conditions Source: RG43 NE 844
11 August 1917	Letter from Henry Miller, Department of State Advisory Commission of Railway Experts to Russia/Petrograd, to Daniel Willard, Council of National Defense

BIBLIOGRAPHY

	Subject: Description of Russian Railway, management, organization of divisions, track, labor conditions; with attachments detailing rates, resources, locomotives, repair shops, engine houses, freight car types, coal and Transbaikal coal mines, etc. Source: RG43, New Entry 844
20 December 1917	Letter from L. Oustrougoff, Commissar/Vladivostok, to J.F. Stevens, Chairman/American Railroad Commission Subject: Quarters for RRSC men to arrive; locomotive shops at Vladivostok
6 January 1918	Letter from F.M. Titus, Vladivostok, to C.M. Muchnic, American Locomotive Sales Corp/New York City Subject: Details of civil/revolutionary governments and activity in Harbin, Irkutsk, Vladivostok, Khabarovsk and Siberia in general Source: RG43, New Entry 844
16 January 1918	Letter from Lieutenant Colonel Frederick Jasperson, Representative/ Baldwin Locomotive Works – Russian Service Corps, Obama to Colonel Emerson, Nagasaki Subject: Forwards 6 January letter from Titus/Vladivostok and 16 January letter regarding equipping erecting shops at Vladivostok Source: RG43, New Entry 844
27 April 1918	Letter (telegram) from Summers, Moscow, to Secretary of State Lansing Subject: Semenov gaining ground; 14 dead Red Guards at Chita Source: State Department File No. 861.00/1810
2 May 1918	Letter (telegram) from Ambassador David R. Francis to Secretary of State Lansing Subject: Intervention, Recognition of Soviet government; German influence and world revolution Source: State Department File No. 861.00/1955
8 May 1918	Letter (telegram), from Secretary of State Lansing to Ambassador David R. Francis Subject: Semenov request for RRSC assistance Source: State Department File No. 861.00/1729
9 May 1918	Memorandum from Major David Barrows, Peking, to General Evans Subject: Advance of Ataman Semenoff's Forces, 20 April–5 May Source: MID File No. 2070-505, RG165, Microfilm M1443
17 May 1918	Letter, from Ambassador David R. Francis to Colonel George Emerson Subject: Journey Vladivostok–Vologda–Moscow Source: RG165, Microfilm M917
June 1918	Report Subject: Type locomotives on Chinese Eastern and Ussuri Railways
6 July 1918	Letter (telegram), from Secretary of State Lansing to Ambassador David R. Francis Subject: Semenov defeated; Kolchak movement toward Vladivostok; Czechs determined to fight Austro-Germans, not fellow Slavs Source: State Department File No. 861.00/2096
28 July 1918	Report No. 15 by Lieutenant Colonel David P. Barrows, US Military Attaché, Peking, Notes on the situation in Manchuria and eastern Siberia, July 1918 Subject: Expert analysis of Semenov, White movement and Japanese influence; OMO composition and order of battle; Semenov and Kalmykov proclamations Source: RG395, File 095 Semenoff, Box 29
24 August 1918	Intelligence diary Subject: 18–24 August, 1918 events Source: RG395, File 095 Semenoff, Box 29

31 August 1918	Intelligence diary Subject: 25–31 August 1918 events Source: RG395, File 095 Semenoff, Box 29
2 September 1918	Simpson telegram from Ataman Semenov's headquarters at Borzya Subject: White liberation of Transbaikalia Source: RG395, File 095 Semenoff, Box 29
2 September 1918	Communiqué No. 14, General Nakajima, Japanese General HQ, Bureau of Information, Vladivostok Subject: Semenov advance guard at Khada-Bulak on 29 August, Red forces near Bikin and south of Khabarovsk; Amur Flotilla Source: RG165, Microfilm M917
3 September 1918	Communiqué No. 16, General Nakajima, Japanese General HQ, Bureau of Information, Vladivostok Subject: Semenov detachments occupied Olovyannaya, Red *broneviki* Source: RG165, Microfilm M917
3 September 1918	Telegram from AP correspondent Simpson at Borzya Subject: Colonel Emerson, Czechs took Sretensk, 'great scoop' Source: RG395, File 095 Semenoff, Box 29
6 September 1918	Intelligence summary No. 1, AEFS intelligence office Subject: Semenov advance; HQ Olovyannaya (with map) Source: RG165, Microfilm M917
6 September 1918	'Vsem russkym grazhdanam, lyubyashchim svoyu rodinu' (Notice to the Russian People Loyal to their Fatherland) Subject: General Otani's Russian propaganda flyer describing Allied intentions Source: Glavnokomanduyushchii Soyuznymi Voiskami, RG165, Microfilm M917
7 September 1918	Telegram from AP correspondent Simpson, Hailar Subject: Gajda's bash at Olovyannaya Source: RG395, File 095 Semenoff, Box 29
7 September 1918	Telegram from AP correspondent Simpson, Bukhedu Subject: Gajda's deathblow to Bolsheviks; Japanese flags Source: RG395, File 095 Semenoff, Box 29
9 September 1918	Military intelligence summary (annotated 'App. #61'), Major David P. Barrows, AEFS Subject: Joint Czech Legion–Semenov Operations at Verkhne-Udinsk 40 Red trains captured Source: RG165, Microfilm M917
21 September 1918	Weekly intelligence summary, AEFS intelligence office Subject: 15–21 September events Source: RG395, File 095 Semenoff, Box 29
27 September 1918	Intelligence summary No. 15, AEFS intelligence section Subject: Blagoveshchensk campaign Source: RG395, File 095 Semenoff, Box 29
28 September 1918	Annual Report, engineer office AEFS 1918 (excerpt: pages 60–70) Subject: 12 July–9 September 1918 Czech Legion/White Russian offensive Source: RG165, Microfilm M917, Roll 11
3 October 1918	Intelligence summary No. 311, AEFS intelligence section Subject: Kalmykov HQ at Pogranichnaya Source: RG165, Microfilm M917
3 October 1918	Communiqué No. 46, Japanese General HQ Vladivostok, Bureau of Information Subject: Alekseevsk and Zeya river actions Source: RG395, File 095 Semenoff, Box 29

BIBLIOGRAPHY

7 October 1918	Intelligence summary No. 19, AEFS intelligence office Subject: British Gun Train Company and French movements Source: RG395, File 095 Semenoff, Box 29
10 October 1918	Intelligence summary No. 318, AEFS intelligence section Subject: Kalmykov and Semenov activity on Chinese Eastern Railway Source: RG165, Microfilm M917
11 October 1918	Memorandum from AEFS intelligence section to chief of staff Subject: 'Friendly Russian Forces in Eastern European Russia and Siberia: Forces of Omsk Siberian Provisional Government', 5th Siberian Corps Source: RG165, Microfilm M917
11 October 1918	Newspaper summary (excerpt) Subject: Siberian Railway System Source: RG165, Microfilm M917
11 October 1918	Report by Captain John Delancey/Contingent No. 12 RRSC Subject: Nikolsk Terminal facilities/capabilities (details) Source: RG43 RRSC, Entry 843/338, Index 1, 79/Nikolsk
14 October 1918	Intelligence summary No. 322, AEFS intelligence section Subject: Railway workers salaries, bribed by Japan; Semenov aims to take Mongolia Source: RG165, Microfilm M917
18 October 1918	Report, AEFS intelligence section Subject: Semenov relationship with Omsk Government (details); Semenov QM and Japanese supplies; Semenov staff Officers; 'partisan division' Source: RG165, Microfilm M917
18 October 1918	Newspaper summary (excerpt) Subject: Railway workers strike at Omsk Kulomzino station Source: RG165, Microfilm M917
18 October 1918	Memorandum for file from Captain F.B. Rives Subject: Prostitution and cocaine Source: RG165, Microfilm M917
20 October 1918	Memorandum from AEFS intelligence section to Major Barrows Subject: Currency conditions; Japanese money: Imperial Japanese province Source: RG165, Microfilm M917
23 October 1918	Newspaper summary, AEFS intelligence section Subject: Order from Colonel Butenko – Kalmykov subordinate, and response from Kalmykov; Skipitrov telegram to Kalmykov Source: RG165, Microfilm M917
23 October 1918	Memorandum from AEFS intelligence officer to chief of staff Subject: General Ivanov-Rinov – background: founder of League of Cossacks, Petrograd, September 1917 Source: RG165, Microfilm M917
25 October 1918	Newspaper summary (excerpt), AEFS intelligence section Subject: Khabarovsk military school renamed after Kalmykov Source: RG165, Microfilm M917
26 October 1918	Newspaper summary, AEFS intelligence section Subject: English–Japanese alliance Source: RG165, Microfilm M917
28 October 1918	Newspaper summary, AEFS intelligence section Subject: Ussuri Cossack Conference presided over by Kalmykov; Semenov interview Source: RG165, Microfilm M917

undated (probably late October 1918)	Report: 'Habarovsk', Major Malcolm Wheeler Nicholson, AEFS Subject: Profile of Khabarovsk Source: RG395, File 095 Semenoff, Box 29
10 November 1918	Translation of 'Semienoff and the Special Manchurian Detachment', Primorskaya Zhizn, 10 November 1918, No. 54, AEFS intelligence office, Vladivostok Subject: Pro-OMO profile Source: RG395, File 095 Semenoff, Box 29
18 November 1918	Telegram from Lieutenant H.L. Hoskin/RRSC Nikolsk, to Colonel Emerson/RRSC Harbin Subject: Austrian and Bolshevik POWs – conditions Source: RG43 RRSC, Entry 843/338, Index 1, 88/POWs, Refugees
19 November 1918	Memorandum from Captain Roger W. Straus to intelligence officer, AEFS Subject: Amur Province under Semenov influence; Colonel Shemelin and troops very brutal (details) Source: RG165, Microfilm M917
20 November 1918	Telegram, from Lieutenant H.L. Hoskin/RRSC Nikolsk, to Colonel Emerson/RRSC Harbin Subject: Austrian and Bolshevik POWs – conditions; Japanese will not assist POWs Source: RG43 RRSC, Entry 843/338, Index 1, 88/POWs, Refugees
22 November 1918	Telegram, from Lieutenant H.L. Hoskin/RRSC Nikolsk, to Colonel Emerson/RRSC Harbin Subject: Austrian and Bolshevik POWs – conditions Source: RG43 RRSC, Entry 843/338, Index 1, 88/POWs, Refugees
22 November 1918	Telegram from author unknown/RRSC to Colonel Emerson/RRSC Subject: 2 Government ministers arrested by Semenov men; Kolchak arrested Semenov men; Semenov ordered Kolchak arrested Source: RG43 RRSC, Entry 843/348, Index 1, 89/Politics, Semenov
26 November 1918	Telegram, from Dugan/RRSC to Colonel Emerson/RRSC, Harbin Subject: Rumor of Red takeover Chita a fabrication; Semenov severed 'connection from Omsk' Source: RG43 RRSC, Entry 843/348, Index 1, 89/Politics, Semenov
26 November 1918	Intelligence summary No. 34, AEFS intelligence section Subject: Japanese–Semenov relationship; advisor Captain Kuroki; prison train – Chita residents forbidden to assist Source: RG165, Microfilm M917
undated (probably December 1918)	Extracts from report on Amur province, Captain Straus, AEFS Subject: Conditions in Amur province Source: RG395, File 095, Box 29
1 December 1918	Intelligence summary No. 37, AEFS intelligence section Subject: Ataman Gamov of Amur Cossacks blames Colonel Shemelin for outrages Source: RG165, Microfilm M917
1 December 1918	Telegram from Captain Schuyler/AEFS Omsk Subject: Conversation with Captain Skladal, Chita Source: RG395, File 095 Semenoff, Box 29
1 December 1918	Telegram from Captain Skladal/AEFS Chita to Colonel Barrows/AEFS Vladivostok Subject: Detailed report of OMO forces; 3 armored trains, Dragulich and Serbs Source: RG165, Microfilm M917

BIBLIOGRAPHY

2 December 1918	Telegram from Captain Skladal/AEFS Chita to Colonel Barrows/AEFS Vladivostok Subject: OMO under Colonel Tierbach; Semenov forces strength Source: RG165, Microfilm M917
2 December 1918	Telegram from Captain Skladal/AEFS Chita to Colonel Barrows/AEFS Vladivostok Subject: rumor – Semenov arrested by OMO Officers; POW train status Source: RG165, Microfilm M917
4 December 1918	Letter from Captain Harold V.V. Fay/intelligence officer – Harbin, to intelligence officer/AEFS Vladivostok Subject: OMO defector Piper; Serbian–Japanese skirmish in Chita; Chinese Generals Gao, Tao, Li and Ma; Gao promotion to division commander; Japanese barracks incident in Manchuli; 40 cars of Japanese supplies daily Source: RG165, Microfilm M917
5 December 1918	Letter, from Colonel Emerson/RRSC, Harbin, to General Graves/AEF Vladivostok and ARC/Vladivostok Subject: Prisoner train in transit 1 month; horrible conditions Source: RG43 RRSC, Entry 843/348, Index 1, 88/POWs and Refugees
6 December 1918	Intelligence summary No. 41, AEFS intelligence section Subject: 2 'leagues' in Semenov's Army; Semenov 'declared war on Kolchak' with Japanese support; Kolchak order removing Semenov as commanding officer/5th Siberian Corps Source: RG165, Microfilm M917
6 December 1918	Message from 'WJB'/RRSC, to Colonel Emerson/RRSC Subject: Chinese Eastern Railway will not service Semenov; Chinese Eastern Railway has own Russian guards; Semenov west of Manchuria Source: RG43 RRSC, Entry 843/348, Index 1, 89/Politics, Semenov
7 December 1918	Intelligence summary No. 42, AEFS intelligence section Subject: Kolchak–Semenov friction linked with restriction of Semenov traffic on Chinese Eastern Railway Source: RG165, Microfilm M917
7 December 1918	Extracts from Lieutenant Yate's Report on Nikolsk Subject: Detailed description of conditions Source: RG395, File 095, Box 29
9 December 1918	Press summary Subject: Serious White opposition on all sides to Semenov; Kalmykov ordered to submit to Semenov Source: RG43 RRSC, Entry 843/348, Index 1, 89/Politics, Semenov
10 December 1918	Intelligence summary No. 44, AEFS intelligence section Subject: Estimates of Semenov and Kalmykov forces (encl.); Semenov forces in Amur region; Bolshevik force on Tom River Source: RG165, Microfilm M917
11 December 1918	Telegram from Captain Scovell, Manchuli, to Lieutenant Colonel Barrows, Vladivostok Subject: Manchuli OMO commandant and garrison strength Source: RG395, File 095, Box 29
12 December 1918	Intelligence summary No. 45, AEFS intelligence section Subject: Semenov purchasing agent Piper at Harbin quit; Kolchak men threaten to blow Sludyanka tunnel; Manchuli forces Source: RG165, Microfilm M917
14 December 1918	Intelligence summary No. 46, AEFS intelligence section Subject: Incident between Kalmykov–Horvath forces at Nikolsk; Personality summaries: Kalmykov, General Gao Source: RG165, Microfilm M917

14 December 1918   Letter from J.R. Hoag/RRSC, Tsitsikar, to Colonel Emerson and Major Winter/RRSC
Subject: Semenov troops forcibly took detained freight cars
Source: RG43 RRSC, Entry 843/348, Index 1, 89/Politics, Semenov

17 December 1918   Telegram from Captain C. Skladal; Chita, to AEFS intelligence officer, Vladivostok,
Subject: 'Personal danger' from Order No. 60
Source: RG395, File 095, Box 29

17 December 1918   Newspaper summary, AEFS intelligence section
Subject: Semenov arrest rumored; 5th Corps troops at Verkhne-Udinsk refuse to obey Semenov; Annenkov and detachment
Source: RG165, Microfilm M917

18 December 1918   Telegram from Lieutenant R. Baggs, Verkhne-Udinsk, to Major Eichelberger, AEFS HQ
Subject: OMO takeover
Source: RG395, File 095, Box 29

18 December 1918   Newspaper summary, AEFS intelligence section
Subject: Semenov–Volkov conflict; anti-Semenov attitude on Chinese Eastern Railway; Gold fields – locations
Source: RG165, Microfilm M917

18 December 1918   Letter from Acting Secretary of State Frank Polk to US Ambassador to Japan Roland Morris
Subject: Japanese policy in Siberia; Kolchak vs. Semenov preference
Source: State Department File No. 861.00/3430 (Microfilm 316, roll 18)

19 December 1918   Letter from Barrows, Chita, to Major Eichelberger, AEFS
Subject: Meeting with General Oba – will ensure railway traffic flows; Report of railway traffic
Source: RG165, Microfilm M917

21 December 1918   Telegram from unsigned, Chita, to AEFS HQ, Vladivostok
Subject: Semenov wounded in bomb explosion
Source: RG395, File 095, Box 29

21 December 1918   Telegram from Barrows, Chita to AEFS HQ, Vladivostok
Subject: Chita quiet, *bronevik* sent to Ingoda; visited Semenov
Source: RG395, File 095, Box 29

23 December 1918   Telegram from Byers/RRSC to Colonel Emerson/RRSC, Vladivostok and Major Tower, Harbin
Subject: 2 bombs thrown at Semenov; railway workers fear Semenov soldiers
Source: RG43 RRSC, Entry 843/348, Index 1, 89/Politics, Semenov

27 December 1918   Memorandum of conversation Major Johnson had with Mr Alex Osheroff
Subject: conditions and attitudes in Siberia (excellent detail)
Source: RG43 RRSC, New Entry 844, Index 2, Box 8, File 224a

undated (probably 1919)   French report
Subject: Detailed report about OMO and personalities from French military mission intelligence sources
Source: RG395, File 095, Box 29

7 January 1919   Letter from 1st Lieutenant Robert J. Scovell, AEFS, Manchuli, to Lieutenant Colonel Barrows, Vladivostok
Subject: Merchandise on which legal duty should be paid
Source: RG395, File 095, Box 29

8 January 1919   Translation of letter from Colonel Katanaief to Captain K. Skladal
Subject: Attitudes about Japan and United States
Source: RG395, File 095, Box 29

BIBLIOGRAPHY

11 January 1919	Telegram No. 7 from Captain Frederick F. Moore, AEFS, Chita, to Lieutenant Colonel Barrows, Vladivostok Subject: Semenov to Harbin; Cossack representatives; colonel arrested Source: RG395, File 095, Box 29
11 January 1919	Extracts from report of Captain Conrad Skladal Subject: Detailed description of conditions at Chita Source: RG395, File 095, Box 29
13 January 1919	Letter from 1st Lieutenant Robert J. Scovell, AEFS, Manchuli, to Lieutenant Colonel Barrows, Vladivostok Subject: Manchuli customs and duty collections Source: RG395, File 095, Box 29
17 January 1919	Telegram (and AEFS translation) from Junior Captain Filippoff, Kultuk, to Division Commander Subject: Major General Volkov's control point at Kultuk Source: RG395, File 095, Box 29
undated (probably 17–18 January 1919)	Telegram (and AEFS translation) from Major General Verigo, Chita, to Major General Volkov, Irkutsk Subject: Major General Volkov's control point at Kultuk Source: RG395, File 095, Box 29
22 January 1919	Report, Captain I.C. Nicholas, AEFS Subject: Towns west of Khabarovsk Source: RG395, File 095 Semenoff, Box 29
29 January 1919	Telegram from Captain Fay, Harbin, to AEFS Vladivostok Subject: Semenov's movements Source: RG395, File 095 Semenoff, Box 29
5 February 1919	Report interview between Major General Graves and Ataman Annenkov, 5 February 1919 Subject: Annenkov's forces Source: RG165, Microfilm M917
7 February 1919	Telegram from Ataman Semenov to President Wilson, Paris Subject: Request intercession for Mongolian representatives at League of Nations Source: RG395, File 095 Semenoff, Box 29
7 February 1919	Telegram, from Ataman Semenov to President of League of Nations, Paris Subject: Request intercession for Mongolian representatives at League of Nations Source: RG395, File 095 Semenoff, Box 29
9 February 1919	Report from Captain Harold V.V. Fay, AEFS intelligence officer, Harbin Subject: Visit to Semenov's train Source: RG395, File 095 Semenoff, Box 29
10 February 1919	Report 'Ataman Semenoff and his officers', Captain F.F. Moore, AEFS, Vladivostok Subject: Staff personalities; meetings with Mongol leaders; General Shemelin Source: RG395, File 095 Semenoff, Box 29
11 February 1919	Telegram from Lieutenant Baggs, Chita, to Colonel Barrows, Vladivostok Subject: Shemelin replaces Afanasiev Source: RG395, File 095 Semenoff, Box 29
12 February 1919	Telegram from Captain Schuyler, Omsk, to AEFS intelligence officer, Vladivostok Subject: YMCA men in army officer uniforms Source: RG395, File 095, Box 29

21 February 1919	Letter from Lieutenant Colonel Barrows, AEFS Vladivostok, to AEFS intelligence officer, Harbin, and attached report, 'Ataman Semenoff', by Nicholas Romanoff Subject: Romanoff's visit with Semenov Source: RG395, File 095 Semenoff, Box 29
21 February 1919	Letter/Report from 1st Lieutenant H.F. Cauthard/27th Infantry Spasskoe, to Commanding Officer, 27th Infantry/Spasskoe Subject: Brutal behavior of Horvath and Kalmykov's troops Source: RG165, Microfilm M917
1 March 1919	Report on northern Manchuria in general and Harbin in particular, Captain Harold V.V. Fay, AEFS Subject: Manchuria and Harbin background and conditions Source: RG395, File 095, Box 29
3 March 1919	Letter from Major General Ivanov-Rinov to CINC Allied Forces in Far East Subject: Russian forces Vladivostok Source: RG165, Microfilm M917
8 March 1919	Newspaper summary, AEFS HQ intelligence section Subject: Major General Ivanov-Rinov order to preclude rumors; 28 February Cossack Conference at Khabarovsk, Cossack mobilization, drunkenness and smuggling by Cossacks Source: RG165, Microfilm M917, Roll 5
11 March 1919	Telegram from Robbins, Peking, to Barrows, Vladivostok Subject: Peking newspapers report Barrows sent telegram on behalf of Semenov Source: RG395, File 095, Box 29
13 March 1919	Telegram from Major General S. Graves, Vladivostok, to US Military Attaché, Peking Subject: Barrows' telegram for Semenov Source: RG395, File 095, Box29
16 March 1919	Letter from James W. Blair/British Military Mission Vladivostok, to Major General Graves Subject: Red HQ at Sakhatino, Amur province; January 1919 Red atrocity at Sukhotona, River Zeya
18 March 1919	Report No. 1945 from HA, conditions between Harbin and Omsk Subject: Economic, political and military conditions Source: RG395, File 095, Box 29
20 March 1919	Extract from engineers office report on Chita Subject: Detailed city description Source: RG395, File 095, Box 29
22 March 1919	Regulations promulgated by John F. Stevens Subject: Regulations referring to restrictions against the use of special service trains, formulated by the IATB and confirmed by Interallied Committee Source: RG43, New Entry 844
April 1919	An account of the AEFS, August 1918–March 1919 (excerpt) Source: RG165, Microfilm M917
undated (probably spring 1919)	Extracts from the report of Lieutenant Byrnes re the town of Beresovka Subject: Details about Beresovka Source: RG395, File 095, Box 29
undated (probably spring 1919)	Extracts from the Report of Lieutenant Byrnes re the town of Posol'skaya Station Subject: Details about Posol'skaya Station and Posol'skaya Source: RG395, File 095, Box 29

BIBLIOGRAPHY

28 April 1919   Letter from chief inspector (unidentified) to D.P. Kasekavitch, Assistant General Manager/Chinese Eastern Railway, Harbin
Subject: 2 unauthorized Semenov specials (No. 102 and No. 8) from Tsitsihar to Manchuli causing several delays
Source: RG43, New Entry 844

28 April 1919   Wire, from Colonel Emerson, Harbin, to Major Egber, Hailar
Subject: Advise fully regarding Semenov specials delaying echelon 2156
Source: RG43, New Entry 844

29 April 1919   Wire from Major Egber, Hailar, to Colonel Emerson, Harbin
Subject: details of arrivals/departures regarding delays caused by Semenov's No. 102 and No. 8 between Oogoonor and Wangun
Source: RG43, New Entry 844

6 May 1919   Letter from chief inspector (unidentified), to John F. Stevens, President/Technical Board
Subject: 28 April delays to all freight trains, unauthorized movements by Semenov's specials
Source: RG43, New Entry 844

11 May 1919   Verkhne-Udinsk Report, 1st Lieutenant Ralph L. Baggs, US 27th Infantry Regiment, USAT Sherman
Subject: Verkhne-Udinsk conditions November 1918–February 1919
Source: RG395, File 095, Box 29

13 May 1919   Telegram No. 32 from Major Shamotulski, Khabarovsk, to AEFS Vladivostok
Subject: Kalmykov to execute 50 pro-Kolchak officers
Source: RG395, File 095, Box 29

14 May 1919   Telegram No. 33 from Major Shamotulski, Khabarovsk, to AEFS Vladivostok
Subject: Kalmykov executed 2 pro-Kolchak officers; Tashima threat
Source: RG395, File 095, Box 29

17 May 1919   Telegram No. 139 from Allderdice, Spasskoe, to AEFS chief of staff, Vladivostok
Subject: Kalmykov distributing arms near Ussuri
Source: RG395, File 095, Box 29

1 June 1919   Telegram No. 55 from Major C. Shamotulski, Khabarovsk, to AEFS, Vladivostok
Subject: Pro-Kolchak officers executed
Source: RG395, File 095, Box 29

2 June 1919   Telegram No. 55 from Baldwin, Tokyo, to Major General Graves, AEFS, Vladivostok
Subject: Order No. 60 cancelled 27 May
Source: RG395, File 095, Box 29

3 June 1919   Letter from W.H. Blaine, Vladivostok, to US Consul, Vladivostok
Subject: Conditions in Verkhne-Udinsk: Gdali Itzkovich businesses forced to buy Japanese merchandise shipped in Red Cross boxes; frequent executions by Semenov (confidential)
Source: RG165, File No. 1766-1107/2

4 June 1919   Letter from US Consul, Vladivostok, to US Secretary of State
Subject: Conditions in Verkhne-Udinsk: W. H. Blaine, Japanese merchandise shipped in Red Cross boxes; increase in Japanese shipping; frequent executions by Semenov (confidential)
Source: RG165, File No. 1766-1107/1

6 June 1919   Memorandum for AEFS chief of staff from Lieutenant Colonel Eichelberger, AEFS intelligence officer
Subject: Increase Chanan Silverman pay to $100 per month
Source: RG395, File 095, Box 29

9 June 1919	Letter from Captain Montgomery Schuyler, Vladivostok, to AEFS chief of staff Subject: General report on Omsk Source: RG395, File 095, Box 29
12 June 1919	Circular No. 6, John Stevens/President Technical Board, Harbin (Russian original, English translation) Subject: Regulations regarding movement of special trains Source: RG43, New Entry 844
15 June 1919	Paraphrase of cipher to Consul General Harris and to American Legation Peking for Department of State Subject: Events surrounding Colonel Morrow's ultimatum for immediate removal of *broneviki* from Verkhne-Udinsk to Chita; Japanese threat Source: RG43, New Entry 844, Box 8, File 226
16 June 1919	Memorandum from author unknown/Irkutsk to Mr Thompson Subject: Colonel Medi, OMO Superintendent of Military Transportation, orders; 11 June whippings at Birka by drunken Vosnesensky; armored train inventory: 9 locomotives, 27 passenger cars, 160 freight cars, 4 armored trains
20 June 1919	Letter from Colonel George H. Emerson, Verkhne-Udinsk, to Colonel C.H. Morrow/Commanding Officer, 27th Infantry, Verkhne-Udinsk Subject: Daily reports from Colonel Lantry that Semenov controlling train movement and operations; Emerson 30 May trip to Vladivostok: IATB ordered allied force to prevent railway interference; Semenov *broneviki* Manchuli–Mysovaya a menace; 'reign of terror' Source: RG43, New Entry 844, Box 8, File 226
22 June 1919	Report from Commanding Officer, Hospital Train No. 1 to chief surgeon, Vladivostok Subject: Trip No. 2 in June 1919 of Hospital Train No. 1 Source: RG165, Microfilm M917
4 July 1919	Telegram from Colonel Lantry, Irkutsk, to Colonel Emerson, Omsk Subject: East of Verkhne-Udinsk Semenov constantly violating Circular No. 6 regarding movement of special trains; 9 locomotives and shops/roundhouse tied up with work for Semenov; 20 June delay at Khilok due to drunk *bronevik* commander taking locomotive, threatened UK Officer with knife Source: RG43, New Entry 844
11 July 1919	Telegram from Colonel Lantry, Irkutsk, to Colonel Emerson, Omsk Subject: 7 July Semenov *bronevik* took Chinese Eastern car 322 at Chita, moved to Adrianovka, repainted it Source: RG43, New Entry 844, Box 8, File 226
11 July 1919	Letter from Marley, Handaohedzy, to Major Winter Subject: July *hunghutze* destruction of 3 bridges and extortion Source: RG43
14 July 1919	Letter from Lieutenant B. Twaddle/Assistant Traffic Engineer, Borzia, to Major Gravis Subject: 12–13 July 1919 taking of RRSC Car 5 at Dauria by Colonel Jukovsky Source: RG43, New Entry 844, Box 8, File 226
15 July 1919	Telegram from Colonel Lantry, Irkutsk to J.F. Stevens, Harbin Subject: Car 5 passed through Manchuli still attached to *bronevik*; Japanese promise help; *broneviki* operating without staff unsafe Source: RG43, New Entry 844, Box 8, File 226
15 July 1919	Telegram from Colonel Lantry, Irkutsk to J.F. Stevens, Harbin Subject: Lantry told all allied inspectors Verkhne-Udinsk– Manchuli to remain in quarters until military protection provided Source: RG43, New Entry 844, File 226

BIBLIOGRAPHY

18 July 1919	Telegram from Major Gravis to Colonel Emerson and Lantry (with copy of original Russian telegram) Subject: Japanese War Mission informed Gravis that Zhukovski dismissed, ordered to Chita to explain Source: RG43, New Entry 844, File 226
20 July 1919	Report on Manchuria station, Captain H.V.V. Fay, Hailar Subject: Details of conditions in Manchuli Source: RG395, File 095, Box 29
23 July 1919	Letter from J.F. Stevens, Harbin to Colonel G.H. Emerson, Omsk Subject: 'move inspectors from Semenov territory until proper protection can be given' Source: RG43, New Entry 844, File 226
July 1919	Notice 'To the Russian Women of Trans-Baikal' Subject: Example of anti-US propaganda Source: RG43, New Entry 844, File 226
5 August 1919	Translation from Russian of Report on Semenoff Subject: Verigo and Ukrainian regiments; General Lovtsov and Cossack affairs staff in Maritime province Source: RG395, File 095, Box 29
8 August 1919	Letter from District Inspector Transbaikal Railway to Colonel G.H. Emerson, Chief Inspector, Harbin Subject: Car 5 returned evening of 23 July; Japanese will not protect inspectors; 'Officers in constant danger' may be 'done away with' Source: RG43, New Entry 844, File 226
12 August 1919	27th Infantry Base Map: Verkhne-Udinsk to Mysovaya Source: RG165, Microfilm M917
13 August 1919	Message from Lieutenant B.N. Twaddle, Borzia to Major Gravis Subject: Passenger engine used on *bronevik*; master mechanic threatened with whipping to perform repairs Source: RG43, New Entry 844, File 226
14 August 1919	Message from J.R. Hoag, Olovyannaya to Major J.C. Gravis Subject: 11 August delays due to *broneviki* bullying on line Source: RG43, New Entry 844, File 226
14 August 1919	Translation Subject: Killings by Kalmykov at Iman Source: RG395, File 095, Box 29
15 August 1919	Letter from Colonel Hawkins, Omsk to Captain J.M. Sundheimer, Irkutsk Subject: 'keep off line as much as practicable'; General Oba operating under instructions from Tokyo Source: RG43, New Entry 844, File 226
16 August 1919	Letter from Colonel Lantry, Irkutsk to Colonel Emerson, Omsk Subject: General Oba praises Semenov; 13 August US interpreter arrested Adrianovka; Gravis demanded removal/Stepanov; Japanese mission promised improved conditions in Emerson's 31 July telegram Source: RG43, New Entry 844, File 226
22 August 1919	Letter from Major Gravis/4th Division inspector to General Oba, Commanding Officer/3rd Division Subject: Complaint of Semenov interference; 15 July–14 August: 15 whippings of railway workers at Olovyannaya; threats by OMO at Chita shops; delays to train of wounded soldiers; OMO locomotive killed 2 horses on Chita river bridge in unsafe operations (includes copy of 8 August 1919 letter from Lieutenant McDonald to Gravis regarding drunk OMO Officer on train at Mogzon) Source: RG43, New Entry 844, File 226

28 August 1919	Telegram from Blunt, Vladivostok to Colonel Jones, Harbin Subject: Semenov and Kalmykov holding engines out of service at Vladivostok and Nikolsk Source: RG43, New Entry 844, File 226
2 September 1919	Telegram from Colonel Lantry, Irkutsk to J.F. Stevens, Harbin Subject: Recommend moving all inspectors out of Transbaikal; Railroad Agreement ignored by all but United States Source: RG43, New Entry 844, File 226
3 September 1919	Report, AEFS intelligence office – Chita to AEFS chief intelligence officer Subject: Adrianovka slaughter yard – 19 August prisoner trains; local people terrorized; Captain Raynor/British representative is apologist for Semenov Source: RG165, Microfilm M917
5 September 1919	Telegram No. 234 from Colonel Lantry, Irkutsk to Colonel Emerson, Omsk Subject: Mongol mutiny at Dauria; *bronevik* ditched Source: RG43, New Entry 844, File 226
6 September 1919	Telegram No. 239 from Colonel Lantry, Irkutsk to Colonel Emerson, Omsk Subject: Mongol mutiny at Dauria; line cleared Source: RG43, New Entry 844, File 226
10 September 1919	Letter from M.K. Jones, district inspector, Harbin, to D. Kazakevich, Assistant General Manager – Chinese Eastern Railway, Harbin Subject: Train to be ready for arrival of Japanese Ambassador 22 September; train composition, etc. Source: RG43, New Entry 844
19 September 1919	Telegram from Captain Sundheimer, Irkutsk to Colonel Emerson, Omsk Subject: 3 armored trains ditched 16 September; Reds very active; rumor Sretensk taken Source: RG43, New Entry 844, File 226
29 September 1919	Letter from Cantrell (?), district inspector Transbaikal Railway, Irkutsk to Colonel Emerson, Irkutsk Subject: Delays caused by orders of Colonel Medi; *bronevik* commander Colonel Jardovsky threatening whippings; Dauria: refusal to accommodate Russian Officer with typhus Source: RG43, New Entry 844, File 226
3 October 1919	Intelligence summary No. 311, AEFS intelligence section Subject: Kalmykov takes hotel at Prograннichnaya, General Rozanov's 'hooligan element', Semenov–Merlin, Kulesha and Gajda conspiracy against Kolchak Source: RG165, Microfilm M917
3 October 1919	Telegram from Major Colby/RRSC, Verkhne-Udinsk to Lieutenant Colonel Cantrell/RRSC, Irkutsk Subject: Semenov with special and armored train arrived last night; Semenov gave Colonel Morrow a banquet! Source: RG43 RRSC, Entry 848, File 526, District Inspector Records
6 October 1919	Letter/report from 1st Lieutenant Justis S. Davidson, chief intelligence officer/AEFS intelligence section (Confidential) Subject: Transbaikal situation report; 1,800-man Mongol expeditionary force funded by Japanese for march on Urga; deserted at Dauria Source: RG165, Microfilm M917
6 October 1919	Translation from the summary of information No. 1116 issued by offices of commander of the Pri-Amur military district Subject: American grenades and revolvers given to Reds Source: RG395, File 095, Box 29

BIBLIOGRAPHY

8 October 1919   Letter from J. Gravis/RRSC Inspector 4th Division, Adrianovka to Lieutenant Colonel T.S. Cantrell/RRSC, Irkutsk
Subject: Semenov's stationary train HQ here has 2 US box cars
Source: RG43 RRSC, Entry 848, File 526, District Inspector Records

9 October 1919   Report on interview with Mr Braude, assistant chief of the Russian information bureau
Subject: Yugolewski, chief of counter-espionage, etc.
Source: RG395, File 095, Box 29

10 October 1919   Intelligence summary No. 318, Lieutenant Colonel R.L. Eichelberger, AEFS intelligence section
Subject: Operations on Chinese Eastern Railway; Russian military movements in Maritime province; Japanese relations with German POWs; British gold shipment
Source: RG165, Microfilm M917

11 October 1919   Letter from district inspector/Transbaikal Railway to Colonel G.H. Emerson, Irkutsk
Subject: Sludyanka dispatcher Novikov threatened by Russian rail guards who want to use phone
Source: RG43 RRSC, Entry 848, File 526, District Inspector Records

14 October 1919   Report from intelligence officer Spaskoye, to chief intelligence officer, Vladivostok
Subject: summary of railway traffic 6–12 October
Source: RG165, Microfilm M917

14 October 1919   Letter from 2nd Lieutenant W.A. Kelley/RRSC, Borzia, to Major J.C. Gravis/RRSC, Adrianovka
Subject: 'Mstitel'' sentry shoots switchman in yard; 'Mstitel'' searched No. 22 for all booze
Source: RG43 RRSC, Entry 848, File 526, District Inspector Records

14 October 1919   Letter from 2nd Lieutenant W.A. Kelley/Borzia to Major J.C. Gravis/Adrianovka
Subject: Delays at Dauria due to inspections; summary of all traffic
Source: RG43 RRSC, Entry 848, File 526, District Inspector Records

14 October 1919   American Red Cross Photograph No. 07207
Subject: Armored dining car of Volunteer Army 7th Division commander
Source: Kuban Command of American Red Cross, Library of Congress, Still Picture Division, ARC Lot 2918 F

17 October 1919   Letter from Cantrell/district inspector Transbaikal Railway, Irkutsk to Colonel Emerson, Irkutsk
Subject: Railroad workers so scared that they ignore railway rules when ordered by Semenov
Source: RG43, New Entry 844, File 226

18 October 1919   Letter from Major J.C. Gravis/RRSC Adrianovka, to Major General W.S. Graves/AEF Vladivostok
Subject: 15 October *semenovtsy* to take US supply train
Source: RG43 RRSC, Entry 848, File 526, District Inspector Records

24 October 1919   Letter from district inspector, Transbaikal Railway, Irkutsk to Colonel Emerson, Irkutsk
Subject: Stepanov threatens to whip 25–50 lashes dispatcher who followed procedures on phone
Source: RG43, New Entry 844, File 226

25 October 1919   Letter [handwritten] from Foster/RRSC Verkhneudinsk, to 'STC' [Cantrell]/RRSC
Subject: Serious incident with Semenov: try to take supply train; RRSC plans in case of trouble
Source: RG43 RRSC, Entry 848, File 526, District Inspector Records

25 October 1919	Message (handwritten transcript by Major Gravis), Ataman Semenov to Colonel Morrow, Verkhne-Udinsk Subject: 'I shake your hand' Source: RG43 RRSC, Entry 848, File 526/District Inspector Records
28 October 1919	Message from Major J.C. Gravis, Adrianovka to Major General Graves Subject: Details regarding Semenov attempt to take 15,000 rifles from Lieutenant Ryan's supply train at Chita; armed confrontation Source: RG43, New Entry 844, File 226
30 October 1919	Letter from 2nd Lieutenant W.A. Kelley, Borzia to Major J.C. Gravis, Adrianovka Subject: Delays at Dauria resolved by discussion with station commandant Source: RG43 RRSC, Entry 848, File 526, District Inspector Records
1 November 1919	Letter from 1st Lieutenant W.A. Kelley/RRSC, Borzia, to Major J.C. Gravis/RRSC, Adrianovka Subject: 'Battle of Hadabulok'; 'Don't concern yourself about my welfare'
1 November 1919	Message from man on duty, Shestopalov, to RRSC [handwritten Russian note, typed English translation] Subject: Colonel Stepanov's threatening behavior Source: RG43 RRSC, Entry 848, File 526, District Inspector Records
4 November 1919	Telegram from Gravis to Lieutenant Colonel Cantrell, Irkutsk Subject: 'Only protection – 1 armored train'; Friday morning trouble a frame up Source: RG43 RRSC, Entry 848, File 526, District Inspector Records
5 November 1919	Letter District Inspector Transbaikal Railway, Irkutsk, to Colonel G.H. Emerson/Chief Inspector, Irkutsk Subject: 25 October incident: Semenov try to take US supply train Source: RG43 RRSC, Entry 848, File 526/District Inspector Records
6 November 1919	Letter from DMI (MI5-1) to Lieutenant Colonel B.B. McCroskey Subject: Detail as military observer with armies of Admiral Kolchak Source: RG165, MID-2663-2
6 November 1919	Letter from Major J.C. Gravis/inspector 4th Division, Adrianovka, to Lieutenant Colonel S.T. Cantrell, Irkutsk [on YMCA stationary] Subject: Colonel Stepanov's character (forwards 1 November message) Source: RG43 RRSC, Entry 848, File 526, District Inspector Records
7 November 1919	Letter from district inspector Transbaikal Railway, Irkutsk, to Colonel G.H. Emerson/Chief Inspector, Irkutsk Subject: Battle of Khada-bulok', General Ungern Source: RG43 RRSC, Entry 848, File 526/District Inspector Records
14 November 1919	Report from 1st Lieutenant Albert E. Ryan/31st Infantry, to chief of staff Subject: 25 October incident (1st hand details) Source: RG165, Microfilm M917
17 November 1919	Letter from Lieutenant Colonel S.T. Cantrell/District Inspector, Transbaikal Railway, Verkhne-Udinsk, to Colonel G.H. Emerson/Chief Inspector, Irkutsk Subject: Adrianovka theft of flour by Semenov soldiers Source: RG43 RRSC, Entry 848, File 526, District Inspector Records
20 November 1919	Letter from Lieutenant Colonel S.T. Cantrell/district inspector Transbaikal Railway, Adrianovka, to Colonel G.H. Emerson/Chief Inspector, Irkutsk Subject: Colonel Stepanov departed for 'the East' Source: RG43 RRSC, Entry 848, File 526, District Inspector Records

BIBLIOGRAPHY

15 December 1919	Letter from Commanding Officer/HQ, China Expedition Tien Tsin, to Commanding Officer/Philippine Department, Manila Subject: Chinese army, description of troops Source: MID 156-141
16 December 1919	Memorandum for chief of staff, from DMI Subject: Siberia (controversial extract from Siberian Monograph) Source: RG165, MID File 2663-8
22 December 1919	No. 73, Meeting Minutes: Inter-Allied Railway Committee Subject: Disorder of Omsk evacuation – Semenov charges, Czechoslovak countercharges; congestion on Vladivostok and Transbaikal lines Source: RG43, NE844
24 December 1919	Telegram from Major General Ataman Semenoff (Translation) Subject: Order of the commander-in-chief of all the armed forces in the Far East, Chita No. 2 Source: RG395, File 095, Box 29
25 December 1919	Letter from Lieutenant General Inagaki, chief of staff, Japanese forces in Siberia, Vladivostok, to Major General Graves, AEFS Subject: Japanese troop movement to Mysovaya Source: RG395, File 095, Box 29
25 December 1919	Telegram from Parker, Irkutsk to J.F. Stevens, Harbin Subject: Irkutsk revolution on 24 December 1919; Semenov Officers, men arrested, *bronevik* captured without bloodshed Source: RG43, NE844, File 238
26 December 1919	Order of Lieutenant General Semenov to commanding officer/Irkutsk military district (original poster and translation) Subject: Orders to hold out until arrival of Major General Skipetrov and Wild Division Source: RG43, NE844, File 238
26 December 1919	Letter from Lieutenant Colonel F.B. Parker, Irkutsk to Colonel B.O. Johnson, Irkutsk Subject: Irkutsk revolution: events 25–26 December: Japanese–Czechoslovak tension; 2 Semenov *broneviki* at Sludyanka awaiting Cossacks Source: RG43, NE844, File 238
29 December 1919	Telegram from Sundheimer, Irkutsk to J.F. Stevens, Harbin Subject: Irkutsk revolution: events 27–29 December: fighting continues; Socialist-Revolutionaries taking city on north side of river Source: RG43, NE844, File 238
31 December 1919	Telegram of Czech Dennik, Irkutsk Subject: Irkutsk revolution: events 26–31 December: *bronevik* activity Source: RG43, NE844, File 238
31 December 1919	Telegram (encoded) from Sundheimer, Irkutsk, to J.F. Stevens, Harbin Subject: 10 Czechoslovak trains at Chernorejinskaya; Bogotol; coal lacking; trains out of food, fuel; wounded soldiers freezing to death; wood buildings destroyed for firewood; Socialist-Revolutionaries drove Semenov 23 *versts* east of Irkutsk; temperature $-11°$ Source: RG43, New Entry 844
1 January 1920	Telegram from Sundheimer, Irkutsk to Colonel Johnson, Harbin Subject: Irkutsk revolution: events – Semenov losses, 4 Czech Legion killed trying to clear line Source: RG43, NE844, File 238
2 January 1920	Letter from 1st Lieutenant C.G. Grigg, Adrianovka to Major A.S. Merz Subject: The 'Punisher' whipped station masters 31 December because of 20-minute delay Source: RG43, New Entry 844, File 226

3 January 1920	'To All Who Work' flyer (translation), Central Bureau of Professional Unions of Vladivostok Subject: Executions of Gaida uprisers; 'Down with Atamans!' Source: RG43, NE844, File 238
5 January 1920	Letter from Lieutenant H. Rattach, Olovyannaya to Major Merz Subject: 26–27 December whippings; 1 January 32 men and women taken and shot; town terrorized Source: RG43, New Entry 844, File 226
5 January 1920	Letter from Lieutenant R.S. Ashby, Mogzon to Major A.S. Merz, Chita Subject: 'The Destroyer' took 9 people for 'deportation Source: RG43, New Entry 844, File 226
6 January 1920	Letter from Lieutenant R.S. Ashby, Mogzon to Major A.S. Merz, Chita Subject: 9 bodies found near Taidut; Mogzon girl among bodies Source: RG43, New Entry 844, File 266
6 January 1920	Telegram from Sundheimer, Irkutsk, to J. F. Stevens, Harbin Subject: Movements of Czech Legion, Red Cross, Con Gen Harris; Kolchak–SR armistice; soldiers arresting Officers; co/Semenov troops tried to take gold from state bank last night Source: RG43, New Entry 844
7 January 1920	Letter from Major F.A. Flanagan to Colonel B. B. McCroskey Subject: detailed observations: 25 June 1919–7 January 1920, Krasnoyarsk–Irkutsk: conditions; New Siberian Army; evacuations; Red POWs freed; Social Revolutionaries behave decently with Americans; 30 December 1919 Semenov attack on Irkutsk – details Source: RG43, New Entry 844
8 January 1920	Letter from Major A.S. Merz, Inspector 4th Division/Chita to Colonel B.C. Johnson, Chief Inspector/Harbin Subject: 2 railway men whipped severely Source: RG43, New Entry 844, File 226
8 January 1920	Telegram from Sundheimer, Irkutsk to J.F. Stevens, Harbin Subject: Japanese bribed Railway Minister into secret treaty; Socialist-Revolutionaries took Verkhne-Udinsk, Shilka, Petrovsky Zavod Source: RG43, NE844
8 January 1920	Letter to Colonel B.O. Johnson, Harbin Subject: Irkutsk revolution: events 29 December 1919–8 January 1920 Source: RG43, NE844, File 238
10 January 1920	Letter from Lieutenant Colonel F.B. Parker, Irkutsk to Colonel B.O. Johnson, Harbin Subject: Battle at Sludyanka between Semenov and Czech Legion: 4 *broneviki*, 700 men captured Source: RG43, NE844, File 238
12 January 1920	Letter from Lieutenant Colonel F.B. Parker, Irkutsk to Colonel B.O. Johnson, Harbin Subject: Line clear of Semenov to Hilok; only rumors regarding 30 Socialist-Revolutionaries taken by Skipetrov Source: RG43, NE844, File 238
12 January 1920	Opening Meeting of the Siberian Soviet of national government, Irkutsk Subject: Proceedings of Soviet; main objective of Political Center: liquidation of counterrevolutionaries Source: RG43, NE844, File 238
14 January 1920	Telegram from Colonel Johnson to Lieutenant Retzer, Manchuli Subject: Colonel Medi embargos US messages into Transbaikal; see ataman and protest

BIBLIOGRAPHY

15 January 1920	Letter from Colonel B.C. Johnson, Harbin to J.F. Stevens, Harbin Subject: forwards messages from Major Merz regarding 'brutal atrocities' Source: RG43, New Entry 844, File 226
15 January 1920	Letter from M.K. Jones, District Inspector/Harbin, to J.F. Stevens, Harbin Subject: Unauthorized armored train 106 of 4 coaches, 6 boxcars from Manchuli at Harbin; 1st (?) border crossing by *bronevik* Source: RG43, New Entry 844
15 January 1920	Telegram from J.M. Sundheimer, Irkutsk to Major Colby, Verkhne-Udinsk Subject: 3 January Socialist-Revolutionaries took over government; status of RRSC Officers in area Source: RG43, NE844
1? January 1920	Newspaper summary, AEFS intelligence section Subject: General Skipetrov actions at Irkutsk Source: RG165, Microfilm M917
16 January 1920	Telegram, Grammes, Vladivostok to Mr Stevens, Harbin Subject: Japanese emperor's special train with armored cars authorized to move on Chinese Eastern Railway Source: RG43, New Entry 844
16 January 1920	Memorandum from Colonel B.O. Johnson, Harbin to J.F. Stevens Subject: Semenov will allow US cipher telegrams through again Source: RG43, New Entry 844, File 226
17 January 1920	Intelligence summary No. 17, AEFS intelligence section Subject: 1st US echelon left Verkhne-Udinsk; Czech Legion disarms Semenov troops at Beresovka Source: RG165, Microfilm M917
18 January 1920	Intelligence summary No. 18, AEFS intelligence section Subject: Trustworthy Semenov troops; Czech Legion arrested Semenov troops at Verkhne-Udinsk Source: RG165, Microfilm M917
19 January 1920	Intelligence summary No. 19, AEFS intelligence section Subject: Kalmykov *bronevik* wrecked at Shmakovka; soldiers taken prisoner Source: RG165, Microfilm M917
21 January 1920	Weekly Report, Inter-Allied Railway Committee, prepared by Captain R.A. Grammes, Vladivostok Subject: General Hosino is President/IA Military Transportation Board; Semenov ordered all Russians not to interfere with Czech Legion
22 January 1920	Military Attaché, China (HA) report (4 pages) Subject: Forces of Ataman Semionov Source: Microfilm M1444, Roll 6, MID 2009-82
27 January 1920	Intelligence summary No. 27, AEFS intelligence section Subject: Kalmykov *bronevik*, location; fall of Nikolsk (details)
28 January 1920	Minutes of meeting, Japanese Staff HQ, Chita Subject: Discussion regarding transportation problems between generals Hosino and Suzuki, Semenov representatives, B.B. McCroskey, Major Merz etc. Source: RG43, NE844
28 January 1920	Newspaper summary, AEFS intelligence section Subject: Vladivostok situation report; Semenov order not to punish Red POWs; Red–Czech Legion clash at Irkutsk
30 January 1920	Letter from Colonel B.O. Johnson, Harbin, to J.F. Stevens, Harbin Subject: Transbaikal coal situation Source: RG43, NE844

undated 1920	Telegram from author unknown/RRSC to Colonel Emerson/RRSC
Subject: Rumor Bolsheviks took Chita untrue; Semenov denies telegraph use to RRSC
Source: RG43 RRSC, Entry 843/348, Index 1, 89/Politics, Semenov
0? February 1920	Newspaper summary (excerpt), AEFS intelligence section
Subject: Kalmykov (details); Semenov's wife
Source: RG165, Microfilm M917
?? February 1920	Telegram (encoded) to MID, from McCroskey (undated, unnumbered, Chita, received 17 February)
Subject: Arrested on train to Irkutsk by Colonel Morrow
Source: RG165, File 2663-13
6 February 1920	Intelligence summary No. 37, AEFS intelligence section
Subject: 3rd US echelon left Verkhne-Udinsk; Colonel Butenko enemy of Kalmykov; Japanese try to bribe officers to fake an attack on Japanese troops
9 February 1920	Telegram (encoded) to MID, from 1st Lieutenant John James, acting adjutant, 27th Infantry and Colonel Charles Morrow, Chita
Subject: Semenoff using McCroskey for political purposes
Source: RG165, MID File 2663-13
1? February 1920	Newspaper summary, AEFS intelligence section
Subject: Kalmykov quote: 'I shall hang all of you'
Source: RG165, Microfilm M917
17 February 1920	Intelligence summary No. 48
Subject: Kalmykov did not resist Khabarovsk takeover; Japanese give up Kalmykov officers
Source: RG165, Microfilm M917
17 February 1920	Excerpt from RTA Bulletin No. 53
Subject: Major General Tumbair, new provisional government supreme ruler in Harbin; gold transport via Chang Chun
Source: RG395, File 095 Semenoff, Box 29
18 February 1920	Letter from Major F.A. Flanagan, Manchuli to Lieutenant Colonel M.K. Jones, Harbin
Subject: Ungern-Shternberg took 40 Russians from Manchuli to Dauria for execution; Japanese General Hosano prevented executions
Source: RG43, New Entry 844, File 226
18 February 1920	Letter from James E. Hood/inspector, Harbin to Lieutenant Colonel M.K. Jones, Harbin
Subject: 4 cars of quartz gold from Semenov to Japanese/Chang Chun left Harbin today under heavy guard; 'looks irregular'
Source: RG43, New Entry 844
18 February 1920	Memorandum for chief/personnel branch of Operations Division, from DMI
Subject: McCroskey detailed as Assistant Military Attaché Peking
Source: RG165, File 2663-12
19 February 1920	Letter from Sundheimer forwards telegram from Colonel Johnson, Chita to J.F. Stevens, Harbin
Subject: 8 Russian and 3 Japanese *broneviki* around Chita; Czech Legion movement; conditions; flour shipments
Source: RG43, New Entry 844
2? February 1920	Excerpt from weekly intelligence summary, AEFS
Subject: Prince Tumbaef, 'Dictator at Harbin,' leaves for abroad on mission for Semenov
Source: RG395, File 095 Semenoff, Box 29

BIBLIOGRAPHY

20 February 1920 — Letter from Smith, Chita, via Captain Sundheimer to General Graves and Dr Girsa
Subject: Japanese actions 'unjustifiable' regarding Czech Legion movement interference; Russian workmen will not provide locomotives for *broneviki*
Source: RG43, New Entry 844

20 February 1920 — Letter from Sundheimer forwards message from Colonel Johnson, Chita to J.F. Stevens, Harbin
Subject: Semenov evacuated train (message from Sludyanka/Messovaya area?)
Source: RG43, New Entry 844

20 February 1920 — Memorandum for chief of staff, from Brigadier General M. Churchill, director of military intelligence
Subject: Controversy between Colonel Morrow and McCroskey
Source: RG165, File 2663-13

20 February 1920 — Newspaper summary, AEFS intelligence section
Subject: Lieutenant General Starkovski attempt to prosecute Kalmykov; Kalmykov's torture chamber at Nikolsk
Source: RG165, Microfilm M917

2? February 1920 — Newspaper summary (excerpt), AEFS intelligence section
Subject: Transbaikal villages in revolt against Semenov; US troops only restraint in Verkhne-Udinsk against Semenov
Source: RG165, Microfilm M 917

21 February 1920 — Telegram from Colonel Johnson, Chita, to Captain Sundheimer, Harbin
Subject: Colonel Medi refused concessions; appealed to Semenov himself this morning
Source: RG43, New Entry 844, File 238

21 February 1920 — Telegram from Colonel Johnson, Chita, to Sundheimer, Harbin
Subject: Japanese evacuating Messovaya, gathering at Verkhne-Udinsk; 'bad feeling' developing between Japanese and Semenov; *broneviki* 'to stop operating'
Source: RG43, New Entry 844, File 238

22 February 1920 — Letter from Lieutenant Colonel B.B. McCroskey, military observer, en route to Vladivostok, to commanding officer, AEFS Vladivostok
Subject: Illegal and forcible arrest
Source: RG165, MID File 2663-23

23 February 1920 — Telegram from Colonel Johnson, Chita, to Captain Sundheimer, Harbin
Subject: Czechoslovak workmen still not allowed Chita shops; Japanese evacuating unannounced; 'final blowup Semenov army... very funny'
Source: RG43, New Entry 844, File 238

23 February 1920 — Intelligence summary, AEFS HQ
Subject: Ussuri Cossack Conference
Source: RG395, File 095 Semenoff, Box 29

26 February 1920 — Telegram from Johnson, Chita, to Captain Sundheimer, Harbin
Subject: SGT EN Davis, 27th Infantry, deserted to Reds at Verkhne-Udinsk; captured by Semenov forces; bridge blown east of Verkhne-Udinsk 24 February
Source: RG43, New Entry 844

27 February 1920 — Telegram from Johnson, Chita, to Captain Sundheimer, Harbin
Subject: Japanese interfering with all movement at Mogzon; Japanese 'guilty of high handed unnatural work'; Reds cooperative
Source: RG43, New Entry 844

2? February 1920 — Newspaper summary (excerpt) AEFS intelligence section
Subject: Monarchist paper accuses US–Jewish–Bolshevik conspiracy; anti-Kalmykov partisans
Source: RG165, Microfilm M917

27 February 1920	Intelligence summary No. 58, AEFS intelligence section Subject: Japanese participation in Gaida uprising; Semenov power waning in Chita; N. Romanov is Semenov representative in Washington DC; Kalmykov's departure from Khabarovsk – murdered *droshkie* drivers Source: RG165, Microfilm M917
27 February 1920	Newspaper summary, AEFS intelligence section Subject: Shipment of rifles for Semenov at Vladivostok railway station Source: RG165, Microfilm M917
29 February 1920	Telegram from Colonel Johnson, Chita, to Captain Sundheimer, Harbin Subject: 'Semenov entirely eliminated...replaced by Voshkovsky...' Semenov evacuation Chita–status near complete; Semenov forces nearby menaced by Reds; Semenov followers request US aid to escape Source: RG43, New Entry 844
2 March 1920	Intelligence summary No. 62, AEFS intelligence section Subject: Japanese burn bridge to cover Kalmykov's escape from partisans Source: RG165, Microfilm M917
2 March 1920	Telegram from Johnson, Chita to Sundheimer, Harbin Subject: Ungern commanding officer/Dauria tried to delay Czechoslovak movement; Japanese mobilize in Chita, fear Czechoslovak takeover; Japanese evacuating Verkhne-Udinsk Source: RG43, New Entry 844, File 238
3 March 1920	Telegram from Colonel Johnson, Chita, via Sundheimer, Harbin, to J.F. Stevens, Harbin Subject: Battles east of Verkhne-Udinsk today; Semenov *bronevik* captured; Semenov troops Verkhne-Udinsk disarmed by Japanese; Japanese detachment cut off by Reds at Verkhne-Udinsk Source: RG43, New Entry 844, File 238
3 March 1920	Telegram from Major Clarke, Vladivostok to Harbin Subject: Japanese diplomats in Riga trying to reach evacuation agreement with Trotsky; Semenov telegrams Irkutsk *zemstvo* seeking alliance Source: RG43, New Entry 844, File 238
4 March 1920	Telegram from Colonel Johnson, Chita, to J.F. Stevens, Harbin Subject: Flour/food distribution Source: RG43, New Entry 844, File 238
4 March 1920	From the Russian Telegraphic Agency, AEFS HQ Subject: Khabarovsk 1 March Korean independence celebrations Source: RG395, File 095 Semenoff, Box 29
5 March 1920	Telegram from Sundheimer, Harbin, to Colonel Johnson, Chita Subject: Major Flanagan's nervous breakdown at Manchuli; epidemics in Vladivostok; 'Grammes...taken to Manila' for trial Source: RG43, New Entry 844, File 238
5 March 1920	Untitled report, AEFS HQ Subject: March 4 Communist–Bolshevik Party meeting under Mr Gubelman at People's Hall; Nikolaevsk-on-Amur events Source: RG395, File 095 Semenoff, Box 29
5 March 1920	Report, telegram received from Mr Smith, AEFS HQ Subject: Information from French officer just returned from Irkutsk Source: RG395, File 095 Semenoff, Box 29
5 March 1920	Telegram from Colonel Johnson, Chita, to J.F. Stevens, Harbin Subject: Japanese interference at Chita continues; Reds at Verkhne-Udinsk very cordial Source: RG43, New Entry 844, File 238

BIBLIOGRAPHY

5 March 1920	Summary of news article from *Dalnivostochnoye Obozreniye* Subject: Japanese support for General Rozanov during Gaida uprising Source: RG165, Microfilm M917
6 March 1920	Intelligence summary No. 66, AEFS intelligence section Subject: Kalmykov arrested by Chinese Source: RG165, Microfilm M917
6 March 1920	Letter from Lieutenant Kotrba/Czech Legion to J.F. Stevens, Harbin Subject: Semenov army summary Dauria, Olovyannaya, Adrianovka, Karymskaya; *broneviki* and 'Oosmirityel' (Suppressor) Source: RG43, New Entry 844, File 238
6 March 1920	From the Russian Telegraphic Agency, AEFS HQ Subject: Information and disinformation re: Red drive on Verkhne-Udinsk and OMO Source: RG395, File 095 Semenoff, Box 29
7 March 1920	Telegram from Johnson, Chita, to S.F. Stevens, Harbin Subject: Czechoslovak workmen now in Chita shops; Petrovsky Zavod taken by Reds; 2 *broneviki* derailed near Hilok Source: RG43, New Entry 844, File 238
7 March 1920	Newspaper summary Subject: Articles in *Voennyi Nabat, Golos Rodini, Krasnoe Znamya, Dal'nivostochnoe Obozrenie*: Japanese support to Semenov: Red Army occupied town 10 kilometers north of Olovyannaya, Semenov troops withdrew, Japanese 59th Infantry Regiment attacked Source: RG43 RRSC, Entry 843/338, Index 1, File 73/Press
8 March 1920	Intelligence summary No. 68, AEFS intelligence section (excerpt) Subject: Japanese–partisan trouble at Nikolsk; Reds have 2 armored trains there; Semenov left Chita for Harbin Source: RG165, Microfilm M917
8 March 1920	Telegram from Johnson, Chita, to J.F. Stevens, Harbin Subject: Semenov only a figurehead; Kappel Army in Chita, brought typhus; great unrest and harsh rule in Red territory Source: RG43, New Entry 844, File 238
9 March 1920	Summary of events Subject: Russian railway men stymie Japanese attempt to take tunnel, warn Reds; new government Nikolsk has 2 *broneviki* Source: RG43, New Entry 844, File 238
9 March 1920	Cablegram to Adjutant General, from General Graves Subject: McCroskey mentally unsound Source: RG165, File 2663-20
9 March 1920	Letter from Lieutenant Colonel B.B. McCroskey, military observer, Vladivostok, to director of military intelligence, Washington Subject: Illegal arrest and prevention of carrying out instructions Source: RG165, MID File 2663-23
10 March 1920	Newspaper summary Subject: Articles in *Dal'nivostochnoe Obozrenie*: Harbin, 8 March: Semenov's gold; Colonel Shadrin; detained from wife's car Source: RG43 RRSC, Entry 843/338, Index 1, File 73/Press
10 March 1920	Letter from Lieutenant Colonel F.B. Parker, Manchuli to Colonel Johnson, Chita Subject: Chinese government attitude to armed Russian troops entering Manchuria; General Semenov – Ataman's uncle Source: RG43, New Entry 844, File 238
11 March 1920	Letter to Secretary of State, from Newton D. Baker, Secretary of War Subject: McCroskey to return to US Source: RG165, File 2663-20

11 March 1920	Intelligence summary No. 71, AEFS intelligence section Subject: Voitsekhovskii outranks Semenov; anniversary of revolution; request Horvath turn over authority Source: RG165, Microfilm M917
13 March 1920	Record of daily events, from Major D.S. Colby, Verkhne-Udinsk to Colonel B.O. Johnson, Chita Subject: Events of 13 March–10 April: Irkutsk starvation; SGT Davis; relations with Reds; *broneviki* in area
13 March 1919	Message, Colonel Emerson, Harbin, to General Graves, Vladivostok Subject: General Knox arrived Harbin for conference with Semenov Source: RG43 RRSC, Entry 843/348, Index 1, File 89/Politics, Semenov
13 March 1919	Message (deciphered), Colonel Emerson, Harbin, to Colonel Lantry, Vladivostok Subject: Horvat made up with Semenov; Horvat refuses Kolchak orders, leaves for Vladivostok 14 March Source: RG43 RRSC, Entry 843/348, Index 1, File 89/Politics, Semenov
14 March 1920	Telegram from Smith, Chita, to Major Clarke, Vladivostok Subject: Russian troops deserting trains at Dauria; anti-Jewish proclamation by Semenov; discipline in Red Army Source: RG43, New Entry 844, File 238
15 March 1920	Memorandum from Chairman Medvedev, provisional government Maritime Provincial Zemstvo Board, administration of foreign affairs to Chinese High Commissioner, No. 259 Subject: Horvath's special authority illegal; Semenov crimes in Manchuria; Semenov robbing gold etc.; armed refugees Harbin, etc. Source: RG43, New Entry 844, File 238
15 March 1920	Telegram from Smith, Chita, to Major Clarke, Vladivostok Subject: Verkhne-Udinsk government peace proposal to General Voitshoffsky; guarantee safety to all but Semenov; typhus epidemic Source: RG43, New Entry 844, File 238
16 March 1920	Telegram from Parker, Hailar, to Colonel Johnson, Chita Subject: Socialist-Revolutionaries takeover Russian settlement; Semenov Cossacks went over; General Skipetrov under Japanese protection Source: RG43, New Entry 844, 238
16 March 1920	Telegram from Smith, Chita, to John Stevens, Vladivostok Subject: Semenov concessions for Japanese; Semenov *bronevik* captured at Olovyannaya 15 March Source: RG43, New Entry 844, File 238
17 March 1920	Letter from Major D.S. Colby, Verkhne-Udinsk to Colonel Johnson, Chita Subject: High tension between Czech Legion and Soviet commanders regarding movement of Red echelons into Messovaya Source: RG43, New Entry 844, File 238
17 March 1920	Letter from Major D.S. Colby, Verkhne-Udinsk to Colonel Johnson, Chita Subject: Czech Legion–Soviet tension at Messovaya; Commissar Semenov Source: RG43, New Entry 844, File 238
17 March 1920	Telegram from Sundheimer, Harbin, to Colonel Johnson, Chita Subject: Chinese commission requests *broneviki* entering Chinese Eastern Railway be sealed at Manchuli; Japanese claim Hosino–Smith friction Source: RG43, New Entry 844, File 238

BIBLIOGRAPHY

17 March 1920	Reports from the Russian Telegraph Agency regarding the program of the strike of the Chinese Eastern Railway Subject: Chinese Eastern Railway strike: Semenov troops at Boohedoo and Hailar join strikers Source: RG165, Microfilm M917
18 March 1920	Telegram from Parker, Hailar to Colonel Johnson, Harbin Subject: Socialist-Revolutionaries and Semenov troops in Hailar agree to disarming by Chinese; General Hosino takes Czechoslovak locomotive at Borzia Source: RG43, New Entry 844, File 238
18 March 1920	Telegram from Johnson, Chita to J.F. Stevens via Sundheimer, Harbin Subject: Mogzon-Borzia still Voitshoffsky territory; Olovyannaya taken twice by Reds, who went back to hills Source: RG43, New Entry 844, File 238
18 March 1920	Telegram from Chita to Sundheimer, Harbin Subject: Semenov officers threaten arrest of General Syrovy because *bronevik* captured at Olovyannaya; *bronevik* crew mutinied Source: RG43, New Entry 844, File 238
19 March 1920	Telegram from Parker, Hailar via Sundheimer, Harbin, to Stevens, Harbin Subject: Repeats 17 March telegram Source: RG43, New Entry 844, File 238
?? March 1920	Protocol of a citizen of the village Olovyannaya, Ivan Gerasinov-Sovenkov Subject: Robbery and whipping by Semenov Lieutenant and 6 Cossack soldiers on 19 March Source: RG43, New Entry 844, File 238
20 March 1920	Letter from Ernest L. Harris/American Consul–Harbin, Vladivostok, to Lieutenant Colonel McCroskey Subject: Full approval for McCroskey activity Source: RG165, MID 2663-23 (Encl. 3)
20 March 1920	Telegram from Colonel Johnson, Chita, to J.F. Stevens Subject: 3,000–5,000 Reds with officers of main Soviet Army approaching Mogzon; no Semenov strength this territory; Verkhne-Udinsk conditions very bad Source: RG43, New Entry 844, File 238
21 March 1920	Telegram from Smith to Major Clarke, Vladivostok Subject: Meeting of Kappel Officers Chita – want to leave, only 3,000 men; Semenov must stay, fight; Verigo going Olovyannaya; Annenkov arrived Source: RG43, New Entry 844, File 238
21 March 1920	Intelligence summary No. 81, AEFS intelligence section Subject: No Semenov *broneviki* permitted on Chinese Eastern Railway; Stanicnik captured; Japanese ¥2,000,000 loan to Semenov for workers; Reds captured Semenov *bronevik* at Olovyannaya Source: RG165, Microfilm M917
24 March 1920	Letter from Major G.H. Hazzard, Olovyannaya to Colonel B.O. Johnson, Chita Subject: Japanese interference: blocking tracks with *bronevik*; Japanese workmen replaced Czechoslovaks by order Colonel Medi Source: RG43, New Entry 844, File 238
24 March 1920	'The Japanese and the Czechs', translation of pro-Japanese– Semenov article from *Vladivo Nippo* reprinted by *Golos Rodini* Subject: Czech Legion disarmed Semenov troops 9 January between Baikal and Messovaya; Czech Legion gave Reds opportunity to attack Verkhne-Udinsk 2 March Source: RG43, New Entry 844, File 238

25 March 1920	Telegram from Major Hazzard to Colonel Johnson, Chita Subject: Colonel Gronye de Pol arrived; terrorizing workmen, threatening execution by drowning in Onon river Source: RG43, New Entry 844, File 238
25 March 1920	Intelligence summary No. 85, AEFS intelligence section Subject: Japanese and Chinese reinforcements; Red and partisan movements; Japanese holding Chita; 10 Red echelons at Hilok
26 March 1920	Intelligence summary No. 86, AEFS intelligence section Subject: Japanese surround Nikolsk station; Reds concentrate at Zagarin to cut off Semenov *broneviki* Source: RG165, Microfilm M917
26 March 1920	Letter from Major C.H. Hazzard, Olovyannaya to Colonel Johnson, Chita Subject: Japanese stealing horses from railway men; 14–15 March invasion by Reds Source: RG43, New Entry 844, File 238
28 March 1920	Telegram from Mr Smith, Chita, to Major Clarke, Vladivostok Subject: Japanese guard Semenov, run armored trains; 'their petty demeanor'; food very scarce
29 March 1920	Military Attaché China (HA) Report Subject: Student movement Source: Microfilm M1444, Roll 6, MID 2657-I-108
31 March 1920	Military Attaché China (HA) Report No. 2484 Subject: Semeonoff's agents in Peking; Colonel Kroupsky; McCroskey message Source: Microfilm M1444, Roll 6, MID 2657-I-101
31 March 1920	Memorandum for J.F. Stevens from Colonel B.O. Johnson, Harbin Subject: Major Hazzard harassed by Japanese soldiers at Olovyannaya regarding red signal cloth in windows Source: RG43, New Entry 844, File 238
5 April 1920	'The Taking of Nikolsk by the Japanese' by H. Van Vechten Fay Subject: detailed Report (11 pages); Kalmykov officers work with Japanese against fellow Russian officers Source: RG43, New Entry 844, File 238
6 April 1920	Telegram from Major Merz, Chita, via Sundheimer to J.F. Stevens, Harbin Subject: Red aeroplane dropped literature on Chita; 9 echelons and *broneviki* to the west; Japanese interference continues Source: RG43, New Entry 844, File 238
9 April 1920	Letter from Colonel B.O. Johnson, Harbin to J.F. Stevens, Harbin Subject: Reds captured letters at Verkhne-Udinsk including letter summary of Japanese troops and supplies Source: RG43, New Entry 844, File 226
10 April 1920	Letter from Dr Blagosh, Czechoslovak Representative, Hailar, to Commanding Officer, Chinese Troops, Hailar Subject: Request to release men arrested by Japanese command Hailar Source: RG43, New Entry 844, File 226
14 April 1920	Letter from Major D.S. Colby, Hailar, to Colonel B.O. Johnson, Harbin Subject: Events at Hailar 13 April; role of Major Colby Source: RG43, New Entry 844, File 238

BIBLIOGRAPHY

14 April 1920	Military Attaché China (HA) Report (2 pages) Subject: 'Russian Group', General Situation, Manchuria and eastern Siberia; request information on McCroskey Source: Microfilm M1444, Roll 6, MID 2657-I-125
15 April 1920	Letter from Lieutenant Colonel Kopal, chief, military mission of the Czechoslovak Ministery of National Defense, Harbin, to Lieutenant Colonel Engineer Clupek, Czechoslovak Legion, Harbin Subject: Events at Hailar 11–13 April; role of Czechs
16 April 1920	Memorandum from Colonel Johnson, Harbin, to J.F. Stevens Subject: Anti-Red forces between Chita–Mogzon; last Semenov garrison at Dauria; Japanese–Red battle near Mogzon, 200 WIA; Major Merz; British 'relief' train carrying munitions Source: RG43, New Entry 844, File 238
16 April 1920	Translation of letter from Prosecutive Attorney Sotchin, Russian Vice Consul, Hailar, to chief of military mission, Japanese Consul, certified by Lieutenant Colonel Klupek, Harbin. Subject: 9 April Japanese arrested several Russian officials at Hailar; request turnover to Russians Source: RG43, New Entry 844, File 238
17 April 1920	Letter from office of Czechoslovak representative–IATB (signed by Czech Lieutenant Colonel, 'C.R.T.B.') to J.F. Stevens, Harbin Subject: Events at Hailar 11–13 April; detailed accounts Source: RG43, New Entry 844, File 238
17 April 1920	Military Attaché China (HA) Report (1 page) Subject: Russian and Japanese political movement in Manchuria Source: Microfilm M1444, Roll 6, MID 2657-I-111 (?)
19 April 1920	Military Attaché China (HA) Report Subject: Chinese students in Siberian affairs Source: Microfilm M1444, Roll 6, MID 2657-I-112
21 April 1920	Memorandum from Colonel Johnson to Mr Stevens Subject: Semenov troops moving into Manchuria and Hailar; threatened Manchuli dispatchers Source: RG43, New Entry 844, File 238
22 April 1920	'The Hailar Incident', *Peking and Tientsin Times* Subject: Events at Hailar 11–13 April Source: RG43, New Entry 844, File 238
22 April 1920	Telegram (encoded) from Lieutenant Colonel B.B. McCroskey, S.S. Great Northern to DMI Subject: Unjustly removed from duty; Russian situation Source: RG165, File 2663-21
23 April 1920	Military Attaché China (HA) Report (8 pages) Subject: Japanese, British and Semenoff; atrocities; US withdrawal Source: Microfilm M1444, Roll 6, MID 2657-I-129
23 April 1920	Military Attaché China (HA) Report (7 pages) Subject: 'Conditions in Siberia and Manchuria' Source: Microfilm M1444, Roll 6, MID 2657-I-130
27 April 1920	Report (C), ONI OP-16-B Subject: Mongolia: Urga outlook; OMO pirates on Kyakhta road Source: RG165, MID 156-130/2
28 April 1920	Telegram (plain) to DMI, from McCroskey, San Francisco Subject: Request investigation of Colonel Morrow Source: RG165, File 2663-22
3 May 1920	Letter (handwritten), from Lieutenant Colonel B.B. McCroskey, San Francisco, to Brigadier, General Churchill, DMI

	Subject: Incident with Colonel Morrow, details, personal feelings Source: RG165, MID 2663-24
5 May 1920	Letter from Lieutenant Colonel McCroskey to DMI Subject: Incident with Colonel Morrow: request for impartial investigation Source: RG165, MID 2663-23
12 May 1920	Report No. 312 from Agent 'K', Marine detachment, American Legation Peking Subject: Mongolia: conditions in Urga; Little Hsu; caravan freight; 20 Russian prostitutes at Chinese HQ Source: RG165, MID 156-130/2
24 May 1920	Letter from Congressman Hugh S. Hersman, to Secretary of War Newton D. Baker Subject: Court of inquiry for B.B. McCroskey Source: RG165, MID 2663-38
24 May 1920	Letter from J.M. Sundheimer to Mr Stevens, Harbin Subject: Reds burned Onon river bridge east of Olovyannaya Source: RG43, New Entry 844, File 238
24 May 1920	Report, 'The Local Situation', Vladivostok Subject: Transbaikal Railway from Sretensk to Chita to 'fighting front' under Semenov protégé Kislitsyn; Japanese promise to liquidate Semenov adventure if representatives put into Vladivostok provisional government; Amur river bridge near Khabarovsk unpassable Source: RG43, New Entry 844, File 238
26 May 1920	Letter from Benjamin F. Fiery/Private Secretary to Secretary of War, to Congressman H.S. Hersman Subject: Court of inquiry for B.B. McCroskey Source: RG165, MID 2663-39
28 May 1920	Memorandum of Lieutenant F.B. Byers, Harbin Subject: Vladivostok situation report: Japanese returned 1,000 rifles to Militia; heavy patrols on empty streets; Kalmykov coup rumored Source: RG43, New Entry 844, File 238
25 November 1920	Report (C), ONI Section B Subject: Mongolia: Chinese troops move into Urga, some on buses Source: RG165, MID 156-130
8 February 1921	Intelligence report, ONI (Marine detachment, American Legation– Peking) Subject: Mongolia: October 1920 conditions; detailed description of Urga Source: RG165, MID 156-130/5
18 February 1921	Questionnaire for Oriental language detail Subject: B.B. McCroskey personal data Source: RG165, MID 2663-45
10 March 1921	Report MID 2657-I-159 Subject: Capture of Urga; Ungern Source: Microfilm M1444, Roll 6 from 405
17 March 1921	Report No. 180, ONI File No. 810-200 Subject: Ungern's troops; situation report from Urga Source: Microfilm M1444, Roll 6 from 502
30 March 1921	Report No. 212 from Agent 'K', ONI File No. 810-200 (MID 2657-I-158) Subject: Capture of Urga Source: Microfilm M1444, Roll 6 from 407
12 April 1921	Report No. 229 from Agent 'K', ONI File No. 103-100 (MID 2657-I-171) Subject: Government of Manchuria influenced by Japanese and Semenov representatives Source: Microfilm M1444, Roll 6 from 503

16 April 1921	Letter MID 156-130/8 Subject: Mongolia: 3rd Mixed Brigade killed/driven into Siberia by Ungern Source: RG165
19 July 1921	Report No. 427 from Agent 'K', ONI File No. 103-100 (MID 2657-I-189) Subject: Mukden: preparation for Mongolian expedition Source: Microfilm M1444, Roll 6 from 618
22 March 1922	Questionnaire for Oriental language detail Subject: B.B. McCroskey personal data Source: RG165, MID 2663-59
1942	*Byuro po delam rossiiskikh emigrantov, Razdel VII, No. 29, (Spravka sostavlennaya v UKGB po Khabarovskomuo krayu na osnovanii materialov sbornika 'Belaya emigratsiya v Man'chzhurii' (razvedotdel UNKVD po Chitinskoi oblasti, 1942 g.), a takzhe pokazanii arestovannykh K.V. Rodzaevskogo, M.A. Matkovskogo, M.V. Potapova* Subject: Bureau of Emigration Source: Rossiiskii gosudarstvennyi istoricheskii arkhiv Dal'nego Vostoka, Vladivostok
1942	*Dal'nevostochnyi Soyuz Voennyikh, Razdel III, No. 9, Spravka sostavlennaya v UMVD Khabarovskogo kraya, na osnovanii materialov sbornika 'Belaya emigratsiya v Man'chzhurii' (razvedotdel UNKVD po Chitinskoi oblasti, 1942 g.)* Subject: Union of Servicemen; GBREM; Kislitsyn; General Yanogita; Chita Military School, etc. Source: Rossiiskii gosudarstvennyi istoricheskii arkhiv Dal'nego Vostoka, Vladivostok
10 June 1943	Reference Card, Siemeonov Subject: General Vlasov's appeal to Russian patriots Source: OSS File OB-1344, RG226, Entry 14, Box 18, NM54
11 September 1944	Interview report No. 324 from M.A. ID CSD 9SC, Fort Douglas, UT Subject: Political situation in Manchoukuo as of 1941 Source: OSS File XL-1674, RG226, Entry 19, Box 21
22 July 1944	Reference card, Russia Subject: Russia and Far Eastern settlement; may invade North Manchuria when Japan's defeat is near Source: OSS File XL-1081, RG226, Entry 17, Box 100
26 October 1944	Intelligence report No. 604, headquarters 9th SC, Fort Douglas, UT Subject: Who's Who – Dairen Source: OSS File XL-2139, RG226, Entry 19
15 August 1953	*Ob'edinenie Kazakov, Razdel V, No. 26, Spravka sostavlennaya v UMVD Khabarovskogo kraya, o Soyuze kazakov na Dal'nem Vostoke* Subject: Union of Cossacks; Cossack State; A. Baksheyev; K. Biryukov; *rossizm*; relationship to fascists; Conference of Stanitsa Atamans; Cossack leaders Source: Rossiiskii gosudarstvennyi istoricheskii arkhiv Dal'nego Vostoka, Vladivostok

Newspaper articles

Trotsky, Leon, 'Order Concerning Prisoners of War', *Izvestia*, 21 April 1918.
'Reports Korniloff and Semenoff Dead', *New York Times*, 22 April 1918, p. 1:2.
'Semeneff Active Again', *New York Times*, 14 May 1918, p. 2:3.
'Semenoff Sets Up Independent State', *New York Times*, 24 May 1918, p. 5:1.
'General Semenoff Reported in Flight', *New York Times*, 8 June 1918, p. 5:1.
'Bolsheviki Can't Get Siberian Grain; Gen. Semenoff Defeated', *New York Times*, 22 June 1918, p. 3:3.

'Semenoff Defies Siberian Dictator', *New York Times*, 26 November 1918, p. 2:4.
'Semenoff's Arrest Ordered by Kolchak', *New York Times*, 9 December 1918, p. 3.
'Kolchak Decries Siberian Council', *New York Times*, 9 December 1918, p. 3:1.
'Semenoff Now Offers to Recognize Kolchak', *New York Times*, 26 December 1918, p. 3.
'Bomb Wounds Semenoff', *New York Times*, 27 December 1918, p. 6:7.
'The March of the Red Cross', *Red Cross Magazine*, 14, 4, April 1919.
'The March of the Red Cross', *Red Cross Magazine*, 14, 5, May 1919.
'US Consul Train Held Up in Siberia', *New York Times*, 31 May 1919, p. 2:5.
'Intrigue and Force in Siberia: Semenoff's Aspirations', *The Times*, 11 November 1919, p. 13.
'Red Menace to the Far East', *The Times*, 8 March 1920, p. 13.
'Chino-Japanese Agreement', *The Times*, 18 March 1920, p. 15.
'The Hailar Incident: Eyewitness's Account', *Peking and Tientsin Times*, 22 April 1920.
'Semenoff, Cossack Chief, is Arrested on Arrival Here', *New York Times*, 7 April 1922, pp. 1 and 3.
'Routed Chita Troops', *New York Times*, 8 April 1922, p. 3.
'Move to Deport Semenoff Begun', *New York Times*, 9 April 1922, p. 13.
'Semenoff Silent as to Bank Theft', *New York Times*, 11 April 1922, p. 9.
'New Bail Bond or Jail for Semenoff', *New York Times*, 13 April 1922, p. 21.
'Japanese Attack Chita Forces', *New York Times*, 13 April 1922, p. 24.
'Semenoff in Jail; East Side Throngs Hiss Cossack Chief', *New York Times*, 14 April 1922, pp. 1 and 4.
'Seek Allies' Part in Semenoff Case', *New York Times*, 14 April 1922, p. 4.
'Japanese Prevent Chita Army Advance', *New York Times*, 14 April 1922, p. 3.
'Semenoff, Freed, Called Bigamist', *New York Times*, 20 April 1922, pp. 1 and 2.
'Semenoff Departs to Rejoin His Army', *New York Times*, 10 June 1922, p. 12.
'Semenoff's Departure a Relief to Officials', *New York Times*, 11 June 1922, p. 24.
'German Mission in Chita', *New York Times*, 24 June 1922, p. 15:8.
'Gen. W.S. Graves Dead, A.E.F. Leader', *New York Herald-Tribune*, 28 February 1940.
'Velikii Knyaz Mongolii, Kavaler Ordena Proroka Magomeda', *Pravda Buryatii*, Ulan Ude, 25 July 1992, p. 3 (courtesy of Dr Chingis Andreev).
Aprelkov, V., 'Zoloto Atamana', *Ekstra (Chitinskaya Oblastnaya Gazeta)*, 4 October 2000, Chita.
Aprelkov, V., *'Vernet li Yaponiya Russkoye Zoloto?'*, *Ekstra*, 4 October 2000, Chita.
Yur'ev, Anton, 'Chto prines "veter peremen"?', *Zabaikal'skii Rabochii*, Chita, No. 1. 242 2001, (23524).
'Reminders of Russian Legacy Linger in Harbin', *St Petersburg Times*, No. 658, 3 April 2001.
'China turns Battlefield into Tourist Resort', *People's Daily* (Beijing), 9 May 2001.
'Cruel Torture Recorded in Tibet', *People's Daily* (Beijing), 14 May 2001.
Aprelkov, V., 'Zabaikal'skoe kazach'e voisko', *Ekstra*, Chita, No. 79, 25 July 2001.
Kulikov, Anatolii, 'Mnogo sdelal ya dobra...', *Zabaikal'skii Rabochii*, Chita, No. 1, 12 (23539), August 2001.
Barinov, Aleksandr, 'Zabytyi pisatel', ili "piarshchik" atamana', *Zabaikal'skii Rabochii*, Chita, No. 65 (23593)/No. 54 (23582), 9 April 2002.
Barinov, Aleksandr, 'Zabytyi pisatel', ili "piarshchik" atamana', *Zabaikal'skii Rabochii*, Chita, No. 65 (23593)/No. 59 (23587), 9 April 2002.
Barinov, Aleksandr, 'Tsyganka Masha', *Zabaikal'skii Rabochii*, Chita, No. 65 (23593)/ No. 239 (23521), 9 April 2002.

Books

Ablova, N.E., *Istoriya KVZhD i rossiiskoi emigratsii v Kitae (pervaya polovina XX v.)*, B.G.U., Minsk, 1999.
Academy of Sciences-Mongolian People's Republic (ASMPR), *Information Mongolia: The Comprehensive Reference Source of the People's Republic of Mongolia*, Pergamon Press, Oxford, 1990.

BIBLIOGRAPHY

Alexander, Roy, *The Cruise of the Raider Wolf*, Yale University Press, New Haven, CT, 1939.
Anderson, Jesse A., *A Doughboy in the American Expeditionary Force Siberia*, J.A. Anderson, CA, 1983.
Asakawa, Kan'ichi, *The Russo-Japanese Conflict, Its Causes and Issues*, Houghton Mifflin, Boston, MA, 1904.
Baerlein, Henry, *The March of the Seventy Thousand*, Leonard Parsons, London, 1926.
Balfour, G., *The Armoured Train: Its Development and Usage*, B.T. Batsford, London, 1981.
Barron, John, *KGB: The Secret Work of Soviet Secret Agents*, Bantam Books, New York, NY, 1974.
Batchelor, John, *Rail Gun*, John Batchelor, Broadstone, Dorset, 1973.
Bawden, Charles R., *The Modern History of Mongolia*, Weidenfeld & Nicolson, London, 1968.
Bell, James Mackintosh, *Side Lights on the Siberian Campaign*, Ryerson Press, Toronto, 1922.
Beloborodov, Afanasii Pavlantrevich, *Proryv na Kharbin*, VoenIzdat Ministerstva oborony SSSR, Moscow, 1982.
Borisov, B., *Dalnii Vostok*, Izdaniye Novoi Rossii, Vienna, 1921.
Borodin, A.V., *History of Russia's Pacific Fleet*, Institute of History, Archaeology and Ethnography of the Peoples of the Far East, Vladivostok, 1998.
Boyd, Alexander, *The Soviet Air Force Since 1918*, Stein & Day, New York, NY, 1977.
Bradley, J., *Allied Intervention in Russia*, Basic Books, New York, NY, 1968.
Braudel, Fernand, *The Structures of Everyday Life: The Limits of the Possible; Civilization and Capitalism, 15–18th Century, Volume I*, Harper & Row, New York, NY, 1979.
Brenner, Lenni, *Zionism in the Age of the Dictators*, L. Hill, Westport, CT, 1983.
Brovkin, Vladimir N. (ed.), *The Bolsheviks in Russian Society: The Revolution and the Civil Wars*, Yale University Press, New Haven, CT, 1997.
Brown, Arthur Judson, *New Forces in Old China; An Unwelcome but Inevitable Awakening*, F.H. Revell Company, New York, NY, 1904.
Budberg, Baron Aleksei Pavlovich, *Dnevnik Byelogvardeitsa*, Leningrad Priboi, Leningrad, 1929.
Burkova, Valentina Fedorovna, *Dal'nevostochnaya Magistrali Rossii'*, Chastnaya Kollektsiya, Khabarovsk, 1997.
Caiti, Pierangelo, *Artiglierie Ferroviarie e Treni Blindati (Atlante Mondiale delle Artiglierie)*, Ermanno Albertelli Editore, Parma (Italy), 1974.
Chwialkowski, Paul, *In Caesar's Shadow: The Life of General Robert Eichelberger*, Greenwood Press, Westport, CT, 1993.
Crone, Allia, *East Lies the Sun*, Dell, New York, NY, 1982.
Curtin, Jeremiah, *A Journey in Southern Siberia*, Arno Press, New York, NY, 1909 (1971 reprint).
Daurets, N.P., *Semenovskie Zastenki*, N.P. Harbin, 1921.
Deacon, Richard, *Kempei Tai: The Japanese Secret Service Then and Now*, Charles E. Tuttle, Tokyo, 1990.
Degras, Jane (ed.), *Soviet Documents on Foreign Policy*, vol. I, Oxford University Press, New York, NY, 1951.
de Hartog, Leo, *Russia and the Mongol Yoke*, British Academic Press, London, 1996.
Deriabin, A. and Palacios-Fernandes, P., *Grazhdanskaya Voina v Rossii 1917–1922: Byeliye Armii*, Izdatel'stvo AST, Moscow, 2000.
Deriabin, A. and Palacios-Fernandes, P., *Grazhdanskaya Voina v Rossii 1917–1922: Natsionalniye Armii*, Izdatel'stvo AST, Moscow, 2000.
Deyatelnost' Osobago Man'chshurskago Otryada, Atamana Semenova, Tip. Kharbininsatsu-sho, Harbin, 1919.
Digby, George Bassett, *Tigers, Gold and Witch-Doctors*, Harcourt Brace & Co., New York, NY, 1928.
Dobson, C. and Miller, J., *The Day We Almost Bombed Moscow: The Allied War in Russia 1918–1920*, Hodder & Stoughton, London, 1986.
Dotsenko, Paul, *The Struggle for Democracy in Siberia 1917–1920*, Hoover Institution Press, Stanford, CA, 1983.

Dvornichenko, Nikolai Egorovich, *Putevodit'el'po Chitye*, Vostochno-Sibirskoye Knizhnoye Izd-vo, Irkutsk, 1981.
Dyboski, Roman, *Seven Years in Russia and Siberia (1914–1921)*, Warsaw, 1922 (Library of Congress Call No. D627.R8 D913).
Dziak, John J., *Chekisty: A History of the KGB*, Lexington Books, Lanham, MD, 1988.
Facts about Korea, Samhwa Printing Company, Seoul, 1984.
Fedyuninskii, Ivan Ivanovich, *Na Vostoke*, VoenIzdat Ministerstva oborony SSSR, Moscow, 1985.
Fleming, Peter, *The Siege at Peking*, Oxford University Press, Oxford, 1959.
Fleming, Peter, *The Fate of Admiral Kolchak*, Harcourt, Brace & World, New York, NY, 1963.
Forsyth, James, *A History of the Peoples of Siberia: Russia's North Asian Colony 1581–1990*, Cambridge University Press, New York, NY, 1992.
Fraser, John Foster, *The Real Siberia*, Cassell, London, April 1902.
Ginzton, Edward L., *Times to Remember: The Life of Edward L Ginzton*, Blackberry Creek Press of Berkeley, CA, 1995.
Gitelman, Zvi, *A Century of Ambivalence: The Jews of Russia and the Soviet Union, 1881 to the Present*, YIVO Institute for Jewish Research, New York, NY, 1988.
Goldhurst, Richard, *The Midnight War: The American Intervention in Russia, 1918–1920*, McGraw-Hill Book Company, New York, NY, 1978.
Graves, Major General William Sidney, *America's Siberian Adventure 1918–1920*, Jonathan Cape & Harrison Smith, New York, NY, 1971 (reprint).
Grondijs, Lokewijk-Hermen, *La Guerre en Russie et en Siberie*, Editions Bossard, Paris, 1922.
Guins, G., *Sibir', Soyuzniki i Kolchak: Povorotnyi moment russkoi istorii, 1918–1920 g.g.; vpechatlieniya i mysli chlena Omskago pravitel'stva*, vol. I, Peking, Tipo-lit. Russkoi dukhovnoi missii, 1921.
Gunther, John, *Inside Asia*, Harpers, New York, NY, 1939.
Gutman, Anatoly Gan, *The Destruction of Nikolaevsk-on-Amur: An Episode in the Russian Civil War in the Far East, 1920*, Limestone Press, Fairbanks, AK, 1993.
Hane, Mikiso, *Peasants, Rebels & Outcastes: The Underside of Modern Japan*, Pantheon Books, New York, NY, 1982.
Heald, Edward Thornton, ed. by Gidney, James, *Witness to Revolution: Letters from Russia 1916–1919*, Kent State University Press, OH, 1972.
Hilditch, A. Neville, *Battle Sketches 1914–1915*, Clarendon Press, Oxford, 1915, available at greatwar2.topcities.com/Tsing_Tao/Tsing_Tao_Text_01.htm
Hirschfeld, Dr Magnus (ed.), *The Sexual History Of The World War*, Panurge Press, New York, NY, 1934.
Holmes, Burton, *The Burton Holmes Lectures*, vol. 8, The Little-Preston Co., Battle Creek, MI, 1901, available at www.burtonholmes.org
Hopkirk, Peter, *Setting the East Ablaze: Lenin's Dream of an Empire in Asia*, Kodansha Globe, New York, NY, 1984, p. 129.
Johnston, Mamie, *I Remember It Well: Memories of China 1923–1951*, Presbyterian Chruch in Ireland, Belfast, 1981.
Jukes, Geoffrey, *Carpathian Disaster: Death of an Army*, Ballantine Books, New York, NY, 1971.
Karan, Pradyumna P., *The Changing Face of Tibet*, University Press of Kentucky, Lexington, KY, 1976.
Kerensky, Alexander, *Russia and History's Turning Point*, Duell, Sloan & Pearce, New York, NY, 1965.
Khvostov, Mikhail, *The Russian Civil War: The Red Army*, Osprey Military, Oxford, 1996.
Khvostov, Mikhail, *The Russian Civil War: White Armies*, Osprey Military, Oxford, 1997.
Knyazev, Lev, *'Doch' Atamana'*, from *Morekhody 3: Skazaniya o Moryakakh Rossiiskikh*, Dal'nevostochnaya Gosudarstvennaya Morskaya Akademiya, Vladivostok, 1999.
Kopenhagen, Wilfried, *Armored Trains of the Soviet Union 1917–1945*, Schiffer Military History, Atglen, PA, 1996.
Korol'kov, Yurii Mikhailovich, *Sovershenno Sekretno: Pri Opasnosti Czhech'!*, Izd-vo Belarus', Minsk, 1986.

BIBLIOGRAPHY

Krasheninnkov, Stefan P., *The History of Kamtschatka, and the Kurilski Islands, with the Countries Adjacent*, printed by Robert Raikes for T. Jeffreys, Geographer to His Majesty, Gloucester, 1764, reprinted by Quadrangle Books, Chicago, IL, 1962.
Krist, Gustav, trans. Lorimer, E.O., *Prisoner in the Forbidden Land*, Faber & Faber, London, 1938.
Kropotkin, Prince Peter, *In Russian and French Prisons*, Ward & Downey, London, 1887.
Krupskaya, Nadezhda K., *Reminiscences of Lenin*, International Publishers, New York, NY, 1970.
Kuranov, V., *The Trans-Siberian Express*, Sphinx Press, New York, NY, 1980.
Lenin, Vladimir Ilyich, *Collected Works*, vol. 28, Progress Publishers, Moscow, 1965.
Lincoln, Bruce, *Red Victory: A History of the Russian Civil War 1918–1921*, Da Capo Press, New York, NY, 1989.
Lloyd's Register of Shipping, The Register, London, 1918.
Longworth, Philip, *The Cossacks: Five Centuries of Turbulent Life on the Russian Steppes*, Holt, Rinehart & Winston, New York, NY, 1970.
Louis, Victor and Jennifer, *The Complete Guide to the Soviet Union*, St Martin's Press, New York, NY, 1976.
Luckett, Richard, *The White Generals*, Viking Press, New York, NY, 1971.
Lyandres, Semion and Wulff, Dietmar (eds), *A Chronicle of the Civil War in Siberia and Exile in China: The Diaries of Petr Vasil'evich Vologodskii, 1918–1925*, Hoover Institution Press, Stanford, CA, 2002.
Maclean, Fitzroy, *To the Back of Beyond: An Illustrated Companion to Central Asia and Mongolia*, Little, Brown & Company, Boston, MA, 1975.
Maddox, Robert James, *The Unknown War with Russia: Wilson's Siberian Intervention*, Presidio Press, San Francisco, CA, 1977.
Manusevich, A.Ya., Birman, M.A., Klevanskii, A.Kh., Khrenov, I.A., *Internatsionalisti: trudyashchiyesya zarubyezhnykh stran – uchastniki borbi za vlast sovietov*, Izdatel'stvo Nauka, Moscow, 1967.
March, Francis A., *History of the World War: An Authentic Narrative of the World's Greatest War*, United Publishers of the US and Canada, Chicago, IL, 1919.
March, General Peyton C., *The Nation at War*, Greenwood Press, Westport CT, n.d.
Marks, Steven G., *Road to Power: The Trans-Siberian Railroad and the Colonization of Asian Russia, 1850–1917*, Cornell University Press, Ithaca, NY, 1991.
Massie, Robert K., *Nicholas and Alexandra: An Intimate Account of the Last of the Romanovs and the Fall of Imperial Russia*, Atheneum, New York, NY, 1968.
Meakin, Annette, *A Ribbon of Iron*, Arno Press, New York, NY, 1901 (1970 reprint).
Meyer, Karl E. and Brysac, Shareen Blair, *Tournament of Shadows*, Counterpoint Press, Washington, DC, 1999.
Morley, James William, *The Japanese Thrust into Siberia, 1918*, Columbia University Press, New York, NY, 1954.
Moynihan, Brian, *Comrades: 1917–Russia in Revolution*, Little Brown & Company, Boston, MA, 1992.
Murray, John, *A Memoir of the Life of Peter the Great*, William Clowes, London, 1832.
Naayem, Joseph, *Shall This Nation Die?*, Chaldean Rescue, New York, NY, 1920.
Newby, Eric, *The Big Red Train Ride*, Weidenfeld & Nicolson, London, 1978.
Nilus', Ye. Kh. (ed.), *Istoricheskii Obzor' – Kitaiskii Vostochnii Zheleznoi Dorogi 1896–1923*, Tipografii Kit. VoSt Zhel. Dor. & T-va Ozo, Harbin, 1923.
North, Robert N., *Transport in Western Siberia: Tsarist and Soviet Development*, University of British Columbia Press/Centre for Transportation Studies, Vancouver, 1979.
Okudzhava, Bulat, trans. Sonia Melnikova, *Unexpected Joy*, Rosen Publishing, New York, NY, 1992.
Ossendowski, Ferdinand, *Beasts, Men and Gods*, E.F. Dutton & Co., New York, NY, 1922.
O'Toole, G.J.A., *Honorable Treachery: A History of US Intelligence, Espionage and Covert Action from the American Revolution to the CIA*, Atlantic Monthly Press, New York, NY, 1991.
Paal, Jaanus, *Kamchatka Story*, Tartumaa Muusemumi Toimetised, Tartu (Estonia), 1993.
Paleologue, Maurice, *An Ambassador's Memoirs*, George H. Duran, New York, NY, 1925.
Parkin, P.I. (ed.), *Razgrom Kolchaka*, Boennoe Izdatel'stvo Ministerstva Oborony, Moscow, 1969.

Pearce, Brian, *The Military Writings and Speeches of Leon Trotsky*, vol. 3, *How the Revolution Armed*, New Park Publications, London, 1920.
Pearlstein, Edward W. (ed.), *Revolution in Russia! as reported by the New York Tribune and the New York Herald, 1894–1921*, Viking Press, New York, NY, 1967.
Petrov, Fedor N., *Geroicheskiye godi borbi i pobed*, Izdatel'stvo Nauka, Moscow, 1968.
Potseluyev, V.A., *Bronenostsi Zheleznikh Dorog*, Molodaya Gvardiya, Moscow, 1982.
Powell, David E., *Antireligious Propaganda in the Soviet Union*, MIT Press, Cambridge, MA and London, 1975.
Putevodit'el'po Chitye, n.p., 1951.
Quested, R.K.I., *Sino-Russian Relations: A Short History*, George Allen & Unwin, Sydney, 1984.
Radkey, Oliver Henry, *The Election to the Russian Constituent Assembly of 1917*, Harvard University Press, Cambridge, MA, 1950.
Rasputin, Maria, *Rasputin: The Man Behind the Myth*, Warner Books, New York, NY, 1977.
Reitzel, Gail Berg and Raymond J., *Shifting Scenes in Siberia* (Book 2 of biography of Raymond J. Reitzel), self-published (Library of Congress Call No. D639.Y7 R44).
Roberts, Fred M., *Assignment Siberia 1917–1919: Russian Railway Service Corps*, FMRoberts Enterprises, Dana Point, CA, 2000.
Savin, S. and Tarasov, G., *Za Baikalom*, Izdatel'stvo Sovietskaya Rossiya, Moscow, 1963.
Sayers, Michael and Kahn, Albert E., *Sabotage! The Secret War against America*, Harper & Brothers, New York, NY, 1942.
Schapiro, Leonard, *The Russian Revolutions of 1917: The Origins of Modern Communism*, Basic Books, New York, NY, 1984.
Seaton, Albert Warner, Phillip (ed.), *The Soviet Army*, Osprey Publishing, Reading, 1972.
Semenov, G.M., *O Sebe*, Harbin, 1938; reprinted by Izdatel'stvo AST, Moscow, 2002.
Sergeyev, M., *Irkutsk: Putevodit'el*, Raduga Publishers, Moscow, 1986.
Severin, Tim, *In Search of Genghis Khan*, Atheneum, New York, NY, 1992.
Shambarov, Valerii Evgen'evich, *Belogvardeishchina*, Izdatel'stvo EKSMO-Press, Moscow, 2002.
Shaw, Robert B., 'The Railroad War', Veterans AEFS So. Western Div. #1 (Reprinted by permission of Federation for Railway Progess), undated. The Jos. B. Longuevan Papers, Box 1, Folder: Robert B. Shaw, 'The Railroad War', MHI Carlisle Barracks, PA.
Shereshevskii, B.M., *Razgrom Semenovshchiny*, USSR Academy of Science, Siberian Division, Novosibirsk State University, Science Publishing House, Novosibirsk, 1966.
Shishkin, S.N., *Grazhdanskaya voina na Dal'nem Vostoke 1918–1922*, Moscow, 1957.
Sigachyov, Sergei, *Trans-Siberian Web Encyclopedia*, Russkii Ekspress, Moscow, 1998.
Silverlight, J., *The Victor's Dilemma: Allied Intervention in the Russian Civil War*, Weybright & Talley, New York, NY, 1971.
Skrilov, A. and Gubarev, G.V., *Kazachi Slovar-Spravochnik (The Cossack Dictionary)*, vol. 1 (Abramov–Zyavlovski), Tipografia Kazachevo Natsiyonalnovo Obshchestva Pyechati, Cleveland, OH, 1966.
Smele, Jonathan D., *Civil War in Siberia: The Anti-Bolshevik Government of Admiral Kolchak, 1918–1920*, Cambridge University Press, New York, NY, 1996.
Smith, Canfield Ferch, *Vladivostok Under Red and White Rule 1920–1922*, University of Virginia, VA, 1972.
Snow, Russell E., *The Bolsheviks in Siberia 1917–1918*, Fairleigh Dickinson University Press, Madison, NJ, 1977.
Spector, Ivar, *An Introduction to Russian History and Culture*, D. Van Nostrand Co., New York, NY, 1949.
The Story of the Great War, vol. 15, P.F. Collier & Son Company, New York, NY, 1919.
Storry, Richard, *A History of Modern Japan*, Pelican Books, Harmondsworth, 1960.
Sutton, Antony C., *Wall Street and the Bolshevik Revolution*, n.p., 2001.
Taft, William Howard, (Chairman of editorial board), *Service with Fighting Men: An Account of the Work of the American Young Men's Christian Associations in the World War*, vol. 2, Association Press, New York, NY, 1922.

Trotsky, Leon, *My Life*, Charles Scribner's Sons, New York, NY, 1930.
Trotsky, Leon, *The History of the Russian Revolution*, London, Sphere Books, 1967.
Trotsky, Leon, *Military Writings*, Merit Publishers, New York, NY, 1969.
Tsypkin, S., *Oktiabrskaya Revolutsia i Grazhdanskaya Voina na Dal'nem Vostokye: Khronika Sobitii 1917–1922*, Dal'giz, Moscow and Khabarovsk, 1933.
Tuchman, Barbara W., *The Zimmermann Telegram*, Ballantine, New York, NY, 1958.
Turnbull, S.R. and McBride, Angus, *The Mongols*, Osprey Military, Oxford, 1980.
Unterberger, Betty Miller, *America's Siberian Expedition 1918–1920: A Study of National Policy*, Greenwood Press, New York, NY.
US Department of the Army, *China Area Handbook*, 1994.
US Department of the Army, US Army Forces Far East, Military History Section, *Political Strategy Prior To Outbreak Of War*, Pt. 1, Japanese Monograph No. 144, 1952.
US Department of State, *Papers Relating to the Foreign Relations of the United States (FRUS)*, Government Printing Office, Washington, DC, 2004.
US House of Representatives, *Events Leading Up to World War II: Chronological History of Certain Major International Events Leading Up to and During World War II with the Ostensible Reasons Advanced for Their Occurrence*, 78th Congress, House Document No. 541, Government Printing Office, Washington, DC, 1944.
US Senate Committee on Education and Labor, *Deportation of Gregorie Semenoff: Hearings Relative to the Deporting of Undesirable Aliens, April 12–18, 1922*, Government Printing Office, Washington, DC, 1922 (reprint by Beamur International Limited, Hong Kong, 1972).
Varneck, Elena and Fisher, H.H. (eds), *The Testimony of Kolchak and Other Siberian Materials*, Hoover War Library Publications, No. 10, Stanford University Press, Stanford, CA, 1935.
Vasilevskii, V.I., *Ataman Semenov, Voprosy gosudarstvennogo stroitel'stva: Sbornik dokumentov i materialov*, Knizhnoe Izdatel'stvo Poisk, Chita, 2002.
Vernadsky, George, *The Mongols and Russia*, Yale University Press, New Haven, CT, 1953.
Vespa, Amleto, *Secret Agent of Japan*, Little, Brown & Company, New York, NY, 1938.
Volkov, Sergei V., *Tragediya Russkogo Ofitserstva*, Izd-vo 'Fokus', Moscow, 1999.
Vrangel, Petr N., *The Memoirs of General Wrangel*, Duffield & Co., New York, NY, 1930.
Ward, Colonel John, *With the 'Die-Hards' in Siberia*, Cassell & Company, London, 1920.
Wenyon, Charles, *Across Siberia on the Great Post-Road*, C.H. Kelly, London, 1896.
White, John A., *The Siberian Intervention*, Greenwood Press, NY, 1950.
Wieczynski, Joseph L. (ed.), *The Modern Encyclopedia of Russian and Soviet History*, vol. 7, 'Chinese Eastern Railway', Chita Operation of 1920', 'Chita Republic', 'Civil War in Russia'; vol. 34: 'Semirech'e Cossack Host'; vol. 53: 'Siberia under Soviet Rule', Academic International Press, Gulf Breeze, FL, 1990.
Woodward, David, *Armies of the World 1854–1914*, G.P. Putnam's Sons, New York, NY, 1978.
Woods, Alan, *Bolshevism: The Road to Revolution*, Wellred Books, London, n.d.
Worden, Robert L. and Savada, Andrea Matles (eds), *Mongolia: A Country Study*, Federal Research Division, Library of Congress, Washington, DC, 1989.
Zalesskii, K.A., *Imperiya Stalina: Biograficheskii entsikolopedicheskii slovar'*, Beche, Moscow, 2000.

Magazines, journals and other sources

12th Armored Division Memorial Museum and Abilene Christian University, 'Organization of the ASTP', Abilene, Texas, 2002, available at www.acu.edu/academics/history/12ad/astpx/org.htm
27th Infantry Regimental Historical Society, Inc., 'Colonel Charles H. Morrow', Schofield Barracks, HI, 2003, available at www.kolchak.org/History/Whos2/Regiment/Col%20Morrow%201918.htm
Ablazhei, Natal'ya, 'V sostave edinoi i nedelimoi: sibirskoe oblastnichectvo v emigratsii', Rodina, 2001.
Ablova, Nadezhda E., 'Politicheskaya Situatsia na K.B.Zh.D. nolse Krusheniya Rossiiskoi Imperii', *Belorusski Zhurnal*, 98, 4, 1998.

Ablova, Nadezhda E., 'Rossiiskaya Fashistskaya Partiya v Man'chzhurii', *Belorusski Zhurnal*, 99, 2, 1999.
Allen, Jonathan, 'A Long Road Home: The Czechoslovak Legion in Russia', *Command Magazine*, 24, September–October 1993, p. 38.
Antropov, Oleg K., 'Kharbin kak Kul'turnyi Tsentr Zarubezhnoi Rossii (1920–1930s)', Rossiiskii Gosudarstvennyi Gumanitarnyi Universitet, Istoriko-Arkhivnyi Institut, 2002, available at zaross.rsuh.ru/kult/zs5_hrbk_g.html
Army and Navy Journal, 'Trial of Japanese Map Thief', 16 October 1920.
Balkarei, Boris, 'Svidetel' stvo podpolkovnika Eikhel'bergera', *Novoe Vremya*, 34, 19 August 1988, pp. 34–7.
Balkarei, Boris, 'The Past and the Present: Lieutenant Colonel Eichelberger testifies: A 55-year-old American intelligence report declassified (interview with D.Sc. (HiSt) Victor Malkov)', *New Times*, 40.88, 1988, pp. 34–7.
Barber, Laurie, 'Checkmate at the Russian Border: Russia-Japanese Conflict before Pearl Harbour', University of Waikato, 1997, available at www.waikato.ac.nz/wfass/subjects/history/waimilhist/1997/lhb-folder/lhb-p1.html
Barinova, Aleksandra, 'Taina Shumovskogo Dvortsa', Chita, 2001, available at www.chita.ru/~barinov/9.html
Belikov, Vasilii Valerianovich, 'Evenki Buryatii', Ulan-Ude, 1994.
Belov, E., 'Kak Byla Likvidirovana Avtonomiya Vneshnei Mongolii', Aziatskaya Biblioteka, 2001, available at asiapacific.narod.ru/countries/mongolia/avtonomia_v_ mongolia.htm
Berzin, Alexander, 'Exploitation of the Shambala Legend for Control of Mongolia', Berlin, 2003, available at www.berzinarchives.com/kalachakra/exploitation_shambala_legend_mongolia.html
Blinoff, Michael, 'Civil War in China. Russian Division of Armored Trains 1924–1928', Tank Museum of Kubinka, 2003, available at www.tankmuseum.ru/index_e.html
Bragin, A.P., 'Krovavoe prestuplenie zhido-bol'shevikov na rekov Khor', *Nashe Otechestvo, Sankt Peterburg*, 73–4, August–September 2001, available at www.nashe-otechestvo.spb.ru/173/hor.html
Bragin, A.P., 'Vozrozhdenie russkoi gosudarstvennosti', Vladivostok, 1997, available at sotnia.8m.com/t1997/ts00.htm (site no longer active).
Brown, Scott J., 'Neanderthals and Modern Humans: A Regional Guide', 2001, available at www.neanderthal-modern.com/
Bukin, Andrei G., 'Ivan Afanasevich Butin', Project ZAO-EKT, Chita, 2002, available at www.oldchita.megalink.ru/
Bukin, Andrei G., 'Sergei Lazo', Project ZAO-EKT, Chita, 2002, available at www.oldchita.megalink.ru/
Bukin, Andrei G., 'Sokol-Nomokonov V.M.', Project ZAO-EKT, Chita, 2002, available at www.oldchita.megalink.ru/
Bukin, Andrei, 'Pokushenie na Atamana Semenova', Chita, 2002, available at megalink.ru/~sps/differ/pokushen.htm
Bukin, Andrei, 'Zabaikal'skaya Militsiya na Sluzhbe Boennogo Rezhima', Chita, 2002, available at megalink.ru/~sps/differ/sem_mil.htm
Caplovic, Miloslav, 'French Military Mission in Czechoslovakia 1919–1938', *Slovak Army Review*, Autumn 2001.
Commandeur, Marc, 'Red Star Cats II', *The Catalina Chronicles*, vol. 2, PBY Catalina Foundation, 2002, available at www.catalina.demon.nl/pby/redstar.htm
Cordier, Henri, 'Mongolia', *The Catholic Encyclopedia*, vol. 10, Robert Appleton Co., New York, NY, 1911.
Croner, Don, 'Avenger Lama: The Life and Death of Dambijantsan', Ulaan Baatar, n.d., www.doncroner.com/MONGOLIA.HTML
Crush, Peter, 'The Chinese Eastern Railway: A Glimpse of History', Hong Kong Railway Society, 2002, available at www.hkrs.org.hk/members/crush/CER_1.htm
Daly, Jonathan W., ' "Storming the Last Citadel": The Bolshevik Assault on the Church, 1922', in Brovkin, V.N., *The Bolsheviks in Russian Society; The Revolution and the Civil Wars*, Yale University Press, New Haven, CT, 1997, pp. 235–68.

BIBLIOGRAPHY

Davis, Dr Geo W., IV, Photo Album: 'Harbin Cholera Epidemic 1919' etc., Liberty Memorial Museum, Kansas City, MO.

Denisov, S.V., 'General-Leutenant A.I. Dutov', n.p., 2001, available at www.geocities.com/terek_kaz/dutov.html

Dinets, Vladimir, 'Brown Bears of Russia', n.p., 2001, available at dinets.travel.ru/russianbears.htm

Dovbnya, Anatolii, 'Klady samozvanykh atamanov', Kladoiskatel'stvo, 2001, available at www.tvplus.dn.ua/column.php?div=chrono&art=0001.

Earns, Lane R., 'Where Do We Go From Here: The Russian Railway Service Corps in Nagasaki', *Crossroads: A Journal of Nagasaki History and Culture*, 6, Showado Printing, Nagasaki, 1999.

Federal Bureau of Investigation, 'Famous Cases: Vonsiatsky Espionage', 2002, available at www.fbi.gov/libref/historic/famcases/vonsiatsky/espionage.htm

Fic, Victor M., 'Book Review: *Tibetsky buddhismus v Burjatsku*', *Journal of Global Buddhism*, 4, 2003.

Footman, David, 'Ataman Semenov', St Antony's Papers on Soviet Affairs, St Antony's College, Oxford, February, 1955.

Fridman, Aleksandr, 'Evreiskie pogromy... v Mongolii', *IJC*, Nizhne Novgorod, 2002.

Gentes, Andrew, 'Review: *Iakutiia v sisteme politicheskoi ssylki Rossii 1826–1917* [and] *Politicheskaia ssylka v Sibiri: Nerchinskaia katorga*', *Kritika: Explorations in Russian and Eurasian History*, 3, 1, 2002, pp. 140–51.

Giffin, Frederick C., 'An American Railroad Man East of the Urals, 1918–1922', *The Historian*, 60, 4, 22 June 1998, p. 812.

Great War, The Standard History of the World-Wide Conflict, vol. 13, 'From the Armistice to the Peace'.

Grigoryan, V., 'Chelovek s poslednego parokhoda: Dve sud'by pevchego "Man'chzhurtsa" Vasiliya Nikolaevicha Molchanova', *Vera: Khristianskaya Gazeta Severa Rossii*, 409, March 2002.

Hallman, Andrew L., 'Battlefield Operational Functions and the Soviet Campaign Against Japan in 1945', US Marine Corps Command and Staff College, Quantico, VA, 1995, available at www.globalsecurity.org/military/library/report/1995/HAL.htm

Hillman, Tom, 'Polish Legion in Siberia', n.p., 2002.

History of the Temple of Kalachakra', St Petersburg Temple of Kalachakra, St Petersburg, 2000, available at datsan.newmail.ru/history_e.html

Iouzéfovitch, Leonid, 'Il ne doit rester graine ni d'homme ni de femme', *Bulletin de l'Association Anda*, 40, January 2001.

Ivanov, V.D. and Sergeev, O.I., 'Ussuriiskoye Kazachestvo b Revolyutsiyakh 1917 goda u Grazhdanskoi Voine na Dal'nem Vostoke', Institute of History, Archaeology and Ethnography of the People of the Far East, DVO RAN, 1999, available at www.fegi.ru/primorye/kazaki/kazak2.htm

Kandidov, B., 'Tserkovnye shpiony yaponskogo imperializma', *Sputnik Agitatora*, 14, 1937, pp. 24–7.

Karpenko, S.V., 'Kazach'i Stanitsy v emigratsii (1921–1930s)', Rossiiskii Gosudarstvennyi Gumanitarnyi Universitet, Istoriko-Arkhivnyi Institut, 2002, available at zaross.rsuh.ru/kazak/zs36_kazastan_kp.html

Kaufman, Linda Fay, 'Harold Van Vechten Fay', Fay Family [Genealogy] Page, www.fayfamily.org, April 2003.

Khatuntsev, Stanislav Vital'evich, 'Ungern fon Shternberg: Buddist s Mechom', Voronezh State University, Historical Faculty, 2003.

Kolbenev, E.K., 'Drug Mongol'skogo Naroda, Chekist Gridnev', *Ocherki Istorii Rossiiskoi Vneshnei Razvedki*, vol. 4, n.p., 1992.

Komissarova, Tamara, 'A Library Legend', *We/Myi – The Women's Dialogue*, 4, 20, 1999, available at www.we-myi.org/issues/20/library.html

Kroupnik, Vladimir, 'With the White Russians in Siberia', Perth, 2000, available at www.argo.net.au/andre/latchfordENFIN.htm

Kurlat, F.L. and Studnikov, L.A., translated by Gebhardt, James F., 'OMSBON: Independent Special Purpose Motorized Brigade', *Voprosy istorii*, 10, 1982.
Lackenbauer, P. Whitney, 'Why Siberia? Canadian Foreign Policy and Siberian Intervention 1918–19', University of Waterloo (Canada), April 1998, available at www.rootsweb.com/~canmil/siberia/siberia1.htm
Lafferty, Brian, 'Going Back to the Future in Tibet', *Columbia East Asian Review*, Spring 1998.
Lapidus, Mikhail and Golovin, Yuri, 'Sud'ba Zolotogo Zapasa Tsarskoi Rossii', 23 November 1999.
Leifheit, Daniel A., 'America's Secret War', n.p., 2003, available at secretwar. hhsweb.com/.
Limonov, Edward, 'Whips and Castration: A Guide to Russian Cults', *The Exile*, 5, 10–23 April 1997.
Luzianin, Sergei, 'Soviet Russia's Policy towards Mongolia 1919–1924', *IIAS Newsletter*, 9, Summer 1996, International Institute for Asian Studies, Leiden University, Netherlands.
Mahoney, Tom, 'When Yanks Fought in Russia', *American Legion Magazine*, April 1978.
May, Timothy M., 'Banditry in Inner Mongolia', University of Wisconsin, Madison, WI, 1998, available at userpage.fu-berlin.de/~corff/im/Landeskunde/im-bandits-1.html
McCormack, Gavan, 'Manchukuo: Constructing the Past', *East Asian History*, 2, December 1991, pp. 199–121.
Merzliakova, Irina and Karimov, Aleksei, 'A History of Russian Administrative Boundaries (XVIII–XX Centuries), International Workshop on Historical GIS, 25 August 2001.
Michelson, Henry, 'The Trans-Siberian Railroad', *Scientific American*, 26 August 1899.
Miller, Lyubov trans. Nabatova-Barrett, Irina, 'Holy Martyr of Russia, Grand Princess Elizaveta Fedorovna', n.p., available at www/fatheralexander.org/booklets/english/princess_elizabeth.htm
Morozova, Irina Yu., 'Japan and its Influence on Pan-Mongolism and Pan-Buddhism', Nordic Institute of Asian Studies, Copenhagen, 1999, available at www.iacd.or.kr/archive.htm
Naletov, Petr Ivanovich, 'Pedagogicheskoi Eksperiment: Vospominaniya Uchastnika Splava 1923 goda' Irkutsk, 1985, available at www.megalink.ru/~zabscout/leto23.htm
Narangoa, Li, 'Educating Mongols and Making "Citizens" of Manchukuo', *Inner Asia*, 3, 2001, pp. 101–26.
Narangoa, Li, 'Japanese Geopolitics, Manchuria and the Mongol Lands 1905–1945', Nordic Institute of Asian Studies, Copenhagen, 2001, available at www.uoregon.edu/~iwata/_private/GEACS/new_page_33.htm
New Red Cross Magazine, June 1919, p. 82.
Nederlands Mongoolse Cultuurvereniging & Mediarctic, 'Buddhist and Mongolian Persons and Terminology', 2004, available at mongoluls.net
Nun Seraphima, 'Bury Me Like a Christian', *Orthodox Life, Brotherhood of Saint Job of Pochaev at Holy Trinity Monastery*, 47, 6, November–December 1997, pp. 29–31.
Odigon, Sarangerel, 'History of Buryatia', n.p., 1997, available at www. buryatmongol.com/
Old Fort Niagara Association, 'Old Fort Niagara', Youngstown, NY, 2004, available at www.oldfortniagara.org/americanhistory.htm
Omsk State Archive, Description of Personal Collection of G.E. Katanaev, f.366, op.1, 488 d., available at www.ic.omskreg.ru/~omskarchive/section2_2_4.html
Österreich Lexikon, AEIOU Kulturinformationssystem, Austrian Federal Ministry for Education, Science and Culture, Vienna, 1996.
Pereira, Norman, 'Atamanshchina i belaia vlast' v vostochnoi Sibiri vo vremia grazhdanskoi voiny', *Sibir'*, XX vek vyp. 3, Kemerovo: Kuzbassvuzizdat, 2001, pp. 57–63.
Pereira, Norman, 'Siberian Atamanshchina: Warlordism in the Russian Civil War', in Brovkin, V.N., *The Bolsheviks in Russian Society: The Revolution and the Civil Wars*, Yale University Press, New Haven, CT, 1997.
Pereira, Norman, 'Siberian Atamanshchina: Warlordism in the Russian Civil War', in Brovkin, V.N., *The Bolsheviks in Russian Society: The Revolution and the Civil Wars*, Yale University Press, New Haven, CT, 1997.
Petrov, Leonid A., 'Out of the Frying Pan, Into the Fire: Russian Immigrants in China', Asian Studies Association of Australia, Hobart, 2002, available at north-korea. narod.ru/immigrants.htm

BIBLIOGRAPHY

Phillips, John A., III, 'Thomas H. Lantry on the Trans-Siberian Railway', Northern Pacific, Auburn, WA. 20 March 2002.
Piskunov, Sergei, 'Sovetsko-kitaiskii vooruzhennyi conflict na KVZhD 1929 g.', 2003, in Rumyantsev, Vyacheslav (ed.), *Khronos*, www.hrono.ru, Moscow, 2003.
Podalko, Petr E., 'Pavel Vaskevich: Uchenyi, Diplomat, Puteshestvennik: k 125-letiyu co dnya rozhdeniya', Hokkaido University, Slavic Research Center, Sapporo, 2001, available at src-h.slav.hokudai.ac.jp/publictn/acta/19/podalko.pdf
Pro Patria Press: Newsletter of the 31st Regiment Association, *From the Past*, 9, February 1998.
Reed, John, 'Liar or Just Doesn't Know', *Revolutionary Age*, 19 August 1919.
Rice, C.R., 'Pravda', RRSC Reunion, 11 November 1932.
Rumyantsev, Vyacheslav (ed.), *Khronos*, www.hrono.ru, Moscow, 2003.
Sabin, Burritt, 'The Pianos Fall Silent: The Tragic End of the Yokohama Colony of the Russian Diaspora', *The East*, 37, 4, November/December 2001.
Schmidt, Juergen, 'The Diversionary Operation of a German Military Attaché in China in 1915', *Arbeitskreis Geschichte der Nachrichtendienste e. V. Newsletter*, 7, 2, Winter 1999.
Shishkin, Vladimir I., 'State Administration of Siberia from the End of the Nineteenth Through the First Third of the Twentieth Century', *Proceedings of Summer 1998 Symposium: Regions: A Prism to View the Slavic-Eurasian World*, Slavic Research Center, Hokkaido University, Sapporo, 2000, available at src-h.slav.hokudai.ac.jp/sympo/98summer/98summer-contents.html
Sigachov, Sergei G., 'Transsiberian Historical Background 1857–1891', *Trans-Siberian Web Encyclopedia*, 1998, available at www.transsib.ru/Eng/history-review.htm
Sotskov, Vadim, 'General i Ataman: Sud'ba generala Semenova po materialam Tsentralnogo Arkhiva FSB', *Zavtra* (Moscow), 2, 371, 1 September 2001.
Sotskov, Vadim, 'Zoloto Imperii: obespechit li protsvetanie Rossii eë byvshii Verkhovnyi Pravitel'?', *Ekonomist*, January–February 2001.
Stolberg, Eva-Maria, 'Siberia and the Russian Far East in Japanese Strategic and Economic Conceptions, 1890s–1920s', Institute of Russian History, University of Bonn, n.d, avilable at nias.ku.dk/Neighbours/StolbergPaper.htm
Taylor, Virginia Westall, 'Bull Kendall in Siberia', *The Blue Devil* 38, 2 (publication of the 88th Infantry Division Assoc., Inc.), POB 925, Havertown PA 19083, May 1987 (excerpted from *Military Review*). The Jos. B. Longuevan Papers, Box 1, Folder: A Soldier's View, MHI Carlisle Barracks, PA.
Tumina, Apollinaria, 'Trup Pyatiletiya: Aktual'noe Interv'yu', n.d, n.p., available at imperium.lenin.ru/EOWN/eown4/ungern.html
US Department of Justice, Federal Bureau of Investigation, 'Famous Cases: Vonsiatsky Espionage', 2002.
Ungern-Shternberg, R.F., *'Prikaz No. 15: Prikaz russkim otryadam na territorii sovetskoi Sibirii'*, 15 May 1921, Urga; State Archives of the Russian Federation, F. Varia, d. 392, l. 1–6; reproduced by Radio Islam, 2002, available at abbc.com/russ/ungern.html
Vajda, Edward J., 'The Ewenki', Western Washington University, Bellingham, WA, 2001, available at pandora.cii.wwu.edu/vajda/ea210/ewenkiewen.htm
Ventugol, Nicolas, 'Les officiers à titre Etrangers', n.d.
Vertyankin, V.V., 'Istoriya Ledokola "Angara"', Irkutsk, 1991.
Vlasov, Artem, 'Kuda Ischezlo Chitinskoe Zoloto?', zona.com.ru, Provintsiya, BG, Moscow, 2000, available at www.zona.com.ru/news/press_8.shtml
Wigowsky, Paul J., 'Collection of Old Believer's History and Tradition', Hubbard, OR, 1978, available at www.geocities.com/Athens/Agora/2827/collection.html
Wood, Junius B., 'The Far Eastern Republic', *National Geographic Magazine* 41, 6, June 1922, pp. 565–92.
Yaponiya Sevognya, 'Vitalii Guzanov: Rasstrelyan kak yaponskii shpion, Vostochnaya odisseya krasnogo komkora', n.d.
Yasutomi, Ayumu, 'Money and Finance in Manchuria 1895–1945', Nagoya University, 1998.
Yates, Athol and Karachevtsev, Ilya, 'The History of Russian and Soviet Armored Trains', Academic International Press, Gulf Breeze, FL, available at www.cix.co.uk/~nrobinson/railgun/Armoured%20Trains/Russian/russian_history.html

YMCA personnel record: Charles W. Riley, forwarded by YMCA of the USA Archives letter of 13 January 1994, University of Minnesota, 2642 University Ave, St Paul, MN 55114 (courtesy of David Carmichael).
Young Sik Kim, 'The Sacrificial Lamb of the Cold War: The Nationalists of Korea', Seattle, available at www.kimsoft.com/2001/abook.htm, 2000.
Zaloga, Steven J., 'Soviet Armoured Trains', n.p., 2001, available at www.aopt91.dsl.pipex.com/railgun/Content/Armoured%20Trains/Russian/russian_1.html

INDEX

Adagiri, General 246–7
Adrianovka 47, 70, 159–60, 163–4, 178, 184–5, 191, 196, 217–18, 240, 264, 293, 390
Advisory Commission of Railway Experts 61, 82, 94–5, 314–16
Afanas'ev, Mikhail, Lieutenant General 138, 217, 261–2, 300
Aga 66, 69–71, 164
Aivazov, M.E. 287–9, 396
Aksenov, G.N. 166
alcoholism 11–12, 21, 28, 55, 67, 78, 85, 121, 132, 135–6, 138, 143–5, 149, 155, 160, 171, 176, 186, 230, 285
Aleksandra, Empress 238
Aleksandrovskii Zavod 88, 167, 205
Aleksandrovskoe 121
Alekseevsk 102, 155, 238
Alioshin, D. 272, 275, 392
Al-Kadir, Prince 41, 201, 317
Altan Bulag *see* Maimachen
American Expeditionary Force, Siberia 93, 99–101, 109, 138, 148–9, 152–3, 170–4, 177–8, 196–8, 203–4, 225–30, 289, 313
American Legion 288, 290
American Red Cross 90, 115, 126, 152–3, 182, 225, 366
Amur Cossack Host 8, 69, 102–3, 119, 122, 140
anarchists 31, 38, 58, 70, 84–7, 102–3, 105, 121, 140, 167, 259, 349–50
Ando, Colonel 302
Andreev, Commander 246–7, 259, 387
Angara (icebreaker) 81–3, 214, 258, 263, 377
Angara River 5, 51, 208–12
Anichkov, V. 260
Annenkov, B.V. 50, 113, 148, 155, 241, 279, 311, 361, 385
Antonov, V.G. 282, 394
Anuchino 283–4

Aquitania, RMS 290–1
Araki Sadao, General 305
Argun Cossack Regiment 52, 73, 110
Argun River 140, 169, 296, 298, 304
armored trains 65, 72–3, 77–9, 81–3, 88, 91–2, 98–9, 102–3, 109, 112, 120, 137, 140, 145, 147–8, 154, 156, 157–66, 169–73, 178, 182, 184, 191, 201, 204, 207, 210, 212, 216–18, 222–3, 237–40, 245–6, 250–4, 263, 283, 318, 322–5, 356, 374, 378, 390, 398; Ataman 159, 164–6; Atamanovskaya 78; Bezposhchadnyi 159, 162, 170–3, 177–8, 184; Bi-Yats 159, 164; Edinenie Rossii 245, 323; Groznyi 158–9, 163–4, 324, 367; Istrebitel' 159–60, 216, 221–2, 324; Khrabryi 264; Mstitel' 159, 164–5, 195–6, 325; Orlik 240, 252–5; Spravedlivyi 264; Stanichnik 240
Artem'ev, Lieutenant General 193, 208, 212
Artomonov, General 208
Asano Detachment 308
Ataman Kalmykov Khabarovsk Military School 118
Ataman Semenov Military School 111, 301
Atkinson, J.S. 136
aviation 99, 107, 109, 111–12, 182, 211, 239, 264, 280, 282, 291, 298, 306, 310, 326, 356, 390

Badam-Dorzhi 190, 268
Badmazhanov, T. 189
Baerlein, H. 193, 223, 281, 335
Baggs, R.L. 147, 168
Baikal (icebreaker) 13, 81–3, 258
Baker, N.D. 93
Bakhmet'ev, A.A. 289
Baksheev, A.P., General 185, 304, 308, 310–11
Baldwin Locomotive Company 94

441

INDEX

Balyabin, F. 52
Bank of Chosen *see* Chosen Bank
Bao Huit-sing, General 239–41
barakholka 292–3
Baratov, N.N. 29–30, 336
Bargut Mongols 48–51, 188–90, 271, 276, 292, 372
Barrett, W.S. 137
Barrows, D.P. 61, 63–6, 69, 72, 78–80, 98–9, 103, 107, 122, 130, 132, 137, 190, 288, 344–5
Bashkirs 271
Bazilevskii, V.G. 82, 258
beggars 154–5, 193
Bell, J.M. 54–6, 67, 90–1, 96–7, 100, 139, 165, 342
Berenbaum, M. 133
Beresovka 170, 172–3, 177, 208, 369, 386
Berezovskii, C. 40–1, 317, 338
Bezrodnov, Captain 276
biological warfare 305
Black Squadron 137, 362
Blagosh, Doctor 252, 388
Blagoveshchensk 16, 28, 51, 59, 69–70, 85, 88, 101–3, 120–2, 133, 155, 158, 169, 180, 186, 194–5, 208, 223, 231, 245, 248–9, 279, 298, 311, 354, 373, 393
Blyukher, V.K., General 283, 297–8
Bochkarev, V.I., Captain 259, 284–5, 394
Bochkarevo 121
Bodoo, D. 280, 292, 391, 397
Bogdat' 195, 199
Bogdo Khan *see* Khutuktu
Bogomolets, N., General 160, 221–2
Bogomyag, G. 52
Bogomyagkov, S.G. 166
Boldyrev, V.G., General 234, 245, 265, 357, 383
Borah, W.E., Senator 290–2, 313
Borisov, B. 27, 334
Borodin, M.I. 167–8
Borzya 47, 52, 64–5, 73–4, 86, 88–9, 106, 180, 184, 195–6, 199–201, 218, 233–5, 250, 264, 348
boutiques 116, 135
Boxer Rebellion 16, 41, 333, 342
Breitner, B. 137, 312
BREM 307–8
British Army: 25th Middlesex Battalion 93, 99, 124–5, 175; British Gun Train Company 158–9
British Military Mission 60, 113, 378
Brooklyn, USS 153
Broz, Major 228
Brusak, I.N. 211–14, 225, 359, 377

Budberg, B.A.P. 63, 78, 115, 136, 138, 140, 189, 311, 344–5, 431
Bukhedu 49, 126, 153, 240
Bulgakov-Bel'skii, I.G. 230
Bulgun River 281
Burikov, Colonel 115–16, 135, 344
Business Cabinet 91, 98, 105, 323
Butenko, Colonel 114, 119, 123, 196, 224
Butin, I.A. 51, 62, 85, 186, 349
Byers, F.B., Lieutenant 229

C.B. Richard & Company 287–8
Canadian Siberian Expeditionary Force 147, 183, 364
Cassini Convention 15–16, 41, 270, 297
Central Bureau of Military Organizations 196
Chang Ching-hui, General 270, 273
Changchun 18, 116, 124–5, 232, 250, 285, 296, 299, 309–10, 312, 322, 359, 388
Chang Kuan-hsiang, General 78
Chang Kui-Vu, General 79
Chang Tso-Lin, Marshal 41, 54–5, 181, 199, 237, 256–7, 267, 273, 279–80, 284, 286, 296–7, 312, 342
CHEKA 37–8, 47, 49, 80, 117, 236, 238, 258, 281, 285, 301, 323, 340, 346, 395
Chelyabinsk 76, 158, 197
chemical warfare 77
Cherven-Vodali, A. 209, 215
Chicherin, G.V. 249
Chinese Army 16, 22, 43, 48, 53–4, 73–4, 78, 97, 120, 129, 144, 159, 179, 181, 191, 231, 237, 239, 241, 246, 250, 252–5, 262, 268–70, 278–81, 298–9; 1st Heilong Jiang Brigade 239; 1st Kirin Brigade 239; 1st Mukden Brigade 239; 3rd Mixed Infantry Brigade 181; 19th Mukden Mixed Brigade 179; 28th Division 280; Armored Train Division 398
Chinese Eastern Railway 13–14, 16–18, 32, 41–5, 48–9, 53–7, 61–3, 68–74, 89, 95, 98, 115, 127, 129, 146, 148, 150, 156, 169, 179–83, 240–1, 243, 250, 255–7, 279, 297, 302, 305–7, 311–12
Chinese Eastern Railway Board 61, 67–8, 74, 241
Chinese Eastern Railway Militia 42, 44–5, 55, 61, 67, 121, 257
Chita 1, 7, 8, 10, 18–19, 23–5, 33, 35–8, 45–7, 51–3, 62, 66, 84–9, 104–9, 116, 132–3, 218, 239, 249–51, 256–8, 261–4, 282, 292–3, 295, 313, 355
Chita police 84–5, 105, 142, 167, 368
Chita Republic 19, 35, 36–7, 107
Chita stopper 249, 264, 387

INDEX

Choibalsan, K. 269–70, 276, 292, 294, 387
cholera 182, 193, 218, 317
Chosen Bank 89, 257, 306, 313
Chu Chi-hsiang, General 273
Churchill, M., Brigadier General 227
Clark, B.P. 35, 78, 87
Cohen, M. 304
Colby, D.S., Major 229, 236–7, 242, 250, 252–4
Coltman, C.L. 272
Comintern 273, 294–5, 396
Compatangelo, Lieutenant Colonel 287
Concordia Society *see* Manchukuo
Constituent Assembly 19, 34–6, 46–8, 50, 52, 55, 80, 96–8, 108, 117, 132, 196, 214, 217, 285, 320–1, 361
Cossack League 106, 113, 129
Counterintelligence: Japanese 305; Soviet 306, 310, 327; White 55, 109, 133, 139, 142–3, 150–1, 167, 211, 251, 276, 277, 283, 284, 294, 325, 376
currency 51, 120, 123, 127, 150, 194, 210, 236, 257, 258, 293, 322, 325, 328, 364
Czechoslovakians: 1st Infantry Battalion, Czechoslovakian Red Army 150; 1st Penza Czechoslovakian Revolutionary Regiment 150
Czechoslovak Legion 75–7, 79, 81–4, 86–7, 90–3, 98, 147, 150–2, 173, 203–4, 206–8, 215, 232–3, 236, 240, 254, 256, 258, 262, 312–13, 347, 376, 383; 2nd Division 98; 3rd Division 237, 252–3; 5th Regiment 99; 6th Regiment 213; 7th Regiment 81–2, 90, 106; 12th Regiment 254; Artillery Regiment 246

Dairen 18, 21, 55, 116, 255, 284, 295–307, 310, 323
Dalai Lama 19–21, 271, 281, 324
Dauria 28, 37, 40–5, 53, 63, 78, 84–7, 142–3, 186–7, 189–91, 200–1, 250, 256, 262–4, 266–7, 289
Davidson, J.S., First Lieutenant 115, 122, 185, 190, 198, 207
Davis, E.N., Sergeant 229–30, 421, 424
Death trains 125–7, 211, 359
Denny, R.B. 60, 63
Derber, P.Y. 50, 91
Derber Government *see* Provisional Government of Autonomous Siberia
disease 10, 11–12, 21, 93, 126, 149, 182, 193, 218, 243, 317
Diterikhs, M.K., Major General 89–90, 98, 150, 153, 262, 285, 351
Dockray, Major 270, 275, 277, 392

Doihara Kenji, General 298–9, 399
Dom Nikitin 106, 239
Domrachev, A.V. 133, 142–3, 294
Dorzhiev, A.L. 19–20, 23, 334
Dotsenko, P. 105, 192, 208, 210
Dovgal, Madame 165
Dragulich, Colonel 151, 406
droshky 323, 365
Dutov, A.I., Lieutenant Colonel 37, 113, 155, 187, 311, 364, 400
Dyboski, R. 93, 100–1, 400
Dzham Bolon 271

Earle, E. 114–15, 290
Easter 11, 154, 251–2
Eichelberger, R.L. 148, 197, 198, 244
Elmsley, J.H., Major General 147
Emerson, G.H. 82–3, 94, 348
Empress of Russia 287
Engineer Report 1918 348
Eruchina 165–6
Evenks 2, 6, 8–9, 35
Evetskii, A., Colonel 248

Fainberg, M. 289, 396
Far Eastern Republic 237, 248–9, 260–1, 263–5, 273, 277–9, 284–5, 291, 293, 387, 395
Far Eastern Union of Servicemen (DVSV) 301
Farvater 204
Fay, H.V.V., Captain 138, 147, 190–1, 246–7, 387
Fedorov, S.A., Grand Duke 18, 238
Fedorovna, E., Grand Princess 238, 262, 286
field courts 42, 141, 182, 328
Field Police Service 151, 218
Flanagan, F.A., Major 193, 205, 235
Flegontov, A.K. 108, 311, 355, 387
Fleming, P. 34, 55, 68, 71, 104, 132, 203, 243, 264, 342
Footman, D. 24, 137, 334–5
forest communes 88, 163, 166, 195, 325, 350
Fowler, H., Consul 201–2, 221
Freiberg, E.N. 258
Freiburg, Lieutenant Colonel 161, 163, 166, 368
French Military Mission 56, 60, 128, 147, 197, 364, 376
Frunze, M. 35, 311
Fu Chia Tien 53–4
Fujii, General 86–8, 90, 129–30, 360
Fukuda, General 254
Fukushima Yasumasa, Captain 14
Fussenge, General 190–1, 267

443

INDEX

Gajda, R. 82, 86, 90, 106–7, 150, 152, 183, 203–5, 312, 349, 355
Gamov, A. 102–3, 121–2
Gao Fin Tonen, Major General 120, 358
Gao Sin Shan, Major General 120, 407
Gazimurskii Zavod 167
Ghengis Khan 3, 330
Girsa (doctor) 89, 383
Gludkin, Colonel 282
gold 84–5, 105, 108, 121, 135, 137, 140–1, 176, 187, 190, 202, 205, 212, 230, 232, 237–8, 239, 244, 255, 259, 261, 264, 270, 276, 280, 283, 288–9, 293, 300, 306, 312–13
Goloustnoe 81–2
Gongota 251, 259–61
Gospolokhrana 285, 324, 395
Grant, Captain 109, 111, 165, 214
Graves, W.S. 93, 112–13, 144–5, 153, 156–7, 173–4, 183, 193–7, 201, 204, 222, 224–5, 227–9, 242, 288, 290, 295, 313
Gravis, J.C., Major 177, 201–2
Great Northern, USAT 229, 242, 245
Great Northern and Western Railroad 82, 94, 314
Gridnev, V.V. 301
Grishin-Almazov, A.N. 50, 77, 113, 347
Grodekovo 26, 91, 97–8, 187, 197, 230–1, 248, 263, 265, 282–4, 286, 319, 335, 390
Grondijs, L.H. 89, 135, 165, 350
Guptill, A.M. 274–5, 277, 391
Gusinoozersk 281, 394

Hailar 43, 45, 48–9, 57, 63, 80, 179, 181, 232–3, 239–40, 251–6, 271, 299, 301
Handaohedzy 182
Hankow 270, 308, 342
Harbin 17–18, 28, 41–4, 50, 53–6, 58–75, 78–9, 91, 97, 115–16, 119, 122–3, 141, 147, 182, 201, 232, 237–41, 250, 255–7, 296–312
Harris, E.L., Consul General 171, 174, 208–10, 226–7
Hata Shunroku, General 305
Heald, E. 92, 126, 131–3, 153–4, 174, 184
Hersman, H.S., Congressman 288
Hiroyama, Colonel 271
Hitachi Maru 56, 342
Hizen 205
Hoffmann, General 218
Horvath, D.L. 44–5, 48–9, 53, 55–6, 59–63, 67, 69, 72–4, 77, 90–1, 95, 97–8, 113–14, 129, 141, 144, 146, 156, 174, 176–7, 180, 197, 208, 239, 241, 295
Hoshino, General 235, 254, 256
Hotel Dauria (Chita) 85, 264

Hotel Selekt (Chita) 85, 105, 109–10, 135, 138, 147–8, 264, 295
Hsingan Bureau 302–3
Hsui Shu-cheng, General 267
Hungarians 39, 52, 57, 62, 64, 66, 76, 81–3, 85–6, 88, 92, 103, 116, 146, 211, 247
hunghutze 25, 54, 56, 140, 181, 194, 257, 278, 282, 284, 302

Iman 96–7, 100, 145, 187–8, 196, 230, 248
Imyanpo 182
Inagaki, Lieutenant General 128, 209
Ingoda River 107, 140, 185, 202, 249–51
Innokentii 81–2
insignia 112–13, 152, 205–6, 218, 248, 262
intelligence: Allied 57, 80, 92, 99, 106, 110, 254, 342, 354; Czechoslovak 228; Japanese 21–2, 54, 58–9, 69, 79, 188, 198, 207, 299, 301–2, 308; Manchukuo 299–300, 305; Soviet 168, 214, 229, 301, 307, 311; US 99, 109, 122, 128, 130, 135, 138, 147–8, 190, 197, 226–7, 246, 287, 288, 353; White 55, 56, 57, 63, 109, 110, 113, 118, 161, 201, 229, 270, 273, 308, 318, 327, 349
Inter-Allied Railway Agreement 155–6
Inter-Allied Technical Board 155–6, 179, 246, 290
internationalists 38–9, 47, 51–2, 57–8, 64–5, 70, 76, 79, 81, 84–6, 88, 91–2, 101, 116, 150–1, 167, 238, 247, 276, 280, 309, 312, 350, 354
interventionists 91–3, 152, 211, 231, 242, 245
Irkutsk 6–7, 9–10, 13, 18–19, 33, 36–40, 47, 50–2, 60, 79, 81–2, 129–30, 134–5, 183, 192–3, 207–20, 223, 225–7, 235–7, 263, 273, 278–80
Irtysh River 4, 117, 134, 202
Ishikawa, Major 100, 231, 382
Ishimitsu Makiyo, Major 102
Isome, Colonel 261
Italians 4, 45, 124–5, 146–7, 168, 217, 271, 287, 309, 364
Itzkovich, G. 33, 123–4
Ivanov, V. 282
Ivanov, V.F. 300
Ivanovka 91, 298
Ivanov-Rinov, P.P. 50, 106, 113–14, 132, 148, 154, 192, 284, 311, 365

Janin, M. 75, 128, 147, 207, 209, 215, 217, 233, 287, 364
Japanese Imperial Army 14, 59, 85, 87, 105, 109, 112, 116–18, 122–7, 129–30, 145, 149–50, 165, 169, 172, 179, 184, 187,

INDEX

191, 194, 198, 201, 210, 221, 231, 235, 240, 242–3, 247–60, 262–3, 264, 271, 279, 282, 285, 298, 305, 308, 343; 3rd Division 198, 287, 373; 5th Division 122, 198, 249; 7th Division 61, 80, 86–7, 90, 122; 12th Division 90, 98, 100–1, 119; 13th Division 217, 220, 246; 14th Division 246; Kwantung Army 59, 102, 299, 302–3, 305–6, 309, 399; Unit 731; *see also* biological warfare
Japanese intelligence *see* intelligence: Japanese
Japanese Military Mission-Harbin 59, 70, 123, 135, 302, 305, 308
Japanese volunteer battalion 78, 80, 348
Japanese war effort 56
Jews 19, 33, 53, 98, 111, 134, 136–7, 147, 187, 239, 258–9, 261, 276, 280, 288, 291, 297, 303–4; anti-Semitism 98, 136–7, 187, 239, 258–9, 261, 276, 304; Hebrew Association of Manchuria 303
Johnson, B.O., Lieutenant Colonel 202, 232, 235, 313

Kaigorodov, A.P., Colonel 278–9, 281, 311, 393
Kaka-Kashi 306–7, 310, 400
Kalmykov, I.P. 35–6, 69, 73, 92, 96–101, 113–14, 118–20, 122, 143–6, 148, 152, 155, 169–70, 187–8, 195–7, 204, 208, 223–4, 230–2, 247, 263, 319–21, 324, 326
Kalmykov Detachment *see* OKO
Kamennov, A.M. 109
Kansk 49–50, 219
Kanzan So 21–2, 188, 324
Kao Tsai-ting, General 271
Kapanov, Captain 164–5
Kappel, V.O., General 213, 225, 234
Kappel Army 213, 232, 240, 242, 251, 260, 262–5, 282, 388
Karachen Mongols *see* Mongols
Karaul Khathyl 279
Karymskaya 13–14, 47, 66, 70, 87, 112, 133, 163–4, 176, 186, 235, 240, 263–4, 293, 361, 370
Kaspe, S. 303–4
Katanaev, G.E., Lieutenant General 141–2, 286
Kato Kanji, Admiral 62, 90
Kaufman, A. 303–4
Kazagrandi, Colonel 271, 276, 278–9, 281, 392
Keller, B.A.A., Colonel 25, 335
Kelley, W.A., First Lieutenant 196, 200–1
Kendall, P.W., Lieutenant 222, 313
Khabarovsk 14, 37, 39, 59, 70, 79, 87, 91, 96, 98–102, 118–20, 135, 143–6, 148–50, 152, 167, 169, 187–8, 196–7, 206, 223, 230–1, 244–8, 257, 259–61, 282–3, 298, 310–11, 353
Khada-Bulak 88, 166, 199–201, 264
Khalkin Gol River 306
Kharanor 53, 63–4, 85–7, 263, 390
Kharashibersk 220
Khilok 178, 237–8, 249, 386
Khor 170, 248, 261
Khreshchatitskii, B.R., General 45, 97–8, 109, 140, 261, 263, 311, 339
Khutuktu, J. 21–2, 24, 189, 267–70, 272–3, 276–9, 294, 325
Kim, A.P. 58, 101, 353
Kirgizov, S.S. 168, 234
Kiselev, Major General 26
Kislitsyn, V.A., General 308
Kiyakovskii, V.S. 295, 397
Klukvennaya 219
Knights of Columbus 152–3, 225
Knox, A.W.F., Major General 60, 113–15, 119, 127, 138, 141, 147, 198, 204, 343, 357
Ko, General 278
Kobdo 22, 28, 189, 278–9, 281, 325, 334
Kolchak, A.V., Admiral 66–74, 97, 114–15, 117, 119, 127–32, 135, 138, 141, 145, 147, 154–5, 163, 170, 175–7, 179–81, 183, 192–3, 198, 201, 202–4, 206–7, 212–15, 217, 225, 228, 241, 251, 261, 286, 345
Kolesnikov, V. 51
Kolusatai 62–3, 65
Kopal, Lieutenant Colonel 253
Koreans 9, 15, 38, 57–8, 61, 78, 80, 101, 146, 167, 206, 271, 305, 353, 368
Kornilov, L., General 35, 40
Kos'min, V.D. 300, 398
Kraevski 91–2, 98–9, 158
Krakovetskii, A.A., Colonel 33, 50, 108, 224–5, 245
Krasilnikov, I.N. 117, 155, 193
Krasnoshchekov, A.M. 37, 54, 100, 103, 223, 236, 242, 248–9, 255, 259–61, 263–5, 279, 282, 294, 311, 338, 384, 386, 389, 400
Krasnov, P.N., General 45, 310
Krasnoyarsk 5, 38, 52, 117, 124, 147–8, 155, 158, 193, 197, 205–6, 213, 215, 219, 386
Kronstadt 76, 111, 282
Krugobaikalets 81–2
Krupskii, G., Colonel 226, 288, 290–1, 380, 396
Krymov, A.M., General 27, 35
Kudashev, N.A., Prince 41, 48, 60, 67–8, 189, 262, 267, 295, 343, 390
Kulikov, E.D. 233–4
Kulikov, I.I. 43

INDEX

Kultuk 135, 209
Kunst and Albers 237, 384
Kuo Tsung-hsi 69
Kurizawa, Captain 255
Kuroki Chikayochi 61, 72, 80, 124, 127, 135–6, 138, 161, 198, 318, 348
Kurozawa Jun, Lieutenant Colonel 59
Kurunzulaya 166, 168, 369
Kuznetsov, Ataman 208, 223
Kuznetsov, I.A. 220
Kuznetsov Museum 24
Kyakhta 6, 14, 25, 35, 76, 188–9, 221, 223, 266–7, 269, 271, 274–8, 325, 328

labor unions 19, 195, 297
Lake Baikal 2–6, 8–9, 11, 13, 34, 81–4, 127–9, 135, 156, 172, 206, 209, 215, 258, 278, 293, 311, 322
Lake Buyr Nur 280, 301
Lake Khasan 305
Lake Tulba 281
Lake Urmia 29–30, 39, 336
Lantry, Colonel 122, 160, 163, 180, 183, 207
Lapta, Commander 231
Lazo, S.G. 38, 52–3, 62, 65–6, 70–4, 77–8, 80, 85, 87–8, 102, 111, 224–5, 234, 241, 244–5, 258–9, 305, 325, 341, 345
Lebedev, E.V. 220
Lebedeva-Kyashko, N.P. 243, 260–1
Leckie, R.G. 288, 395
Lenin, V.I. 19, 34, 36, 39, 42, 44, 46, 49, 52, 57, 62, 76, 92, 157–8, 248–9, 261–2, 320–1
Lepushanski, Lieutenant 121
Levitskii, General 206, 208, 220–3
Li, Doctor 393
Likin 134–5
Lin Fu-Man, Major General 53
Ling Sheng 303
Listvinichnaya 17–18, 81–2, 210, 214
Lithuanians 27, 62, 146, 305
Little Hsu *see* Hsui Shu-cheng
Lobanov (Miss) 164–5
Loubignac, Colonel 252
Lutskii, A. 244–5, 259
Lvov, Colonel 208
Lyuskov, G. 305

McCroskey, B.B., Lieutenant Colonel 225–31, 242, 288
McDonald, J.F., Lieutenant 164, 166, 184–5, 368
McNutt, G.I., Lieutenant 160, 163–4, 179–80, 184, 367
Madievskii, Sub-Lieutenant 40, 44
Madras 153

Magdeburg 92, 351, 367
magistral 12–13, 16, 157–91, 203, 207, 213, 218–19, 314–16, 325
Magocha 89
Magruder, J., Major 272
Mahagala 272
Maimachen 189, 277–8, 325
Makeev, Captain 281, 392
Maketno, Captain 280, 301, 313
Makkaveevo 109, 164, 184–6, 195, 300
Malinovskii, General 255
Manchukuo 295, 299–312, 322, 324–6, 357, 387–8, 398–9; Concordia Society 299, 305, 325
Manchuli 17, 42–9, 53, 55, 59–64, 68–9, 71, 73–4, 76, 78–80, 85–7, 89, 104, 110, 112, 116, 122, 123, 124–5, 127–30, 134–5, 140, 160, 175, 178–81, 184, 191, 199, 200, 216, 235–6, 239, 250, 252, 255–6, 262–5, 277, 279, 281, 298, 299, 300, 317, 318, 325
Manchuria 5, 13–18, 21, 41–2, 46, 48, 53–6, 58–9, 62, 67, 90, 110, 114, 116, 124, 125, 150, 181, 188, 225, 239, 240, 257, 279, 296, 299, 302, 303, 305; Manchurian Incident 299; Three Rivers settlements 296; Toogenskii settlements 296, 298
Manstein, H.V. 262, 287–92
Marconi Radio *see* radio communications
Mariinskii Theatre 33, 132–3, 136, 294
Matkovskii, M.A. 215, 308
Matsievskaya 53, 77–9, 87, 264
Matsievski, Major General 66, 86
Medi, Colonel 162, 170–1, 179, 301, 318
Medvedev, A.S. 224–5, 234, 245, 248–9, 255, 257, 259, 261–5, 282, 384
Mendebayar, N.G. 190
Merkulov, N. 282–4
Merkulov, S.D. 282–5
Merritt, USS 395
Mezhak, Major General 49, 170, 172
Mikasa 199
Mikhailov, M.M., Lieutenant Colonel 278–9
Mikhailovski Hunting and Fishing Society 117
Military Intelligence Division 287
Miller, H. 314–16
Miller, W.C., Lieutenant Colonel 156, 170
Mills, E.W. 272
Minami Jiro, General 302, 399
Ministry of Ways and Communications 94, 183, 314
von Mirbach, W., Ambassador Count 80, 238, 342
Mirovskii, V. 150
Missyuri, General 208
Mogzon 84, 87, 129–30, 217, 237–8, 249

INDEX

Mongol–Buryat Regiment *see* Russian military units
Mongolia 6, 19–26, 28, 56–8, 108, 175, 188–91, 266–81, 294–5, 301–6, 308
Mongolian Alliance League 302
Mongolian Army 3–4, 22, 267–9, 306, 309
Mongolian People's Party 276–7, 294
Mongolian State Internal Security 295, 301, 324
Mongolian Trading Company 272–3, 391
Mongols 2–4, 6, 9–10, 19–23, 48, 78, 181, 188–91, 267, 269–71, 278–9, 302–3; Bargut Mongols 48–9, 51, 188–90, 271, 276, 292, 372; Buryat Mongols 1–3, 5–6, 8, 9–10, 18–20, 26, 27, 33, 46, 52, 65, 85, 107, 111, 188–91, 271, 274–5, 276, 279–81, 292, 294, 295, 298; Chahar Mongols 220, 269–72, 276, 278, 279, 302; Karachen Mongols 48; Khalka Mongols 6, 18, 21, 24, 181, 269
Moore, F.F., Captain 104, 109, 115, 121, 135, 138, 178, 189
Morris, R.S., Ambassador 107, 130, 163, 185, 193–4
Morrow, C.H., Colonel 100–1, 156, 163, 170, 172–4, 177, 183–4, 220–3, 225–9, 242, 288, 290–1
Motono I., Foreign Minister 59, 61–2, 344
Murav'ev, N.N. 8, 12, 14, 38, 81, 330–1
Murav'evo-Amurskii 100, 259, 325
Murphy, J.K. 289
Muto Nobuyoshi, General 61–2, 68, 72, 78, 116, 123, 299, 346
Mysovaya 13, 17–18, 83, 156, 168, 171–2, 209, 215, 232–3, 237, 239, 325, 332, 383

Nakajima Masatake, Major General 59–62, 68, 70–3, 96–7, 102, 122, 127, 346
Nakhabov, N. 287
Naletov, P.I. 186, 341
Natsvalov, N.G., Major General 63, 65, 140–3, 175, 318
Natsvalova, Z.A. 141–2
Nechaev, K.P., Lieutenant General 297, 312, 398
Nedorezov, K.G. 36
Nerchinsk 5, 7–8, 14, 23, 70, 88–9, 129, 133, 135, 165, 167, 195, 233–4, 251, 262–3, 333, 345, 373
New Siberian Army *see* Russian military units: Siberian Army
Nicholas II, T. 12–13, 15, 18–21, 26, 30–1, 67, 79–80, 206, 304
Nikiforov, P.M. 225, 234, 245, 260–1, 263, 380
Nikolaevsk-on-Amur 187, 203, 223, 231, 243–4, 248, 258–61, 294–5, 344

Nikolsk-Ussuriisk 14, 69, 90–2, 96–9, 101, 104, 119–20, 126–7, 144–5, 150, 153, 161, 182, 187, 223–5, 230–2, 239, 245–8, 256–7, 259, 261, 265, 282, 285, 351, 358, 387
Nikonov, M.P., Lieutenant General 63, 105, 118
Nizhne-Udinsk 77, 208, 212–13
NKVD 295, 298, 301, 305, 310, 324
Nomonhan 306, 308
Noriyoshi Yokoo, Captain 96
Novo-Dmitrievka 280–1
Novo-Doronino 202
Novonikolaevsk 50, 76, 124, 207, 215, 281, 326, 378
Novo-Selengensk 281
NRA *see* Russian military units

Oba, General 122, 130, 172, 198, 287
Ogata, Major General 220–1, 223
Oi, General 98, 101–2, 118, 145, 201–2, 248, 258–61, 265
Okabe, Captain 118–19
OKO 73, 97–100, 118, 143–5, 169, 187–8, 223–5, 230–2, 246–8, 259, 293, 324
Okumura Naonari, Captain 78, 348
Old Believers 8–9, 19, 107, 113, 327, 331
Olga 248, 284
Olovyannaya 43, 47, 65–6, 72, 86, 88–90, 106, 122, 126, 158–9, 164, 168, 178, 184, 199, 216–17, 240–1, 258, 340, 390
Olympia, USS 93, 151
OMO 46–53, 59–74, 76–80, 85–9, 104–16, 122, 127–30, 132–42, 147–8, 150–2, 156, 159–63, 167, 170–5, 177–80, 182–91, 197, 200–2, 205–6, 208, 210–22, 226, 230, 232, 234, 236–42, 249–52, 254–8, 262–4, 269, 271, 273–4, 282–4, 286, 291, 298, 301, 310, 313
Omsk 49–50, 74, 76–7, 91, 106, 112–14, 117, 123–5, 127, 131–4, 141, 147–8, 150, 152–5, 171, 177, 193, 197–8, 201–7, 215, 228, 236, 305
Onon River 2–3, 23, 47, 61, 65–6, 69–73, 76, 86, 88, 159, 216, 258, 263, 345, 350
Oparin, Staff Captain 41, 317
orders of battle 78, 86, 99, 110, 114, 169, 218, 275, 318, 336
Orenburg Cossacks 24, 187, 251, 311
Orlov, A.A. 268
Orlov Detachment *see* Russian military units
Oshima Ken'ichi, War Minister 57, 342, 346
Ossendowski, F. 28, 139, 271–2, 276–9
Ostroumov, B.V. 297, 314
Ostrovskii, Colonel 277, 281
Otani, General 89, 101, 106, 119, 353, 404

447

Palestine 262
Pan-Mongol movement 19, 108, 181, 188–91, 205, 255, 267–8, 303, 372
Pao Kwei-ching, General 255
von Pappenheim, W.H.K., Captain 56–7
partisans 35, 86–8, 99, 109, 112, 140, 145–6, 148, 154–5, 161, 163, 165–70, 174, 178, 181–2, 187–8, 194–6, 199–203, 205–6, 211–13, 215, 219–24, 229–40, 242–5, 247, 249–51, 258–60, 263–4, 266, 276, 281, 283–5, 297, 300–1, 311, 325
Pavlunovskii, Chairman 281
Pearl Harbor attack 308
Pechanga 205
Pepelyaev, A.N. 50, 213
Pepelyaev, V. 213, 225
Perezhogin, E. 84–5, 102–2, 313
Petrov, L. 310, 312
Petrovskii Zavod 220, 234, 326
Pleshkov, M.M., General 59, 61–3, 67–8, 73–4, 79, 97–8, 114, 311
Podogaev, F.A. 234
Pogranichnaya 17, 49, 62, 73, 97, 120, 122, 182, 197–8, 241, 248, 256–7, 265, 285, 298, 358
pogroms 136–7, 276, 278, 258–9
poison 3, 77, 87, 189–90, 199, 223, 235, 294, 340, 372
Poles 9, 38–9, 53, 57, 79, 92–3, 100, 125, 128, 139, 146, 149, 151–2, 203, 219, 342, 351, 364, 378–9; 1st Polish Infantry Battalion 151–2
Polish Legion 92–3, 151–2, 351, 379
Political Center 208–14, 217, 219, 235–6, 376–7
Pontovich, Lieutenant 63
Popov, N.L., Captain 96
Port Arthur 14–15, 17–18, 23, 55–6, 67, 123, 265, 282–3, 296, 310, 326
Port Baikal 81, 83, 214–15
Posol'skaya 83, 171–2, 221–2, 226, 289, 313, 379
Post 159 186
prisoners-of-war 36, 38–41, 47, 51–3, 57–8, 62, 64, 66, 70, 73, 76, 79, 81–2, 89, 92, 99–102, 107, 117, 120, 123, 125–7, 131, 137, 139, 145–6, 151–2, 159–60, 170, 174, 201, 204, 211, 218, 222, 248, 272, 305, 312, 317, 321, 338, 342, 346
prostitution 11, 54, 112, 149, 171, 244, 298–9, 331
Provisional Government of Autonomous Siberia (PGAS) 50, 69, 77, 91, 341
Provisional Government of Pribaikalia 236
Provisional Priamur Government 282, 284

Provisional Siberian Government (PSG) 77, 91, 95, 106–7, 112–15, 117–19, 123, 127–9, 142, 181, 192, 361
Puntsag 276
Pu-Yi, H. 299, 324

radio communications 62, 158, 214, 236, 238, 256, 258, 270, 275, 277, 300, 374, 386
railway workshops 107, 157, 162, 178, 239, 315, 320–1
rats 154–5, 366
Rattach, H., Lieutenant 216–17
Razdolnoe 265, 282
Red Terror 40, 49–53, 105, 107–8, 117, 183, 311, 395
Reed, J. 95
refugees 29, 38–9, 54, 107, 110, 116, 131, 142, 149, 153–5, 182–3, 202–3, 205–7, 213, 218, 232, 236, 239, 256–7, 260, 265, 267, 270, 279, 281, 284–6, 292–3, 296–7, 300, 307, 336, 346, 395
Regional Popular Assembly 257–8, 262, 382
Reitzel, G.B. 148, 150, 155, 183, 363
Rice, C.R. 161
Rinchino, E. 292, 294, 396
Riutin, M.N., Ensign 42, 53, 182, 339
Rodzaevskii, K.V. 300, 302–4, 308–11
Romanov, N. 121, 135–6, 140, 147, 154, 175–6
Rozanov, S., General 137, 177, 193, 195, 197–8, 203–5, 224, 244, 371, 380
Rumanians 57, 62, 90, 111, 116, 128, 146, 151–2, 203, 211, 219, 235, 280
Rumsha, K., Colonel 151–2, 219, 379
Russian All-Military Union (ROVS) 301, 311
Russian Fascist Party 300, 302
Russian military units: 1st Amur Anarchist-Communist Regiment 259; 1st Argun Cavalry Regiment 86; 1st Argun Cossack Regiment 52, 73, 87; 1st Ataman Semenov Cavalry Regiment 176; 1st Chita Cossack Regiment 47, 86–7; 1st Chita Internationalist Detachment 280; 1st Infantry Battalion, Czechoslovakian Red Army 150; 1st International Partisan Division 86; 1st Irkutsk Soviet Division 237–8, 249–50; 1st Irkutsk Territorial Brigade 208; 1st Khabarovsk International Partisan Detachment 99; 1st Khabarovsk Ussuri Cossack Regiment 144; 1st Manchurian Ataman Semenov Regiment 218; 1st Manchurian Regiment 77; 1st Nerchinsk Regiment 25–7, 31; 1st Penza Czechoslovakian Revolutionary Regiment 150; 1st Revolutionary Transbaikal Cossack Division 52;

INDEX

1st Semenov Infantry Regiment 110, 318; 1st Separate Transbaikal Cossack Brigade 234; 1st Transbaikal Corps 264; 1st Transbaikal Cossack Regiment 169, 177; 1st Transbaikal Semenov Regiment 195; 1st Verkhne-Udinsk Cossack Regiment 51; 2nd Amur Rifle Division 263; 2nd Argun Cavalry Regiment 86; 2nd Ataman Semenov Cavalry Regiment 218; 2nd Chita Cossack Revolutionary Regiment 51; 2nd Daurski Mounted Regiment 78, 318; 2nd Daurski Regiment 110; 2nd Manchurian Ataman Semenov Regiment 218; 2nd Manchurian Infantry Regiment 110; 2nd Nerchinsk Cossack Regiment 51; 2nd Verkhne-Udinsk Revolutionary Regiment 86, 133; 2nd Zargol Detachment 86; 3rd Irkutsk Territorial Brigade 208; 3rd Tomsk Regiment 88; 3rd Transbaikal Cossack Regiment 169, 223; 3rd Verkhne-Udinsk Cossack Regiment 29, 31, 39; 4th Semenov Regiment 206; 4th Transbaikal Cossack Regiment 169; 5th Military-Revolutionary Regiment 195; 5th Pri-Amur Independent Army Corps 127, 141, 175; 6th Eastern Siberian Army Corps 218; 7th Partisan Cavalry Regiment 234; 7th Special Detachment 281; 8th Transbaikal Cossack Division 110; 9th Infantry Division 114; 9th Siberian Division 170; 29th Troitskosavsk Infantry Regiment 169, 233–4; 30th Nerchinsk Infantry Regiment 169; 31st Chita Regiment 169; 32nd Regiment 114; 33rd Regiment 114, 145, 247–8; 36th Regiment 114; 38th Transbaikal Infantry 208; 53rd Siberian Regiment 208–9, 236, 376; 54th Siberian Regiment 212; 104th Brigade 208; 106th Sakhalin Regiment 280; 618th Tomsk Infantry 44–5; Aboriginal Mounted Corps 169; Anarchist Cavalry Regiment 86; Armored Train Division 159–66, 184, 210, 218, 240; Asiatic Horse Division 143, 176, 267, 280, 289; Chita Cossack Regiment 110; Chita Internationalist Battalion 70; Chita Red Guard 36–7, 46–7, 51–3, 64–6, 77–8; Combined Manchurian Division 218; Composite Ataman Semenov Division 234, 370; Far East Red Guard 73; Irkutsk Red Guard 38; Jaeger Cavalry Regiment 114, 145, 212, 223, 247–8; Japanese Volunteer Battalion 78, 80, 348; Jewish Cossack Company 136–7; Kalmykov Detachment see OKO; Kappel's Army 213, 225, 232, 234, 239–42, 251, 258, 260, 262–5, 282–5, 298, 324, 382, 388, 394; Khabarovsk Red Guard 39; Krasnoyarsk Red Guard 38; Listvenichnoye Red Guard 81; Local Manchurian Division 218; Manchurian Ataman Semenov Division 140, 169; Mongol–Buryat Regiment 30–2, 34–6, 40, 48–9, 318; New Siberian Army see Siberian Army; Onon Cossack Regiment 110; Orlov Detachment 59, 61, 63, 65, 73, 79, 97, 344; People's Komuch Army 92–3, 151; Piskulich Detachment 151, 218; Priamur Mounted Regiment 169; Samara People's Army 213; Separate Eastern Siberian Army 127, 171, 176, 218, 326; Serpukhov Regiment 205, 375; Shevchenko's Detachment 97, 99, 223–4; Siberian Army 81, 113–14, 196–7, 204, 213; Tomsk 1st Internationalist Battalion 70; Tomsk 2nd Internationalist Battalion 70; Transbaikal Cavalry Division 263; Transbaikal Cossack Brigade 234, 251; Transbaikal Cossack Division 251; Transbaikal Internationalist Detachment 70; Transbaikal Railway Red Guard 52; Ufa Regiment 251; Ussuri Cossack Division 45, 97; Wild Division 377; Yakimov Division 169, 240; Zolotukhin Detachment 62–4, 66

Russian National Fascist Revolutionary Party 302
Russian Orthodox Church 9, 113, 150, 165, 294, 307, 365
Russian Railway Service Corps 61–2, 94–5, 170, 179–80, 182–3, 217, 225, 235, 239, 242, 252, 256, 313, 316
Russo-Asiatic Bank 15, 67, 205
Russo-Japanese War 17–18, 23, 28, 54, 67, 109, 181
Ryan, A.E., Lieutenant 201–2
Rychkov, V.V. 300, 308
Rydzinski, A. 38

sabotage 54, 56–7, 83–4, 87, 166, 168–9, 181–2, 194, 200, 275, 283, 298, 302, 305, 308
Safron, B. 107, 294–5, 355
Saito Kijiro, Major General 74, 191, 344, 353, 373
Sakabe Tosuho, Lieutenant Colonel 59, 62, 97
Sakharov, K., General 213, 229, 295, 311
Salnikov, General 301
Samarin, Major General 33, 36

INDEX

Samoilov, M.K., General 61
Sando 21, 270, 391
sanitary trains 153, 193, 203, 207, 215, 232, 239
Sato Naotake, Consul 59, 61, 72–4, 343, 346
Savel'ev, Captain 47, 119
Savel'ev, N.I., Lieutenant Colonel 187, 265, 282
Savitskii, Zh. A., Colonel 231
Schuyler, M., Captain 111, 152
Selenga River 9, 88, 140, 171–2, 178, 190, 206, 219–21, 279, 292
Semenov, G.M.: 1918 April offensive 62–6, 68–74, 76; 1918 August offensive 85–90; 1918 January offensive 46–9, 50–3; 1918 July defeat 77–80; assassination attempts 132–3, 138, 142–3, 287, 294, 296; as ataman 101, 105–6, 174, 176, 304; in Canada 287–8; capture 310; childhood and youth 23–4; in China 287, 296; corruption 115–16, 123–4, 130, 134–5, 140–3, 160, 194, 205, 220, 232, 237, 239, 295; counter-revolution 40–6, 55, 59; debauchery 135–7, 185; departure from Russia 286–7; departure from Transbaikalia 264–6; elections 108, 257; execution 311; family 23, 25, 136, 199, 262, 292, 296, 306–7, 309–10, 313; ideology 304; in Japan 287, 295–6; in Korea 287; in Manchuria 295–6, 298–1, 304–8, 310; military education 24; Mongolian assignment 24–5; Napoleonic delusions and comparisons 104, 251; negotiations with Reds 261, 263; October Revolution 36–7, 40; political administration 69–70, 75, 89, 105, 108, 110, 257–8, 262; Port Arthur exile 282; Provisional Government commissar 31–5; relations with China 74, 78–9, 129–30, 190, 239, 267, 270, 287; relations with Czechoslovak Legion 75–7, 87, 89–90, 106, 150, 207, 223, 240; relations with Great Britain 60, 63, 73, 114–15, 175, 177; relations with Horvath 61, 63, 74, 141, 144, 176–7; relations with Japan 59–62, 70, 72–4, 78–80, 86, 89, 94, 112, 116, 122–4, 126, 138, 198, 233, 235, 251, 257, 260, 283, 301, 304–5; relations with Kalmykov 97, 119; relations with Kolchak 66, 70–4, 114, 127–31, 141, 155, 163, 170–1, 175–6, 179, 198, 207, 217; relations with Merkulov Government 282–4; relations with Mongolia 24–5, 189–91, 238, 267, 270, 303; relations with Serbia 176; relations with Ungern-Shternberg

27–9, 31, 185, 205, 267, 271–2; relations with United States 64–6, 95, 107, 138, 156, 170–4, 179–80, 190, 196, 198, 201–2, 204, 225–30, 313; staff 63, 109, 111–13, 138–9, 151, 160, 218, 304, 317, 318; trial 310–11, 313; in United States 286–92; First World War 26–30
Semenov, M. 23
Semenov, V. 25, 292
Semenova, Elena 287, 296, 307, 310, 313
Semenova, Elizaveta 296, 310
Semenova, H. 262, 287–92
Semenova, T. 296, 310, 313
Semenova, Z. 25, 33, 136, 199, 262, 292, 307
Semenov-Merlin, General 198, 203–4
Seraphim, Father 238, 262
Serbians 51–2, 60, 66, 78, 92, 111, 129, 132, 134, 146, 151, 176, 183, 218–19, 235, 364
Serov, V.M. 36, 109
sex 10–11, 21, 298, 299
Shadrin, Colonel 237
Shamotulski, C.A., Major 169–70
Sharaban, M. 136–7, 140–2, 199, 238, 286, 312
Sheinman, Doctor 276
Shemelin, General 121–2, 138
Sheraldai 220
Shevchenko, G.M. 97, 99, 224
Shevtsov, I. 81, 349
Shikunts, D.I. 133, 294
Shilka River 174, 293
Shil'nikov, I.F., Major General 33, 69, 109, 284
Shilov, D.S. 100, 166
Shin-naikai 58
Shiroki, Captain 63, 66, 318, 349
Shiromidzu, General 231
Shiryamov, A. 211–12
Shirzhaev, A.G., Captain 187
Shishkin, V.P. 283
Shmakovka 99, 223
Shtiller, A. 38
Shtrombakh, Y. 150
Shumov, V.K. 140–3, 175, 286
Shumovskii Palace 62, 141, 313, 344
Shumyatskii, B. 38, 260, 387
Siberian Army *see* Russian military units: Siberian Army
Silverman, C. 228, 381
Sipailov, Colonel 138–9, 185, 214, 277, 280, 301
Skipetrov, Major General 46, 104, 107, 114, 119, 138–40, 209–12, 214–15, 240, 291
Slaughter, H.H., Lieutenant Colonel 228–9, 369
slaughter yards 160, 165, 183–8, 361

450

INDEX

Sludyanka 82, 129, 162, 229, 233, 383
Slutskii, I.V. 306–9, 400
Smith, C.H. 290
Socialist-Revolutionaries 34, 38, 42, 46–7, 49–51, 54, 77, 80, 102, 108, 113, 117, 131, 133, 167, 207, 211, 214, 223–5, 231, 239, 241, 245, 249, 263, 337, 361, 384
Sofronov, A.P. 133, 363
Sokol'nitskii, V. Yu., Colonel 279, 281
Sokol-Nomokonov, V.M. 35
Sorge, R. 304–5
South Manchuria Railway 58, 123–4, 250, 253, 301, 398
Spasskoe 145, 156, 237, 248, 257, 259, 282, 284–5
Sretensk 7, 51, 70, 85, 88–9, 142, 167, 171, 191, 208, 233–4, 240, 249–50, 262, 345, 388
Stark, I.K., Admiral 284, 395
Stepanov, Colonel 44, 49–50, 140–1, 160–1, 165, 184–5, 196, 286, 291, 317, 367, 395
Stevens, J.F. 61–2, 82, 94–5, 155–6, 163, 173, 180, 233, 314, 352
Straus, R.W., Captain 121
Suchan 148, 174, 195, 284
Suffolk, HMS 38, 99, 147, 159, 364
Sukhe Bator, N. 268–70, 273, 276–81, 292, 294
Sulevich, General 119
Summer Car 137, 161
Sungari River 41, 53, 239, 256, 309–10, 342
Suzuki, Captain 271
Suzuki, Major 190
Svoboda, L., Lieutenant 312
Swedish Red Cross 101, 152, 353
Swiss Red Cross 179
Sychev, Major General 208, 210, 212, 214
Syrobiarskii, General 207
Syrovy, J., General 207, 210, 240, 251, 254, 312, 375
Sze Sheo-Chang 42, 44

Tachibana, General 285, 287
Taishet 169
Tanaka Gi'ichi, Lieutenant General Baron 59, 72, 343, 346
Tankhoe 82–3, 332, 349
taplushki 43–4, 126, 135, 163, 206, 215, 232, 248, 327
tarasun 11, 328
Taskin, S.A. 33, 46, 69, 105, 217
Taube, Major General Baron 70, 346
tayang p'iao 257, 328
Tea Road 2, 6–7, 21, 34, 57, 181, 189
Teh Wang 303

Teusler, R., Dr 153
Thomas, USS 95
Tibet 13, 19–21, 23, 188, 190, 270–1, 274–6, 281, 295
Tientsin 16, 60, 270, 287, 295–6, 307–8, 312, 342, 364, 397
Tierbach, Colonel 46–7, 109–10, 139–40, 169, 185, 195, 218, 300
Tikhon, P. 50, 340
Timireva, A.V. 202
Togtakhu Taiji 181
Togtokh-gun 271, 276, 280, 292
Tola River 266, 274, 275, 277
Tomlovskii, Colonel 170–2
Torchinov, V., Captain 142, 390
torture 1–2, 49, 52–3, 105, 108–9, 111, 117, 125, 133, 137, 139–40, 145–6, 148, 161, 163, 185–8, 206, 222–5, 231, 248, 266, 273, 276, 292–4, 303, 305, 312, 329
Tower, G.W., Colonel 183
trakt 6–8, 10–12, 203, 218–19, 234, 316, 328
Transbaikal Cossack Host 8, 23–5, 28, 33, 48, 50, 69, 78, 106, 111, 136–7, 174, 215
Trans-Siberian Railroad 12–13, 17, 19, 38, 57, 70, 75–7, 79, 95, 148, 152, 155, 158, 178, 195, 205, 207, 218, 233–4, 249, 264, 314–16; *see* Advisory Commission of Railway Experts
Treaty of Brest–Litovsk 52, 75–6, 95, 151, 338, 347
Treaty of Kyakhta 35, 267
Treaty of Shimonoseki 15, 73
Triapitsyn, Y.I. 148, 203, 206, 231, 243, 248, 259–61, 382
Trilisser, M.A. 81, 86, 311, 395, 401
Troitskosavsk 24–5, 88, 114, 166, 169, 208, 220–1, 233–4, 240, 269, 273, 280, 325, 328
Trotsky, L. 10–11, 30, 57, 76, 136, 158, 216, 231, 235, 263, 311, 321
Tsao Kun, General 273
Tsentrosibir' 40, 52, 70, 84–5, 103, 311, 328, 354
Tsing-Tao 15, 56, 58, 296, 353
Tsitsihar 43, 57, 74, 130, 181–2, 189, 281, 296, 306, 309, 333, 388
Tsu Jui Fu, General 271
Tumbair, Major General 238–9
Tungpei 301
Tungus 2, 80, 111, 203, 330
Twaddle, B.N., Lieutenant 180
typhus 11, 143, 153–4, 187, 193–4, 211, 218, 236, 239, 393

Uehara Yusaka, General Baron 59, 344
Ugol'naya 148, 224, 232, 282

INDEX

Ukhtomsky, P.E. 20, 310–11, 333, 400
Uliastai 20, 22, 189, 276, 278, 281, 334, 393
Ungern-Shternberg, Roman Fedorovich von, Baron 27–31, 40, 43–4, 47, 49, 51, 142, 186–7, 190, 200–1, 205, 217–18, 235, 250, 256, 266–7, 271–82, 284, 287, 289, 292, 296, 317, 335, 338, 363, 391–3
uniforms 61, 75, 95, 112–13, 138, 152, 157, 174, 179, 184, 196–7, 208, 265, 271–2, 298–9, 305, 307, 309, 363
Union of Cossacks in the Far East (SKDV) 301
Union of Far Eastern Cossack Armies 101, 119
Urga 5, 6–7, 20, 22–5, 35, 85, 189–91, 266–80, 294, 325, 328, 334
Urul'ga 87, 166, 350
US Army: 8th Division 93; 27th Infantry Regiment 93, 100, 145, 148–9, 156, 170–2, 178, 183–4, 220, 222, 225, 228–9, 352; 31st Infantry Regiment 93, 148, 174, 195, 201
Ushumun 90, 350
Ussuri Cossack Host 8, 45, 62, 69, 89, 96–8, 111, 118–19, 144–5, 187, 223, 230–1, 265, 304
Ussuri Railway 206, 223, 257, 284
Ussuri River 25, 98–100, 149, 305
Ustrugov, L.A. 94, 345

Vagin, P.T., General 209
Vagzhanov, A.P. 167, 185, 368, 372
Vandalov, Captain 276
Vangdanov, Colonel 281
Vaskevich, P.Y. 300, 306–7
venereal disease 21, 93, 149, 193, 194
Verigo, Major General 63, 109, 111, 135, 138–9, 177, 224, 241, 355, 362–3, 380, 385, 409, 413, 425
Verkhne-Udinsk 6–8, 19, 33–4, 36–9, 51, 70, 78, 83–6, 88, 105, 123–4, 129–30, 133, 136, 147–8, 156, 160, 162–3, 168, 170–4, 184, 190, 195, 208, 219–23, 229, 233–7, 242, 248–51, 259–63, 281, 292, 328
Verkhne-Udinsk Democratic Republic 389
Versailles Peace Conference 190, 372
Verzhbitskii, General 265, 283, 285
Vespa, A. 286, 300, 303, 308, 357
Vladivostok 8, 12–15, 32, 38–9, 41, 62, 90–5, 97, 114, 123, 125–6, 128, 135, 139, 142, 146–55, 183, 188, 195, 198, 203–5, 217, 223–30, 234, 237, 242, 244–5, 260–1, 282–7, 296, 310, 314–15
Vlasov, A.A., General 309, 310
Voitsekhovskii, S.N., Major General 226, 232, 234, 242, 263, 380, 383, 424
Volkov, B.N., Colonel 189

Volkov, V.I., Major General 50, 128–30, 135, 155
Vologodskii, P.V. 77, 91, 106
Vonsiatskii, A.A. 302, 399
Voropaev, S.I. 133, 294
Vrangl, P.N., General Baron 27–9, 53, 260, 284
Vrashtel, V., Colonel 63, 65, 144, 146, 180, 182, 223–4, 248, 345
Vsevolozhskii, Colonel 129

Waldorf-Astoria Hotel 289–91
Walker, E. 147
Wang Tsao-tsun 278
Ward, J., Colonel 93, 124–5, 150, 175, 177
Warden, J.W. 288
Wheeler, M., Major 118
White diaspora 286
White movement 91, 140, 217, 228, 234, 283, 287
Wilson, Woodrow 93, 153, 190, 361, 372, 376, 409
wireless *see* radio communications
Wood, J.B. 292

Xinjing *see* Changchun

Yakovleva, V., Sister 238, 262
Yakushev, P. 204–5
Yamada Yoshimi, General 56
Yanogita, General 308, 429
Yarborough, L., Lieutenant 242, 402
Yasue Norihiro, Colonel 304
Yermak Timofeyevich 4–5, 158
Yi Dong Whi 167
YMCA 92, 124, 126, 132, 146, 152–3, 182, 184, 225, 409
Yokohama Specie Bank 296, 306, 313
Yoshi, General 172
Youroveta Home and Foreign Trading Company 289–90, 292, 396
Yuan Shih-Kai 272, 392

zaibatsu 58, 60, 329
Zemskii sobor 196
zemstvos 38, 62, 93, 98, 223–5, 230, 242, 257, 265, 282, 329
Zeya River 101–3, 145–6, 194, 350
Zhevchenko, Lieutenant 41, 59, 67, 317, 345
Zhugalin, Y. 51
Zhukov, G., General 306
Zhukovski, Colonel 161, 179–80, 194, 413
Zhuravlev, Commander 195
Zinkovka 146
Zubkovskii, Colonel 201, 218, 360
Zum Kuren 273
Zurbrick, J.L. 288

LaVergne, TN USA
19 January 2010
170479LV00001B/51/P